The Venetian Bride: Bloodlines and Blood Feuds in Venice and Its Empire

The Venetian Bride: Bloodlines and Blood Feuds in Venice and Its Empire

PATRICIA FORTINI BROWN

OXFORD
UNIVERSITY PRESS

OXFORD
UNIVERSITY PRESS

Great Clarendon Street, Oxford, OX2 6DP,
United Kingdom

Oxford University Press is a department of the University of Oxford.
It furthers the University's objective of excellence in research, scholarship,
and education by publishing worldwide. Oxford is a registered trade mark of
Oxford University Press in the UK and in certain other countries

First Edition published in 2021
Impression: 1

Published in the United States of America by Oxford University Press
198 Madison Avenue, New York, NY 10016, United States of America

British Library Cataloguing in Publication Data
Data available

Library of Congress Control Number: 2020949094

ISBN 978-0-19-289457-1

DOI: 10.1093/oso/9780192894571.001.0001

Printed and bound by
CPI Group (UK) Ltd, Croydon, CR0 4YY

This book is dedicated to Paul, John, and Anton—my own bloodline

Contents

Acknowledgements ix
List of Illustrations xi
Note on citations and abbreviations xvii
Preface xxi

PART ONE: BIRTHRIGHTS

1. A Future Bride 3
2. A Bitter Bequest 19
3. Recovery 48
4. Restitution 66
5. Honour and Disgrace 87

PART TWO: A MELDED BLOODLINE

6. The Venetian Bride 113
7. Exile 136
8. The Capitano Grande 163
9. The Return 188
10. The Sacrifice 222

PART THREE: LINEAGES

11. Wars and Peace 251
12. Suitable Alliances 279
13. The Cardinal 290
14. Retrenchment 307
15. The Legacy 320

Epilogue 353

Appendices 355
I. Francesco Sansovino, Vita delle illustre signora Contessa Giulia Bemba della Torre 355
II. Family Trees 363
A. Bembo 363
B. Della Torre I: sixteenth century 364
C. Della Torre II: seventeenth–eighteenth centuries 365
D. Colloredo 366
E. Savorgnan 367

Bibliography 369
Index 395

Acknowledgements

One incurs many debts for a book that took sixteen years to bring to fruition. Acknowledging them all is a daunting task, and I ask forgiveness from those whom I have inadvertently left out. First, I would like to thank Princeton University for generous institutional support over the years. The chair of the Department of Art & Archaeology, Michael Koortbojian, and the office staff—Maureen Killeen, The late Susan Lehre (before her retirement), Stacey Bonette, Diane Schulte, and Julie Angarone—were most helpful in a myriad of ways. I benefited greatly from grants from the University Committee on Research in the Humanities and Social Sciences, as well as from the Ione May Spears Fund of the Department of Art & Archaeology for research travel and photography. The Department's Barr Ferree Publication Fund afforded crucial support for reproduction fees and the acquisition of photographs. Support from the Program in Hellenic Studies, and its director, Dimitri Gondicas, allowed me to teach a course on Renaissance Crete, with a class trip that allowed me to familiarize myself with the island. In the final phases of manuscript preparation, Luciano Vanni, my talented graduate research assistant, offered much-needed assistance in acquiring images and permissions.

My research over the years was greatly facilitated by the staffs of the Marquand and Firestone libraries at Princeton; in Venice at the Archivio di Stato, Archivio Storico del Patriarcato di Venezia, Biblioteca del Museo Correr, Biblioteca Nazionale Marciana, the Fondazione Giorgio Cini, and the Istituto Ellenico; in Udine at Archivio di Stato, Biblioteca Civica Vincenzo Joppi, and Biblioteche Storiche Diocesane; in Trento and in Trieste at the Archivio di Stato; and at the Biblioteca Seminario Vescovile in Ceneda (Vittorio Veneto).

For practical help, advice, and various kinds of assistance, I would like to thank Bernard Aikema, Christopher Apostle, Benjamin Arbel, Lilian Armstrong, Joško Belamarić, Mauro Bondioli, Giulio Bono, Linda Borean, Donatella Calabi, Lorenzo Calvelli, Federica Caneparo, Giovanni Caniato, Stan Chojnacki, Paula Clarke, Leslie Contarini, Gigi Corazzol, Michela Dal Borgo, Giada Damen, Blake de Maria, Alex Eliopoulos, Peter Fergusson, Joanne Ferraro, Mary Frank, Edviljo Gardina, Paolo Giovannini, Edoardo Giuffrida, Olga Gratziou, Amy Gross, Jim Grubb, Jasenka Gudelj, Johanna Heinrichs, Charles Hope, Kristin Huffman, Frederick Ilchman, Eleni Kanaki, Elizabeth Kassler-Taub, Michelle Komie, Bianca Lanfranchi, the late Patsy and George Labalme, Laura Lepskchy, Margherita Losaccco, Piero Lucchi, Chryssa Maltezou, Rosella Mamoli, Vittorio Mandelli, Lia Markey, Georgios Markou, John Martin, Stefania Mason, Gabriele Matino,

Christine Morley, Reinhold Mueller, Jacki Musacchio, Daniela Omenetto, Susan Nalezyty, Andrea Nanetti, Alessandra Negrin, Giulio Ongaro, Luciana Osti, Gerassimos Pagratis, Nikolas Patsavos, Katja Piazza, Debra Pincus, Dennis Romano, Susannah Rutherglen, Claudia Salmini, Alessandra Sambo Alessandra Schiavon, Richard Schofield, the late Allison Sherman, Emily Spratt, Alan Stahl, Dr. Lucia Stefanelli, Helena Szépe, Giorgio Tagliaferro, Francesca Tamburlini, the late Dottoressa Maria Francesca Tiepolo, Francesca Toffolo, Irina Tolstoy, Eurigio Tonetti, Fra Apollonio Tottoli, Maria Vasilaki, Despoina Vlassi, Tim Wardell, and Marino Zorzi. I am also grateful for the gracious hospitality of Giuliana, Chiara, and Federica at the Hotel Suite Inn in Udine.

I am particularly indebted to Melissa Conn, director of the Venice Office of Save Venice and the Rosand Library & Study Center, for favours too numerous to cite. Special thanks go to Tracy Cooper, my intrepid travel companion to sites in the Veneto and the Friuli, for her insights throughout the process; to my sister Barbara Medwadowski for helping me explore Crete; to Monique O'Connell for sharing the manuscript of her book, *Men of Empire*, in advance of publication; to Nubar Gianighian for organizing a visit to the Castello di San Martino in Ceneda, where we were welcomed by Nice Vecchione and Don Adriano Dall'Asta; to Pallina Pavanini for help with transcriptions and for offering important perspectives on a draft of the first chapter of the book; to Ed Muir for vetting the second chapter; and to Gillian Malpass, Deborah Howard, and Sarah Blake McHam for their friendship, encouragement, and always welcome advice.

Finally, I am especially grateful to Michelle Lovric, who read a draft of the entire manuscript before I submitted it to a press and offered invaluable criticisms and suggestions for improvement; to the anonymous reviewers for Oxford University Press, who gave me further constructive feedback; and, finally, to my editors at Oxford University Press, Cathryn Steele and Katie Bishop, for their ongoing enthusiasm, support, and encouragement.

List of Illustrations

1.1. Valerio Belli, Pietro Bembo (obverse), bronze medal, dia. 3.45 cm, ca. 1532. Washington, National Gallery of Art. Samuel H. Kress Collection, inv. 1957.14.79.a. 6

1.2. Venice, Ca' Bembo on Campiello Santa Maria Nova. Photo: Tony Hisgett. < https://commons.wikimedia.org/wiki/File:Campiello_S._Maria_Nova_(7263292432).jpg> (15 February 2021). 9

2.1. Abraham Ortelius, *Patria del Friuli*, engraving with hand colour, 35.5 × 48 cm, 1573. From *Theatrum Orbis Terrarum Abrahami Ortelii Antverp. Geographi Regii*. Antwerp, Plantin Press, 1601. Photo: www.sanderusmaps.com. 20

2.2. Joseph Heintz il Giovane, attrib., *View of Udine*, oil on canvas, 146 × 233 cm, c. 1650–60. Udine, Civici Musei, Galleria d'Arte Antica, inv. 65. Photo: Fototeca. Civici Musei di Udine. 21

2.3. Earthquake in Udine after the Cruel Carnival of 1511, from MCVe, MS Correr 963, 'Udine saccheggiata l'anno 1511, c. 29', eighteenth century. By permission of Museo Civico Correr, Venice. 42

3.1. Castello di Villalta from the southwest. Photo: Alessandro Steffan. Reflexbook.net. 49

3.2. Castello di Villalta in 1480. BCUd, MS 208, Fondo Joppi. Biblioteca Civica 'Vincenzo Joppi' di Udine. 50

3.3. Castello di Colloredo di Monte Albano. Archivio fotografico della Soprintendenza Archeologia, Belle Arti e Paesaggio del Friuli Venezia Giulia, inv. ts 5749. 53

4.1. Joseph Heintz il Giovane, attrib., *View of Udine* (detail of Figure 2.2). Photo: Fototeca. Civic Musei di Udine. 67

4.2. Udine, Loggia del Lionello, 1448–55, with later repairs and modifications up to 1868. Photo: Udine2312. <https://commons.wikimedia.org/wiki/File:Loggia_del_Lionello_(Udine).jpg> (15 February 2021). 76

4.3. Udine, Piazza Contarena (now Piazza della Libertà). Photo: Sailko. < https://commons.wikimedia.org/wiki/ File:Udine,_piazza_della_libert%C3%A0_00.JPG> (15 February 2021). 78

5.1. Ceneda (Vittorio Veneto), Castello di San Martino. Photo: author. 87

5.2. Ceneda (Vittorio Veneto), Municipal loggia, 1537–8. Now Museo della Battaglia. Photo: author. 88

5.3. Paris Bordone, attrib. *Count Girolamo Della Torre*, oil on canvas, 126.4 × 95.5 cm, c. 1535–45. Private collection. Photo: Courtesy of New Orleans Auction Galleries. 89

5.4. 'Corte del Palazzo Ducale di Venetia' (The courtyard of the Ducal Palace of Venice), from Cesare Vecellio, *Habiti antichi, et moderni di tutto il mondo*, Venice: Giovanni Bernardo Sessa, 1598, c. 101. Amsterdam, Rijksmuseum, obj. no. BI-1938-0066-148. 100

5.5. View of tomb of Alvise II Della Torre, ca. 1549–50. Venice, Chiesa di Santa Maria Gloriosa dei Frari. Photo: Matteo da Fina. Courtesy of Save Venice, Inc. 104

5.6. Andrea Schiavone (attrib.), Tomb of Alvise II Della Torre, oil on panel, 320 × 380 cm, ca. 1549–50. Venice, Chiesa di Santa Maria Gloriosa dei Frari. Photo: Matteo da Fina. Courtesy of Save Venice, Inc. 105

5.7. Andrea Schiavone (attrib.), *Murder of Alvise II Della Torre and Giambattista Colloredo*, detail of Figure 5.6. Photo: Matteo da Fina. Courtesy of Save Venice, Inc. 105

5.8. Andrea Riccio, *The Death of Della Torre*, Bronze, height 37 cm, 1516–20. Paris, Museé du Louvre, OA9155 (orig. San Fermo Maggiore, Verona). Photo: (C) RMN-Grand Palais (Musée du Louvre) / Stéphane Maréchalle. 106

6.1. Titian (possibly after), *Portrait of a Lady*, oil on canvas, 63.5 × 51.8 cm, 1530–60. The Art Institute of Chicago, Max and Leola Epstein Collection, 1954.301. 114

6.2. 'Ordinario (Everyday clothing worn by the entire Venetian nobility)', from Cesare Vecellio, *De gli habiti antichi, et moderni*, 1598, c. 106. Amsterdam, Rijksmuseum, obj. no. BI-1938-0066-81. 115

6.3. *Course of the River Brenta*,, from Giovanni Francesco Costa, *Le Delizie del fiume Brenta nei palazzi e casini situati sopra le sue sponde dalla sua sboccatura nella laguna di Venezia infino alla città di Padova*, I, 1750. Paris, Bibliothèque Nationale de France. © BnF. 118

6.4. 'Spose non sposate' (Brides before their weddings in our time) and 'Spose sposate' (Brides outside the house after they have married), from Cesare Vecellio, *De gli habiti antichi, et moderni*. Venice: Giovanni Bernardo Sessa, 1598, cc. 125, 126. Amsterdam, Rijksmuseum, obj. nos. BI-1938-0066-95 and BI-1938-0066-96. 122

7.1. Carpaccio, *Departure of the Betrothed Pair* (detail), oil on canvas, c. 1495. Venice, Museo Nazionale Gallerie dell'Accademia, cat. 575. © Gallerie dell'Accademia di Venezia, 'Ministero dei beni e delle attività culturali e del turismo'. Photo: Matteo Da Fina, Save Venice Inc. 139

7.2. *Candia*, from Bernhard von Breydenbach, *Peregrinationes in Terram Sanctam*, Mainz, 1486 (1st ed.); 1502 (2nd ed.). Woodcut by Erhard Reeuwich. The National Library of Israel, Eran Laor Cartographic Collection, Shapell Family Digitization Project and The Hebrew University of Jerusalem, Department of Geography—Historic Cities Research Project. 144

7.3. Eucharius Rösslin, *Libro nel qual si tratta del parto de lhuomo*, Venice, 1538, frontispiece. Library of Congress, Rare Book and Special Collections Division, shelfmark RG91.R715. 151

8.1. MCVe, Mariegola 56, Accademia degli Uniti, 1551, cover. Venice, Biblioteca del Museo Civico Correr. 165

8.2. MCVe, Mariegola 56, Accademia degli Uniti, 1551, frontispiece. Venice, Biblioteca del Museo Civico Correr. 166

8.3. 'Bravo [armed retainer] of Venice and other cities of Italy', from Cesare Vecellio, *De gli habiti antichi, et moderni*. Venice: Giovanni Bernardo Sessa, 1598, c. 165. Amsterdam, Rijksmuseum, obj. no. BI-1938-0066-127. 168

8.4. Maneas Klontzas, *View of Candia* (detail), drawing, early seventeenth century. By permission of Malcolm Weiner. Photo: Historical Museum of Crete, Heraklion. 171

8.5. Bembo Fountain, 1552–4. Candia (Heraklion). Photo: author. 174

9.1. Venice, Ca' Morosini (now Hotel Ca' Sagredo) on the Grand Canal in Cannaregio. Photo: Didier Descouens – Own work, CC BY-SA 4.0, <https://commons.wikimedia.org/w/index.php?curid=15794062> (15 February 2021). 190

9.2. *Scodella* (Broth Bowl) on a High Foot: Birthing Chamber Scene, Maiolica (tin-glazed earthenware), h. 10.8 cm, diam. 14.4 cm, 1545–60. Princeton University Art Museum, Museum purchase, y1941–28. 193

9.3. German or Polish artist, Bona Sforza as a widow, oil on canvas, 210.5 × 111 cm, seventeenth century. The Royal Castle in Warsaw—Museum, inv. no. ZKW/60. Photo: Andrzej Ring, Lech Sandzewicz. 202

9.4. Giovanni Merlo, *Vero e real disegno della inclita cita di Venetia* (detail), 1676. Chicago, Newberry Library, Novacco 4F 288. Newberry Digital Collections. 215

10.1. Ceneda (Vittorio Veneto). Marble fountain in the cathedral square, 1555. Photo: author. 224

10.2. Ceneda (Vittorio Veneto). Aerial view of Castello di San Martino. Photo: Reflexbook.net. 225

10.3. Girolamo Romanino (attr.), *Banquet of Bartolomeo Colleoni in honour of Christian I of Denmark in 1467* (detail), fresco, 1520s. Castello di Malpaga. Photo: Giorces. <https://commons.wikimedia.org/wiki/ File:Malpaga28.JPG> (15 February 2021). 230

10.4. Giovanni da Udine, Allegorical frescoes (detail), Studiolo, Castello di Colloredo di Monte Albano. Archivio fotografico della Soprintendenza Archeologia, Belle Arti e Paesaggio del Friuli, inv. Ud_R 867-11. 232

10.5. Commission of Lorenzo Bembo, capitano of Paphos, from Doge Nicolo Priuli, 1558. Houghton Library, Harvard University, MS Typ 330. 234

10.6. Cornelis Cort, *Birth of the Virgin*, engraving after Federico Zuccaro, 32.7 × 20.5 cm, 1568. Amsterdam, Rijksmuseum, RP-P-1888-A-12476. 239

10.7. Master of Ceneda, Coronation of the Virgin, tempera on panel, 283 × 303 cm, 1450. Venice, Museo Nazionale Gallerie dell'Accademia, cat. 1. © Gallerie dell'Accademia di Venezia, 'Ministero dei beni e delle attività culturali e del turismo'. Photo: Matteo Da Fina, Save Venice Inc. 242

10.8. Frontispiece of Francesco Sansovino, *Vita della illustre Signora Contessa Giulia Bemba della Torre* (Venice: Domenico & Gio Battista Guerra, fratelli, 1565). Shelfmark: Misc. 1215.007. Venice, Biblioteca Nazionale Marciana. 244

11.1. 'Lutto' (Mourning clothes outside Venice), from Cesare Vecellio, *De gli habiti antichi, et moderni*. Venice: Giovanni Bernardo Sessa, 1598, c. 166. Amsterdam, Rijksmuseum, obj. no. BI-1938-0066-128. 252

11.2. Commission of Lorenzo Bembo, Provveditore Generale of the Kingdom of Cyprus, from Doge Girolamo Priuli, 1565. Trinity College, Cambridge, MS R.4.30, James no. 659. © Master and Fellows of Trinity College, Cambridge. 263

11.3. Girolamo Romanino (attr.), Hunting scene (detail), fresco, 1520s. Comune of Bergamo, Castello di Malpaga. Photo: Giorces. <https://commons.wikimedia.org/wiki/ File:Malpaga27.JPG> (15 February 2021). 271

11.4. Domenico Zenoi, *Entry of Henri III, King of France and Poland, into Venice*, etching, 19.7 × 27.1 cm, 1574. New York, Metropolitan Museum of Art. Acc. No. 59.570.432. The Elisha Whittelsey Collection, The Elisha Whittelsey Fund, 1959. 273

12.1. 'Spose del Friuli' (Brides of Friuli and places nearby), from Cesare Vecellio, *De gli habiti antichi, et moderni*, 1598, c. 217. Amsterdam, Rijksmuseum, obj. No. BI-1938-0066-149. 280

12.2. Castello di Valvasone. Photo: Ufficio Turismo di Valvasone. 281

12.3. Castello di Valvasone. Frescoes, fourteenth century. Photo: Ufficio Turismo di Valvasone. 281

12.4. Treviso, Ca' da Noal. Photo: Appo92 <https://commons.wikimedia.org/wiki/File:CaDaNoal1.JPG> (15 February 2021). 284

12.5. Castello di Villalta from the east. Photo: Reflexbook.net. 286

13.1. Bartolomeo Carducci [Bartholome Carducho], *Portrait of Cardinal Michael Turrianus* (Posthumous Portrait of Cardinal Michele Della Torre), oil on canvas, 140 × 155 cm, 1608. GASK—The Gallery of the Central Bohemian Region, Kutná Hora. Photo: Oto Palán. 291

13.2. Frontispiece, Adriano Grandi, *Canzone nella morte dell'Illustrissimo Reverendissimo Cardinale di Ceneda, Monsignor Michele della Torre*, Verona: Appresso Girolamo Discepoli, 1586. Shelf mark MISC 2525.008. Venice, Biblioteca Nazionale Marciana. 297

14.1. Palazzo Torriani of 1540, ink drawing made after 1589. Facade on Borgo Strazzamantello. ASUd, Archivio Della Porta, B. 12-3. Photo: author. By permission of the Archivio di Stato di Udine. 308

14.2. Palazzo Torriani compound in 1589. ASUd, Archivio Della Porta, B. 12-3. Photo: author. By permission of the Archivio di Stato di Udine. 309

14.3. Loggia in Palazzo Torriani compound in 1589. ASUd, Archivio Della Porta, B. 12-3. Photo: author. By permission of the Archivio di Stato di Udine. 309

14.4. Veronese and workshop. *Coronation of Hebe*, oil on canvas, 387 × 387 cm, 1580s. Boston, Isabella Stewart Gardner Museum, acc. no. P25c26. 312

15.1. Andrea Vicentino, *Madonna of the Rosary*, with Pope Pius V, St. Dominic, and the Queen of Cyprus, c. 1600. Church of St. Kvirin Museum. Krk, Croatia. 323

15.2. Portrait of Bishop Giovanni Della Torre. Oil on canvas, 1606. Musei Civici di Padova. Inv. 1479. Photo: Ghiraldini Giuliano. By kind permission of the Comune di Padova—Assessorato alla Cultura. 325

15.3. Lucio, Sigismondo, and Girolamo, sons of Carlo II Della Torre. BCUd, Fondo Principale, MS 541, cc. 25, 26, 27. Biblioteca Civica 'Vincenzo Joppi' di Udine. 334

15.4. Villa Pedrina, Azzo Decimo (Pordenone). Photo: Reflexbook.net. 337

15.5. Palazzo Torriani before 1717. Street facade of the main palace (lower left) and three views of the facades facing the interior courtyard. BCUd, Fondo Principale, MS 541, c. 29r. Biblioteca Civica 'Vincenzo Joppi' di Udine. 340

15.6. Column of infamy in Piazza del Fisco and Demolition of Palazzo Torriani in 1717. BCUd, Fondo Principale, MS 541, c. 30r. Biblioteca Civica 'Vincenzo Joppi' di Udine. 340

15.7. Della Torre and Villalta coats of arms, with a banderole inscribed with 'Tranquilité'. Entry portal, Castello di Villalta. Photo: Tracy E. Cooper. 344

Note on Citations and Abbreviations

Printed sources are referred to in the notes by author and year of publication (anonymous works by short title and year). The bibliography at the end of the book, divided into primary and secondary texts, gives full references. The following abbreviations are used in the notes.

Archives and Libraries

ASDUd	Archivio Storico Diocesano, Udine
ASTr	Archivio di Stato, Trento
ASTS	Archivio di Stato, Trieste
ASUd	Archivio di Stato, Udine
AT	*Archivio Torriani-Della Torre*
ADT	*Archivio Della Torre*
ADP	*Archivio Della Porta*
ASVe	Archivio di Stato, Venice
AC	*Avogaria di Comun*
	Barbaro, *Genealogie Miscellanea codici, Storia Veneta*, bb. 17–23 (I–VII), Marco Barbaro, *Genealogie patrizie*
CCX	*Capi del Consiglio di Dieci*
Coll.	*Collegio*
CX	*Consiglio di Dieci*
X Savi	*Dieci Savi alle Decime in Rialto*
LPF	*Luogotenente alla Patria del Friuli*
MC	*Maggior Consiglio*
NA	*Notarile, Atti*
NT	*Notarile, Testamenti*
SAV-MC	*Segretario alle Voci, Elezioni in Maggior Consiglio*
SAV-Sen.	*Segretario alle Voci, Elezioni in Senato*
Sen.	*Senato*
ASVic	Archivio di Stato, Vicenza
BCUd	Biblioteca Communale 'V. Joppi', Udine
MCVe	Biblioteca del Museo Civico Correr, Venice
	Barbaro, *Genealogie* MS Cicogna 2498–2504 (I–VII). Marco Barbaro, *Genealogie e origine di famiglie venete patrizie*

Publications

Bembo/TraviPietro Bembo,	*Lettere*, ed. Ernesto Travi, 4 vols., Bologna, 1987–93.
Cardinals	*The Cardinals of the Holy Roman Church*: http://cardinals.fiu.edu/cardinals.htm
CSP/5	*Calendar of State Papers Relating To English Affairs in the Archives of Venice, Volume 5, 1534–1554*. Edited by Rawdon Brown. London: Her Majesty's Stationery Office 1873. *British History Online*, accessed 4 June 2020, http://www.british-history.ac.uk/cal-state-papers/venice/vol5.
CSP/8	*Calendar of State Papers Foreign: Elizabeth, Volume 8, 1566–1568*. Edited by Allan James Crosby. London: Her Majesty's Stationery Office 1871. *British History Online*, accessed 4 June 2020, http://www.british-history.ac.uk/cal-state-papers/foreign/vol8.
Cicogna, *Ins. Ven.*	Cicogna, Emmanuele A. *Delle inscrizioni veneziane*, 6 vols in 7. Venice, 1824–53.
DBI	*Dizionario Biografico degli Italiani*. 92 vols. Rome: Istituto dell' Enciclopedia Italiana, 1960–[online: http://www.treccani.it/enciclopedia/]
DU	Leonardo and Gregorio Amaseo, with Giovanni Antonio Azio, *Diarii udinesi dell'1508 al 1541*, ed. Antonio Ceruti, Monumenti storici, 3rd ser., vol. 2, Cron*A*Che e diarii, vol. I, Venice: R. Deputazione Veneta di Storia Patria, 1884.
DU, GA	Portion of diary by Gregorio Amaseo (225–492: 1511–41)
DU, GAH	Appendix to diary by Gregorio Amaseo, *Historia della crudel zobia grassa et altri nefarii excessi et horrende calamità intervenute in la città di Udine et patria del Friuli del 1511* (497–544)
DA, LA	Portion of diary by Leonardo Amaseo (1–191: Feb. 1508–10)
Moroni, *Dizionario*	Moroni, Gaetano. *Dizionario di erudizione storico-ecclesiastica da S. Pietro sino ai nostri giorni*. 103 vols. Venice, 1840–61.
Pastor	Pastor, Ludwig Freiherr von. *The History of the Popes from the Close of the Middle Ages*, 40 vols. London, 1891–1953.
Relazioni/Legnago	*Relazioni dei Rettori Veneti in Terraferma. VIII. Provveditorato di Legnago*, Milan, 1977.
Relazioni/Friuli	*Relazioni dei Rettori Veneti in Terraferma. I. Patria del Friuli, Milan*, 1973.
Sanudo, *Diarii*	Sanudo, Marin. *I diarii*. Edited by Rinaldo Fulin et al, 58 vols in 59. Venice, 1879–1903.
Vasari,	*Lives*Vasari, Giorgio. *Lives of the Most Eminent Painters, Sculptors and Architects*. Translated by Gaston du C. De Vere. 10 vols. London, 1912–15.
Vasari, *Vite*	Vasari, Giorgio, *Le vite de' più eccellenti pittori, scultori ed architettori* (1568). Edited by Gaetano Milanesi. 9 vols. Florence, 1878–85.

Other abbreviations

b./bb.	Busta/Buste
c./cc.	Carta/carte (leaf/leaves)
fasc.	Fascicolo
fu	son or daughter of
MS/MSS	Manuscripts/s
n.	Note
q.	quondam (son or daughter of)
r./rr.	Registro/Registri
s. v.	*Sub voce*
v./vols.	Volumes/volumes

Names

The names of Girolamo and Hieronimo were used interchangeably in this period. Gian Matteo Bembo might be called Zuan Matteo, Zan Matteo, Giammatteo, or Giovanni Matteo. The first version is used in this book for consistency. Likewise, Luigi might be referred to in the primary sources as Alvise, or Ludovico or Lodovico; or Jacopo as Giacomo; or Marco Antonio as Marcantonio; and so on. In general, a specific individual will be referred to with the same spelling throughout the book when possible. When the same name is repeated through the generations, the first so-named and his/her successors will be designated as Carlo I, Carlo II, Carlo III, and so on.

The Della Torre surname, generally used throughout the book, also appears in documents of the period with several spellings, including Dalla Torre, a Turre, a Torre, a Turri, Turriani, Torriani, and even delatore.

Patronymics: In primary documents, a living father is typically (but not always) designated by fu; a deceased father by q. (i.e., Gian Matteo Bembo fu Alvise; or Gian Matteo Bembo q. Alvise). The original spelling is retained in the book.

Dates

The Venetian year began on 1 March. Thus, dates in original documents that were cited as *more Veneto* have been changed to normal usage. The Venetian dating system was not used in the Friuli, where the year began on 1 January.

Translations

Unless otherwise noted, all translations are by the author.

Previous publications

In addition to material that was presented in a different context in my book, *Private Lives in Renaissance Venice* (Brown 2004), I have published articles on specific topics that are incorporated into the present book: Brown 2008, Brown 2013a, Brown 2013b, Brown 2013c.

Preface

In exploring Venice's engagement with the ancient past for my book *Venice & Antiquity* (1996), I came across the curious statue of a wild man holding a solar disc inserted in a classical niche on the façade of a palace in Campiello Santa Maria Nova. I learned that the owner and patron, Gian Matteo Bembo (also called Zuan Matteo, Giovanni Matteo, and Giammatteo in the primary documents), had led a consequential life, not only in Venice, but also in its territories in the Terraferma and the stato da mar. Gian Matteo's sculptural pastiche made a cameo appearance in the conclusion to *Venice & Antiquity* as an example of uniquely Venetian self-fashioning that engaged the republic's classical past and imperial present.

Gian Matteo would play a far more important role in my *Private Lives in Renaissance Venice* (2004). I became intrigued by his daughter Giulia's marriage to Count Girolamo Della Torre, a mainland noble with a castle and other properties in the Friuli. A new book, the microhistory of a marriage, was in the making. My working title was *The Venetian Bride.*

Brides were central to the Venetian experience. Bejewelled brides played a major role in Venetian pageantry, put on display for foreign dignitaries as emblems of the city's wealth and, as future bearers of sons, of its continual renewal. Indeed, Venice was itself a bride, its identity grounded in a bridal paradox. On the one hand, the city, its mythical foundation on the day of the Annunciation, was identified early on with the Virgin Mary, the mother and bride of Christ, as *Venetia-Vergine*. On the other hand, in the *Festa della Sensa*, the annual Marriage to the Sea, the city conveniently switched genders. Here, Venice, as represented by the doge, became a husband, espousing the sea as its bride in a metaphor of its dominion over its maritime empire. Over time, the trope of Venice as Virgin (chaste and undefiled) eventually incorporated a notion of Venice as Venus (sensual and fertile). In sum, the ideal bride.

But then what about Giulia Bembo's husband, the feudal lord from Venice's mainland empire? He was the other half of the bridal equation. The Friuli was new terrain for me, and the project entailed a number of trips to Udine to research the Della Torre family archive in the Archivio di Stato and related material in the Biblioteca Comunale. Three books—Edward Muir's *Mad Blood Stirring: Vendetta in Renaissance Italy*; Antonio Conzato's *Dai castelli ai corti*; and Laura Casella's *I Savorgnan*—and a wealth of articles were essential for my understanding of the complex dynamic between the Venetian patriciate, the feudal nobility of the Friuli, and the Holy Roman Empire. But as I carried out my research, the playing field was expanding both chronologically and spatially. For Gian Matteo's career as a 'man of empire', and Girolamo's exile to Crete, were other parts of the story.

Following this line of research brought me into contact with Venice's maritime territories. The publications of Chryssa Maltezou, Maria Georgopoulou, Benjamin Arbel, Monique O'Connell, Lorenzo Calvelli, and Helena Szépe were particularly important for my journey into what was, for me, previously unexplored territory. In the course of two decades of research, I went on to publish several articles on various aspects of the topic, parts of which have been incorporated into this book. More recently, I had the opportunity to review Erin Maglaque's book, *Venice's Intimate Empire: Family Life and Scholarship in the Renaissance Mediterranean.* And I finally accepted the fact that my own book in progress was about more than a bride. It was about the mingling of the bloodlines of two families with contrasting notions of honour and justice in three spatial theaters over three centuries. A study of their lives opened a precious window into a past in which Venetian republican values clashed with the deeply rooted feudal traditions of the mainland. And thanks to an anonymous reader for Oxford University Press, I retitled the book to *The Venetian Bride: Bloodlines and Blood Feuds in Venice and Its Empire*—a far more accurate description of its contents.

And what happened to the notion of a microhistory? I would refer readers to Thomas Cohen's masterful definition of the genre in his essay entitled 'The Macrohistory of Microhistory'. He calls attention to a weariness with 'the Linguistic turn and the rise of theory' and the emergence of a desire for what he calls 'suchness', defined as 'palpable reality, as experienced directly and as understood by its inhabitants'. How do we get at it? Through examinations of individual agency, material things, spaces, places, and time. In sum, a deep dive into the archives. Given the fragmentary nature of surviving evidence, we can only hope to piece together a patchwork of experiences that these inhabitants of the historical past—Girolamo Della Torre and Giulia Bembo and their extended families: past, present, and future—might recognize as their own, and to stitch this patchwork into a matrix that comprises the larger world in which they lived. One can never get it exactly right, but one can try to come close.

What is the significance of the marriage of Girolamo Della Torre and Giulia Bembo? I see it as emblematic of the Venetian experience, with the metropole at the center of a fragmented empire: the union of a Terraferma nobleman and the daughter of a Venetian senator, who raised their family in the stato da mar, in the stato da terra, and in Venice itself. And who, beyond that, established a bloodline that would survive the end of the Venetian republic. In sum, a microhistory embedded in a macrohistory.

PART ONE
BIRTHRIGHTS

1

A Future Bride

Antonia Bembo was not blessed by marital good fortune. Daughter of the humanist diplomat Bernardo Bembo, and sister of Pietro, man of letters and later a renowned cardinal, she had married the noble Sebastiano Marcello in June 1493. On the face of things, his prospects were good. An experienced *sopracomito* (galley captain), he had already served as podestà of Montona (Istria) and castellano and camerlengo of Lepanto. Indeed, he seemed destined to become a prototypical Venetian man of empire. After the marriage, Sebastiano settled down with Antonia for a time, with government positions inside Venice, and Marcella, the first of three daughters, was born in February 1496.[1]

A New Malady

But soon, disquieting news emerges from Pietro Bembo's correspondence. In a letter dated 3 December 1498, he consoles a close friend who had recently contracted the *morbo francese*. He knows how hard this is, because 'the husband of my sister has been suffering from this malady already for many months, now healthy, now sick, and mostly bad'. He counsels his friend to continue with his treatment until it is complete, even though he may think himself healed.[2]

Antonia's husband Sebastiano had fallen victim to a disease of disputed origins that had already been described by the Venetian diarist Marin Sanudo in July 1496, shortly after Marcella's birth:

> Note that due to celestial influences, two years ago, that is, since the coming of the French in Italy, a new malady was discovered in the human body called the *mal franzoso*, which disease has spread throughout Italy, as well as Greece, Spain, and almost the entire world. And it is of such a nature that it overwhelms the limbs, the hands and feet with a type of gout, and makes pustules and inflamed blisters over the entire body and on the face, with fever and arthritic pains…with such misery that the patient calls for death. And this sickness begins first in the area of the genitals; and in coitus it is contagious, otherwise not. It is said that even children have it. Its duration will vary widely, and it is conclusively a filthy disease, but few die of it. Which malady, although many say it came from the French, they also have had it for two years, and they call it the *mal italiano*.[3]

The Venetian Bride: Bloodlines and Blood Feuds in Venice and Its Empire. Patricia Fortini Brown, Oxford University Press (2021). © Patricia Fortini Brown. DOI: 10.1093/oso/9780192894571.003.0001

Striking the highborn as well as the low, the mysterious disease, later called syphilis, swept through the papal court in Rome, infecting Cardinal Cesare Borgia, son of Pope Alexander VI, and at least seven other cardinals. It also seems to have plagued the Este family of Ferrara.[4]

As Sanudo had observed, the disease was not usually fatal, at least in the early stages. After a year or so, it typically entered a latent phase without symptoms, but was still transmittable to others. And herein lay a silent but deadly threat to chaste wives, and, indeed, any future sexual liaison. A tertiary stage, with paralysis, blindness, dementia, and death, might appear only decades after the initial infection.[5]

Perplexed doctors tried a variety of treatments on desperate patients. Those endured by Sebastiano might have included bloodletting, ointments and baths of wine and herbs, toxic applications of mercury, the cauterizing of sores, and sweats in dry heat. None would have been truly effective, but as his disease entered the latent phase, Sebastiano may well have thought himself cured.[6] While he would undoubtedly have contracted the disease from a prostitute or courtesan, his infidelity was thus not the biggest problem facing Antonia. The conjugal debt was enshrined in canon law, and during the periods in which Sebastiano felt himself 'now healthy', it had to be paid.

By June 1499, Sebastiano is serving as podestà of Cologna Veneta, a small commune in Veronese territory, accompanied by Antonia and their second-born daughter, Maria, known as Marietta. Pietro has joined his parents in Ferrara, where his father Bernardo is serving a two-year term as *visdomino* (Venetian consul in residence) at the court of Isabella d'Este. Little Marcella is staying there as well with her grandparents and already learning her letters. Pietro writes Sebastiano an affectionate note, assuring him that 'your sorrows and annoyances are my annoyances and sorrows. I expect that the others of our house are also of this mind.' Unsettling words, suggesting that Sebastiano's maladies continue. Maria could have been born as early as 1497 or as late as early 1499, and thus conceived after Sebastiano became infected. But there is no evidence that he passed on the disease to Antonia or the child, and thus to the Marcello bloodline—a danger to which Pietro seems oblivious. After reporting on rumours of war in Naples and Tuscany, he adds that he is sending Sebastiano a female puppy and signs off cheerfully: 'Be well and kiss the *podestaressa* for me, and kiss Marietta for me. La Marcellina has become a great sonneteer.'[7]

Bernardo has returned to Venice from Ferrara by 1500 and is living with his wife Elena in a rented palace at San Trovaso. The household now includes Pietro, and probably his brother Carlo and half-brother Bartolommeo, along with Sebastiano and Antonia and their children. But then world events intervene. At war with the Ottomans for the past year, Venice loses its fortress at Modon on the tip of the Peloponnese in August, and Sebastiano is dispatched as *sopracomito* (captain) of a war galley to Zara, a Venetian port city on the Adriatic, with money and munitions. He dies in Corfù the following April, leaving Antonia a widow, now with three daughters.[8] The third, Giulia, must have been born in this period and would definitely have been conceived after Sebastiano had been infected with the *morbo francese*.

What was expected of a good wife? Juan Luis Vives, in his treatise *De Institutione Feminae Christianae* [*The Education of a Christian Woman*], published in 1523, praised an innocent young girl whose husband, more than twenty years her senior, was infected with the French pox:

> The doctors advised her not to touch him or go close to him. Her friends gave the same advice... She was not deterred by these words, but cared for both soul and body... So, through his wife's care, his life dragged on for ten years after his first illness in his cadaverous body, or more truly, a living tomb. During this time she bore him two children in addition to the six to whom she had already given birth since her marriage at the age of twenty, never becoming infected with her husband's contagious disease... and her children also were endowed with healthy and clean bodies. From this example it becomes clear how great is the virtue and holiness of those women who love their husbands with their whole heart, as is fitting, and how God rewards them in this life.[9]

Again, we have to ask whether Antonia was equally fortunate or whether she or any of her daughters had contracted Sebastiano's disease. Pietro makes no mention of such a dire consequence in his correspondence, and we can only hope that such was not the case.

Unbeknownst to the family, Pietro was involved in a torrid clandestine love affair at the time with Maria Savorgnan, a young aristocratic widow from the Friuli who was living nearby. Maria was a woman of resolve. Sanudo had recorded the extraordinary appearance before the Collegio on 22 December 1498 of

> the widow of Giacomo Savorgnan, our *condottiere* of one hundred horsemen, dead at Pisa... with two little boys and two little girls, most beautiful creatures, and her brother, Domino Anzolo Francesco da Santo Anzolo, also our *condottiere* and the brother-in-law of Sir Girolamo Savorgnan, in mourning clothes. And throwing themselves at the feet of the Signoria, that lady begged for maintenance and for dowries for her daughters because of her husband's fidelity. The Collegio was moved to compassion and the doge said that he would consider her plea, but she received nothing.[10]

Maria left her four children with relatives back in the Friuli and remained in the palace of friends near San Trovaso, where she met Pietro. Even after she went to

Figure 1.1. Valerio Belli, Pietro Bembo (obverse), bronze medal, ca. 1532 (Washington, National Gallery of Art)
The medal is probably a fair likeness of Bembo in his early 60s. Most surviving painted portraits depict him as a bearded patriarch after his election as cardinal in 1539. The verso of the medal depicts him *all'antica*, as a partially nude figure, reclining beside a stream.

Ferrara for carnival celebrations in December 1500 and stayed on, they continued to carry on a passionate correspondence, complete with exchanges of sonnets. He wrote to her on 1 March 1501: 'Love me, love me, love me and a thousand times love me.' They met for the last time in September, when he wrote: 'I pray the gods that they bring to you, a thousand times doubled, that sweetness which you are now removing from my life. It will always be most sweet to me, above all other sweet things, hearing that heaven advances your every desire.'[11]

Pietro did not remain heartbroken for long. Within a year he was residing in a villa near Ferrara and already in love with the golden-haired Lucrezia Borgia, the bride of Alfonso d'Este (himself reputed to be suffering from the *mal francese*). Their dalliance lasted until 1503, and even beyond, when she took on a new lover, her own brother-in-law, the condottiere Francesco II Gonzaga, Marquis of Mantua, husband of Isabella d'Este.[12] Pietro—cultivated, charming, and cash-strapped—went on to lead the life of the courtier, making the rounds of the courts, Mantua, Ferrara, Urbino, and particularly Rome, in search of benefices (Figure 1.1).[13]

Foeminae innocentissimae

Antonia remarried in 1508, further evidence that she had escaped a disfiguring, and shameful, infection with the *mal francese*. Again, the prospects were bright. Giacomo Marcello fu Giovanni, a distant cousin of Sebastiano's and also a galley captain, was a widower without sons.[14] But the marriage did not go well. Commissioned as capitano of the galleys of Beirut, Giacomo sailed away in September.[15] Unlike most men of the sea, when he returned to Venice the following February it was not to his family, but to a courtesan with whom he had been enamoured all along. Antonia, whose mother would die later that year, was miserable. She tried to regain Giacomo's affections 'with humanity, decency, restraint, and patience, making the greatest efforts without saying anything to anyone, to no avail'. When her father became aware of the situation, he too was unsuccessful in persuading the wayward Giacomo to mend his ways. Pietro, referring to his sister as *foeminae innocentissimae* [the most innocent of women], a description that he had used to refer to his own mother, was appalled to hear of Giacomo's 'unprecedented arrogance' and wrote from Urbino to the Patriarch Antonio Contarini in July 1510. He asked him to intervene with his brother-in-law as 'their last hope, the sacred anchor which can save the family from shipwreck'.[16]

Pietro was himself most susceptible to feminine charms, and his moral calculus was clearly different when the shoe was on the other foot. In 1513, the year that he was appointed secretary to Pope Leo X, he met the beautiful Ambrogina Faustina Morosina della Torre, the love of his life (although not the first), in the Borgo outside the Vatican walls. Although only sixteen and already married, Morosina became Pietro's lover and companion, secretly in Rome, but openly when she accompanied him back to the Veneto as his *de facto* wife. From a little-known family of Genoese origins with aristocratic pretensions, she was said to be charming and cultivated, perhaps like her sister Mariola, a Vatican courtesan who owned at least two houses in the Borgo. If Morosina had not been married off with a dowry at such a tender age, she might well have shared a similar fate. Little is known of her husband, not even his name.[17]

Antonia's three daughters—Marcella, Maria, and Giulia—were probably already safely sequestered in the convent of Santa Caterina as boarding students in those years. The precocious Marcella would remain Pietro's favourite niece throughout his life. Back in 1502 he had written to his brother Carlo: 'I am sending to Antonia a couple of Greek rules [grammars] of messer Costantino [Lascaris] for Marcella.'[18] Heavy reading indeed for a six-year-old. Allowing that she was better educated than most of her teachers in the convent, Marcella would have been instructed along with her sisters in the womanly arts of weaving, sewing, and embroidery, in addition to basic reading and writing.

The convent complex, consisting of a church, a large cloister, and dormitories surrounded by high walls, housed widows, battered women, and *converse* (servant nuns), in addition to professed nuns and *foeminae innocentissimae* like the Bembo girls. A *ruota*, a revolving door like a subway turnstile, 'that only one person can enter', was intended to restrict access. It led to the *parlatorio* in which visitors gathered to chat with cloistered nuns—brides of Christ—who were safely secured behind a double grate in an adjacent room. But a letter written by the Patriarch Antonio Surian in 1505 had told a different story. He complained that many of the nuns were 'accustomed to leaving the convent and wandering about the city at leisure *cum scandolo* of many'. He threatened all such transgressors with excommunication. Without much success, it would seem. The same admonition, now applying to all the convents in the city, was repeated in 1509 by the Patriarch Antonio Contarini, to whom Piero had written the following year.[19]

The gap between religious ideals and actual practice, as well as the special status accorded talented courtesans as well as court ladies, was further highlighted by Marin Sanudo in his diary entry of 16 October 1514:

> This morning Lucia Trivixan, who was an excellent singer, was buried at Santa Catarina. She was the consummate courtesan of her day and was held in much esteem by musicians; all of the virtuosi met at her house. She died last night, and eight days from today, at Santa Catarina, the musicians will have a solemn funeral mass and other offices said for her soul.[20]

Whether or not Antonia's husband had changed his ways and abandoned his own courtesan, a mellowed Pietro was addressing him later that year as his *carissimo cognato*—'dearest brother-in-law'.[21] The next we hear of Giacomo is in 1518, when he sailed off as capitano of the galleys of Beirut for two consecutive terms.[22] During his absence, Antonia may have been living in the convent or, more likely, with her father Bernardo. He died on 27 May of the following year at the age of eighty-seven and was buried in San Salvador three days later. Sanudo writes: 'He was an excellent and most learned patrician and senator, especially in the humanities. He served in many ambassadorial missions and governorships... He dedicated himself to his life, continually writing, until the final hour of his illness, fine and well-composed letters filled with every sort of erudition.'[23]

A Very Good and Virtuous Gentleman

The year 1519 had been difficult for Pietro. In addition to his father's death, a trusted employee had robbed him of 600 florins. And now he was responsible for his three nieces. Writing in October to Cardinal Bernardo Bibbiena, he lamented that a long illness had left him

> not only impoverished, but also in debt. Furthermore, as an additional burden on top of so many problems, I had to marry off my niece with a dowry of 3000 florins, not however of cash, that I could not have found, but with an equivalent sum of my annuities assigned to the husband, with several hundred florins in addition. And two other [nieces] already grown, remain on my shoulders, each to be married... I can tell you that I have never found myself at any time of my life more travailed than I find myself now.

But then he reconsiders: 'Leaving melancholy matters aside, I have given my oldest niece, called Marcella, to a very good and virtuous gentleman not only of my

Figure 1.2. Venice, Ca' Bembo on Campiello Santa Maria Nova, built late fourteenth century.

patria, but also of my family, Messer Giovan Mateo Bembo, not rich, but well off enough, esteemed in this city and much honoured for his age, that is, of 28 years. Of this I am well satisfied.'[24] Patrician dowries were limited to 3000 ducats by law, which meant, of course, that this amount was expected by a prospective spouse.[25] After the wedding, Marcella moved from the convent of Santa Caterina into Ca' Bembo, a modest fourteenth-century Gothic palace on Campiello Santa Maria Nova inherited by Gian Matteo (Figure 1.2).[26]

Ever the courtier, Pietro wrote to Pope Leo X about the newlyweds shortly after the marriage: 'Both of them kiss the blessed feet of your *Beatitudine* and humbly bow and kneel before you in supplication, asking that you deign to give them your blessing.'[27] The pope was quick to comply with a letter directly to Gian Matteo, who thereupon forwarded it to Pietro for perusal. Pietro then wrote another letter thanking the pope, sent it back to Gian Matteo, and instructed him to read it and forward it to Rome along with his own response. He also advised his new nephew to have Marcella visit her two sisters at Santa Caterina and ask the abbess and the nuns to 'devote a prayer to God for the health and happiness of Pope Leo'. In his letter to the pope, Pietro had indicated that his mother Antonia was also staying in the convent and that he wished his sisters to remain there, like Marcella, until they were married.[28] Marcella, then twenty-three years old, had received a classical education, unusual for a young woman of her time. With her family connections, she was an ideal wife for a man aspiring to a career in public life. Indeed, with the marriage—and Pietro's support—Gian Matteo's career took off on an upward trajectory.[29]

Giacomo Marcello, Marcella's misbehaving stepfather, returned from his last galley trip on 11 January 1520. Sanudo observes that he 'came to the Collegio dressed in black velvet for the death of ser Bernardo Bembo, doctor and cavalier, his father-in-law'. Giacomo himself died on 14 March before he could present a full report of his voyage to the Senate.[30]

A Valiant Woman

Leaving Morosina behind in the Veneto, Pietro returned to Rome that spring to shore up his financial situation. He writes to Gian Matteo on 26 June, addressing him as *figliuol caro* [dear son].

> It is precious to me that my sister [Antonia] is with you. You should all live happily and lovingly as much as you can. It pleases me that you are often in my house with Madonna Morosina and that she comes sometimes to be with you. It is true that I am a bit envious of you. The more love you show her the more you will please me, and I will be indebted to you…Marcella, dear little girl, I kiss you from here; you will kiss your sisters for me.

He signs himself *Bembus pater*.[31] Marcella is pregnant, and Pietro writes to Gian Matteo again a month later: 'I am pleased that your Marcella has entered the ninth month because she will be over that burdensome labor so much sooner. The child who is born, if male, I would like to be called Quintilio, if female, Lucina.'[32]

The baby was born right on schedule on 10 August, the feast day of San Lorenzo. Pietro writes again on 28 August:

> I rejoice with you for the son who has made you a father, with good health and little annoyance to Marcella, his mother and my daughter. Nor do I demur in celebrating with you that she is a valiant woman, [and] that our lord God would make both you and all your house and ours (that is one alone, both in love and in name) happy with this baby boy. Take care of him well and kiss him in my name many times, and also his mother.[33]

A new bloodline, Bembo twice over, was begun.

Pietro's preference in names is worth noting. Quintilio referred to the Roman rhetorician Quintilian, whose *Institutio Oratoria* was on the bookshelf of any Renaissance humanist worthy of the name. Lucina, the Roman goddess of child-birth, might seem a suitable name for a first daughter, but, perhaps by coincidence, it was also the name of the eldest daughter of Maria Savorgnan, Pietro's lover of two decades earlier.[34]

The new parents honoured Pietro's wishes, at least technically, and named their first son Quintilio Lorenzo (although thereafter they called him Lorenzo). In doing so, they departed from the traditional Venetian practice that privileged the renewal of the ancestors through repetitive names. The firstborn son was typically, but not always, named after his paternal grandfather. If not that, after another relative. But with no Quintilio evident on either side of the baby's family tree, this would be a new beginning, sanctioned by the addition of Lorenzo, the name of his patron saint.[35]

It would not be long before Pietro would write again to Gian Matteo, in January 1521: 'I am pleased that Marcella is expecting [again] in that children will not be lacking. [But] for her, I am worried that she will grow old too quickly. Take care of yourself, and refrain from those bad practices that take away or shorten or weaken and ruin old age.' We can only speculate as to what practices he referred to.[36] When a daughter was born in July, she would be named Augusta—also a name with a Roman pedigree—not Lucina. Her grandmother Antonia probably died soon thereafter, but her presence at the births of both babies must have been a godsend to Marcella, an inexperienced, if erudite, mother of two infants under the age of two.[37] By the end of the decade, Augusta would be followed by four more brothers: Alvise (named after his paternal grandfather), Marco Antonio, Sebastiano, and Davide.[38]

When Pietro returned from the Vatican in the spring of 1521, he held twenty-seven benefices, including the *commenda* of the Knights of St John of Jerusalem in Bologna. Granted by Julius II in 1508, it had required him to join the Order in six months' time, but he had managed to obtain deferrals from Leo X, who even granted him an additional *commenda* of Benevento and appointed him Prior of Hungary. Pietro settled down contentedly with Morosina in Villa Noniano (or Villa Bozza) at S. Maria di Non, a village north of Padua where the Piovego river flows into the Brenta. They would be joined at some point by Maria and Giulia, his unmarried nieces.[39] But then on 1 December, Leo X died unexpectedly. When he was succeeded in January by the hardliner Adrian VI, Pietro knew that he would finally have to take vows. He had been receiving benefices from the Order of St John for fourteen years. No more deferrals could be expected. Undaunted, although he was living openly with Morosina, he finally joined the Order in December 1522. Supplying the requisite proof of four noble grandparents and taking vows of 'true obedience towards every superior given me by God and this Order', he promised 'to live henceforth without any private property and to observe chastity'. He put on the distinctive black habit with the white eight-pointed cross and returned to the villa and Morosina. Although the rules of the Order strictly forbade a member from keeping a concubine—and Morosina, Pietro's *de facto* wife, definitely fell into that category—Pietro blithely ignored the injunction and seems to have suffered no negative consequences. His first child, Lucilio, was born eleven months later, to be followed by Torquato in 1525.[40]

A Modest Affair

Pietro still had to find husbands for his two unmarried nieces, presumably untouched by the *mal francese*. The matter was of some urgency, since both girls were well past the typical age for a first marriage. Maria, born in 1497/8, was his first concern. She was betrothed, finally, in early 1526, to Bernardino Belegno, 'a Venetian gentleman, very well-mannered, and, for his age, much honoured and loved in the city'. Pietro's letters make clear that Maria was a passive player in a game played out by her male relatives. The major protagonists in the negotiation of the marriage contract were Bernardino himself and the Magnifico Pietro Marcello, a distant but very wealthy and influential relative of the bride's birth father. The two men made the agreement official with a handshake. The witnesses included Bernardino's brother Vincenzo and Maria's brother-in-law, Gian Matteo, the latter standing proxy for our Pietro, who had been involved in the negotiations but seems to have remained in Padua.

Pietro Bembo affirms the engagement in a letter to Gian Matteo on 1 March: 'I pray that the lord god would give his blessing. Since you are so content, I remain very satisfied... I am resolved to obey the Magnifico Pietro [Marcello] in all things.' The wedding itself, as orchestrated by the Magnifico, was to take place as soon as possible. It should also be modest, far from the extravagant multi-week affairs for which Venice was famous. Our Pietro continues:

> So, tomorrow morning, God willing, I will mount the barge with Maria and her sister, and we will be with you tomorrow evening. So that Saturday after dinner, at whatever hour his Magnifico determines, she will be married. It would be good if this affair would take place as secretly as possible. Tell Marcella that she should find some clothes for her... and anything else that is needed, even something like a beautiful string of pearls, or whatever is customary. But do it soon, so that it is not late for Saturday. I don't know what else to tell you. You who are there will know the whole thing better than I know.[41]

Why did the Magnifico Pietro, a very distant relative of the bride, take such an interest in the wedding and essentially manage the entire affair? The answer might lie in his ambitions, his wealth, and the political climate. Having entered the Senate back in 1515 with a payment of 500 ducats, he was accustomed to deploying his assets for political advantage. It is unclear whether he subsidized part of Maria's dowry (perhaps with a loan to her uncle Pietro), but one might conjecture that he had been eager to conclude her marriage as swiftly and privately as possible to avoid drawing attention to untidy aspects of the family tree.

Long concerned with maintaining the purity of the patrician bloodline, the nobility were particularly outraged that spring by a marriage between a patrician and a wealthy and sumptuous courtesan, an event that, according to Sanudo, 'has cast great shame on the Venetian patriciate'. The Council of Ten immediately passed legislation making it difficult for any sons born of such unions, not to mention those born to *de facto* wives, to gain admission to the Great Council when they reached maturity. At stake was 'the honour, peace and preservation' of the state, which rested on the 'immaculacy and purity' of the 'status and order of nobility'.[42] Such attitudes might explain Morosina's absence from the wedding party in Ca' Bembo. Admittedly she had two small children to care for, but she was often a visitor in the house and must have been close to the bride. Indeed, it was perhaps no coincidence that the Magnifico would be elected Procurator of San Marco with a contribution of 16,000 ducats on 13 June, a few months after Maria's wedding. The most prestigious office in the Venetian government next to the doge, this lifetime position came with the right to wear a splendid red velvet toga and involved duties such as the administration of estates.[43] Pietro's son Lucilio would die at the age of eight; Torquato would eventually be legitimized by the pope and become a cleric, but he would never be a Venetian patrician.[44]

It was a time for weddings. Gian Matteo must also have been involved, along with his brothers Davide and Bernardo, in the marriage negotiations for his sister Marina to Francesco Tiepolo in 1526. The wedding took place on 5 July 1527. Already cited in her father's will of 7 December 1492, Marina must have been in her mid-thirties—a most mature bride.[45] And, unlike her brothers, completely absent from Pietro's correspondence.

What Fortune Will Bring

Pietro has a respite of three years before Gian Matteo writes him in April 1529 that a suitor has been found for Giulia, the youngest niece, now living with his family in Ca' Bembo. Pietro, by then the father of a daughter, Elena, responds with little enthusiasm:

> Concerning Giulia, I tell you that these are bestial and dangerous times, such that for now I do not want to make that expense. I would like for you to write me

> a line about who he is. I did have a thought which I did not want to write you, that is, that a rich and very kind and wise man had some desire to be related to me. We will see what fortune will bring.

It is worth noting that Pietro views the thirty-year-old Giulia's desirability in terms that relate to himself and not to her own personal charms.[46]

Pietro ponders the situation further and writes to Gian Matteo again three days later: 'God knows that I would like to do every good thing for all my family; you know from past experience that I am of this mind.' But the world is in tumult, and Pietro has lost much of his income and has taxes and loans to pay. For all that, he comes up with a proposition: 'If that young man will be content with 30 *campi* of land that will count for 600 ducats, and take the rest at so much a year, along with that of her mother [Giulia's share of Antonia's dowry], I will gladly consider it. But I cannot give them money, since I do not have a *soldo*.' He cites a tale of a father who would be content to remain in a Spanish prison if it excused him from marrying off his daughter. Pietro concludes: 'I tell you this, and I say it most truly: that if Giulia were my daughter, I would not have had nor will I have now the burden of marrying her, that I would have her become a nun, and she would have to do it, since I being her father, she would have to obey me.'[47]

Giulia's suitor, Marc'Antonio Longo, hopefully 'a rich, and very kind, and wise man', agreed to the terms. The wedding took place in the convent church of Santa Caterina on 18 November 1529, with Bernardino Belegno and Gian Matteo acting as witnesses for the bride.[48] Pietro sent his regards to the couple three weeks later and wrote to Giulia herself the following March, inviting her and Marc'Antonio to visit him and Morosina in Padua.[49] Alas, Giulia died soon thereafter, perhaps in childbirth.[50] But her name would live on, for Marcella was pregnant yet again.

Pietro writes to Gian Matteo in July 1531 during a heat wave. He is concerned about Marcella, 'who with her great body would be faring badly in her prison'. A month later, he writes: 'I am content that Marcella is relieved [from her burden], and also that she has given birth to a baby girl, since you have already have too many boys. I rejoice with her and with you. Take care to stay healthy, and nourish the *bambina* well.'[51] Marcella's second daughter, her seventh child in eleven years, would be named Giulia, thus renewing her sister's name in the family bloodline.

As we have seen from our brief tour through the marital history of the Bembo and Marcello families, brides were the creations of male agency and mediation. It is telling that in documents and genealogies of the fifteenth and early sixteenth centuries women were typically cited without a first name, and only as wives, mothers, or daughters of named male figures. The latter, by contrast, were invariably referred to by a first name along with a patronymic, attesting to the transcendent importance of male lineage.

At the time of her wedding a girl was truly the central figure in a drama, but one that was fully orchestrated by her father, her new husband, and male relatives on both sides. In theory, a girl had the right of refusal; but, in reality, such refusals seldom happened. A generation later, Lodovico Dolce could still write:

> Since a virgin neither knows nor desires the union with man, our young girl will leave all deliberations in her father's hands, accepting gladly as a husband the one [he] will choose. Apart from the fact that this responsibility does not befit a virgin, she would not be able to make a good choice since she has no experience of the world.[52]

The alternative to marriage was the convent, and again it may not have been a matter of choice or vocation. As Pietro Bembo had put it, if Marcella's sister Giulia had been his own daughter, he would have insisted that she become a nun, and 'she would have to do it, since I being her father, she would have to obey me'. Ironically, it turned out that his own daughter Elena resisted life in a convent, and he would give in, marrying her off to a Venetian patrician at the age of fifteen. She was, like her aunt Marcella, a skilled Latinist whose marriage would restrict her literary activities to personal correspondence. And she would be, like her aunt Antonia, the forgiving wife of an unfaithful husband.[53]

That would not, happily, be the case for Pietro's grandniece, the renewed Giulia, a future bride. She was destined for an eventful marriage that played out in three spatial theatres: Venice, the Terraferma, and the Stato da Mar. But before we encounter her as a bride, we must travel back in time to the early sixteenth century and explore the early life of her eventual husband, Count Girolamo Della Torre, a feudal lord from the Friuli, part of Venice's mainland empire. For our Giulia's destiny was determined not only by her Venetian roots, but also by the feudal and ecclesiastical heritage of the extended family of which she would become a part. A decades-long vendetta between the Della Torre and the Savorgnan families was central to that heritage. And, indeed, two generations later, Tristan, grandson of Maria Savorgnan, Pietro Bembo's former lover, would carry out the very act of vengeance that led to the merging of two noble bloodlines with the marriage between Girolamo Della Torre and Giulia Bembo, his Venetian bride.

Notes

1. Giannetto 1985, 52, 204–7. Antonia must have lost her first child. Pietro writes in September 1494 that he had returned to Venice from Sicily to find his sister pregnant. Bembo/Travi, I: 7 (11 or 22 September 1494). Sebastiano served on the Quarantia

Civil Nuova in 1494 and on the Quarantia Civil e Criminale, and as one of the Signori di Notte in 1495. ASVe, *SAV-MC*, r. 5, 16v, 32v; r. 6, 66r, 79r. 129r, r. 9, 9r.

2. Kidwell 2004, 22; Bembo/Travi, I: 34 (3 December 1498). For the spectacular career of Pietro Bembo, see now Beltramini, Gasparotto, and Tura 2013; Nalezyty 2017.
3. Sanudo, *Diarii*, I, 233–4.
4. Arrizabalaga, Henderson, and French 1997, 47–50, 113; Alfani 2013, 109–10.
5. Arrizabalaga, Henderson, and French 1997, 25; Eatough 1984, 11–13.
6. Arrizabalaga, Henderson, and French 1997, 29, 131–42; Frith 2012, 49–58; Tognotti 2006, 29–59; Cohen and Cohen 2001, 244–6.
7. Kidwell 2004, 21–2; Bembo/Travi I, 37, no. 43 (12 June 1499). Modern studies indicate that untreated syphilis is transmitted to around 60 per cent of sexual partners. A child could receive it from an infected mother in the womb or during the birth. See Garnett 1997, 185–200.
8. Sanudo, *Diarii*, 3: 769, 907; 4: 49. Cf. Kidwell 2004, 192, who confuses Sebastiano di Benedetto (Antonia's husband) with Sebastiano di Antonio.
9. Vives 2000, 200–2.
10. Sanudo, *Diarii*, 2: 245; Kidwell 2004, 28–30. Maria was the daughter of the condottiere Matteo Griffoni de Sant' Angelo of Urbino. For Giacomo's will, written in 1495 before he went off to battle, see Casella 2003, 142. The Signoria, the supreme body of Venetian government, typically consisted of the doge, his six councilors, and the three heads of the Quarantia Criminale (criminal courts). The Collegio, the main executive council, comprised the Signoria, plus the five savi agli ordeni, five savi di Terraferma, and six savi di Consiglio. See Labalme and Sanguineti White 2008, 546, 549.
11. Kidwell 2004, 25–8, 62–8; Bembo/Travi, I, no. 126 (1 March 1501); no. 132 (4 September 1501); Nalezyty 2017, 74–87, 97–8. Pietro kept eighty of her letters until his death in 1547; they were discovered in the Vatican archives only in 1950.
12. Kidwell 2004, 71–98; Quatrocchi 2005, 1–5, 10. Gonzaga also exhibited symptoms of the *mal francese*. See Arrizabalaga, Henderson, and French 1997, 47–9.
13. Kidwell 2004, 113–50. For Bembo's possible portrait by Giovanni Bellini in this period, see Shearman, *Early Italian Pictures*, 41–3.
14. For the two marriages, see ASVe, Barbaro, *Genealogie*, IV, cc. 469, 477; MCVe, Barbaro, Genealogie, IV, cc. 305, 308. See also Giannetto 1985, 256 n296. For the probable death of Marcello's wife and daughter in 1503, see Sanudo, *Diarii*, 5: 65.
15. Sanudo, *Diarii*, 7: 440–1, 461, 628, 741; ibid. 8: 11–12.
16. Quotations from Kidwell 2004, 192, 411n31. For the letter, see Bembo/Travi, II, 299 (7 July 1510), incorrectly naming the patriarch as Domenico Contarini. For Elena's death, see Kidwell 2004, 146; Bembo/Travi, II, 293. Sanudo, *Diarii*, 10: 18, incorrectly refers to the death of a *figlia* of Bernardo Bembo on 4 March 1510. He may be referring to the death of Bernardo's wife Elena in 1509. Gianetto, 253, accepts the date, but cf. Kidwell 2004, 192, noting that Antonia is cited in Pietro's letters up to 1521. BMVe, MS, it. Cl., VII, 8307(=18), Cappellari Vivaro, *Il Campidoglio veneto,* 3:31, cites incorrect names for Antonia's daughters, again disproven by Pietro's letters. See Gianetto, 205n297.

17. Kidwell 2004, 174–5, 199–200. Although he seems to have still been alive in the 1530s, he simply disappeared from the pages of history without any record of an annulment or divorce. For concubinage, see Byars 2019, 22–59, esp. 33–42.
18. Bembo 1564a, 11r–11v (8 October 1502). Cf. Bembo/Travi, I, no. 138, with a misreading of 'Antonia' as 'Antonio'. Pietro had studied Greek with Lascaris, one the greatest Byzantine scholars of the day, in Messina. See Kidwell 2004, 11; Wyatt 2014, 13.
19. Canosa 1996, 47–8; Toffolo, *Art and the Conventual Life*, 1–37; Laven 2003.
20. Labalme and Sanguineti White 2008, 322.
21. Kidwell 2004, 148, 192; Bembo/Travi, II, 345 (4 December 1514). Unaware of Antonia's marriage to Giacomo in 1510, both Kidwell and Travi incorrectly assume that this refers to Sebastiano (who died in 1501).
22. Sanudo, *Diarii*, 26: 386, 437; ibid. 27: 156, 536, 574.
23. Ibid. 27: 324–5. English translation from Labalme and Sanguineti White 2008, 430.
24. Bembo/Travi, II, no. 392 (1 October 1519). See also Brown 2013a, 232–3. Gian Matteo was born on 21 August 1490. His father Alvise q. Zaccaria had died in 1501, and was presented for membership in the Great Council by his mother Pentesilea Michiel. See ASVe, AC, r. 165, 24v (1 December 1511). She also presented his brothers Davide (ibid. 25r; August 1514) and Bernardo (ibid. 26v; 9 October 1516).
25. Chojnacki 2000, 67–72. The limit was raised from 1600 ducats to 3000 in 1505. The wealthiest families frequently violated the limits with dowries of 10,000 ducats or more.
26. ASV, NT, b. 1259, n. 507. For the layout, see Brown 2004, 188–9, 190–6; Maretto 1978, 74–7; Maretto 1986, 115–20.
27. Bembo/Travi, II, no. 393 (4 November 1519).
28. Ibid. No. 394 (15 November 1519).
29. Brown 2013a, 231–49.
30. Sanudo, *Diarii*, 28: 166, 168–9, 352.
31. Kidwell 2004, 194; Bembo/Travi, II, no. 400 (26 June 1520).
32. Bembo/Travi, II, no. 402 (28 July 1520).
33. Ibid. II, no. 404 (28 August 1520).
34. Lucina was born well before her mother Maria's romance with Pietro.
35. ASVe, AC, r. 51, 15r. For naming strategies see Brown 2004, 16–18, 255; Grubb 1996, 42–7. Cf. Klapisch-Zuber 1985, 283–309.
36. Bembo/Travi, II, no. 412. See Bell 1999, 27–33.
37. With the birth of Augusta imminent, Antonia is still living on 5 July 1521. Bembo/Travi, II, no. 417 (5 July 1521). He does not mention Antonia in subsequent letters. She probably died before 10 December 1522, when Pietro sends his love to Marcella and others, but not to his sister.
38. Brown 2004, 94–5.
39. Kidwell 2004, 201–2, Bembo/Travi, II, 417; 670.
40. Kidwell 2004, 198–9, 202. Lucio was born in November 1523, Torquato on 10 May 1525.
41. Kidwell 2004, 265–6; Bembo/Travi, II, 647 (27 February 1526), 648 (1 March 1526), 652 (16 March 1526), 670 (21 April 1526). The Magnifico Pietro shared a common ancestor with Sebastiano Marcello back in the thirteenth and fourteenth centuries.

Andrea di Giovanni (d. 1318) was the fourth great grandfather of the former and the third great grandfather of the latter. ASVe, Barbaro, *Genealogie*, IV, cc. 469, 479; MCVe, Barbaro, *Genealogie*, IV, cc. 305, 309.

42. Sanudo, *Diarii*, 41: 201, 203; Chojnacki 2000, 53–75, esp. 64.
43. Brown 2004, 166–7; Sanudo, *Diarii*, 41: 539–40, 616; ASVe, Barbaro, *Genealogie*, IV, c. 479; MCVe, Barbaro, *Genealogie*, IV, 309. He was a Procuratore di Citra, with jurisdiction over the three sestieri north of the Grand Canal. See Hart and Hicks 2017, 91–2, 192.
44. Kidwell 2004, 257–8.
45. ASVe, *Ospedali e Luoghi Pii Diversi*, b. 236, Processo A, c. 2; ASVe, *AC*, r. 87, 299; MCVe, Barbaro, *Genealogie*, VII, c. 20; ASVe, Barbaro, *Genealogie*, VII, f. 89.
46. Ibid. 266; Bembo Travi, III, 951 (23 April 1529). Pietro's daughter Elena was born on 30 May 1528.
47. Kidwell 2004, 266; Bembo/Travi, III, 952 (26 April 1529). For the burdens that dowries imposed on fathers, uncles, and brothers, see Chojnacki 2000, 132–52, and *passim*.
48. ASVe,AC, r. 87, 22v (10 December 1529).
49. Bembo/Travi, III, no. 1034 (7 December 1529); no. 1047 (2 March 1530); Brown 2004, 95.
50. Marc'Antonio married a second wife in 1532. ASVe, Barbaro, *Genealogie*, IV, c. 300; MCVe, Barbaro, *Genealogie*, IV, c. 190. It is likely that Giulia died before February 1531, when Pietro refers in a letter to Gian Matteo about Marc'Antonio's wish to embark on a ship bound for Candia. Bembo/Travi, III, no. 1197 (11 February 1531).
51. Bembo/Travi, III, nos. 1264 (31 July 1531); 1292 (26 September 1531).
52. Dolce 1547, 31, quoted in Rogers and Tinagli 2005, 117.
53. After Morosina's death in 1535, Pietro's daughter Elena was placed in a convent in Padua. In October 1543, Pietro, by then a cardinal, entrusted Gian Matteo Bembo to negotiate her marriage to the Venetian patrician Pietro Gradenigo. See Ross 2009, 54–66; Kidwell 2004, 346, 352–4. See also Medioli 2000, 122–37.

2
A Bitter Bequest

Girolamo Della Torre would never forget the Cruel Carnival of 1511, when his world would change forever. In a savage orgy of violence on the evening of Giovedì Grasso (*Zobia Grassa* in Venetian dialect), normally the high point of Carnival in Udine, he lost his father, an uncle, two cousins, and his family's closest friends. The memory of this cataclysmic event lived on in the Friuli for centuries. It was recounted in diaries and chronicles in its own time and in articles and books in ours, most notably Edward Muir's *Mad Blood Stirring: Vendetta in Renaissance Italy*. But it is fundamental to our story and must be retold here once again.[1] It was a bitter bequest.

A Gathering Storm

Girolamo, born in 1504 as the second son of the Friulian lord Alvise Della Torre, had led a privileged childhood, divided between a luxurious family palace in the city of Udine and the seignorial castle of Villalta in the countryside seven miles to the west. But what should have been a comfortable life was not a carefree one—for the boy had been born in the eye of a gathering storm. The Patria del Friuli, part of Venice's mainland empire since the 1420s, was in a state of siege (Figure 2.1). It was threatened from without by the Turks, who saw it as the gateway to the west; by other European powers who resented Venice's expansionary policies; and by the Holy Roman Emperor Maximilian I (1459–1519), who eyed it hungrily from north of the Alps as his rightful inheritance. It was threatened from within by a polarized nobility and an increasingly restive mixture of oppressed peasants and discontented townspeople.[2]

Decades earlier, Marin Sanudo had commented on the fragile balance of power in the Patria, split between two 'vigorous and organized factions', following old alignments of Ghibellines and Guelphs. The Strumieri, a consortium comprising most of the castellans—the feudal nobility based in castles in the countryside—was led by the Della Torre family and included the Colloredo, Strassoldo, Spilimbergo, Collalto, Castello, Valvasone, Brazzaco, and Partistagno, among others. Initially resistant to the Venetian takeover of the Friuli and the whittling away of their legal sway over the lives of their peasants, the Strumieri were seen by many (not without reason) as exploiters of the poor. Like their Ghibelline predecessors, they were accused of supporting the emperor. The Venetians, well

The Venetian Bride: Bloodlines and Blood Feuds in Venice and Its Empire. Patricia Fortini Brown, Oxford University Press (2021). © Patricia Fortini Brown. DOI: 10.1093/oso/9780192894571.003.0002

Figure 2.1. Abraham Ortelius, *Patria del Friuli*, 1573, from. *Theatrum Orbis Terrarum Abrahami Ortelii Antverp. Geographi Regii.* Antwerp, Plantin Press, 1601.
The Venetian Terraferma includes Istria and part of the Veneto (colored green) and the Friuli (bordered in yellow). Imperial lands are bordered in red.

aware that the Hapsburgs offered tempting imperial favours to the castellans—pensions, fiefs, posts, debt management, and status—regarded their loyalty with caution, if not suspicion.[3]

The Zamberlani, Guelph counterparts to the Ghibelline Strumieri, were headed by the Savorgnan family. Elected to the Venetian patriciate—an extraordinary honour—in the fourteenth century, the Savorgnan had supported Venice's move into the Friuli with men and arms. Although the wealthiest clan in the Patria in terms of both land and riches, the Savorgnan fashioned themselves as protectors of peasants and the common people and were supported by 'quasi il populo tutto'. They also had allies in Udine among a newly noble mercantile class which resented the swaggering demeanour and superior attitude of the castellans, including the Della Torre, who maintained residences inside the city. Within a society already stratified along lines of hereditary privilege and economic class, the elites were themselves thus profoundly divided.[4]

Udine itself had a split personality. On the one hand, it was the urban hub of a rural hinterland, with roads radiating out from a dozen or so portals to

Figure 2.2. Joseph Heintz il Giovane, attrib., *View of Udine*, c. 1650–60 (Udine, Civici Musei, Galleria d'Arte Antica).

castles and villages dotted throughout the surrounding plain and foothills of the Alps (Figure 2.2). On the other hand, it was inward looking. The city had grown up around the *colle*, a prominent hill surmounted by the Castello, the thirteenth-century palace of the patriarch of Aquileia, who wielded temporal and spiritual authority in the region. It was protected by five circuits of walls that had been built over time. After the Venetian conquest in 1420, the Castello remained the administrative centre of the Patria and served as residence of the luogotenente, a rotating post held by a Venetian noble for sixteen months, with an attendant cadre of officials. The real centre of political authority remained, however, in Venice.[5]

The Serenissima successfully controlled the fractious nobles for a time by playing one group against the other and securing vows of allegiance from both, and yet the internal situation remained volatile. The contentious relationship between the Della Torre and some of the Savorgnan was particularly complicated. A property dispute dating to 1339 had given rise to a feud that would flare up periodically over the next two centuries and beyond. During the last decades of the fifteenth century, the streets of Udine and Cividale, the most important cities in the territory, were filled with partisans brandishing pennants, one side shouting *Savorgnan, Savorgnan* and the other *Struma, Struma* or *Torre, Torre*, and proclaiming their allegiance to one side or the other with special signs such as flowers, foliage, or other insignia attached to their ears, hats, shoes, or other parts of their dress.[6]

There were also more specific provocations. In 1478 the Venetian luogotenente Zuane Emo railed against the Strumieri (and the Della Torre in particular) in a session of the citizen council of Udine:

> At the time of the patriarchs they were accustomed to do what they wished in this city and throughout the Patria. They lament that it is no longer that time: and this is the cause of their rage. But those who took the land in the name of our Illustrious Signoria did badly in that they did not cut off the heads of those who were of that house.[7]

In response, Francesco Della Torre complained bitterly to Venetian authorities that Emo had favoured the Savorgnan from the outset and showed his own family 'capital hatred' and no justice: 'Whereas we are innocent and averse to any discord, he has sought to treat us as guilty and as troublemakers.'[8]

Two years later, Isidoro Della Torre was attacked by assassins and left for dead. His family claimed that the crime was perpetrated by Antonio Savorgnan (who later became their prime enemy), but the evidence was scanty. Although the Council of Ten banished the unknown assailants in absentia, no one was charged, and the Della Torre remained convinced that the Venetian deck was stacked against them.[9] Still, the Republic strove to maintain an even hand. A Venetian order of that year was one of many forbidding the wearing of insignia of factional identity by men, women, and even children. Although penalties ranged from fines to lashes to prison, such rulings had little success. As with sumptuary laws everywhere, new fashions were quickly devised to replace those that had been banned.[10] Public gatherings of the opposing factions were also prohibited, but were held anyway. Sanudo observed: 'And I have seen chains across some streets that can be closed so that one cannot pass', to prevent confrontations.[11]

The large Savorgnan clan boasted a family tree that looked like a thicket, with several branches stemming from a common ancestor in the thirteenth century. By the late fifteenth century, the most significant for our story were the two bloodlines descending from Tristano Savorgnan dello Scaglione, whose father Federico had been granted Venetian noble status in 1385: (1) the Savorgnan del Torre (not to be confused with the Della Torre), led by the brilliant but hot-tempered Antonio Savorgnan del Torre, the leader of the Zamberlani in the last decade of the fifteenth century and a bitter enemy of our little Girolamo's father Alvise; and (2) the Savorgnan del Monte, headed by Antonio's cousin and rival Girolamo, and, by contrast, a Della Torre ally.[12]

Girolamo Savorgnan del Monte had married Alvise's first cousin, Maddalena Della Torre, in 1491, in the third of three Savorgnan–Della Torre marriages in the fifteenth century. Maddalena's father Raimondo having died, Alvise and his brother Isidoro acted as her guardians and guaranteed a dowry of 1500 ducats plus 200 ducats from her mother. It is worth noting that the dowry signing, held in the sacristy of San Francesco in Udine, was attended by members of both the Strumieri and Zamberlani factions in a rare moment of aristocratic unity, but not, it is also worth noting, by Antonio Savorgnan del Torre. The Savorgnan clan was itself thus divided. Although Maddalena would die after bearing four children in four years a decade before the birth of our Girolamo, the relationship between Girolamo Savorgnan del Monte and the Della Torre remained reasonably amicable.[13] And, it might be noted, it was this Savorgnan's brother Giacomo who had been the husband of Maria, onetime lover of Pietro Bembo.[14]

The Turkish incursions of the late fifteenth century had heightened a general sense of insecurity among the castellans and worsened the already tenuous condition of both the peasants, who were forced to pay them higher levies, and the city dwellers, who were faced with higher prices for agricultural products. Antonio Savorgnan del Torre sought to press his advantage. Shrewdly choosing clientage over immediate profit, he distanced himself from most of the other feudal lords, estranged from both their Friulian subjects and their Venetian masters, and set himself up for virtual lordship in the city of Udine. Toward this end, he built up a loyal following among rural militias made up of contadini and rallied urban artisans and small merchants against the Strumieri—most notably Alvise Della Torre—as exploiters of the *popolo minuto* and as lords whose knightly pretensions aligned them more closely to the Empire than to the Venetian republic.[15]

In his earlier years, Alvise had pursued a military career. According to later sources, he had spent several years in France, probably in the 1480s, serving with distinction in unspecified wars and attaining a 'significant rank' in the army of King Charles VIII.[16] Alvise was back in Udine by the beginning of 1494. The following year, in response to an urgent appeal from the Venetian Signoria, he provided one hundred horsemen drawn from his own peasants and villagers to defend the Republic against invasions led by the French king he had once served. But his service was undermined by Antonio Savorgnan's populist strategy, for once Alvise's troops left the confines of the Patria, so many broke ranks to 'serve under another captain' (presumably Savorgnan) that the Venetian doge wrote to his *provveditori* in the field 'that the *disobedienti* should be admonished and reminded of their obligation to recognize Della Torre as their *capo* and no other'.[17]

By August 1499, in an about face, Venice had allied itself with France and made plans to attack Milan, despite reports that the Turks were about to invade the Friuli. Alvise appeared with a delegation before the Collegio in Venice, pleading for improved fortifications, munitions, and men to defend Udine. But Venetian resources were stretched thin and the request was ignored. By the end of September, in an eight-day orgy of violence, the Turks had burned 132 villages and slaughtered or enslaved more than ten thousand people throughout the territory. Although Udine was spared, several castellans holed themselves up in their castles, and ignobly left their subjects to their own devices. Venice's failure to protect the countryside only encouraged peasants and villagers to seek protection from the Zamberlani and for the Strumieri to remain receptive to overtures from the Emperor Maximilian.[18]

A Papal Dispensation

In 1500 Alvise, then around fifty years old, was finally ready to start a family after years on the battlefield. Of his two brothers, Isidoro was not inclined to marry and Francesco had died ten years earlier, leaving only one son, Nicolò. A marriage that produced more sons would better ensure the survival of the family line. Strategic in their marriage arrangements, the Della Torre had created links over the course of the fifteenth century to the most powerful castellan families of the Patria—including the Colloredo, Strassoldo, Spilimbergo, Collalto, Valvasone, Brazzaco, Partistagno, and (as we have seen) even the Savorgnan. Alvise was no exception, but his choice of Taddea Strassoldo as his bride raised several issues. First, there was a great disparity in their ages, probably more than thirty years. This was not the norm in the Friuli, particularly for first-time grooms. While brides might be as young as sixteen, husbands were rarely over twenty-five, and often younger than twenty.[19] But for Alvise, the first imperative was to perpetuate the lineage, and an ideal bride would have many child-bearing years ahead of her. Like most nobility of the time, the two families viewed marriage as a matter of business rather than romance. It is most unlikely that Taddea was consulted in the matter. Second, the dowry was also a matter of concern, but according to the contract signed in the Strassoldo family palace in Udine, Taddea brought a suitable 1400 ducats, to be paid in instalments, and 'alia ornamenta et preparamenta' (other ornaments and preparations—that is, her trousseau) guaranteed by her widowed mother Victoria and her brother Ettore. But third, and potentially more troublesome, Taddea's paternal uncle Ropretto Strassoldo was married to Alvise's sister Anna. Although this was not a close blood relationship, a papal dispensation was still necessary. It was granted on 8 August and confirmed by the patriarchal vicar on 26 August, with the union taking place four days later in the sacristy of the ancestral Della Torre church of San Francesco. Witnesses included close male friends and relatives from the two families.[20] It is worth noting that it was a Sunday wedding—considered auspicious according to popular belief in Venice, but a bad augury in the Friuli.[21] In retrospect, one might suggest that it was a superstition that should not have been ignored.

The Savorgnan family had shrewdly followed a different marital strategy. Although they too married within the Friuli, they also sought to reinforce their privileged status in Venice with marriages to Venetian brides. After the early death of his first wife, Maddalena Della Torre, Girolamo Savorgnan del Monte married a succession of three Venetian widows, thus grafting his family tree to the Tron, the Malipiero, and the Canal, as well as those of their former spouses, the Tiepolo and the Marcello—some of the most distinguished families of the lagoon patriciate. The four marriages produced no less than twenty-four children, more than enough to ensure the perpetuation of the lineage.[22]

After his marriage to Taddea, Alvise turned his attention from the battlefield to domestic and civic affairs. He represented Villalta in the parliament of the Friuli and frequently travelled to Venice on official matters. When Leonardo Loredan was elected doge in October 1501, Alvise was a member of a delegation of six dispatched to congratulate him.[23] But his first duty was to secure the survival of the Della Torre line. His son Raimondo, probably born in 1502, was followed by Girolamo in 1504 and then by Giovanni and Ginevra in close succession. Alvise also increased the family holdings, buying up land with his brother Isidoro, sometimes in competition with Antonio Savorgnan. For the feudal nobility, land was money. The Della Torre family fortune was built largely on payments in kind from villani (sharecroppers and peasants) and rents from villagers.[24]

Living in draughty hovels of wood and straw rather than in sturdy castles of stone, the dour-faced peasants labouring in the fields grumbled that few fruits of the harvest ended up on their own tables. In response to a sustained agrarian crisis of low yields and high prices, the castellans attempted to control the market and to restrict the rights of peasants to farm the land as they saw fit. Matters came to a head in November 1503, when the Friulian parliament passed a law prohibiting tenants from making improvements on their land without their landlord's permission, along with other restrictions of long-cherished rights.[25] In the face of rowdy protest meetings, Francesco Strassoldo, a Della Torre relative, spoke for his fellow castellans:

> Our peasants, daring without fear [and encouraged by Antonio Savorgnan, although this was unstated], have created monopolies, conventicles, and assemblies in various villages and places of this Patria, of five hundred, eight hundred, a thousand or two thousand people and more, where they have among other things, made some very evil and diabolical statements about cutting to pieces prelates, gentlemen, castellans and citizens, and, then, that they will carry out a Sicilian Vespers.[26]

Savorgnan defended the peasants, arguing that they should be helped rather than exploited and called for a return to the paternalism of earlier generations. Aiming to set himself up as 'a prince without a title', he understood the power of clientage and social capital over economic profit. It was a distinction that escaped castellans like Alvise Della Torre, who countered with his own speech against the peasants. In this pivotal moment he became the face of the enemy, setting in motion a chain of events that would culminate in the disaster of 1511.[27]

With the two sides deadlocked, each sent a delegation to Venice, arriving on the last day of December. Sanudo reported that

> six orators representing the castellans and the parliament, along with many other castellans, and also four orators from Udine and many peasants, appeared before the Collegio and spoke of great turmoil in that province. Lord Francesco Strassoldo charged that many peasants, from 500 to 1000, had risen up against their castellans and threatened to kill all of them.

Speaking in defence of the peasants, a Savorgnan ally quoted scripture: '*Infunde iram tuam in inimicis* [Pour out thy wrath upon the enemies] and not the peasants.' The Doge, unsympathetic to such bellicose threats to the established hierarchy, responded harshly: 'The heads of such sedition will be punished, and the peasants should be peasants, nor can they have meetings without the permission of the luogotenente. And he ordered all of them to leave.'[28]

The countryside was in chaos, with raids by imperial mercenaries, as well as the uprisings by emboldened peasants. While the Patria had recovered from the last of four Turkish invasions in 1499, the threat remained and the worst was yet to come, but from another direction. The area—still dotted with imperial enclaves—became a focus of renewed interest for the Emperor Maximilian, who sought to reclaim the rest of territory.

Outside foes created new allies, however reluctant. In February 1508, Alvise—now the father of four young children—strapped on his armour once more, this time in defence of the Republic against the emperor, and rode off to Tolmezzo with Antonio Savorgnan's natural son and closest ally, Nicolò, known as 'Cherubino'. Armed with small cannons and ammunition, they led two hundred soldiers 'both on foot and on horseback' to support the condottiere Bartolomeo d'Alviano, commander of the Venetian armies.[29] In April, Della Torre galloped alongside Antonio Savorgnan himself to defend the fortress at Gorizia against imperial troops, without, however, engaging them. In May the two enemies travelled to Venice together as part of a delegation of six, dispatched by the parliament of the Friuli to celebrate the Venetian acquisition of Pordenone, Gorizia, and Trieste.[30]

The triumph was short-lived. In December, the treaty creating the League of Cambrai was signed by France, Mantua, Ferrara, Spain, the pope, and the emperor, with the aim of taking over Venice's mainland territories. The Empire's share would be the Patria del Friuli. The events of the year 1509 threatened Venice's very survival. On 14 May, after nearly six months of fighting, the Venetian Republic suffered a crushing defeat at Agnadello by the French, losing nearly all its mainland territories. The Emperor Maximilian, ready to press his advantage, proposed taking Venice itself and dividing it into four parts to be distributed to the major powers in the League.[31]

Reports reached Udine in June that 6000 imperial troops had taken back Gorizia and Trieste with great cruelty and were expected to attack Udine itself. Rumours created panic in the city, and the interests of Della Torre and Savorgnan were again aligned. Leonardo Amaseo, a Della Torre partisan, documented events of the time in his diary: 'the city was up in arms . . . those of the Savorgnan, those of the Della Torre . . . and many others escaped with all their movable possessions and wives to Venice, and as a result, Udine is upside down.'[32]

This may have been one of the earliest memories of the four-year-old Girolamo Della Torre. Was he left in the care of servants at Villalta or sent to Venice with his mother? The diarist did not provide further particulars, but in either case, the atmosphere must have been one of impending catastrophe.

A Great Shadow

By early July 1509, the old enemies—Savorgnan and Della Torre—were both back in Udine. It could not have helped matters that their city palaces (both since demolished) were near one another in the same borgo: Palazzo Torriani with its gardens and outbuildings covered a large plot in the area of the present Piazza XX Settembre, while Palazzo Savorgnan was just a few minutes' walk away on the neighbouring piazza behind the church of San Francesco. Amaseo transcribed an anonymous letter written to the luogotenente:

> I inform your Magnificence that there is a great shadow over the commoners of this your most faithful city, because the leading citizens of this city keep armed men in their homes, which causes concern about some [secret] pact and novelty; [about] which thing, in my belief, there is no one, either great or small, who would not be loyal and devoted to our illustrious Signoria. But to dispel the shadows, I recommend to your Magnificence that you should make the magnificent messer Antonio Savorgnan, messer Alvise Della Torre, messer Camillo de Colloredo, and other leading citizens, work closely together daily with righteous fraternal love, to lift that shadow from the commoners of our city, so that it may be known expressly by such discourse, that the citizens as well as the commoners have one will and one mind about the well-being and honour and glory of the state of Messer San Marco.[33]

Again, the plea seems to have fallen on deaf ears. At the end of the month, the castle of Sterpo, an imperial fief belonging to the Colloredo, was pillaged and burned in a savage peasant revolt. Alvise Della Torre was quick to point to Savorgnan as the instigator and accused him and his followers of 'rustic bestiality'. Savorgnan shot back that Della Torre was an enemy of the Republic and ready to betray it.[34] In response, the Council of Ten repeatedly admonished the two adversaries to make peace and settle their differences. Indeed, a letter to the Collegio of 23 August from the Venetian provveditore Francesco Cappello in Udine brought the welcome news of 'the reconciliation between Antonio Savorgnan and his cousin Girolamo, and these were [also] reconciled with lord Alvise Della Torre'.[35] But any suspension of hostilities was superficial and short-lived; populist rage had a quickening pace and its own momentum.

In the following year of 1510, the great shadow of vendetta continued to hover over the countryside as well as the city. Chronicles of the time were filled with a litany of attacks and counterattacks, protests, confrontations, forced truces, and broken promises. On 20 January a delegation of forty-six castellans and Udinese citizens appeared before the Venetian Signoria. Amaseo wrote:

> The subject of their argument was this, that the magnificent messer Antonio Savorgnan wanted to be lord of the Patria, and was not content with his station, but he wished to be both luogotenente and proveditore [military general] and that he wanted to distinguish the faithful from the unfaithful, that is, to label as a rebel whoever he wanted, and to create enmities between the peasants and the castellans.[36]

Jacomo de Castello lamented that 'all the poor castellans have stayed in their castles in great fear, anxious not to be cut to pieces by the peasants and burned out as happened at Sterpo'. He promised the doge that the castellans would willingly defend the Patria from Venice's enemies if 'his sublimity would see to it that messer Antonio Savorgnan would be content with his station, and not engage in seditious or scandalous behavior'. Swearing obedience to the 'magnificent luogotenente, who is a most worthy person, and the magnificent proveditore', the castellans then avowed, 'if his sublimity would do this, everything would turn out perfectly'.[37]

Unfortunately, it was not to be. For the Strumieri could themselves be deliberately provocative, none more so than Alvise Della Torre's nephew Nicolò, labelled 'the most bestial' by Antonio Savorgnan. Ten days after Castello's speech to the Signoria, Nicolò, along with seven henchmen, confronted Savorgnan's nephew Francesco in front of his own palace and beat him severely. When the news spread through the borgo, only the decisive intervention of the luogotenente Antonio Giustiniani prevented Savorgnan partisans from torching the Della Torre palace. On 25 February, Nicolò yet again, this time with fifteen companions on horseback, attacked a group of peasants, accusing them of supporting Savorgnan. On 2 March, Nicolò and his entourage rode provocatively through the streets of Udine shouting 'Torre Torre! Long live the Strumieri!'[38] Savorgnan followers struck back two days later, murdering a Della Torre familiar 'in the piazza in front of the bottega of the spicer Raynaldo'. The assassins ran through the city and quickly attracted a ragtag following of around two hundred. Amaseo recorded the event:

'part of them the most poor and beggarly, and part the major *giottoni* (pigs) of the city, greedy for plunder, ran to the house of the Turriani with the mind to sack it.' They would have succeeded, since the palace was not defended, were it not for the prompt action of Antonio Giustiniani, 'doctor and philosopher, the worthiest luogotenente', with two constables and a company of soldiers.[39]

An alarmed Alvise Della Torre rode off to Venice with a delegation of nine prominent Strumieri and a company of twelve companions and servants. Appearing before the Collegio on 14 March, they complained strenuously about the Savorgnan, especially Antonio, and avowed that they only wanted to live in peace. The Doge immediately summoned Savorgnan from Cormons, where he was commanding Venetian troops.[40]

A week later, Della Torre and the other castellans were back in the Collegio, this time with Savorgnan. The doge admonished both sides to resolve their differences and to remain united against the barbarians in such perilous times. As Amaseo put it, 'after many exhortations, a new reconciliation was made between them, Savorgnan embracing the nobles *alla gattesca*' (in a feline manner). After ordering that the perpetrators in Udine 'who had committed certain homicides should be punished', the doge urged 'these castellans to return to the Patria and especially the lord Antonio Savorgnan who is the *primo* and has the greatest following in that Patria'. The reasons for Venice's obvious bias toward Savorgnan are made plain by a letter that was read out in the same hearing. Written 'in the greatest desperation' by Alvise Dolfin, Venetian commander in the Friuli, it stated that 'since messer Antonio Savorgnan has left, things have gone badly' and that five hundred troops loyal to him were in complete disarray. In short, Venice depended on Savorgnan and soldiers devoted to him to defend the Patria against the imperial armies.[41]

A Fateful Prediction

But before departing Venice, Della Torre made a fateful prediction:

> that there being no other provision made by his sublimity, he held for certain that Savorgnan persevering in his deceits with impunity, one day with some of his machinations, he would have him [Della Torre] murdered; after he died, it would no more be him, but his widowed wife with their little children who would come to plead for justice at the feet of his eminence.[42]

That the situation was already well beyond Savorgnan's control is made evident by an incident on the trip back to Udine. As Della Torre and other castellans rode into the piazza of Mala Zompicchia near Codroipo, they were attacked, pelted with stones, and chased by a mob of armed peasants (between fifty and two hundred, according to differing estimates) led by militia captains who had participated in the Sterpo attack two years before. Those of the Della Torre group who were on horseback fled over the fields to Valvasone, while their familiars in the carriages escaped to Udine.[43]

On 8 June, Sanudo writes, 'the Council of Ten summoned Lord Antonio Savorgnan and Lord Alvise Della Torre to appear before the Signoria'.[44] The reasons were clear. According to Amaseo, 20,000 French soldiers were camped between Verona and Peschiera, only awaiting their king's command to follow the orders of Maximilian. With another 8000 imperial troops in Lubljana (Istria) and more than 500 lancemen at Gorizia, the loyalty of the Venetian castellans was a matter of urgent concern.[45] Sanudo reported that Savorgnan and Della Torre presented themselves on 14 June to the Capi of the Ten and were reminded of their promises to support light cavalry, 'and they spoke in the Collegio for a long time on the matter...and they returned to Udine'.[46] But it would not be long before Savorgnan would again accuse Della Torre of being disloyal and ready to rally the castellans to the side of the emperor. The Council of Ten ordered Della Torre to Venice yet again.[47] Sanudo recorded his appearance in the Collegio on 9 July:

> Lord Alvise Della Torre...summoned here because of his enmity with Lord Antonio Savorgnan...said that that he wished to return home, since he was not a rebel, but most faithful, as he has always demonstrated, sacrificing his private hatreds for the good of the Signoria; he concluded that in these turbulent times, staying here [in Venice] would make it seem that his loyalty was suspect, and that he wished to go [home] and see his [family] and then return. The doge spoke cordially that he held him most dear, and that he had given this order to separate them like two brothers so that they did not kill each other, but he was not convinced that this would be, and that [Alvise] should have the pleasure to stay here; the matter of his going back to Udine and then returning would be discussed and determined.[48]

Two weeks later, Alvise left Venice anyway, risking capture by the Germans at Strassoldo.[49] Although he arrived home safely without any ambushes, his time was running out. On 11 November, the vice-luogotenente in Udine wrote to the Venetian authorities, advising that the young Nicolò Della Torre be retained in Venice: 'since he is *fastidiosetto* (a little irritating), no one will regret it.'[50]

By the end of 1510, thanks to Savorgnan's continued agitation of the locals, resentment of the Strumieri reached fever pitch. Having whipped up patriotic sympathies, he continued to encourage rumours that the already unpopular castellans—most notably, Alvise Della Torre—were traitors to the Serenissima and secretly making deals to deliver the Patria to the Emperor.[51]

On New Year's Day of 1511, the new luogotenente, Alvise Gradenigo, was making his official entrance to the city through the Porta di Poscollo when a cannon misfired, injuring four bystanders and killing another. The event was duly reported by Gregorio Amaseo. Continuing the chronicle of his brother Leonardo, who had died the previous August, he judged that this most unfortunate accident was 'reputed by all to be the worst portent'. And indeed, even worse was yet to come as the flickering flame of unrest travelled ever more quickly along the fuse of vendetta. Five days later, on 6 January, the Feast of the Epiphany and first day of the Carnival season, a sixteen-year-old Strumiero youth, Francesco Candido, unarmed but 'of bold spirit', was wounded and chased by seven Savorgnan *bravi* (hired ruffians) into the courtyard of his father's palace. While the incident was just one of many perpetrated by both factions, the Strumieri nobles feared for their lives, 'seeing that every hour they encountered these *bravi* in crowds; opening their capes and showing their naked swords to frighten them and make them yield the right of way'. It was necessary to fight fire with fire. The nobles dispatched Teseo Colloredo and Sebastiano Monfalcone to Gradisca and Monfalcone, where they put together a private militia of fifty soldiers 'which they divided among themselves according to their resources to resist the traitor [Savorgnan]'.[52] The Venetian authorities, preoccupied with their own problems, failed to respond effectively to complaints from either faction.

Writing to the doge on 25 January, Savorgnan attempted to force the issue: 'It is of the highest necessity that your Serenity either remove my person from this city or remove those four, that is ser Jacomo de Castello, ser Alvise de la Torre, ser Teseo de Colleredo and ser Francesco de Cergneu.' All four, he warned, 'indubitably await the Messiah and the coming of the Germans and are the most hostile enemies of your Serenity; I write this neither though hatred nor rivalry but only for the good of the State.'[53] The Signoria still refused to take sides openly (although it continued to favour Savorgnan secretly) and encouraged them all to stand together against the common enemy. Savorgnan left Udine on 15 February with twenty horsemen while both sides built up their brigades. The castellan Giacomo da Spilimbergo, a Della Torre relative, assembled a private army of five hundred soldiers and fifty horsemen to defend his friends and family.[54] The stage was set for disaster.

As the final week of Carnival approached, the streets of Udine were filled with swaggering bands of armed partisans of both sides, spoiling for confrontation. It was no place for highborn women and children. Like most of the other castellans, the sixty-year-old Alvise Della Torre had secured his family in their well-fortified castle in the countryside. He remained in the Della Torre palace in the centre of the city with his brother Isidoro, his brash young nephew Nicolò, and other relatives and retainers. His family would never see him again.

On Monday 24 February, by order of the Council of Ten, the luogotenente, Alvise Gradenigo, prohibited anyone, whatever his station, from carrying arms in the city under penalty of the gallows. To no avail. On Tuesday, fully armed Zamberlani partisans marched through crowded streets shouting 'Savorgnan, Savorgnan', prompting citizens to run to the Castello and plead with Gradenigo to act against 'imminent scandals'. By Wednesday, Savorgnan himself was back in town and the situation was clearly out of hand. Gradenigo summoned the leaders of the two factions to the Castello, separating Savorgnan with his associates in one room from Della Torre and other Strumieri leaders in another. He exhorted each group 'to reconcile with their enemies', and then brought them together in a third room filled with citizens, commoners, and public officials. Gregorio Amaseo described the event with characteristic bias:

> Then Antonio Scarioth [Iscariot: Amaseo's unflattering epithet for Antonio Savorgnan] with fake obedience embraced and kissed one by one Alvise Della Torre, Zuan and Zuan Battista Candido, Teseo Colloredo, Francesco Cergneu, and Zuan Leonardo Frattina, with the greatest demonstration of true reconciliation and peace on every side, and not without tears of some of them and the sweet tenderness of the presiding official.[55]

Returning to their homes, the newly reconciled adversaries made an effort to celebrate the eve of Giovedì Grasso, the culminating day of Carnival, with traditional festivities. For the Savorgnan, it was a ball in the palace of Maria Savorgnan, widow of Antonio's cousin and onetime mistress of Pietro Bembo. For the castellans it was an all-male banquet in the Della Torre palace, where dancing was not on anyone's mind. Although Francesco Cergneu cautioned the other Strumieri leaders that the peace was fragile and urged them to retire to their castles in the countryside, Teseo Colloredo persuaded them that their honour was at stake and that they should stay in the city. It was a fateful, and fatal, decision.[56]

A Sicilian Vespers

The morning of Giovedì Grasso, 27 February 1511, cavalry forces were sighted outside the walls of Udine and rumours of a German invasion raced through the city. The sputtering fuse of vendetta finally burst into flame, resulting in a savage orgy of violence. While accounts written after the fact by partisans on both sides offered different, self-serving views of who was to blame for the calamitous train of events, there is general agreement on what happened.

According to Giambattista Cergneu, who later recorded his father Francesco's eyewitness version of the events in a chronicle, the melee began when the hotheaded Nicolò Della Torre, clad in armour because of false rumours of approaching Germans, stepped outside the door of the Torriani palace and (according to Savorgnan sources) uttered Strassoldo's prophetic words of 1508, 'today we are going to have a Sicilian Vespers'.[57] They did, indeed, but it did not turn out as he had hoped. One of Savorgnan's most rabid followers, Tempesta da Venzon, approached with four armed companions. When Nicolò did not retreat, they saw his self-confident stance as proof that the hated Strumieri were indeed rebels, just awaiting the arrival of imperial troops to help them take over the city. The aptly named Tempesta ran up and stabbed Nicolò in the underarm between two plates of his armour, 'and would have slashed him from side to side had he not been wearing a cuirass'. Although wounded, the youth stumbled back into the palace and took up his arms, and the deadly game was on. An inflamed mob of peasants began to gather in front of the house. And then, in Cergneu's words, 'Savorgnan partisans stirred them up, saying that the enemy was heedless, that their houses full of riches were in their reach, [and] that they should not fear a solitary man'. The furore could be heard in the Castello atop the hill, where Savorgnan was meeting with the luogotenente. The bells in its campanile began to ring incessantly and were soon joined by others throughout the city. Shopkeepers shuttered their botteghe, and Savorgnan's rural militia joined forces with the common people, shouting *a sacho, a sacho, alla ruina de rebelli* (sack, sack, ruin the rebels).[58]

What had begun as a skirmish between the two factions quickly turned into an all-out attack on the Torriani palace. Around fifteen noble Strumieri, along with their armed retainers, perhaps fifty to sixty in all, were at lunch inside the house. Taken by surprise, they leaped up from the table, grabbed their arms, ran to the doorway, and beat back the crowd, wounding many. But the mob outside swelled to numbers between 2000 and 4000, according to various estimates, 'because the majority of the commoners were up in arms, part to sack the rich, part in high expectation of what would be born from such furor'.[59] The furious fighting went on for four hours, with the mob trying to gain entry by every means possible.

After beating back the first assault, those inside assessed their options. According to Amaseo, they

> almost decided to mount horses and to go at once to Venice since they had the ease of leaving through nine doors of that house...In the discussion, messer Isidoro [Della Torre], who was the oldest of all, tried to persuade them that united together in battle they had defended an assault; retiring at once to the Castello they would save themselves, being more secure with the luogotenente.

But Teseo Colloredo remained adamant; he stuck with his earlier position, to remain and fight, and dissuaded the others from leaving.[60]

In the meantime the rioters, led by Savorgnan's son Nicolò, raced up to the Castello and forced their way into the armoury. Dragging out two *falconetti* (small cannons), along with a supply of powder and cannonballs, they returned to Palazzo Torriani and 'pounded the house with blow after blow to the point that those inside could no longer defend the house'. The luogotenente came down from the Castello and tried to calm the tumult, but in vain. After he left, the artillery bombardment was stepped up. For all their bravado, most of the Strumieri inside were terrified and, 'moved by fear and hope, without knowing where to go', escaped through the gardens and over the rooftops and sought refuge with neighbours, who hid them as best they could.[61]

Savorgnan partisans bombarded the Della Torre house for more than an hour and, seeing no sign of further resistance, began to suspect that no one was inside. Reluctant to enter themselves, they sent in a young boy to search the house. When he found no one, the rioters poured into the palace and the hunt for booty was on. They stripped the house bare of furnishings and anything of value. Then they set it on fire and burned it to the ground. From then on, no noble house was safe, whether belonging to castellan or citizen, and the mob ran from one to another, sacking and burning. Cergneu observed: 'Many of the pursuers were actually beneficiaries of the Della Torre and other gentlemen, with goods and money; and likewise, many peasants were even their own subjects, and generally worked every day as domestics in those houses, and now they persecuted anyone with noble blood with the utmost hatred.'[62]

The rampage continued overnight. Having taken all the goods and money they could find, the rioters began to hunt for the fugitive Strumieri. What specifically, was the fate of the Della Torre and the Colloredo, who will play leading roles in our story? Amaseo's account probably comes close to the 'revenge narrative' that would be repeated over and over by the families in the years to come:

> The Turriani, with their companions... unable to combat such fury any longer, fled through neighboring houses, because they could not go elsewhere with their block entirely surrounded by armed men. All of their followers escaped unharmed in the flight, except Andrea Boccastorta who was killed, and Isidoro [Della Torre] who, fleeing, was shot by an arrow in the shin from the rooftop of the houses that were armed all around, and Alvise his brother, struck in the arm in the battle; and Bernadino Pavona, likewise shot with an arrow, stayed with messer Isidoro; they were among the last to get away even though they were the oldest and the youngest of all. Casa Turriana thus having been abandoned, the mob entered, sacking it and ruining it to the foundations, having set it on fire and burned everything, and pursued them in every direction.[63]

Isidoro Della Torre, the oldest of the Strumieri and little Girolamo's uncle, escaped through the garden to the nearby house of Ascanio Sbroiavacca. The rioters discovered him lying there in bed, and

> attacked him again, and sent another one there who struck him on the head with an axe, and it was rumored to have been Girolamo Arlato [a member of the city council]; as soon as he regained consciousness, he made his last confession and pardoned everyone; on the third day he died, filling the chamber with the sweetest odor, to the extreme amazement of those around him, and of all the [Della Torre] only he was buried in the ancient tomb of his ancestors.[64]

Later histories of the family would record that he had died, like a saint, 'in a state of holiness'.[65]

Girolamo's father, Alvise, suffered a far worse death:

> After around 24 hours, it having been revealed to the traitor [Antonio Savorgnan] how Alvise Turriano was hidden in the house of messer Beltrame Rondolo, patriarchal vicar, he immediately sent his butchers to pull him out of a basement (wine cellar], dragging him forward, where he fell to his knees, with his hands crossed, crying and asking pardon and offering a reward of 4000 ducats for his life to be spared; the assassins turned their backs, having made their own plans, [and] he was cut to pieces by Vergon [a Zamberlani ringleader] and by diverse peasants . . . praying for his persecutors in his final words like a San Stefano, and saying: *God forgive you and also me.* Stripping him bare, they found 400 gold ducats, and leaving him nude on the roadway—a man of 60 years, of a heroic stature with the appearance of a true lord, who had adorned all the city, and Isidoro likewise, wherever they went. His body was trampled, pelted with stones, and dragged through the mud, and wretchedly taken to [the church of] San Tomasso, but one of the fingers of his hand remained there for more than three days to the greatest pity of those who saw it.[66]

And what of Alvise's provocative nephew, Nicolò? He had taken refuge, along with Teseo Colloredo and Zuan Leonardo della Frattina, in the house of Francesco Colombatto. Threatened with fire and flames unless he gave them up, Colombatto was finally persuaded by Savorgnan that they would be freed if he handed them over. When their hiding place was revealed, the once combative Colloredo and Della Torre threw themselves on their knees at Savorgnan's feet, crying and pleading for their lives. 'After having made them arise, he embraced and kissed them. They trusted him, accepting his good words like good brothers.'[67] After persuading Frattina to come out from under an old bed in the kitchen where he had been hiding, Savorgnan told the three that he would send for them that evening in order to take them secretly to his house, avoiding the tumult of the *popolo*. Leaving guards in place so that they could not escape, he reassured them that this was only to protect them against the furore of those outside. But then Savorgnan sought the advice of one of his top allies, the distinguished jurist Francesco Janis da Tolmezzo, who responded tersely: 'a dead man doesn't make war.'[68]

Savorgnan returned to the Colombatto house with a crowd of followers in the middle of the night and summoned the three captives outside. Seeing the mob of armed men, they immediately feared their deaths. Frattina fled and was captured in Piazzola del Borgo del Feno; wounded by a scythe, he was thrown to the ground and 'cut to pieces by numerous blows'. The other two, walking along the road, 'were most cruelly quartered like cattle . . . by Vergon and others, raising yells and screams to the heaven, bloodied the whole street and scattered about bits of flesh, brains, and hair'. Later that evening, one of the assassins was celebrating 'at a gluttonous feast of stolen wine and chickens [and] boasted of having hacked Della Torre with a butcher's cleaver; his face covered with blood and the rings of the dead on his fingers, the fiend took the lighted torches from Zuanne Bianchino and shouted, 'Kill! Kill those that still move!''[69]

Federico Colloredo (a distant cousin of Teseo's) was murdered on Friday morning after his house had been sacked. The assassins 'slashed him with so many wounds that one could see all his insides, that were then eaten by dogs, since they did not permit him to be buried'. The same was true of the other victims. A priest came out at night and dragged their bodies to a mass tomb that had been made inside the door of the Duomo. The luogotenente came down from the Castello that night and examined the bodies one by one but could not easily recognize them since they were so badly stabbed, beaten, and bruised.[70]

According to Amaseo, Vergon and another 'bloody butcher' were strangled in their beds that evening by Luigi da Porto, on command of his uncle Antonio Savorgnan, 'so that they could not reveal their many outrages'; their bodies were thrown in a well, to remain undiscovered for a month. Amaseo charged that Da Porto

> was also motivated by greed for booty hidden by the assassins in several places, because there were carts full of silver and gold and other precious things. However, the major part of it ended up in the hands of the traitor [Savorgnan], and especially, as far as we know, a very large chest, seen to be carried by eight men to his house, extracted from beneath one of the staircases of the Turriani, where there was said to be an ancient treasury of that family. Its location had been disclosed by messer Isidoro who, seeing his death near, asked a trusted servant to reveal it to his brother or nephew, not knowing of their bitter fate. The boy was taken prisoner and when threatened by Savorgnan, revealed all to him.[71]

By the end of the evening, as many as fifty nobles and their retainers had been murdered and twenty-two houses ransacked or burned or both. Savorgnan's followers later claimed that he had given them a list of Strumieri houses, each signed with the letter B., A., or M., indicating whether they were to *bottinare* (loot), *ardere* (burn), or *morte* (kill).[72]

The fury only ended with the arrival of the condottiere Teodoro del Borgo with one hundred crossbowmen, summoned by the luogotenente from Gradisca. The city was saved from further devastation. But even then, grotesque festivities took place on the final Sunday of Carnival while much of the city mourned. As Amaseo put it,

> the bloody associates and followers of the most perfidious assassin had a great celebration, running from one diversion to another, dressed in the silk clothes

> and livery of the betrayed gentlemen, calling one other by the name of those whose clothes they wore. The piper Sebastiano Cornetto, dressed in sumptuous velvets of the Della Torre, played to the people who were frolicking in the square... When the rapacious clods left for their villages in merry gangs, mocking and jeering the miserable nobility, they were dressed even as doctors, and their wives as ladies so that it appeared the world was upside down.[73]

A Desperate Flight

Indeed, the rioters were not through with the Della Torre. Remaining behind in their castle at Villalta were Alvise's pregnant wife Taddea Strassoldo and their five young children Raimondo (ten years old), Girolamo (six), Giovanni (five), Ginevra (four), and Michele (less than a year), as well as Nicolò's wife Giacoma Brazzaco, also pregnant. During the afternoon of Giovedì Grasso, Taddea and Giacoma received alarming reports of rioting and mayhem in the city. Amaseo recounted their desperation: 'Not knowing how much time they had to get out of there, especially because of the commotion of the peasants of their own castle Villalta... not knowing where best to go to, they sent away Raimondo and Girolamo, Alvise's two oldest sons... to Moruzzo, before the evening of Zobbia.'[74] It must have taken the boys some 45 minutes to reach the fortified castle of Moruzzo, about two miles away. The residence of the Arcoloniani family, the castle stood on a hilltop, its keep surrounded by a curtain wall divided by small, crenellated towers. Thus began the first segment of Girolamo's flight over frozen fields.

The following morning, Amaseo continued, Taddea and Giacoma, by then unknowing widows, left the infant Michele with his wet nurse at Villalta and 'abandoned their castle and possessions. Tearful and lamenting, both pregnant, they walked on foot through the mud and snow', also to Moruzzo. With them were Giovanni and his little sister Ginevra, two servants, a teacher, and Pietro Passerino, 'an old cittadino, as familiar as St Joseph'. But arriving at Moruzzo they heard the shouts of the rioters, who were pillaging and sacking at Brazzacco, less than two miles away to the east. Gathering up Raimondo and Girolamo, the women fled north to the Castello di Colloredo di Monte Albano, just over five miles distant. They hurried along, 'looking all around them, constantly expecting to be met with some fury, making laments of the Magdalene, falling and slipping so much that they would move a stone to pity'.[75]

At Colloredo they were reluctantly received by Madonna Pinosa, 'fearing for her own ruin, not yet knowing of the bitter death of her own son, Teseo Colloredo, in Udine'. She cautioned that 'they should not remain because of the danger that persisted; so that as soon as they had eaten, they departed from there and went to Pers [three miles away], where they were similarly admonished by Antonio

Colloredo, padrone of the place'. He insisted (rather ungallantly) 'that they should not remain there since he had secretly been informed that ruin would follow for those sheltering the banned by commandment from the Signoria'. Although Venice had given no such order, and the Della Torre had not been banned or declared outlaws, Taddea still had good cause to fear for the lives of her two oldest sons, inheritors of the family line and—according to the prevailing norms of the feudal nobility—eventual avengers of family blood and honour. She would have been well aware that the aphorism uttered by Francesco Janis da Tolmezzo during the riots—'a dead man doesn't make war'—was used to justify vendetta and might include sons, nephews, and grandsons. But providentially, another Strumiero lord, Andrea Prampero, arrived, promising to take care of the two oldest boys, and fled with them to Gemona, up in the mountains around eight miles distant. The boys had by now covered nearly eighteen miles in two days.[76]

Alvise's cousin Giacomo da Spilimbergo then arrived in Pers with nine horsemen to retrieve the two pregnant women and the younger children. Doubling back and crossing the Tagliamento, they rode the twenty miles to his own castle in Spilimbergo, arriving past midnight. But it was not a safe refuge. As a tumult of rioting peasants and townspeople began to fill the streets around the castle, they fetched Giacomo's wife, Aloisa Candida, and fled to Brugnera. Arriving in the evening after a 25-mile ride, they found themselves in the middle of a gala carnival ball of noble ladies, unaware that some of their husbands had been slaughtered in Udine the day before.[77]

This was an age in which portents were taken seriously, and the women later recalled two great marvels that in retrospect could be understood as ill omens. One was 'that the ladies having retired to costume themselves, every one of them immediately brought back a weapon on her shoulder, as if she would have to defend the men'. The other was that

> in the evening the torches fell to the ground without any cause as soon as they were lit, with everyone becoming overwhelmed by the darkness, as if the light of justice had been extinguished... Moreover, Giuditta Bruno, already the widow of Teseo Colloredo, but not yet aware of it, as if prescient of her ruin began to sob piteously, without knowing the cause of her tears, to the great surprise of the others, who were not able to calm her down.

Such was not the case, however, for Madonna Lucretia, daughter of Soldoniero Soldonieri, whose father had also been murdered. She continued to dance happily and enjoy herself. 'By such an example', Amaseo concluded, 'it thus appeared to all of them that the matrimonial tie was more powerful than the kinship of blood. And so, the music-making and dancing were transformed into tearful exclamations and the most bitter tears.'[78]

The castle of Brugnera was soon to close its own gates to pillaging peasants, and the Della Torre refugees moved on to Pordenone, and then to Venice, where the two pregnant widows gave birth, 'renewing the names of their predeceased husbands with two beautiful posthumous sons.'[79] A letter reaching Venice on 3 March claimed that 'the widow of don Alvise de la Torre was captured and tortured to try to learn the whereabouts of her children.'[80] The allegation is improbable, for even Amaseo did not report such an outrage. The informant, writing in the fog of war, likely confused Taddea with a servant loyal to the family who had been captured and forced to reveal the children's location.

In any case, the castello of Villalta had been thoroughly sacked and partly ruined. Taddea's infant son, Michele, who had been left behind, was torn from the arms of his wet nurse by the rioters, 'and publicly carried to the presence of the Iscariot, who sent the baby to Smeralda Della Torre, wife of Ettore Strassoldo, doctor, to conceal his wickedness, thinking that he could hide his failings under a pile of straw.'[81] In a textbook example of Friulian endogamy—the preference of noble clans to intermarry with one another—Ettore was little Michele's uncle (that is, the brother of his mother Taddea) and Smeralda his first cousin (the daughter of his father Alvise's brother Francesco and sister of his uncle Nicolò, who had shared Alvise's fate in Udine). Thus retrieved by a married couple representing both sides of his lineage, Michele would survive, as noted earlier, to build an illustrious career in the church.[82]

And what of Raimondo and our Girolamo, the two older brothers who had been hidden in Gemona? According to Amaseo, partisans of Savorgnan demanded that the boys be given up, but the Venetian Signoria 'insisted that they be brought to Venice with maximum speed for their protection.'[83] Luigi da Porto saw the matter somewhat differently, arguing that Savorgnan had given refuge in Udine even to some of his enemies, thus saving their lives, and that some of his family had helped others in the countryside escape the fury of the peasants:

> I will tell you of his authority, that I saw one of the ambassadors who came to him on behalf of the community of Gemona to ask him what they should do with the two boys of the Della Torre house, who were in their city with a master, and a nurse brought another to him that she had cared for in the villa. And all were therefore saved, since he was aware that he should, with great pretense, appear to regret the murders and subsequent incidents.[84]

The peasant revolt spread throughout the region. While the Colloredo castles at Pers and Mels were spared thanks to the intervention of a Savorgnan friend, Madonna Pinosa was correct in her fears about Colloredo di Monte Albano, which was sacked and ruined. A number of other castles would also be plundered, burned, or destroyed and their princely inhabitants reduced to the state of refugees: Cergnocco (the family castle of the prudent Francesco Cergneu), Moruzzo, Brazzacco, Arcano, Cusano, Zoppola, Valvasone, Spilimbergo, Susans, Madrisio, San Daniele, Fagagna, Caporiacco, and Salvarolo.[85] Popular insurrections were dangerous for any 'well-instituted Republic', and the Venetian authorities came down hard on the perpetrators. Meeting on 16 March, an enraged Council of Ten (although headed by Savorgnan's longtime supporter, Andrea Loredan) pronounced:

> Having appeared before us representatives of the heirs of the deceased Alvise Della Torre, requesting restoration of their properties and restitution of the goods stolen in the recent disturbance and violently taken away... we will proceed with such a severe manner of punishment against the transgressors that their penalty will be a perpetual example for all others that might presume to disobey the commands of their superiors.[86]

Thus, while Savorgnan was initially found blameless, his ragtag followers were ordered to make restitution and to rebuild the properties they had just destroyed.

Manifest Sign of Vendetta

But populist rage was soon tempered by natural disasters, and the rebuilding of Villalta would have to wait. On 26 March, the entire region suffered a devastating earthquake, only to be followed by a plague that decimated the city and swept through the countryside. The events could only be regarded by the surviving castellans and their supporters as divine judgement. Amaseo opined that Savorgnan might have escaped worldly justice...

> ...but not that of God, who never fails: in demonstration of his ire, as seen by diverse persons, religious and most worth of faith, at the hour of vespers above the top of the campanile of San Francesco near the house of Savorgnan, there appeared a semblance of two angels with bloody swords in their hands, and between them a great flame of fire in manifest sign of vendetta, as was also... the great earthquake of the 26th of March 1511 at around 20 hours, so fearsome that had never been felt by living men, and perhaps since the passion of Christ, in this place; and it lasted for an eighth of an hour, with a terrible roar in the air and horrifying inundation of waters... with the movement and trembling of buildings, collapsing the floors and walls at every turn, with the desolation of many places and oppression of persons, so that everyone remained shocked and terrified, confessing the power of God and the wonder of nature.

Their houses in ruins, people poured into the streets and set up tents in orchards and gardens. Amaseo reported, ominously, that a pinnacle fell from the top of the Duomo, 'breaking the tomb where the innocent murdered ones had been buried, not without exciting comment from everyone, running there immediately from the greatest to the least, asking pardon for the past error to placate the ire of God'.[87]

The luogotenente Alvise Gradenigo, who had fled the Castello and taken refuge in the monastery of San Francesco, wrote to the Signoria on the day after the quake. Reporting that half the Castello had collapsed, he judged that his survival was a miracle: 'It was such a horrendous thing and so frightening that one cannot not say more.' However, he did say more, telling of religious processions and prodigious signs. On the day of the earthquake, as one group marched with the crucifix past a church, a cross mounted on a column above the façade fell to the ground with a great clatter. The next day, the bishop paraded the cross in a great procession with the clergy, the confraternities, and the luogotenente at the head of the line, followed by the popolo. As they passed the ruins of Alvise Della Torre's palace, a piece of the cross broke off by accident. The terrified crowd began to shout and make a commotion. The dignitaries in front, who had turned a corner, did not know what was going on and began to shout *arme, arme*. The bishop cried out 'what is that, what is that?' Running back and forth, he learned the cause of the commotion and calmed everyone down (Figure 2.3).[88] But to many the implications were clear. Cergneu would later note with satisfaction, 'The divine wrath was truly just, and an avenger of patrician blood'.[89] As for Gradenigo himself, he remained neutral, concluding that although 'one sees great travails, everyone is grateful that God has preserved their Patria'.[90]

The Della Torre refugees, still in Venice, would have felt the earthquake there as well. Sanudo reported:

> The chimneys were swaying, the walls bursting open, the bell towers tottering, things on high were tumbling down, and the water in the canals—even the Grand Canal—was boiling as if it had a fire under it. Indeed, people said that, although it was high tide, some canals ran dry when the earthquake struck, as if there were a great drought... Everyone was stunned by this frightful event. Some ran out into the public squares, some into the streets, some began to pray, and some did not know what to do.

To add misery upon misery, heavy rains, high winds, and high tides flooded the city three days later—more than a foot high in Sanudo's courtyard—and many wells were ruined.[91]

Like Amaseo, Taddea and her family would have seen the quake as divine justice for the terrible events of Giovedì Grasso, but their Venetian neighbours interpreted the causes of God's ire from a local perspective. Sanudo reported:

> our Patriarch, don Antonio Contarini, appeared [before the Collegio], saying that the earthquake is a sign from God: it is because of our sins that misfortunes

Figure 2.3. Earthquake in Udine after the Cruel Carnival of 1511, MCVe, MS Correr 963, 'Udine saccheggiata l'anno 1511', c. 29, eighteenth century. (Venice, Museo Civico Correr).

> afflict us... The prostitutes have sent him word that they cannot make a living; no one comes to them so rampant is sodomy... Thus, it was ordered that all preachers assigned to churches should preach, beginning tomorrow morning. The Patriarch ordered a three-day fast of bread and water and processions singing litanies around the campi in the evening and in Piazza San Marco in the morning. I applaud these measures as far as good habits and religion are concerned, but as far as preventing earthquakes, they accomplish nothing, for these are a phenomenon of nature.[92]

By contrast, the 'furor del populo' of Giovedì Grasso, as Francesco Janis da Tolmezzo had put it in defence of Savorgnan, was a phenomenon of human nature, and it would soon become apparent that divine justice was not enough. To the relatives of the victims, it called not for penitence, but for revenge. It is true that 'dead men don't make war', but it was only a matter of time before the living sought retribution.[93]

In Righteous Revenge of Patrician Blood

Udine remained a dangerous place. Aftershocks from the earthquake continued sporadically until mid-February of the following year. The plague continued to claim victims throughout the summer. Amaseo claimed that the deaths quadrupled when Antonio Savorgnan returned on Pentecost (15 June) to swagger round an afflicted city. As even his nephew Luigi da Porto put it: 'Loved and feared as much as he desired, he ran everything in the Patria according to his pleasure.'[94] But that pleasure was short-lived and bittersweet at best. Antonio was tormented by the ongoing inquest on the events of Giovedì Grasso. Initially confident that he would be found blameless, he began to sense that opinion was turning against him. He 'was constantly aware of having above his head a sharp and weighty sword sustained by a weak thread'.[95] As the plague raged on, Antonio returned to the field with a decimated army and inadequate supplies. Responsible for defending the Patria from imperial troops, he complained about the meagre resources coming from hard-pressed Venice. By September the emperor's armies had taken over almost the entire territory and Udine itself was in peril.[96]

Several other castellans, fearing the collapse of Venetian rule, had already switched their allegiance to the emperor to protect their feudal holdings. Fearing for his life, Antonio was incensed that the Republic might not absolve him even though, as he saw it, he was singlehandedly defending the Patria on the battlefield. In contrast to the uncertain outcome of the slow-moving deliberations in Venice, the emperor offered him a permanent alliance and a guarantee that he could keep all his properties. After deliberating for many hours, Antonio did the unthinkable and made the fateful decision to change sides.[97] On 20 September he rode into Udine with imperial prefects and effectively handed over the city to the enemy. At first incredulous when they learned of Savorgnan's betrayal, the Council of Ten declared Savorgnan a rebel and a traitor, confiscated all his possessions in the Patria, and voted unanimously to put a hefty bounty of 5000 gold ducats on his head.[98] To Amaseo, it was no coincidence that the plague ended only with the departure of Savorgnan. By the end of October, in the space of less than six months, around one-third of the population of the city—probably around 5000–6000—had died.[99]

Despite Savorgnan's new allegiance, the imperial forces lost ground in the Patria. By the following April, Maximilian was ready to sign a truce with Venice. No longer in good favour in the north, and a wanted man in the Patria, Savorgnan took refuge in Villach, a city in the Carinthian Alps just inside imperial territory on the road to Vienna. It was time to settle accounts. Armed with a secret assassination contract from the Council of Ten, a posse of Strumieri lords pursued Antonio 'in righteous revenge of patrician blood' and tracked him down nine months later. The Colloredo, whose landholdings in the Friuli were second only to the Savorgnan's, figured prominently in the enterprise: Girolamo Colloredo, son of Albertino, whose castle at Sterpo had been sacked in the peasant uprising of 1510, and brother of the slaughtered Teseo; another brother, Gregorio, whose house at Monte Albano had been burned to the ground; and Agostino Colloredo, a priest from a different branch of the family, who 'wanted to get back a possession of mine'. Supported by a contingent of ten familiars, the noble participants also included Giovanni Giorgio Zoppola—whose country estate had been sacked, with two women of his family raped—and Giovanni Enrico da Spilimbergo, who had lost a brother. Spilimbergo was a shifty character, himself under sentence of perpetual exile for having joined Antonio Savorgnan in switching to the imperial side the year before.[100]

Describing the gory event at third hand, Cergneu reported that the assassins confronted Antonio Savorgnan in Villach on 27 May 1512 as he was leaving church after attending mass. Spilimbergo struck him on the head with a mortal blow of his sword, to be followed by Girolamo Colloredo, who struck him as well. Cergneu elaborated on the event with relish: 'He never arose from that place, where by divine will a pig drank his blood and a dog ate his brains. Such was a just end for the new Judas, who belonged in the lowest circle of hell.' Savorgnan's bloody demise would have been a suitable quid pro quo for the castellans whose bodies had been left to be devoured by dogs the year before on the streets of Udine.[101] Sanudo remarked at the time that 'his cousin don Girolamo Savorgnan [Del Monte]...did not wear any sign of mourning, because this Antonio has brought shame upon his house'.[102] In his *History of Venice* written two decades later, Pietro Bembo delivered the judgment of history: 'Antonio Savorgnan had been responsible for a massacre of citizens at Udine during factional fighting there. Despite being a Venetian noble, he had deserted the Republic and gone over to the enemy, acting against her in a thoroughly ungrateful and malign way. Now Savorgnan was murdered by his enemies in Maximilian's lands and met the death that his many crimes deserved.'[103]

The happy news soon reached Venice, and the assassins were rewarded with a handsome bounty of 3000 ducats and other benefits. Sanudo writes: 'Among other things, [the Senate] absolved from banishment that Giovanni Enrico da Spilimbergo, and the other accomplices, who had been banned from our cities and other places, who murdered Antonio Savorgnan at Villach.'[104] Dead men don't make war, but the living do. And Antonio's death was only the beginning.

Notes

1. This chapter is particularly indebted to Muir 1993 (not to be confused with an abridged version published in 1998) and to Leonardo and Gregorio Amaseo, with Giovanni Antonio Azio, *Diarii udinesi dell'1508 al 1541*, Venice, 1884 (see Abbreviations). Giovedì Grasso is the last Thursday before Lent; a day dedicated to feasting, it is called Fat Thursday in English-speaking territories.
2. Sanudo 2014, 422–3. See also Muir 1993, 89–91; Bianco 1994b, 36–7.
3. Muir 1993, 15–48, 89–90; Ciconi 1861, II, 350; Degani 1900, 3–5.
4. Muir 1993, 37–44, 77–97.
5. Lucchese 2005, 43–54; Tagliaferri 1969, 15–24; Bergamini and Buora 1990, esp. 7–33.
6. Muir 1993, 89–90.
7. ASUd, *AT*, b. 19, cited by Bianco 1994b, 26–7, with the incorrect date of 1497. Emo was luogotenente in 1478–9. See Muir 1993, 93–4.
8. Cited by Muir 1993, 95.
9. Muir 1993, 96.
10. DU, GAH, 425; Cergneu 1895, 6–7; Muir 1993, 89–90.
11. Sanudo 2014, 422–3. See Muir 1993, 92; Bianco 1994b, 27–8.

12. Casella 2003, 142–4, 215–28; Muir 1993, 78–83. For the family tree, see Appendix II, Table E herein.
13. Casella 2003, 142–4; Muir 1993, 312 n16. See Tentori 1988, 44, Fig. 44 for a probable marriage portrait of Girolamo Savorgnan and Maddalena Della Torre. See also Garafolo 2002, 69–97. See Appendix II, Table E.
14. See Chapter 1.
15. Muir 1993, 120–6.
16. *DBI, s.v.* 'Della Torre, Luigi,' 603.
17. ASUd, *AT*, b. 5 (11 September 1495).
18. Muir 1993, 126–9.
19. Sachs 1915, 78–9, 83–4. Taddea is also referred to as Tadea in primary documents.
20. ASUd, *AT*, b. 24, no. 31 (Sunday, 30 August 1500). See also Muir 1993, 327 n32.
21. Sachs 1915, 80.
22. Casella 2003, 210. Orsina Da Canal, the fourth wife of Girolamo Savorgnan del Monte, was the widow of Marcantonio Marcello q. Fantin, a distant relative of Antonia Bembo's first husband Sebastiano Marcello. See MCVe, Barbaro, *Genealogie*, IV, 301.
23. *DBI, s.v.* 'Della Torre, Luigi,' 603.
24. ASUd, *AT*, b. 3; ibid., b. 33.
25. Muir 1993, 136–7.
26. Bianco 1994a, 265 (citing an incorrect date of 1508). The term referred to a popular revolt in Palermo in the late thirteenth century against the Angevin occupation of Sicily. See Runciman 2012.
27. Muir 1993, 126, 137–8, coining the phrase 'a prince without a title'. Francesco Strassoldo was probably the brother of Taddea Strassoldo's grandfather, Giovanni.
28. Sanudo, *Diarii*, 5:632. The speaker was Rizzardo Fontanabuona [Fontebuono]. See also Muir 1993, 120.
29. *DBI, s.v.* 'Della Torre, Luigi,' 603–4.
30. Sanudo, *Diarii*, 7:552. See also *DU*, 31 and 40.
31. Muir 1993, 131–2.
32. *DU*, 88. See also Bowd 2018, 34–40, 104.
33. *DU*, 101.
34. *DBI, s.v.* 'Della Torre, Luigi,' 605; Muir 1993, 135–8.
35. Sanudo, *Diarii*, 9:92 (23 August 1509).
36. *DU*, 144.
37. Ibid.
38. *DBI, s.v.* 'Della Torre, Luigi,' 605–6. Cf. Sanudo, *Diarii*, 9:507, misidentifying Nicolò as the son, rather than the nephew, of Alvise Della Torre.
39. *DU*, 156; DU, GAH, 501.
40. *DU, GAH*, 502 (with an incorrect date of 14 May); Sanudo, *Diarii*, 10:33 (14 March 1510).
41. *DU, GAH*, 502; Sanudo, *Diarii*, 10:52, 53 (20 and 21 March 1510); Savini 1931, 280.
42. *DU, GAH*, 502.
43. Ibid., 502–3 (est. 200 peasants); Cergneu 1895, 33–4 (50 peasants). Cf. Muir 1993, 153, 322 n1: who assumes that this incident happened before the 21 March meeting, but Amaseo, presumably writing in real time, puts it later.
44. Sanudo, *Diarii*, 10:532 (8 June 1510).

45. *DU*, 169 (16 June 1510).
46. Sanudo, *Diarii*, 10:570 (14 June 1510).
47. Ibid., 10:682–3 (1 July 1510).
48. Ibid., 10:741 (9 July 1510).
49. *DBI*, *s.v.* 'Della Torre, Luigi', 606.
50. Savini 1931, 283.
51. *DBI*, *s.v.* 'Della Torre, Luigi', 606; Muir 1993, 155.
52. *DU, GAH*, 504. See also Muir 1993, 154–5. For *bravi*, see Walker 1998.
53. Cited by Savini 1931, 283.
54. Muir 1993, 155–6; *DU, GAH*, 505.
55. *DU, GAH*, 505–6; Muir 1993, 157–8.
56. *DU, GAH*, 506; Muir 1993, 158–9. For Maria Savorgnan, see Dionisotti 1950 and Clough 1993, 119.
57. Cergneu 1895, 41; Savini 1931, 303; *DU, GAH*, 509; Muir 1993, 4, 161.
58. *DU, GAH*, 509; Cergneu 41. See *DU, GAH*, 497–521; and Muir 1993, 4–12, 160–9, for a full account.
59. Cergneu 1895, 42; *DU, GAH*, 510.
60. *DU, GAH*, 512.
61. Cergneu 1895, 42–3.
62. Ibid., 43–4.
63. *DU, GAH*, 513. For the concept of the 'revenge narrative', see Muir 1993, xxvii–xxviii, 200–14.
64. *DU, GAH*, 514.
65. ASUd, *AT*, b. 2, colto 5, Fasc. 1, 'Persone morte in concetto di santità', 43.
66. *DU, GAH*, 514.
67. Ibid., 516.
68. Ibid.: 'homo morto non fa Guerra.' Cf. Muir 1993, 167, 326 n27.
69. *DU, GAH*, 517. English transl. from Muir 1993, 9.
70. *DU, GAH*, 517–8. See also Cergneu 1895, 46.
71. *DU, GAH*, 518–9. See also Muir 1993, 162, citing BCUd, MS Joppi 592, f. xlvii (recto). Cf. Da Porto 1857, 277–9, for Luigi's own account of the affair. His mother Isabetta was the sister of Antonio Savorgnan. Antonio was the brother of Da Porto's mother Isabetta.
72. Muir 1993, 98; Ciconi 1861, II, 350. Estimates of the number of deaths ranged from twenty-five to fifty and those of damaged or destroyed houses from seventeen to twenty-two.
73. *DU, GAH*, 521. Eng. transl. Muir 1993, 10.
74. *DU, GAH*, 521. See also Muir 1993, 11, for an admirable summary of the Della Torre flight.
75. *DU, GAH*, 521–2.
76. Ibid.
77. Ibid. Cf. Muir 1993, 11.
78. *DU, GAH*, 521–2.
79. Ibid.
80. Sanudo, *Diarii*, 12:15 (3 March 1511). Engl. trans. from Labalme and Sanguineti White 2008, 99–100.

81. *DU, GAH*, 522–3; ASVe, *CCX*, Lettere di rettori e pubblici rappresentanti, b. 169 (15 March 1511) . For Savorgnan's version of the incident, see Savini 1931, 304.
82. For Friulian marriage patterns, see Muir 1993, 42–9, 84–9.
83. *DU, GAH*, 523.
84. Da Porto 1857, 279.
85. Bianco 1995; Muir 1993, 169–38.
86. Zucchiatti 1989, 309 n592. The term 'well-instituted republic', coined by Domenico Morosini in his treatise written 1497–1509, soon became an essential element of Venetian historiography. See Morosini 1969; Chojnacki 2000, 65–6; Cozzi 1970, esp. 408–13.
87. *DU, GAH*, 528. See also Muir 1993, 204–8.
88. Sanudo, *Diarii*, 12:90–1. Cf. Muir 1993, 207.
89. Cergneu, 50.
90. Sanudo, *Diarii*, 12:90–1.
91. Ibid., 12: 79–82, 89.
92. Ibid., 12: 84–5, 109. See also Labalme and Sanguineti White 2008, 376–7; Hacke 2004, 177–8.
93. Muir 1993, 200–14. For Janis da Tolmezzo, see Sanudo, *Diarii*, 26: 109 (8 April 1511); *DBI, s.v.* 'Janis, Francesco (Francesco da Tolmezzo)'.
94. Da Porto 1857, 280; *DU, GAH*, 533.
95. Da Porto 1857, 280. See Savini 1931, 300–5 for a transcription of Antonio's fifty-two-point declaration (undated), presumably addressed to the Signoria, protesting his innocence.
96. Muir 1993, 216–17; Sanudo, *Diarii*, 12:535.
97. Da Porto 1857, 280–1. Muir 1993, 216–18; Sanudo, *Diarii*, 12:555.
98. ASVe, *CX*, Criminale, r. I, c. 168v (29 September 1511); *I Savorgnan e la Patria del Friuli* 1984, 129–30; Muir 1993, 216–22, 342 nn2–4.
99. *DU, GAH*, 533–4; Muir 1993, 207–8.
100. Cergneu 1895, 59; *DU, GAH*, 231–4, 541–4; Colloredo, 'Cronache Friulane, 1508–18', 5–6; Muir 1993, 171–2, 174, 219–22. Girolamo and Gregorio di Albertino I belonged to the Terzo Ramo of the Signori di Colloredo, See Custoza 2003, Tav. VIII. Cf. Crollalanza 1875, Tav. V, labelling this line the Secondo Ramo.
101. Cergneu, 59. See also Muir 1993, 222–38, with a fine analysis of the symbolic importance of dogs devouring human victims. See also *DU, GA*, 259.
102. Sanudo, *Diarii*, 14:282–3. See also ibid., 12: 576–7.
103. Bembo 2009, Book XII: 75.
104. Sanudo, *Diarii*, 14:282–3 (27 May 1512); and 14:284 (4 June 1512).

3
Recovery

Back in the Friuli, despite the plague and alarming aftershocks from the quake, shattered lives were already being rebuilt by the summer of 1511. Taddea Della Torre had likely given birth in Venice to her fifth son by 4 July, when she was declared legal guardian of her minor children.[1] The newborn was named Alvise after his murdered father; to avoid confusion, let us henceforth call him Alvise II (and his father Alvise I). It is questionable whether Taddea had returned to Udine by that date, with the plague still in full fury, killing 150 people a day according to some accounts.[2] But at some point she did return to the city with Alvise II and her four older children, to be reunited with little Michele, then in the care of Taddea's brother Ettore and his wife Smeralda. The expanded household would also have included Giacoma, widow of the murdered Nicolò I (Alvise I's nephew), and her own infant son Nicolò II, also born in Venice and also named after his father. The babies bearing the paternal names were living reminders of the terrible circumstances of their births.

Taddea's world had collapsed around her. The first order of business was finding a place to live. The castle of Villalta, stripped of its furnishings, was still partly in ruins from the earthquake, as well as the damages inflicted by the peasants. Even worse, the family palace in Udine had been razed to the ground, with only a pile of rubble left on Via Strazzamantello where it had once stood. Initially, the Della Torre survivors must have stayed in the Strassoldo palace nearby while their castle at Villalta was being repaired and refurnished.

A Rebuilt Villalta

Taddea would have recalled her first view of the castle situated atop a mound surrounded by vineyards and fields of grain when she was brought there as a young bride by Alvise I in the late summer of 1500 (Figure 3.1). Its name—*villa alta*—signified its elevated position overlooking the countryside with views south all the way to the Adriatic on a clear day.

Near the road linking Udine and Spilimbergo, the castle also surveyed the flood plain of the braided channels of the meandering Tagliamento river eight miles to the west and the wooded hills of the lower Alps to the north.[3] Villalta had seemed a secure refuge in a dangerous world. And now, along with a husband 'of a heroic stature with the appearance of a true lord', it was gone.

The Venetian Bride: Bloodlines and Blood Feuds in Venice and Its Empire. Patricia Fortini Brown, Oxford University Press (2021). © Patricia Fortini Brown. DOI: 10.1093/oso/9780192894571.003.0003

Figure 3.1. Castello di Villalta from the southwest.
The watchtower served for defense and storage (and the confinement of prisoners at times) rather than habitation. On the right, the mastio or keep served as the family residence. Three stories high, it was modeled on military architecture and constructed for maximum defense in an era before firearms. It featured canted walls and a polygonal floor plan called a sperone (buttress) on the lower level. The four-story structure in the center was probably added in a later period.

The rebuilding of Villalta had begun soon after its partial destruction. On 16 March 1511, less than a month after the riots, representatives of Alvise I's heirs had appeared before the Council of Ten, 'requesting reintegration of the jurisdictions of their properties and restitution of the possessions sacked from them and violently taken in the recent disturbances'. The Ten ordered that the heirs should be given back their possessions and declared that 'we will proceed with such a severe form of punishment against the disobedient ones, that their penalty will be a perpetual example to all others who may presume to go against the commandments of their superiors'.[4] And in fact, all the able-bodied peasants of the Della Torre jurisdictions, even those not involved in the mayhem, would have been diverted from their farming to reconstruct the castle, heavy stone by heavy stone.[5] What had taken just two evenings to bring to ruin—first by man and then by nature—took months to restore. And that was only the beginning.

The chronicler Amaseo had written that 'the major part' of Villalta 'was looted and ruined' in 1511.[6] But what was the actual extent of the damage? First mentioned in documents in 1216, the castle had already been demolished by hostile forces and rebuilt no less than three times in the fourteenth century. The Della

Figure 3.2. Castello di Villalta in 1480. BCUd, MS 208, Fondo Joppi. (Udine, Biblioteca Civica "Vincenzo Joppi").

The drawing depicts the complex from the south, with the imposing watchtower, the mastio, and two circuits of fortified curtain walls and battlements *alla ghibellina* atop a mound. The inner wall displays the Villalta coat of arms between two portals. The secondary walled area in front, labeled Borgo, was accessed by the main entry portal and a drawbridge on the south side. The entire compound was further protected by a moat.

Torre family gained possession of the property in a series of land transfers beginning in 1433 and had acquired nearly all the rights by the time that Alvise I and his brother Isidoro inherited it in 1473. The basic layout at the time of the Cruel Carnival of 1511 is captured in a drawing, dated 1480 but possibly made at the time of an earlier property division (Figure 3.2). It consisted of a watchtower, a *mastio*—the residence—and upper and lower courtyards.[7]

The present state of the complex suggests that the top third of the watchtower had been toppled in the earthquake and was rebuilt with bricks atop the original stone walls. Likewise, remains of Gothic window openings on the upper level of the *mastio* indicate that it had not been completely razed to the ground. Its ground floor was occupied by a large cavern-like kitchen dimly lit by two small, barred windows on the west wall and a storeroom in the *sperone* on the south end. The *sala magna*, a space of representation and entertainment analogous to the portego of a Venetian palace, occupied the first floor (i.e., second level), above the kitchen, along with a smaller chamber in the *sperone*, probably a study or office. The second floor above must have been divided into bedchambers.[8] The kitchen, with its *fogolar*, a huge fireplace with a raised hearth for cooking and heating, was probably the centre of day-to-day family life in a draughty home. This was Taddea's world. As the wife of a castellan she was not expected to be an ornamental court lady, but the manager of a domestic establishment. During Alvise I's frequent absences, she would have been responsible for running the house, with a foreman overseeing the larger estate and agricultural holdings.

The high curtain walls that extended around to create the upper courtyard, were topped by crenellations and furnished with arrow loops, remnants of an age before arquebuses had replaced longbows and crossbows. In the early life of the family, this was the children's playground. The courtyard created by the second circuit of walls lower down the hill contained the *borgo*, a tiny rural village with twenty-two wooden huts that housed peasants and provided storage for farm equipment and agricultural products. With only a single portal providing access to the outside, the enclosure could be used for refuge by the peasants from the countryside in times of danger. The close proximity of lordly masters and disaffected peasants, with minimal separation afforded by the upper bisecting wall with its two entrance portals, may well have facilitated the devastating events of 1511.[9]

By 9 September 1512 the family had moved back in, when Taddea signed documents in the *sala magna castri Villaltae*, granting her a lifetime pension from feudal holdings, even though the peasants had burned the rent-rolls.[10] With all the adult Della Torre males dead, Taddea's brother Ettore, whose title of *dottor* indicated a university education, became the de facto head of the family and father figure for the children. Records show that he supervised their financial affairs and kept accounts of the rents that continued to come in from feudal property until Taddea's sons came of age.[11]

With Villalta again in habitable condition, it was time to attend to more permanent accommodations for the family inside the city. On 10 March 1513, acting in the name of the Della Torre heirs, Ettore purchased a house for Taddea and her children from the Cuccagna family, Strumieri allies, close to the original family palace, as well as to his own.[12]

Taddea's children grew to adulthood in a time of continuing unrest, most likely following a typical pattern of winters in the city and summers in the country. While neither place could be considered safe, the castle was not a military target and remained unscathed in 1514, when the imperial troops retook the Friuli and even occupied Udine for three months.[13]

Reprisals and Pacification

The revenge narratives were a work in progress that grew in the telling and were enriched from time to time as Venetian authorities continued to punish those held responsible for the uprising. On 13 October 1513 the Council of Ten put out a contract on the head of the hated Nicolò Cherubino, cleric of Aquileia and Udine and bastard son of Antonio Savorgnan. Those who apprehended and killed him were promised a bounty of 600 ducats, but more importantly, following Venetian custom, they were offered absolution from previous sentences of banishment. This was a powerful incentive to those who had been banned from specific territories—a typical penalty for violent behaviour by mainland nobles and their associates. Nicolò's days were numbered.[14]

Sanudo reported in August 1515 that two of the rioters, already held in prison for four years for murdering Alvise I and others, were finally sentenced by the Council of Ten to be executed in Piazza San Marco. Five days later they 'were beheaded and then quartered and hung all night on the gallows until the following evening'.[15] They were punished in Venice and not in Udine, for their crime was not considered a local infraction but one of *lèse-majesté*, an offence against the dignity of the Venetian state.

That very same month, the Signoria awarded all the goods and property belonging to the murdered Antonio Savorgnan del Torre and his deceased brother Giovanni to his cousin and rival Girolamo Savorgnan del Monte, the castellan who had married a Della Torre bride back in 1491. Giovanni Savorgnan's sons (that is, Antonio's nephews) Francesco and Bernardino, who had fled to Flanders with their mother after their uncle's assassination, were effectively disinherited, at least for the moment. Their branch of the family protested, and the luogotenente, Leonardo Emo, was called in as a mediator. He suggested a marriage between Francesco, then twenty-three years old, and one of Girolamo Savorgnan del Monte's many daughters, with the youth receiving the inheritance due him from his father and uncle. Such a union would join together two branches of the family that had long been at odds. But Girolamo was not enthusiastic: 'I responded that I did not wish to give him my daughter, and that the Serenissima Signoria has given me this faculty and could also take it away, but certainly never with my consent.'[16]

Just as ambitious as his cousin Antonio, Girolamo Savorgnan sought to replace him in the affections of the popular classes. But, less talented politically, he was frequently guilty of overreach. Despite his strategic marriages to both Venetian and Friulian brides and his distinguished military service to the Republic, his arrogant manner offended important people in both spheres and he never gained the devotion of either. Beyond that, the Venetians, now vigilant about the rise of a new demagogue, managed to hem him in over the following decade by supporting the rights of the Udinese nobility.[17]

It was not long before the Colloredo were again on the attack. The luogotenente, Giacomo Corner, wrote to the Senate in October 1516 that Giambattista Colloredo and Ercole della Rovere, an Udinese comrade in arms, had wounded Giovanni Battista Savorgnan, the nineteen-year-old 'son of our gentleman Giacomo' (and of Maria, Pietro Bembo's former mistress), while he was riding horseback, and left him for dead on the road. Corner requested permission to banish the perpetrators from the Patria. The Senate voted 138 to 22 to allow him to impose the ban along with a bounty of 4000 ducats should they violate it, and the two were sentenced to confinement in Padua.[18] The attack must have put a strain on the relationship between the Della Torre and the Colloredo clans, given that Giovanni Battista's older sister Giulia was married to Giovanni Strassoldo, a brother of Taddea Della Torre.[19]

By 1517, the city of Udine was beginning to heal. Construction finally began on a new palace for the Venetian luogotenente to replace the thirteenth-century castello that had been badly damaged in the earthquake six years before. Designed in a Renaissance classical style by the Lombard architect Giovanni Fontana, it would later be embellished with a grand double-branched staircase on the northern façade designed by native son Giovanni da Udine.[20] The parliament of the Friuli—a tripartite body made up of noble castellans, the clergy, and representatives of the larger communities—which had been in recess since 1511 also began to meet again, with the young Raimondo Della Torre, now sixteen, representing Villalta along with a certain Mainardus, one of the Caporiacco heirs that still owned a share of the property.[21]

Nicolò Cherubino was tracked down the following year, again in Villach, and murdered along with two of his six familiars inside the church of San Marco on Good Friday (2 April 1518). Agostino Colloredo would note in his chronicle: 'whereas this Antonio and his son Nicolò might have believed that they had ruined the house of Colloredo, it was their house that was ruined.'[22] This time the assassins included Nicolò Colloredo, another son of Albertino, and the castellans Francesco Candido and Giovanni Giacomo Caporiacco.[23] Amaseo commented drily that 'Who wounds by the sword, dies by the sword'. Two exiles were also involved: 'At their request, messer Giambattista Colloredo and messer Ercole della Rovere were liberated from two years of confinement in Padua for having wounded messer Giovanni Battista Savorgnan.' They were now allowed to travel throughout the Patria, but not to return to Udine until the peace treaty with the emperor was publicly proclaimed—an event that took place on 17 June, thus ushering in an era of relative quiet in the countryside.[24]

In Udine the struggle between the nobility and the popular classes continued, but in the councils rather than on the streets. And within the nobility itself, the nature of the conflict between the Zamberlani and the Strumieri changed. With the leaders of the two factions—Della Torre and Savorgnan—both dead, discord between the clans was driven more by personal hatreds and grievances than by politics.[25]

An Ancient Pedigree

Taddea, probably less than forty years old, died in 1519, after which her brother Ettore settled her dowry account with her sons.[26] On 4 January 1520 all five boys, now ranging in age from eight to eighteen years, were invested with the feudal lands of their father Alvise I.[27] Even before their father's death, the older children would have learned about the ancient pedigree of the family, which included four Patriarchs of Aquileia. Their uncle Isidoro had been obsessed with lineage and was something of an amateur genealogist. Back in 1484 he had written to a certain Giovanni Francesco Della Torre, son of Giacomo, who belonged to a branch of the Della Torre family in Milan, consoling him on the death of his brother, Monsignor Giacomo Antonio, Bishop of Cremona, the year before. Isidoro proposed a meeting to fill in the gaps in the family tree. The record is silent as to whether it ever took place. Correspondence over the years suggests a sense of grievance over lost ancestral holdings. In 1507, Isidoro wrote to Ambrogio di Maino, a Milanese knight, lamenting the wrongs suffered by the Torriani in the past and expressing his hopes for restitution of some property—perhaps a castello, he suggested—once owned by the family before they were expelled from Milan in the late thirteenth century. Isidoro and Alvise I were both in correspondence with the Count of Misoch, imperial prefect in Goldestain, in 1509, about a possible common ancestry. The prefect suggested that they meet in Venzone to compare the family trees, but the brothers invited him to Udine instead. Again, there is no record of a family reunion of that sort in those turbulent times, and it probably never took place.[28]

In the Friuli, as in Venice, the firstborn son was typically named after his paternal grandfather. But Alvise I, whose father was named Nicolò, did not follow this practice, perhaps to avoid confusion with Nicolò I, his nephew who was living with the family at Villalta. Instead Alvise I's oldest son, Raimondo, was given the name of his father's brother, the same as that of the Patriarch who had established the Della Torre in the Friuli after being driven out of Milan two centuries earlier. As to Alvise I's other children, Girolamo renewed the name of his maternal grandfather. Giovanni bore the name of two uncles, one on each side of the family. Ginevra's name honoured her paternal grandmother, Ginevra di Spilimbergo. The source of Michele's name, uncommon among the Friulian nobility, is puzzling. It does not appear in his direct ancestral line, but a distant Della Torre cousin in Gorizia did bear the name, and the naming may have been intended as a gesture to that branch of the family. And, as we know, Alvise II was named after his murdered father, Alvise I himself.[29]

The insistence on lordly prerogatives and an alertness to affronts to familial honour was as much a part of the children's patrimony as their feudal properties. They were all too aware that a noble line, vast wealth, and ancient vendettas in the Patria del Friuli restricted the circle of friends one could trust. Over the years even the younger ones would hear gruesome stories about the deaths of their father, uncle, and other relatives, keeping alive the desire for revenge and retribution. As the Della Torre sons came of age, there were troubling signs that the vendetta with the Savorgnan was beginning to resurface.

Discords and Urgent Conflicts

Francesco Janis da Tolmezzo, an advisor to Antonio Savorgnan, returned to Udine after years of confinement in Venice.[30] It was only a matter of time before the spilling of patrician blood would again be avenged. Amaseo's diary entries for 1522 tell the tale:

> On the 21st day of August the news spread through all of Udine that the new pope [Adrian VI] had reached Italy with many sails…and on the same day messer Francesco Janis da Tolmezzo was assaulted and wounded on the head and on the hand in Udine near the Porta di San Antonio, by ser Gerolamo, son of ser Federico Colloredo, because he considered ser Francesco to have been the chief cause of *Zobia Grassa*, when so many in Udine and the Friuli—and among others ser Federico—were killed, burned, and sacked by Antonio Savorgnan.[31]

Francesco's wounds were slow to heal, and the old jurist remained confined to his house, with time to ponder his injudicious remark to Savorgnan back in 1511 that 'a dead man doesn't make war'.[32] The following year, Nicolò Colloredo, brother of Teseo who had also died in the 1511 massacre, tracked down another Savorgnan associate, Giovanni Monticolo, in Monza and killed him on 9 December. Upon hearing of the death on the 18th of the month, Janis di Tolmezzo took to his bed and died the next day. The notary Antonio Belloni noted in the civic death register that Janis had died on the 19th, 'wounded, but not from the wounds'.[33]

On 19 January 1523, the Council of Ten ordered Nicolò Colloredo along with Girolamo Colloredo, 'who promised for his brother' to make peace with Nicolò Monticolo, brother of the murdered Giovanni.[34] But accounts were by no means settled, and the vendetta continued to fester under the surface. Only six months later, on 11 June, because of 'discords and urgent conflicts between Giovanni Battista Savorgnan and those of the Colloredo, that is, Domino Giambattista and Nicolò; Ercole della Rovere; [and] Raimondo and Giovanni Della Torre, brothers', the Venetian luogotenente admonished the two factions to abstain from offending one another with words and deeds or in any other way under penalty of confiscation of all their property. The main protagonists were old enemies: for this was the Giovanni Battista Savorgnan who had been wounded and left for dead by Giambattista Colloredo in 1516.[35]

While Venice's support of a reform-minded civic oligarchy in Udine kept the old noble factions in check, hostilities between the nobility and the popular classes continued.[36] An official census carried out back in 1518 had offended the (often wealthy) commoners, since it was restricted to the nobility and included only 111 families. In response, the luogotenente ordered a general census of all the inhabitants of the city in March 1522. Class identification was a particular concern, and the Consiglio del Comune voted that a noble citizen or knight should be designated by the title of *magnifico*, a doctor (that is, a university graduate) as *domino*, and a commoner as *ser*.[37]

No family was more aware of its place in the social hierarchy than the Della Torre. One thing that particularly rankled was the Savorgnan claim to Venetian patrician status. Amaseo reported that rumours were circulating in Udine of 'how the excellent Council of Ten had confirmed an ancient privilege of 160 years earlier that these gentlemen Della Torre of Udine were gentlemen of Venice, [a title of] Venetian nobility the Della Torre had never used nor enjoyed after the Signoria took over the Patria. It was not true.'[38] The source of the rumours could only have been the family itself. Assertion of the purity and antiquity of its noble lineage would have come to the fore in 1523, when the twenty-two-year-old Raimondo became a Knight of the Order of St John of Jerusalem following the fall of Rhodes to the Ottoman Turks. Pietro Bembo was inducted the same year, and one wonders whether their paths crossed at the time. And like Pietro, Raimondo had to provide documentary proof of his noble ancestry, not that it was ever in question.[39] Now head of the family, he began to use the title of cavalier. The year before, at the age of sixteen, his brother Giovanni had entered the Venetian army under the command of the Duke of Urbino, Francesco Maria I della Rovere.[40]

New Alliances

Marriages were, as always, favoured ways to create new alliances and cement old ones. In 1518, Pagano, the brother of Giovanni Battista Savorgnan who had been wounded by Giambattista Colloredo two years earlier, took a Venetian bride, Chiara Priuli. The same year, Pagano's sister Lucina gave birth to the child of Francesco Savorgnan del Torre, the disinherited nephew of Antonio Savorgnan.[41] This was an alliance that Girolamo Savorgnan del Monte had rejected for one of his own daughters. He seems to have looked upon it more favourably for his ward, Lucina, daughter of his deceased brother Giacomo. This was the Lucina who had sung so sweetly at the ball given by her mother Maria Savorgnan on the eve of Giovedì Grasso in 1511. And this was the Lucina with whom Luigi da Porto, soldier, writer, and nephew of Antonio Savorgnan, had fallen in love. The hopeless prospects of their union are thought to have provided the inspiration for his *Historia novellamente ritrovata di due nobili amanti*, an autobiographical novella set in Verona. Writing it while nearly paralyzed from war wounds, Luigi completed the book sometime before June 1524 and dedicated it to Lucina. Published in 1530, it later took on new life as the basis for Shakespeare's *Romeo and Juliet*, but that is another story for another time.[42]

Lucina's marriage, formalized only in 1522 and probably not one of her choice, may have joined together two branches of the family, but it did not resolve the question of the inheritance, which remained a matter of contention throughout the 1520s. More importantly, her union and that of her brother Pagano produced sons who would be raised in the poisonous atmosphere of vendetta and who, as we shall see, became the eventual bloody avengers (or victims) of family honour.[43]

Following a family pattern of late marriages for Della Torre males, no plans seem to have been made in those years to perpetuate the bloodline with a marriage into another Friulian family, and the other three sons—Girolamo, Michele, and Alvise II—prepared to enter the priesthood. But when their sister Ginevra turned sixteen around 1524, she was ready for marriage. What better choice than Giambattista Colloredo, a longtime ally? A military man who rode in the imperial army of Charles V, he was now in his mid-forties. It was high time to settle down and raise a family, as had Ginevra's own father Alvise I two and a half decades earlier. And as with Ginevra's mother Taddea, the dowry contract was negotiated with Colloredo by her brothers and Uncle Ettore. It provided for 1000 ducats to be paid out at 50 ducats per year, plus another 800 ducats to be satisfied by an annual payment of 80 stara of grain.[44]

Ginevra moved from the protection of her brothers to the care of her husband and the responsibilities of a wife. First and foremost, she should perpetuate the lineage, a duty that she would fulfil and then some. Her first child, Sertorio, was born in the 'camera abbasso' (lower chamber) of the Colloredo family palace in Udine on 17 June 1525. Andriana followed in 1526. Although Ginevra's husband Giambattista must have been away a good amount of time in military service of the emperor, the next four children were born one after the other: Girolamo in 1527, Fulvia in 1529, Marzio in 1530, and Curzio in 1531, all in the Castello di Colloredo di Monte Albano (Figure 3.3).[45]

Indeed, life went on. Despite prognostications of torrential rains, devastating floods, and catastrophic earthquakes forecast by some astrologers for the month of February 1524, the year turned out to be a good one overall for the family and the city.[46] In April, the Venetian luogotenente, Andrea Foscolo, moved into his new apartments in the castello, reconstructed and refurbished after a seven-year campaign.[47] In July, Carlo Contarini, the Venetian orator to the Archduke Ferdinand of Austria, passed through Udine on his way to Vienna. From a lengthy account of his journey, duly summarized by Sanudo in his Diaries (but curiously ignored by Amaseo), we learn that the Della Torre brothers were living together in the city and that the extended clan enjoyed the good graces of the Republic. Contarini's delegation was met at the city gates by the luogotenente, 1500 horsemen, and 'a great number of gentlemen of the town'. Contarini was lodged at the house of the brothers' uncle, Ettore Strassoldo. The guests dined with the luogotenente, 'where they were treated most superbly with diverse dishes'. The following day 'they went to mass together at the Duomo, then to the loggia where lord Gregorio Amaseo, dottore [our chronicler], gave a Latin oration in his praise, and he responded to the orator with the greatest elegance. After dinner together they

Figure 3.3. Castello di Colloredo di Monte Albano before the earthquake of 1976. The castle is still undergoing reconstruction.

went on horseback to see the city, both inside and outside.' In an admirable showing of civic unity, they were joined by the governor 'with all his light cavalry and many gentlemen and castellans of the patria, and [referring to the castello] saw some buildings made by the luogotenente'.[48]

The third day featured a shooting contest in honour of the visitors, but no one won a prize. 'Then this orator went to supper at the house of Lord Raimondo de la Torre, cavalier, where there are five brothers.' With the old Della Torre palace yet to be rebuilt, the men were probably still living in the house bought for their mother back in 1513. It was obviously a venue suitable for a banquet. The brothers 'offered a beautiful meal, which lasted more than four hours, with a copious number of dishes'. Leaving Udine, the delegation travelled a short distance to the Castello di Colloredo, where they lunched on 'a beautiful meal of fish' as guests of Giambattista Colloredo and his brothers, and continued on to Venzone, where they spent the night before proceeding on over the Alps, arriving in Vienna two weeks later.[49]

That fall, the Patriarch Marino Grimani transferred his residence to Udine from Aquileia, still in the hands of the Austrians. After a solemn entry on 1 November, he celebrated the mass in Piazza del Mercato with 'extraordinary pomp and concourse'. Five bishops and three Venetian procurators of San Marco, with their wives dressed in cloth of gold, sat in a loggia specially constructed in front of the church of San Giacomo. Amaseo estimated 30,000 in attendance, along with the luogotenente and all the Udinese nobility, filling the piazza and the windows all around, 'and if there had not been torrential rains, without doubt there would have been more people'. Grimani declared the city *Aquileia Nova* and the metropolitan city of the Patria, a designation that was proclaimed on an official seal. But for Amaseo, the most impressive event was yet to come: 'Afterwards, I, Gregorio Amaseo, on Sunday, November 6th… in the pulpit of the cathedral in the presence of all the citizenry of the city and many other worthy persons, gave a very long panegyric for more than two and a quarter hours, with the greatest admiration and attention by everyone.'[50]

Honour Defended

By 1526 Girolamo was studying law in Bologna and displaying the quick temper and readiness to take offence typical of a Friulian lord. According to Sanudo, he was about to fight a duel, a perilous event that his relatives sought to prevent:

> Some members of the Della Torre family, citizens of Udine, came before the Collegio [in Venice], saying that a dispute had arisen at the University of Bologna between Girolamo Della Torre and the Venetian patrician Marco Michiel, son of Alvise, who is in exile… [Della Torre's relatives] do not want them [Girolamo and Marco] to do what they have decided to do: to battle it out on February 18th in Mantuan territory.

But then Sanudo corrected himself:

> And it should be noted that although I wrote that they have appeared before the Collegio, it is actually the case that they have *not* appeared yet. And arguing against them, the Venetian patrician Marin Michiel, the brother of the aforementioned Marco, wants to block [their appearance] saying that he [Girolamo] is lying in his throat about what he says about the Venetians and that he should be slapped as he slapped my brother.

And yet, confident that Venetian distaste for duelling would prevail, Sanudo predicts: 'And peace will be made.'[51]

Girolamo did indeed show up in Mantua to defend his honour, but Michiel did not. A notarial document in the Della Torre family archive in Udine, labelled 'Fede legalizata, ed autenticha fatta in Mantova', attests:

> I, Giovanni Rigala, notary of the aforementioned magnifico Lord Collalto, state on my word… [that] the presence… [of] the Magnificent messer Hieronymo

della Torre, nobleman of the Patria del Friuli and law student, did occur on the aforementioned day in Mantua and at the office of the aforementioned Magnificent and Generous Count Lord Marc'Antonio at the office of the Magnificent Lord Collalto, which location is a gathering place for nobles, and that he was waiting for a time for a Venetian, a Messer Marco de Connichelle (Marco Michiel), and, not seeing him, he had me, the notary, draw up a document attesting to his presence and to the absence of the said ser Marco: in the presence of the Magnifico Messer Zuan Lodovico Gonzaga, citizen of Mantua...and the magnifico messer Giacomo Aliprando, university laureate and citizen of Mantua...and the magnifico messer Paullo Luchisco a captain in the Marquis's army, witnesses called by the aforementioned messer Girolamo.

[Signed:] I, Zuan, son of Artusi [Arturo] dei Rigali, citizen of Mantua and public notary.[52]

The existence of the notarized document, with reputable witnesses, indicates that Girolamo's legal training had already taken hold. The incident suggests that challenges to honour, verbal or otherwise, were beginning to be addressed by the formalized ritual of the duel rather than bloody ad hoc confrontations in the streets.[53] Michiel's failure to appear also reminds us that a Venetian would be at a considerable disadvantage in duelling with a feudal lord who had grown up with a sword in his hand. The matter would soon be forgotten, with most of Italy engulfed in war.

The Church and the Army

The Della Torre sons pursued the two most desirable career options open to feudal lords: the church and the army. Girolamo must have completed his legal training, typically a two-year course in Bologna, when he was stood up by Michiel in Mantua. Three weeks later, on 7 March 1526, at the age of twenty-one, he was appointed a *chierico* (cleric) of the Diocese of Aquileia. Pope Clement VII named him his familiar and conferred on him the office of *scrittore apostolico*—a scriptor responsible for preparing briefs in the papal chancery.[54] A promising career in Rome was on the horizon. But politics intervened. Two months later, Venice was again at war. On 22 May 1526, the Republic joined France, Milan, and Pope Clement VII in founding the League of Cognac (and later joined by Henry VIII of England). An anti-imperial alliance, it aimed to contain the ambitions of Charles V and prevent him from taking over Italy. Gian Matteo Giberto, a confidant of Clement VII, wrote the following month to the Bishop of Veroli 'it is not a war that concerns a point of honour, a petty vengeance, or the preservation of a single city, but the deliverance or the eternal slavery of all Italy.'[55] Four years of war, famine, and pestilence would ensue.

In Udine, Girolamo's brother Raimondo continued to represent the family in civic matters. At the end of the year, he joined a delegation of some forty nobles who appeared before the Council of Ten and successfully blocked Girolamo Savorgnan del Monte from sitting amongst the deputies of the Udine city council. Amaseo reported that Savorgnan received this decision with displeasure: 'he had already begun…to make himself the signore, as these Savorgnans were accustomed to do in the city of Udine, having little by little usurped a manifest tyranny.'[56] But Savorgnan's support in Udine was falling away, and in 1528 he moved to Venice where he died the following year.[57]

Amaseo began his diary for the year 1527 with grim statistics: 'At the beginning of January it was said that there were in Italy more than 60 thousand persons representing the emperor, between Germans, Spaniards, and Italians, in Lombardy, Romagna, Tuscany, and Naples, and also many more representing the league against them.'[58] Girolamo Della Torre was still seeking a position in Rome, and a second papal bull issued in February 1527 authorized him to fill any office in the Roman Curia.[59] But just three months later, such a prospect looked decidedly less attractive. On 6 May, Rome was devastated by the Sack: three bloody days of murder, rape, and pillaging by more than 30,000 Imperial troops. To the Della Torre, the disastrous event must have been grimly reminiscent of the Giovedì Grasso massacre in Udine writ large.[60] Notwithstanding the Sack, with Pope Clement VII still barricaded in Castel Sant'Angelo, the two posthumous orphans of 1511—Alvise II and cousin Nicolò II—received their first tonsures on 14 May at the age of fifteen and joined Girolamo in the priesthood. Michele must have also been tonsured in this period.[61]

Less than three months later, the family was struck by personal tragedy. While serving in the Venetian army under the Duke of Urbino, Giovanni died on 15 August in Perosa, a village near Turin, at the age of twenty-one, having suffered from 'a continuous fever'—possibly typhus. According to family records, his body was brought back to Udine on 12 September, 'despite great peril of war and the plague, and was most sumptuously buried three days later in San Francesco in the tomb of his ancestors'.[62] Amaseo delivered an extemporaneous funeral oration that lasted an hour and a half, 'in the presence of the whole city, to the fervent applause of all'. In his eulogy he reiterated Della Torre claims that the house had descended from Charlemagne, the Dukes of Milan, and the Patriarchs of Aquielia. But not everyone applauded. Amaseo later wrote of being persecuted by those who complained that he that had exalted the Della Torre above all others.[63]

Famine and Pestilence

The remainder of 1527 was marked by a severe famine throughout the region. In mid-December, although ships filled with grain were arriving from Cyprus, Sanudo wrote that

> everything is expensive, and every evening in Piazza San Marco and in the streets and in Rialto there are children crying, 'I want bread—I am dying of hunger and of cold,' and it rends your heart. And in the morning, bodies are found under the portico of the Palazzo Ducale. Yet no steps are being taken.

By the following February, the situation had worsened:

> And so many have come from the countryside around Vicenza and Brescia, that it is stupefying. You cannot go to hear Mass without ten poor people coming up and asking for alms; you cannot open your purse to buy anything without poor people asking for a coin, and until late in the evening people go about beating on doors and crying out in the street, 'I am dying of hunger.' Still the government has made absolutely no provision to deal with this.

In March, Sanudo observed wryly that amid all this misery, Carnival celebrations continued, with banquets and dancing until dawn, and noted wryly: 'it would have been better to give alms.' The following month, the Quarantia finally acted, voting to register the indigent, to house the sick and weak in emergency shelters, to give a quarter-ducat to the healthy and, if peasants, to send them back to the mainland.[64]

Italy remained a battlefield, with the situation going from bad to worse. In Udine, the prolific Amaseo had run out of paper in mid-October 1527 and discontinued his writing until February of 1529, when he summed up the events that had happened in the meantime. In the summer of 1528, he reported that,

> having survived the great heat, all the encampments of the league began to get sick, not only from the plague that raged in diverse places, but much more from the *mal de petecchie* (typhus), a little less venomous than the plague, which illness ruled all of Italy, with the consequence that an infinite number of persons of every condition died from such infirmity, so that from hunger, as well as from war, plague, and *petecchie*, many villages, castles and cities remained desolate. The famine and scarcity of grain throughout Italy was the greatest ever known in human memory.[65]

The cost of wheat was four times higher than usual—if one could find it—and meat doubled in price. The poor survived on grasses and roots and even ate the grapevines. Even then, Amaseo allowed that 'the Patria di Friuli suffered less than the rest of Italy from these three great scourges, that is, from war not at all and from hunger and *petecchie* less than in other places.'[66]

And yet, Udine remained a dangerous place, even for tonsured clerics with connections in high places. In 1528 Girolamo was granted a licence to bear arms in Venetian territories as well as the city of Venice by the Council of Ten, but 'only for his defense, as he humbly requests.'[67] And that was only the beginning.

Notes

1. ASUd, *AT*, b. 17, c. 207. See Grubb 1996, 91–3, on the appointment of widows as governors of their children.
2. DU, GAH, 533–4; Muir 1993, 208.
3. Tockner 2003, 239–53.
4. Zucchiatti 1989, 12.
5. Ibid., 18.
6. DU, GAH, 522; Muir 1993, 172.
7. Zucchiatti 1984, 65–8; Zucchiatti 1989, 13–17.
8. Zucchiatti 1989, 13–17, 22–9; Miotti 1977, 401.
9. Zucchiatti 1989, 7–36; Ulmer 1997, 278–309; Miotti 1977, 399–407; Maffei 2005, 274–5. For Venetian palace layouts, see Brown 2004, 53–89.
10. Muir 1993, 172, 327n34: ASUd, *AT*, b. 17, c. 207; ibid., b. 33.
11. ASUd, *AT*, b. 24, no. 31.
12. Ibid., b. 22, no. 35. It was purchased from Bernardino q. Zanutti di Cuccagna and his brothers.
13. DU, GA, 239.
14. See Savini 1931, 298, citing BCUd, Fondo Joppi, MS 592. On this practice, see Cozzi 1973, 293–5, 318–19, 338–9. See also ASVe,AC, r. 32, cc. 3v-4 (26 June 1524).
15. Sanudo, *Diarii*, 20:505 (9 and 13 August 1515).
16. Casella 2003, 134.
17. Muir 1993, 238–43.
18. Sanudo, *Diarii*, 25: 14–15 (6 October1516). Cf. Degani 1900, 76; Conzato 2005, 30 and 58 n66; and Casella 2003, 112, who assume incorrectly that Savorgnan was killed.
19. See Casella 2003, Tav. 3; BCUd, MS. Del Torso 162, 'Enrico Del Torso, Genealogie nobiliari', for the Strassoldo family tree.
20. Bergamini and Buora 1990, 70–5; and further references in Kassler-Taub 2010, 5–6.
21. ASUd, *AT*, b. 47.
22. Colloredo 1889, 6.
23. DU, GA, 250; , Muir, 1993, 244; Casella 2003, 110–11.
24. DU, GA, 250: 'Qui de gladio ferit, de gladio perit.' See also Conzato 2005, 58 n66.
25. Casella 2003, 113; Bianco 1994a, 267–9; Bianco 1995, 34–5.
26. ASUd, *AT*, b. 24, no. 31.
27. Ibid., b. 17, fasc. 1, 'Prove storico-genealogiche della famiglia Della Torre', 130–3; Conzato 2005, 30–1; ASVe, *LPF*, b. 279, Ducali, 22v–23.
28. ASUd, *AT*, b. 13. For the family tree, see Appendix II, Table A herein.
29. Ibid., b. 16 and b. 17. See also Appendix II, Table B; Gélis 1991, 212l; Brown 2004, 16–19. Alvise I's distant cousin, Giovanni Della Torre, capitano of Gorizia, who had died in 1505, had sons named Michele, Giorgio, and Nicolò, later knights in the imperial army.
30. Muir 1993, 244. After his house arrest in Venice, he also represented Venetian interests in Spain before returning to the Friuli.
31. DU, GA, 268. Adrian VI was regent of Spain when elected pope on 9 January 1522; he sailed to Italy, reaching Genova on 19 August and making his solemn entry into Rome ten days later.

32. Ibid., 269 (for the aphorism see 257 and 516). This Girolamo Colloredo belonged to the Primo Ramo of the family and should be distinguished from his homonym, son of Albertino, who had participated in the assassination of Antonio Savorgnan. Cf. Muir 1993, 245, who conflates the two Girolamos. For the lineage of this Girolamo q. Federico, see Custoza 2003, Tav. V; Crollalanza 1875, Tav. V.
33. BCUd, MS Joppi 423, 'Antonio Belloni, Necrologium et Flaminio de Rubeis, Chronica Defunctorum', 2: 'obijt vulner*at*us sed non ex vulneribus.' See also DU, GA, 269; DU, GAH, 498n; Muir 1993, 244–5; Fulin 1881, 64. Cf. Antonini 1877, 87–8; Mandelli, 'Francesco Janis'.
34. DU, GA, 270; Muir 1993, 245.
35. ASVe, *LPF*, b. 275, Ducali, 1516–23, c. 94 (11 June 1523).
36. Muir 1993, 215, 241–3.
37. Battistella 1932, 17–19.
38. DU, GA, 268.
39. Kidwell, 2004, 123–4.
40. ASUd, *AT*, b. 17, cc. 158–9.
41. Casella 2003, 134–7.
42. Clough 1993, Muir 1993, 158–9; Lavarda 2007, 64.
43. Casella 2003, 134–7, noting that the belated marriage of Lucina and Francesco four years after the birth of their first child would be repeated in 1555 by their son Giovanni with his first cousin Maria, the daughter of Lucina's brother Pagano. See also Clough 1993, 122.
44. ASUd, *AT*, b. 22, no. 38, 'Quittance for dowry of Ginevra q. Alvise Della Torre' (24 February 1565). My thanks to Reiny Mueller, Bianca Lanfranchi, and Gigi Corazzol for assistance in interpreting this document. For Friulian marriage traditions, see Sachs 1915, 108–14.
45. BCUd, Fondo Joppi, MS 84, fasc. 27. See also Appendix II, Table D; Custoza 2003, 139 and Tav. VI; Crollalanza 1875, Tav. VII.
46. For the dire, but erroneous, predictions, see Cergneu 1895, 75–6; and Sanudo, *Diarii*, 35: 483–4, noting that towns in central Italy near Urbino did suffer heavy rains and flooding on the sixteenth of the month.
47. Bergamini and Buora 1990, 65.
48. Sanudo, *Diarii*, 36: 574 (573–81 for a full account). See also Bergamini and Buora 1990, 70–5.
49. Sanudo, *Diarii*, 36: 574.
50. DU, GA, 276; Ciconi 1861, II, 353–4.
51. Sanudo, Diarii: 40: 726 (26 January 1526). I am grateful to Linda Carroll for assistance with the translation and interpretation of this passage.
52. ASUd, AC, b. 6, colto 11: Bolle pontificie varie, no. 1 (18 February 1526).
53. An early example of a trend that would take on momentum toward the middle of the century. See Muir 1993, 247–72; Povolo 2015, 195–244.
54. ASUd, *AT*, b. 6, colto 11, 'Bolle pontificie varie', no. 2 (7 March 1526). On Bologna, see Grendler 2002, 447, 453, 455, 515.
55. Ruscelli 1573, 193.
56. DU, GA, 288 (24 December 1526). See also Sanudo, *Diarii*, 43: 416, 425, 667.

57. Muir 1993, 242–3.
58. DU, GA, 289.
59. ASUd, *AT*, b. 6, colto 11: Bolle pontificie varie, no. 3 (7 February 1527).
60. Chastel, *The Sack of Rome, 1527*; Partner, *Renaissance Rome, 1500–1559*, Berkeley, 1976, 33; Hook, 'The Destruction of the "New Italia"', 10–30.
61. ASUd, *AT*, b. 5, no. 13. Michele's patent of first tonsure is missing from the busta.
62. Ibid., b. 17, c. 159. For plague and typhus afflicting the troops, see Corradi 1867, 52–60. See also Alfani 2013, 52–6, 85–6, 88–9.
63. DU, LI-LII. See also Muir 1993, 213–14.
64. Sanudo, *Diarii*, 46:380, 512; ibid., 47:83–4; translations Labalme and Sanguineti White 2008, 326, 327.
65. DU, GA, 298. *Petecchie* was a pestilential fever accompanied by spots resembling flea bites all over the body. It is now thought to have been epidemic typhus, spread by body lice, with a 60 per centmortality rate in the pre-antibiotic period. See Bechah, 'Epidemic typhus', 417–26; Byrne, *Encyclopedia of Pestilence*, I: 181, 732; Cohn 2010, 49–53, 97, 173–4.
66. DU, GA, 298–9. For the interaction between war, famine, and disease, see Alfani 2013, esp. 43–6.
67. ASUd, *AT*, b. 11, cartella XI, colto 21, fasc. 20 (1 August 1528).

4
Restitution

The Della Torre children had grown up in a city ravaged by riots, earthquakes, occasional famines and pestilence, wars, and threats of war. The Sack of Rome of 1527 was a turning point, ushering in a period of urban renewal. One of its major architects was Giovanni Ricamatore, known as Giovanni da Udine, a native son who had enjoyed a brilliant career in Rome in the second and third decades of the century. One of the pioneers of *grotteschi*, a style of fanciful painted and stuccoed ornament based upon the decoration of ancient buildings, he had worked with Raphael on the Villa Farnesina, as well as the Vatican Logge and the Loggia of Pope Leo X in the Vatican Palace, and took over the decoration of Villa Madama after Raphael's death.[1] He continued to work for Clement VII, but fled Rome after the Sack. His return to Udine gave him the opportunity to demonstrate his skills as an architect with a commission to construct a clock tower in Piazza Contarena. Completed in 1528, it would house the city's first public clock and herald a civic building boom parallel to the *renovatio urbis* taking place in Doge Andrea Gritti's Venice.[2]

Civic attention soon focused on two spaces near the clock tower at the foot of the hill crowned by the Castello: the *piazza del comun* and the *piazza del vin.* Adjacent to Mercatovecchio and the fifteenth-century Loggia Comunale, popularly called the Loggia del Lionello, the squares were bustling centres of citizen life (Figure 4.1). But between them stood the partially ruined Trecento church of San Giovanni Battista that had been badly damaged in the 1511 earthquake. In 1530 the Venetian luogotenente, with the citizen council, decided to raze it to the ground and create an expansive new piazza in the space.

By 1531 the luogotenente could write: 'In the entire time I've been here, no one has died nor been mortally wounded in this city and territory, a rare thing. May God see that it would continue to the end.'[3] His optimism was premature. Old wounds had not yet healed.

Redress of Grievances

The vastly wealthy Girolamo Savorgnan del Monte died in Venice in 1529 after giving up his dream of becoming lord of Udine. Providentially, as far as the Della Torre and the other castellans were concerned, his earlier wills had been destroyed by fire, and he had neglected to make a new one. His death intestate revived old claims and presented new opportunities, for it fell to the Venetian government to

The Venetian Bride: Bloodlines and Blood Feuds in Venice and Its Empire. Patricia Fortini Brown, Oxford University Press (2021). © Patricia Fortini Brown. DOI: 10.1093/oso/9780192894571.003.0004

Figure 4.1. Joseph Heintz il Giovane, attrib., *View of Udine* (detail of Figure 2.2) c. 1650–60 (Museo Civico, Castello di Udine).

The Castello, palace of the Venetian luogotenente, sits on a hill looking over the city. Piazza Contarena is below it to the right, where Giovanni da Udine's clocktower (1527) rises behind Bernardino da Morcote's church and Porticato di San Giovanni (1535). On the elevated platform in front are two tall columns, one topped with a statue of Justice (1614) and the other with the lion of Saint Mark (1539). Giovanni da Udine's fountain (1542) anchors the right-hand corner. The Loggia del Lionello is the square, hip-roofed building opposite. To the right are the Duomo and tall tower of the baptistery. The arcaded facade of Palazzo Torriani is visible between the two bridge towers at the bottom right of the detail. The church and monastery of San Francesco are situated next to the moat to the right. The open expanse of Piazza San Giacomo, with a column and another fountain (1542) by Giovanni da Udine, is clearly visible on the left.

settle the estate. First in line were the heirs of Girolamo Savorgnan himself and the sons of Antonio Savognan's deceased brother Giovanni; but not close behind were the Strumieri families that had suffered losses in 1511. On 30 April 1530, Doge Andrea Gritti ordered the Savorgnan heirs to pay the Strumieri a total of 30,000 ducats over a fifteen-year period. He admonished both sides 'to live in peace and not offend' one another.[4] It may have been no coincidence that Alvise II Della Torre and his cousin Nicolò II were granted licences to bear arms on 9 July, 'lest they fall into manifest peril'.[5] The Strumieri claimants protested that the settlement was woefully insufficient, and a board of arbitration was appointed to examine detailed claims for compensation.[6]

This would open the door to further adjudication. A detailed petition to the Venetian authorities, written in a chancery hand on behalf of Raimondo, Girolamo, Michele, Alvise II, and Nicolò II Della Torre, was begun, taking two years to compile.[7] In the meantime, there were setbacks. In May 1532 Raimondo stood for election to the position of Collateral General of the Venetian armies, a highly prized position filled by the Venetian Senate in a secret election. Sanudo listed seventeen contenders. The post went to Francesco da Porto of Vicenza, with 175 votes out of 236. Bonifacio di San Bonifacio of Verona came in second with an unstated number of votes, and the Venetian Giovanni Amadi came third. Raimondo did not even come close.[8]

Even worse, Raimondo died on 25 November, but his name remained on the petition of redress when it was presented to the Council of Ten on 13 January 1533. Recounting 'the immense and infinite damage suffered by us in that horrendous event of unhappy memory of *Zobia Grassa*', the claimants concede that they cannot provide complete documentation,

> because as your lordships know well, part of us were of minor age, and part were in our mothers' wombs. But constrained to do like the others, we will now state that on that horrendous occasion three houses were burned, the Castello of Villalta ruined, put to sack and all the goods stolen, that is, wheat and other grains, wine, silver, and all the furniture of the house, which in everyone's judgment, was of the greatest value. And we do not intend nor wish to prove or justify any of this, since this is a well-known matter, manifest, and clear to everyone.

They are confident that the Signori will exercise their usual prudence and sense of justice and do what their conscience demands.[9]

A list of nine points follows. From it we learn that a chest was found in the basement of one of the houses occupied by the family and that it was carried away to the house of Antonio Savorgnan: 'And in this chest it is common opinion that there were coins and items of the greatest value.' Their uncle Isidoro 'had said over and over that in this house where we now reside, that there were a great number of coins and things of the greatest price and value'. Indeed, Isidoro's corpse had been robbed of 3000 ducats that he had hidden in his sleeves on the day of the riots. In addition, because of the wars of that time, their father Alvise I had buried in their garden 'certain chests with many coins'. These too were gone. Moreover, before all this happened, Isidoro had intended to buy the feud (fief) of Castelnovo that year for 5000 ducats, a sure sign that the family had a good amount of cash on hand. Furthermore, Alvise I had kept a sack full of promissory notes recording loans made to many people, 'that were of great value'. With it missing, debts owed to the family would never be repaid. Finally, they conclude with three points to clinch the argument: 'That it is publicly known and famous that our house was very wealthy; that everything was taken away and sacked, that nothing else remained other than the clothes on our backs; and that in the judgment of all, our house has suffered damages of more than 50,000 ducats.'[10]

A Noble Lineage

But the family's concern was not only financial redress. Girolamo, now head of the family, presented a second petition, elegantly written in a chancery hand, on behalf of himself, his two surviving brothers, and his cousin Nicolò II. Declaring themselves 'most devoted servants' of the Serenissima, they fill in the blanks of a genealogical record that provides the family with a specifically Venetian provenance. Gastone (Cassono) Della Torre, Archbishop of Milan, was chased out of that city with his brothers by the emperor Henry VII [1311] and 'deprived not only of their patrimony, but of every honour, degree, and preeminence'.[11]

Subsequently appointed Patriarch of Aquileia [1317], Gastone died in 1318 before he could settle in that Friulian city, and his brother Moschino moved to Venice with his sons. Over the course of thirty years, they ungrudgingly made forced loans of 30,000 ducats to the Monte Vecchio, the state loan office celebrated in official documents as 'the life and health of this blessed Signoria'. Such loans were a form of indirect taxation akin to a modern-day municipal bond. Usually paying around 5 per cent annual interest, they were not a bad investment.[12] In recognition of this service to the Republic, Doge [Giovanni] Dolfin had conceded to Moschino's sons Nicolino, Ottolino, and Cassono, and to their descendants, the privilege and grace of being 'sons and heirs, citizens and Venetians of this illustrious dominion' in 1356.[13] However, the petition argues, 'considering the grandeur and nobility of the house of the Della Torre at that time', it must actually have been intended that they 'be made nobles of Venice as one sees by other similar concessions'—a veiled reference to the privilege enjoyed by the Savorgnan for a century and a half.[14] The supplicants, whose faith and merit are second to none, reiterate that many other subjects, both inside and outside the Patria, have received similar concessions. Their own concession was thus far more restrictive than it should have been, 'for one immediately sees that their long-lasting gratitude and faithful service for 200 continuous years, was accompanied with infinite merits and was never remunerated in any way'.[15]

Still addressing the doge, the Della Torre are certain that 'it would be pleasing to him to concede the gift and similar grace of being confirmed or admitted and aggregated into the consortium of your other nobles'. This would go a long way toward repairing 'so much damage, fires, and killings suffered on that horrendous and most unhappy day of *Zobia Grassa*, so cruel and hellish, of which the memory alone should move everyone to compassion'. Now raising the estimate of their losses to '100,000 ducats or more', they add that their father, Alvise I, had also spent at least 10,000 ducats as a cavalry captain in the Venetian army at Novara [1495] 'with no small damage to his house'. Likewise, their brother Giovanni had spent another 10,000 ducats of family resources in his five years of faithful service to the Duke of Urbino, capitano generale of the Venetian army. Passing over the fact that Giovanni's death near Turin was associated with a fever and not military exploits, they assert that 'he died in the most important events in Rome in the year 1527'.[16]

For all their avowals of fidelity, humility, and sacrifice, the Della Torre conclude their petition with words that convey a sense of entitlement that may not have sat well with Venetian officials: 'And in conclusion, the said supplicants, obtaining from your sublimity such a *grazia*, will be satisfied for every damage and inconvenience that they, and their progenitors, have always suffered, in their persons and in their own faculty, for the comfort and service of this illustrious dominion.'[17] Alas, the Venetian authorities declined to accept the Della Torre as 'true gentlemen of Venice', despite their wealth and noble antecedents and despite those 'other similar concessions'—a slight that would remain a source of discontent and help to keep alive their rivalry with the Savorgnan for years to come.[18]

Imperial Honours

But there were compensations. The emperor Charles V had reconciled with the pope and was crowned emperor in Bologna on 24 February 1530, after the Turks had withdrawn from the siege of Vienna. Despite the failure of the Della Torre to achieve patrician status in Venice, the Peace of Bologna of 1530 had brought relative peace to Italy and a new opportunity for the family to burnish its noble credentials.[19] By early 1532, when Raimondo lost his bid to command Venetian forces, the Turks had also withdrawn from Hungary, and the emperor planned a triumphal progress over the Alps through Italy to Rome, and then back to Genoa, whence he would sail to Spain. On 1 October he summoned the Venetian ambassador, Marcantonio Contarini, to his court and informed him that he wished to travel through the Friuli since it was the shortest and quickest route. His entourage would include Spanish troops and four to five thousand Germans, 'for the honour and security of our person'. Judiciously, Charles reassures Contarini that

> I do not wish to enter inside any city in order not to create any suspicion by the Signoria; I will lodge in open places, and I desire that the necessities of life be provided for these people and for my court...Nor should the Signoria worry that our people would create any inconvenience, as had happened in coming here, that I will send them with these gentlemen who will have this responsibility, and where my person will be, there will not be any disorder.[20]

Only on the last count was he, strictly speaking, correct.

Charles trusts that Contarini will also inform the Signoria of his intentions and asks that two Venetian senators meet him at the border to accompany him through the Patria. The imperial company would cross into Venetian territory over a stone bridge at Tarvisio and proceed on to Pontebba, then Venzone, and then to San Daniele, where there was lodging in case the Tagliamento was frozen over. And on to Spilimbergo, Sacile, Conegliano, Bassano, and finally to Erbe, where the company would enter Mantuan territory. His schedule? He intends to leave Vienna in just two days' time. By the time the Signoria had received his letter, he had already been on the road for a week.[21]

The Signoria sprang into action, and the pages that follow in Sanudo's diaries track the progress of men and food. In addition to Venetian officials in Udine, Treviso, Vicenza, and Verona, the castellans along the route were ordered to provide grain, wine, meat, and fodder and to make sure that the roads in their lands were in good repair.[22]

But good intentions were frustrated by the short time frame and realities on the ground. Letters poured in from the Friuli that although wine was plentiful, there was a shortage of wheat, little cheese, and insufficient fodder for the horses. Venice promised to send supplies, and yet, more disquieting reports began to proliferate. From Venzone came reports that the company of Guido Rangoni, with two hundred horsemen, had arrived and been given lodging, but 'there is no fodder for the horses nor victuals for the troops'. Worse yet, Rangoni offered alarming news that another 6000 soldiers were on their way, 'sacking and raping women in disrespect of the emperor', and 'they want fodder for horses and other victuals'. The community is 'in the greatest fear'.[23] From Gemona came reports of 12,000 unpaid soldiers in mutiny, who had murdered two or three of their captains and were looking for others. With a great shortage of bread, they were desperate and travelling 40 miles and more per day. That evening they would reach Villach, which had locked its gates and prepared artillery and arms to keep them out of the city. From Verona came reports that the castellans of Chiusa and Crovara had pulled up the bridges, barges, and rafts from the Adige to keep the troops from crossing into their territory.[24]

For all that, the emperor moved along sublimely above the fray. He arrived in Spilimbergo on 25 October with more than a thousand horsemen and stayed for three nights in the house of Odoardo di Spilimbergo. The Spanish general, Antonio de Leva, so tormented by gout that he had to be carried on a litter, was lodged in the house of the chronicler Roberto di Spilimbergo, 'with more than 100 mouths'. They consumed 1766 pieces of bread and ten *orme* of wine, costing more than 58 ducats, but 'they gave me only 16 scudi'. To honour his hosts, Charles knighted three of the lords of Spilimbergo after attending Sunday mass under a baldaquin of cremesino damask. Among the new *cavalieri aureati* (knights of the golden spur) was little Bartolomeo, a baby of seven months, suitably attired in a long gown of cremesino silk, adorned with gold cloth and a gold necklace valued at 50 ducats. When he started crying during the ceremony, his wet nurse—'tall and beautiful'—was summoned and gave him her breast. As to the emperor, 'he ate alone and he ate quickly…he drank well and ate well; he said that as much time as he has spent in Italy, he had not eaten better bread than here. He ate many oysters…he ate without a fork.' [25]

The Emperor was generous in appointing *cavalieri aureati*. Amaseo could not get the numbers straight, writing in one place that the emperor had created seven *cavalieri* in Spilimbergo and in another that it was ten, but he did not name them.[26] For Roberto di Spilimbergo it was three in the first instance, as cited previously, and eight later. He reported that one of the Spilimbergo youths was wearing his sister's sandals and white hose that were ragged and dirty, and concluded: 'the other knights remained with low reputation for being in such a crowd.'[27]

Amaseo reported that many citizens from Udine had gone to Spilimbergo to see Charles and praised his admirable appearance:

> full of benignity and an Italian manner with most humane gestures, such that he obliged everyone to love him and to revere him…they had never seen a more beautiful spectacle of so many squadrons on foot and on horseback so well ordered, accompanied by more than six thousand women of every sort, and among the others of the most noble lords and very well adorned with silk, gold, and jewels, and there were many with little babies at the breast, born in the field, so that it was an amazing thing to see, and that such had not happened for centuries in Italy.[28]

But the troops from Gorizia were a problem. Like the contingent in Venzone, 'they made great damage of every sort, robbing, beating, and shaming women on the 29th and 30th, so that the peasants fled day and night to Udine'. Such outrages happened in villages throughout the territory, so bad that Amaseo judged the perpetrators to be worse than the Turks.[29]

After moving on to Mantua and Bologna, where Titian painted his portrait, Charles travelled to Rome, then Genoa, and finally Barcelona. And once there, he created yet more *cavalieri aureati*. Among them was Titian, who was granted the title on 10 May 1533.[30] But that was not all. Two weeks later on 26 May, Charles also conferred on Girolamo, Michele, and Alvise II Della Torre, along with their cousin Nicolò II, the titles of Counts of Valsassina and *cavalieri aureati*.[31] As counts palatine, a hereditary title of nobility that would pass on to their legitimate male descendants in perpetuity, they were allowed to appoint notaries and to legitimize children born out of wedlock among other privileges and distinctions. Perhaps just as importantly, as *cavalieri aureati*, they had the right to wear insignia such as golden spurs, gilded armour and sword, and a gold collar or chain around the neck.[32] Whether or not Charles's generosity in granting the distinction had eroded its prestige, such visible signs of nobility set the Della Torre apart from the patricians of Venice.

But why the Della Torre and why at that time? Relatives of the Lords of Spilimbergo, they might well have been among the Udinese citizens who had been part of the throng enthralled by Charles's gracious presence during his visit there. But another possibility is more credible. According to a nineteenth-century source, Michele had joined the court of Charles V at a very young age and had travelled with him through the Friuli to Barcelona, where he was present to receive the diploma of knighthood on behalf of himself and his male relatives. Only then, clad in imperial privilege, did he go to Rome to pursue a career that took him to the upper echelons of the church.[33]

In Udine the following year, there were signs of disquiet. The Ten were besieged with requests from the Savorgnan heirs for permission to arm themselves. In July 1534, the sons of Girolamo Savorgnan del Monte (Mario and his brothers) were granted licenses to carry arms, each with two armed servants, since their brother Costantino—defenceless, innocent, and without armed servants—had recently been assassinated on the streets of Venice. Their cousins, the sons of Giovanni Savorgnan del Torre—Francesco and Bernardino—were granted the same privilege the following February, and Mario's brother Giulio a month later.[34]

In the meantime, and perhaps not coincidentally, the indemnification appeals dragged on and would eventually be settled only in September 1535. The Della Torre claim of 100,000 ducats had been the greatest by far among the fifty-three that were presented to the adjudicators. Next in line were their Spilimbergo relatives at 25,648 ducats, to be followed by the Colloredo with 18,100 and the Brazzacco at 10,279, and others on down to the widow of Alessandro Spilimbergo at 25, for a total of 158,369 ducats. In the end, the Savorgnan heirs were ordered to pay out just 80,000 ducats in all, slightly more than half the amount requested over a period of fifteen years. The Della Torre were awarded 20,000 ducats, substantially less than their claimed losses.[35] But there were consolations. Just a month later, on 22 October 1535, following the death of Raimondo, the Luogotenente Francesco Venier invested the Della Torre with full feudal rights to Villalta and other country properties, and on 29 March 1536, with the support of Doge Andrea Gritti, with the patrimony of the contado of Valsassina.[36]

The Della Torre were moving on with their lives, enjoying the title of Conte di Valsassina, as well as rents from their feudal holdings and the benefices they received as clerics. Alvise II and Nicolò II remained in the Friuli for the most part but Girolamo increasingly spent time in Venice, while continuing to attend to family affairs in Udine and Villalta. As to Michele, his ecclesiastical career in Rome was on an upward trajectory, a circumstance that would bring both triumph and tragedy. And eventually, for Girolamo, a Venetian bride.

Papal Connections

Further commissions from Clement VII had lured Giovanni da Udine back to Rome in 1531, when he competed with Sebastiano Luciani and Benvenuto Cellini for the lucrative post of pontifical keeper of the lead seals—'frate del Piombo'. Vasari wrote that the pope,

> thinking that the talents of Sebastiano deserved it, ordained that Sebastiano should have the office, but should pay out of it to Giovanni da Udine an allowance of three hundred crowns. Thus Sebastiano assumed the friar's habit [and name of Sebastiano del Piombo], and straightway felt his soul changed thereby, for, perceiving that he now had the means to satisfy his desires, he spent his time in repose without touching a brush, and recompensed himself with his comforts and his revenues for many misspent nights and laborious days; and whenever he happened to have something to do, he would drag himself to the work with such reluctance, that he might have been going to his death.[37]

Fortunately, Giovanni's more modest pension did not have the same effect. He carried out several commissions from the newly elected Pope Paul III, moving back and forth between Rome and Udine. In 1534, he expanded the family home on Via Gemona with a new porticoed façade extending over the sidewalk. The following year, at the age of forty-eight, Giovanni married the twenty-year-old Costanza de' Becaris, who brought him a modest 100-ducat dowry.[38] His first child (of an eventual ten) was born in February 1536; by that fall he had moved back to the Friuli and actively pursued commissions in Udine, Venice, and the Veneto. A shrewd businessman, with an ever-growing portfolio of real estate in Udine and its environs, he had to work out a reliable way to collect his income from Rome, not an operation to be left to chance in an age of perilous travel.

Enter the Della Torre family. With the election of Alessandro Farnese as Pope Paul III in 1534, the Della Torre brothers cemented their relationship with one of the most powerful families in Italy. Michele quickly earned the affection of the pope and was appointed *Referendario apostolico*. This was a position in the papal chancery responsible for examining requests for favours in the Signatura gratiae and petitions for justice in the Signatura justitiae and passing them on to the pope for his signature. As one of the first steps in the cursus honorum at the papal court, the appointment boded well for a bright future in the upper ranks of the church.[39]

Michele's responsibilities at the papal court also brought him into close contact with Giovanni da Udine. The artist named Baccio della Croce, a papal *banderaro* (standard-bearer), as his procurator in Rome, and authorized him to collect the salary 'for my office of cavalier and pension of the Piombo'. Baccio would pass the funds on to Michele Della Torre, by then a well-regarded figure at the court. Michele thereupon dispatched the monies to his brother Girolamo in Udine for payment to the artist. The arrangement was already in force by October 1536 when Giovanni recorded his first receipts.[40] Further payments are noted for 1538 and 1539, a period when Giovanni was decorating the ceilings of two rooms in Palazzo Grimani at Santa Maria Formosa in Venice.[41] He is now calling Girolamo Della Torre *mio compare*—my friend—a term also used for godfather. Indeed, when Giovanni's third child, Raphaiello, was baptized in the Duomo of Udine on Palm Sunday, 30 March 1539, Girolamo was one of the godfathers.[42]

A Beautiful Construction

The urban space of Udine was becoming ever more attractive. In 1533, after contentious negotiations with church authorities, the council accepted a proposal from Bernardino da Morcote, a Lombard stonemason, to rebuild the church of San Giovanni Battista on the expanded square on front of the civic loggia. He envisioned a new church incorporated in a long portico that created a monumental frontispiece for the Castello atop the hill behind.[43] Well regarded in the city for his recent completion of the new façade of the church of San Giacomo (1525–33) in Mercatonuovo, a large market square to the west, Bernardino married Giovanni da Udine's sister Antonia in 1535 and continued his work on the new project for another four years.[44]

Morcote's church of San Giovanni, adjacent to his brother-in-law's belltower, was framed by a triumphal arch portal in the centre of the Porticato di San Giovanni—a long arcaded walkway set upon an expansive stone platform three steps above street level. The latter was no small amenity. Most of the streets and piazzas in the city centre were unpaved—dusty or muddy, depending on the weather—and after a heavy rain, those on an incline became conduits. This unpleasant result was particularly true of the streets that led down from the Castello, which channelled swiftly running water into Mercatovecchio and areas around the Loggia. The Porticato was completed in 1539 with the erection of a *columna magna* surmounted by the Lion of San Marco on the southeast corner. And now the citizens could carry out business on the elevated piazza without wading through rising waters (Figure 4.1).[45]

The newly created Piazza Contarena, named after the fifteenth-century luogotenente who had first envisioned such a project, was bounded on the southwest by the municipal loggia, called the Loggia di Lionello. The legislative centre of the commune, the building featured a large hall on the piano nobile for meetings of the Consiglio Maggiore and an expansive arcaded loggia on the elevated ground floor, where citizens mingled and festivities took place (Figure 4.2).[46]

Figure 4.2. Loggia del Lionello, Udine, 1448–1455, with later repairs and modifications up to 1868.

Upon leaving office in November 1539, the luogotenente Gabriel Venier reported to the Collegio:

> Udine is a beautiful city, but not well fortified. The people are obedient and respectful to the rector and number 13,345 persons, including 46 dottori and 40 notaries... A beautiful construction in the piazza was built to adorn the city and this cost a great deal of money.[47]

The private sector also shared in the project of civic renewal, for the patronage of architecture afforded a constructive and durable means to express personal magnificence. With the settlement of 1535 in hand, the three surviving Della Torre brothers—Michele, Alvise II, Girolamo—had appeared before the notary Antonio Belloni in 1538, and signed wills that left their shares of the family estate to each other if any should die without a legitimate male heir, 'because it is decent and honourable that the faculties remain in the family'. A few months later, their cousin Nicolò II did the same.[48] It was time to build a city residence suitable to their new titles and investitures. Despite complaints of financial distress in several petitions to the Venetian doge, the Della Torre were wealthy by any measure. When Girolamo posted a bond guaranteeing a grain shipment by the noble Udinese merchant Beltrame Susanna to the government of Bologna in 1539, he had claimed 10,000 scudi of income. This was more than double the yearly revenue of the city of Udine.[49]

The family began to rebuild the old Palazzo Torriani that had been destroyed in 1511. Work on the palace was already underway on 1 July 1540, when Girolamo petitioned the city council for a concession of public land facing Borgo Strazzamantello on the road leading to Porto Grazzano. The Della Torre wished to continue the construction of their palace up to the corner leading to the church of San Francesco and promised that 'it will be an ornament of this magnificent city'. Their petition was approved by an 83–18 vote.[50]

The new palace contained some twenty rooms. Behind it was a large courtyard with additional buildings and an orchard and gardens on a large property that occupied a full city block (see Figure 4.1).[51] The family must have moved in as soon as it was built. Aside from servants and retainers, the household included the widowed Giacoma Brazzaco Della Torre, now the lady of the house, and four clerics: her son Nicolò II, and nephews Girolamo and Alvise II, as well as Michele when he was not in Rome or on assignments for the pope.

Who was the architect of the palace, 'an ornament of this magnificent city'? No documentary evidence survives, but Giovanni da Udine has been suggested. As we have seen, he was closely connected to the Della Torre and was in Udine at the time. Several of the spaces in the palace were described in a later inventory as *grottesca* and some had gilded or painted cornices, probably of stucco: a *scalone* (stairwell), a *camera da letto* (bed chamber), a *studiolo* (study), two rooms facing the courtyard, a room in the loggia. If Giovanni was not the architect of the building, he could well have been responsible for its interior decoration.[52]

The new palace was built to impress. Indeed, the young counts were sublimely indifferent to an old Italian proverb inscribed in gold letters on the corner of some houses owned by the sons of the noble Ettore Strassoldo, their uncle and former guardian. It counselled: 'Chi non se mesura non dura' (He who fails to keep the measure of himself, does not endure). But the aphorism did capture the attention of the notary Belloni, who copied it down in his journal in 1540, the year when construction began on Palazzo Torriani.[53] In the years to come, the Della Torre might well have wished to have heeded that admonition.

The rebuilding of Udine continued, despite a drought in 1540, followed two years later by a plague of voracious locusts that prompted the commune to order three propitiatory processions by confraternities.[54] Fountains designed on Roman models by Giovanni da Udine were inaugurated in Piazza Contarena in 1542 and Piazza San Giacomo the following year.[55] The clock tower, refurbished in 1542 with the lion of San Marco on its face, would be fitted up in 1544 with two wooden figures clad in lead that beat the hours on the model of the Torre dell'Orologio in Piazza San Marco in Venice (Figure 4.3).[56]

Figure 4.3. Udine, Piazza Contarena (now Piazza della Libertà), with the Porticato of San Giovanni, clock tower and fountain, with the lion of Saint Mark atop a column.

Family Business

The Della Torre now had a new palace suitable to their station, but challenges remained. The family was lacking in male heirs, enemies still lurked on the streets of Udine, the patrimony required prudent management, and honour demanded constant vigilance. The three brothers remained in close contact, each playing a separate role in the service of family affairs. Alvise II took care of business in Udine and Villalta, representing the family in the parliament and disbursing the pension payments to Giovanni da Udine.[57] Michele continued his cursus honorum in Rome as a valued member of the papal court. He wrote to his cousin Canon Claudio Colloredo in 1540, requesting 'a very fast horse... healthy and honourable, because I certainly have need of one for the comfort of my life, to follow our Lord (the pope), who rides very fast; as you well know. With the horses I have at present... it is necessary that I always trot, and the trotting ruins me.'[58]

As to Girolamo, he was spending considerable time on family business in Venice. On 14 March 1542, he petitioned the Council of Ten on behalf of himself, his brothers, and his cousin, for restitution of funds that their great grandfather Nicolino Girolamo Della Torre had deposited in the Monte Vecchio in the fifteenth century. He complained that the Rason Vecchie had demanded documentation that they could not supply because of the events of 1511 when they had 'clearly suffered losses of 100,000 ducats'. Beyond that, despite an agreement calling for 4 per cent interest negotiated by their father Alvise I and uncle Isidoro back in 1497, the funds were earning only 2 per cent. The shortfall would 'bring about the total ruination of their house'. Justice and piety demanded that the family should not lose funds that were left on deposit in good faith for forty-five continuous years. He now humbly (but firmly) requested a copy of the original documents and an accounting of the principal and accrued interest held in the Monte Vecchio under the name of the Della Torre. The Ten voted unanimously, 15–0, to order the officials of the Rason Vecchie to provide Girolamo with a copy of the original agreement—the *madre della camera*—accounting for the capital and the interest due them.[59] While the resolution of the issue is not clear, the dispute would surely have renewed attention to the Della Torre in the councils of Venetian government.

Michele had sent his brother a chatty letter from Rome in January, revealing his awareness of problems back home. He is displeased to hear of a disagreement between their aunt Smeralda (wife of their maternal uncle Ettore Strassoldo) and Count Nicolò II. But he is pleased to know that Girolamo is urging them to settle their differences amicably without further litigation and counsels patience with an aphorism: 'because in fact it is a question more of the shirt than the doublet.' On balance, he thinks that Smeralda is in the wrong and urges Girolamo to use every means to persuade her to change her mind. On the day after tomorrow, Michele will go 'with our lord [the Pope] to the most beautiful *cazze* (country house) in his state', where they will stay fifteen or twenty days.[60] He might have been referring to the fortified residence at Caprarola before it was turned into a proper villa.[61] Michele was ever closer to the Farnese pope, whose twelve-year-old grandson Ranuccio had arrived in Venice that year as prior of the Knights of Malta and had his portrait painted by Titian.[62] At the end of July, the pope was in Assisi, where he named Michele his Cameriere Segreto and Scalco Segreto: 'Count, for your nobility as well as your goodness, we have decided to make such election of your person, so that we wish to put our life in your hands.'[63]

Girolamo was residing in Venice in the monastery of San Nicolò della Lattuga at the Frari on 9 January 1543, when the Procuratori di Citra ordered him to leave, 'together with all his servants', by the end of the month. The guardian Marcantonio Foscari responded two weeks later that Girolamo and his retainers would be out in three days and agreed that 'never would another foreigner be accepted in that place' without permission from the procurators, who had jurisdiction over the convent.[64] The tiny convent church, accessible only through the second cloister of the Frari, had been rebuilt in 1512–14 and featured a handsome altarpiece by Titian—*Virgin and Child in Glory with Six Saints*, painted 1533–5—and other works.[65] It is unclear whether the procurators' decree was specifically directed at Della Torre or if it was aimed more broadly at any unapproved lodger.

While Girolamo was probably still a tonsured cleric when he was housed in the little convent, his thirty-two-year-old cousin Nicolò II had already left the priesthood and was on his way toward providing a male heir for the family fortunes. His nickname, 'Il Gobbo de la Torre', indicates that he had a hunched back or some kind of spinal deformity, but on 22 February 1543 he married the wealthy Elena Valvasone. One of four daughters of Enrico Valvasone and Vittoria Strassoldo, Elena was heiress to one-fourth of the paternal estate—a property at Fratta.[66]

A few months later, on 7 July, Giambattista Colloredo, Ginevra's husband, 'with twelve children who are all living at present', petitioned the Signoria for 'the benefit of an exemption customarily conceded to all those who are burdened by so many children, for his loyalty and merits toward our republic and the nobility of his blood so dear to our state'. This exemption 'from every *angaria* real and personal' was granted, 'as has been conceded to many others for similar reasons'.[67] In feudal law, an *angaria* was a service exacted by a lord of his tenant. In Colloredo's case it might have been tax levies or the requirement to provide a number of peasants living on his property for military or other service. Aided by the exemption, Giambattista was able to provide a suitable dowry to marry his seventeen-year-old daughter Andriana to Giulio Sbroiavacca, Dottore, a promising young attorney, on 31 December. The lawyer Cornelio Frangipane, who had defended several Savorgnan in court and was a rival of Sbroiavacca's, observed morosely:

> My reputation has been in a [bad] state because I lost a number of cases, and through the revolution of the heavens, I now have little hope for esteem, because of the wedding last night of the daughter of M. Battista di Colloredo, especially in matters of the Patria, because it would favor the son-in-law and leave me out.[68]

When Giovanni da Udine's fifth child, Apollonio, was baptized in Duomo on 13 February 1544, one of the godparents was Nicolò II's wife Elena, who carried the infant back home to Palazzo Torriani afterwards for the celebration.[69] She was likely a new mother herself, since she would give birth to three healthy children—a son, Guido, and two daughters, Diadema and Virginia—before she and her husband both died of smallpox in January 1546.[70]

An Ominous Backdrop

Family affairs, whether joyous or sad, played out against an ominous backdrop of the threat and reality of violence. The deliberations of the Council of Ten in those years reveal that the insults and injuries of the past continued to fester among the castellan families. The settlement reached in September 1535 had settled nothing. Neither side was happy with it: the Della Torre and other injured castellans for what they considered an inadequate restitution, the Savorgnan heirs for being required to pay much at all. More importantly, it did not repay blood with blood.

Antonio Montereal and Alberto Cisternin de Spilimbergo, both adherents of the Della Torre–Colloredo faction, had petitioned the Ten in July 1537. They reminded them that after Girolamo and Nicolò Colloredo had assassinated the traitors Antonio and Nicolò Savorgnan back in 1512–14, they—Antonio and Alberto—had 'gone to the city of Monza where Giovanni Monticolo of Udine, also a rebel, resided, and killed him'; they did this not for money, 'but only to demonstrate the capacity of their good hearts for doing things agreeable to the illustrious dominion'. Regrettably, although each had been granted a licence to bear arms, they had failed to get it in writing. And now, after some twenty years, the capitano of the Signoria had confiscated their weapons. They wished to reconfirm their licences now, 'so that they could defend themselves from the followers and relatives of that rebel Giovanni Monticolo'. The luogotenente confirmed that they had indeed murdered Monticolo in 1522, and the licences were granted by a vote of thirteen in favour, two against, and two undecided.[71]

Precedents were quickly established. On 28 May 1539, the four sons of Pagano Savorgnan—Giacomo, Tristano, Giovanni Battista, and Scipione —had petitioned the Ten for the right to carry arms, noting that their relative Francesco and his sons already had that privilege and that it would be scandalous not to grant the same to them. Pagano, described as infirm and rarely leaving the house, was the brother of the Giovanni Battista who had been wounded by Giambattista Colloredo and Ercole della Rovere back in 1517.[72] We will remember that he was also the son of the beautiful Maria Savorgnan who had so charmed Pietro Bembo four decades earlier. The Ten approved the request by a vote of thirteen in favour, two against, and none undecided.[73] Three months later a cousin, Mario Savorgnan del Monte (who had been granted a licence to bear arms in 1534), and our Girolamo Della Torre were ordered to appear before the Ten and admonished to respect each other's right to the road, 'which after all belongs to the Signoria for the common use of all, and to live quietly and modestly and avoid arrogant behavior'.[74]

In September 1541, an alarmed Ten discussed the many injuries and homicides that took place during *feste* in towns throughout the territory and banned the carrying of firearms—*schioppi* and *schioppetti* (guns and muskets)—on all such occasions in cities and castles in the dominion.[75] Alas, if guns were not allowed, daggers and swords were at the ready. Ercole della Rovere, banned from the Venetian Terraferma for having killed Giovanni Battista Savorgnan in concert with Giambattista Colloredo back in 1516, had been rewarded with a reprieve when he helped kill the fugitive Nicolò Savorgnan at Villach two years later. He returned to the Friuli and became one of the leaders of the castellans and worked tirelessly to consolidate the unity of the clans.[76] Still a close friend of Giambattista's, Della Rovere was stabbed by unknown assassins on the evening of Carnival Sunday, 15 February 1545, and left to die on an Udine street. Suspicion fell on Jacopo or Tristan Savorgnan or their familiars, but no one was arrested.[77]

A flurry of requests for licenses to bear arms ensued by members of the opposing faction. On 7 March 1545, three sons of Ettore Strassoldo and their cousin Marco Antonio were granted licences to bear arms, each with a servant, 'for the security of their persons'. Ettore, they claimed, had lost all his wealth in more than ten years of continuous wars, from 1511 to 1523, spending more than 1000 ducats a year on behalf of the Venetian forces to maintain the Castello di Strassoldo and to buy all sorts of munitions, even though the imperial agents had tried to recruit him and his brother. They lamented that they were constrained to leave the Friuli and to live in Venice, where they stayed for a long time with the loss and ruin of their houses. This dire fate may have inspired the proverb on the corner of their houses in Udine recorded by the notary Belloni in 1540: *Chi non se mesura non dura.*[78]

Fatefully, Girolamo Della Torre made his own request to the Ten on the very same day. He reminded the council that he had previously been conceded a licence to bear arms, but for him alone, without servants. Furthermore, his brothers Raimondo (now deceased), Michele, and Alvise, and their cousin Nicolò, had also been given the licence but with only one servant each, not with two, which was the norm 'in similar cases'. Now he requested that each of them should be allowed to have two servants with arms. The petition was quickly approved by a vote of 11–3.[79] Four days later, the signoria authorized Vittore Barbarigo, luogotenente of the Patria, to offer a bounty of Lire 800 di piccolo to anyone who turned in the murderer of the Ercole della Rovere, citizen of Udine.[80]

Great confederations of families were involved in these blood feuds, with bonds of fidelity and the solidarity of vendetta that obliged everyone pertaining to the clan to defend against, and react to, offences of the rival faction.[81] And yet, although ever suspicious of fractious mainland nobles, the Venetian authorities seemed to hold the Della Torre in high repute during this period. On 21 March, the Venetian orator to Rome presented a glowing Ducale to the papal curia from Doge Pietro Lando, commending Count Michele Della Torre, as well as his family, to the pope for their singular virtues and good qualities, and for Michele's continuous services in Rome on behalf of Venice. He asked His Serenity to favour and embrace the Count.[82]

The doge died on 9 November and was replaced two weeks later by Francesco Donato.[83] Michele, then in Rome, lost no time in currying favour with the new doge and dispatched two letters to Venice on 5 December with the Venetian orator Venier. The first went to Donato, fulsomely congratulating him on his election. The second went to Girolamo. Celebrating that he had been the first person at the papal court to inform the pope of the happy news, Michele added that they had had a lengthy conversation about how good this would be for all Christendom.[84]

The situation remained volatile in the Friuli. The following April Giambattista Colloredo requested a licence to carry arms for himself and his sons. Reminding the Council of Ten of the service of his uncle Camillo against the German army, he allowed that he had seven sons. However, he reassured the Ten not to fear arming such a great number of men, since his oldest sons Sertorio and Girolamo were studying in Padua and Marzio in Rome, while the others were still of tender age and living in Udine. After the luogotenente, Maffeo Michiel, endorsed the petition, attesting to the courtesy, calmness, and modesty of Giambattista and his sons, on 15 April 1546 the Ten granted the licence to him and all seven sons, each with a servant. The same privilege was granted to Giulio Sbroiavacca (Giambattista's son-in-law) and his brothers three weeks later.[85]

Attempts were made at reconciliation between the feuding families. Later in the year, two canons, Francesco Manini and Claudio Colloredo, persuaded Giambattista to make peace with Tristan and Giacomo Savorgnan. All three, as heads of two warring factions, swore a solemn oath at the foot of the high altar in the Duomo of Udine 'to quiet the ancient rancours and live in peace'.[86] Venetian republican values of prudence and restraint should surely prevail on the streets of Udine.

Notes

1. Saccomani 1970–1, 331; Custoza 1996: Villa Farnesina (1518–19); Vatican Logge (1517–19); Loggia of Leo X (1518–19); Villa Madama (1520).
2. Prampero de Carvalho 2003, 33–4; Dacos, Furlan, and Cargnelutti 1987, 135–8; Bartolini 1987, 66–7.
3. Bianco 1995, 81; ASV, *CCX*, Lettere Rettori, b. 169 (21 February 1530) [Antonio Savorgnan].
4. DU, GA, 304; *I Savorgnan e la Patria del Friuli* 1984, 129–30. ASUd, *AT*, b. 11, cartella XI, colto 26 (3 April 1530); Casella 2003, 117.
5. ASVe, *CX*, Comuni, Filze, b. 11, no. 60 (30 April 1530) and no. 158 (9 July 1530).
6. Muir 1993 202–4, 288–90, 338nn21–2.
7. ASUd, *AT*, b. 19, cartella 19 colto 26, 'Supplica alli Rattatori del la Robba de Savorgnani;' BCUd, Fondo Principale MS 1247, cited by Casella 2003, 117n100.
8. Sanudo, *Diarii*, 56:273–4 (24 May 1532).
9. ASUd, *AT*, b. 19, cartella 19, colto 26; Ibid., b. 33, 'Raccolta di istrumenti di Villalta e Ville Annesse, 1337–1831', fasc 1, no. 28.
10. ASUd, *AT*, b. 19, cartella 19, colto 26. Castelnovo was a commune around 35 km northwest of Villalta on the other side of the Tagliamento River. See also Muir 1993, 203–4, 289. For the system of feudal property ownership see ibid., 32–48.
11. Ibid., b. 11, Cartelle 11a, colto XXI, no. 19. The petition is undated but would have been written between Raimondo's death on 25 November 1532 and 26 May 1533, when the brothers were granted knighthood by Charles V.
12. For the Monte Vecchio, see Mueller 1997, 457.
13. ASUd, *AT*, b. 11, Cartelle 11a, colto XXI, no. 19. For the concession of Cives Veneciarum granted to 'NICOLINUS ET OTULINUS ET CAPPONUS FRATRES DE LA TURRE QD MUSCHINI' on 14 July 1356, with a lead seal, see http://www.cives-veneciarum.net/dettaglio.php?id=2757, versione 56/2017-02-01.

14. Most notably, Federico Savorgnan, whose concession 'per privilegio', granted membership in the Maggior Consiglio to himself and his heirs on 3 April 1385, with a gold seal: http://www.civesveneciarum.net/dettaglio.php?id=1205, versione 56/2017-02-01.
15. ASUd, *AT*, b. 11, Cartelle 11a, colto XXI, no. 19.
16. Ibid.
17. Ibid.
18. Thirty-three foreigners—primarily *condottieri,* high church functionaries, and rulers of other states—were inducted into the Venetian nobility in the sixteenth century. Pietro Alvise Farnese, so honoured on 7 October 1537, was the eighteenth since 1500. This was primarily an honorific title; the new nobles were not expected to attend the Maggior Consiglio and vote. See ASVe, Miscellanea codici, Storia veneta, b. 44, I–IIIv.
19. Eisenbichler 1999, 430–9.
20. Sanudo, *Diarii*, 57: 47.
21. Ibid., reporting that the letter was received on 9 October.
22. Ibid., 47:63, 67–9.
23. Ibid., 47:85.
24. Ibid., 47:86.
25. Occioni-Bonaffons 1887, 103–4; Spilimbego 1884, 28–31; see also Molmenti 1898, 192–3.
26. DU, GA, 330, 332.
27. Quoted by Molmenti 1898, 194.
28. DU, GA, 330–1.
29. DU, GA, 331.
30. Emiliani 1881, 7; Beltrame 1852, 99–103. See also Wethey 1969, 22; Wethey 1971, 4 n20; and Hope 1979, 7–10.
31. ASUd, *AT*, b. 7, cartella 7, colto 15, no. 1 (26 May 1533); ibid., b. 17, fasc. 1, c. 132. See Occioni-Bonaffons 1877–78, 66–73. Without citing a date, the author states that Girolamo was given a dispensation by the pope to marry following the near extinction of the family in 1511. This must have happened after 1540, when he was still referred to as 'reverendo'.
32. For *cavalieri aureati*, see Bergamaschi 1695; Grendler 2002, 184.
33. Bernardi 1845, 240–1.
34. ASVe, *CX*, Delib, Comuni, filze, b. 18, no. 149 (24 July 1534); no. 346 (13 February 1535); ibid., b. 19, no. 17 (20 March 1535); Tassini 1866, 192–3.
35. Muir 1983, 203–4. ASVe, *LPF*, Ducali, b. 278, vol. I, cc. 55v–56.
36. ASUd, *AT*, b. 11, cartella XI, colto 21; ibid., b. 33, 'Raccolta di istrumenti di Villalta e Ville Annesse, 1337–1831', fasc. 11. On 11 May 1527 the Della Torre brothers and their cousin Nicolò II had bought part of the Castello of Villalta from Jacopo q. Valentino and Giorgio q. Domenico Valentino di Villalta (also known as Caporiacco) and his brother Bernardo for 20 ducats; on 24 December 1530, they bought the remaining share from Battista di Villalta.
37. Vasari 1912–15, 188.
38. Bartolini 1987, 81–2.
39. Capodagli 1665, 473.
40. Cargnelutti 1987, 59.

41. Dacos, Furlan, and Cargnelutti 1987, 165–73.
42. Cargnelutti 1987, 80, 81, 87, 233. Giovanni's life remained closely intertwined with the Della Torre and their relatives and associates for the next two decades. Elena Della Torre, wife of Nicolò II, was godmother of Giovanni's fifth child, Apollonio Zuan Battista Josepho, baptized on 9 February 1544; and on 18 August 1551, Michele Della Torre, by then bishop of Ceneda, held Michelangelo, Giovanni's tenth child and his namesake, at the baptismal font. The last payment from Rome via Michele is recorded in the Libro dei Conti (ibid., 379) in 1558.
43. Buora 1986, 140–2 (dating the commencement of construction of the Porticato to 1535); Kassler-Taub 2010, 46–9; Bergamini and Buora 1990, 72.
44. Bergamini, 'Bernardino Da Morcote (1450–1542)'.
45. Battistella 1932, 108.
46. Maniago 1839, 3–14, 57–8, citing the *Annales Civitatis*, vol. 46, 262. It was named after Girolamo Contarini, lugotenente in 1484, and an ancestor of Marcantonio Contarini, the luogotenente in 1529–30. See also De Piero 1983, 26–7.
47. Venier 1858.
48. ASUd, *AT*, b. 56, f. 1 (5 April 1538 and 13 September 1538).
49. Battistella 1903, 131–3; ASVe, *Coll.*, Relazioni (secreti), b. 49 [Udine]; Venier 1858.
50. BCUd, Annales civitatis Utini, vol. L (1540), fol. 39. See also Battistella 1932, 119–20 Faccioli and Joppi 2007, 52, citing Annales Civitatis, t. 4, fol. 35 [1540 1 July].
51. Joppi 1890, 124–6. See also ASUd, *ADP*, b. 12; Prampero de Carvalho 2003, 48–53. For further improvements by Antonio Marchesi in the 1590s, see Chapter 14.
52. Prampero de Carvalho 2003, 48–53; Prampero de Carvalho 2005, 7–14. The author's argument that Giovanni designed the complex according to Vitruvian principles is intriguing, but inconclusive.
53. Faccioli and Joppi 2007, 63.
54. Emiliani 1881, 7; Battistella 1932, 267.
55. See Faccioli and Joppi 2007, 81–2.
56. De Piero 1983, 80.
57. ASUd, *AT*, b. 47: Both Alvise II and Girolamo served in the parliament in 1537, Alvise II alone in 1541, 1542, 1543, 1546. Pension payments were made by Alvise II on 18 Jan 1541, 23 January 1542, 23 May 1542. Cargnelutti 1987, 117, 146, 152.
58. Archivio Paolo di Colloredo, Lettere, colto VI (10 August 1540). cited in Bertolla 1901, 47.
59. ASVe, *CX*, Delib., Comuni. filze, b. 31, no. 32.
60. ASUd, *AT*, b. 2, colto VI, fasc. 10 (8 January. 1542): 'perche in fatto tocca piu la camisa che il giuppone.' A version of an Italian proverb: 'che più tocca la camiscia, che non fa il giuppone.'
61. Paul II vacationed in several such properties in addition to Caprarola when he was not in the Vatican. These include the Rocca of Bagnaia and a vineyard on the Gianicolo (later turned into a villa by one of his descendants). My thanks to Federica Caneparo for this information.
62. Wethey 1971, 98–9.
63. Capodagli 1665, 476 (30 July 1542). Cf. Bernardi 1845, 241, with the date of 1543. For the offices of Cameriere Segreto and Scalco Segreto, see Moroni, *Dizionario*, 62: 85–93.
64. ASVe, San Nicolò della Lattuga, b. 2, n. 3, 4r–5.

65. Humfrey and Sherman 2015. The church also contained Donato Veneziano's *Crucifixion with Saints Francis and Bernardino*, recorded by Boschini in the chapter house, but moved to the sacristy before the convent was destroyed by fire in 1746. The church was destroyed after 1797.
66. Strassoldo 1895, 85; ASUd, *AT*, b. 25, no. 34.
67. ASVe, *LPF*, Ducali, b. 279, 22v-23.
68. Antonini 1881, 53. For Frangipane, see also De Vivo 2007, 21–8.
69. Cargnelutti 1987, 232–3.
70. BCUd, MS Joppi 423, Antonio Belloni, 'Necrologium et Flaminio de Rubeis, Chronica Defunctorum', cols. 10, 14: 'Nicolò Della Torre, variolis Helena uxor et nara povis diebus ante variolis pariter.' The children were raised by Nicolò II's mother Giacoma Brazzaco until her own death in 1551.
71. ASVe, *CX*, Comuni, filze, b. 21, no. 178 (30 July 1537).
72. See Chapter 3. Pagano was son of Giovanni, brother of Girolamo Savorgnan del Monte. See Casella 2003, Tav. 3.
73. ASVe, *CX*, Comuni, Filze, b. 25, no. 120.
74. ASVe, *LPF*, Ducali, b. 278, 78, 90. Mario was the son of Girolamo Savorgnan del Monte, whose heirs were ordered to pay compensation to the Della Torre and other families that had suffered losses in 1511. See Casella 2003, 156–9, tav. 4.
75. Ibid., b. 30, no. 46 (28 September 1541).
76. Bianco 1995, 82; Degani, 1900, 78–79.
77. Antonini 1877, 86; ASVe, *LPF*, Ducali, b. 279, 93v; Antonini 1881, 49 n1. See Casella 2003, 116, stating that Tristan di Pagano Savorgnan murdered Ercole, in revenge for killing his uncle back in 1517.
78. ASVe, *LPF*, b. 279, Ducali, 91v–93v. ASVe, *CX*, Delib, Comuni, filze, b. 37, no. 9. Approved 11 in favor, 2 against, 1 undecided. Ettore Strassoldo, Dr, died in Udine on 19 August 1545: BCUd, MS Joppi 423, Antonio Belloni Necrologium and Flaminio de Rubeis, Chronica Defunctorum, col. 10. For the proverb, see Chapter 3.
79. ASVe, *CX*, Delib, Comuni, filze, b. 37, no. 17 (7 March 1545); ASUd, *AT*, b. 11.
80. ASVe, *LPF*, b. 279, c. 93v (11 March 1545).
81. Bianco 1984, 268–269; Bianco 1995, 79–83.
82. ASUd, *AT*, b. 11, colto XXI, no. 16; Capodagli 1665, 476.
83. Da Mosto 1960, 249, 252: 24 November 1545.
84. ASUd, *AT*, b. 2, fasc. 10.
85. ASVe, *CX*, Delib. Comuni, Filze, b. 40, nos. 40, 73.
86. ASVe, *LPF*, b. 279, c. 93v; ASUd, *AT*, b. 11, fasc. 7, c. 5.; Antonini 1877, 86; BCUd, MS. Joppi 166: Contese Cavallaresche, Bianco 1995, 82. Crollalanza 1875, 91–92.

5
Honour and Disgrace

Indeed, peace did seem possible for a time. Auspiciously, Michele Della Torre was named Bishop of Ceneda by the pope in February 1547.[1] Situated in the Veneto on the site of an ancient Roman castrum, Ceneda had been an episcopal see since the tenth century. The community had voluntarily put itself under Venetian protection in the early fifteenth century, but it was still ruled by a count-bishop appointed by the pope. Not surprisingly, the question of Venetian sovereignty and the relationship between the count-bishops and Venice had remained a source of friction.[2]

The Castello di San Martino, the seat of the bishop, was built into the mountainside overlooking the citizen loggia in the cathedral square (Figure 5.1). A

Figure 5.1. Castello di San Martino, Ceneda (Vittorio Veneto).
The castle complex comprised two towers built in the Longobard era on earlier remains, a large courtyard, and the bishop's palace, rebuilt and expanded in the fifteenth and sixteenth centuries. Ceneda would disappear from the map after 1866 when it was joined to the adjacent city of Serravalle and rechristened Vittorio Veneto (after King Vittorio Emanuele II) when the Veneto was annexed to the Kingdom of Italy.

The Venetian Bride: Bloodlines and Blood Feuds in Venice and Its Empire. Patricia Fortini Brown, Oxford University Press (2021). © Patricia Fortini Brown. DOI: 10.1093/oso/9780192894571.003.0005

Figure 5.2. Municipal loggia, 1537–8. Now Museo della Battaglia, Ceneda (Vittorio Veneto).

The Renaissance-style building features a plain stucco façade pierced by three round-headed bifora atop a five-bay portico supported by rusticated piers. A sculpted relief of the Lion of Saint Mark stands guard above the central windows of the ringhiera on the piano nobile. Three of the four stemme in the spandrels of the ground-floor loggia were chiseled off when the Contea of Ceneda fell to the troops of Napoleon in 1786. Only the figure of San Tiziano, symbol of the city of Ceneda (on the right) remains.

clear statement of the dominance of ecclesiastical over secular authority, the arrangement was unusual, perhaps unique, by that time in the Veneto and Friuli. Typically, when Terraferma cities came under Venetian rule, its podestas were moved into preexisting citadels, maintaining a visual hierarchy between Venetian protectors and citizen councils.[3] In Ceneda, the two centres were linked by the Via Brevia, a winding road a half-mile long, cut into the side of the mountain. Now, and probably then, it leads through a lush mixed forest of pine trees, roverella oaks, hazelnuts, and poplars, with vineyards covering the slopes below the castle.

The Grimani family had held the bishopric of Ceneda (and indeed the patriarchate of Aquileia) as a virtual fiefdom for the previous forty years. Through canny machinations both in Venice and at the papal court, Domenico Grimani and his nephews Marino and Giovanni exchanged the seat among themselves like a personal sinecure.[4] Only Marino left a substantial imprint on the cityscape. Like his uncle and brother, he was rarely in residence, but he understood the importance of visually evocative symbols of rule. He was responsible for the construction and decoration of the municipal loggia, designed (according to local tradition) by Jacopo Sansovino (Figure 5.2), and the reconstruction of the thirteenth-century campanile of the cathedral—two structures at the centre of civic life.[5]

Figure 5.3. Paris Bordone, attrib., *Count Girolamo Della Torre*, c. 1540s? (Private collection).

The painting was long attributed to Titian, but more recently was assigned to "the circle of Titian." An attribution to Paris Bordone is suggested by two smaller portraits by him that appear to be of the same sitter.

But despite Marino's efforts to link Ceneda's venerable past to a glorious present, the city was in turmoil during his final term, with the old Cenedese nobility in a furore over what they saw as an outsider's attempts to meddle in their affairs. Situated within the Venetian republic, the city was ruled by communal magistrates who were, however, subject to the temporal authority of the bishop. In 1546 Marino took away the right of appeal, and the citizens complained vociferously to the Venetian Senate, decrying his governance as 'insolent and harsh'. They declared themselves 'oppressed in various ways... and reduced to the utmost desperation' because of his 'fervid and arrogant attitude'.[6] The Venetian government had long been concerned about the extensive Grimani ecclesiastical preferments in northern Italy and gave the citizens of Ceneda a sympathetic ear. The Senate referred the matter to the Great Council, which promptly removed all temporal authority from Grimani, expelled the ministers and judges that he had appointed, and installed a Venetian patrician as podestà, a secular office customary in other cities in the Venetian dominion. As one local chronicler put it, 'He was driven away, Cardinal

Grimani of Ceneda, a Venetian gentleman, for being a tyrant, and the illustrious Signoria took possession there and sent messier Giacomo Surian.'[7]

In protest over what he considered an arbitrary and illicit action, Marino set his revenge in stone. He ordered four coats of arms to be sculpted in the spandrels of the arches of the loggia (undeniably the seat of temporal power): one of the pope, one of the city of Ceneda, and two (one as cardinal and the other as bishop) of Grimani himself. A third Grimani coat of arms, this countersigned with a large 'M' for Marino, was affixed below the clock on the campanile, asserting ecclesiastical—and Grimani—authority over civic time as well as space. Defiantly, he even removed the lion of San Marco from the entrance to the Castello. He then rode off to Rome to ask Paul III to intervene, but died at the end of September without a resolution of the controversy.[8]

Giacomo Surian, the podestà, moved swiftly to assert Venetian political hegemony. The coats of arms of Doge Francesco Donato, the comune of Ceneda, and Surian were mounted on the loggia in the pendentives of the central bifora above—and superior to—the Grimani reliefs below. Surian remained in control of civic affairs until Michele Della Torre was appointed bishop on 8 February 1547.[9]

The pope was confident that Della Torre was the right candidate to restore Ceneda to the temporal fold of the Vatican. Indeed, he was even acceptable to the Venetian senate, which jealously guarded its prerogatives to approve appointments of bishops and patriarchs in Venice and the Veneto. Given the resentment of the Grimani monopolization of clerical appointments, it may well have been to Della Torre's advantage to be a member of the Friulian nobility and not a Venetian patrician. Describing him in dulcet terms as 'our most faithful [subject] and a person honoured with singular virtue', the Senate voted almost unanimously (146–6) that Michele, 'or his legitimate procurator, should be given the holdings and corporal possession of this bishopric, with the payment of the fruits, income, and revenues as in similar matters it is customary to be done'. Considering Michele's reputation, it observed, 'one must hope for every good action'.[10] This posed a problem. The church insisted on its ancient right to exercise temporal authority in Ceneda and did not recognize Venice's warrant to bestow it on anyone else. The Senate, by its action, virtually made the Bishop of Ceneda equivalent to a podestà, whose tenure could be terminated at its will.

The thirty-six-year-old Michele was walking into a complicated and delicate situation, but he had been a member of the papal court for the past decade and knew what was at stake. On 3 March he postponed any resolution of the issue of temporal authority by appointing Girolamo as his procurator to take care of his administrative duties in Ceneda. The move had the added advantage of removing his brother from the troubled streets of Udine to the Castello di San Martino, sixty miles distant. Along with his brothers, Girolamo was also granted honorary Roman citizenship and named a Nobile Romano, but he never assumed the title. Michele stayed in Rome, presumably to attend to ongoing assignments. Then on

20 August, the pope dispatched him as his nuncio to the King of France, a post that he would hold for the next three years.[11]

Girolamo assumed his position with enthusiasm and was soon involved in negotiating jurisdictional disputes with the podestas of Treviso and Serravalle. It was likely during this period that he had his portrait painted, perhaps in recognition of his new role (Figure 5.3).[12] Soberly dressed in aristocratic black, softened by the white ruffs at the wrists, Girolamo is every inch a nobleman. An inscription above his head asserts his aristocratic credentials as Count of Valsassina and a knight of the Holy Roman Empire: 'HIERONYMVS A TVRRI S.R.I & VALSASS. COMES.'

One gets the impression of a complex individual, whose personal passions are controlled by a strong sense of decorum. His sensuous lips and reddish-brown forked beard soften a dignified, even stern, demeanour. Holding his cap in one hand and gloves and a dagger topped by a pommel in the other, Della Torre gazes directly, even defiantly, at the onlooker. A dagger or sword was a typical courtly accessory at the time, carried for defence not only by feudal lords but indeed by many, if not most, gentlemen of means. In Girolamo's case, it was an ominous portent of troubles, and violence, yet to come.[13]

The Visitor

But that was for the future. Count Girolamo settled down in his new position and was soon to welcome an important visitor. It was a matter of being in the right place at the right time. Tiziano Vecellio, Venice's most renowned painter, had been summoned by the Emperor Charles V to the imperial court at Augsburg in the autumn of 1547. It was an invitation that Titian—ever the businessman—could not refuse. At stake was not only the emperor's favour and patronage, but also the prospect of a payment of 1000 gold scudi, the possibility of further commissions from members of the court, and a favourable business deal for the timber business that the artist ran on the side. At more than seventy years old (if one believes the artist and his contemporaries), or ten years younger (if one prefers the modern consensus), Titian finally set out in early January.[14]

Such a journey in the dead of winter was arduous, and careful preparations were in order. According to Carlo Ridolfi, Titian's seventeenth-century biographer, the artist travelled on horseback with 'an honourable retinue of young men and servants', a considerable entourage that included his son Orazio, his young cousin Cesare Vecellio, the Dutch painter Lambert Sustris (then working in Titian's studio), and two or three workshop assistants. To them one must add men to handle the horses and a cart carrying painting materials and at least two paintings: an *Ecce Homo*, painted on slate, and a *Venus* on canvas, 'so unusual that it seemed to be alive'.[15]

Titian would retrace a familiar route as far as Pieve di Cadore, his birthplace, but this was his first time crossing the Alps. The January trip of some 400 miles would have taken at least three weeks, with overnight stops every 20–30 miles.[16] Leaving behind the flat Veneto countryside of dormant cornfields and frosty vineyards, with a probable stop in Treviso and a crossing of the Piave River, the travellers would enter a landscape that might have been painted by Titian himself: the Prealpi Trevigiani, a mountainous area of light and shadow dotted with castles, terraced vineyards on steep hillsides, deep ravines, swift rivers, small lakes, and grassy meadows alternating with mixed forests—a transition zone between the Veneto plain and the snow-covered peaks of the Dolomites. The hills of the Cenedese rose up toward the west.[17]

Not only a convenient rest stop halfway to Pieve di Cadore, the area was also a source of visual inspiration for the painter and a nearby retreat from the cares of the city. Indeed, Titian had begun to acquire land near Ceneda as early as 1539. Local commissions soon followed for altarpieces in the duomo of Serravalle and the church of Castel Roganzuolo, a few miles south. He soon made plans to build a *caseta* in nearby Col di Manza. The pivot point of his visual world, the country house would offer a sweeping view of the Alps to the north and of Venice itself to the south.[18] Titian's personal connections to the area would be further strengthened in 1555 when he married his daughter Lavinia to Cornelio Sarcinelli, a nobleman of Serravalle;[19] and more so in the early 1560s, when his *caseta* was finally completed.[20] But that was for the future.

Returning to that first week of the year 1548, we find Titian and his entourage passing the city of Conegliano, the Castello of Roganzuolo, and the building site at Col di Manza. As they rode by the Cistercian monastery at San Giacomo di Veglia, the rocky promontory and wooded slopes of Colle San Paolo abruptly rose up ahead to the left, with three castles visible on the ridge and flanks; below, a cluster of red tiled rooftops and a prominent campanile revealed the presence of the city of Ceneda. Instead of staying on the main road that led through Serravalle, possibly Titian's usual overnight stop, the company turned west toward Ceneda and rode up the Calle Maggiore, flanked by porticoed palace facades, to reach the main square. On the right was the Romanesque cathedral of San Tiziano—Titian's namesake, a happy coincidence that would not have gone unnoticed—with the new municipal loggia directly ahead. Inside its portico were three monumental frescos depicting acts of justice, featuring Trajan, David, and Solomon, painted in a many-hued palette of colours by Pomponio Amalteo, a celebrated local painter.[21] Titian must have taken the opportunity to examine the frescoes on one of his trips north, but his destination this time was not the city centre but the Castello di San Martino. And as we know, the bishop was not at home. Awaiting the travellers instead was Girolamo Della Torre, firmly in place as his brother's procurator and pleased to offer hospitality to the most famous artist in Venice.[22]

A Courtly Gesture

Girolamo was in a good position to promote Titian's fortunes at the imperial court. Acquainted with high-ranking clerics through his brother Michele, as well as through his own short-lived career in the priesthood, he remembered a powerful family friend then in Augsburg. Using the flowery language of clientage of the period, Girolamo dictated a letter of introduction to Cardinal Cristoforo Madruzzo, Bishop of Trent:

> I hear that your Lordship has left Rome and returned to the court of His Majesty. I therefore take this opportunity of presenting to your Lordship Titian, the painter, the first man in Christendom. I have wished to honour messer Titian by recommending him to you with this letter and asking that you might grant him favor, assistance, and comfort. I ask you to treat him as you would treat myself, which would give me the greatest pleasure. This messer Titian is coming at His Majesty's bidding to make some works for him. Otherwise, I ask nothing, except to commend myself to your good graces, asking that I might serve you on any occasion, as your least servant ... Girolamo Della Torre.[23]

We know that Titian delivered the letter to Madruzzo, since it survives in the Corrispondenza Madruzziana in the state archive in Trento. And it seems to have resulted in a commission. According to Ridolfi, Titian 'on his return to Italy visited the Cardinal of Trent, who wished Titian to paint him, where he executed other paintings; and... he returned to Venice with eleven thousand scudi's worth of gifts'.[24] Indeed, Titian's superb full-length portrait of Madruzzo, inscribed (in three places) with the date 1552, survives in Sao Paulo, Brazil, seemingly a visual document of the encounter in Ceneda.[25]

Della Torre's letter may well have been not a first-time introduction but simply a courtly gesture by an important man, presenting the famous painter to an old (and powerful) friend. In the formalized world of Renaissance patronage, such letters created relationships of obligation. Noblemen granted grace and favours and opened doors, but these were not one-way acts of generosity, for in so doing they also burnished their own credentials as men of taste, in this case putting an artist in their debt and sharing in the glory of his talent—a commodity that money and ancestry could not buy.[26]

For Girolamo Della Torre, the letter was an opportunity to assert his noble prerogatives in a Venetian milieu that had not always been accommodating to his family. He may have become acquainted with Titian through the painter Giovanni da Udine, a longtime friend who had worked on the decoration of the Palazzo Grimani in Venice during the 1530s and 40s. Girolamo's brother Michele would almost certainly have met Titian in 1545–6 when the painter was in Rome executing paintings for Paul III.[27]

Titian would remain in Augsburg, painting portraits of the Emperor and members of the court, until mid-September, when he moved on to Füssen in the entourage of Cardinal Otto von Truchsess, Prince-Bishop of Augsburg. Documented in Innsbruck on 20 October, the painter was back in Venice again three weeks later. His workshop busy with multiple commissions, he had little time to rest. But the emperor ordered him to Milan in mid-December to paint portraits of his son, Philip II. Remaining there for around three weeks, Titian was paid the considerable sum of 1000 gold scudi on 29 January 1549 for 'certain portraits'.[28] He returned to Augsburg in November 1550, but this time Della Torre would not be in Ceneda to offer hospitality during the journey. The count was, instead, in disgrace, exiled by the Council of Ten to the island of Crete. Despite the rising fortunes and eminence of his family, he had not been able to escape his past.

For all was not well in the Patria. The peace sworn at the high altar of the Duomo in 1546 had fallen apart just a few months later when Germanico Savorgnan managed to overcome and kill some Strumieri in a wooded area.[29] The following year, Girolamo Colloredo, Della Torre's nineteen-year-old nephew and namesake, home from his studies in Padua, was riding through the streets of Udine with an entourage of friends, relatives, and servants when he encountered Tristan Savorgnan. According to the Venetian luogotenente, Colloredo provoked Savorgnan first with words, then fought with him, wounded him, and put him to flight. Savorgnan vowed in turn to kill the young Colloredo's father, Giambattista.[30] A new generation had come of age, and the stage was set for disaster.

A Great Offence to Justice

Chroniclers record the winter of 1549 in Venice as very severe. The chill began on 21 January, when the lagoon froze over and the traghetti had to be pulled across the ice with ropes.[31] There may have been a break in the weather around 1 March when Girolamo Della Torre mounted his horse in Ceneda and rode back to Udine during the last days of Carnival. There he was joined by the young Girolamo Colloredo, spoiling for a fight, and they set out on horseback to Padua with an entourage of twenty well-armed retainers. Their expressed intention was to participate in the carnival jousts, but as it turned out, they had a different agenda. Dismounting at Lizza Fusina, the mouth of the Brenta Canal, they were met by a Venetian official, Pietro Diedo. He had been alerted that Della Torre and Colloredo were looking for trouble and, aware that Giovanni Savorgnan was also going to be in Padua, Diedo cautioned the two to avoid a confrontation. According to a Savorgnan partisan, Della Torre responded with the arrogance typical of Friulian castellans: 'You have spoken to me with respect, so I am content, but if Giovanni Savorgnan survives this time, he will not survive another.'[32]

The Della Torre group boarded a barge and proceeded on to Padua toward an almost inevitable confrontation. Nicolò Savorgnan, admittedly not an impartial observer, later described the event in colourful detail:

> Count Girolamo left the Santo and was walking along the Strada Larga toward Ponte Corbo when he saw my brother Giovanni coming toward the church under the porticoes... the said Count Girolamo left the street and ran under the porticoes and encountered my brother; [the Count] demanded the right of way, and my brother yielded it to him; and nonetheless, Count Girolamo with his companions and followers surrounded him with unsheathed swords, and dealt with him as one knows.

Giovanni Savorgnan was injured and two of his companions killed, while his cousin Tristan escaped only by hiding in a house nearby.[33]

A week later, on 11 March, the rectors of Padua reported to the Council of Ten that Savorgnan had been gravely wounded on Monday of Carnival (4 March). The Ten immediately claimed jurisdiction and ordered those involved to report (or be sent) to Venice for trial. They were further ordered to surrender their arms and those of their servants, whether inside Venetian lands or not.[34] Two days later, the Ten (actually numbering seventeen members including the doge and Signoria), voting with the Zonta (additional senators who voted with the council on major issues), formally charged Girolamo Della Torre and Girolamo Colleredo with a 'wicked and audacious' assault on Giovanni Savorgnan, having stabbed him and caused many wounds, 'with the greatest offense to justice, scandal, and disturbance of this city'. Their examination with torture was authorized, a pro forma threat, and they were ordered to present themselves to the council within eight days. Although the vote passed nineteen in favour, two against, and nine undecided, it is worth noting the lack of unanimity.[35]

The trials took place in late May. There is no evidence that torture was necessary, given that the facts were clear. Such an ordeal, an unpleasant reality of Venetian justice, would have taken place in the Camera del Tormento, adjacent to the meeting room of the Council of Ten. It consisted of the *strappado*, also called the *corda*, a procedure where the victim's hands were tied behind his back and attached to a lifting rope. He was hoisted to the ceiling and then lowered using a jerking motion that often resulted in the painful dislocation of the shoulder joints.[36]

On 22 May, by a vote of 24–6, the young Girolamo Colloredo was banished for life from Venice, Padua and its territories, and the entire Patria, including Udine. The next day, the Council moved on to the most serious matter at hand: the guilt or innocence of Count Girolamo Della Torre. The pope had weighed in on Girolamo's behalf at the behest of his brother Michele, but to no avail. Despite Girolamo's impassioned plea that he was only defending himself from the Savorgnan brothers, he was found guilty 'of so much wickedness and audacity' by an incensed Council of Ten. Observing that the Della Torre party of twenty greatly outnumbered the Savorgnan contingent of eight, the Ten voted unanimously, 22–0, to sentence the forty-five-year-old count to ten years of exile in Candia (Crete), where he would be required to report in person each month to the Venetian rectors. A pardon would be possible only by a unanimous vote of the Ten. Adding insult to injury, Della Torre was ordered to compensate Giovanni Savorgnan for his injuries with a fine of 1000 ducats: 500 to be paid immediately and the remaining 500 in a year. A proposal by Bartolomeo Pesaro and Lorenzo Priuli to reduce the sentence to banishment from Venetian territories for ten years, but without exile to Crete, got just five votes. Caterino Zen proposed reducing it to banishment only from Padua, Treviso and the Trevisano, Ceneda and the Cenedese, Udine, and the Patria del Friuli, without exile to Crete. He got only three votes.[37]

The surprisingly stiff sentence, considering the positive reputation hitherto enjoyed by the Della Torre family in Venice, reflected the exasperation of the Venetian authorities with its unruly mainland nobility. The Ten wanted to send a clear message that vendetta and blood feuds would not be tolerated in its territories. Beyond that, aside from the severe winter, it was not a good year for the region. Chroniclers wrote of an 'extreme famine': 'The peasants left their villages because of hunger and fled to Venice to beg because of the great shortage of grain, so that the city was full of the poor.'[38] The Ten were in no mood to be merciful to a privileged, and contentious, Friulian lord.

Della Torre appealed the sentence, and Bishop Michele even persuaded the pope and the King of France to petition the doge directly, but again to no avail, and indeed, the pressure from outside parties seems to have hardened the determination of the Ten to stand firm.[39] Della Torre was relegated to quarters in the Palazzo Ducale to await his transport to Crete. The family prepared for the inevitable, and Michele appointed his brother Alvise II to replace Girolamo as his vicar in Ceneda.[40]

A Problematic Balance Sheet

Girolamo, declaring himself 'the oldest of our house', made up a *Memoria delle cose di casa nostra*, a list of the family's financial obligations, carefully noting which items applied to each of the brothers and to their deceased cousin's son Guido. A *scrittoria* (writing desk) purchased in Rome in Girolamo's name, but from funds drawn from the Monte Vecchio in Venice—two-thirds creditable to the three brothers and one-third to Guido—had been sold by him for 1550 scudi and spent for '*mia particolarità*' (my personal expenses). Presumably, Girolamo would reimburse the others with 1220 scudi of these proceeds. A loan of 351 ducats from Calimano Ebreo shows that Girolamo was availing himself of the money-lenders in the Ghetto. The three brothers still owed their brother-in-law Giambattista Colloredo 915 ducats for their sister Ginevra's dowry. All four Della Torre also owed Colloredo an additional 1800 ducats, most of it used to rebuild the family palace in Udine. Alvise II had borrowed 1000 ducats from a messer Nadal Riccio, but this sum was assignable to Michele, who used the funds for his mission to France as papal nuncio.[41]

Alvise II had also borrowed 500 scudi from Livio Podocataro, the Bishop of Cyprus, to pay the initial instalment of Girolamo's indemnification to Giovanni Savorgnan. Girolamo was obliged to pay this back eventually from his own share of the family income.[42] But with characteristic resourcefulness, he worked out a way to augment that income, even as an exile in Crete. A few days before his scheduled departure, he would finalize an agreement with representatives of Ranuccio Farnese, Cardinal of Sant'Angelo and Latin Patriarch of Constantinople, to collect rental income for the next three years from the patriarchate's properties in Candia.[43]

On 16 July Giambattista Colloredo petitioned the Council of Ten. Declaring that he just wanted to live quietly, he requested a special *grazia* for his son Girolamo, now banished from the Friuli, Padua, and the city of Venice. So that his son would not fall into greater error—as well as for his safety, since his life was continually threatened—he asked that the youth be allowed to go on the galleys of Alexandria to Candia, where he would remain far from conspiracies and not cause other disturbances to his father's old age. Toward this end, he requested that the young Colloredo be allowed to pass through Venice and present himself to the captain of the galleys. He would be confined to the ship until it set sail and be subject to the strictest penalty if he should disobey. Specifying that the youth should come to the city on 27 July to board the galley, the Ten approved the plan with a vote of twenty-five in favour, three against, and one unsure. If he disembarked before it set sail, he would be sentenced to three years in the strong prison and fined 2000 ducats.[44]

A Band of Butchers

Around a week before the scheduled departure of the galleys on 2 August, Della Torre's family made plans to travel to Venice to see him off. The group included his brother Alvise II; his sister Ginevra, with her husband Giambattista Colloredo (whose son was to be on board the ship); Giacomo Zorzi, a canon of Cividale; and three servants. Tristan Savorgnan had been waiting for just such an opportunity to exact revenge for the events in Padua. Alerted by friends that the Della Torre relatives planned to travel through the Cenedese and Trevisano for greater security, rather than taking the direct route, Tristan devised his own plan, with the cooperation of his relatives, the Collalto, the Signori di San Salvatore. Only too glad to help, they erected an improvised toll station at a passage point over the Piave River near Lovadina on a much-frequented commercial route. On the pretext of imposing a new special toll, they installed there a guard of ten lancers with a knight in command. Once the Della Torre party had passed through, the soldiers were to alert Tristan and his associates in time to capture the travellers before they reached Venice. However, the Della Torre contingent had their own informants and were alerted in time to change their route. When they did not cross at Lovadina, the shack and guard disappeared, and the toll was removed.[45]

Arriving safely in Venice on 1 August, the Della Torre group believed themselves secure, under the protection of Venice's ever-vigilant government. They were mistaken. As their gondola was rowed past San Marcuola on the Grand Canal, two large fruit barges pulled up alongside. Hiding inside them under reed mats was Tristan Savorgnan with a gang of heavily armed rowdies. Two mercenaries, Cesare da Roma and Gerolamo da Ferrara, jumped up, firing their archibuses, and murdered Alvise II Della Torre and Giambattista Colloredo, as well as the noble canon from Cividale and two servants. The other servant was badly wounded. Tristan and his associates immediately fled the city.[46]

Ginevra seems to have survived unscathed physically; emotionally was another matter. She was left with eleven children ranging in age from five to twenty-two. With two sons already deceased, her oldest daughter married, and her son Girolamo in exile, she would now depend upon eighteen-year-old Marzio to assume the role of family protector. He eagerly embraced the obligation of the vendetta and later had the motto 'mihi vindictam' (vengeance is mine) engraved on his sword. The blood feud had received a new infusion, once again.[47]

The Venetian authorities were outraged by the multiple murders on the Grand Canal in the heart of the city. Although not involved directly in the attack, the brothers Nicolò and Giovanni Savorgnan were arrested on suspicion for their involvement and held for trial. Tristan and his henchmen were indicted in absentia. Still in confinement in the Palazzo Ducale, Girolamo Della Torre drew upon his legal training and once again appealed his sentence of exile to Crete, asking for mercy because of the devastating insult to his family. According to his theory of the case, the two Savorgnan brothers had inspired Tristan to commit the dastardly act:

> The atrocious assassination perpetrated by the Savorgnan on the person of my brother, the unfortunate Count Alvise Della Torre, [and] on Baptista Colloredo and others, clearly reveals what has always been their animus toward the Della Torre family, most faithful and sincere servants of this most just republic; our family has been persecuted continually by these Savorgnans with every sort of ruin, homicide, calamity, and conflagration…These crimes and enormous

excesses as a legacy are not only unheard of, but also [now] executed by the brothers, Giovanni and Nicolò Savorgnan, with the firmest intention to extirpate and eliminate us from the world with all their might; and how many infinite times the two have contrived to take the life of myself, Girolamo Della Torre, as confided to friends, relatives and their authority, as documented by the cited processes; never however did they succeed to execute their spirit of malicious cruelty against my person.

So that seeing that I defended myself against their machinations with the help of God, they drove Tristan Savorgnan, executor of their most unjust appetites and desires, to murder my poor unarmed brother, and in a boat, far from any such suspicion, and above all most innocent, for whose death there were assembled in number perhaps 20 persons in two armed boats in the middle of the Grand Canal of this city, the head of which was the cited Tristan, by commission, however, and order of the above cited Savorgnan brothers, who, claiming themselves to be offended by me for the event that happened in Padua, and knowing that my poor brother and my sister with my brother-in-law had come here to accompany me to the galley, had made an insidious plot; they expected to assassinate all of them, but seeing that they could not execute their depraved design against all, they directed their arms against my brother to revenge themselves, and here one sees [that this was clearly ordered by them], because Tristan had never been offended by us; indeed none of the Della Torre have ever held any enmity toward Tristan, so he would have not had cause to be moved to commit such an assassination, one might say in the eyes of the Prince [Doge]...

Regarding this case, however, I, Girolamo della Torre, hold for certain that it will be adjudicated by the excellent Council of Ten with the severe justice merited by a crime so cruel and so horrendous that, in truth, never has anything similar been committed in Venice: that in armed boats a band of butchers equipped with firearms [that are] prohibited in the middle of Venice, have massacred subjects of this Illustrious Dominion in the eyes of all the world, even in gondolas, as one might say in their own home.

Therefore, your illustrious lords, seeing the importance of this miserable case, seeing that these Savorgnans try to extirpate and send into ruin the afflicted family of the Della Torre, [and] seeing that in our house after the death of my brother there is no one who could repair such ruin, I, Girolamo on bended knee supplicate your excellent lords for justice and piety to suspend my departure to my exile, so that I can provide for the conservation of my life and jointly be able to provide for my calamitous family, in which no one remains to govern except for my person, [and] wish for your clemency so that I could repair so many misfortunes in that brief time that would seem appropriate to your illustrious lords, to whom I humbly prostrate myself on the earth [and] recommend myself.[48]

The Council of Ten granted Girolamo's petition to delay his departure to Candia, but only with a vote of nineteen in favour, six against, and three undecided that

Figure 5.4. "Corte del Palazzo Ducale di Venetia," from Cesare Vecellio, *Habiti antichi, et moderni di tutto il mondo,* 1588, c. 101 (Rijksmuseum, Amsterdam).

narrowly met the two-thirds requirement. The split decision suggests that Della Torre had some sympathy but also considerable opposition in the highest councils of government:

> Count Girolamo Della Torre being about to depart with the present galleys to go to Candia, according to his sentence, with the death of his brother having occurred, it is held that his departure will be postponed up to the passage that will appear appropriate to this council. During this time he has to stay in the chamber assigned to him in the courtyard of the Palazzo [Ducale], and not to leave it in any way, and is obligated to renew the *piezara* (pledge) of not leaving this chamber until he will depart for Candia.[49]

Girolamo was likely housed in a chamber in the Scuderia del Doge, a row of rooms, each with its own door, on the ground floor of the west side of the *corte del palazzo* (later replaced by a long arcade). Although assigned to the squires of the doge, the rooms were often rented out to affluent prisoners who had surrendered voluntarily. These detainees do not seem to have been heavily guarded: thus the *piezara*, which might be a sum of money or even simply the swearing of an oath, to ensure compliance (Figure 5.4).[50]

A Manhunt

The Council of Ten immediately began diplomatic initiatives, and the hunt was on. They informed the Mantuan ambassador of the assault, the immediate arrest of Giovanni Savorgnan, and the mandate of capture for his cousins.[51] They also wrote to the Alfonso II d'Este, Duke of Ferrara, on 7 August that they had heard that Tristan and the other fugitives were hiding in Ferrarese territory. Trusting in the mutual love and respect shared by Venice and the duke, they asked him to send the criminals to the border of his state, where Venetian authorities would arrest them.[52] Two days later the secretary of the Council of Ten went to Ferrara himself. Wanting to capture Tristan at all costs, he reminded the duke that no one, not even the pope or emperor, would have been disposed to protect a bandit in such an atrocious case. Credible reports had already arrived in Venice, however, that Tristan had left Este territories and repaired to Mirandola.[53]

Or perhaps he had taken refuge elsewhere. Pietro Morosini, luogotenente of the Friuli, had written to the Ten on 6 August that he had heard rumours that Tristan was holed up in Pinzano, the castle of Bernardino Savorgnan. But, he cautioned, it was perched high on a crag overlooking the Tagliamento River, with several passes that provided means to escape. A great number of men would be necessary to apprehend the fugitive. Five days later, Morosini wrote again, informing the Ten that he had employed many spies, but had not been able to ascertain whether Tristan was in fact at Pinzano. Morosini did not want to mount an attack without being sure and reminded the Ten that the castle was high in the mountains and the villagers residing in the village below rarely went up to it. He told them he would stay attentive and monitor the situation.[54]

The news quickly spread through the Friuli. Francesco Della Torre, a relative from another branch of the family, wrote to his nephew Mattia Hofer on 7 August: 'This inhumane event is displeasing to the entire world and there are great laments over the death of the poor innocent count.' Complaining that the Venetian authorities never punished the Savorgnan sufficiently, Francesco did allow that they were hunting for Tristan.[55] Hofer received a more neutral letter from his brother-in-law Giulio Manin. All his pity was for the poor Alvise II, but he expressed a certain admiration for the audacity of Tristan, who had been able to flee even though surrounded by barges on the Canal Grande. Manin was also worried about how much the conflict would involve the several branches of the extended family. It would seem to him that the blood feud was diluted. How would they know how to reconfigure the alignments? These were not times to join hands with everyone: 'I do not live sincerely and sympathetically next to everyone; I attend to my little family.'[56]

By 17 August word of the assassinations had spread to Rome. Matteo Dandolo, the Venetian ambassador to the pope, wrote two letters to the Senate. In the first he reported the arrival of Marin Corner, who told him that Giacomo Zorzi, the canon who had been mortally wounded in the affair on the Grand Canal, had renounced his canonry, knowing that he would also die. In the second letter, Dandolo reported that the pope asked the Signoria to share his love for Count Girolamo and his great affection for the house of the Della Torre, especially considering the service he had received for years by Girolamo's brother, the reverend of Ceneda.[57]

The fugitives were judged in absentia on 27 August. Although the wily Tristan had managed to elude his pursuers thus far, he was sentenced to the most severe punishment ever meted out by the Republic to a Friulian noble. He was banished from all Venetian territories forever more; his membership in the Venetian patriciate, and that of all his descendants, was revoked; his palace in Udine would be razed to the ground, never to be rebuilt on that spot; and the remainder of his possessions were to be confiscated. If ever captured, he would be taken on a barge to San Marcuola, where he would be given thirty lashes and his right hand would be amputated. From there he would be taken to Santa Croce, where he would be tied to the tail of a horse and dragged to Piazza San Marco; there he would be decapitated, drawn, and quartered between the two columns on the Piazzetta. A bounty of 4000 ducats plus an annual pension of 300 ducats was offered to anyone who took him alive; 2000 ducats if dead. As to his fellow perpetrators—Cesare da Roma, 'who has a scar on his face', and the capitano Gerolamo da Ferrara—they would be banned in perpetuity from Venice and all its possessions and would suffer the same punishment as Tristan if ever apprehended. While a bounty of 2000 ducats was put on their heads, the first perpetrator (other than Tristan) who turned in his accomplices before 20 September would receive 4000 ducats and be absolved of the present condemnation.[58]

On the one hand, Venice dealt harshly with vendetta and vigilante justice. On the other, as we have seen with those who had assassinated the perpetrators of the 1511 massacre, Venice rewarded *banditi* (banished persons) who killed fugitives from Venetian justice with cash rewards and pardons. They were, in a sense, the unofficial state executioners in Venetian territories outside Venice. Old enemies became new friends when they disposed of newer enemies.[59]

The news spread rapidly throughout Michele Della Torre's ecclesiastical networks. Cardinal Otto Truchsess von Waldburg wrote to Doge Francesco Donato on 17 September from Dillingen, Germany. He was most distressed to hear of the terrible fate of Count Alvise and his relatives, but pleased with the swift action taken by the doge and the senate against the perpetrators, 'because of the great love I have had for many years for that most noble house of the Della Torre'. He particularly wished to put in a good word for Count Girolamo, whose appeal he hoped would be treated with generosity and kindness, 'trusting most certainly that this Lord Count would not do any act that would not be a thing of honour, obedience and satisfaction of your Illustrious lordship. And I would regard every favor and accommodation that he would receive from you as if it were made to my own person.'[60]

Still in France as papal nuncio, Michele was kept apprised of the situation. At the end of September he wrote from Compiègne to Antonio Elio, the Bishop of Pola, acknowledging a packet of letters that he had just received and commenting on the poor quality of the wax seals, which melted in the heat. He has already heard of the death of his relatives, which came on top of the bad situation of his brother Girolamo.[61] Calamity upon calamity. But Michele has other things on his mind. Two days later he follows up with a letter about his finances. Reminding Elio that he had already written to him about the excessive expenses that constrained him from living according to his rank at court, he complains that he has not received a response. And now he insists, adding that he is not making any superfluous expenditures, and cannot get along on the 200 *ecùs* per month heretofore sent to him by his brother Girolamo. 'Nonetheless, whether everything is expensive because of the great famine or because of the concourse of many foreigners who come to my house, the provision that I have from your lordship is not sufficient.' Moreover, he has had to rescue his family, and above all his brother.[62] Whether Michele's pleas brought financial relief is not recorded.

The Council of Ten had extended its offer of a reward for information on the whereabouts of Tristan and his accomplices through the month of October.[63] Gian Francesco Barbo, podestà and capitano of Cremona, reported that he had put up posters about the crime perpetrated by Tristan Savorgnan in public places in the city and surrounding places.[64] On 8 October, the Venetian secretary Febo Capello wrote to the Capi of the Council of Ten that Tristan was under the protection of a Gonzaga.[65] The branch of the Della Torre family in imperial territories then got involved. Francesco and Nicolò Della Torre, Captains of Gorizia and Gradisca, wrote to Ferrante Gonzaga, governor of Milan, that they had heard that Alvise Gonzaga has given the perpetrators refuge in his state and argued that anyone guilty of such atrocities merited no refuge and should be returned to Venice for trial. They reminded Ferrante that Tristan was also a rebel from the Imperial armies, having gone over to the French.[66] The hunt continued.

In Honoured Storage

After the assassination, the body of Girolamo's brother Alvise II had been taken to the church of Santa Maria Gloriosa dei Frari and stored in a wooden casket to be later transported for burial in the family tomb in the church of San Francesco in Udine. Instead of this, the body remained in Venice, with the casket incorporated in a modest tomb monument. Even if temporary, it would keep the memory of the event alive, while avenging Alvise II's death in a notably peaceful way.[67]

Although humble, the monument did not escape the notice of Francesco Sansovino, who would cite it in 1581 in his guidebook to the city: 'Luigi [Alvise] dalla Torre, brother of Count Girolamo, placed in honoured storage above the door through which one descends into the cloister.'[68] It remains there to this day: a casket mounted high on the wall at the end of the right-hand aisle of the church and framed by a large painting depicting a pavilion-type canopy with curtains pulled back by two winged putti to reveal a skull, on a red pedestal above the casket. Suspended from the cupola of the canopy are five coats of arms, and above

Figure 5.5. Tomb of Alvise II Della Torre. ca. 1549–1550 (Venice, Chiesa di Santa Maria Gloriosa dei Frari).

them a narrative painting in grisaille that resembles an entombment of Christ (Figures 5.5, 5.6, 5.7).[69]

But upon closer examination, it becomes clear that the grisaille depicts not an entombment of Christ, but the aftermath of the assassination on the Grand Canal. The iconography—the representation of the actual death of the deceased (not to mention a murder)—seems to have been unique at the time on tomb monuments in Venice.[70] But a close parallel is found on a tomb in the Franciscan conventual church of San Fermo Maggiore in Verona. It too commemorated men who carried the Della Torre surname—Girolamo (d. 1506) and his son Marcantonio (d. 1511), both distinguished university professors of medicine and members of the intellectual elite of Verona. Marcantonio's surviving brothers commissioned the monument from the Paduan artist Andrea Riccio, who probably created it in the period 1516–21. It consisted of a free-standing raised marble tomb chest decorated with eight bronze narrative reliefs that depict a professor's teaching, illness, death, and afterlife. The iconography has been linked, most notably, to writings on the immortality of the soul by the physician Giovanni Fracastoro, an old friend of Cardinal Pietro Bembo. Riccio's panel of the *Death of the Professor*, with mourning figures surrounding the dying man, is not only reminiscent of images of the lamentation of Christ; it is also prescient of the tomb painting in the Frari (Figure 5.8).[71]

What might be the connection to the Della Torre of Villalta? The occupants of the Veronese tomb, although city dwellers and not feudal lords, shared a common ancestor with Alvise II and his brothers, in Pagano II Della Torre (d. 1241).[72] Given the genealogical pursuits of the former's uncle Isidoro (see Chapter 3), they would have been well aware of, and even in touch with, the Veronese branch of the family.

Figure 5.6. Andrea Schiavone (attrib.), Tomb of Alvise II Della Torre, ca. 1549–50 (Venice, Chiesa di Santa Maria Gloriosa dei Frari). The monument was restored in 2011–12 by Save Venice, Inc.

Figure 5.7. Andrea Schiavone (attrib.), *Murder of Alvise II Della Torre and Giambattista Colloredo*, Tomb of Alvise II Della Torre (detail), ca. 1549–50 (Venice, Chiesa di Santa Maria Gloriosa dei Frari).

Figure 5.8. Andrea Briosco, known as Il Riccio, *The Entombment* (*The Death of Della Torre, Bronze*, height 37 cm, 1516–20 (Paris, Musée du Louvre)).

Further questions remain. Who might have been the artist responsible for the tomb painting of Alvise II in the Frari? The Dalmatian painter Andrea Meldolla, called Schiavone, is a likely candidate. He was completing the fresco decoration of the chapel of Marcantonio Grimani in the church of San Sebastiano in Venice during the same period.[73] The Della Torre lunette displays striking similarities with the Grimani frescoes and with several of Schiavone's drawings and paintings.[74] But given his confinement in the Palazzo Ducale, how did Girolamo arrange for the commission? As we shall see in the next chapter, the answer may lie in a new alliance that would cement his ties with important members of the Venetian patriciate.

Important News

Let us return to Girolamo's young nephew, Girolamo Colloredo, who had been given permission to serve out his own sentence of exile close to his uncle, in Candia. Already on board a galley and ready to set sail, following the dictate of the Council of Ten, he must have been allowed to disembark after the assassination of his father and uncle—for he was still in Venice at the end of October when he wrote to his cousin Pompeo with important news: 'These past days the adversaries made a great attempt to free Nicolò [Savorgnan] from prison because he was ill; but they have not succeeded in anything. I am hoping that we will marry Count Girolamo to a daughter of the Magnificent Gian Matteo Bembo. Although a final agreement has not yet been made, I think it will happen shortly.'[75]

With letters from highly placed foreigners falling on deaf ears in Venetian councils, it was time to pursue a new strategy to overturn the sentence of exile. Girolamo Della Torre, once a tonsured cleric, was soon to wed a Venetian bride.

Notes

1. ASUd, *AT*, b. 2, colto 5; ASVe, *Sen.*, Terra, r. 34 (18 February 1546 m.v.); Tramontin 1990, 29–46; *DBI, s.v.* 'Della Torre, Michele', 619–21.
2. Cozzi 1962, 176–88. See Pianca 1997, 6–14.
3. For example, Udine, Conegliano, and Brescia.
4. Marino Grimani exercised spiritual and temporal authority over the diocese (with his uncle Domenico as administrator) from 1508 to 1517, his uncle Cardinal Domenico from 1517 to 1520; Marino's brother Giovanni (as administrator) from 1520 to 1531; Marino, by then a cardinal himself, a second time (as administrator) from 1531 to 1540; Giovanni a second time (as administrator) from 1540 to 1545; and Marino a third time from 1545 to 1546. See Faldon 1993, 131–5; Sartori 2005, 106–15; Tomasi 1998, I, 117–19.
5. Cozzi 1997, 320 n84; Marson 2005. The loggia is not included in Sansovino's oeuvre in Morresi 2000, the most recent monograph on the architect's architecture. For loggias in the Venetian domain, see Sexton 2015, 258-78.
6. Cited by Tramontin 1990, 29–30; Paschini 1960, 77–8.
7. Tramontin 1990, 29–30; Cicogna, *Ins. Ven.*, I, 363; Cozzi 1962, 185.
8. Pianca 1997, 13; Sartori 2005, 113; Biblioteca del Seminario Vescovile di Ceneda, Giovanni Battista Mondini, *Storia della citta' di Ceneda e dei Cenedesi*, MS 2E7, c. 138r-146v, 859–67; Paschini 1958, 79–88; Zamperetti 1991, 275–7.
9. Pianca 1997, 13; Sartori 2005, 106–13.
10. Tramontin 1990, 30; ASVe, *Sen.*, Terra, r. 34 (1545–6), 185v–186 (18 February 1546 m.v. [=1547]; ASVe, *MC*, Deliberazioni, Registri, Novus, 20 June 1546.
11. Tramontin 1990, 31; Bernardi 1845, 243. For Michele's activity at the French court, see Bonner 2002, 60–78. For the Castello, see Cortelletti 2005, 185–200; Bechevolo 1982.
12. Sold for $112,500 in Lot 158 in the winter sale of the New Orleans Auction House, 20 December 2017. The painting had been gifted to Friends University, Wichita, Kansas by the Sam and Rie Bloomfield Foundation, Newport Beach, CA. See https://www.liveauctioneers.com/item/57938653_circle-of-titian-ca-1535-1545 (with incorrect information about the Della Torre family). The Fondazione Zeri, Fototeca, no. 40739, attributed the painting to 'Anonimo veneziano sec. XVI', with an alternate attribution to Paris Bordone by A. Morassi (https://w3id.org/zericatalog/oaentry/40739). The

latter proposal is tenable; two portraits by Bordone of a red-bearded gentleman strongly resemble the figure in the New Orleans portrait, perhaps at a younger age. See Donati 2014, 378–9, nos. 174, 174.1 (dating the latter works to c. 1535). Cf. Lucco 1985, 185–7, identifying the sitter as Marco Serravalle. But Fossaluzza 1987, 193 n51, rejects such an identification as improbable.

13. 'S. R. I.' stands for Sacro Romano Impero. The pommel of the dagger is just visible to the left of his index finger.
14. Martin 2006, 99–108; Mancini 1998, 35–8, 165–7; Wethey 1969, 31. For Titian's age, see Joannides 2001, 8–9.
15. Ridolfi 1996, 94. For the *Ecce Homo*, signed and dated 1547, now in the Prado, see Wethey 1969, 86–7; cat. 32, for the *Venus*, see Wethey 1975, 196–7, cat. 48. See also Martin 2006, 99; and Meijer 1999, 500 n35.
16. See Ohler 1995, 98; Coolidge 1908, 189; Edler 1938, 132.
17. See Gilbert 1869, 25–50; Mazzotti 1982, 107–15; Williams 1911, 244–5.
18. Giorgio Tagliaferro, catalogue entry in Mazza 2007, 54–60; Wethey 1971, 100, 145–6, 499–502; Wethey 1969, 112–13, cats. 70 and 71.
19. Hope 2008, 30–2; Puppi 2004, 39.
20. Svalduz 2007, 48; Svalduz 2008, 129–36.
21. Furlan and Casadio 2006, 30–2; Truant 1980, 76–9; Cohen 1996, 481–5.
22. Sartori 2005, 117.
23. Archivio di Stato, Trento, Archivio del Principato Vescovile, Corrispondenza Madruzziana, b. II, fasc. VIIa, no. 22 (6 January 1548). Trans. from Crowe and Cavalcaselle 1877, II, 167, 502–3.
24. Ridolfi, *Titian*, 100.
25. Ibid. For the dating of the painting, see Wethey 1971, 116–17, cat. 62; Camescasa 1987, 82–91; Hope 1993, 177–8. See also Dal Prà 1993, 57.
26. See Kent with Simons 1987, 1–9; and Landé 1977, xiii–xxxvii.
27. Humfrey 2007, 145–6.
28. Wethey 1971, 8, 41–5. Titian was presumably present during Philip's entire stay in Milan (20 December 1548 to 7 January 1549).
29. *ASU, AT*, B. 19, fasc. 7, c. 5; Muir 1993, 248; Bianco 1995, 82.
30. Antonini 1877, 86; Degani 1900, 80.
31. BMVe, MS It. VII 134 (=8035), c. 313r. See also MCVe, MS P.D. C 815/3, c. 16; Camuffo 1987, 60.
32. ASUd, *AT*, b. 19 (deposition by Antonio Savorgnan, brother of Giovanni).
33. Ibid. See also BCUd, MS. Joppi 166. Giovanni and Nicolò were from the Savorgnan del Torre line, while Tristan was a Savorgnan del Monte. See also Degani 1900, 81; Casella 2003, Tavs. 3, 7.
34. Antonini 1877, 86; ASVe, *CX*, Criminali, r. 7, f. 91.
35. ASVe, *CX*, Criminali, r. 7, f. 91v (13 March 1549).
36. Franzoi 1997, 18–19; Grendler 2015, 55–6.
37. Antonini 1877, 86, 154–5; ASVe, *CX*, Criminali, r. 7 (1546–51), ff. 143–143v, 146v-147; ASVe, *LPF*, b. 279, cc. 118v-119; BCUd, MS Joppi 166, cc. 206–9.
38. BMVe, MS It. VII 134 (=8035), c. 313v; MCVe, MS P.D. C 815/3, c. 23.

39. Lestocquoy 1966, 433–4 (no. 231), 444 (no. 242); Gaeta 1967, V, 65–8 (nos. 29, 30), 70–2 (nos. 32, 33), 75–6 (no. 36), 80 (no. 43), 186 (no. 124).
40. ASUd, *AT*, b. 6, colto 11, nos. 5 and 10.
41. Ibid., b. 2, colto VI, no. 5, fasc 4. All told, the family debts added up to the substantial sum of around 10,000 ducats.
42. Ibid., b. 2, colto VI, no. 5, fasc 4.
43. Ibid., b. 6, colto 11, no. 10. Notary: Marcantonio de Cavanis of Venice. Witnesses: Donato de Bardi, canon of Florence, and Jacobo Giorgio de Strassoldo, canon of Cividale for a three-year period: 1 October 1549–April 1552. The document was reviewed by Giulio Sbroiavacca , the husband of Girolamo's niece. It was signed in the convent of San Giovanni di Tempio, property of the Knights of Malta, of which Farnese was grand prior.
44. ASVe, *CX*, Comuni, Filze, b. 43, no. 219.
45. Degani 1900, 82–4, confusing Girolamo Della Torre with Girolamo Colloredo.
46. Strassoldo 1895, 84–5. Casella 2003, 118; Muir 1993, 249–50. Cf. Hoby 1902, 15–16, with a garbled account of the affair, based on hearsay. Although Hoby switches the identities of the Della Torre with the Savorgnan, his statement that the bodies of the dead were taken to Palazzo Querini on the corner of the Grand Canal and the Canale di Cannaregio near San Marcuola is credible.
47. ASUd, *AT*, b. 19, cartella 19, colto XVI: 1 August 1549; Conzato 2005, 33–4. Bianco 1995, 87. Cf. Muir 1993, 268, stating that Tristan Savorgnan had the phrase engraved on *his* sword.
48. ASVe, *CX*, Comuni, Filze, b. 43, no. 245.
49. Ibid.
50. See Scarabello 1979, 10, 18; Franzoi 1997, 31; Zanotto 1853, I, Tavs. X-Xbis; Lorenzi 1868, 497–8, 501, 606; Rosenthal and Jones 2008, 153.
51. Conzato 2005, 38.
52. ASVe, *CX*, Secreti, r. 6, 37v. (7 August 1549).
53. Conzato 2005, 37–8, 62 n100.
54. ASVe, *CCX*, Lettere di Condottieri, b. 308 (Filza Savorgnan).
55. Conzato 2005, 31–3, 59 n73.
56. Ibid., 33, 59 n76.
57. ASVe, Secreta Archivi Propri Ambasciatori, Roma, r. 7, 61r and 63v.
58. ASVe, *CX*, Criminali, r. 7, ff. 102r-103v, 106 [154r-155v, 158]; Cantù 1874, 154–6; MCVe, MS Cicogna 1363, 261; Antonini 1877, 86; ASVe, *LPF*, b. 279, cc. 132-132v; ASUd, *AT*, b. 19.
59. Molmenti 1898, 88–9.
60. ASDUd, MS Bartoliniana 151, c. 191.
61. Lestocquoy 1966, 444, no. 242 (24 September 1549).
62. Ibid., 445, no. 244 (29 September 1549).
63. ASVe, *CX*, Criminali, r. 7, f. 158 (25 September 1549).
64. ASVe, *CCX*, Lettere di Condottieri, b. 308 (Filza Savorgnan).
65. ASVe, *CCX*, Lettere degli ambasciatori, b. 16, fasc. Milano, 'Dispacci 1549–8 ottobre—12 Decembre', fol. 195 (8 October 1549).

66. Text in Cantù 1874, 153–6. See also Conzato 2005, 38–40.
67. The present discussion is drawn from my essay: Brown 2013b, 137–59. The tomb painting was restored by Save Venice in 2018.
68. Sansovino 1581, cc.69v (1663 ed., 92).
69. Brusegan 2005a, 610–11; Lorenzetti 1994, 591. The canopy type called *paviglione* or *padiglione* was used on doge's tombs in the fifteenth century. See Wolters 1976, 131–3, 239–40, 292–4; Pincus 1976, 402–35; Schulz 1978, 9–35; Romano 2007, 322–9; Brown 2013b, 149–50.
70. The only comparable depiction on a surviving Venetian tomb is the monochrome fresco on the monument of Marcantonio Bragadin, heroic defender of Famagusta in 1571, in SS. Giovanni e Paolo (1596). Attributed to Giuseppe Alabardi or Cosimo Piazza, it depicts Bragadin's flaying alive by the Turks. See Marinelli and Mazza 2002, 40–1, 44; Calvelli 2012, 32.
71. See Carson 2010, 13–25, 200–2, and *passim*; Radcliffe 1984, 373–4. The tomb is still in the church, but the bronze reliefs are now in the Louvre, Paris. I am grateful to Sarah Blake McHam for pointing out the similarity between the Riccio panel of the *Death of the Professor* and the Frari tomb painting.
72. Pagano II Della Torre was fifth great grandfather of Girolamo (d. 1506) in the Verona line and sixth great grandfather of our Girolamo in the Udine line (http://genealogy.euweb.cz/torre/torre6.html).
73. Ranieri 2002, 65–74; Richardson 1980, 44, 179–80 (cats. 299–302). Cf. Pignatti and Pedrocco 1966, II, 91.
74. For example, Richardson 1980, 127–8 (cat. 182); 130–1 (cat. 190); 134 (cat. 205); 144–5 (cat. 236); Hochman 2015, 111–20. For the full argument, see Brown 2013b, 151–6.
75. ASUd, *AT*, b. 19, fasc. 7. Colloredo's letter, dated 31 October 1549, is cited by Domenico Ongaro in a letter to Sigismondo Della Torre on 19 January 1782. Colloredo later made his way to Rome, where he became a Jesuit. See Degani 1900, 107; Crollalanza 1875, Tav, VII, identifying him as a *sacerdote*; and, Muir 1993, 250–1. See also Chapter 9.

PART TWO

A MELDED BLOODLINE

6
The Venetian Bride

From his place of detention—a chamber in the Corte del Palazzo of the Ducal Palace—Girolamo Della Torre wrote to Nicolò Della Torre, a distant cousin, on 3 November 1549:

> It seems to me that I would be lacking in my debt to your lordship if I did not share with you [news of] my every fortune, however good or bad it may be. Therefore, you should be advised by this [letter] of mine that I have concluded a marriage [*ho concluso matrimonio*] in the name of the Holy Spirit with a daughter of the Clarissimo messer Giovanni Matteo Bembo, a gentleman much honoured in this city of Venice, and tomorrow with the help of God I will give him my hand [*li daro la mano*]. This oath gives me the greatest peace of mind, and it is also of advantage in my travails.
>
> Thus knowing that your lordship will rejoice in my happiness, I wished to give you this news, and if these nuptials [*le nozze*] had called for some outward demonstration of celebration, I would have invited your lordship as my principal and honoured relative, but for the reasons that you know this cannot be. But let us save it for a better occasion. In the meantime, stay well and tell me if I can be of service, and to you and your beloved consort I recommend myself, and with her ladyship celebrate my happiness with me.[1]

Nicolò, capitano of Gradisca, had served in the imperial army as a cavalry commander during the wars of the League of Cambrai and was no friend of Venice. He must have been less than thrilled by Girolamo's marriage to a Venetian wife, but the ancestral solidarity of the Della Torre clan was paramount. And considering the perilousness of Girolamo's situation, Nicolò would have understood, albeit begrudgingly, the attractiveness of such an alliance.[2]

With Such Noble Breeding

The bride's name was Giulia. Eighteen years old, she was 'tall in stature, of healthy and strong complexion, beautiful in all her actions, happy in expression, and gracious in manner and affable in every way'. She was, moreover, 'raised with such

The Venetian Bride: Bloodlines and Blood Feuds in Venice and Its Empire. Patricia Fortini Brown, Oxford University Press (2021). © Patricia Fortini Brown. DOI: 10.1093/oso/9780192894571.003.0006

Figure 6.1. Titian (possibly after), *Portrait of a Lady*, oil on canvas, 63.5 × 51.8 cm, 1530–60 (Art Institute of Chicago).

The sitter's shoulders are modestly covered with a *bavero*, a veil of fine silk. The *lattuga*, ruffled cuffs of white lace, at her wrists were a common feature in both male and female dress. The absence of a pearl necklace and the dark clothing suggests that she is as yet unmarried or, less likely, a widow.

noble breeding, that at a most tender age she gave the clearest indication in all her actions of her high and singular intelligence'. The description comes from the biography written after her death by Francesco Sansovino, son of the sculptor-architect Jacopo. While we might not expect him to be an impartial witness, his account is the best source we have for the uncommon life of a Venetian noblewoman.[3]

No known portrait of Giulia survives, and it is possible that none was ever made. But we might take the liberty of suggesting a portrait of a young woman in the Art Institute of Chicago as a proxy (Figure 6.1). The identity of both sitter and artist are unknown. The work was once identified as a portrait of Giulia Gonzaga Colonna, a proposal now held to be untenable. Attributions have ranged from Titian to Tintoretto to Irene of Spilimbergo, but the present consensus points to an artist in Titian's circle, with the museum settling on 'Titian (Possibly after)', with an equally imprecise date of 1530/60. Given the attribution and dating, the image may be considered a plausible surrogate for another Giulia—a suitably refined partner for the dignified presence projected in Girolamo's portrait of the same period (Figure 5.3). Indeed, the sitter's strong features and direct, even appraising, glance bespeak the determination, lack of affectation, and secure sense of self attributed to our Giulia in Sansovino's biography.[4]

But Giulia's personal attributes, while important, would have been of less interest to Girolamo Della Torre than her noble and influential parentage. Indeed, we met

Figure 6.2. "Ordinario" (Everyday clothing worn by the entire Venetian nobility)," from Cesare Vecellio, *De gli habiti antichi, et moderni*, 1588, c. 106 (Amsterdam, Rijksmuseum).

Vecellio writes: "the dress ordinarily worn by the Venetian nobility is the ancient Roman toga, and its uniformity is perhaps no small reason for the harmony and concord with which this immense Republic has always been governed."

her parents in the opening pages of this book: Gian Matteo Bembo and Marcella Marcello, niece of Pietro Bembo. Appointed cardinal in 1539 by Paul III, Pietro had died only recently, in 1547. Girolamo, and particularly his brother Michele, would have known the cardinal personally, as fellow clients of Paul III and the Farnese family.[5]

Gian Matteo had remained close to Pietro since his marriage to Marcella in 1519 and went on to fill a succession of important posts in the Venetian government. Sansovino elaborated:

> In the bosom of the most noble and magnificent city of Venice, among those families who for nobility are the most famous and illustrious, resides the Bembo, no less for the valor of many excellent gentlemen, both in civil government and in arms, who are celebrated and famous for their antiquity, and also for the honoured memory of the most noble subjects living in the documents, nevertheless we have the most renowned Signor Gian Matteo Bembo, Senator, second to no other in our times, in whose breast so must prudence and so much valor resides.[6]

In the absence of surviving portraits of Bembo, we must again rely on a surrogate, this in the form of an engraving of a typical Venetian nobleman (Figure 6.2).[7]

A capable administrator in Venice's outlying territories during perilous times, Gian Matteo was celebrated for defending Cattaro against an assault by the Turkish pirate Barbarossa when he served there as rettore and provveditore in 1539. His impressive portfolio of elected offices also included Count of Zara, podestà of Capodistria, podestà of Verona, and most recently capitano of Famagusta in Cyprus.[8] He was demonstrably a man of influence who would surely be helpful in sorting out Girolamo's present travails.

Advantageous Alliances

By the time of Giulia's marriage in 1549, her parents had eight surviving children—six sons and two daughters—ranging in age from sixteen to twenty-nine.[9] Only two had already been married off. The marriages of the children were not a matter left to chance. Arguably the most important transactions in the life of a family, they had to bring in money or advantageous alliances or, preferably, both.

Back in November 1534, when Giulia was only three years old, her older sister Augusta was betrothed at the tender age of thirteen to Febo Arnaldi, a Vicentine noble. Augusta's immaturity, atypical for a Venetian bride in those years, suggests that the marriage was made for compelling strategic—almost certainly economic—reasons. Febo, also known as Deifebo, was the natural son and only male heir of Andrea Arnaldi, who had died in 1521 when the boy was still a minor.[10] The Arnaldi family, originally wool merchants and notaries, had amassed a great fortune, with extensive properties in and around Vicenza, and had risen from citizen to noble status by the end of the fifteenth century. No longer actively engaged in trade, they were living off their investments by that time and marrying into the highest levels of Vicentine society.[11]

Febo's marriage to Augusta Bembo was his clan's first such alliance with the Venetian patriciate. But what of his illegitimate birth? It mattered less in Vicenza than it would have in Venice. In addition to Febo, Andrea Arnaldi also had a natural daughter, Cinzia. Both had been born of an extra-marital dalliance, in all likelihood with a household servant, while their father was still married to a certain Dorothea. She had given birth to a son who had died at the age of two in 1508 but left no other children. That Andrea had no other legitimate heirs, male or female, would have been to Febo's advantage. Legitimized by his father, he became ipso facto a noble.[12] Andrea left him a specific bequest of 5000 gold ducats in his testament, a distinction noted in family genealogies, and essentially made him his residuary heir. He also provided, albeit less generously, for Cinzia, with a bequest of 300 gold ducats. Andrea further specified that the patrimony should pass on down to both legitimate and illegitimate descendants. Lacking them, the estate would revert to his mother, Elena, and then to his married sisters. Such stipulations, while not unheard of in Vicenza, were uncommon in Venice, where legitimacy and male succession—through collateral lines if direct descendants were lacking—were privileged above all.[13]

Gian Matteo lacked the resources to marry off Augusta with a large dowry. His wife Marcella had given birth to her ninth child just two months earlier, and he was about to take up his post as Count of Zara, a Venetian post equivalent to a podestà.[14] By marrying Augusta to a wealthy Veneto noble, he could ensure that her financial future would be secure. It was an opportunity that could not be passed up. Indeed, in her testament of 1547, Marcella would describe her daughter as *molto ricca*.[15] The couple most likely lived in one of the two Palazzi Arnaldi, adjacent Gothic residences on Contra' Pasini, a five-minute walk from the Piazza della Signoria, in the heart of Vicenza.[16]

But how had Gian Matteo become acquainted with the prosperous Arnaldi family of Vicenza in the first place? Marcella's uncle, Pietro Bembo, was a likely intermediary, his correspondence with Gian Matteo indicating an ongoing familiarity with Febo and the Vicentine milieu.[17] Furthermore, Gian Matteo had already put down roots in the Veneto. His tax declaration of 1538 lists a *casa di villeggiatura* with ten campi at Ponte di Brenta, along with four additional campi outside Padua. Now known as Villa Bembo-Boldù, the building may have been constructed around 1530 when he held the Venetian office of provveditore sopra le fabbriche (supervisor of public works) for Padua. It was around ten miles downriver from Pietro's Villa Noniano. A sure sign of Gian Matteo's aristocratic aspirations, Villa Bembo would have served several practical functions: a source of food, a refuge in time of plague, and a welcome retreat for the family during the summer and autumn months (Figure 6.3).[18]

Gian Matteo's oldest son Lorenzo, elected *sopracomito* of a galley in 1539 at the age of nineteen, was already an experienced seaman when he married Laura Foscarini in 1546 in her family palace at San Marcuola. She brought him a handsome dowry of 6000 ducats, two galley captain brothers, and a wealthy and influential father-in-law. The dowry exceeded the 4000-ducat limit decreed in 1535, as well as the 5000-ducat limit that would be passed in 1551. By the time of Giulia's marriage in 1549, Lorenzo and his wife already had two sons and were expecting a third.[19]

Inspired by the Majesty of God

The decision to marry Giulia to Girolamo Della Torre was fraught with complications. He was not a Venetian noble; he was under sentence of exile to Crete; he had influential enemies in Venice. With other suitors already seeking Giulia's hand, Gian Matteo was faced with a difficult decision. He could not make it alone. In company with his two oldest sons, Lorenzo and Alvise, he set off for the church of San Francesco della Vigna. During mass, Gian Matteo was 'inspired by the Majesty of God to put the Signor Conte before any other'. Equally inspired, his sons concurred with the decision.[20]

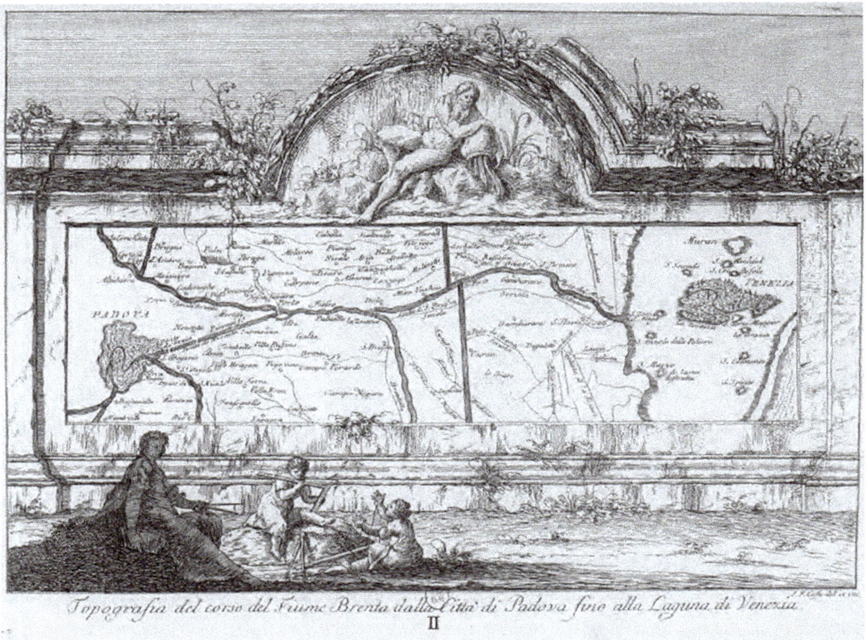

Figure 6.3. *Course of the River Brenta*, from Giovanni Francesco Costa, *Le Delizie del fiume Brenta* . . . 1750 (Paris, Bibliothèque Nationale de France, Département Estampes et Photographie)

Gian Matteo Bembo's villa was located at Ponte di Brenta, just south of the river between Codeneghe and S. Vido on the left side of the map. Pietro Bembo's Villa Bozza, upriver at S. Maria di Non, was outside the boundary of the map.

Aside from divine inspiration, what might have persuaded Bembo to agree to the union? As with Augusta's marriage, a wealthy son-in-law was an optimal way to ensure the future security of his daughter. Beyond that, the lure of having a titled count with an unimpeachable pedigree in the family was hard to resist. When Gian Matteo had taken up the two-year post of Count of Zara in 1535, the cardinal Pietro had written to him: 'I am pleased that Marcella would make an admirable countess, nor have I believed otherwise: she will be a countess of majesty.'[21] As would Giulia, her father must have thought.

Furthermore, just as Girolamo resented the fact that the Della Torre were not accepted as 'true gentlemen of Venice', Gian Matteo himself had suffered the indignity of not being given the honorary title of Cavaliere by the Senate after heroically defending Cattaro from the Turkish pirate Barbarossa back in 1539. Cardinal Pietro had written to him at the time: 'Comfort yourself to endure patiently this injury of fortune, which could never, I think, take away from you so much that you would not be regarded as a great and wise and honoured and spirited and most virtuous citizen of our country.'[22] Gian Matteo, still aggrieved, responded a few months later, citing a long list of other men who been rewarded for far less. He asked why 'that I alone, without being able to understand the reason, would be the son much loved, much praised, and little—or to put it better—in no way recognized'.[23] A marital alliance with feudal nobility would surely offer a degree of distinction that set him apart from his fellow patricians. As to Girolamo's present travails, Gian Matteo had never hesitated to take on challenging projects and may have seen this one as admirably well suited to his diplomatic skills.[24]

About to be shipped off to Crete, Girolamo had at least two reasons to contract the marriage. The first was political. He was certainly counting on Bembo's influence to help overturn his ten-year sentence of exile. The second reason was dynastic. Girolamo had just celebrated his forty-fifth birthday in his place of detention in the Palazzo Ducale, and the family was still lacking in heirs. And yet, his choice of a Venetian bride was contrary to Friulian (and family) tradition. Most castellan families, including the Della Torre, contracted marriages within the Friuli, preferring wealthy Udinese commoners over Venetian patricians as spouses for their children.[25] The Savorgnan were a notable exception. From the fifteenth century on, as we have seen, they had made strategic marriages to Venetian noblewomen to cement their influence in Venice—a practice that may have accounted in part for Della Torre's severe sentence. Paradoxically, the marital calculus of his old enemies could now serve Della Torre as a model in dealing with the true gentlemen of Venice.

Girolamo's decision was not made lightly. Sansovino writes that Della Torre's

> dearest friends and relatives had urged him to choose among three of the most noble ladies in Italy; it was the will of God that he did not consent to this...Indeed, as it happened, none of the three ladies who had been proposed was ever blessed with children after they married, a principal defect of unhappiness in marriage. It would have been particularly unhappy in the illustrious house of the Signor Conte, who had remained the only one [of his line] from whom one could hope for a legitimate posterity of children.[26]

This would not, as we shall see, be a problem in his marriage to Giulia Bembo. No information on the amount of the dowry survives, but it was probably modest, like most of those in the Friuli.[27] Della Torre needed influence more than money.

Without Outward Demonstration of Celebration

This was not the wedding that every noble daughter dreamed of. It was private, swift, and devoid of the extended public festivities that were ideally part of such an event. As far as one can tell, there was no ritual showing of the bride, led around the portego of the family palace by a *ballarino* (dance master), to the assembled guests; no visits by the bride and her attendants in gondolas to relatives in convents; no dancing on specially fitted up barges on the Grand Canal; no lavish banquets; no theatrical entertainments; no procession of the bride from the house of her father to that of her new husband. Indeed, the full Della Torre marriage ritual seems to have taken less than a week and involved only the immediate families and perhaps a few close friends.[28]

As Girolamo himself had put it, given his travails, these nuptials did not call for an outward demonstration of celebration. But it must be said that the lack of festivities was not new in the Bembo family, for it recalls the marriage of Giulia's aunt, Maria Marcello, married to Bernardino Belegno back in 1526, as quickly and as privately as possible.[29]

The complete nuptial sequence on this occasion consisted of just three steps. The first—the finalizing of the marriage contract referred to in Girolamo's letter of 3 November (*ho concluso matrimonio*)—must have taken place in his chamber of confinement facing the courtyard of the Palazzo Ducale. Such documents had the weight of law and were carefully guarded by the families concerned. Indeed, the contract is cited in a *busta* labeled 'Doti entrate nella famiglia Della Torre, 1495–1643' in the family archive in the Archivio di Stato of Udine. Although the dreaded phrase 'questo instromento manca' (this document is missing) is written next to the citation, a short summary of the agreement is included. It anticipates, in sum, a transfer of property: Gian Matteo promises to give his most noble daughter Giulia as a legitimate wife and bride to Count Girolamo, who promises to accept her, 'according to the commandments of the Holy Mother Catholic Church'. An attestation at the end of the original document is copied out in its entirety: 'I Giovanni Antonio Venier, Cavaliere, relative and friend of the parties, made and wrote the present contract with my own hand.'[30] A lawyer and art collector, Venier was Gian Matteo Bembo's first cousin by marriage and had been a close friend of Pietro Bembo. He had also served as luogotenente of the Patria del Friuli in the period 1539–41, when the Della Torre palace was being rebuilt in Udine and would have been well known to Girolamo. Now around seventy years old, Venier would have been trusted by both parties and was an ideal choice to provide counsel on a marriage that required tact and diplomacy.[31]

The second step, the touching of the hands (*dar le mano*) accompanied by a verbal promise (*verba de futuro*), referred to the public announcement that made the betrothal (*sponsali*) official. Although sometimes made in the home of the bride, it often took place in the Corte del Palazzo, where the groom received the congratulations of relatives and friends and the bride was not present. Given Girolamo's situation, the principals may well have chosen the latter option. If all went according to plan, it took place on 4 November.

One more hurdle remained before the third and final step—the true and proper wedding ceremony (*le nozze*)—could take place: the permission of the Council of

Ten. It was granted on 8 November, a few days after the public announcement of the betrothal:

> That Count Girolamo Della Torre would be permitted, as he has requested, to be transported to the house of his bride to conclude the marriage, going secretly by *barca*; and after having made this marriage, he must return on the evening of the same day to the place where he is presently residing.

The vote was, as always, not unanimous: twenty-three in favour, two against, and one undecided.[32]

The *nozze* took place the very next day, on Saturday 9 November. Leaving the Palazzo Ducale through the water entrance on the east side, Girolamo would have boarded a *barca* (probably a gondola equipped with a *felze*, or covered cabin). Gliding north along the Rio di Palazzo, the boat followed a zigzagging route under numerous bridges and into Rio San Giovanni Grisostomo to reach the water entrance at the rear of Ca' Bembo. The trip would have taken less than ten minutes.[33] Disembarking and walking through a narrow alley to a private courtyard, Girolamo could enter the side entrance of the palace and mount the stairs to the portego on the piano nobile. All this without public gaze.

It was there that he and Giulia would see each other for the first time. Such would probably have been the case even if Girolamo had been free to move about the city. Cesare Vecellio, cousin of Titian, later observed:

> The greatest and most remarkable modesty characterizes the method and tradition of bringing up noble girls in Venice, for they are so well guarded and watched over in their fathers' houses that very often not even their closest relatives see them until they marry…These maidens, when they begin to grow up, very rarely, indeed, almost never, leave home unless to go mass or other church services.[34]

During the negotiations, Girolamo would have relied on descriptions from trusted friends and family, Giulia on the counsel of her father and brothers. Did Giulia have any choice in the matter? Not as an obedient daughter. But from all accounts, neither party was disappointed. Girolamo's first view of his bride would have been of a stately figure, her unbound hair falling to her shoulders, resplendent in a white satin gown and adorned with a pearl necklace (Figure 6.4).[35]

Sansovino described her as no 'less the true and legitimate heir of her mother in the singular gifts of her mind than in the considerable beauty of her body'.[36] As to Girolamo, although almost the age of Giulia's father, his portrait speaks for itself: a tall, imposing figure with a reddish-brown beard and a compelling gaze (Figure 5.3). We cannot know Giulia's thoughts, but her later actions bespeak an intense loyalty that formed over the months that followed.

Figure 6.4. "Spose non sposate" (Brides before their weddings in our time) and "Spose sposate" (Brides outside the house after they have married), from Cesare Vecellio, *De gli habiti antichi, et moderni. De gli habiti antichi, et moderni*, 1588, cc. 125, 126 (Amsterdam, Rijksmuseum).

Vecellio writes of unmarried girls, "when they are fully grown, they dress entirely in black, with a *fazzuolo* called a *cappa* of very delicate silk, very full and ample, and *stoccato* [crimped] and of great value, which covers their face so that they are unseen but can see others. But girls of the nobility and high ranks go out rarely, only on principal festivals and holy days." At her wedding, the maiden was transformed. Typically dressed in white satin, signifying her fidelity and chastity, she wore her hair down to her shoulders.

Despite Giulia's passive role in—indeed, absence from—the marriage negotiation, Sansovino took pains to stress the equivalence of the bride and groom:

> Thus, all who knew them could reasonably believe and hold that this most happy union was ordained in heaven in demonstration of a proportionate correspondence of one to the other. For those who with the same good will and the same sincerity of mind were joined together, would likewise be of equal valor, of equivalent virtue, and with compatible beautiful qualities balanced between them.[37]

Although the gathering was private by design, the relatively small portego could well have been filled with close family and friends. On Giulia's side, these would include her parents, six brothers and a sister-in-law, and possibly her sister Augusta, who might have made the trip from Vicenza with her husband Febo. And then there were Giulia's aunt Maria and her husband Bernardino Belegno, with whom Gian Matteo remained close. Gian Matteo had at least one brother as well, Davide, recently married with a pregnant wife. And Giovanni Antonio Venier, who had drawn up the contract, was surely present.

But who else supported Girolamo? His brother Michele was still in France, and Alvise II was now dead. His cousin Nicolò II had recently died of smallpox and his son Guido was only two years old. Otherwise, Girolamo's next closest kin were the Colloredo. His nephew Girolamo, who had written from Venice to a cousin about the marriage on 31 October, must have remained in the city for the marriage before going into exile. But it is unlikely that Ginevra or any of her other children made the journey from Udine. Memories of the tragic events on the Grand Canal were still fresh; the Colloredo clan and their banished allies, like the Della Torre of Gradisca, remained hostile to Venice for years to come.[38]

With the witnesses assembled, the couple would pronounce their vows of mutual consent—words of the present (*verba de praesenti*)—with a second touching of hands, and Girolamo gave Giulia her wedding ring (*annellamento*). In these years before the Council of Trent, a priest may have been present or there may have been a blessing in the nearby church of Santa Maria Nova, but neither was required.

It is fair to suppose that any banquet following the wedding would have been modest. At the same time, it had to be sufficient for family honour. In conformity with Renaissance tastes, it would have been heavy on meats and sweets. A sumptuary law of 1542 restricted meat courses—veal, lamb, goat—to one dish of roasted meat and one of boiled on such occasions, in addition to capons, hens, or chickens, and soup and salad. For fish meals, there was one dish each of roasted, boiled, and fried. And for dessert, cake, marzipan, and *confetti* (sweetmeats) were served 'after the meal as usual'.[39]

After the banquet the marriage would have been consummated in one of the bedchambers, and Girolamo boarded a gondola, returning that evening to his place of confinement in the Palazzo Ducale. For the time being, he was a husband in absentia.

Setback in Rome

Elation over the wedding was soon muted by grief and, perhaps, apprehension. Pope Paul III, protector of Michele Della Torre and his brothers for a decade and a half, died on Sunday 10 November 1549, the day after the wedding. The Della Torre family had lost a powerful ally. According to the Venetian ambassador Matteo Dandolo, who wrote frequent dispatches to the doge, the Pope had fallen ill a few days earlier. Fearing the loss of Farnese influence if the pope were to die, the cardinal-nephew Alessandro Farnese had seized control of Castel Sant'Angelo and closed the gates of Rome. On the evening of the 10th, Dandolo wrote: 'I am assured from several quarters, that his Holiness has just now expired. May God give rest to his soul, and may his successor prove no less friendly to the Republic than he was.'[40] The interregnum began, with the cardinals beginning to assemble and with large numbers of French and Spanish troops roaming the city. But Dandolo wrote three days later: 'As compared with former vacancies of the Apostolic See it is nevertheless singular how few outrages are committed, although everybody is in arms, both at home and abroad, with wheel-lock harquebuses in their hands instead of handkerchiefs, everyone relying on himself.' Referring to Venice's struggles with its obstreperous mainland feudal nobility, he added: 'But I am very sure that those who do not approve of your Highness's [the Doge's] regulations, were they to see those of this city, would perhaps change their minds, for they are no better than those of the Friuli used to be.'[41]

The city was abuzz with intrigue. Dandolo wrote: 'The wagers at the bankers' shops are twenty-four in favour of England [Cardinal Reginald Pole], nor does any other cardinal get near him; but the Pope, please God, will be created in conclave [and not in the marketplace?] by a majority of two-thirds of the cardinals.'[42] By the time the conclave convened on 29 November, the horse trading had begun in earnest. The cardinals were already split into two factions: the French versus the Imperialists, with the Farnese a third force that supported the Emperor. Some cardinals had not yet arrived, and each side dug in their heels. Dandolo wrote on 14 December: 'Never were the times more perilous, nor the Conclave fuller, nor more divided (*disordinato*). The number of candidates for the Popedom is great; the members of very opposite opinions (*diversissimi*), and powerful.'[43]

By 24 December, a Conclavist—an attendant to one of the cardinals—wrote: 'there have been 19 scrutinies without any decision whatever; day after day they continue uniform.'[44]

The new year began with Dandolo writing: 'In order to do all that can be done to make the Cardinals hasten the election, they only allow one single dish, either roast or boiled, to be taken into them by their carvers (*schalchi*).'[45] To no avail. With the daily scrutinies yielding no results, a week later he observed: 'both factions have again taken oath not to yield one to the other.'[46] And on 29 January: 'The Conclavists, who yesterday and today quitted Conclave, declare, apart one from the other, that there they consider the election of a Pope hopeless.'[47] But finally, on 8 February, Cardinal Alessandro Farnese turned his back on the Imperialists and made a deal with Cardinal de Guise, the head of the French faction, and a dark horse candidate, Giovanni Maria del Monte, was elected as Pope Julius III.[48] After nearly three months the vacant see was finally filled. As Ludwig Pastor, the great historian of the papacy, put it, 'As in numbers it was most considerable, this conclave was also the longest in the memory of man.'[49] With Michele Della Torre still in France, papal support for Girolamo's cause was an open question.

Matters of Life and Death

During the long interregnum in Rome, Giulia's family was caught up with matters of life and death, attributable to divine providence or to human agency, depending on one's point of view. Litigation continued on Girolamo's formal appeal to his sentence, while Gian Matteo worked behind the scenes. The events of the past six months must have reminded him of his own mortality. Only fifty-five years old at the time, he purchased a modest floor tomb in the center of the Cappella di San Nicolò (now long gone) in the church of SS Giovanni e Paolo. The inscription read: 'Joannes Mattheus Bembus sibi vivens posuit 1550' (Giovanni Matteo Bembo, living, placed [this] himself).[50]

The timing of the acquisition suggests that it was he, and not his new Della Torre son-in-law, who might have been responsible for the creation and installation of the tomb of Alvise II in the Frari. We can make a circumstantial case if we remember that the grisaille painting above the Frari tomb had a precedent in a tomb in Verona that housed deceased members of another branch of the Della Torre family who were close to the physician Girolamo Fracastoro. He may have suggested the novel iconography of the Frari tomb, for Gian Matteo had come to know the old physician well when had served as podestà of the city in 1543–4 Fracastoro had written to Pietro Bembo at the time that Gian Matteo was much loved in the city and that it was shameful that he had not been made a cavaliere by the Venetian Senate for his impressive achievements.[51]

Gian Matteo had already demonstrated an understanding of the powerful role of the visual arts in conveying a political message during his tenure as capitano of Famagusta.[52] The grisaille depicting the grisly assassination suggests an attempt to push a personal family agenda by creating a secular martyr and restoring the good name of the Della Torre. What better way than to model the composition on an entombment or lamentation of Christ?

By the time Julius III was finally elected, Giulia was pregnant with Girolamo's first son, who would be born on 9 October. The time and place of conception are matters of conjecture. A date around the first of the year is most likely. In any case, by the end of Lent, Giulia would have been aware of her condition—a cause for relief and celebration on both sides of the family. And she would have enjoyed the comforting presence—and benefited from the experience—of her mother Marcella, who had long ago forsaken the study of Latin and the writing of sonnets for motherhood.[53]

But where was the baby conceived? Girolamo was officially confined to his quarters in the Palazzo Ducale, while Giulia remained in the family palace. No documentation survives granting Girolamo permission to pay conjugal visits to his bride in Ca' Bembo, less than ten minutes away by gondola, but such is possible. Alternately, Giulia may have visited her new husband, again by gondola, in his place of detention. As Vecellio would later remark on the comfort of Venetian gondolas: 'It is also a great advantage that married women and noblewomen, when leaving home, have the convenience of arriving directly at the doors of the palaces and churches to which they are going, and from there of returning to the doors of their own houses.'[54] Although such a scenario may seem implausible, given the scant presence of noble women in Venetian public space except for festive celebrations, Giulia was now a married woman and no longer a maiden, and there is at least one suggestive precedent.

A Prisoner of Consequence

During the wars of the League of Cambrai, Cristoph Frangipane, the Count of Veglia, Senia, and Modrusa in Dalmatia, was a commander of the Emperor Maximilian's forces fighting Venice. Captured by Venetian troops in 1514, he was imprisoned in the Torresella, the corner tower of the Palazzo Ducale near the Ponte della Paglia. The facility had been used for 'prisoners of consequence' since the fourteenth century. Frangipane, though confined, was treated with considerable respect. Marin Sanudo described him as 'young, 32 years old, handsome and large of person, and slender'. Recently married, Christoph was allowed to correspond with his new wife, Apollonia Lang: the beautiful widow of the Count of Lodron, sister of the cardinal of Gurk, Matthias Lang, and formerly a maid-in-waiting of the Emperor Maximilian. Their affectionate letters were read by the state censors and (fortunately for us) recorded in Sanudo's diaries.[55]

Apollonia, with the support of the Emperor, petitioned the Signoria for a safe conduct to travel to Venice to visit her husband. Although twice denied, she forced the issue, arriving without notice at the edge of the lagoon on 13 January 1517 with four maids-in-waiting, her *maestro di casa*, her physician and twenty-two servants. The Council of Ten dispatched a flotilla of twelve barges and a small reception committee to meet her: Giovanni Antonio Dandolo, the patrician superintendent of the ducal prisons, and two highborn 'German' prisoners of war—a certain capitano Rainer and Nicolò Della Torre. The latter two had been captured in Pordenone while serving in the imperial army. Given their rank, they were allowed to stay in the Fondaco dei Tedeschi after posting a bond to ensure that they would not leave the city.[56] It is worth noting that this was the same Nicolò Della Torre to whom Girolamo would write about his impending marriage some thirty-five years later.[57]

Dandolo housed the countess's entourage in his family palace, now the Hotel Danieli, on Calle delle Rasse. Facing the *bacino*, it was just a bridge away from the Torresella. Apollonia was allowed to visit her husband the next morning and stayed with him until evening. She speedily dispatched a letter to her brother, the cardinal, asking him to post a bond—*una segurtà*—of 50,000 ducats demanded by the Collegio to free her husband. A week later, Apollonia appeared before Doge Leonardo Loredan with her full retinue, along with the reception committee that had welcomed her to the city. She thanked the Doge for the courteous treatment accorded her husband, and asked permission to visit him twice a week. Loredan and his councilors, charmed by a determined high-born woman, gave their approval.[58]

Apollonia visited Christoph in his quarters that very afternoon. And refused to leave. Dandolo reported that he found her in bed in the Torresella the following morning, and that the count had used *gran parole* (great words), insisting that she remain with him. The Collegio was no longer charmed and reacted with *gran mormorio* (much whispering). But remain she did, for over a year, with two excused absences to visit the healing springs at Abano. After a foiled attempt to escape, Christoph was finally released from the Torresella in January 1519. But he was not freed and travelled under guard to further imprisonment in the Castello of Milan. Apollonia, who was forced to part with him at Lizza Fusina, followed him to Milan and died there in September. Despairing of ever being released, Christoph escaped the Castello a month later and returned to his estates in Dalmatia and a military life.[59]

Did the Collegio's indulgence of Apollonia provide a meaningful precedent for visits by Giulia Bembo to her Della Torre spouse? More than it might seem on the face of it, allowing that the circumstances between a highborn prisoner of war and an unruly Friulian noble, punished for pursuing a family vendetta, were different. In the first place, both cases concerned titled mainland nobility—persons *da conto* (of account)—to whom certain courtesies might be extended. Count Girolamo's residence in a chamber in the *corte del palazzo* suggests that he had some degree of freedom, for he was required to pledge a bond—a *piezara*—against an attempted escape. In a sense he was under house arrest, from which he had already been granted leave in order to finalize the marriage.

In the second place, Girolamo almost certainly received visitors in his place of confinement. He continued to conduct family business, and his marriage negotiations had required repeated personal contact with Gian Matteo Bembo and other familiars. Later on, his new bride could well have been one of them. Indeed, the Collegio had had little problem in allowing Apollonia to *visit* her husband once she was in the city; the conflict occurred when she herself became his roommate and a resident of his prison. Even then, the authorities gave in and allowed her to remain. It is unlikely that Giulia would have wished to remain overnight in Girolamo's chamber, and in fact, there would have been no advantage to it. Her intention would have been to perform her wifely duties, paying the conjugal debt, and to provide Girolamo with an heir. On this count, one aspect of Girolamo's marriage strategy was successful.

The Continuing Quest for External Favours

With the papal election settled, the Della Torre supporters resumed their Roman initiative. Bishop Lodovico Beccadelli, the new papal nuncio, was now the point man in Venice.[60] The appeal procedure was dragging on, and Tristan Savorgnan remained a fugitive. Finally, on 7 May, after prolonged investigations, the Council of Ten identified seven of his accomplices in the attack on the Grand Canal and offered bounties for their capture. More importantly, it acknowledged the complicity of Giovanni Savorgnan, sentencing him to exile in Zara for five years, and that of his brother Nicolò, banishing him from Udine and the Patria del Friuli for two years.[61] The situation for Girolamo—about to be a father—looked more promising.

On 17 May, Cardinal Girolamo Dandino wrote to Beccadelli from Rome, informing him of Pope Julius III's desire to see Della Torre liberated from his banishment, 'for the great respect that he should receive for his rank, and principally for being the brother of the Monsignor of Ceneda, nuncio in France, so well regarded by this Holy See and a prelate of so many rare qualities'. As soon as the pope's ambassadors arrived in Venice, Beccadelli should remind them to make 'every warm office with the Signoria and with whoever else would seem to be necessary. The pope wishes to be informed about this.' But Dandino covered his bets. He also asked Beccadelli to give Della Torre a copy of the *procura* (proxy) from Cardinal Alessandro Farnese, finalized the previous year, commissioning Della Torre during his exile to collect rents due his brother, Cardinal Ranuccio Farnese, for the properties that he held in Crete as titular Latin Patriarch of Constantinople. A copy of the *procura* should also be given to the Signoria.[62]

On 24 May, Beccadelli reported back to Dandino about his appearance before the Collegio the previous morning:

> I made the most strenuous argument that I could for [Girolamo's] liberation and had the most gracious audience and response from those lords. They told me that out of respect for your holiness they would always do what they could, but that the banishment was so rigorous and strict that it could not be dismissed if not with all the ballots of the Council of Ten with the Gionta, and that this was impossible. So, it is thought that the best service to the count would be to take another road and to speak of moderation and not of total absolution. [63]

Beccadelli affirmed that he would not stint in continuing to do what he could in the name of the Pope, especially when the Bishop of Ceneda returned. Michele had been recalled from France on 25 April, a normal change at the beginning of a new pontificate. But then he was asked to remain until a new nuncio was in place and it was some time before he would return to Venice.[64]

Dandino responded to Beccadelli's letter on 31 May, declaring that his holiness had heard with great satisfaction the office that Beccadelli had made with those lords on behalf of Count Girolamo, and that in the future he should do the same any time an occasion presents itself, however, maintaining the respect that is owed to the dignity of his sanctity and the place that he holds.[65]

But Dandino's response crossed in the mail with another letter from Beccadelli written on the very same day. Expanding on his letter of the 24th, he reported that he had now been to the Collegio twice and made the strongest case possible for the count's release. He had heard that the most Christian king, Henri II, had also written on Della Torre's behalf. Again, the authorities spoke nicely and paid the 'reverence which is appropriate to your grandeur', but excused themselves for not being able to change anything.

For what I get out of it, both from the Heads of the Council of Ten and others, this business is very difficult because of the rigorous language of the ban of the said count, and I believe there is nothing else to be done here for now, also because here their humors are governed by diverse brains that always cannot be reconciled together.[66]

The decision came on 9 June. The Council of Ten voted that Girolamo Della Torre should go to his confinement in Candia with the trireme galleys of Alexandria, scheduled to depart on the first of August, 'and before then if he would have a good passage'. The vote was sixteen in favour, four against, and three undecided.[67]

Beccadelli reported the unwelcome judgment to Dandino:

To satisfy Count Girolamo Della Torre, who implored me with great urgency, I returned to the Collegio and summoned the Heads of the Ten with whom I again argued in the best way that I knew and with due gravity, the desire of our Lord [the pope] that a reprieve should be given in all or in part to the said count in respect to the many merits of his honoured brother with the Apostolic Seat. I was listened to courteously, but they responded to me in the same way: that is that they would remain united to serve their laws, which they could not alter, saying a thousand good and honoured words about our holiness and the Apostolic Seat, turning to me to make the point they had also written the past Saturday and celebrated the creation of the reverend and illustrious del Monte [as pope], while again they made testimony to our holiness of how the greatest pleasure this state took of every joy of His Holiness, and that they celebrated that with all their hearts.[68]

All this was to no avail. Beccadelli continued:

The following day I heard how they had voted that Count Girolamo would go in any case to his confinement, appearing to these lords, as much as I could

> understand, that the said count would have wished to benefit too much from external favors, the ambassador of France having already made a similar office, so that what has happened here, and, in the judgement of those who understand these practices, the count can do no better now than to obey and then at an opportune time, request a reprieve from his confinement; and that [to persist] in this way it is to beat his head against the wall. Your lordship will be content to make Monsignor Montemerlo [secretary to Cardinal Alessandro Farnese], who is in Rome, understand how much I desire the consolation of the Monsignor of Ceneda and his brother.[69]

Dandino responded: 'I informed Montemerlo what you wrote in your letter of the 14th, and he said that he is satisfied with everything that has been done in the case of Count Girolamo, about which I cannot think of anything else to say.'[70]

The strategy of urging foreign princes, such as the pope and the King of France, to pressure the Council of Ten to reconsider its decision had backfired. The Ten resented outsiders, no matter how distinguished, who attempted to interfere in local affairs. Nor were they swayed by the good reputation of the defendant's brother. Girolamo now faced certain exile in Candia. But it did not take long before he sought to cut his losses. On 13 June he filed another appeal, arguing that he should not have to pay Giovanni Savorgnan the remaining 500 ducats of his 1000-ducat fine, considering that Giovanni was responsible for the murders of Alvise II Della Torre and Giambattista Colloredo. The matter was remanded to November, when it would be reconsidered after other depositions had been taken.[71]

Memoria delle cose di casa nostra

Resigned to his fate, Girolamo put his affairs in order. On 17 June he executed a power of attorney, naming three relatives as his main procurators: Bernardo Colloredo and Dottore Giulio Sbroiavacca (respectively, brother and son-in-law of the deceased Giambattista), and Bernardo Strassoldo (Girolamo's first cousin), all nobles of Udine, *absentes tamquam prasentes* (absent, as if present). The document was signed in the chamber of Marco Antonio Venier, *scribae carcerum*, a distant cousin of the lawyer who had drawn up Girolamo's marriage contract.[72]

Three days later, on 20 June, Girolamo compiled a new *Memoria*, updating the one that he had written the year before. Some of the debts had been paid off, others had been paid down, and some were new. He also expanded his list of procurators to a veritable army. In the Friuli, to Giulio Sbroiavacca, Bernardo Colloredo, and Bernardo Strassoldo, he added two first cousins, Girolamo Partistagno and Strassoldo's brother Francesco. For matters of the Michele's bishopric in Ceneda, Giulio Sbroiavacca was his factor until the arrival of the bishop. For matters relating to the bishopric in Venice: Giovanni Battista Feretto,

Sebastiano Bravo, Alfonso Bidernuccio Dottore, and his new brother-in-law Lorenzo Bembo, the latter 'to take care of my affairs'. In Venice to receive the family's rents and other income, he appointed Alvise Dalla Gatta and also Madonna Giacoma, widow of his cousin Nicolò II, in the name of her son Guido, the only male Della Torre heir at this point. He entrusted little Guido, then around five years old, and the family palace in Udine to Madonna Giacoma and was confident that she would not be lacking in teaching letters and good manners to the boy so that he would become a *homo da bene* (a worthy man).[73]

Girolamo wrote a second memo that day to Lorenzo Bembo, thirty years old at the time. In it he trusts that Lorenzo can work with the other procurators and gives him a detailed list of instructions that are direct and, indeed, imperious:

> On the first of every month you should check in with the Council of Ten to avoid paying the 500 ducats that I still owe Giovanni Savorgnan and press my case, which is under appeal...
>
> The conductor (bursar) of the bishopric of Ceneda will bring you in September, December, March, and June, the payments that come from the bishopric, that is, 293 gold scudi. Computing what will have been spent of these monies, from every payment you will give 6 scudi to Giovanni Battista Feretto for his provision; the remainder you should send me in *zecchini* in Candia.
>
> If messer Febo di Rinaldi forwards certain monies to my account having sold my horses, send them to me in Candia in so many *zecchini*.
>
> If messer Hercole dale Maniche gives you some monies on account of 146 scudi that he and Capitano Hanibale, his brother, owe me—that is Hercole 114 and his brother 32—you should keep them with you until you have another order from me, but do not request anything other than 32 scudi from his brother, which he should pay at the end of this month.
>
> If the procurators, messer Hercole dale Maniche and messer Alfonso Bidernutio, assigned to collect 160 scudi from Giacomo Savorgnan, collect the monies, they should give them to you and you should keep them with you until my further order.
>
> You will be content to have the duty of writing to me often of all my affairs and of the affairs of the world and forward to me all the letters that are sent to me, and it would please me if you are diligent and write to me frequently.
>
> You will remember to attend to my liberation so that I would soon return home, and when it seems the right time, you should advise my brother the bishop in Rome to come to negotiate such a thing.[74]

Girolamo's *memorie* of 20 June are our last dated records of his presence in Venice. Indeed, they may well have been written on the eve of his departure, for he arrived in Candia on 16 July.[75] He must have secured a 'good passage' on a merchant galley, at least a month before the scheduled departure of the less comfortable triremes of Alexandria. With sailing times averaging thirty-three days according to one estimate, this would be a relatively speedy trip of perhaps three weeks.[76]

Not being a merchant, Girolamo's cargo was minimal; but his responsibilities were great. For what of Giulia, Girolamo's pregnant bride? Hopeful that his exile would be brief, he had planned to leave her behind, but did not reckon with a strong-willed woman, reminiscent of Apollonia Frangipane. As Sansovino writes, Giulia

> had a soul so invincible and a constancy so strong, that at the same time she surpassed her youthful age and the fragility typical of her sex. She gave an example of this when the Signor Conte had to go to Candia, because not only was she not dismayed to go among so many travails and perils of the sea, including corsairs, but rather she opposed with the greatest efficacy the plan that the Signor Conte had to leave her at home, imploring him that he should take her with him, because she gladly faced with him every fortune [and] she did not want to stay in any sort of comfort without him.[77]

Indeed, disposing of her gold chains, jewels, and embroidery, Giulia 'dressed herself in simple clothing, it appearing appropriate to her, that since her mind was in travail on that unfortunate occasion, the clothing of her body should also be modest and re-worn'.[78]

Giulia's relatives and friends tearfully accompanied her to the galley, lamenting her departure. By contrast, 'she was always cheerful, and with dry eyes showed her joyful mind, and her disposition to suffer major accidents of ill fortune, that were not the present ones, as she soon demonstrated with great liberality on the voyage'.[79] The second chapter in the married life of Girolamo's Venetian bride was about to begin.

Notes

1. ASTS, Archivio della Torre di Valsassina di Duino, b. 62, fasc. 1 (1525–57), Nicolò di Giovanni di Febo, Corrispondenza.
2. Girolamo and Niccolò were sixth cousins once removed who shared a common ancestor in Pagano II Della Torre, Duke of Milan (d. 1241). See Morelli di Schönfeld 1855–56, I, 358–61; Conzato 2005, 28–30, 33.
3. Appendix I: Sansovino, *Vita*, f. 4v. See Brown 2008.
4. Art Institute of Chicago, Ref. no. 1954.301. Lloyd 1993, 246–8. Wethey 1971, 169, cat. X-60. Giulia Gonzaga Colonna lived c. 1513–66.
5. Kidwell 2004, 296, 320–1, 359.
6. Appendix I: Sansovino, Vita, ff. 3r–3v.
7. Rosenthal and Jones 2008, 158. See Chapter 11 for portraits of Gian Matteo in the Palazzo Ducale that would be destroyed by fire.

8. Mazzuchelli 1760, II:II, 731–2; *DBI, s.v.* 'Bembo, Giovanni Matteo' (1966), 124–5; Brown 2004, 94–5, 190–1 (with his name spelled as Zuan Matteo); Brown 2013a, 240–1; Calvelli 2012, 19–66.
9. Brown 2004, 191–5. Two sons, Bernardo Andrea and Paolo, had died in infancy.
10. Bembo/Travi, III, 551, no. 1638 (26 November 1534). On Febo's Vicentine identity, see ASVic, Arnaldi, b. 109, 'Genealogie', citing the marriage of Deifebo [Febo] and Augusta. Chojnacki 2000, 180, 185–91, observed that families favoured marriage in the early teens for their daughters in the fourteenth century, but that the preference had risen to the mid to late teens by the late fifteenth century.
11. Grubb 1996, 6–7, 156–7, 180–4; Grubb 2002, 3–24.
12. See Grubb 1996, 38–9.
13. ASVic, Arnaldi, b. 51, Testament of Andrea Arnaldi q. Silvestro (9 December 1521). See also Grubb 1996, 38–9; and Appendix II, Table E.
14. On Marcella's pregnancy, see Bembo/Travi, III, 527–9, nos. 1610, 1611 (15 September 1534). On Gian Matteo's election as Conte di Zara, see ibid., III, 531–3, no. 1616 (4 October 1534); and no. 1619 (17 October 1534); and ASVe, *SAV-MC*, r. 1 (1526–40), 146. He served from 19 March 1535 to 18 November 1537.
15. ASVe, NT, b. 1210.716 (Antonio Marsilio): Testamento of Marcella Marcello, wife of Gian Matteo Bembo: 23 February 1546 m.v. [=1547].
16. Cevese 1964, 201–3, and Fig. 91; Grubb 1996, 183. They are now called Palazzo Godi Arnaldi Segala ora Bertevello and Palazzo Arnaldi Tretti ora Piccoli, dating to the mid and late fifteenth centuries, respectively. Other extant Arnaldi palaces were built in the late sixteenth century.
17. Bembo/Travi, III, 638, no. 1739 (3 January 1536) and 643–4, no. 1750 (Sunday of Carnival 1536); ibid., IV, 423–4, no. 2338 (13 July 1542) and 428, no. 2344 (5 August 1542).
18. De Checchi 2005, 9–12. For Pietro's villa at Santa Maria di Non, also known as Villa Bozza, see Kidwell 2004, 204–5; Nalezyty 2017, 42, 192–3.
19. Laura's father was Alvise Foscarini q. Andrea q. Bernardo. Her brother Marcantonio was a *sopracomito*, as was Giacomo, who later became capitano da Mar and purchased a magnificent palace opposite S. M. del Carmine, where he was buried in a lavish tomb. See MCVe, Barbaro, *Genealogie*, I, cc. 209–10; ibid., III, cc. 297–8; ASVe, Barbaro, III, 552; ASVe,AC, b. 9, 160v; Cicogna, *Ins. Ven.*, II, 408–9; Sforza 1745, 8. For dowry legislation, see Bistort 1912, 106–13.
20. Appendix I: Sansovino, *Vita*, f. 5v.
21. Bembo/Travi, IV, 584–5, no. 1635 (24 April 1535).
22. Ibid., 262–3, no. 2126 (30 September 1539).
23. Ibid.
24. See Brown 2013a, 231–49.
25. Conzato 2005, 33; Sachs 1915, 79–80; Muir 1993, 85–92. Garafolo 2002, 69–97, states that all the Della Torre marriages in the fifteenth century, except by noble daughters who married Veneto husbands outside the Friuli and one illegitimate daughter, were contracted with the Friulian nobility.
26. Appendix I: Sansovino, *Vita*, 5v–6.
27. Sachs 1915, 86–107.

28. For sumptuous marriages, for which Venice was famous, see Molmenti 1905–8, 2:329–35; Labalme and Sanguineti White 1999, 43–72; Labalme and Sanguineti White 2008, 303; Krohn 2008, 12–13.
29. See Chapter 1.
30. ASUd, *AT*, b. 15: Carte varie, fasc 9, no. 5; ibid., b. 25: Doti entrate nella famiglia Della Torre, 1495–1643, no. 35.
31. Battilotti and Franco 1978, 58–86; Battilotti 1994, 211–12; Lauber 2004, 11–30; Lauber 2013, 441–54; Szépe 2018, 178–80; *Relazioni/Friuli*, LX; BCUd, Annales civitatis Utini, vol. 50, fol. 39 (1 July 1540). Venier was married to Pierina Michiel, whose paternal aunt, Pentesilea, had married Gian Matteo's father, Alvise Bembo. MCVe, Barbaro, *Genealogie*, c. 269.
32. ASVe, *CX*, Comuni, Filze, b. 49, no. 93.
33. Piamonte 1992, Itinerario IV, 59, 69–80; Itinerario V, 87.
34. Rosenthal and Jones 2008, 177–8.
35. Sansovino 1581, 148v; Cohen and Cohen 2001, 204.
36. Appendix I: Sansovino, *Vita*, 4v.
37. Appendix I: Sansovino, *Vita*, 4v.
38. Conzato 2005, 33–4.
39. Bistort 1912, 211; Labalme and Sanguineti White 2008, 299, 303–4.
40. *CSP*/5, no. 587 (10 November 1549). Alessandro Farnese (1520–1589), cardinal-nephew, was the grandson of Paul III.
41. Ibid., no. 588 (13 November 1549).
42. Ibid.
43. Ibid., no. 600 (14 December 1549).
44. Ibid., no. 604 (24 December 1549).
45. Ibid., no. 613 (1 January 1550).
46. Ibid., no. 618 (8 January 1550).
47. Ibid., no. 635 (29 January 1550).
48. Ibid., no. 642 (8 February 1550).
49. Pastor, 13: 3.
50. MCVe, MS Correr 406, Giovanni Giorgio Palfero, Memorabilia Venetiarum Monumenta Antiquis., Part I, 71, no. 376; MCVe, MS Correr 201, Giovanni Giorgio Palfero, *Palferis Memorabilia Venetiarum monumenta*, 357; BMVe, Marc. Lat. X 144 (3657). The Cappella di San Nicolò, located on the north side of the second cloister of the monastery, was replaced by the sala del capitolo in the seventeenth century. See Alberghina 2016, 20–2.
51. Brown 2013a, 241–3.
52. Ibid., 243–4, 249 nn73–4; Calvelli 2012, 19–66.
53. If the couple obeyed Church commandments ordering abstinence from sex during Advent (1–25 December 1549) and Lent (19 February to 6 April 1550), the baby must have been conceived between 26 December and 18 February. See Grubb 1996, 35; Brundage 2009, 91, 158, 198, 242, 503–5. For awareness of a pregnancy, see Sánchez 2015, 449–54.
54. Rosenthal and Jones 2008, 175–6.

55. Thode 1900. See also Brown 137, II, 98–106, 234–7; Crawford 1907, 490–9; Franzoi 1966, 101, XXVI; Cicogna, *Ins. Ven.*, 6:2, 777–8; Sanudo, *Diarii*, 18:256–8, 261, 489–95; 19: 467–9; 20 187–90.
56. Thode 1900, 11–14. Sanudo, *Diarii*, 18: 91–2, reported that 132 German prisoners, captured in Pordenone, had been imprisoned in the cabioni or gabioni in Terra Nova prison (formerly on the site now occupied by the Giardini Reali) on 2 April 1514. Of these eleven were 'da conto', including the brothers Nicolò and Michele da la Torre.
57. Conzato 2005, xx; *DBI, s.v.* 'Della Torre, Niccolò'.
58. Sanudo, *Diarii*, 18: 256, 449, 470, 490; Thode 1900, 78. The couple were depicted as their namesake saints in Jan van Scorel's *Frangipane Altarpiece* (1519–20) in the church of St. Martin zu Obervellach in the Tyrol (less than 100 miles north of Udine).
59. Sanudo, *Diarii*, 18: 505–6; Thode 1900, 80, 112–25.
60. He served from 17 March 1550 to mid-1554. *DBI, s.v.* 'Beccadelli, Ludovico'.
61. ASVe, *CX*, Criminali, r. 7, f. 168v–169r.
62. Gaeta 1967, V, 65–6, no. 29. For the Farnese, see Robertson 1992; and http://www2.fiu.edu/~mirandas/bios1545.htm#Farnese. Curiously, Ranuccio was given the patriarcate title on 10 August 1546 but resigned it on 19 March 1550. He held the title a second time from ca. 1554 until his death on 19 October 1565. The original contract with Della Torre was drafted in 1549, but it is unclear why it should have been reaffirmed on 17 May 1550 when Ranuccio no longer held the title. A procura is a legal document authorizing one person to act as the agent of another.
63. Gaeta 1967, V, 67–8, no. 30
64. Ibid.; Lestocquoy 1966, 34–6 (13 August 1550).
65. Gaeta 1967, V, 71–2, no. 33
66. Gaeta 1967, V, 70–1, no. 32
67. ASVe, *CX*, Comuni, Filze, b. 50, no. 125; ASVe, *CX*, Comuni, r. 19c. 115v. For the scheduled departure of the triremes, see ASVe, *CX*, Comuni, Filze, b. 50, no. 228 (30 July 1550).
68. Gaeta 1967, V, 75–6, no. 36 (14 June 1550).
69. Ibid.
70. Ibid., 80, no. 43 (21 June 1550).
71. ASUd, *AT*, b. 19.
72. Ibid., b. 6, no. 10 (17 June 1550).
73. Ibid., b. 6, no. 10 (20 June 1550).
74. Ibid. It is possible that Febo di Rinaldi is actually Febo Arnaldi, Girolamo's new brother-in-law.
75. ASVe, Duca di Candia, b. 8, no. 6, 188.
76. Braudel 1976, 1:360–2. See also Sardella 1948, 56–55, citing fifty-six examples of voyages from Venice to Candia ranging from nineteen to eighty-one days.
77. Appendix I: Sansovino, *Vita*, 9v.
78. Ibid., 10r.
79. Ibid.

7
Exile

Sailing was a fact of life for Venetian men of the sea, but the thought of several weeks on the ocean in various degrees of discomfort, in addition to a plethora of life-threatening dangers—most notably corsairs—was a daunting prospect to men of the land. This would have been particularly the case for Girolamo, a feudal lord who was more at ease on horseback than in a rocking boat and whose young wife was expecting their first child. But while this may well have been Girolamo's maiden voyage on a seagoing vessel, it was not the first time for Giulia. As the daughter of a professional 'man of empire', she was more traveled than most patrician girls her age. In 1534, when only three years old, she had sailed with her parents to Zara, a port city on the Dalmatian Coast, for her father's assignment as Conte or count (the Venetian administrator) and returned to Venice by ship when she was six. And again, at the age of ten she sailed to Capodistria and lived with her family in the Palazzo Pretorio for more than a year while Gian Matteo served as podestà and capitano. But these were short voyages—a matter of a few days at most—and probably on smaller vessels.[1]

Giulia might also have been part of the entourage in 1547, when Gian Matteo was posted to Cyprus as capitano of Famagusta. We know from his correspondence with Pietro Bembo that his wife Marcella planned to accompany him 'with some of the children'.[2] But which children? This is one of those intriguing mysteries for which archival records are inconclusive. Giulia's oldest brothers Lorenzo and Alvise, ages twenty-seven and twenty-four, were already *sopracomiti* on ships. Marco Antonio was twenty-three, Sebastiano twenty, Davide seventeen, and Pietro fourteen. Giulia was sixteen years old at the time, a sensitive age for a girl. As we know, most patrician girls of marriageable age were carefully guarded, closely watched, and kept inside the family palace until safely married. The family thus had two options. On the one hand, they might have left Giulia behind in a convent in Venice for her education—and her protection. For this there was family precedent. We will recall that her mother Marcella was residing in the convent of Santa Caterina along with her two sisters when she married Gian Matteo at the age of twenty-three.[3] And Giulia, as we shall learn, was a notably pious young woman, her character perhaps shaped by prolonged residence in a religious environment during her adolescence. On the other hand, she may well have travelled with the family. Sansovino tells us that Marcella had put her daughter 'in the constant governance of the house as she came out of her childhood'.[4] And indeed,

The Venetian Bride: Bloodlines and Blood Feuds in Venice and Its Empire. Patricia Fortini Brown, Oxford University Press (2021). © Patricia Fortini Brown. DOI: 10.1093/oso/9780192894571.003.0007

Marcella may have wanted Giulia as a companion on the long sea voyage, as well as in the household, for a two-year stay on a faraway island. As Pietro Bembo had commented of Marcella at the time, 'She is a wise and good wife.'[5]

Giulia would follow this model in her own marriage to Girolamo, accompanying him into exile and later on to a succession of residences. She was praised for being capable and resourceful, as well as pious—attributes that could well have been shaped by helping her mother cope with the challenges of living in the small Venetian community in Famagusta. Such an experience would certainly have been good preparation for what awaited her in Crete. The question remains open.

Sailing into Dangerous Waters

Gian Matteo was well aware of the uncertainties of sea travel and the perils that awaited his daughter. He could recall his heroic defence of Cattaro against the Ottoman admiral Hayreddin Barbarossa back in 1539. After leaving his family at home in Venice and preparing the small Dalmatian town for war as its Venetian rettore and provveditore, Bembo had written confidently to the admiral Vincenzo Cappello: 'I have so effectively emboldened these people and soldiers that they do not fear the time when the enemy would show himself.'[6] Barbarossa pounded the city with volleys of cannon balls without result, and tried to demoralize Bembo with threatening letters: 'To you Rector of Cattaro…Do not think that I have come here only for Castel Nuovo, rather, I have come in order not to leave a hand-length of land from here to Constantinople.'[7] After a fusillade of letters back and forth, Bembo had ordered a Venetian ship to be sunk in the bay to prevent the Turks from approaching from the sea, and the town stood firm. After two weeks Barbarossa gave up and withdrew his fleet.

Bembo was praised throughout Europe as the town's defender, but unfortunately, his triumph was short-lived. After Barbarossa captured several Christian outposts in the Ionian and Aegean Seas, Venice finally signed a humiliating peace treaty with the Sultan Suleiman the Magnificent on 2 October 1540, recognizing Ottoman territorial gains, ceding Monemvasia and Nauplion, and paying an indemnity of 300,000 gold ducats.[8]

While the treaty bought relative peace to Venetian shipping for a time in relation to the Ottoman navy, freelance corsairs still ravaged ports and attacked ships of all nations with impunity. Their booty was not only grain and merchandise; it was also slaves. Captives were sold in the slave markets in Algiers and Constantinople or, if affluent, held hostage, sometimes for years, until desperate families could raise enough money to ransom them.[9] Fernand Braudel, the historian of the Mediterranean, observed that 'June was a good month for corsairs.'[10] Gian Matteo knew that his daughter and her new husband were sailing into dangerous waters.

No record of the passage survives, but Girolamo and his bride probably sailed on a type of round ship, possibly a carrack (*caracca*), similar to the vessels on which Alessandro Magno sailed a few years later on three voyages to Cyprus and Alexandria (1557–61). Designed for trade rather than warfare, carracks featured high forecastles and sterncastles and three or four masts and were powered by the wind. Like the Alexandria triremes, they were armed with cannons and other defensive weaponry. But unlike the triremes, they sailed in all seasons.[11]

The discomforts of sea travel recounted by Felix Fabri, the German priest who twice traveled to the Levant on great galleys in the 1480s, would have been little different in the 1550s. He cautioned:

> A journey by sea is subject to many hardships. The sea itself is very injurious to those who are unaccustomed to it, and very dangerous on many accounts; for it strikes terror into the soul; it causes headache, it provokes vomiting and nausea; it destroys appetite for food and drink... it causes extreme and deadly perils and often brings men to a most cruel death.

Aside from the sea, he continued, the wind—too strong, adverse, or none at all—posed other dangers, as did defects of ship or crew.[12]

On his return trip from Cyprus in 1483, Fabri made note of the presence of the shipmaster's pregnant sister-in-law, whose husband was a counsellor to Caterina Cornaro, the Queen of Cyprus. It was not an easy trip for her. Fabri reported a three-day layover at Lesina, a village north of Bari on the Apulian coast:

> because the wind at sea was very strong, although it was a fair wind for us; we waited also in order to recruit the strength of the pregnant lady who had suffered much and become very weak during the gale; indeed, it is a wonder that both she and her infant did not perish during that terrible time.[13]

In sum, a voyage to the Mediterranean was not a happy prospect for any Venetian bride, and even less so for one in the sixth month of pregnancy. Probably over the discomforts of the first trimester—morning sickness, fatigue, and cramping—our Giulia faced the possibility of seasickness, back pain, and difficulty in sleeping. She would have begun to feel the baby's movements in her swelling belly and would have been desperate not to lose this precious heir.

When the day of departure arrived, the couple would have taken leave of Giulia's tearful family in a moment reminiscent of Saint Ursula's leave-taking (albeit without the 11,000 virgins) in Carpaccio's famous narrative painting cycle.[14] But how and where did they board the ship? As indicated in the painting, it may not have been a matter of simply walking up a gangway from the dock. Saint Ursula's carrack was anchored in deep water. She and her entourage were rowed out to it in a small boat and boarded ship by climbing a ladder (Figure 7.1).

Figure 7.1. Carpaccio, *Departure of the Betrothed Pair* (detail), c. 1495 (Venice, Gallerie dell'Accademia).

Girolamo and Giulia were almost certainly accompanied by servants, at least one each, although none are named in the primary documents. However they might have boarded the galley, their possessions would have been loaded on board in advance and duly recorded by the purser. In addition to clothing and personal items, as well as a strongbox for valuables, they were required to supply their own mattresses and bedding for the voyage—furnishings that would also be useful when they reached their destination. Giulia must have had a chest of her own packed with linens, indispensable items in every bride's trousseau.

No two voyages were alike, but a handful of near-contemporary accounts allow us to sketch out the probable features of their voyage. Setting sail was always a dramatic moment for veteran sailors and first-time passengers alike. When the captain deemed the winds favourable, the trumpets sounded, and the crew moved to their stations. As Magno put it, the helmsman blew a whistle on his pipe and prayed for God's blessing, in the name of the Virgin, San Marco, and all those saints 'who protect this blessed world, that they accord us a favorable and profitable voyage'. The assembled crew responded: 'As God wills.' The sails were hoisted, and the ship moved swiftly into the turbulent waters of the Adriatic under the protection of the heavenly hosts.

The same ritual was repeated in each port from which Magno's ship set sail. Every evening around the second hour of night (this varied according to the time of sunset), the *bona parola* was sung. This was an antiphonal chant between the officers and the crew, consisting of the Pater Noster and the Ave Maria, along with special supplications and prayers to the Virgin and a plethora of saints for safe passage, with good tailwinds, and calm seas, and for good health and (eventually) profit.[15]

As they sailed down the Adriatic, probably well offshore, the galleys tacked back and forth with the wind and took advantage of favourable currents while avoiding the rocky outcroppings of the Dalmatian and Italian coasts. The round ships typically made few stops on this leg of the journey in this period; the great galleys of Alexandria and Beirut sailed directly to Corfù. With the visible horizon only three miles distant, land was often out of sight, it seeming to the passengers as if they were in the middle of a vast ocean.[16]

A Temporary Microcosm

For descriptions of living conditions on board ship in the mid-sixteenth century we are indebted to Magno, as well as to Elijah of Pesaro, a Jewish merchant who sailed with his family to Famagusta on a state galley in 1563. Elijah called it a galleass, an enlarged version of the traditional great galley used for trade—but its general layout would have been similar.[17] Like present-day cruise ships, Elijah's galleass was like a small city. In addition to the crew and passengers (four hundred in all, according to his estimate), his vessel carried two doctors, one a surgeon; also a barber, a secretary, a priest, a tailor, a blacksmith, a carpenter, a rope maker, a butcher, and, not least, a cook and a baker. But unlike present-day cruise ships, most of the space was filled with cargo. Elijah's ship also carried a substantial menagerie of live animals to be slaughtered for meals en route: '35 or 40 sheep, 2 or 3 oxen, 5 or 6 veal calves, numerous poultry of all kinds.'[18]

In addition to a crew of mostly non-Venetian sailors, the voyagers comprised people of diverse religious, cultural, and economic backgrounds, forced into close proximity. The paying passengers included merchants, diplomatic envoys, and Venetian officials travelling to posts abroad, along with their families and servants. As Benjamin Arbel observes of the galley experience: 'This isolated capsule constituted a temporary microcosm, functioning under particular circumstances, quite different from those in which these men and women were accustomed in their daily life on land.'[19]

The hierarchy of role, class, and caste in society at large was reflected in the sleeping accommodations. On Elijah's ship, they ranged from small cabins only 5 feet in height, with a 5 × 7 foot floor plan, lining the sides of the level below the deck like prison cells and costing 4–5 ducats for the voyage; to officer's cabins in the stern, subletting for 8–12 ducats; to slightly larger quarters with individual storage areas in the prow. Elijah rented one of the latter for 32 ducats for himself and his family. Conceding that an average-sized man could not stand in the chamber upright, he still considered it comfortable. Above the officers' quarters in the stern was the captain's cabin—relatively spacious, but dark—that went for the considerable sum of 50 ducats—the annual rent of a moderate-sized palace back in Venice.[20]

Arnold Van Harff, a German knight sailing on one of the state galleys of Alexandria in 1496, was particularly impressed by the captain's quarters: 'He had a fine cabin in the ship with a bed gilded over and furnished as in a prince's court.'[21] But even in the best of conditions, passengers complained of fleas, lice, mice, rats, unpleasant odours, and constant noise that made it difficult to sleep. Arbel described ships loaded with grain and other foodstuffs as 'a virtual mice-paradise' and characterized the ship's cat as 'an important personality'.[22]

The order of dining arrangements, with several classes of service, mirrored the sleeping accommodations. Joining the captain at his table on Elijah's ship were the pilot, the purser, and other important crew members, along with Venetian nobles, wealthy merchants, and distinguished passengers who paid extra for the privilege.[23] He observed that any Christian passenger paying 10 ducats could eat at the captain's table, with a good meal served morning and evening that included wine and entertainment by musicians. There was a second seating for passengers paying 5 ducats and a third seating for 3 ducats at a table set up in the servants' saloon. But Elijah's family—perhaps because they were Jewish—and many of the passengers prepared their own meals, with a shop aboard ship where they could purchase a wide range of provisions, including wine, cooking oil, eggs, salt fish, smoked meat, fruit, vegetables and biscuit.[24]

The tedium of long days at sea was often relieved by the sound of music. Aside from musical entertainment at the captain's table, travellers noted a wealth of musical instruments—lutes, flutes, trumpets, violins, drums, harps, and even organs and clavichords—played by the passengers themselves, and dancing and singing by the crew.[25]

Whether or not this was the first long sea voyage for both Girolamo and Giulia, it must have been the first time they were together under one roof for any length of time. Given their status and Girolamo's wealth, they would have travelled in relative comfort.[26] Were they housed together, or did he sleep with the 'noble comrades' and she, separately, with other 'noble ladies'? Whether together or apart, they must have occupied the equivalent of one or more of the officer's cabins in the stern. In the absence of any accounts of women dining with the crew and male passengers on board the galleys, it is possible that the pregnant Giulia remained in her cabin for much of the time, with at least one maidservant, and took her meals with other women.[27] These would have included the handful of wives and other female relatives of merchants and Venetian officers who were typically on board such ships.

Girolamo was another matter. Albeit under sentence of exile, he was a titled count and ready to prove himself equal to any Venetian noble. Invariably referred to as *Conte* in official documents, he had been accorded the respect due his rank during his detention in the Palazzo Ducale, and his wife's patrician pedigree was impeccable. It is hard to imagine him *not* at the captain's table.

On one occasion during the voyage Girolamo would even arm himself to help defend the galley when some corsairs were sighted near Sasino, an Ottoman island off the Albanian coast, 'which put not a little fear into everyone on the ship'. Those present at the time of the incident were impressed with Giulia's bravery when she beseeched her husband 'that for the love that he had for her she asked a special grace: that she would rather suffer death at his own hand, if by chance they fell into the hands of the enemies, than for him to allow her to go into such a vile servitude'. A young pregnant woman, she would have been prize merchandise to be held for ransom, or for the slave markets of the Barbary Coast and Constantinople.[28] Fortunately, the ship moved on down the coast to Corfù without further incident.

The Sentinel of the Adriatic

After a week at sea, all on board would have rejoiced when Corfù's distinctive fortress atop two peaks on a promontory finally came into view. In all likelihood, this was their first landfall, with a flotilla of large rowing galleys guiding them into port.[29] Under Venetian control since the late fourteenth century, the island in 1550 was still recovering from the devastating siege by the Turks in 1537. Although the Venetian fortress had remained secure, as many as 20,000 Corfiotes were killed or taken as slaves from the countryside and the unprotected town. Known as the borgo, it was separated from the fortress by the spianada—a broad plain that had been cleared of most buildings to create a buffer zone.[30] In response to the siege, the Venetians had immediately embarked on a campaign to further strengthen the citadel, with an extensive plan of fortification drawn up by the military architect and engineer Michele Sanmicheli. By 1550 Girolamo and his bride would have seen two huge bastions flanking a 560-foot-long curtain wall under construction along the moat on the western side of the Venetian citadel.[31] Provveditore Generale Alvise Gritti remarked at the time that Sanmicheli's expertise would make the island 'the key to Christianity from the side of the sea'.[32]

After a week at sea, crew members were always eager to disembark. Although not allowed to spend the night on shore, some made extra money by buying and selling goods from their personal storage lockers. Others patronized prostitutes, many reputed to be afflicted with the *mal francese*, for which the town was notorious.[33] As to the Della Torre, whether or not they dined at the captain's table or sat with the officers, it is unlikely that they had to shop for their own supplies. Girolamo may well have disembarked, if only to look around; Giulia almost certainly stayed on the ship, with servants taking care of provisions.

The next port of call for the Della Torre would have been the lush island of Zante (Zakynthos), called 'the flower of the Levant' by Venetians. The southernmost of the Ionian islands, it was a short journey of perhaps three days further down the coast past the Venetian islands of Paxos, Santa Maura (Lefkada), and Cefalonia. As the last market stop before the week-long voyage to Candia, Zante was much frequented by ships of all nations. The main city was spread out on a plain at the foot of a mountain topped by a small Venetian fortress. Elijah of Pesaro found the island 'good and agreeable, rich above all in vineyards and fine oil, in superior honey…in sugared fruits, and fish and eggs in abundance; in sum, nothing lacks there that one could desire'. That said, he complained that 'everything that is sold is very expensive, and I even heard it said that the arrival of the galley has caused this increase'.[34]

That Other City of Venice in the Levant

Zante was the last likely stopover before the ship carrying the Della Torre set out for Candia, again through waters plagued by corsairs. Moving cautiously down the coast, the galley rounded Cape Matapan, the westernmost point of the Peloponnese, and sailed past the Venetian island of Cerigo (Kythira). The voyagers were again on the open sea, with little to look at but the horizon, rising and falling with the action of waves, but in a day or two the western tip of the island of Crete came into view. Sailing past the harbors of Canea (Chania) and Rettimo (Rethymnon), the ship finally approached the city of Candia (Heraklion). From a distance it resembled a jewel mounted in a setting of fields and low rolling hills. Its skyline punctuated with campaniles of churches, the town spread up a gently sloping rise, with the distinctive profile of Mount Juktas visible in the distance. And in the foreground, the Rocca al Mare—the Fortress on the Sea—stood sentinel at the end of a long mole that defined the western side of the harbour (Figure 7.2).[35]

After some seventeen days, mostly at sea, Girolamo and Giulia were finally able to step foot on dry land. But Candia, often called 'that other city of Venice in the Levant', might not have been what they expected.[36] In contrast to the Serenissima,

Figure 7.2. *Candia*, from Bernhard von Breydenbach, *Peregrinationes in Terram Sanctam*, Mainz, 1486 (1st ed.); 1502 (2nd ed.). Woodcut by Erhard Reeuwich (The National Library of Israel, Eran Laor Cartographic Collection).

The pinnacle atop the campanile of the church of San Francesco is the tallest structure in town. On the right, the mouth of the port is flanked by a small fortress and the Rocca al Mare.

protected by an expansive lagoon, with a sweeping panorama of palace facades and public buildings proclaiming its civic identity, Candia presented itself first and foremost as a port, its harbour and shipyards creating a frontispiece—both portal and barrier—to its urban space. It was, after all, Venice's most important port in the eastern Mediterranean, with a thriving import and export trade. In addition to mundane local products such as honey, beeswax, cheese, fruit, cotton, and salt, high quality Cretan wines were exported to Europe, Constantinople, and Alexandria. Wool and silk fabrics, iron tools, paper, and glassware were imported from Venice, caviar and salt fish and meat from Constantinople, and spices from Alexandria and other Middle Eastern ports, to be transshipped elsewhere. [37] And, far from serene, the city was *disordinatissima*: chaotic, messy, noisy. For even more than Corfù, Candia was a vast construction zone.

As Girolamo and his bride approached the port of Candia, the sounds of the lapping waves were replaced by the sharp tapping of stone masons. Directly ahead as they entered the harbour, work was beginning on the *arsenali vecchi*, a project that would add a four-vaulted shipyard for the refitting and construction of ships adjacent to the five vaults of the *arsenali antichi* to the east. In addition, the crumbling Byzantine-era enclosure of square towers and low curtain walls that had long protected the old city near the port was being replaced.

Modern warfare required modern fortifications, and a growing Greek population in the borgo, the sprawling suburbs toward the south, and the Venetians and the Cretan elite who lived in the old city required protection. Accordingly, the Republic, alarmed by the increased activity of corsairs and Turkish pirates, had ordered the engineer Michele Sanmicheli to take time off from his assignment in Corfù in 1538 and turn his attention to Candia. The architect formulated a master plan for an expansive enceinte embracing both the old city and the suburbs. The job was massive, and the work, largely carried out by reluctant Cretan conscripts from the countryside, had continued in fits and starts in a piecemeal manner over the following decade, with delays caused by lack of funds and manpower and opposing views from other experts. In 1548 the engineer Gian Girolamo Sanmicheli, the son of a cousin of Michele's, had been brought in to advise on the way forward. He called for several substantial modifications, but the governor general, backed up by the duke and the capitano grande, disagreed with some of his suggestions, causing further delay. By 1550, only a few sections of the new fortifications had been completed.[38]

The sense of disorder was compounded by the fact that the city had suffered a damaging earthquake less than a year before. The Duke of Candia had reported on 14 September 1549 that 'the palaces of the duke and capitano are affected and open in some parts, since they are old buildings, and especially that of the capitano, and if means are not provided to restore them, there could be some damage and great inconvenience'.[39] The piles of rubble and partly ruined buildings may well have brought back Girolamo's earliest childhood memories of Giovedì Grasso in 1511 and the earthquake that had occurred shortly thereafter. The murder of his father and other relatives and the destruction of the family palace in Udine and castle at Villalta were the very foundations of the vendetta that had led to his exile in Crete. To make matters worse, the island had experienced a very poor harvest, and there was a great shortage of wheat and grain and few galleys available to bring it in.[40]

These grim thoughts may have been in Girolamo's mind on 16 July as he proceeded up the Ruga Maistra, lined with palaces and government offices in both good and bad condition. When he reached the main square, 600 metres from the port, he entered the palace of the Duke of Candia. A message to the Council of Ten dated 9 August 1550 copied into the *Liber secretorum* (secret correspondence) of the Duke recorded his arrival: 'On the 16th of the past [month], Count Girolamo Della Torre presented to me the letters of your excellencies with the decision taken by the excellent Council of Ten…on 23 May 1549, by which he would be confined for ten years on this island.'[41] His exile had begun.

A new reggimento was about to take over administration of the island. Although overlapping terms were the norm to ensure continuity, almost all of the important offices were being turned over on this occasion to a new cast of noble Venetians. Sebastian Venier, the Duke of Candia, and Alvise Da Riva, the capitano, were completing their terms. Of the two counsellors, Bartolomeo Zorzi was about to begin his second year in office, and Gabriel Valaresso had arrived just two months earlier. Giovanni Lando, the new capitano grande, would take office at the end of the month, along with two of the three treasurers, Carlo Bono and Francesco Contarini. Perhaps the latter three had dined with Girolamo at the captain's table on the voyage.[42] It was time for a new beginning.

Another Count Girolamo

The top military officer was also on his way out. Count Girolamo Martinengo di Padernello, Governor General of the Militia, having served on the island for two years, had recently been granted permission to return home to Brescia to marry.[43] The timing was fortuitous, for Della Torre appeared before the authorities on 18 August and declared that he and Giulia had not yet found a residence and were forced to move every day. It was proposed that they be given the house where Martinengo was residing, since he was about to leave and was only awaiting the arrival of his replacement. Della Torre should pay an appropriate rent—whatever the owner, Nicolò Querini, would wish. But since Nicolò was out of town on business, the reggimento dispatched the comandador, Zuan Russea, to Nicolò's brother Marco Querini to ask whether he would rent the house to Della Torre. Russea reported back that Marco did not wish to meddle in his brother's affairs, but that he was content if Nicolò's wife Madonna Palma approved. The reggimento then sent Russea to Palma, who responded that 'being a woman, she does not know what to say other than she trusts that the excellent lords would do what seems right to them as long as it is for the benefit of Zuane, her and Nicolò's son, who is not yet of legitimate age'. The duke, the capitano, and the counsellors discussed the matter and determined that as soon as Martinengo had vacated the house, Della Torre [and his household] could move in, paying an annual rent of 40 ducats—that is, 20 ducats every six months—as long as he remained there.[44]

The two Girolamos had much in common. The wealthy Martinengo belonged to one of the most powerful and distinguished families of Brescia, with a long history of military service to the Venetian republic. Like Della Torre (and many mainland lords), his background was one of violence and vendetta. In 1522, when Martinengo was still a child, his father Antonio had murdered his mother on suspicion of infidelity. Her death was avenged six years later when her brother, with the help of some other noble Brescians, murdered Antonio. One of the perpetrators was Scipione Martinengo from a different branch of the family, and another blood feud was on. In 1533 the orphaned Girolamo Martinengo, either fourteen or twenty-one years old (the sources are ambiguous) and with a band of some forty armed retainers, encountered Scipione, with an entourage of only sixteen. In the ensuing brawl, the outnumbered Scipione was killed.[45]

As in the Della Torre affair of 1549, the Council of Ten had exiled the young Girolamo Martinengo to one of Venice's Mediterranean outposts—on this occasion not to Crete, but to Zara on the Dalmatian coast. He would have had frequent contact there with Giulia's father Gian Matteo, Conte di Zara from 1535 to 1537, but already in the city in 1534.[46]

Martinengo would redeem himself in 1539 by fighting off an Ottoman incursion with a small army of forty horsemen that he had assembled at his own expense. In recognition of his courage, and after he had 'paid money to be liberated', the Council of Ten freed him from his confinement and allowed him to return to Brescia. Once there, after completing the renovation of one of the grandest palaces in the city, Martinengo would marry Eleonora Gonzaga, daughter of Lodovico, Duke of Sabbioneta, in a sumptuous wedding in 1543. The Saletta delle Dame, one of three rooms especially decorated for the occasion, featured frescos on all four walls of 'six beautiful Brescian gentlewomen' set against a landscape.[47] Following Eleonora's untimely death in childbirth two years later, Martinengo left the comforts of the palace to again become a man of arms in the Venetian stato da mar. Appointed Governor General of the Militia of Crete in 1549, he soon established himself as an expert on fortifications. Although his proposal for the walls of Candia was not followed, the Martinengo Bastion was named after him, and later on another one in Corfù as well.[48]

Martinengo was accustomed to living well, even as a military man, and Ca' Querini must have been comfortable, even if without rooms frescoed with portraits of gentleladies. Residences of the elites in Candia—and the Counts Martinengo and Della Torre were certainly elites, although not members of the Venetian nobility—were comparable to those in Venice. The house probably featured a stone façade and consisted of two storeys, with the residence on the upper floor, or piano nobile. A few decades later, an unnamed Venetian official in Candia would report that 'there are also many beautiful palaces with very grand details, and although they are not too satisfying from the outside for not being built in the Italian manner, nevertheless inside they are copious with beautiful and spacious chambers decorated with the finest ornamented textiles and coats of arms as in the city of Venice'.[49] It is fair to say that Della Torre, castellan at Villalta and Ceneda and builder of a seigneurial family palace in Udine, would have been satisfied with nothing less.

We do not know the location of Ca' Querini, but given Martinengo's assignment it was probably close to the civic centre, or even on the Ruga Maistra, the equivalent to Venice's Grand Canal and lined by the most important palaces in the city.[50] The Querini clan was among the original group of noble Venetians sent to colonize Crete in the early thirteenth century. Three centuries later, they had become one of the four most influential and powerful feudatory families on the island. Their descendants had extensive landholdings and business interests, and, importantly, maintained their status as noble Venetians.[51]

Life in Candia

The social and political hierarchy in Candia was similar to that in Venice, with a relatively small caste of hereditary nobles; a slightly larger group of educated commoners who earned a living as notaries, physicians, lawyers, merchants, and the like; and a large lower class with its own hierarchy, including artisans, shop owners, manual labourers, fishermen, seamen, and peasants. But there was an important distinction. In Crete, unlike in Venice, there were two levels of nobility. At the top were Venetian nobles of the colony. With the single exception of the Greek Calergi (Kallergis) family, these were the Catholic descendants of the ninety-four noble families sent from Venice in 1210 to replace the old landed nobility of Byzantine *archontes* (provincial governors).[52] In return for receiving feudal rights to tracts of land, the new feudatories were required to provide for the military defence of the island. Over the generations, they secured the same status for their posterity through the *prova*—an examination of credentials required to grant full noble status to their sons in Venice as well as in Crete. Their names were inscribed in the Libro d'Oro in Venice, thus according them the highly prized right to sit in its Great Council in the mother city, as well as in that of Candia. They were thus of equal status to the top officers of the reggimento—Venetian nobles residing in Venice who were sent in to govern the island.[53]

Cretan nobles were a step lower in the hierarchy. They were, by contrast, noble only in the colony, not in Venice. Descendants of the Greek archontes as well as commoners of Venetian origin who had acquired Cretan noble status for military, financial, or other services to the Republic (or who had lost their noble status in Venice for some reason), they could be either Catholic or Orthodox, and many would have been feudal lords as well. They had the right to sit with Venetian nobles of the colony and feudatories in the Greater Council, the body that ran daily affairs on the island, subject to the oversight of the Venetian authorities.[54]

Zuanne Papadopoli, a Cretan who worked in the Venetian chancery in Candia, would describe the main piazza of the city in the mid-seventeenth century. Given the Venetian predilection to maintain traditions over time, it was probably much the same a century earlier: 'On both sides the street was paved with stone. In the area where the Venetian Nobles would take their walk, it was not forbidden for Cretan Nobles or even commoners to go and talk to them, and people were allowed to pass by or stop at will, without causing offence.'[55] Thus, although the Venetian and Cretan nobles walked in separate groups, they spoke freely to one another, reflecting a society characterized by mixed marriages, partial assimilations, and linguistic and religious ambiguities. Indeed, some Venetian nobles of the colony were more Greek than Latin. In the late sixteenth century, Provveditor General Giacomo Foscarini would remark:

> Among the noble Venetians, many are those who have no memory of their noble descent...who preserve nothing but their surname and their few remaining fiefs...They have completely forgotten the Italian language and, since there is no possibility of hearing mass according to the Latin rite in any of the island's villages, they are obliged, while staying in their village...to baptize their children, to marry and to bury their dead in accordance with the Orthodox rite and Greek customs. And these are the Venieri, Barbarigi, Morosini, Boni, Foscarini—families in all respects Greek.[56]

Many such families must have signed their marriage contracts in Greek, just as they petitioned in Latin or Venetian for noble status back in Venice for their sons and grandsons in Crete.

Where did Girolamo Della Torre fit into this complicated social mix? As a titled count from the Friuli, and neither noble Venetian nor noble Cretan, he occupied an ambiguous space, akin to that of Girolamo Martinengo. He moved freely throughout the city, as he had in Venice before (and even perhaps during) his year of detention in the Palazzo Ducale. In Candia, he employed Italian-speaking Greek notaries for his business affairs and would have associated with Venetian nobles and citizens. Although he exercised no direct power politically, his wealth, his title, his legal training, and his noble Venetian bride earned him respect and a place in the social life of the city, as would be evident at the baptism of his son.

A Firstborn Son

Giulia was in the last trimester of her pregnancy. The unavoidable discomforts of the voyage and the stress involved in finding a new home in a strange land went counter to all advice given to pregnant women of the time. They were counselled to get adequate rest and to shun excesses in all things: avoiding air that was too hot or too cold; loud sounds like thunder or artillery fire; violent movement such as dancing, jumping, running, traveling in carriages, and climbing and descending stairs too quickly (not to mention finding their footing on a pitching galley). They should also not eat too much or too little. Preferred foods were 'well-cooked bread, chicken, veal, birds, but not aquatic [ones]; wine not red, not white, but *rossetto*'. No legumes, walnuts, chestnuts, onions, leaks, scallions, and greens. No fresh fruit. No salted or spicy meats or fish or anything pickled in vinegar, among other prohibitions. Given the limited provisions available on-board ship and the state of near famine prevailing on the island, it was fortunate that herb broths and boiled food (unspecified) were on the approved list. Above all, the expectant mother should remain even-tempered 'and happy and of good mind in every honourable way'.[57]

Less than three months after setting foot in Candia, Giulia gave birth to her first child. She had just turned nineteen and did not have her own family around her. But she did have a concerned husband. Girolamo, about to turn forty-six, could finally start compiling a list entitled *Fedi Battesimali delli Conti Della Torre*. The first entry reads:

> 1550, on Monday 9 October, at the fifth hour of night in Candia, in the house of the physician Scillini, my first son was born to me, and on the 16th he was baptized in the church of Saint Titus by the Reverend Deacon Bonfio da Luca, and he was named Lodovico. There were present twenty godfathers, all gentlemen.[58]

Was Girolamo present in the birthing chamber? The space was typically the province of women, but there were exceptions. Nobles at the Hapsburg court often attended the births of their heirs. Such was the case with Philip II of Spain, who was present when his third wife Elisabeth of Valois gave birth to twin girls in 1564. Indeed, the correspondence of their daughter Catalina Micaela indicates that she 'expected and wished more than anything' that her husband Carlo Emanuele would be present at the births of their children, ten in all.[59] We do not know whether Girolamo was inside the room, but his precise designation of the fifth hour of the night—at that time of year around 2am—suggests that at least he had been waiting anxiously outside the door.

That Giulia gave birth in the house of an Italian physician rather than at home may have been inspired by an abundance of caution, but there is evidence that physicians and midwives sometimes worked together at a birth, particularly in upper-class homes in northern Italy.[60] Little Lodovico was almost certainly delivered by a midwife, with the doctor standing by in case of complications. That doctor may well have been armed with a copy of Eucharius Rösslin's *Libro nel qual si tratta del parto de lhuomo*, the 1538 Italian translation of a treatise written by a German doctor. Originally published in 1513, the text had become the standard obstetrical manual for the instruction of midwives throughout Europe (Figure 7.3).[61]

Midwives were typically older married or widowed women who had borne children themselves. Practising their professions with the skill of their hands, they usually came from humble backgrounds, but were respected members of the local community.[62] In Candia they might well have been Greek-speaking, and the Della Torre, reassured by the presence of an Italian physician, would have relied upon referrals from other Venetian women who had given birth there.

Following common practice, Giulia would have remained at home while the midwife carried the baby to the church and Girolamo presented him at the baptismal font. The 'twenty godfathers, all gentlemen' in attendance attest to Della Torre's ability to establish a substantial network of aristocratic support and clientage soon after his arrival in the city. Most of these *compadri* must have been Venetian nobles or high-ranked citizens. As an outsider, Della Torre was not constrained by a Venetian rule that forbade patricians to serve as godfather to the offspring of other patricians. The rationale for this was that the relationship established a degree of consanguinity that might prevent a marriage alliance in the future.[63]

The church of Saint Titus, appropriated from the Greeks when the Venetians took over the island in 1210, was the Latin cathedral of Candia. Like San Marco in Venice, it was Byzantine in form and Catholic in practice. The church was described in the early sixteenth century as 'a large, tall structure with innumerable columns of various styles made of rare marble; it was adorned with the tombs and coats of arms of famous noblemen and with precious altars and chapels decorated

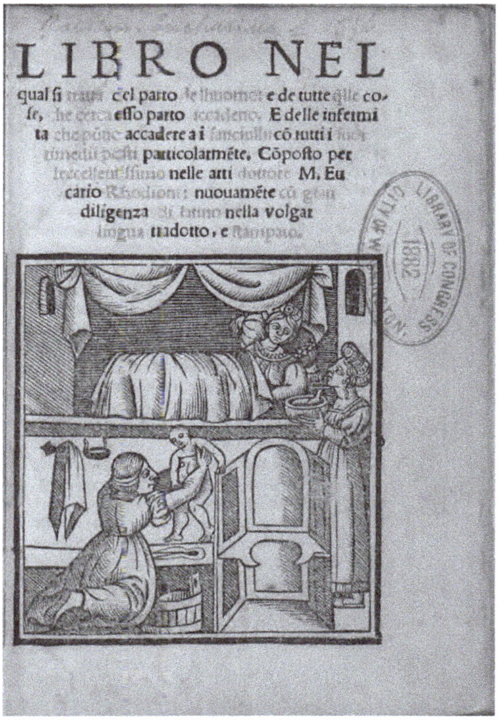

Figure 7.3. Eucharius Rösslin, *Libro nel qual si tratta del parto de lhuomo*, Venice, 1538, frontispiece (Library of Congress, Rare Book and Special Collections Division). Rösslin counseled: "The midwife must instruct and preserve the mother: not only to fortify her with food and drink, but also with words to console and offer hope for a happy birth, or for a male child, which would make most women rejoice."

in such a way that all these were an eternal ornament to the city'.[64] It was also the home of the *Virgin Mesopanditissa*, a miraculous icon that was displayed in a casket every Tuesday and carried in procession by six Greek priests to the Orthodox Cathedral of St Mary of the Angels outside the old city wall.[65] Girolamo could not have had a more prestigious venue in which to establish the Della Torre line in Candia.

Sansovino later explained the infant's name: 'The first born was called Lodovico, his name referring to the two Alvise's, one the father and the other the brother of the Signor Conte, both of saintly habits and truly exemplary kindness.'[66] Alas, as we know, the two Alvises had died untimely deaths, and the name was not propitious. The infant lived for only two weeks. With infant mortality estimated as perhaps 30 per cent in the first year of life in that period, such an outcome was not unusual.[67]

Giulia and Girolamo would at least have been comforted that the baby had been baptized. The loss would have been felt bitterly, nonetheless, since little

Lodovico embodied their hopes and dreams and represented the continuance of the bloodline. He deserved a burial appropriate to the rank of the Della Torre.[68] Girolamo's notation continued: 'he died on the 23rd of the month, and was placed in a marble tomb in San Francesco on the right-hand side as one enters the church in the wall between the Chapel of the Madonna and that of Saint Barbara; may he always pray for us to the Almighty God.'[69]

The choice of a Franciscan church for the burial was in line with family tradition.[70] Moreover, San Francesco (now destroyed) was the wealthiest and most prominent of the twelve mendicant churches in Candia. It was also the most visible; built atop the only hill in the city, it was the first structure inside the walls that came into view to travellers approaching the city by ship. According to legend, the monastery had been founded by Saint Francis himself on an early visit to the island. By the sixteenth century, it possessed a wealth of relics, including a piece of the True Cross in a gilded silver and crystal container, a fragment of the column of the Flagellation in a silver capsule decorated with enamels, and four reliquary busts of the 11,000 virgin martyrs who accompanied Saint Ursula. The walls of the nave were covered with frescoes painted in the Byzantine style, but the high altar was adorned with a *Virgin and Child with Eight Saints* by Giovanni Bellini. Altarpieces by Bellini were also installed in the Chapels of Saint Anthony of Padua and Saint George. Other chapels featured an icon of the Madonna painted by Saint Luke, an altarpiece by Palma Vecchio, and a marble relief of the Annunciation by Jacopo Sansovino. Like the cathedral of Saint Titus, the interior of the Franciscan basilica thus acknowledged both the Latin and Greek residents of the island. And like the Frari and SS. Giovanni e Paolo back in Venice, San Francesco had become a civic pantheon—housing at least eight tombs of dukes who had died in office, more than any other church in the city. It was a most suitable resting place for the remains of the Della Torre's infant son.[71]

Giulia's Domain

The city celebrated the arrival of the new Duke of Candia, Alvise Renier, on 18 November. Giulia was probably still recovering from childbirth and grieving the death of Lodovico, but given its political importance, Girolamo could well have been part of the throng that lined the sides of the Ruga Maistra that day. The ceremony was well choreographed, as befitted the entry of the supreme Venetian authority on the island, a colonial counterpart to the Doge of Venice. After disembarking from his galley, Renier proceeded to the Porta del Molo, where he was greeted by the outgoing duke, Sebastian Venier, whose entourage included his ducal court, his chaplain, the Greek Protopapas, and the nobility, all lined up in a prescribed order. Led by a contingent of drummers and pipers, they marched together in procession up the Ruga Maistra to the ducal church of San Marco in the civic centre. The incoming duke marched to the left of his predecessor, with his insignia—standard, shield, helmet, and sword—carried at the head of the procession. After a prayer and the reading of the Doge's letter of appointment, Venier positioned Renier, his successor, to his right. The new duke received the ducal scepter and keys to the prisons as signs of his political and judicial authority and was escorted by the cortege across the square to the palace.[72]

Ca' Querini would have been Giulia's domain for much of the time she lived on the island. Her world was centred on the household, her husband, and her eventual children. And yet, while a woman's sphere was circumscribed by gender and geography, we know from testamentary bequests that bonds of affection forged outside the caste system with women of lower status were typical. Giulia's social circle would have been composed of other Venetian women of similar rank, but it also included her own servants and close neighbours, and eventually midwives and wet nurses.[73]

Even back in Venice, upper-class women typically remained in the house while their servants or husbands did the marketing. The unfamiliar streets of Candia presented additional challenges. Filled with merchants and sailors from all over the Mediterranean and a cacophony of tongues, they were not unlike Venice at Rialto, but now with Greek competing with Venetian dialect as the dominant language. And yet, deeply religious, the strong-willed Giulia must have ventured forth to attend church and to socialize with other Venetian wives living in the city.

Papadopoli wrote that most patrician women in Candia left the house only in the early morning or in the evening 'per non esser vedute' (in order not to be seen). Clad in long cloaks and shawls that revealed only the face, they might go out to visit the homes of other women or to go to church but were always accompanied by servants or other women of the house. Attractive maidservants were sent to the public fountain only in the evening to avoid undue attention from men who could see them there in the daytime.[74]

When Magno passed through the city in 1559 he declared that the island 'produces fearless and courageous men', in contrast to the timid men of Cyprus. As to the Cretan women, he had his own views on the evening forays: 'they are almost all beautiful, but very licentious, and most of them go out, especially at night. They wear black mantles, under which they conceal everything, and they are annoyed to be looked at by Italians, whom they call Franks; nevertheless, they look [back] at them willingly, but secretly.'[75] It is fair to say that this was not true of Giulia Bembo Della Torre.

The Rent Collector

Even before the birth of Lodovico, Girolamo had begun to collect annual rents for around twenty *casali*, rural villages owned on Crete by Ranuccio Farnese, Latin Patriarch of Constantinople. The contract was originally for three years, beginning on 1 October 1549 and ending in April 1552. With the postponement of Girolamo's departure because of his brother's murder, he actually began the job a year late. As a *conduttore* he was required to collect rents from eleven tenants in October, with five of them allowed to defer half their payment to a second collection the following April. With most of his activity taking place only two months a year, Girolamo would have found it an attractive arrangement to bring in extra income and occupy his time in exile. The total annual receipts amounted to 1053 ducats, a *grosso* of millet, and a *botta* of malvasia wine (a large cask holding around 751 litres). Out of this sum, Girolamo paid the salaries of certain Catholic priests on the island, as well as his own stipend of 70 gold ducats—payable in Venetian gold *zecchini*, half at Christmas and the other half in the month of June.[76] The original agreement had called for Girolamo's brother Alvise II to act as his agent in Venice to transmit the payments to the cardinal's representative, but after Alvise's death this duty was transferred to his brother-in-law Bernardo Colloredo. The arrangement was similar to that begun two decades earlier, wherein an agent of the pope transferred funds drawn from the pension of Sebastiano del Piombo to Michele Della Torre in Rome to be sent on to Girolamo or Alvise II in Udine and then paid out, finally, to the artist Giovanni da Udine.[77]

We do not know whether Girolamo travelled in person to the various *casali* or if the tenants or their agents brought the monies into Candia to be paid there. The properties were inland and not easily reached by a boat travelling along the coast. Girolamo was a capable horseman and could have dealt with roads that were sometimes no more than trails without too much trouble. But surviving receipts show that each payment was notarized, with witnesses. Unless Girolamo made his rounds in company with a notary, it is probable that the transactions were made in the city, where most of the feudatories had their main residences.[78] It is important to note that Girolamo's role as *conduttore* of funds was an acceptable noble occupation according to the norms of the day. Venetian patricians did not disdain mercantile or financial activities, so long as the individual did not engage in an *arte meccanica* that required working with his hands. Some of the tenants on Girolamo's rent-list had the titles of domino or magnifico, indicating their status as Venetian or Cretan nobility. Even if they did not own the land, they were not farmers themselves, but proprietors who gained their income from the labour of their villani or peasants.

No Place to Hide

Crete was an island of well-armed men, and Girolamo must have felt vulnerable without a sword or dagger. Back in 1545 he had been conceded the privilege of carrying arms in the city of Venice 'and the other cities and places of our dominion' with two armed servants; presumably the permission was revoked when he was arrested, and he now sought its reinstatement. In mid-December 1550, the heads of the Council of Ten advised the duke and capitano of Candia that, 'this concession seeming honourable', it should again be allowed and observed on Crete as well. Della Torre was required to submit the names of his servants to the chancery and to be responsible for their expenses and salaries.[79]

It was none too soon. The capitano Giovanni Lando reported on 29 January of the following year that he had heard rumours that Tristan Savorgnan had been trying to board ship in Ragusa to sail to Crete, to take revenge on Della Torre. He cautioned that all possible precautions be taken to protect the count, both for his security and for the honour of the reggimento.[80] Girolamo shared another version of the news with a Colloredo relative in a letter of 1 February: 'Tristan Savorgnan has been seen in Ragusa: I think that he is going to Constantinople, either to be aided in being freed from his banishment with the help of that Signor or to carry out some evil plot against me.'[81]

Savorgnan was not Della Torre's only security concern. Roger Bodenham, an English ship captain sailing a galley to Chios, stopped over in Candia in April 1551. There he was alarmed to see some Turkish vessels called *skyrasas* that had brought in a much-needed shipment of wheat. Lacking a safe conduct, he waited until the Turks departed the following morning and set sail to Chios in the evening. As he left that harbour for his return trip after delivering his cargo, he narrowly escaped capture by seven Turkish corsairs. Then, nearing Candia, he was alarmed to catch sight of a huge Turkish fleet sailing past the island toward the Adriatic Sea. He kept his distance until the ships had moved on. When he was able to get into port, he learned that the local population was already on the alert:

> Preparation was made as though the Turks would have come thither. There are in that island of Candia many banished men, that live continually in the mountains. They came down to serve, to the number of 4,000 or 5,000. They are good archers. Everyone was armed with his bow and arrows, a sword and a dagger; and had long hair, boots that reached up to the groin, and a shirt of mail hanging, the one half before and the other half behind. These were sent away again as soon as the army was past. They would drink wine out of all measure.[82]

And, one can imagine, noble women would have been kept safely inside the house until this informal security detail returned to the mountains.

The Turkish fleet that had unsettled the city would have been an awesome sight: two galleasses and some 112 galleys in full sail—an anxious Bodenham had estimated 250—commanded by the Ottoman admirals Dragut Reis and Sinan Pasha. Sailing past the island toward the Adriatic Sea, the vessels carried 12,000 Janissaries. Fortunately, Candia was not their destination. Despite the treaty of 1540, they moved on to attack Sicily and a number of Venetian ports and wreaked havoc on Venetian shipping. Failing to capture Malta, stronghold of the Knights of Saint John, they sacked the nearby island of Gozo, taking 5–6000 prisoners, and then sailed on to take over Tripoli in August.[83] It was a matter of good timing that the Della Torre galley had not fallen into their path the year before.

Against the backdrop of war and peace, family life went on. Girolamo's brother Bishop Michele had returned to Udine by August and was appointed dean of the Cathedral Chapter of the city by Pope Julius III. But, soon back on the road, he participated in the opening session of the Council of Trent on 11 October.[84] And yet he still found time to return to Udine on 18 October to hold Giovanni da Udine's tenth child at the baptismal font in the Duomo. The infant was named Michelangelo after his noble godfather.[85]

A Prodigious Birth

Just ten days later, in Candia, Girolamo and Giulia also had cause to celebrate a birth. Girolamo's entry in his *Fedi Battesimali* tells the tale:

> On Wednesday the 28th of October 1551 at the hour of around 15:30, my second son, named Sigismondo, was born to me. He was baptized on the 4th of November in Saint Titus by the Reverend Deacon Bonfio with the assistance of twenty godfathers and two godmothers. May God make him good.[86]

The circumstances of Sigismondo's birth were particularly memorable. In his *vita* of Giulia Bembo, Sansovino would allude to 'certain signs outside the natural order' attending the births of three of the eventual Della Torre children:

> This was observed in the second son born in the kingdom of Candia, and called Sigismondo, to renew the names of the Reverend Patriarch of Aquileia with the lordship of all the Patria del Friuli, and of the illustrious brother of the Signor Conte, because during his birth the right arm came out first, before any other part of his body, and then with his face all covered with something like a veil, and with a great mass as large as the infant.[87]

If Sansovino's description is accurate, the birth may have been an ordeal for Giulia, and it was perhaps a miracle that both mother and child survived. Rösslin defined the shoulder presentation as 'against nature' and stressed that it required special care.[88] *De Secretis Mulierum* (On the Secrets of Women), a late medieval treatise published in Venice in 1508, cautioned:

> Certain women have more pain in childbirth than others, because sometimes the fetus presents its hand and sometimes its feet, and these are dangerous

> situations. In these cases, the midwives carefully thrust back the hand or feet, and this causes great pain, weakening many women and causing death except to the very strong.[89]

In Giulia's case, the midwife's ministrations were successful, but the faulty presentation was not the only problem. Sansovino's reference to 'a great mass as large as the infant' is curious. The placenta, or afterbirth, expelled after every birth, would probably not have occasioned such a comment, and one is tempted to hypothesize. Is it possible that Giulia had a twin pregnancy, with a mole—a growth of abnormal tissue—inhabiting the uterus along with the healthy foetus? Scipione Mercurio, in his treatise of 1595, devoted a full chapter to the *mola*, which he called a 'useless and deformed piece of flesh.'[90] Nearly all such false pregnancies result in miscarriages in the fourth to sixth month and rarely go to full term. But twin pregnancies such as Giulia's—if, indeed, that is what she had—are even more rare, occurring once in 20,000 to 100,000 pregnancies, with perhaps one-fourth resulting in a live (and usually premature) birth. The risk to both mother and child is significant even today, calling for close surveillance of an ongoing pregnancy to detect potential signs of complications. In Giulia's case, such a condition would have come as a surprise, revealed to her midwife (and her doctor) only at the time of the birth.[91] That it resulted in a healthy baby was a prodigious event in itself—indeed, a sign of divine providence. And entering family lore to be recorded by her biographer.

There was a further sign. Sansovino also noted that little Sigismondo was born 'with his face all covered with something like a veil'. He was almost certainly referring to a caul, a piece of the amniotic membrane covering the baby's face. Caul births were also very rare, occurring in less than one out of 80,000 births, but not dangerous if the midwife carefully removed the membrane immediately after the birth. Given their rarity, it is possible that Sigismondo's midwife had never seen one before. Fortunately, she—or the doctor—had the knowledge, skill, or common sense to deal with it properly. It was considered a miracle of nature, with both good and bad connotations. In his *Occulta naturae miracula*, first published in 1559 in Latin, the Dutch physician Levinus Lemnius complained:

> There is an old opinion, not onely prevalent amongst the common and ignorant people, but also amongst men of great note, and Physitians also, how that children born with a caul over their faces, are born with an omen, or sign of good or bad luck…Wherefore old Wives say, this skin when it covers the face, is a helmet, of which they speak many fabulous things, and fright or cheer the childbearing woman.[92]

For most of Giulia's contemporaries, however, a caul was a most favourable sign, presaging good fortune for the child and even his family. Among the peasantry of

Girolamo's native Friuli in the sixteenth century, some of these children were called Benandanti, endowed with special gifts that benefited the entire community: the ability to detect sorcerers, to lift evil spells, and to protect the harvest. It was widely thought that babies born with a caul would be protected from drowning, a belief that would be put to the test several decades later.[93] Although Lemnius and others scoffed at such superstitions, and the Church inveighed against them, they were often believed by pious church-goers and even ordained priests.[94] In the case of little Sigismondo, the caul may well have been credited by the family with the favourable outcome of the birth, despite the other complications.

The rhythms of daily life continued. Girolamo was the head of a growing family. And again, twenty godfathers—presumably all gentlemen—stood with him in the church of Saint Titus at the baptismal font of his son. They were now joined by two godmothers, evidence that Giulia's social circle was also growing. Girolamo continued to collect the rents for the Patriarch's feudal holdings, reported monthly to the authorities, and now moved freely through the streets of Candia with two servants—all three carrying arms for their defence. The public world was his domain.

Giulia's was inside the walls of Ca' Querini and her parish church. With the urgency—indeed, necessity—of producing a son and heir now diminished, she was finally able to fulfil her destiny. She had already proven herself a loyal wife, accompanying her husband into exile in a strange land. She would now have the opportunity to become an exemplary mother, putting 'great study and infinite diligence into raising her children'.[95] She attended mass daily, devoted herself to little Sigismondo, socialized with other women, and managed the household. Her life had achieved a degree of normalcy, but for one thing: she was still far from her birth family. That unhappy situation was soon to change.

Notes

1. Bembo/Travi, III, 584–5, no. 1679; ibid., III, 651, no. 1760; ibid., IV, 73, no. 1883; ibid., IV, 386, no. 2287, et al.
2. Ibid., IV, 594, no. 2571 (13 November 1546). See also ibid., 592, no. 2567. Gian Matteo was elected capitano of Famagusta on 17 October 1546 and took office on 6 May 1547. ASVe, *SAV-MC*, r. 2, 190 (=193). Marcella declared that she was drafting her will on 23 February 1547, because Gian Matteo had just drafted his: ASVe, NT, b. 1210.716 (Antonio Marsilio). But she was still in Venice on 16 June 1547 when her will was witnessed in her home at S. Maria Nova. According to this document trail, if Marcella did in fact go to Cyprus, she must have sailed to the island later than her husband. Perhaps the transaction on 16 June was made in anticipation of her departure on one of the galleys of Beirut, typically around 1 August, or even sooner on a merchant ship.
3. Bembo/Travi, II, 140, no. 395. See also Romano 1989, 339–63.

4. Appendix I: Sansovino, *Vita*, 4v.
5. Bembo/Travi, IV, 594, no. 2571: 'Fa di savia e da buona mogliera'.
6. Ibid., IV, 138 (6 August 1539).
7. Bembo/Travi, IV, 139v (14 August 1539).
8. See Brown 2013a, 231–49; Gluzman 2014, 29–78; Setton 1984, 431–4, 446.
9. Setton 1984, 448–9, 529–36; Davis 2004.
10. Braudel 1976, 2: 907.
11. For galleys, see Lane 1934, 17–53; Lane, 1973, 379–84; Lane 1968, 22–46; Ercole 2006, 85–101; and the essays by Sergio Bellabarna, Ulrich Alertz, and Mauro Bondioli in Beltrame 2003, 201–27. During these years, the great galleys were being retrofitted as warships and replaced for the mercantile trade by the round ship or the carrack. Cf. Judde de Larivière 2008, 83, stating that although the number had declined, five great galleys were still in use in 1550.
12. Fabri 1892, 121–3.
13. Ibid., 41; Arbel 2017, 190.
14. Brown 1988, 272–82 and *passim*.
15. Magno 2002, 49–50, 52–9, 530–5. In addition to God and the Virgin, the saints specifically named in Magno's account were Mark, Nicholas, Anthony, the apostle James, John the Baptist, Christopher, Helena, Marta, Alvise, Segondo, and Chimento.
16. Arbel 2017, 183–220; Gluzman 2010, 264–94. The Adriatic Sea is a maximum of 120 miles wide.
17. The length and width of the great galleys grew over the years, and the Venetian galleazze played a major role in the Battle of Lepanto. Ercole 2006, 67, cites a galea da Mercanzia, built in the Arsenale in 1520 that was 47.8 metres long and 8 metres wide.
18. Barnby 1970, 310; Elia de Pesaro 1879, 210.
19. Arbel 2017, 184; Lane 1973, 343.
20. Barnby 1970, 310; Megna 1991, 279.
21. Von Harff 2011, 73.
22. Arbel 2017, 195, 202.
23. Lane 1973, 343–45. There might also be a separate chief navigator's table for top deck officers and other members of the crew, including the ship's carpenter.
24. Barnby 1970, 309–14.
25. Arbel 2017, 212; Magno 2002, 535.
26. Girolamo arrived in Candia with around 228–78 ducats: ASU, AC, b. 6, no. 10, 'Questi sono tutti li denari ch'io ho havuti dapoi ch'io son in Candia'. Della Torre corrected the amount in ink, and the final number is unclear, either Duc. 228.2.10, 238.2.10 or 278.2.10. I am grateful to Mauro Bondioli for his help with this transcription.
27. Arbel 2017, 190.
28. Appendix I: Sansovino, *Vita*, 10r. For slave narratives, see Davis 2009.
29. Based on Barnby 1970, 314 the ships in Elijah of Pesaro's convoy were met by twelve large rowing galleys, some with 200 rowers, that towed them into port.
30. Bacchion 1956, 69–72; Concina 1986, 184; Yotopoulou-Sicilianou 1994, 49; Miller 1908, 559–63.
31. Comescu 2016, 143–58.
32. Pagratis 2008, 80.

33. Fincati, 'La nobiltà veneziana', 9; Lane 1973, 345.
34. Elia da Pesaro 1879, 218. See also Magno 2002, 61, 69, 540–1; Miller 1908, 550–4.
35. See Tzobanaki 1998; Gertwagen 2000, 177–241.
36. Thiriet 1958–61, 3:205–6, no. 2994: 'alia civitas Venetiarum apud Levantem.' See also Maltezou 1995, 272.
37. Tzobanaki 1998, 39–40.
38. Gerola 1905–32, I:2, 316; Concina 1986, 184–96.
39. Gerola 1905–32, III, 18; Ambraseys and Karcz 1992, 263.
40. ASVe, Duca di Candia, b. 8, no. 6, 183, 186.
41. Ibid., 186. For the Ruga Maistra, see Thiriet 1959, 268.
42. ASVe, *SAV-MC*, Reg.2 (1541–52), 183 (=186).
43. ASVe, *Sen.*, Mar, r. 31, 10 (29 April 1550); and 28v (5 July 1550).
44. ASUd, *AT*, b. 19 (18 August 1550), 'Exemplum ex Memoriali Cancellerie Maioris Cretae'.
45. *DBI, s.v.* 'Martinengo, Girolamo', 154, states that Martinengo was born 'con tutta probabilità', in 1519; but cf. Norris 2012, 115 n4, with the date of 1512. Given Martinengo's sentence of exile in 1533, the earlier date seems more likely.
46. *DBI, s.v.* 'Martinengo, Girolamo', 154; Guerrini 1930, 276–8; Bembo/Travi, 584–5, no. 1679 and *passim*.
47. For the palace and the wedding, see Norris 2012, 115–34; Lechi 1974, 235–82, esp. 236–50.
48. *DBI, s.v.* 'Martinengo, Girolamo', 154. See also Promis 1874, 103–26.
49. BMVe, Ms. Ital. VII, 569 (7946), ff. 70r–v; Georgopoulou 2000, 96–7.
50. Georgopoulou 2000, 101.
51. McKee 2000, 40, 44, 79–80, 181, 183. The other three were the Corner, Gradenigo, and Muazzo families. See also Parry 2008, 1:202–206.
52. Maltezou 1991, 24, states thatthe privilege of Venetian nobility granted to Georgios Kallergis, son of Alexios, in 1381 is the 'single instance of Venetian nobility being bestowed on a Greek, unparalleled in the whole period of Venetian rule'. But cf. Mueller 1998, 174–5. For the tangled Calergi family tree and their marriages into high-ranking Latin feudatory families in the 14th century, see *MC*Kee 2000, 74–83, 130. See also Tedesco 1989, 119–64. For archontes, see Kazhdan 1991, 160–1.
53. Miller 1964, 179.
54. Papadopoli 2007, 275–6, 336–7; Maltezou 1991, 25–6; Thiriet 1959, 270–302; Lambrinos 2014, 57–70; Arbel 2013, 193–8.
55. Papadopoli 2007, 58, 277. For a similar view of social stratification written in 1612–14, see Gerola 1908, 275. For walking in Venice, see De Vivo 2016.
56. Cited by Maltezou 1991, 33–4.
57. Mercurio 1595, 80–2; Gélis 1991, 82–3.
58. ASUd, *AT*, b. 17, fasc. 1, 'Prove storico-genalogiche della famiglia Della Torre, Conti di Valsassina', f. 196. Schillini is the surname of a noble Brescian family, but I have not been able to identify this doctor. See Capretti 1912, 302–5. A physician named Zuan Antonio Schillini lived in the contrada of San Moisè in Venice in 1568 and was still alive in 1578: ASVe, NT, b. 195.522 and b. 195.649 (M. A. Cavani).
59. Sánchez 2015, 448–9, 457.

60. Green 2008, 250–8, esp. 258; Musacchio 1999, 22–3.
61. Rösslin 1538; Rösslin, *Der schwangeren Frauen und Hebammen Rosengarten* [*The Rosegarden of Pregnant Women and Midwives*], Strassburg, 1513. The Italian edition comprises sixty-four folios with twenty woodcuts and was based upon a Latin translation published in Venice in 1536. The Library of Congress possesses one of the very few surviving copies and has made it available online: http://hdl.loc.gov/loc.rbc/General.32863.1. See also Hellman, *Collection*; and Green 2009.
62. Filippini 1993, 153–7.
63. Sansovino, *Venetia città nobilissima*, 1581, 260; Bistort 1912, 201–3.
64. Cited by Georgopoulou 2001, 117.
65. Brown 2016, 48–9.
66. Appendix I: Sansovino, *Vita*, f. 6.
67. Gélis 1991, 251. For mortality rates, see Filippini 1993, 172 n52.
68. See Lambrinos 2012, 96.
69. ASUd, *AT*, b. 17, fasc. 1, f 196.
70. The ancestral tombs of the Della Torre were in the church of San Francesco in Udine, and the remains of Girolamo's brother Alvise II resided in the wooden casket in the Frari in Venice.
71. Georgopoulou 1992, 191–200; Gerola 1932, 311–18; Hoffman 1944, 221. The church was badly damaged by an earthquake in 1865 and demolished in 1867 by the Turkish government.
72. Papadaki 2005, 23–4; Brown 2016, 57.
73. Lambrinos 2012, 95.
74. Papadopoli 2007, 115, 117, 118–19; Lambrinos 2012, 89–96.
75. Magno 2002, 584.
76. ASUd, *AT*, b. 6, colto 11, no. 10. For Cretan agricultural products, including wine, see, Papadopoli 2007, 339–47. Spanakes 1940, 12, states that there were 1087 *casali* on the island in 1589. Other reports range from 1000 to 1070. See also Greene 2000, 46–52. For the arrangement with Farnese, see Chapters 5 and 6.
77. See Chapters 3 and 4.
78. See, for example, ASVe, Notai di Candia, b. 283 [Zorzi Vasmullo], fasc. 1, 254, documenting a payment on of 250 hyperperi on 1 October 1550 from Andrea Rocco q. Michele for Casal Ligortino. For Cretan money and prices, see Papadopoli 2007, 339–43.
79. ASUd, *AT*, b. 11, cartella XI, colto 21 [16 December 1550].
80. Ibid., b. 19, cartella 19, colto 25 [29 January 1551].
81. Archivio Paolo di Colloredo, Lettere, colto VI, cited in [Bertolla] 1901, 57.
82. Bodenham 1903, 1–5.
83. On 14 August 1551. Setton 1984, 553–5; Braudel 1976, 2:918–23; https://en.wikipedia.org/wiki/Dragut.
84. Capodagli 1665, 477; Lestocquoy 1966, 34–6. Michele participated in the Council from 11 October 1551 to 28 April 1552.
85. Cargnelutti 1987, 331. Other godparents included Jacomo Valvasone, and Francesco Strassoldo's wife, Alda.
86. ASUd, *AT*, b. 17, fasc. 1, f. 313.

87. Appendix I: Sansovino, *Vita*, 6–7. Sansovino seems to have been mistaken about the origin of the child's name, and its source remains a mystery. There is no record of a Patriarch of Aquileia named Sigismondo, whether in the Della Torre blood line or not, as of that date, nor is there evidence that Girolamo ever had a brother with that name. An eighteenth-century genealogy of the family appears to be correct in calling the newborn Sigismondo as 'the first of the name' in the family line: 'Sigismond De La Tour, Premier du Nom, Comte de la Tour, et Valsassine.' See ASUd, *AT*, b. 17, fasc. 1, f. 312, citing Flacchio 1709, 1: 67.
88. Rösslin 1538, f. C. See also Green 2009, 167–70; Dunn 1998, 77–8; Bell 1999, 108–18; Mercurio 1595, 122–3.
89. Lemay 1992, 107.
90. Mercurio 1595, 233: 'un pezzo di carne inutile, e diforme, chiamasi mola.' See also McClive 2002, 219–23; Gélis 1991, 165–72, 200–2, 258–9.
91. See, for example, Freis et al. 2016, 819–22; Vimercati et al. 2013, 1–4; Kushtagi and Hegde 2008.
92. Lemnius 1658, 105 (a close translation of the same passage in the French edition: Lemnius 1574, 134). For a full discussion, see Belmont 1971, 19–26.
93. Forbes 2003, 125. See Chapter 15.
94. See Ginzburg 1983, 16–20; Gélis 1991, 200–2; Forbes 2003, 119–32; Lemnius 1574, 134–6.
95. Appendix I: Sansovino, *Vita*, f. 8v.

8
The Capitano Grande

The search for the assassins of Alvise II Della Torre and his companions had continued back in Venice. On 21 October 1550, the Council of Ten offered safe conduct to anyone, even if under a sentence of banishment, who had information on the perpetrators of the crime. Some observers were predicting the ruin of the entire Savorgnan house.[1]

Vindicated with Our Blood

On 26 November, the Ten finally considered Girolamo's appeal of 13 June to be relieved of his obligation to pay the remaining 500 ducat fine to Giovanni Savorgnan. Briefs supporting his case were presented by Giulia's father Gian Matteo and by Giacoma Brazzaco Della Torre, the widow of Girolamo's uncle Nicolò I. Giacoma was still living in Palazzo Torriani in Udine with her orphaned grandson, Guido, the only living male heir of the present generation of the Della Torre line.[2] She and Gian Matteo argued that Girolamo's sentence was divided into two parts, the public and the private. His exile to Candia satisfied the public part, his offence against the state. The second part was the fine of 1000 ducats to be paid to Giovanni Savorgnan for his offence against a private individual. Girolamo has already paid half of this, but he should not be required to pay the remainder, they asserted, since the Savorgnan brothers—Giovanni and Nicolò—had violated the sentence, albeit indirectly, with the assassination of Alvise II Della Torre and Giambattista Colloredo. Even though the crime had been committed by Tristan Savorgnan, they maintained, it was to avenge his brothers: 'The matter is thus clear, both by the sentences as also by public voice and universal opinion, that the said brothers were vindicated with our blood.' On a practical note, Giacoma added that she was being hounded by the luogotenente in Udine to pay the fine herself and that she had no means to do it.[3]

Nicolò Savorgnan made a counterargument on behalf of himself and his brother Giovanni, the latter already sentenced to exile in Zara for his role in the assassination of Alvise II. Nicolò reproached Gian Matteo for continuing to support his son-in-law and claimed that the argument that the sentence was divided into two parts was specious, and indeed pure chicanery, since the sentence was for a single case alone. Nicolò also rejected out of hand the charge that his brother Giovanni had orchestrated the assassination of the count's brother Alvise II.

The Venetian Bride: Bloodlines and Blood Feuds in Venice and Its Empire. Patricia Fortini Brown, Oxford University Press (2021). © Patricia Fortini Brown. DOI: 10.1093/oso/9780192894571.003.0008

Giovanni appended his own declaration, reasserting that he was innocent of any crime and condemning—by the way—Della Torre's 'use of princes' (referring to the appeals by the Pope, the French king, and highly placed churchmen) to alter his sentence. Lamenting that Della Torre was determined to persecute him to the ruination of his finances, he concludes: 'And because I am resolved to continue in my first intention, and in every way and mode that I can to seek, to live quietly and peacefully, I have resolved to take with me to Zara my brother with his wife and family.' Nicolò grumbled that the Della Torre family, having all kinds of resources and an income of more than 2000 ducats, was well able to pay the fine. Their behaviour, he added in a clinching argument, was an affront to the dignity of the Council.[4]

After considerable discussion, the Ten voted on whether to enforce the original fine. Support for Della Torre was lukewarm at best: twelve voted in favour of letting the sentence stand as is, seven against, and five unsure. Failing to get the required two-thirds vote to reaffirm the fine, the Ten discussed the matter further and voted again. But no minds were changed, and the vote was the same. The matter was remanded to the following January when further arguments would be heard. The delay only eroded Della Torre's support. On 15 January 1551 the Ten voted that Girolamo must still pay the remaining fine, with sixteen now in favour, six against, and three unsure.[5] Giacoma died three weeks later, perhaps worn down by the lawsuit, and young Guido, then around six years old, was sent to live with his maternal grandmother, the widowed Vittoria Valvasone.[6]

Giovanni Savorgnan was already causing problems in Zara. The Venetian authorities reported to the Council of Ten that the Turk Bosdogan Cadì had arrived in the city and that Savorgnan had offered him lodging. The Ten responded that the Turk should be provided with another place to live, 'and you should inform this Savorgnan that he must abstain from these dealings with Turks and attend to live quietly'.[7]

The Most Ardent Desire for Immortality

Frustrated in his efforts to obtain a reduction in Girolamo's sentence of exile and the fine that he was required to pay the Savorgnan, Gian Matteo turned his attention to civic affairs. In December 1551, he was elected president of the Accademia degli Uniti, a society of high-minded gentlemen dedicated to cultural and charitable activities.[8] It had been founded six months earlier by the patrician Pietro da Mosto, 'with the involvement of a very large number of Venetian nobles and other lords', most of whom had twenty or more years of experience in the governing of the Republic. Its main predecessor in Venice was the short-lived Neacademia (New Academy) founded by Aldus Manutius in 1500 to support Greek studies, with a membership that included Pietro Bembo and other learned Venetian patricians, as well as Erasmus and notable Greek scholars. But it had disbanded after Aldus's death in 1515, and its mission was more literary than civic, with the Greek language required at all meetings and banquets held on the model of Plato's symposia.[9]

The Uniti was different. While also inspired by Platonic ideals, it had a more distinctly Venetian character, with stated goals of community and public service. Its principles were summed up in a handsome Mariegola—a bound manuscript of its rules and procedures—with its motto inscribed in gold on the leather cover: FOELICISSIMI GENII on the front, and VNITORVM ETERNITATI on the back—'Most favorable guardian spirits' and 'To the eternal life of the united'—each inside an octagram, an eight-pointed star formed by two interlaced squares (Figure 8.1).[10]

The academy's mission is spelled out inside the book:

> Now that we have created our most happy Academy toward the sole end of raising ourselves to Heaven by means of gracious works of virtue and intelligence, it is a very just and holy thing that we are already showing the results that confirm such a beautiful intention; and therefore, with everyone inflamed with the most ardent desire for immortality we will strive to interact with one another in fraternal love, respect, and reverence.[11]

The 'gracious works of intelligence' cited in the mission statement included learned orations and debates on such opposing themes as 'Servitude versus Liberty' or 'Discord versus Concord.' The 'gracious works of virtue' consisted of 'the defense of poor orphans, widows, minors, and every sort of miserable person

Figure 8.1. MCVe, Mariegola 56, Accademia degli Uniti, 1551, cover (Venice, Biblioteca del Museo Civico Correr).

in the [Ducal] Palace' and the ecclesiastical courts. 'To ensure that all this is to the glory of God, the honour of this State, and the succor of the poor oppressed, it is necessary to assume such duties without any reward.'[12]

A handsome frontispiece illuminates these noble intentions. In the central cartouche, Mercury, symbolizing Eloquence and Reason, stands atop a column and receives a flaming bowl from Saturn as Father Time (Figure 8.2). The flames may symbolize Saturn's role in enflaming 'the most ardent desires of immortality' in the hearts of the members.[13]

When Gian Matteo, then sixty years old, was elected president, he was also chosen to be one of the Dodici Nobili—a newly established panel of twelve perpetual conservators responsible for ensuring the 'quiete e unione' (peace and unity) of the group, which seems to have experienced some recent disturbances. Francesco Venier, Gian Matteo's exact contemporary, was another conservator. Celebrated for his erudition and his moral integrity, Venier had—like Gian Matteo—served the Republic in important assignments abroad.[14] Their service together in the Uniti would bode well for the future of the Bembo and Della Torre families.

For the Vendetta of My Father

While Gian Matteo was burnishing his reputation as a protector of the poor and promoter of peace and unity in intellectual circles in Venice, the search for the assassins of Alvise II dragged on. Informed that the Pope had detained two accomplices of Tristan Savorgnan in Ravenna, the Ten voted on 30 January 1552

Figure 8.2. MCVe, Mariegola 56, Accademia degli Uniti, 1551, frontispiece (Venice, Biblioteca del Museo Civico Correr).

The coats of arms of the four top officers in the first months of the academy's existence anchor the corners of the frontispiece (counter-clockwise from upper left): Francesco Loredan, a celebrated jurist, as the first president; Pietro da Mosto, "famous for his eloquence and other brilliant gifts," as founder and riformatore; Dottore Sebastian Bravo, as riformatore; and probably an unidentified member of the Mella family as the second president.

to ask His Sanctity to extradite them to Venice, for the crime was 'the most atrocious and of worse quality than others that had happened in many years'.[15]

The honour culture of the feudal families of the Friuli stood in sharp contrast to the Venetian culture of civil law.[16] With Tristan still at large, the streets of Udine remained perilous. Girolamo Della Torre's young nephew Marzio Colloredo, whose sword was engraved with the motto *mihi vindictam*, was not alone. The extended Colloredo clan was enormous, with three sprawling branches of the family tree dating back to a certain Liabordo di Mels in 1205. By the mid-sixteenth century, Liabordo's male descendants numbered in the dozens, with the same first names repeated again and again over the generations. Sorting them out is an exercise in frustration, with published genealogies of the family sometimes assigning the same individual to different fathers and even to a different branch.[17] But it is important to note that the extended Colloredo clan tended to stick together, even if only sharing an ancestor six or seven generations back. Whether first cousins or second or third cousins once removed, an insult to one was an insult to all. Bloodlines ensured the survival of blood feuds.

On the feast of San Bernardino in May 1551, several Colloredo partisans led by the eighteen-year-old Marzio had brawled on an Udine street with Marco da Carpi, a Savorgnan supporter and head of the militia of Portogruaro. The Council of Ten dealt gently with the hot-headed Marzio on this occasion and upon the advice of the luogotenente, Francesco Michiel, transferred da Carpi to another post outside the region. Michiel tried in vain to persuade the Colloredos to reduce their personal escorts, which ranged from four to as many as twenty armed men or bravi (Figure 8.3).[18] But numbers per se were not the problem.

In February 1552, Marzio met up with a relative, Girolamo Caporiacco, and two Colloredo cousins—Federico, son of Mario, and Giovanni, son of Iseppo—in the Udine home of Pompeo, yet another Colloredo, whom Federico later referred to as his uncle. 'Inspired by a demonic spirit', they armed themselves 'with archibuses, prohibited firearms, and other sorts of weapons' and lay in wait at the Portello di Poscolo, an entrance to the city from the west, for the approach of Antonio Savorgnan. He was the grandnephew of the infamous Antonio who had initiated the Giovedì Grasso massacre of 1511.[19]

Needless to say, the Savorgnan clan was just as cohesive as the Colloredo, with debts of honour also passed on down through the generations. The young Antonio, then twenty-six years old, had become the leader of the Savorgnan faction after Tristan's flight from Venetian justice. Like other contentious feudal lords, Antonio did not walk through the city alone, and he strolled confidently toward the city gate with his cousin and several retainers, 'not thinking that anyone would wish to offend them'. They were wrong. Marzio and his followers took them by surprise and, in the ensuing fight, slaughtered Antonio and two of his associates, 'cutting their bodies into little pieces' and throwing them into a

Figure 8.3. "Bravo [armed retainer] of Venice and other cities of Italy," from Cesare Vecellio, *De gli habiti antichi, et moderni*. 1588, c. 165 (Amsterdam, Rijksmuseum).

Vecellio cautions: "they serve no one man, now another, for money, swearing and threatening people without cause, causing all sorts of scandals and committing murders . . . They carry a sword and dagger in their belt, and they go around talking about duels and quarrels."

nearby brook. Having wounded several others, the perpetrators fled the city, with Marzio making his way to Gorizia and then Milan and beginning a life on the run.[20]

After the fugitives failed to turn themselves in as ordered by the Council of Ten, their properties were confiscated and they were banished in absentia from Venetian territories in perpetuity with a bounty of 1000 ducats put on each of their heads.[21] Marzio later wrote in his own defence:

> If it is said that Federico Colloredo and I have killed Antonio Savorgnan . . . and some others of his company, I will allow that it was true; but that it was for the vendetta of my father, and given that they were in number of twenty and we were [only] seven, it was their fault if they let many of their own be killed, many get injured and some jump off the bridges in the water.[22]

Once again, the feudal code of honour had prevailed. After all, the Colloredo cousins had behaved no differently from Tristan Savorgnan, still at large after fleeing justice for his attack on the Grand Canal in August 1549.

In other words, vendetta justified murder, and in any case, the Savorgnan group was at fault; with its greater number, it should easily have beaten back the Colloredo assault. It is important to recall the different response of Girolamo Della Torre and his young nephew Girolamo Colloredo when ordered to turn themselves in after their street fight with the Savorgnan in Padua back in 1549. By subjecting themselves to Venetian justice, even if punished with exile and a fine, they signalled a break with the feudal culture of violence and perpetual vendetta and a willingness to abide by the rules of a more civil society.

But the streets of Udine remained a war zone. Francesco Sanudo, the incoming luogotenente, reported to the Ten soon after arriving in the city in August 1552:

> I have seen born here a great enmity, and very perilous, between the noble families of Masari and their adherents on one side, and those of the Codroipo and Maniago on the other, involving the citizens, in which they have perpetrated many wounds, vices, and various bad incidents, but beside that [there is the enmity between] the Savorgnan and the Torresani [sic = Torriani]; this is the principal one.[23]

His words must have echoed prevailing beliefs among the citizenry that even though none of the Della Torre remained in the city, their vendetta with the Savorgnan had been continued by the Colloredo.

Indeed, Antonio Savorgnan's father Bernardino was not satisfied with the sentence meted out to Marzio and his accomplices and claimed that they were actually carrying out a homicide ordered by more senior Colloredos. The Council of Ten ordered an inquest and sent a notary to Udine to collect evidence. The Ten closed the inquiry after four months without any charges and summoned Bernardino Savorgnan and Marzio's uncle Claudio—a cleric—and brother Carlo to Venice as representatives of their respective families, where the Ten exhorted them to make peace.[24] The entreaty was, as it turned out, wishful thinking.

An Overwhelming Vote of Confidence

In the meantime, the personal lives of the Bembo family in Venice and the Della Torre family in Candia were changing for the better. On 20 March 1552, the Great Council had elected Gian Matteo to the prestigious post of capitano grande of Candia almost by acclamation—1192 in favour and only 182 against—in an unusual and overwhelming vote of confidence. Gian Matteo's extensive experience abroad, as well as his participation in civic affairs, had given him the opportunity to join his daughter and her husband in Crete. He must have sailed off to Candia at the beginning of August on one of the regular galleys of Beirut or Alexandria, for he made his official entry to the city on the 29th of the month.[25]

As usual, the seas were dangerous, but particularly so that summer. As we have seen, the humiliating peace treaty of 1540 was not always honoured by the Ottoman navy and did not apply, in any case, to freelance corsairs, who could be Greeks, Uskoks, or Portuguese, as well as Turks and pirates of all ethnicities based on the Barbary Coast. The Senate had just written to the Sultan Suleiman in May 1552 about an outrageous act of piracy by Sala Beg, one of his admirals. Encountering the *Barbara*, a Venetian galley en route to Alexandria, Sala Beg had made the *segno di segurtà*, symbolizing safe passage. The Venetian captain responded with the *contrassegno* and confidently took no defensive measures.

That was a lapse of judgement. Sala Beg seized the ship and sailed it into a Cretan harbour, captured a number of Venetian subjects, and robbed it of 60,000 ducats of goods 'to the total ruin of the Venetian nobles, citizens, and other subjects who had invested their resources in the cargo'. An incensed Senate ordered Domenico Trevisan, the newly appointed Bailo (ambassador to the Ottoman court), to present himself immediately to the Grand Vizier Rustem Pasha upon his arrival in Istanbul, 'and make the greatest complaint you can... [and] you will tell him that this offense has been committed not only against us, but also against his Majesty and the Sublime Porte'. The Sultan and Rustem Pasha responded in July, but only with the promise of a full investigation.[26]

In the meantime, other disquieting news had reached Venice. A Turkish armada of some 216 ships had passed through Corfiote waters in the last week of June on its way to lay siege to Naples. After attacking Gaeta and plundering the surrounding countryside, the fleet began its voyage back to the Levant in mid-August. An awesome sight, it was reported to have reached Santa Maura (Lefkada), an island around 60 nautical miles south of Corfù, around the end of the month. The timing was fortunate. Assuming that Gian Matteo's galley had left Venice on 1 August as scheduled, it would have passed through the straits of Corfù well before then and been safely anchored in Candia.[27]

By early September, although Suleiman had not yet punished Sala Beg, who was enjoying his spoils in Algiers, he did remind Dragut Reis to respect the treaty of 1540 and to regard the Venetians as friends and their cargoes as off-limits. Trevisan wrote optimistically to the Senate in November:

> As for our complaints... about the losses sustained on the *Barbara*,... we cannot but believe that the most serene lord [Suleiman] with his sense of justice will give the order to make up these losses, in keeping with his greatness and the peace which exists between us.

While restitution proved elusive, the Senate continued to pursue a policy of watchful diplomacy. As the historian Kenneth Setton put it, 'The Venetians scanned the seas with the eyes of Argus. Relentless vigilance was the price of security for the Republic's ships and shipping.'[28]

Gian Matteo assumed the office of capitano grande in Candia on 29 August. His formal entry was similar to that of the duke, with a procession to the church of San Marco on the main square. There his predecessor handed over the keys to the city and other officials escorted him to the *luoco suolito della salzada*, a street paved with stone that led to his residence.[29] While the duke was responsible for the civil administration of the island, with the judicial and financial offices under his supervision, as capitano grande Gian Matteo oversaw military defence and public order, with fortifications, public works, and police functions as part of his portfolio.[30]

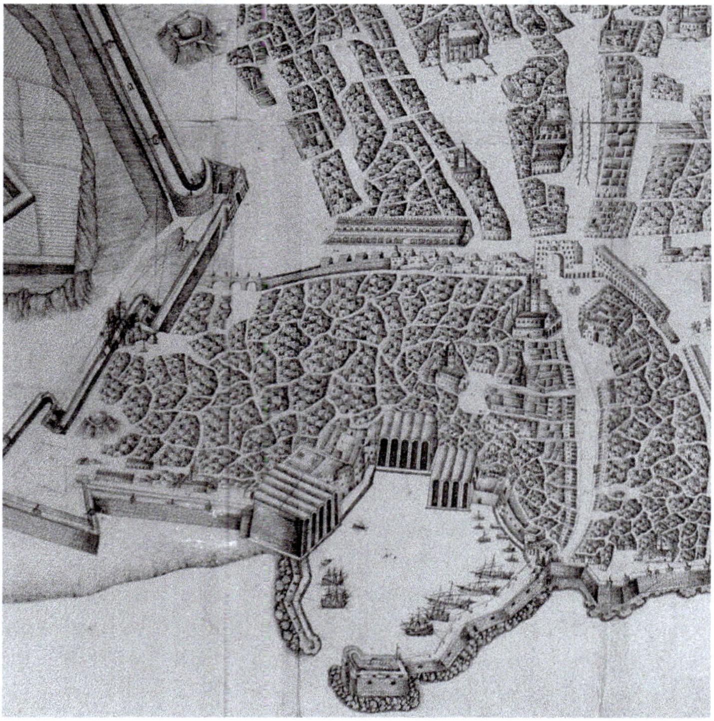

Figure 8.4. Maneas Klontzas, *View of City of Candia* (detail), early 17th century (Collection of Malcolm Wiener).

The map is oriented with south at the top. Gian Matteo Bembo's four-vaulted Arsenale Vecchio protrudes into the harbor to the right of the five-vaulted Arsenale Antichi; the five-vaulted Arsenali Nuovi and Nuovissimi on the left would be built in 1580 and 1620. The Sabbionara arrowhead bastion and Cortina Bembo are on the far left. Bembo's new portal is on the far right of the harbor linking the *sperone* to the Ruga Maistra that leads to the Ducal Palace and the city center. The Bembo Fountain is visible in front of the church of San Salvatore at the top of the detail.

Almost certainly accompanied by his wife Marcella, Gian Matteo moved into the aging palace of the capitano. It had presumably been repaired after the ruinous earthquake of 1549, but there is no record of its layout or its condition. It was located on the main square of the city near the palace of the duke, with the ducal church of San Marco, the citizen loggia, and the grain market close by (Figure 8.4). It would also have been within walking distance of the home of their daughter Giulia.

The Capitano Grande at Work

Gian Matteo's first view of the island was not much different from that of Giulia's and her husband two years earlier. As the debate between the Venetian authorities on how to proceed had continued, the ragged profile of partly finished city walls—stone bastions in various stages of completion, linked by mounds of pounded earth—still dominated the landscape.[31] But while not an engineer, Gian Matteo was an experienced project manager. As Count of Zara (1535–7), he had had dealings with Michele Sanmicheli, who spoke highly of him. As rettore and provveditore of Cattaro (1538–40), he had built up the city's defences and constructed a sea wall along the Skurda River and the Porta Bembo, which still carries an escutcheon with his initials. As capitano of Famagusta (1547–9), he had excavated columns and other antiquities from the Roman ruins at Salamis, begun an extensive programme of urban renewal in the market square, drained the swamps, and attempted to build a water system.[32] In sum, Gian Matteo was up to the challenge.

He got to work immediately. Although some of his projects did not come to fruition before he completed his term, he left a mark on the island that remains to this day. He focused first on the walls. Writing a detailed report at the end of October, he rejected Gian Girolamo Sanmicheli's proposal of an outward projecting *piattaforma* (gun platform) near the church of San Francesco. He recommended instead a *piattaforma rovescia* that would project inside the walls—an ingenious solution that preserved sight lines for artillery and would eventually be built years later.[33]

Bembo then tackled the Sabbionera Bastion on the northeast corner of the enceinte near the shore. It had required special attention, since nearby springs and the sandy earth that gave it its name called for deeper foundations. He lowered the projected height and awaited approval from Venice and the arrival of an engineer. In the meantime, on the south side of the bastion he built a new section of curtain wall, eventually named the Cortina Bembo. His efforts were memorialized by a stone incised with his name and the date of 1553. Upon its completion, he wrote again to the authorities back in Venice, reminding them of a promise to send 1000 ducats. Even though the funds had not yet arrived, he complained, they were already spent. To continue the work, he warned, would require *desine di migliara* (tens of thousands) of ducats.[34]

It would also require the labour of Cretan *villani*—mostly poor peasants who lived outside the city. Like the peasants in the Friuli, their fragile livelihoods were subject to the whims of nature. Indeed, the correspondence of the Venetian reggimenti is replete with warnings of incipient famine and appeals to the homeland to authorize the importation of grain to ward off mass starvation. That said, every able-bodied male in the territory of Candia from fourteen to sixty years of age, numbering around 12,000 at the time, was still subject to the obligation of *angaria*. An ancient tradition of forced labour, it required each to serve for six days a year without pay on public works. Not surprisingly, compliance was erratic, and a good number managed to avoid serving by hiding out in the countryside. And many of those who did serve were too weak to be of much use.

Bembo, whose concern for the poor was not confined to the city of Venice, proposed that workers should be paid eight *marchetti* per day, at least during the four winter months, with the trade-off being that they would be required to work eight days a year instead of six. His appeal fell on deaf ears until 1561, long after he had left the island. He was compelled to work with a reluctant labour force.[35]

While the walls were necessary for the city's security, the port was essential to its economy, not to mention its strategic importance as a naval base. It too required Bembo's immediate attention. Strong winds and waves battering the port month after month meant that projects were no sooner finished than they had to be repaired. The Rocca al Mare, the castle on the sea that protected the harbour entrance, is a case in point. Completed around 1540, it was already in peril less than a decade later. Stones had fallen from the tower and sections of the breakwater that extended beyond it to the north had collapsed, endangering the fortress and the harbour itself. Although new stones were brought in from the nearby island of Standia to repair the damage, little had been done by the time Bembo arrived in 1552. He came up with an ingenious solution, proposing to rebuild the castle in deeper water atop new foundations constructed from two sunken galleys filled with stones. Although the Republic speedily agreed and appropriated 500 ducats along with the galleys, Bembo's term as capitano ended (yet again) before he could carry out the plan and he was forced to shore up the old Rocca without really solving the problem.[36]

The harbour itself also required maintenance, with silting a recurrent, even constant, problem. Like his predecessors (and successors), Bembo had limited success with dredging operations, but he did have the opportunity to transform the south side of the port, where new construction was already underway on the *arsenali vecchi*. Completed shortly after the end of his term, the new yards came to be known as the Arsenali Bembo, with the Bembo coat of arms prominently affixed to the city's new gateway to the sea.[37]

Water for Candia

Crete was a dry island, and careful water management was necessary for agriculture, provisioning ships, and, indeed, daily life. When the Della Torre and Bembo families had arrived, there was no running water in the city of Candia.[38] The situation was much the same back in Venice. There, too, water had to be brought in from outside sources during times of inadequate rainfall. Although both cities collected rainwater in public and private cisterns, in Candia these were augmented by a few springs and wells, but they often ran dry or produced undrinkable water. The difference is that Venice sat in the midst of a salty lagoon, and had to ship water in from the mainland on special barges, while the city of Candia had a reliable source of fresh water nearby—the wells at Cazamba (Katsambas) fed by the River Kairatos, near the ancient port of Knossos, around 1500 metres east of the city. Water vendors gathered there daily to fill barrels of water and carted it back to sell on the streets of Candia. But although three large cisterns had been constructed inside the city to store rainwater, the situation remained one of the daily annoyances of life in Candia.[39]

Enter Gian Matteo Bembo. The Venetian authorities ordered him to find a way to bring fresh water for the first time directly into the city. Frustrated in a similar attempt in Famagusta when he had served there as capitano, he now seized the opportunity to employ his hydraulic skills.[40] The result was an aqueduct leading to a conduit under the new walls that brought water from springs outside the city to a large cistern in front of the Augustinian monastery of San Salvatore. Situated halfway between the old town and the new southern wall embracing the suburbs, the new cistern was an amenity that improved the lives not so much of the Venetian elites, but rather of ordinary, mostly Greek, residents. Even then, a simple unadorned receptacle providing water to the public was not sufficient for Bembo. He was guided by Venetian civic values admirably stated in an inscription on a well head back in Venice: *COMMODITATI PUBLICAE NEC NON URBIS ORNAMENTO* (For the convenience of the people as well as an ornament of the city).[41] Faced with the imperative to combine beauty with utility, Bembo built a monumental wall-type fountain on the north side of the cistern and also indulged in his love of antiquities (Figure 8.5).

Gian Matteo's passion for relics of the ancient past was already evident during his time in Famagusta.[42] The Paduan chronicler Marco Guazzo described Gian Matteo in glowing terms:

> When this gentleman was captain of the kingdom of Cyprus, being of great intelligence,... he sent out people to look diligently for ancient marbles in

Figure 8.5. Bembo Fountain, 1552–54. Candia (Heraklion).

A pastiche of ancient spolia and newly carved marble reliefs, the fountain was assembled from large slabs of gray marble, separated by marble columns and framed by pilasters on the sides and an architrave on top. The coats of *arms* of Alvise Gritti, as duke, and Gian Matteo Bembo, as capitano, flank the headless statue of Aesclepius atop a classical pedestal fitted up as a fountain. Photo: author.

> several places in order to make that place worthy of its dignity. On this occasion they found underground the sepulchre of the goddess Venus carved out of beautiful marble, which is known through letters that are carved in it and that have not been worn out by time. This find brought great pleasure to that rare gentleman, who had it brought to the middle of the square in Famagusta and put in an eminent place between two [ancient] columns, a great embellishment for that city both in terms of the beauty and of the antiquity of the sepulchre.[43]

Bembo was thus no stranger to archaeological appropriation when he approached the project in Candia. As with the market square in Famagusta, the fountain at San Salvatore celebrated both Candia's classical roots and its Venetian present. The centrepiece was a headless Roman statue of Aescleplius standing on a plinth provided with a spout from which water flowed into an antique sarcophagus. According to an early source, the fountain was once crowned by a statue of Cupid, in a triumph of Venetian sculptural eclecticism.[44]

We learn the source of the antiquities from Francesco Barozzi's description of the island in the 1570s:

> Where the Castello of Ierapetra is now, there are infinite columns made of marble of different colors, and also a great number of marble statues buried underground, some large and some small. From this site in the past and still to this day, many illustrious Rettori have had excavated and carried away many statues and marble columns; here they find heads, legs and arms which belonged to broken statues and also some figures of animals. From this place was also taken the large marble statue without head and right arm up to the elbow that is on the fountain of San Salvatore in the town of Candia; this statue was taken from Ierapetra and installed on that fountain built by the illustrious Gian Matteo Bembo, Capitano Generale of Candia in the year 1558 [sic].[45]

Barozzi's contemporary, the Vicentine naturalist Onorio Belli, also described the fountain, indicating that an additional piece of spolia once stood in front of it: 'This is the stone where public announcements are made. It was a most beautiful ancient octagonal altar of white marble.'[46] The fountain thus served as both frontispiece of the cistern and backdrop for official proclamations. We might also see it as an example of Bembo's wit: a headless (and thus speechless) physician standing in front of a water source, in a site where public announcements were made. Bembo was later praised by Giordano Ziletti as 'particularly expert on these matters of water'.[47]

Celebrations and Censorship

The Venetians were aware of the power of pageantry, and Candia had a full ritual calendar, partly in imitation of Venice and partly specific to the island. In addition to his duties as director of public works, Gian Matteo as capitano grande was required to don a red silk toga—a *vesta ducale*—and participate in the most important celebrations of the year, in addition to attendance at the usual Sunday services.[48]

Even though only Latin saints (in addition to Saint Titus) were accorded obligatory feast days, fifty-four such annual observances were included on a list published by the Duke of Candia in 1519. These were in addition to the movable feasts of Pentecost, Easter, Corpus Domini, and the Ascension, as well as the periodic ceremonial arrivals and departures of Venetian officials.[49]

On the afternoon before each feast day, the pealing of the bells in the campanile of the ducal church of San Marco alerted all the inhabitants of the city to the upcoming observance: a mandatory holiday if the *bandiera* of San Marco was also raised, a workday if not. The balconies of the ducal palace were decorated and the ducal standards displayed. Those who dared to sell merchandise in the piazzas of the city on Sunday and other feast days 'when the *bandiera* of San Marco was raised' had their goods confiscated.[50]

The most important celebration was the feast of Saint Titus on 2 October. The Latin and Orthodox clergy and Venetian officials were all out in force, attending services and marching in processions between Saint Titus, San Marco, and the ducal palace. The latter was adorned with carpets, flower garlands, and coats of arms of the Venetian authorities, along with the standards, shield, helmet, and sword of the duke.[51]

The carnival season featured balls and jousts, but also a less attractive festivity on Giovedì Grasso that was modelled after an ancient custom in Venice. It involved the symbolic slaughter of a bull and three pigs under an awning of galley sails set up in the main square. The Venetian authorities viewed the proceedings from the balcony on the ducal palace. Again, Gian Matteo had a role to play. As the musicians began to play their pipes, a line of *bombardieri* (cannoneers) marched into the piazza, blowing trumpets and shooting off fireworks. A bull was then led in, was baited into a frenzy and tormented by dogs, and was finally ceremoniously decapitated by a butcher. He cut the animal into four pieces, with each of the officials receiving a specific part. To the butcher and the contestabile of the capitano grande went the forequarters; to the duke and the gastaldi the hind parts; to the capitano grande himself the head and the stomach; and to the cavalier of the duke the skin and hoofs. The pigs were given to the monasteries of San Pietro, San Salvatore, and San Giovanni. 'And the excellent lord duke is obligated to serve dinner to all the excellent lords for the feast of Giovedì Grasso.'[52] It was a bloody affair, and the irony would perhaps not have been lost on Girolamo Della Torre, whose own father had been slaughtered during the Cruel Carnival in Udine in 1511.

Gian Matteo's duties as capitano included even more dubious tasks. In August 1553, Cardinal Gian Pietro Carafa, head of the Inquisition and an ardent anti-Semite, persuaded Pope Julius III to issue a papal bull ordering the seizure and destruction of Hebrew books. The Talmud and other texts were burned in a great bonfire in the Campo dei Fiori in Rome on 9 September, the day of Rosh Hashanah. The papal nuncio in Venice, Ludovico Beccadelli, pressured the Venetians to do the same. Although prone to stay out of doctrinal disputes, the Council of Ten gave in. Beccadelli reported approvingly on 21 October: 'Without prior notice they seized all the remaining Talmuds [in the stock of a Christian publisher of Hebrew texts], which were then publicly burned at the Rialto, and the copies belonging to Jews were set apart so that this morning a lovely burning was held in St. Mark's Square.'[53]

The Ten would soon follow suit in the stato da mar. In March 1554 they ordered Gian Matteo to confiscate all the books in the Jewish quarter of Candia. Two months later, the island's Greater Council reported back that agents of the University of the Jews, 'displaying the highest obedience to the present edict', had presented their Hebrew books to the capitano Gian Matteo Bembo and Duke Alvise Renier and his councilors, 'to the end that not any book remained in this Zudeca'. The books were examined by 'two Jews made Christians [one named Nicolò and the other Marino], there not being anyone else in this city who would have knowledge of this sort of book'—that is, literate in Hebrew and able to discern 'discrepancies from the truth'. The books were then sorted into three groups. The first group, 'a quantity of books called the Talmud, with their comments and questions', was burned in the main piazza between the Duke's palace and the ducal church of San Marco. The second included other versions of the Talmud to be retained for further examination. The third was comprised of Bibles, vocabularies, and 'books of diverse sciences, that is, philosophy, grammar, medicine astrology, the Kabbalah, etc'. These volumes were returned to the Jews. The Great Council pronounced them 'its most faithful and obedient servants'.[54]

A Cretan Bride

Aside from Gian Matteo's impressive public works projects and participation in both happy and unhappy civic events, the Bembo family strengthened its connection to the island in a more personal way. On 26 November 1552, just months after Gian Matteo's arrival, his son Alvise, a twenty-nine-year-old galley captain, married Magdalena Pasqualigo. The young widow of Benedetto Cornaro, Magdalena had a distinguished Veneto-Cretan pedigree. Her parents were Giovanni Pasqualigo, by then deceased, and Caterina Calergi, daughter of Andrea. We may recall that the Calergi, although Greek, were Venetian nobles of the colony, not just Cretan nobles—an important distinction. Magdalena brought with her a handsome 9000-ducat dowry. The terms were fairly straightforward, with 1000 ducats to be paid immediately and the remainder paid in movable goods, silver, gold, clothing, gems, and other ornaments, to be supplemented, as necessary, by real property at the Casali Melidoni, Agra', and Camarioti. But the contract also contained a curious clause: 'the above cited magnificent spouse promises that he cannot take or have taken to Venice, the above mentioned magnificent lady Magdalena for the next fifteen years under the penalty of two thousand ducats in case of violation, to paid from the proceeds of his own property in this city.'[55] Perhaps Magdalena did not wish to leave Candia; perhaps she spoke little Italian, let alone Venetian dialect; perhaps the real property was entailed by her *dimissoria* (a bequest in addition to her dowry);[56] perhaps her family did not want her to leave. In any case, with Alvise at sea much of the time, where his wife resided may not have made much of a difference. The aim of the union was not so much domestic tranquillity as it was political and social advantage to both families.

Alvise finalized the formal agreement in the presence of 'his father, the famous lord capitano, in a chamber of his magnificent father's palace'. It was an all-male affair. Serving as witnesses were three Venetian nobles from leading families of the colony: Andrea Venier, Pietro Cornaro, and Giovanni Dandolo. Like Magdalena herself, all were descendants of the original noble Venetian settlers of the island. Also present were 'several other magnificent nobles'. Alvise's brother-in-law Girolamo Della Torre was presumably in the latter group. At the same day and hour, Magdalena pledged her troth—separately—in the palace of her Cornaro in-laws. Although one hopes that Marcella and Giulia, as well as Magdalena's own female relatives, were present, the marriage contract lists only three male witnesses: Pietro Augustino, a notary in the camera fiscali of the reggimento, Antonio da Crema, and Thomas da Modone, the latter two an engineer and scribe engaged in Gian Matteo's projects. None would have been familiar with the bride.[57]

For a time, there was only celebration. But the following January it came to the attention of the Senate that Alvise, who was *sopracomito* of one of the four galleys of Candia, part of the Venetian war fleet, had remained in the city with his new bride, while his twenty-three-year-old brother Davide took his place as master of his galley. Permission for the substitution had been given by Alvise Renier, the Duke of Candia, but not by Stefano Tiepolo, the captain general of the sea—a violation of protocol. An outraged Senate ordered Alvise to return to his galley as soon as it reached Candia and serve on it for the entire month of May, 'and not returning in the cited period, he will be removed from his post of *sopracomito*, and forfeit the remainder of his pay'. In the future, no *sopracomito* would be allowed to leave his galley without permission from the head of the armada, and this could not be granted for any reason other than a public cause or grave infirmity. Transgressions would bring a 500-ducat fine and a ten-year ban from serving as a *sopracomito*.[58]

The order got Alvise's attention. He left his bride and returned to his galley as directed. In August the Senate reassessed the situation: 'having obeyed the order of this council... [and] this being an honourable request', Alvise would be allowed to remain in Candia when it was time for his galley to be disarmed, with his brother Davide 'a person practiced and sufficient for such a duty', sailing it back to Venice for that purpose.[59]

Alvise's marriage also brought other difficulties. While it initially expanded the network of influential family and friends, it would eventually create adversaries as well as allies. A few years later, Magdalena's inheritance would be embroiled in a lawsuit filed by her relatives. Referring to Alvise as his 'avversario', her great uncle Matteo Calergi contested her right to some country properties under the laws of primogeniture in a litigation that would continue over the next decade.[60]

A Firstborn Daughter

But, to return to celebrations, there was another cause to rejoice. With little Sigismondo only a year old, Giulia was already seven and a half months pregnant with another child. The young bride's experience of childbirth during the past two years had been a mixed one of grief, fear, and pain, but also joy and relief. Her first baby had died when just two weeks old, and—as we have seen—the survival of the second one was deemed a miracle, given the complications attending his birth. Without the support of her mother and close women friends during these years, Giulia had taken solace in a religiosity characterized by supernatural visions, signs, and portents. But now she had the reassuring presence of her mother Marcella, an educated woman who had herself given birth to ten children, including at least one miscarriage and one stillbirth.

Six weeks after Alvise Bembo's marriage, Girolamo made a third entry in his *Fedi Battesimali*:

> 1553, on Saturday, the 7th of January at the hour of 18:30 in Candia, Taddea, my first daughter, third [child] in order, was born to me. She was baptized in Saint Titus by the Reverend Deacon Bonfio in the presence of 20 godfathers and a godmother; may God make her good.[61]

Sansovino later wrote that the child was named after Girolamo's mother, and importantly, again, that the birth was marked by unusual circumstances: 'one month before she was born was heard (I vow that it seems incredible but it is true) her voice from her mother's womb, with the greatest admiration of those persons worthy of faith who heard it.'[62] Perhaps only the pious were privileged to hear the cries of the unborn child, but such cases had been recorded in medical literature as early as 1546 and as recently as modern times. The phenomenon is called *vagitus uterinus* (crying in utero): 'a cry or joyous exclamation heard from the abdomen of a pregnant woman.' According to ancient tradition, it was a mark of a special destiny. Zarathustra and Mohammed had reputedly cried out from the womb before their births, as had Saint Bartholomew (later to be flayed alive). These rare events usually occurred shortly before the baby was born, although Martin Weinrichius, a German physician, cited a case in 1551 where a child was heard crying fourteen days before birth. In 1596 Andreas Libavius, another German doctor, 'saw a case where the cry from the womb could be heard from quite a distance'. In the nineteenth century, a prominent French physician would conclude: 'Since men of good faith have heard it, I believe it; but [even] if I had heard it myself I would doubt it.'[63] Giulia's personal engagement with dreams and 'signs outside the natural order' would last her entire life.

Back in the Friuli

The situation in Udine had not improved, even after the banishment of Marzio Colloredo. The outgoing luogotenente, Francesco Sanudo, wrote to the Council of Ten at the end of his term in May 1553. He lamented that he had laboured to bring together the opposing groups of nobles and commoners in the city and urged them to settle their differences, 'but found that one part and the other [were] very set in their opinions'. Devoting every day and every hour to this problem, he had finally proposed a vote in the city council that the citizens should live together in peace and quiet. With the help of God, he reports, the measure passed with 175 yea and only 13 nay votes.[64]

Best intentions were well and good, but old enmities died hard. Reports of new outrages continued to trickle in during the following year. In February, three servants of Bernardino Savorgnan were arrested in Venice for attacking some Colloredo associates.[65] In April the luogotenente reported unrest in the city over the elections.[66] On 15 May, Marzio Colloredo had sneaked back into the city and tried to kill Bernardino, who barricaded himself in his house. A frustrated Marzio shot an arquebus at the window of another Savorgnan relative instead. His ban and the bounty of 1000 ducats were promptly renewed in Venice. One member of the Ten even proposed that the bounty be increased to 3000 ducats plus a 300-ducat yearly annuity.[67] The measure failed, but the equation was about to change.

A Rare Thing

Michele Della Torre had returned to Ceneda from Trent by September 1552, but would be dispatched as papal vice-legate to Perugia and Umbria a year later, again leaving the administration of his bishopric in the hands of a procurator.[68] And yet, he had not forgotten his brother in Crete. Although appeals by foreign princes had been counter-productive back in 1550, it was time to try again. On 26 May

1554, Domenico Morosini, the Venetian ambassador to Rome, wrote to the Capi of the Council of Ten:

> This morning the Pope [Julius III] informed me that he had been requested to make a petition to his serenity [the doge]. Declaring that he did not know much about the matter personally, he recommended to his serenity the request of the Bishop of Ceneda, whom he knew to be an honoured person and who had been much loved and esteemed by Pope Paul of holy memory, who had made him his majordomo and had then given him the legation of France in which he was well esteemed by many, and was presently serving the governance of Perugia. Because [Bishop Michele] was not a man to abandon, [the pope] would therefore be greatly pleased if his serenity would free [the bishop's] brother, and that if this could be done, he would accept such service as if it were conferred on the person of the Cardinal del Monte [the pope] himself.[69]

The pope's appeals were not acted upon immediately, for Doge Marcantonio Trevisan was ill and would die just six days later. The timing was possibly advantageous for the Della Torre case, for Trevisan was a man of notable rectitude. While he would surely have been attentive to an appeal from the pope, he was admired—and resented by some—in Venice for his sanctimonious attitude and strict adherence to moral principles. Having accepted the office of doge only reluctantly at the behest of his relatives, Trevisan wore a hair shirt under his ducal robes, subjecting himself to perpetual mortification of the flesh, and had never married 'per non peccare' (in order not to sin). He might not have been sympathetic to a count from the Friuli, no matter how well connected, who had forsaken his priestly vows to marry. During his brief one-year term in office (4 June 1553 to 31 May 1554), he persuaded the Great Council to prohibit theatrical performances, balls, and other frivolous entertainments after midnight. Weakened by fasting, he refused medical attention as a perversion of God's will and collapsed while praying before an altar in the Sala delle Teste in the Palazzo Ducale. In a twist of fate, this devout Christian died at the age of seventy-nine on 31 May 1554, surrounded by the collection of pagan Roman busts left to the Republic by Cardinal Domenico Grimani.[70]

On 11 June, Francesco Venier was elected doge, 'beyond the expectations of many'. He had never held the office of Procurator, an unofficial prerequisite for the dogeship; he was only sixty-five, with septuagenarians (and older) generally favoured for the office; and he was in such poor health that he could only walk when supported by two attendants. Still, he had many friends and was greatly admired for his learning. Beyond that, he had served as a rettore in Brescia, Udine, Padua, and Verona. But most importantly for our story, he was already well acquainted with the Bembo and Della Torre families. As luogotenente of the Patria del Friuli in 1534 he would have come into frequent contact with the Della

Torre brothers; as ambassador to Rome in 1543–4 he would have come to know Michele Della Torre, then chamberlain of Pope Paul III; and as one of the Dodici Nobili of the Accademia degli Uniti in 1551 he would have socialized with Gian Matteo Bembo on a weekly basis and would have had firsthand knowledge of the Della Torre situation.

A few days later, Beccadelli, still the papal legate in Venice, wrote to Cardinal Innocenzo del Monte, the Pope's secretary, acknowledging the receipt of a letter from the Pope asking for a *grazia* for Count Girolamo Dalla Torre.

> I was in the Collegio and presented the letter with the best words I knew...His Lordship had the letter read and responded very amicably, saying that they would meet and let me know what they have decided. They have not yet done this, there being much business to take care of in these days, but I hope to write about it to your lordship in the coming week.[71]

On 23 June, Beccadelli wrote again to Innocenzo, informing him that he had appealed directly to the Doge:

> I have not failed and will not fail to recommend and urge the case of Count Girolamo Della Torre, having entreated his Serenity to do me this favor to expedite it, but up to now I have not yet heard about it. But I hope that given the strict orders that they observe, I should soon have news.[72]

Finally, two weeks later, on 7 July, the Council of Ten announced its decision:

> That in gratification of the high pontiff, a safe conduct will be granted to Count Girolamo della Torre for the next five years, who for that period must live and stay in this city only, notwithstanding his relegation to the island of Candia by deliberation of this council of May 1549, with the condition that he cannot leave this city without license from this council under the penalty contained in his sentence.

The vote was solid: twenty-two in favour, four against, and one undecided.[73] While the decision was made by the Ten, the support of Doge Venier, Gian Matteo's old friend, would have weighed heavily.

Beccadelli wrote to Innocenzo the same day with the happy news. Although Della Torre was not granted a full pardon, the *grazia*, this was 'a rare thing and perhaps not ever done in a similar case, where there are such powerful adversaries; but the respect of doing a thing agreeable to His Holiness has superseded every difficulty. I now leave most content, God always be thanked.'[74] Beccadelli's term as nuncio had ended on a high note and he would soon leave the city well satisfied that papal appeals that had fallen on deaf ears four years earlier had finally been heeded.

The Family Regroups

In the meantime, perhaps unaware that such efforts were in the works, the Della Torre family in Crete had grown once again. Girolamo opened the *Fedi Battesimali* and wrote: '1554 on the 4th of June at the thirteenth hour on Monday in Candia in Ca' Querini, Giulio was born to me, my third son, fourth in order; he was baptized on the 14th.'[75] The baby was named after his mother, 'who highly desired it... because this would perpetuate her name in the house of the [Della] Torre'.[76] The circumstances of the birth were presumably uneventful, occasioning no special note by Giulia's biographer.

As soon as the decision of the Council of Ten reached Candia (by the end of July at the earliest), the families prepared to leave the island. Girolamo, ever methodical, drew up his accounts. During the first three years, he had collected a total of 3159 ducats of rental income for the Patriarchate of Constantinople and forwarded the sums to Venice. For his own account, in addition to the 228 ducats he had carried with him on the voyage to the island, Giulia's brother Lorenzo, as one of Girolamo's procurators in Venice, had forwarded another 1700 ducats in increments by July 1551. Gian Matteo brought with him another 500 ducats from Girolamo's brother Michele in August 1552. A certain Sebastian Boza had arrived in March 1553 with an additional 220 ducats that had been given him by Lorenzo. Another 300 ducats were credited that year, which seems to have been come from properties in the Friuli. Finally, there was a credit of 200 ducats for 'chains of gold and women's dresses of velvet and damask and other things sold'. This must have been the sum raised by the sale of the jewellery and fine clothing that Giulia had renounced before their departure to Candia in 1550, her mind being 'in travail on that unfortunate occasion'. All told, the funds available to the family amounted to almost 3000 ducats during their four years of exile. With only 160 ducats going to rent during that period, they had ample means to lead a comfortable life, even on an island plagued by shortages of grain and other commodities.[77]

Gian Matteo completed his term as capitano grande on 28 August 1554, and, in all likelihood, the Bembo and Della Torre families returned to Venice together on the same galley. The seas were more dangerous than ever. In July, Dragut Reis, with a fleet of fifty galleys, had laid siege to Vieste, a prosperous little town on the coast of Puglia across the Adriatic from Ragusa. His troops sacked and burned the city, slaughtered the elderly and disabled, and took 7000 residents as slaves. By summer's end, Dragut had taken his fleet inside the Gulf and was staging assaults on Venetian ships (despite Venetian protests and the Sultan's directives of two years earlier). Back in Venice, the galleys of Beirut and Alexandria that ordinarily departed on the first of August remained at the dock. Venetian merchants faced a dilemma. Remembering the fate of the *Barbara*, they were fearful of losing expensive cargo—not to mention the passengers and crews—on the one hand, but fearful of losing a season of profits on the other. After weeks of hand-wringing and futile complaints to Dragut himself, a proposal was made and rejected in the Senate on 1 September to cancel the convoys altogether. The galleys were loaded a week later and finally ready to set sail, five weeks after their normal departure. The captains were instructed to be extra vigilant and to steer clear at all cost of Dragut's armada, which, it later became known, was lying in wait in the straits of Corfù.[78]

Despite all the hazards, shipping went on, and the galley carrying the Bembo and Della Torre families sailed back to Venice through pirate-infested waters. The homeward journey could not have been easy, even with prayers chanted and sung three times a day aboard the ship. Giulia's charges now included a three-month-old infant and two toddlers under the age of three. She must also have been accompanied by several servants, including a wet nurse, as well as her mother Marcella. It is unlikely that the women and children ever left their cabin below decks. Whether in the city or on board a ship, their place was inside the walls, protected as much as possible from the perils of public space.

Gian Matteo and Girolamo, by contrast, would have stood outside on deck as the ship slipped out of the harbour of Candia. A veteran of many sea voyages in equally dangerous waters, Gian Matteo could look back with satisfaction at a cityscape that he had transformed in significant ways: the Bembo coat of arms now emblazoned on the walls, the new entrance at the port, the new arsenals, and the first public fountain in the city.

The equation was different for Girolamo. More concerned with family survival than public acclaim, he probably did not look back at his place of exile. Gazing watchfully out to sea, his armour and weapons near at hand, he had even more to lose now than he had on the voyage to the island four years before, when he stood ready to defend the ship and his young bride from marauding corsairs in the Adriatic. His honour as a feudal lord, and now his very posterity, were at stake.

Notes

1. ASVe, *CX*, Criminali, r. 7, ff. 180, 181v; Conzato 2005, 32–3, 59 nn75, 76.
2. See Chapter 4.
3. ASVe, Consiglio dei Dieci, Co. muni, Filze, b. 52, no. 38. Giacoma's eloquent appeal was clearly written by a lawyer—possibly Giulio Sbroiavacca, the husband of Girolamo's niece (and his procurator in the Friuli).
4. Ibid.
5. Ibid. See also ASUd, *AT*, b. 19.
6. BCUd, MS Joppi 423, Antonio Belloni Necrologium and Flaminio de Rubeis, Chronica Defunctorum, col. 14.
7. ASVe, *CX*, Secreti, r. 6, 61 (28 January 1550 m.v. [=1551]. Bosdogan was sent by the Sultan to deal with boundaries in Zara. See the relazione of Alvise Renier, the Venetian Bailo in Constantinople, in *Monumenta spectantia* 1877, 186–7.
8. Monacelli 2008, 46–50; Pilot 1912, 193–207; Battagia 1826, 19.

9. MCVe, Mariegola 56, Accademia degli Uniti, 1551, frontispiece. See Vanin and Eleuteri 2007, 41, cat. 56; Geanakoplos 1960, 116–18.
10. My thanks to Sarah Blake McHam for help with the translation from the Latin. The octagram has been defined as a Hermetic symbol of regeneration or as a Cabalistic symbol of the 'union of positive and negative forces through the medium of intelligence.' Greer, *Circles of Power*, 352. Cf. Battagia 1826, 18–19, who seems to be unaware of the Correr Mariegola and states that the group's motto was 'Vicissim nectuntur'. He was probably referring to a second Uniti founded in the late seventeenth century, as suggested by Maylender 1926–30, 5:410.
11. Pilot 1912, 198–9.
12. Monacelli 2008, 49, 199.
13. Pilot 1912, 199. See also Smith, 'Heraclitus and Fire', 125–7, suggesting that the flames may also refer to Heraclitus's notion of fire as the Logos or the origin of all things. For the coats of arms, see Monacelli 2008, 46, 49.
14. Pilot 1912, 203–6; Monacelli 2008, 46–9. Venier's dates are 1489–1556; Gian Matteo's 1490–1570.
15. ASVe, *CX*, Criminali, r. 7, f. 132.
16. Muir 1983, 255–6, 279–80, and *passim*; Cooney 1998, 131–2.
17. For example, Crollalanza 1875; Custoza 2003; http://www.genmarenostrum.com/pagine-lettere/letterac/Colloredo/COLLOREDO1.htm.
18. Muir 1993, 251; Conzato 2005, 59 n81; ASVe, *CCX*, Lettere di Condottieri, b. 308 (Filza Savorgnan). See also Walker 1998.
19. Muir 1993, 251–2.
20. Ibid.; ASUd, *AT*, b. 19 (6 February 1552); MCVe, MS Cicogna 1363, 261–2; ASVe, *CX*, Criminali, r. 8, 50r-v (2 March 1552). Corbanese 1983, 172: 'minutatimque concisi.' Cf. Casella 2003, 119, with the date of 1551 without citation.
21. Muir 1993, 251; ASVe, *CX*, Criminali, r. 8, 60r-v (4 July 1552); Conzato 2005, 60 n83; Antonini 1877, 86; MCVe, MS Cicogna 1363, 261–2; Corbanese 1987, 172.
22. Vollo 1856, 139. My thanks to Giada Damen for help with this translation.
23. ASVe, *CCX*, Lettere dei Rettori, b. 170, no. 168 (4 September 1552).
24. Conzato 2005, 60 n83; ASVe, *CX*, Criminali, r. 8, 67v (29 October 1552).
25. BMVe, MS VII 824 (=8903), Consegi (3 March 1551–23 February 1555 mv), 74; ASVe, *SAV-MC*, Reg.2 (1541–52), 183 [=186].
26. Setton 1984, 586–8, citing ASVe, *Sen.*, Secreti, r. 68, ff. 24–5 (44–5).
27. Setton 1984, 582–4.
28. Ibid., 587–8.
29. Papadaki 2005, 28, 170; Papadopoli 2007, 58.
30. O'Connell 2009, 41–2, 48–9, 177.
31. Gerola 1905–32, I:2, 313–24; Steriotou 2003, 45–6.
32. Bembo/Travi, IV, 73, no. 1883 (20 September 1537); Arbel 2001, 651–6; Calvelli 2012, 23–4; Brown 2013a, 236–41; Brown 2015, 108–11.
33. Gerola 1905–32, I:2, 325.
34. Ibid., 322–6.
35. Ibid., I:2, 327–9. A *marchetto* was equivalent to a Venetian *soldo* (124 *soldi* = 1 ducat). See Vincent 2007, 276, 317, 320. In 1549, the Venetian rector of Chania had proposed a daily wage of 3 Venetian soldi (7.5 Cretan soldini) for compulsory labour (*angaria*) on

the fortifications, noting that during the war with the Turks of 1537–8 they received 8 soldini. For the eventual walls, see Steriotou 2003, 42–56; Comescu 2016, 85–108.

36. Gerola 1905–32, I:1, 135–48. A repair campaign was launched again in 1556, only to be followed by a succession of similar projects over the ensuing decades.
37. Ibid., IV, 90–1, 125–6; Tzobanaki 1998, 35–50.
38. Gerola 1905–32, IV, 10 (9–63).
39. Calabi 1986, 103–4; Strataridaki et al. 2012, 471–2; Gerola 1905–32, IV, 24–5; Brown 2015.
40. Calvelli 2012, 51–6.
41. On a wellhead in Campo San Leonardo, 1518: Rizzi 1981, 163.
42. Calvelli 2012, 19–66.
43. Guazzo 1554, 413v. Engl. transl. from Calvelli 2012, 19.
44. Brown 2004, 191; Calvelli 2009, 140–5; Calvelli 2012, 51–2; Damen 2012, 252–4, 246–7.
45. Barozzi 2004, 192–3. Engl. transl. by Damen 2012, 254.
46. Calvelli 2012, 52. Cf. Damen 2012, 252, who suggests (rightly in my view) that Belli refers to a separate stone and not the fountain itself.
47. In his dedication to Gian Matteo in Piccolomini 1561: 'particolarmente intendentissima di queste cose dell'acque.' Gian Matteo eventually assembled a notable collection of antiquities. See Sansovino 1561, 19 (first published in 1556 under the pseudonym of Anselmo Guisconi). See also Damen 2012, Ch. 3; Brown 2013a, 243–4, 249.
48. Papadaki 2005, 54, 71–2, 84–5, 105, 170–5.
49. Brown 2016, 43–50, 57–8, 63.
50. Papadaki 2005, 7–11.
51. Ibid., 51–64.
52. Ibid., 83–5, 172.
53. Calimani 1989, 60; Ravid 2001, 25.
54. ASVe, *CCX*, Lettere dei Rettori, b. 285, nos. 73–4.
55. ASVe, Archivio Privato Grimani S. Maria Formosa, b. 5, filza 547 [no. 2776] (26 November 1552).
56. Chojnacki 2000, 278–81.
57. Ibid. See also Gerola 1905–32, I:2, 314.
58. ASVe, *Sen.*, Mar, r. 32, c. 63v [6 January 1552 m.v. [=1553].
59. Ibid., cc. 94v, 101 (4 August 1553; 6 September 1553).
60. ASVe, Archivio Privato Grimani S. Maria Formosa, b. 5, filza 547, 26 November 1552.
61. ASUd, *AT*, b. 17, fasc. 17, ff. 139–40.
62. Appendix I: Sansovino, *Vita*, 6v.
63. Weinrich 1595; Gélis 1991, 51–3; Ryder 1943, 867–72 (with review of the literature); Blair 1965, 1164–5; Pinkerton 1969, 482.
64. ASVe, *CCX*, Lettere dei Rettori, b. 170, no. 170; Antonini 1877, 86; *Relazioni/Friuli* 51.
65. Released on 5 April. Conzato 2005, 60 n83 (who cites the date as 1555); ASVe, *CX*, Criminali, r. 8, c. 112v; 115v (20 February 1554).
66. ASVe, *CX*, Secreti, r. 6, 120–120v (19 April 1554).
67. ASVe, *CX*, Criminali, r. 8, c. 149v–150r (15 May 1554). Cf. Conzato 2005, 34, 60 n85 (with the date of 1555).

68. 26 September 1552: Michele Della Torre wrote to Giovanni da Udine from Ceneda about accounts. Cargnelutti 1987, 339; Tomasi 1998, I, 121, 141; ASTr, A. P. V. Correspondenza Madruzziana, b. IV, f. XI, 218–19.
69. ASVe, *CCX*, Lettere degli ambasciatori, b. 23 [Rome: 1539–54], c. 187.
70. Da Mosto 1960, 254–9; Bertolizio, *Dogi*, 264–6; Laugier, *Storia*, 9: 258; Sansovino, *Venetia citta nobilissima*, 1663, II, 601; Cicogna, *Inscrizioni*, IV, 566.
71. Gaeta 1967, VI, 346, no. 411 (16 June 1554). See *DBI*, *s.v.* 'Del Monte, Innocenzo'; Burkle-Young and Doerrer 1997.
72. Gaeta 1967, VI, 370, no. 415.
73. ASVe, *CX*, Comuni, Filze, b. 63, no. 5.
74. Gaeta 1967, VI, 376, no. 417 (7 July 1554); ASUd, *AT*, b. 11, cartella XI, colto 21, no. 8.
75. ASUd, *AT*, b. 17, fasc. 1, f. 167.
76. Appendix I: Sansovino, *Vita*, c. 6.
77. ASUd, *AT*, b. 6, no. 10, 'Questi sono tutti li denari ch'io ho havuti dapoi ch'io son in Candia'. Della Torre corrected in ink the amount of the money that he brought to the island, and the final number is unclear. It was probably Duc. 228.2.10, but could have been 238.2.10 or 278.2.10. I am grateful to Mauro Bondioli for his help with this transcription.
78. Setton 1984, 607–8; Monacelli 2008, 50–1.

9
The Return

The vessel carrying the Bembo and Della Torre families arrived in Venice by mid to late September 1554. Leaving the turbulent waters of the Adriatic behind, the galley sailed through the port at Malamocco and entered the lagoon. By great good fortune, they were arriving in the city ahead of an outbreak of the plague that would appear the following year, and since they were not coming from an infected port, their ship would not likely have been subject to quarantine. The approach could not be more different from that to Candia, where the small harbor functioned as a defensive vestibule, difficult to enter in stormy weather, with high stone walls and the arsenals closing off the city. By contrast, the expansive lagoon was Venice's welcoming vestibule, presenting the city as open and approachable. Disembarking the ship, Giulia, now with three young children, must have felt truly safe for the first time in four years. But the weary travellers were not yet firmly on dry land. They would have immediately boarded small boats or barges that probably took them directly to the Bembo palace at Santa Maria Nova.

A New Beginning

Slipping through the gently lapping waters of the lagoon, the boats moved swiftly past the Riva degli Schiavoni, past the Palazzo Ducale and the Piazzetta, and then into the Grand Canal. As the travellers looked up at the three and four-storey palaces lining the sides, they knew that they had finally returned to a city that was like no other. But its face was changing. For like Candia, mid-century Venice was also a construction zone.

On the west side of the Piazzetta, the ceremonial entrance to the city, Jacopo Sansovino's new Zecca or mint, a rusticated structure that looked like a fortress, stood between butcher shops and the fondaco—a large grain warehouse where the public gardens are now located. Nearly complete shortly before the Della Torre's departure in 1550, the Zecca was being provided with an 'honourable' doorway, flanked by male herms, on the south facade. To its right, Sansovino's two-storey Libreria (now the Biblioteca Nazionale Marciana) stood partially built, now with fourteen bays—seven more than when Girolamo had left with his young bride, but with seven yet to go. The Beccaria, the cluster of butcher shops

The Venetian Bride: Bloodlines and Blood Feuds in Venice and Its Empire. Patricia Fortini Brown, Oxford University Press (2021). © Patricia Fortini Brown. DOI: 10.1093/oso/9780192894571.003.0009

on its south end next to the Zecca, would block its completion for another three decades.[1]

New classically inspired residences were also rising up on both sides of the Grand Canal. Most notable among them were two new palaces designed, again, by Sansovino: Ca' Dolfin, completed shortly after 1547, and his massive Ca' Corner della Ca' Grande, begun in 1545 and still under construction. These buildings marked the addition of the Roman Renaissance style to the eclectic sequence of Byzantine, Gothic, and Lombard-style residences featuring painted facades and marble incrustations, each more splendid than the next, that gave Venice its special charm. Francesco Sansovino cited twenty *palazzi maravigliosi* in his 1556 guide to the city, twelve of them on the Grand Canal.[2] Passing under the wooden drawbridge at Rialto, the Bembo and Della Torre flotilla would have rowed past the Fondaco dei Tedeschi and turned into the narrow Rio San Giovanni Grisostomo to arrive at the water entrance of Ca' Bembo.

If Sansovino's palaces represented Venice's future, Ca' Bembo represented its past. The modest Gothic palace was charming, but less than grand.[3] Gian Matteo still had four unmarried adult sons, and the space was probably tight. Girolamo soon found more commodious accommodations for his growing family nearby in Ca' Morosini at Santa Sofia. A ten-minute walk (or a short gondola ride) from Ca' Bembo, the palace faced the Grand Canal, separated by just one house from Ca' d'Oro. And like it, it was very grand indeed. An imposing building of Veneto-Byzantine origins with a colourful frescoed facade, it had been remodelled and expanded over the centuries. We do not know how much of the building was occupied by the Della Torre, but given its size, it may have been no more than a single floor. In any event, it was a most suitable residence for a wealthy Friulian count, even if under house arrest in the city, and his noble Venetian wife (Figure 9.1).[4]

Aside from its prestigious position on the Grand Canal and its close proximity to Ca' Bembo, Ca' Morosini was in an optimal location for the needs of the family. It was only a few steps away from the small church of Santa Sofia, which now became the Della Torre family parish church and probably one of the few places that Giulia frequented outside her home other than, perhaps, her parents' palace. As she walked to daily mass, she could observe an inspiring collection of wall frescoes painted by the school of Giovanni Bellini covering the façade of the house of the parish priest next to the church: the *Creation of Adam and Eve*, the *Savior Preaching*, and *God the Father with Saints Sebastian and Rocco*.[5]

The church, its interior featuring a chapel with an altarpiece by Gentile da Fabriano, attracted artists and craftsmen from all over the city, for it also housed the altar of the Arte de Depentori, the painters' guild, whose meeting house was next door. Titian himself was active in the guild, along with other easel and fresco painters, as well as draftsmen, gilders, sign painters, playing card painters, leather decorators, painters of chests, miniaturists, and even embroiderers.[6]

Figure 9.1. Ca' Morosini (now Hotel Ca' Sagredo). Cannaregio, Venice.
The palace's Byzantine pedigree is most evident in the row of tall windows with stilted arches on the mezzanine level. On the piano nobile above, the four-light trefoil window, surmounted by quatrefoils with polychrome marble disks in the intrados, was probably inspired by the Palazzo Ducale. The façade was once frescoed with crimson quatrefoils and winged cherubs.

Another desirable feature of Ca' Morosini was its access to the traghetto based at Campo Santa Sofia—one of thirteen that ferried passengers crossed the Grand Canal—linking it directly to the Rialto market opposite. Girolamo, who managed the finances of his extended family, likely spent considerable time at Rialto, not shopping for fish and vegetables—a task that would have been delegated to servants—but frequenting sites such as the Loggia dei Mercanti, a meeting place that was popular with nobles and wealthy merchants alike.[7]

No Coincidence

News of Girolamo's partial reprieve soon spread around, and his old enemy Giovanni Savorgnan swiftly petitioned the Doge and Council of Ten for similar treatment. We will recall that Savorgnan had been exiled to Zara for five years for his presumed role in the murders on the Grand Canal in 1549. He now asks that he be allowed to serve out the last ten months of his sentence in Venice, 'where I, a poor cripple, could live out my life less uncomfortably'. Belonging to the branch of the Savorgnan family that had been granted patrician status in Venice several centuries earlier, Giovanni was a noble twice over. In his petition, he appealed at first to the sympathy of the Venetian authorities. He is not well, he complains, and has suffered much from the cold climate during his exile, particularly during the winter—which is now approaching. (This from a native of the Friuli, where the weather was much harsher than on the Dalmatian coast.) He then entreats the Doge to extend to him the clemency 'that you have extended to many others'. (The subtext here is obvious.) He does not need to remind the doge of the merits of his ancestors and of the many services made by his family to the Republic, 'nor have I wished to [resort to] those means of princes which others have been accustomed to use in similar cases, and which would also have not been lacking to me'. Although Savorgnan does not cite Della Torre by name, the Doge and the Council would have read between the lines: he too has important princely friends, but he did not call upon them to intervene on his behalf. Savorgnan concludes with another appeal to their sense of compassion: 'I ask you on bended knee for the pity, the clemency, and the mercy that you have been accustomed to exercise toward all those who have obeyed and that have need, as have I, your most faithful servant.' After two ballots, the Council Ten approved his request on 28 September. It is tempting to think that he and Girolamo sailed into the port of Venice at around the same time.[8]

There was little cause for concern about the presence in the city of both Della Torre and Savorgnan. The latter was in poor health, and Della Torre had a growing family to care for. The vendetta would be pursued by younger relatives in the Friuli. But there is more to the story. Giovanni also had a family, for his injuries had not prevented him from fathering a child while in exile. An unformalized relationship with his first cousin, the widowed Maria Savorgnan (sister of the notorious Tristan), had resulted in the birth of a daughter, Elisabetta, in 1553. Now here we come to one of those complicated family entanglements that need sorting out. Maria's father Pagano and Giovanni's mother Lucina were brother and sister, born to the Maria Savorgnan with whom Pietro Bembo had been enamoured a half century earlier. Although the union between Giovanni and his cousin Maria was, as yet, unsanctioned by the church, it was not a question of a clandestine marriage, and the situation was not as scandalous as it might seem. As we have seen, births less than nine months after a formal wedding were common in that period. What counted was the contract, not the nuptial ceremony or blessing by a priest. The de facto marriage would have been considered valid with mutual consent and a formal contract, with the official celebration only awaiting a papal dispensation because of the first degree of consanguinity between the couple.[9]

Indeed, there was precedent for such an arrangement within the immediate family. As noted earlier, Giovanni himself had been born in 1518, well before the official wedding of his own parents, Francesco Savorgnan Del Torre and Lucina Savorgnan Del Monte, in 1522. But while each of these endogamous marriages over the two generations united the Del Torre and Del Monte branches of the

Savorgnan family, they served different ends. The earlier union had reinforced the internal cohesion of the Savorgnan clan. The second promoted family solidarity toward the outside. Giovanni's close ties with Maria's brother Tristan had already wreaked havoc upon the family; the marriage only reaffirmed a united front against adversaries like the Della Torre and the Colloredo.[10]

The union was a mixed blessing, for Tristan was not the only problematic member of Maria's family. Her father Pagano, who had died in 1539, had been adjudged insane.[11] Her brother Tristan, as we know, had been sentenced to permanent exile and brought about the destruction of the family palace in Udine for the incident on the Grand Canal in 1549. And more recently, in March 1554, her older brother Giacomo had engaged in a violent argument with their widowed mother, Chiara Priuli, in the family castle in Ariis. He wounded her and inadvertently murdered yet another brother, Scipione, who was trying to defend her. Giacomo was thereupon banished from the Patria in perpetuity.[12] Another legacy of blood and tears.

Following the favourable decree of the Council of Ten, Giovanni settled down to life in Venice with his wife and child, presumably not crossing paths with Girolamo Della Torre more often than necessary. Both parties had every reason to avoid attracting the attention of the Council of Ten.[13] For Giovanni, as we shall see, that would soon change.

Life and Death

Giulia's return to Venice was bittersweet. With three young children, the youngest only six months old, she was pregnant again by the end of the year. It was comforting to be back home with family and friends, but would another baby so soon be viewed as a burden or a blessing? We cannot hear from her directly, but let us read between the lines of Sansovino's biography. She was from all accounts of a naturally happy disposition, and thus well disposed to meet any challenge with an optimistic attitude. With a strong sense of duty, she knew that Girolamo's greatest wish was to ensure the continuance of the Della Torre line—a wish so strong that it had impelled him to leave the priesthood. Given the short intervals between her pregnancies to date, we can surmise that Giulia had employed wet nurses for all her children for precisely the same reason. Although not a reliable means of birth control, breast feeding tends to suppress fertility and allows greater spacing between children. The practice of using wet nurses was strongly criticized by many clergymen in this period, but the upper classes, however pious, clung to it tenaciously. The desire for an enduring bloodline overcame religious scruples. And, we may assume, the birth of yet another child would be met with elation as well as resignation (Figure 9.2).[14]

On a practical level, Giulia was also praised for her prudent household management and for her kindness to her servants, with whom she had strong bonds.

Figure 9.2. *Scodella* (Broth Bowl) on a High Foot, with a Birthing Chamber Scene, 1545–60 (Princeton University Art Museum).

The bowl was part of a set probably consisting of 5 to 7 pieces and included a cover and tray. It is unlikely that Giulia possessed such a set, but the scene would have been familiar to her. It reveals the confinement room as a social space, with a maidservant bringing broth to the new mother who sits up in a canopied bed. While the wet nurse attends to the newborn, the infant's older brother is playing in the corner.

She was thus not without help and companionship inside the home, the staff likely comprising at that point at least one wet nurse and several servants to help with household chores. Other than daily mass at Santa Sofia, Giulia would have spent most of her time inside the walls and courtyard of Ca' Morosini. Any visits back and forth to her mother or other friends would have been accomplished by gondola, since patrician women rarely walked through the streets outside their own parish. This would have been particularly true that spring, since cases of the plague began to appear in Venice in March 1555, the first such outbreak since 1528.[15]

By early August, another entry into the *Fedi battesimali* was in order. Girolamo writes:

> On Friday, 2 August 1555 at around 14 hours in Ca' Morosini in Venice, Marcella, my second daughter, fifth in order, was born to me. And on the 10th she was baptized by the reverend priest of Santa Sofia in the presence of 15 godfathers and godmothers. May God make her good.[16]

Fears of the plague were not severe enough to discourage a church baptism, and the Della Torre newborns were never lacking in godparents. Sadly, the baby's grandmother and namesake, Marcella, was not present, for she had died on 4 August, just two days after the birth. She had been ailing for at least five months, according to the civic death register—not from the plague, which would have been noted—and had perhaps willed herself to stay alive just long enough to support Giulia through the birth. Like her daughter, she was known for her piety. During her final months, she would have sought solace not only from her family, but also from the church. The mother of ten children herself and 'a matron of the highest virtue', Marcella was only fifty-nine years old.[17]

Marcella's testament, written in 1547 before Giulia's marriage, gives us a sense of what was important to her. In it, she had cited two churches close to home:

> I wish and allow that in our church of Santa Maria Nova there be said 500 masses for the dead with its sequence for my soul, and another 500 masses for the dead... be said in the church of the Madonna dei Miracoli here near our house; and I wish the 1000 masses to be completed within a month after my death.

Such a stipulation was common in testaments of this period, but there was a further slightly more generous request, which attests to the spiritual power of female monasteries: 'I also leave 5 ducats to the church and nuns of the Madonna dei Miracoli with the condition that there be said one time the *psalmista* and one time the office of the dead for my soul, as is said when one of these nuns dies.' Filled with ex-votos, the convent church had been built to house a painting of the Madonna credited with numerous miracles.[18]

Santa Maria Nova, once just across the campo from Ca' Bembo, was the parish church of the Bembo family. The church had collapsed to the ground in 1535 but must have been rebuilt by the time the will was written. Titian's altarpiece of *San Girolamo in Penitence*, datable to 1552, may already have been installed above the first altar on the left by the time of Marcella's death.[19] It might well have drawn the attention of Girolamo Della Torre. Not only did it depict his patron saint; it was also painted by 'the first man in Christendom', whom he had once recommended to the Bishop of Trent.[20] In fact, Titian himself lived close by in his *casa da statio* at Biri Grande near Rio dei Gesuiti at the northern edge of the city. His own parish of San Canciano, just a few steps away from Ca' Bembo, was contiguous to that of Santa Maria Nova. Marcella and her family would have frequented it while the latter was being rebuilt. Given that a patrician woman's public world was generally defined by her parish boundaries, is it possible that our Giulia was acquainted with Titian's daughter Lavinia? Although there is some uncertainty over Lavinia's birthdate, according to a long tradition she was born in August 1530, when her mother, Cecilia, died in childbirth.[21] If such is the case, Lavinia would have been just a year older than Giulia. Titian's sister, Orsa, raised her niece in the family home until her death in 1549, the year of Giulia's marriage.

Lavinia, then nineteen, was also of an age to run a household. Perhaps this new responsibility accounts for her relatively late marriage at the age of twenty-five in June 1555 to Cornelio Sarzinelli, a nobleman from the Veneto (more of this later).[22]

Marcella's testament also reveals the presence of two female servants, one a slave, in the Bembo home in 1547:

> I leave *la mia Moreta* (my Moorish girl), whom my son Lorenzo sent me, liberated and free... and thus I ask my magnificent consort to give her the manumission papers immediately after I die, and if by chance my consort would not be here, I ask my sons to do it; or whoever is here at my death.

She also leaves *la Moreta* 20 ducats and a furnished bed in case she wishes to leave the house and get married, and asks her to pray for her soul. The other servant, a free woman, was treated differently: 'To Mariza, whom my magnificent consort brought from Cattaro, I leave 16 ducats if she is in the house at my death, and if she remains wise and honourable; otherwise I leave her nothing.' Marcella looked upon both women as wards, as it were, for whom the extended Bembo family was responsible:

> And I recommend both *la Moreta* and Mariza to my magnificent consort and to my dear children, [and ask] that they take care of them and keep them in their house, for my soul, so that they do not go wandering through the world, and this I say if they will live honorably.[23]

Such stipulations were common in Venetian wills. As we shall see, Giulia would feel a similar sense of obligation toward her servants when she was contemplating her own death.[24]

The distinction that Marcella makes between the two servants is suggestive. She speaks of *la mia Moreta* or *la Moreta*, while omitting the pronoun from Mariza's name. Does *la mia* simply signify her ownership of *la Moreta* or is it a sign of affection? Perhaps both, but the latter seems more likely, given that her bequest to *la Moreta* is unconditional, while her lesser gift to Mariza depends on good behaviour. Domestic slavery was unfortunately a fact of life in Renaissance Venice. Most slaves were white, from the Black Sea area and the Balkans, but a small percentage were from sub-Saharan Africa, traded through Portuguese, Spanish, and North African ports. As a galley captain, Lorenzo would have acquired *la Moreta* on one of his voyages, perhaps in Alexandria. By the mid-seventeenth century, slavery would die out in Venice, with the descendants of the freed slaves absorbed into the general population.[25] The Barbary pirates would, however, continue to capture and enslave unfortunate Venetian subjects until the early nineteenth century.[26]

Marcella's assets consisted primarily of 2000 ducats (the two-thirds portion of her dowry that would legally revert to her if she were predeceased by Gian Matteo), plus 1400 ducats from her deceased sister Giulia's dowry. Marcella made two charitable bequests that recalled her brief role as countess of Zara a decade earlier: 'I also order and wish that ten ducats would be sent to Zara to be dispensed for my soul, of which I would like five to be dispensed to the poorest artisan of Zara; the other five ducats I wish to be sent and dispensed to the poorest islands that are under Zara.'[27]

The remainder of Marcella's bequests benefited her children.

> If Giulia is not married or in a convent before my death, I wish that she would have 500 ducats from all my assets, including my dowry, as well as [my inheritance] from my sister Madonna Giulia (her daughter's namesake) and whatever other assets should come to me, with this condition: that she marry one of our noble Venetian gentlemen or an honourable foreigner, with the consent of my magnificent consort and her brothers, and if she is married before my death, she will not receive anything [further].

Having indeed married 'an honourable foreigner' two years after the will was written, Giulia received nothing when her mother died, since her dowry was considered her share of the family patrimony. But Marcella did leave 100 ducats to her other daughter, Augusta, even though long married and wealthy, 'in sign of love'. Was the phrase only a convention or does it indicate less maternal affection for Giulia? The latter seems unlikely, but we will never know.

The remainder of Marcella's estate went to her six sons in equal portions, to be passed on to their male descendants in *fedecommesso*. 'But as [also] written by my magnificent consort in his testament, if my sons do not have heirs, I wish that Augusta and Giulia, my daughters, would have everything of mine. Declaring above all that if my sons would have bastards, they can never leave them anything of mine.'[28] Marcella's will was a textbook example of Venetian family economics, with daughters receiving their share of the patrimony in their dowries and sons inheriting almost everything else in equal portions.[29]

In sum, in the gendered geography of patrician Venice (as in Crete), Giulia's world was mostly delimited by the walls of Ca' Morosini, Ca' Bembo, and her parish church.[30] The men of the family, by contrast, moved freely in public spaces. Giulia's father Gian Matteo, the man of empire par excellence, was busily engaged in cultural and political affairs inside the city, as well as in the larger Venetian dominion. As to Giulia's husband Girolamo, although under a type of house arrest for the next five years, from his base in Venice he could again personally attend to business and family interests that extended to the Veneto and the Friuli, as well as to Rome.

A Perpetual Candidate

The management of Gian Matteo's career required constant diligence. Although noble, he was not wealthy and relied in part on his official postings to support his family. In that city of frequent elections, a public man was a perpetual candidate, always running for office. Indeed, many nobles in similar circumstances lived off a succession of minor assignments within Venice and in backwater towns throughout Venetian territories. Gian Matteo had already been elected to prestigious posts in Zara, Verona, Cyprus, and Crete, attesting to his ability to cultivate enough supporters to win elections.[31] And yet, such positions carried risks. The management of large sums of state money put him under close scrutiny. His expenditures were subject to audit by the camerlenghi di comun (custodians of public funds) before he could stand for election—*andar a cappello*—to other posts.[32]

On 30 January 1555, five months after Bembo's return to the city from Candia, the Council of Ten had voted against permitting him to *andar a capello* until a shortfall in his accounts was resolved. It seems that he had used some money left over by his predecessor, Giovanni Lando, for his construction projects. The Ten called for a six-month moratorium to allow for a response from Candia.[33] In the meantime, in March, the outgoing Duke of Candia, Alvise Gritti, would praise Bembo's accomplishments:

> The magnificent messer Zuan Matthio Bembo, who was capitano during my time, used much diligence in those building projects and delighted many; he completed four vaults of the Arsenale to allow the galleys to be put under cover, a work well regarded and useful; he also constructed a warehouse nearby in which to put oars and other things, very convenient to the Arsenal, [and] closed the city [wall] on the side of the Sabbionera conjoined with that bastion....[34]

But that glowing report did not address the problem of possibly misused funds.

By early July the moratorium was over. Marcella was gravely ill, and Bembo appealed to the Ten once again. He argues that Lando had left funds in the treasury of Candia,

> according to custom,...which monies were spent in the time of my reggimento as stated in the present letters of the Reggimento of Candia . . and [these had] been spent necessarily, because otherwise the vaults of the Arsenal would have remained unfinished and I would have left the city open in one part at Sabbionera.

He adds that such use of the funds was 'honest and has been done by others'. He again requests that he be granted the *bollettino* that would allow him to stand for office. His appeal is backed up by a favourable opinion of the Provveditori sopra monti (supervisors of state bond funds): 'We declare it with our oath to be a just thing that ser Gian Matteo has spent that sum of 450 ducats in the building projects of Candia as he narrates [and recommend] that . . . his *ballottini* can be made, as he requests.'[35]

Alas, to no avail. On 30 July the Ten voted twice, with Bembo's case losing ground between the two ballots. The first vote was sixteen in favour, seven against, and six undecided. After what must have been a contentious debate, the second ballot came in at twelve in favour, ten against, and seven undecided. The Ten could reach no agreement. Without achieving the requisite three-quarters of positive votes, the matter was left hanging.[36] How it was eventually resolved is unclear, but the mixed decision suggests that Gian Matteo had staunch enemies as well as friends among the Ten. He was known for a direct manner that had probably cost him a knighthood for his bravery at the siege of Cattaro fifteen years earlier. Fracastoro had written to Pietro Bembo at the time:

> . . . that nature of our [Gian Matteo] Bembo, that I have said to be a little too sincere, and a little too frank, without knowing how to dissimulate, or to make like a fox, is now damaging to him, . . . it can perhaps be interpreted by some as prideful, so he should always strive to make himself better regarded in the eyes, ears and minds of others, and to make himself be recognized and be loved as a nature truly sweet and amiable in every way.[37]

Gian Matteo must have worked on his public persona, given that he had been elected to prestigious posts in the meantime. But it seems that not all were persuaded, and he now had fences to mend.

The Majordomo

During this period Girolamo continued to run the family's business interests by proxy, now using Venice as his base. He no longer needed procurators in the city but retained an agent in Crete to continue collecting the rents for the country properties of Cardinal Ranuccio Farnese. As with the pension of Giovanni da Udine in Rome, the funds were transmitted to Girolamo in Venice to be sent on to Farnese's agent in Italy. Records in the family archives indicate that these transactions would continue until Farnese's death in 1565.[38]

Girolamo could now respond more quickly to concerns of his procurators and factors in the Friuli regarding property owned there by the family. And he was closer to Rome. Pope Julius III, his benefactor of the year before, died on 29 March 1555. Pope Marcellus II was swiftly elected on 10 April but lived for just three weeks. Another conclave on 23 May elected Giovanni Gian Pietro Carafa as Pope Paul IV.[39] The fanatical head of the inquisition when cardinal, he was a hardliner who had little tolerance for Renaissance arts and letters.[40] After the sack of Rome in 1527, he had fled to Venice where he helped to establish the Theatine order at San Nicolò dei Tolentini with a programme of preaching and propaganda against heretics. Moving back to Rome in 1536, Carafa would criticize Paul III's elevation of Pietro Bembo to the cardinalate in 1539 with the dismissive comment: 'Holy Father, the College of Cardinals has no need of men who know how to write sonnets.'[41]

In Carafa's view, what the church did need was a different type of reform, with a return to the strict orthodoxy of earlier times. His election to the papacy, at first opposed and then supported by the Farnese faction, was bad news for Jews, Protestants, readers of heretical books, and lovers of Renaissance art, but good news for Girolamo's brother Michele. Carafa may have encountered the young Michele in Venice, as well as at the court of Paul III. The Neapolitan pope immediately appointed him as his majordomo, perhaps with Farnese support. Prospects for the Della Torre family seemed bright.

Michele had been serving as Pope Julius III's vice-legate in Perugia for the past two years. Still no closer to his episcopal seat in Ceneda, he would now be back at the centre of papal power.[42] And not only at the center, but at the top of a sprawling and complicated papal bureaucracy. Michele was in Rome by the beginning of June. As chief prelate of the pope's household, he oversaw the administration of, and regulated access to, the Apostolic Palace. He also helped form a new papal *famiglia* upon the succession of the new pope. This consisted of no fewer than 734 members, from blood relatives of Paul IV to chancery officials, chamberlains, and ambassadors, on down to gardeners and stablemasters. On 10 July 1555 Michele presented the pope with the *Ruolo*, listing the new papal family. At the top of the hierarchy was Michele himself as maestro di casa, another term for majordomo. He was a conspicuous figure at court. Not only was he allowed to wear distinctive dress and reside in the papal palace, but he was also one of *four prelati di fiocchetto* who had the right to ornament their horses with violet and peacock-coloured feathers.[43]

Although Carafa had led a notably ascetic life as a cardinal, according to Theatine principles, he was fully aware of the political demands of his new office. When Michele had asked him how he wished the external appearance of his court and person to be presented, the pope responded 'magnificently, as is suitable for princes'.[44] Balancing austerity with magnificence was the challenge, for Carafa's rule was a study in contrasts. While begging was strictly forbidden, church services were celebrated with increasing pomp and circumstance. Carafa railed against nepotism, but appointed members of his own family to high positions in the church.

On the personal side, Carafa was notoriously exacting, with a mercurial disposition. As Pastor observed:

> The very arrangement of the day betrayed his hot-blooded temperament. He did not like to be disturbed in the morning, as he wished to say mass and recite his office slowly and with great devotion. He would not be tied down to any fixed hours for his meals, though he wished his table to be served very generously, in accordance with his high position.[45]

The Venetian ambassador Bernardo Navagero observed: 'In dealing with him, as much patience as adroitness is necessary.'[46] Indeed, Michele's appointment was a mixed blessing that must have taxed the graciousness and tact which had endeared him to the French court when he served there as envoy of Paul III. As a Farnese protégé, he had learned the art of 'knowing how to dissimulate, or to make like a fox'—those qualities that had not come easily to his brother-in-law Gian Matteo Bembo.

Navagero described stormy tirades that summed up Paul IV's agenda: 'He never spoke of his Serene Majesty [Philip II] nor of the Spanish nation, without calling them heretics, schismatics, and accursed of God, seed of Jews and Moors, scum of the earth.' The new Pope would eventually launch a disastrous—and unsuccessful—crusade against Philip II, and he wasted no time in moving against the Jews. One of his first acts was the bull, 'Cum nimis absurdum', promulgated on 15 July 1555, that created the Roman ghetto. Carafa also strengthened the Roman Inquisition and used it to control (and intimidate) prelates that he claimed were sympathetic to protestants and, thus, heretical.[47]

Michele was later quoted as saying that he found life stressful at the courts, since the 'uomo civile' lived in continuous servitude to his own ambitions, not knowing that true happiness lies in leading a virtuous life.[48] Indeed, Filippo Archinto, the papal nuncio in Venice, would write a chatty letter to Cardinal Carlo Carafa, a papal nipote, in 1556 suggesting that Michele had been reluctant to accept the majordomo appointment, but it was an honour that he could not refuse. Michele stepped down from his appointment in 1557, undoubtedly with relief, and was back in his diocese in Ceneda by Spring 1559.[49]

Famine and Feasting

Michele might well have been content to have remained in Ceneda during these years, for Udine, where the family still had a palace, continued to face challenges. Domenico Bollani, the incoming luogotenente in May 1555, had inherited a city, and indeed a province, that required a firm hand to pacify the various factions: the ever-feuding castellans; a rising citizen class; a restive popolo—artisans, labourers, and small shopkeepers; an overtaxed peasantry. Licences to carry arms were still requested with tedious regularity as each generation of a family came of age. Beyond that, he also had to ensure that people in the capital city of Udine had enough to eat. Such was the case that year when the harvest was poor. Bollani took extraordinary steps to keep the Fondaco, or communal granary, supplied with enough capital to keep the prices stable and filled with enough grain to distribute to the poor if necessary. When a Venetian merchant unjustly accused him in August of deliberately delaying the mandated grain exports to Venice, Bollani wrote: 'I have never felt unhappier in my entire life.'[50]

But even as the famine continued, Bollani was required to fulfil the ceremonial duties of his office. By the end of 1555, elaborate preparations were underway for the passage of Bona Sforza, Queen of Poland, through the Friuli the following spring. Daughter of Gian Galeazzo Sforza, Duke of Milan, and mother of Sigismond II, the reigning king of Poland, the sixty-two-year-old Bona would depart her son's kingdom with a large entourage on 4 February 1556 to travel to her dukedom at Bari. After a stopover in Padua to visit the thermal baths nearby, and a short stay in Venice, she wished to sail to Apulia on a Venetian galley. The Senate agreed and rose to the challenge by orchestrating a grand ceremonial progress through the Venetian Terraferma.[51]

The journey was not without its challenges. Padua was just recovering from a severe epidemic of the plague, which had spread to the city from Venice in early 1555, as though 'made by ants carrying food', as one writer put it. It had reached the 'monstrous proportions of a wild animal' in Padua by June 1555, with people fleeing the city for the countryside. By September, the empty streets were prowled by dogs, cats, and chickens, and crime was rampant. Providentially, the plague would die out in Padua by the end of the year. Even though cases were still appearing in Venice itself, the disease seemed to be contained by strict quarantine measures.[52]

It was time to celebrate, and the queen's visit would be a welcome respite to famine and pestilence. One of the signal events of the decade, it was recounted in fulsome detail in two published pamphlets.[53] The cortege would follow an age-old route over the Alps from Germany, entering Venetian territory at Gemona and travelling south through Spilimbergo, Pordenone, and Treviso to Padua (see Figure 2.1 above). The Venetian Senate ordered Bollani and the Venetian rettori of towns along the way to greet the queen appropriately as she passed through their jurisdictions. The logistics were daunting. Courtly welcomes, with impressive numbers of nobles and soldiers, had to be planned. Princely accommodations had to be secured. Goats, calves, lambs, capons and hens had to be ordered for meals. Local residents had to provide horses and men. Roads had to be repaired for the Queen's 'carriages, carts and horses.' A special bridge had to be built for

Figure 9.3. Polish or German artist, *Bona Sforza as a widow*, 17th century (The Royal Castle in Warsaw – Museum)

comfortable passage over the Tagliamento River 'not unlike that over which the emperor Charles V had passed' in 1533.[54]

All was in order by 20 March when Bona arrived in Venzone, just north of Gemona, and spent the night in the palace of the noble Mantica family. The queen had been on the road over six weeks. She was described as 'not very tall, and more fat than lean; she looks jovial and cheerful, and is very prudent; she has many languages; she speaks very good Italian, and Latin even better, and does not go searching for words nor express her ideas verbosely; rather she uses the correct words for everything that she wishes to say, which is a most noble thing and worthy of admiration by literati' (Figure 9.3).[55]

Bona's entourage consisted of '400 persons, both men and women, and among them eight damsels from Poland of extraordinary beauty, and two older ones from Italy.' The queen 'traveled in a *seggietta* (sedan chair) covered with black velvet and lined with *pavonazzo* (purple) velvet decorated with crystals. There were [also] diverse barons of that kingdom, superbly dressed, with linings of ermine and other precious furs.' The carriages and carts numbered eighty or more, each drawn by six or eight horses in pairs '*alla Tedesca*', being similar to a galley in length, and 'covered with black cloth so that nothing inside could be seen.'[56]

The royal company made overnight stops at the Savorgnan castle at Osoppo and the house of the noble Portinari family in San Daniele, with a courtly reception in Spilimbergo and formal greetings along the way by the Venetian governors of Sacile and Conegliano before arriving in Treviso on 25 March. There the queen was met outside the gates by Giovanni Cappello, Venetian cavaliere and savio di Terraferma, 'sent by the Senate to receive her majesty with much pomp, with a most honourable company of light cavalry and men of arms and an infinite number of gentlemen of Treviso and Venice'. She was then escorted to Palazzo Brazza (the city residence of a Della Torre relative) to spend the night.[57]

The royal entry to Padua unfolded the next day. Departing Treviso in the morning, the entourage reached Porta Portello, the northern gateway in the city walls, where they were met by 'Venetian Gentlemen and Gentleladies who had come to see Her Majesty in a great number, adorned with jewels and gold'.[58] Our anonymous informant continues: 'Nor do I neglect to tell you that when her Majesty entered at the Portello…so many cannonades of very large pieces of artillery were fired from that stretch of wall between the Portello and the portcullis of Porcia, that it seemed that Padua would be destroyed.' Then came the Queen in her litter,

> carried by two beautiful mules, with black velvet trappings of great price…her Majesty, dressed in black widow's weeds, her head swathed with the purest white veil of bombazine, like those worn by our nuns of Venice, saluted everyone most benignly. And in truth, people truly saw in that royal aspect a certain prerogative that invited them absolutely to revere her.[59]

After entering the city, the royal cortege passed under a triumphal arch erected at the bridge of Santa Sofia. Constructed of wood on the model of the ancient Arco dei Gavi in Verona, it had been designed by Michele Sanmicheli, diverting his attention from fortifications in the Stato da Mar. The arch was elaborately decorated with laudatory inscriptions and allegorical figures honouring Poland, the Queen, the Sforza family, the house of Aragon, the city of Padua, and the Venetian republic. Having dismounted to the sound of fusillades from the arquebusiers, the queen and her court were comfortably lodged in Ca' Cornaro (now destroyed) next to Falconetto's Loggia and Odeo.[60]

With the Easter season approaching, the Collegio prepared a suitable gift and ordered the Venetian rettori to present it to the queen the next morning, 'with the appropriate formulation of words'. The consignment included 40 barrels of Malvasia moscatella; 1000 pounds of torches and candles of white wax; 200 fine sugared breads in two chests; a wealth of spices; 12 fresh sturgeons; salted fish roe from Constantinople; 12 large pieces of Piacentine cheese; and 1000 pounds of Salami, 'that is, prosciutto, tongue, salcizzoni, sopressada'.[61] In sum, enough fixings for several royal banquets. No famine here. As it happens, Bona stayed in Padua for only a month, during which time she visited the baths at Abano, before proceeding on to Venice.

Pestilence and Prejudice

While the Paduans were celebrating the queen, Domenico Bollani was facing another challenge. The plague had left Padua, but now it was Udine's turn. The first documented victim in the city was a Jewish woman who fell ill on 14 March 1556, just a week before Bona entered the territory. Bollani may not even have been aware of the danger until 8 April, by which time six had died (and the queen was safely in Padua). The infection was widely attributed to contact with some bedding brought into the city by the unfortunate woman's husband, Gioseffo da Muggia, a secondhand dealer. Bollani and the city council ordered the contents of his house and two others occupied by his relatives to be burned.[62] Emilio Candido, an Udinese citizen involved in the preventative measures, enumerated

> tapestries, velvets, damasks, silks, infinite garments of every sort, bedding, coverlets, cloaks; today we burned 26 carts of goods, without a doubt worth 2000 ducats and more…and note that closed strongboxes which we did not want to open, were [also] burned, full of women's dresses, beautiful clothing and silver items among other things, which had been pawned.

All went up in flames. The surviving inhabitants of the houses were moved to the Lazzaretto at San Gottardo outside the walls, while the other Jews in the city were sequestered and forbidden from selling their goods.[63]

Over the past century calls for the expulsion of the Jews from the city, typically for religious reasons, had been rejected on several occasions, most recently in 1524. Indeed, as moneylenders and second-hand dealers, Jews were essential to the economy, particularly for the poor, but also for the rich. These included Girolamo Della Torre, whose *Memoria* of 1549 had listed a debt to a moneylender in the Venetian Ghetto.[64] At the same time, Jews were increasingly the victims of anti-heretical zeal during the Counter-Reformation. They were convenient scapegoats when things went wrong: famine, pestilence, droughts, floods, and the like.[65]

To make matters worse, despite the poor harvest of the previous year, grain shipments from Germany had been halted because of the plague. Bollani reported to the Venetian authorities on 24 April that these combined problems 'had put this most faithful people in the greatest fear that they would be lacking in means of sustenance'. Lamenting that he had to deal 'with civil discord, with hunger and with the plague', he hoped that in the present 'travagliosissimo stato' (most travailed situation) the Venetian authorities would not make him order grain to be shipped out of the city to Venice as had been the case in the past.[66]

Hunger and plague were a combustible combination. On 29 April the city council elected three orators to travel to Venice and request the expulsion of all the Jews from the city. One of the emissaries was Giulio Sbroiavacca, Girolamo Della Torre's nephew-in-law. The Venetian Senate agreed but allowed the leaders of the Jewish community in Udine to have a voice in the terms of their own removal. They were given six months to settle their affairs before leaving and allowed to move to 'an outside place of their choice, chosen by the luogotenente'.[67]

The expulsion of the Jews was finalized by the council on 9 June. The decision included Bollani's plan to reform the Monte di Pietà by transforming it from a charity into a communal savings bank that would replace the Jewish system of lending to the poor. At Bollani's request, none other than the Bishop of Ceneda—that is, Michele Della Torre—interceded with the pope, whose permission was required to approve of the reform, 'as in all the other cities where the Jews were wisely expelled'.[68] The council gave thanks that the plague was nearly over. Too soon. It recurred with a vengeance in July, and 827 deaths would be recorded by the time it had quieted down by the end of the year.[69]

Splendid Orations

The year 1556 had also begun in an unpromising way for Gian Matteo Bembo. At the end of January, his son Alvise was nominated for provveditore of the Arsenal by his brother-in-law, Giovanni Pasqualigo, but he received the least number of votes of the four candidates.[70] But then in April Bona Sforza arrived in the city. Her entry was the most important social event of the year and arguably the most notable event of the reign of Doge Francesco Venier. Our anonymous chronicler recorded it in loving detail. At dawn on Sunday 26 April, one hundred Venetian gentlemen 'all dressed *alla ducale* in crimson damask departed in their gondolas covered with the finest tapestries woven with much silk and gold' to meet the queen at Lizza Fusina, the port at the mouth of the Brenta on the edge of the lagoon. The queen, conveyed down the Brenta in the *burchiello* (barge) of the Cavaliere Matteo Dandolo, was accompanied by the Cardinals of Ferrara [Ippolito II d'Este] and Augsburg (Otto Truchsess von Waldburg, a Della Torre friend) and the emperor's ambassador, Don Ferrante Gonzaga, and his wife. Arriving at the port at 8pm, the royal party was greeted with 'a beautiful and splendid Latin oration' by Giovanni Dandolo.[71] But that was only the beginning.

The burchiello was then escorted by the assembled Venetian gondolas and barges to the Isoletta of San Giorgio d'Alga, the Franciscan monastery in the middle of the lagoon, for a second 'beautiful oration'. After mass, the queen and her party boarded 'ducal barges covered with the finest scarlet' and sailed on to the Benedictine convent of S. Biagio on the western end of the Giudecca. Waiting on the embankment was the Signoria with the vice-doge Francesco Foscari standing in for Doge Francesco Venier, who was, as usual, ill.[72]

Amidst 'an infinite clamor of artillery from the galleys and *fuste*', the queen's entourage boarded the Bucintoro. Again, the order was precisely choreographed.

First, came the most beautiful noblewomen in the city, 'three by three, dressed all in white satin, with infinite jewels of the greatest price, and pearls, their heads adorned, and with much gold'. They were followed by the queen's ladies in waiting, numbering twenty-four; then the secretaries of the Senate, dressed in purple togas, together with the secretaries of her Majesty and her court. This group formed the advance guard for the queen. Flanked by the two cardinals, she then boarded the vessel together with the vice-doge and the papal nuncio. They were followed by 'an endless number of noblemen and nobleladies'; then came the ambassadors of the emperor, the king of Spain, and the king and queen of England, and other princes and lords. Then came the principal officials of the Venetian Signoria, followed by foreign lords. Finally came

> the remaining members of the Signoria, two by two, with the most beautiful order and great majesty, behind which followed all those lords dressed in crimson who had gone that day to receive her majesty, some at Lizza Fusina... others at San Giorgio, the youngest always in the rear, that they made in truth a very beautiful and honourable spectacle.[73]

The Giudecca canal was so full of gondolas, barges, galleys, fuste, and brigantines that one could walk from one side to the other 'without any danger of falling in the water'. The Bucintoro joined 'an almost infinite armada... with five galleys carrying all sorts of musicians playing songs of peace and war' as it moved along the Giudecca canal and rounded the Punto della Dogana to enter the Grand Canal. On board the Bucintoro during this sojourn, the queen was honoured with yet another Latin oration, delivered in a quavering voice by Cassandra Fedele, upon order of the Senate. Having mastered Latin and Greek by age twelve, at the age of twenty-six, in 1491, Cassandra had been proclaimed the 'ornament of Italy' by Angelo Poliziano. She would finally marry in 1499, but had no children. After her husband died in 1520, she was reduced to living in destitution until 1537, when Pope Paul III persuaded the Venetian Senate to appoint her as prioress of the orphanage attached to the church of San Domenico di Castello. Now ninety-one years old, she had been living in obscurity, but became once again—for a moment in time—the famed Virgo Veneta. The Queen was so delighted with the oration that she 'took a gold necklace from the neck of one of her damsels and placed it on that of our Cassandra'. The aging humanist would die two years later.[74]

We are reminded of Giulia's mother Marcella, another learned maiden who had mastered Latin and Greek as a young girl. Although her uncle Pietro Bembo was proud of her scholarly abilities, he had encouraged her to follow the alternate path of marriage and motherhood. It is perhaps not surprising that Marcella chose the same future for Giulia, given the difficulties faced by the talented Cassandra.

The anonymous chronicler continued:

> The palaces on each side had beautiful carpets and tapestries at all the windows and were filled with such a number of gentlemen and gentleladies of every sort, such that it brought pleasure and infinite marvel to all onlookers...Every house, there not being enough windows for all the spectators, had loaded the rooftops in another way: I leave out the innumerable balconies and platforms that would have even a little view of the canal, to the end that on that day you could really say that you had seen the greatness and magnificence of this City entirely.[75]

The marine spectacle played out directly in front of Ca' Morosini at Santa Sofia, where the Della Torre family was living. Whether participant or spectator, each member had a defined role to play. Gian Matteo Bembo, as a member of the Venetian Senate with a reputation to uphold, must have been on board one of the boats. Whether Girolamo was among the foreign lords who had gone to greet the queen is an open question. Giulia was again pregnant, now with her fourth child. She was almost certainly not one of the gentleladies on board the Bucintoro, but she could well have been with her children at one of the windows of the palace.

The Bucintoro delivered the queen to the Palace of the Duke of Ferrara, guest residence of the republic, at 23:00 hours. She 'dismounted to the sound of many pipers, trumpets, and drums that sounded through all that contrada, and...of artillery fire, part from the galleys and part from the piazzas of the nearby churches'. Each of the eight days that Bona stayed in Venice was filled with religious observances, banquets, and festivities.[76]

Finally, on Sunday 3 May, the queen informed the Signoria that she would appear in the Palazzo Ducale the next day to take her leave. Laborious preparations had been underway for her passage to Bari since she had arrived in Padua. The Collegio ordered that the Venetian fleet that would accompany the queen to Bari would be composed of five galleys under the command of the capitano del Golfo. They would carry 280 passengers: 60 persons 'of respect' and 220 'servants and others'.[77]

Although gravely ill, Doge Francesco Venier took part in the solemn departure. On Monday morning he was carried in a litter to the foot of the Ponte della Paglia to greet the queen, who had been escorted from her residence by a contingent of senators. Together they entered the Palazzo Ducale, where in the Sala del Collegio 'her Majesty thanked all these lords for the demonstrations made to her'. Escorted back to the molo of San Marco by the doge, the queen boarded the galley of the capitano del Golfo. Followed by the other four galleys which the remainder of the entourage had already boarded, the ship crossed the basin, passed the island of Sant'Elena, and stopped at San Nicolò at the extreme north end of the Lido. The queen descended and spent the day in the fortress of San

Nicolò as the guest of the Council of Ten. Finally, at three hours in the evening, the queen departed for Bari, her dukedom in Puglia.[78]

No Hour without Its Mark

Venier's health only worsened after Bona's departure. The doge died on 2 June at the age of sixty-seven. It was a sad conclusion to a festive spring. But Gian Matteo's old associate in the Academia degli Uniti had a mixed reputation and not everyone mourned. On the positive side, Venier was characterized by a chronicler as a man 'of great intellect, cultivated, learned, of subtle ingenuity, and endowed with every wisdom'. His motto was *audaces iuvat*—'[fortune] favours the bold'. Although known for his piety and austere lifestyle, he was aware, like Paul IV, that the splendour of the ruler represented the magnificence of the state. When the Signoria decided to enhance the ducal ceremonial corno at the beginning of his dogate, Venier chose a model embellished with 290,000 ducats of jewels, three times the value of its predecessor. Likewise, he had commissioned a sumptuous ducal tomb in San Salvador before his death. But Venice, like Udine, had been cursed with shortages of grain during his dogate, and Venier had not endeared himself to the common people when he proclaimed that it was not a true famine as long as the wives of merchants still wore their marriage rings on their fingers. This from a man who had embellished the ducal corno to a level of imperial opulence.[79]

But a new doge would bring a new day, and the elaborate Venetian election system kicked into gear. Just two weeks later, on 14 June, Lorenzo Priuli was elected doge from a field of twenty-two aspirants on the twenty-sixth scrutiny. Gian Matteo was one of his forty-one electors. Priuli promised to be an active doge, unencumbered by the poor health of his predecessor. He too had served as rettore of principal cities of the Venetian state and as an ambassador, and had been knighted by Charles V. His impresa was a sun at its zenith with the motto *nulla hora sine linea*—'no hour without its mark'.[80]

It was not long before Giulia could again make her own mark. Less than a year after the birth of Marcella, Girolamo could add yet another name to the ever-growing *Fedi Battesimali*: 'On Monday 20 July 1556 at around 14 hours in Ca' Morosini in Venice, Giovanni, my fourth son, sixth in order, was born to me, and he was baptized on the 24th at home since he did not feel well.'[81] Although the notation lacked Girolamo's customary appeal for God's benevolence, little Giovanni's birth was preceded by an extraordinary incident similar to that which had occurred before the birth of his daughter Taddea in Candia. Sansovino later attests: 'and he was also heard to speak in a loud voice from inside his mother's body a few days before his birth, which rendered those present shocked and confused by the novelty of the event.'[82] The child was named after Girolamo's brother Giovanni, 'a valiant warrior, who was nurtured and brought up under the most happy military discipline of the illustrious and famous Francesco Maria, Duke of Urbino.'[83] Sansovino does not mention that the first Giovanni had died three decades earlier, at the age of twenty-one, from a fever and not from valorous action in battle.[84] The baptism might have been held in the palace through an abundance of caution, for the plague was now a serious problem in Venice as well as in Udine.

Of Universal Benefit to Everyone

On 6 July 1556 the Council of Ten again issued desperate edicts to prevent the spread of the plague in the city.[85] Most physicians thought the disease was caused by putrefied matter. Some argued that it was spread through miasma or corrupt air; accordingly, bonfires were, futilely, burned throughout the city. Others insisted that it was communicated through direct contact with afflicted persons or contaminated goods. No one thought of fleas. The Magistrato alla Sanità (magistracy of public health) had swung into action the year before with a three-pronged approach. Following the putrefaction theory, it had cleaned up stagnant wells and garbage in the streets. The measure, while laudable, was probably of little use. But the other two initiatives were more helpful. The first sought to prevent infection from entering the city; ships arriving from infected ports, or with afflicted passengers on board, were quarantined, thus limiting the opportunities for contagion. The second was intended to limit its spread inside the city. Doctors were required to report all suspicious deaths or sicknesses and citizens alerted to do the same. If a case of the plague was discovered in a dwelling, it was immediately evacuated and fumigated. Its inhabitants, if not yet infected, were sent to barges moored at the Lazzaretto Nuovo for observation, or, if already ill, to barges at the Lazzaretto Vecchio—hospital islands in the lagoon. Close neighbours and other contacts were examined as well. The quarantines lasted between twenty-two and forty days. The scrivener of the Sanità pronounced the protocol 'un ordine Santo' (a holy mandate) and claimed that 99 per cent of the families so evacuated survived in perfect health. And yet such measures were only partially effective, and they had not prevented the spread to Padua in 1555, and later on to Udine.[86]

With adversity came opportunity, and Giovanni Savorgnan grasped it. Like his old enemy, Girolamo Della Torre, he was still in Venice serving out the remainder of his sentence of exile. Also like Della Torre, his family was growing. A son had been born in the city the previous July and his wife Maria was pregnant again.[87] But he was concerned about Maria's brother, Giacomo, who had been banished from the Friuli and Venetian territories for wounding his mother and killing his brother. Giovanni thus noted with interest the Council of Ten's edict of 6 July. It proclaimed that those who denounced anyone who was receiving or disseminating or selling clothing and other goods from a 'casa amorbata' (infected house) could free a *bandito* from a sentence of banishment.[88]

On 29 July, Giovanni appeared in the offices of the Provveditori alla Sanità with a denunciation:

> It being my intention to benefit this most singular city, and also to devote my own life to its conservation, I have not wished to be remiss on those occasions presented [to act] for the common good. Therefore, suspecting by some signs seen by me that a woman placed by the office of the Sanità in governance of an infected house gave suspected goods to her husband during the night, with obvious danger to the city, I, Giovanni Savorgnan, ordered my men to set a watch on them for many nights. Having discovered their transgression, I personally denounced this husband and this wife to the above office.

The man in question was a certain Fantin Galinetta, a *barcarolo* at the traghetto of Riva San Biasio. His wife Menega had been given custody of an eight-year-old girl who was orphaned after her parents had died of the plague. The charge was serious, and the agents of the Sanità moved fast. When they attempted to apprehend the boatman, he threw himself in the water. After he was captured, they searched his barge and found two men's cloth *zoccoli* (house slippers), inside of which was sewn a quantity of gold and silver coins. Faced with the evidence, Fantin and his wife confessed to have stolen the property from the infected house. The judgment was harsh. The couple were condemned to death, with Savorgnan's report deemed to be of 'universal benefit to everyone'. But that was not the end of the matter.[89]

On 17 August, the five Sopraprovveditori della Sanità (superintendents of the health magistracy) endorsed Giovanni's request to free one *bandito*—namely, his brother-in-law Giacomo—considering 'the great benefit and utility that he had brought to the city'. With twenty-eight of the Council of Ten voting, the proposal received twenty favourable votes, but did not reach the required four-fifths threshold of twenty-three. Giovanni renewed his request on 19 October, this time making a careful legal argument. He observes that the edict of 6 July had declared that such a denunciation could free one person who had been banished for homicide, and if the denounced person were an agent of the office of the Sanità, as was the unlucky Menega, then—as he understood it—two additional *banditi* could be freed. But in this case, he argues, he asks only for the pardon of a single *bandito*, and one who was banned not for homicide but only for assault. He then adds a clinching argument: 'I promise and obligate myself to give 1000 lire from my own resources to the three children of the condemned; since they are deprived of their father and mother by my own action and for public benefit; and being of a tender age and not able to sustain themselves, they can be raised with my help.' Alas, the Council was still not convinced, and the vote remained the same.[90] But the case was reconsidered on 20 November, undoubtedly after considerable lobbying. With two of the Council absent, Savorgnan picked up one more positive vote and reached the four-fifths threshold with a vote of twenty-one in favour, two against and three undecided. Four days later the Council finally freed Giacomo Savorgnan from his ban, with the proviso that Giovanni would pay the 1000 *lire piccoli* (ca. 161 ducats) for the maintenance of the children. But there was one more hurdle. Chiara Priuli, as the injured party, was required to execute a *carta della pace*—an act of absolution—forgiving her son. She did this on 8 December in front of a notary and the luogotenente in Udine; Giacomo was finally freed from his banishment on 14 December. Presumably he moved back into the family castle at Arris and, chastened, made peace with his mother.[91]

A Patrician of Age and Honour

As to Gian Matteo, with his *bollettino* finally restored, he had been elected on 4 October as one of three governatori delle entrate, a powerful post with a sixteen-month term and regular meetings at Rialto.[92] He was again in a position of authority. Marin Sanudo had written that these magistrates were 'patricians of age and honour' and 'esteemed in the city'. Responsible for the oversight of the state financial system, they had a wide range of fiscal responsibilities with voting rights in the Senate; were responsible for auditing and controlling state revenues; oversaw the collection of taxes and expenditures in Venice, as well as in its maritime and Terraferma territories; took action against public debtors and smugglers; denounced crimes to the Avogadori; and oversaw auctions of contraband.[93] It must have been of some comfort to Bembo, who had had to suffer the indignity of an audit of his expenses on Crete, that he was now part of a body that oversaw the finances of state. In sum, he had prevailed in the end with his honour intact.

It was during these years that the façade of Ca' Bembo received a handsome new feature: a classical tabernacle containing a statue of Chronos or Saturn in the form of a wild man holding a solar disc. Beneath it was an explanatory Latin inscription celebrating Gian Matteo's exploits abroad: 'As long as this [sun] rotates, the cities of Zara, Cattaro, Capodistria, Verona, Salamis (Famagusta), and Candia will give testimony to his deeds. P[aolo] G[iovio]. S[ebastian] M[unster].' The cities are those in which Zuan Matteo had served as podestà or capitano of the Venetian republic. The authors were those who had praised Gian Matteo in their writings. In all likelihood, he had composed the assemblage as a personal impresa that spoke to posterity, possibly with a collateral function as totem to protect the house and its inhabitants.[94]

A New Dogaressa

By September 1557, the plague had finally died down, the granaries were replenished, and Pope Paul IV and Philip II of Spain signed a peace treaty, negotiated in part by the Venetian government. The city was ready for another celebration: the first ceremonial entry and coronation of a dogaressa in a century. The formal coronation of Zilia Dandolo, wife of Doge Lorenzo Priuli, had been postponed for a year because of the plague and famine. The triumphal entry of Bona Sforza the previous year provided the script. It is no coincidence that Zilia's family had been deeply involved in those festivities. Her brother Matteo Dandolo had conveyed the queen in his burchiello down the Brenta all the way to the Giudecca. Her husband Lorenzo Priuli—now doge—was one of the ducal councillors who had greeted the queen at San Biagio, and Zilia herself would have been among the two hundred gentleladies who accompanied her on the Bucintoro. Now the city had the opportunity to celebrate Venice's version of a queen. And yet, unlike the welcome given the Queen of Poland, it had a populist character that was distinctly Venetian, with citizens, artisans, and the guilds playing an official role along with the patriciate. Foreign lords were pushed to the periphery.[95]

The festivities began on 19 September, with the Bucintoro docking at a floating platform in front of the palace of Lorenzo's brother, Girolamo Priuli, at San Barnaba, across from Ca' del Duca. Zilia had moved there temporarily to allow for a proper ceremonial itinerary on the Grand Canal. The improvised dock was described as 'a most pompous apparatus of tapestries of gold and silk of extreme beauty'.[96] Resplendent in a golden mantle, Zilia was greeted by a delegation of ducal councillors and senators and escorted onto the boat. She was seated on the ducal *sedia* (throne) and surrounded by 250 of the most beautiful ladies in the city, both noble and cittadino, dressed in satins or white damask. With sumptuary laws suspended, they wore pearls and gold necklaces, with jewels and yet more pearls woven into their hair. The canal was filled with boats of all types, with spectators along the sides in every window and campo, and on every rooftop, but the aquatic spectacle was different from that which honoured Bona Sforza. For Zilia, it featured a parade of festively decorated brigantines, small warships manned by the twenty principal guilds of the city, each flying the guild banner. Most carried fifers and drummers, filling the air with music, and each fired a salute as it passed the Bucintoro.

As each brigantine arrived at the Piazzetta, the guildsmen disembarked and passed under a temporary triumphal arch built by the butchers' guild near the Beccaria and the Zecca at the corner of Sansovino's Biblioteca Marciana. This contingent of guildsmen made up the first segment of a procession that led around Piazza San Marco under white cloth canopies like those used on the feast day of Corpus Christi. The Bucintoro was the last boat to dock. All the ladies, excepting Zilia, disembarked. Following the guilds, they walked under the arch and formed the second segment of the procession. Even among the ladies, hierarchy prevailed. Escorted by twenty-five young patricians, dressed in black togas, 235 younger women marched first, most dressed in white. Then came twenty-five wives of senior officials, all dressed in black, and finally the only wife of a procurator, wearing long sleeves *alla ducale*.

The third segment of the parade was based upon the ducal procession: first came the ducal officials, then the secretaries, then the pages, and then the grand chancellor. They were followed by the families of the doge and dogaressa and finally Zilia herself, accompanied by a page, between the two oldest ducal councillors. Behind her were her brother Matteo, clad in a golden mantle; her brother-in-law Girolamo Priuli, in deep purple like the other procurators; and finally the most prominent patricians and senators in crimson togas. The windows and arcades around the perimeter of the piazza were packed with onlookers, with foreign ambassadors sitting in the Loggetta, which served as a reviewing stand.[97]

After her coronation in the basilica, the dogaressa ascended the stairs to the loggia on the piano nobile of the Palazzo Ducale. There, each guild had a table covered with delicacies, and some displayed objects that they had produced: goldwork, silver, precious fabrics—an exuberant expression of the abundance of the republic. The balustrades were draped with carpets and festooned with garlands with the Priuli arms, presenting a courtly display to the spectators below. After passing through the loggias and greeting the officers of each guild in turn, the dogaressa joined the nobles and high-placed cittadini, both male and female, for a sumptuous banquet in the Sala del Maggior Consiglio on the floor above. After dining, the assembled guests danced the night away. Inside the courtyard, a pyramid had been constructed featuring a statue of Cupid standing on a globe atop a spinning wheel of fireworks. Such an elaborate device, a popular feature at court festivals, was new in Venice. The carefully choreographed entry of the dogaressa allowed the new doge to have it both ways: it created the image of a well-ordered republic headed by a doge with limited powers in which even the trade guilds played an essential role, as well as the image of a powerful empire with a display of magnificence worthy of any court in Europe; and, importantly, it gave respectable women—guarantors of the patrician bloodline—an officially sanctioned public presence in that patriarchal society.[98]

As a senator and perennial office-seeker (and elector of the doge), Gian Matteo was almost certainly among the celebrants. His daughter Giulia was almost certainly not. Pregnant yet again, she would give birth to a son—her seventh child in seven years—less than a month later. Girolamo probably stayed close to home as well. While he would have had a role as a feudal lord in the celebrations for Bona Sforza, Zilia's coronation was a more distinctly Venetian affair. Foreign ambassadors were guests of honour but confined to the reviewing stand and not part of the procession. But again, the Della Torre could have watched the festivities from their palace window. They had moved to Ca' Barozzi, also on the Grand Canal, and would have been on the route of the water parade.

A new house and another baby

Girolamo wrote in the *Fedi battesimali* once again: 'On the 14th of October [1557], at the 9th hour on a feast day in Venice in Casa Barozzi, my Alvise was born to me, the fifth son in the seventh degree, and on the 18th he was baptized by the Reverend priest of San Moisè in the house, since he did not feel well, with two godparents; may God make him good.'[99] Sansovino later tells us that the infant was given the name of Luigi (Alvise) 'for the venerated memory of his uncle, the excellent and religious brother of the lord count, who was in his times most lovable and an example of true goodness.'[100] The baby's uncle was, of course, the Alvise II who had been assassinated on the Grand Canal in 1549 and whose funerary monument was mounted high on the wall in the Frari.

Ca' Barozzi was located in arguably an even more prestigious location than Ca' Morosini. Situated on the west side of Rio San Moisè at the mouth of the Grand Canal directly opposite the Punto della Dogana, it was only a few steps (or a short gondola ride) away from Piazza San Marco, and close to the family's new parish church of San Moisè.[101] Originally built in the thirteenth century, the palace had been expanded over the years into a large complex which could house several families, including two new houses built on the campo in front in the 1540s.[102] It is possible that one of the latter was occupied by Girolamo Della Torre and his large household. Proximity to Santa Maria Nova was no longer essential after Marcella's death, and the lure of a new freestanding palace, even if relatively small, in a prominent position on the Grand Canal could well have been hard to resist (Figure 9.4).

Stormy Weather in the Friuli

Girolamo was coming to the end of his virtual house arrest. The following February (1558), Pietro Sanudo, the outgoing luogotenente, wrote his final report to the Senate. He advised:

> It will be of great importance for the affairs of Your Sublimity to keep a colonel in Udine, because in truth it is a bad thing that in an open Patria like Friuli, and in the city of Udine, it would not be secure without a captain of war, since when there is one there, outsiders have more respect about acting insolently, and it would be a brake on the discords and sedition of the inhabitants of Udine; especially now there is a need for it, since the Savorgnans are freed from their banishments and can live in that city, and Count Girolamo Della Torre will soon end the time of his ban and can return to Udine.[103]

Despite the luogotenente's warning, Giovanni da Udine's son Raphaiello had been seriously wounded in an attack near the palazzo comunale in February 1559, and two nobles were detained at the beginning of May for threatening a duel over perceived insults during a planning session for the annual May Day tournament and

Figure 9.4. Giovanni Merlo, *Vero e real disegno della inclita cita di Venetia* (detail), 1676 (Chicago, Newberry Library).

Ca' Barozzi, set back from the Grand Canal by a large open campo that contains two narrow Renaissance-style houses, is visible on the left bank of Rio San Moise, the canal furthest to the left in the detail. The main façade of the palace, facing the campo, featured an arcaded ground floor and a piano nobile with a gallery of stilted arch Veneto-Byzantine-style windows across its width and merletti cresting.

joust.[104] At some point during that spring, Girolamo's brother Michele had finally taken up residence in the bishop's palace in Ceneda. In anticipation of her husband's release, Giulia had moved there with the children, probably no later than mid-May. She was expecting another baby in July, and the road trip must have been made before the pregnancy was so far advanced as to make travel dangerous. Michele could temporarily assume the role of head of the household, and the Castello di San Martino was a safer place than the palace in Udine. The Della Torre family would do well to stay out of that world, but, given family ties, it would not stay far from them.

A Letter from London

For Girolamo was not alone in Venice. On 5 June, Federico Colloredo, then at the court of Elizabeth I in London, addressed a letter to Pompeo Colloredo 'in Venice at San Moisè at Ca' Barozzi in the house of Count Girolamo Della Torre'.[105] Federico, we will recall, had been banished with Marzio Colloredo and several accomplices for the murder of Antonio Savorgnan in 1552. Although the perpetrators had plotted the attack in Pompeo's house in Udine, he had not been charged. Federico had fled and taken refuge at the court of Charles V in Vienna. There he would learn to replace the swaggering vengefulness of a feudal lord with the refined manners of a court functionary.[106]

After the Emperor Charles V abdicated in favour of his brother Ferdinand I in 1556, Federico remained a *cameriere* (courtier) of the new emperor. He arrived at the English court 'after a long travail at sea' in the entourage of the Archduke Charles II, less than a year after Elizabeth I's ascent to the throne. After a 'beautiful *festa* of all the principal ladies of the Kingdom, so beautiful and so well adorned that it was a marvel to see them', he was introduced to the new queen. Upon hearing his surname, she immediately recalled that she had already met another Colloredo—a certain Girolamo—when she was still a princess.[107] She was referring to Girolamo Della Torre's nephew and namesake (and son of his sister Ginevra), who had been banished in 1549 for the incident in Padua. Although he had stayed in Venice for a short time after his father's assassination on the Grand Canal, he eventually left Venetian territories and wandered through Italy in search of the perpetrators, most notably Tristan Savorgnan. He seems to have ended up in Rome, where he had a religious awakening. He became a Jesuit and wrote to his brother Marzio, urging him to reconcile with their enemies. His council was neither welcome nor heeded.[108] From Federico's letter we learn that the young exile had eventually found his way to the English court and that he was now deceased. Federico writes that Elizabeth, 'hearing of his death, was very sad, chatting with me about him very affectionately for a long time'.[109]

Federico himself was well travelled, declaring the English court to be the most magnificent he had ever seen—not equalled by 'the court of the emperor my lord, nor of the king of Spain, nor of the Kings of Bohemia and Hungary, nor of the many dukes and princes of German and Italy'. Federico praises the young queen as 'bellissima, cortese et savia' and observes that 'she speaks our Italian language as I do, and also speaks Latin, Greek and French very well, which seems to me a miraculous thing in a woman'. He is tempted to remain in London, but offers advice to his cousins instead:

> I find myself in the service of such a great prince that I would be wrong to leave him for any other, but I would council some of the brothers of the poor Signor Girolamo [Colloredo] to continue the service that he had begun with this lady before she was Queen, who truly shows that she has taken him into account, and Signor Camillo seems to me suitable for this office, since he is a cavalier, [capable] of serving ladies in every manner of service.

Federico concludes with greetings to Pompeo's brothers and a sister-in-law and says that he will be returning to Flanders in a few days.[110] Girolamo Della Torre, and probably Pompeo as well, would soon be on the road themselves.

A Chapter Concluded

On 9 June, just days before Pompeo would have received Federico's letter at Ca' Barozzi, Girolamo had dictated a detailed petition to the Council of Ten:

> On 23 May 1549, I Girolamo Della Torre...was relegated by this excellent Council to the island of Candia for 10 years, but because the galleys (on which I should go to Candia) were to depart in the month of August that followed, there was consigned to me (that month) a chamber in the court of the Palazzo, where I made my obedience, posting a bond that I would not leave from there. Then occurred the horrendous case of the death of my unfortunate brother Count Alvise, because of which your illustrious lords in this excellent council postponed my departure, with the [proviso] however that I should continue my said obedience in the same chamber with renewal of the bond to not leave it; from which I did not leave until the order to transfer myself to Candia.
>
> It then appeared to your illustrious lords with the greatness kindness to give me a safe conduct to return and stay in Venice until (up to the 23rd of May past) I finished the ten years of my relegation. Now, desiring that I go with good grace to meet the Monsignor, my brother, and my consort and children who are in Ceneda, I kneel at the feet of your illustrious lordships who would be content (in sign of all my due obedience) to make note of and publish (just as usual) the completion of my relegation, certifying that I, with the same obedience and submission, will continue always at its service also with my own life, as I am obligated, and I recommend myself to your illustrious lordships.

We may note that Girolamo does not mention the excused absence for his wedding day and possible conjugal visits outside the palace. But, easily meeting the three-fourths threshold, the Council voted twenty-six in favour, two against, and two undecided, 'that the time of his relegation is understood to be completed, and the order should be given to the luogotenente of the Friuli and wherever it would be necessary that it should be made public'.[111]

Bishop Michele was present in Venice on 13 June, probably to accompany Girolamo on the trip north to Ceneda, when the Council of Ten granted him permission to visit the treasury of San Marco and the armoury of the Council of Ten in the Palazzo Ducale. The vote was thirteen in favour, one against, and one undecided. Given that such visits were pro forma for visiting dignitaries, it is worth noting that two officials declined to support what should be an uncontroversial visit of a powerful bishop from Venice's Terraferma empire.[112] But despite lingering resentments in the Venetian patriciate, a new chapter in the life of the Della Torre family was about to begin.

Notes

1. Johnson 2010, 190–205; Howard 1975, 10–47.
2. Sansovino 1561.
3. Brown 2004, 188–9, 190–6.

4. Valcanover et al 1991, 47, no. 73; Bassi 1976, 544–9. The palace was purchased in the early eighteenth century by Gherardo Sagredo, grandnephew of Doge Nicolò Sagredo, who died in 1676. He modernized the interior with stuccoes and frescoes. The building is now Hotel Ca' Sagredo, separated from Ca'Oro by Ca' Giustinian Pesaro, now also a hotel.
5. Valcanover et al 1991, 4, no. 72.
6. The church would be rebuilt in the seventeenth century and suppressed in the nineteenth. Zorzi 1984, 355–6; Rosand 1978, 138–9; Moncada 1988, 111; Manno 1995, 84–5, 165.
7. Calabi and Morachiello 1987, 16–40.
8. ASVe, *CX*, Comuni, Filze, b. 63, no. 136.
9. The younger Maria was the widow of Benedetto de' Carli di Sacile. See Casella 2003, Tavs. 3 and 9 (before p. 229). See Appendix II, Table E. See also Hacke 2004, 184–5.
10. Ibid., 137–9; and see Chapter 2. See also Casella 2008, 89–128.
11. De Conti 2016, 101–2.
12. Conzato 2005, 67 n131; Casella 2003, 137–9. See ASVe, *CX*, Comuni, Filze, b. 56, no. 148 (1552), for litigation over the compensation paid by Venice to Giacomo and his other brothers for their share of the family palace destroyed in Udine.
13. Casella 2003, 136–7, Tavola 7.
14. Ferraro 2012, 66; Musacchio 1999, 53, 113–14.
15. Comune di Venezia 1980, 106–10; De Vivo 2016, 138–40.
16. ASUd, *AT*, b. 17, fasc. 1, ff. 217–18.
17. ASVe, Provveditori alla Sanità, Necrologia, b. 797 (1555–6), 17; Appendix I: Sansovino, *Vita*, 7.
18. ASVe, NT, b. 1210.716 (Antonio Marsilio), 23 February 1546 m.v. [=1547]. See also Rosenthal and Jones 2008, 148; Piana and Wolters 2003.
19. Zorzi 1984, 248–9; Corner 1758, 272–3. Cf. Morresi 2000, 290–1, with a suggested date of ca. 1555 for the reopening; for Titian's painting, now in the Brera, see Wethey 1969, 135, cat. 105.
20. See Chapter 5.
21. Puppi 2004, 37–8, 132–3 n91. Cf. Hope 2008, 30, whose argument for a 1535–40 birthdate is unconvincing. It is not the case that a marriage at the age of twenty-five was 'highly unusual', as Hope states. Marcella was twenty-three when she married Gian Matteo, and the five daughters of Girolamo and Giulia would be married at twenty, twenty-one (in two cases), twenty-eight, and twenty-nine.
22. Schulz 1982, 73–82. For vertical relationships of women within their parishes, see Hacke 2004, 23–4; Romano 1987, 131–40.
23. ASVe, NT, b. 1210.716.
24. Romano 1966 , 191–226; Romano 1987, 135–8. See also Chapter 10.
25. Lowe 2013, 412–45; McKee 2008, 305–26.
26. Davis 2004; Davis 2009.
27. ASVe, NT, b. 1210.716 (Antonio Marsilio), 23 February 1546 m.v. [=1547].
28. Ibid.
29. See Chojnacki 2000, esp. 95–111 and 132–52. See Grubb 1996, 101–2, for an admirable explanation of *fedecommesso*. It required that the core of the estate must pass

within the patriline, with sons inheriting equal shares; estates without legitimate male heirs within the patriline must pass to other branches of the patriline. The aim was to keep the patrimony from being dispersed over generations. It was a different mechanism from primogeniture, where the bulk of the estate goes to the oldest son.

30. See Romano 1987, 131–40; Brown 2004. Cf. Davis 1998, 19–38, with a more restricted view, based primarily on seventeenth-century sources.
31. Brown 2013a, 231–4. See also O'Connell 2009, 40–2: in 1540, 117 maritime and 78 mainland offices were available outside Venice for a total of 195. The most important offices in the maritime state were the governors and capitani of Zara, Corfù, Crete, and Cyprus. On patrician office-holding see Zannini 1995, 415–63.
32. The cappello was the urn into which votes were deposited in elections in the Senate and Great Council.
33. ASVe, *CX*, Comuni, Filze, b. 64, no. 136 [30 January 1554 m.v. (=(1555)].
34. ASVe, *Coll.*, Relazioni, Secreta, b. 62, c. 46v [28 March 1555].
35. ASVe, *Coll.*o, Relazioni, Secreta, b. 66, no. 34 (12 July 1555). For the Provveditori sopra monti, see Besta, 'Il senato veneziano', 161–2.
36. ASVe, *Coll.*, Relazioni, Secreta, b. 66, no. 34 (30 July 1555).
37. Ruscelli 1573, 159r. See also Brown 2013a, 240–3.
38. ASUd, *AT*, b. 6, no. 10.
39. Pastor, 14:56–65; Von Ranke 1913, 1:221–5.
40. Von Einem 1959, 159.
41. Cited by Nagel 2000, 188. See also Vanni 2010, 123–77; Santarelli, 'Paolo IV', 1164–66.
42. *DBI, s.v.* 'Della Torre, Michele'; *Cardinals*: http://webdept.fiu.edu/~mirandas/bios1583.htm#Torre. He served in Perugia from 15 September 1553 to 31 May 1555.
43. Moroni, *Dizionario*, 23: 66–73; Baumgarten 1910; Visceglia 2011, 239–64.
44. Moroni, *Dizionario*, 41:258.
45. Pastor, 14:66. Cf. Pattenden 2013, 8–9.
46. Cited by Pastor, 14:68. Michele attended the annual closing exercises of the Collegio Romano, the Jesuit school established by Ignatius Loyola, in October 1555. With him in the audience were Navagero; Cardinal Otto Truchsess of Augsburg; Giovanni Carafa, nipote of the pope and many bishops; as well as Ignatius Loyola. See Garcia Villoslada 1954, , 39–41.
47. Von Ranke 1913, 1: 225–6; Oryshkevich 2016, 23–8.
48. *DBI, s v.* 'Della Torre, Michele'.
49. *Cardinals*: http://webdept.fiu.edu/~mirandas/bios1583.htm#Torre.
50. Cited by Cairns 1976, 66.
51. Cini 1964, 27–65; Palladio degli Olivi 1660, 175.
52. Cohn 2010, 145–7.
53. *La venuta della serenissima Bona Sforza* 1556; Bassano 1556.
54. Cini 1964, 31. See also Werner 2000, 168–93; Zagonel 2016, 66–72.
55. Zorzi 1962, 23.
56. Cini 1964, 40.
57. Zorzi 1962, 25; Cini 1964, 39–40.
58. Zorzi 1962, 25.
59. Cini 1964, 42–4.

60. Ibid., 44–8; Zorzi 1962, 22–8.
61. Cini 1964, 49. In Venice, 1 *libbra grossa* = 477 grams or 1.0516 lbs, and 1 *libbra sottile* = 301 grams or 0.66 lbs. The translation assumes that the weights referred to were *libbre grosse*.
62. Tamburlani 2016, 43–4. See also Susannis 1899, 106–8; Giusti 1900, 122–6; Faccioli and Joppi 2007, 62.
63. Candido 1886, 18–21. The Lazzaretto was a plague and quarantine hospital. It had three sections: for the already afflicted; for those under suspicion; and for poor beggars. See Cohn 2010, 255.
64. See Chapter 4 n132.
65. Tamburlani 2016, 48; Pullan 1971, 510–15.
66. Cairns 1976, 65.
67. Tamburlani 2016, 41, 44; Cairns 1976, 77 nn53–4.
68. Cairns 1976, 69, 72, 77 nn53–4.
69. Candido 1886, 18–21. See also Carmichael 1988, 135–9.
70. BMVe, MS VII 824 (8903), Consegi, 361 (31 January 1555 m.v. [=1556]).
71. Cini 1964, 51.
72. Da Mosto 1960, 259. For Venetian ceremonial entries, see also Brown 1990, 136–86.
73. Cini 1964, 51. *Fuste* were long ships, smaller than galleys. See Lane 1934, 13.
74. Ibid., 58. See King 1991, 199–201; Ossa 2015; Haraguchi 2003.
75. Cini 1964, 54.
76. Ibid., 58, 62.
77. Ibid., 63.
78. Ibid.
79. Da Mosto 1960, 259–61; Tondro 2001, I, 41.
80. Da Mosto 1960, 262–8: twenty-six scrutinies with thirty-five votes in the end. See *DBI*, *s.v.* 'Priuli, Lorenzo'.
81. ASUd, *AT*, b. 17, fasc. 1, f. 160.
82. Appendix I: Sansovino, *Vita*, 7-7v.
83. Ibid., 7-7v.
84. See Chapter 3.
85. BMV. MS It. VII 134 (=8035): Cronaca Veneta di Girolamo Savina sino al MDCXV, 315v; ASVe, *CX*, Comuni, Filze, b. 69, no. 163.
86. Comune di Venezia 1980, 106–7. For the *lazzaretti*, see Crawshaw 2012, 1–75.
87. Casella 2003, 136–7 and Tavola 7. The Savorgnan couple's papal dispensation finally came through, with their first son Francesco born on 13 July 1555. His second son Federico was born on 16 September 1556, and a daughter Giovanna in 1559.
88. ASVe, *CX*, Comuni, Filze, b. 69, no. 163.
89. ASVe, *CX*, Comuni, Filze, b. 69, no. 163, all. I; ASVe, *LPF*, b. 281, 24–5.
90. ASVe, *CX*, Comuni, Filze, b. 69, no. 163, all. II.
91. ASVe, *LPF*, b. 281, cc. 24–5; Casella 2003, 138. For the *carta della pace* see *Leggi Criminali* 1751, 39–40.
92. ASVe, *SAV-MC*, r. 3, c. 11 (=15).
93. Da Mosto 1937, I, 132; Sanudo 1980, 106–7, 245.
94. 'DVM. VOLVITVr. ISTE IAD. ASr. IVSTINOP. VEr. SALAMIS. CRETA. IOVIS. TESTES. ERVNT. ACTOr. PA. IO. SE. MV.' See Brown 1996 , 285–6; Brown 2013a,

243; Cicogna, *Ins. Ven.*, III, 318–19, 323; Ruscelli 1566, 433–4; Rizzi 1987, 321; Tassini 1915, 390.

95. The following description of the 1557 entry is indebted to Tondro 2001, I, 41–63. For transcriptions of the primary documents, see ibid., II, 41–76.
96. Cited by ibid., II, 45.
97. Ibid., I, 46–8.
98. Ibid., I, 48–51.
99. ASUd, b. 17, c. 211. It is unclear as to what feast day Girolamo referred to. It is not cited in Renier-Michiel 1829, and none of the saints honoured on 14 October would appear to be celebrated in Venice.
100. Appendix I: Sansovino, *Vita*, 7v.
101. Vianello 1993, 95–7. Built in the twelfth century, the church was razed to the ground in the seventeenth century and replaced by the present Baroque confection.
102. Schulz 2004, 114–31, Figs 126–32; Brusegan 2005b, 29–31.
103. *Relazioni/Friuli* 60 (6 February 1558).
104. Cargnelutti 1987, 266 (3 February 1559); Muir, 262.
105. Braida 1914, 70–7. See also Conzato 2005, 107–8. Cf. Colloredo Mels 2016, 13, attributing the letter to Federico's brother Lodovico.
106. Conzato 2005, 103–14.
107. Braida 1914, 71. See also Conzato 2005, 107–8. Elizabeth was crowned on 17 November 1558.
108. Degani 1900, 107; Conzato 2005, 107–8.
109. Braida 1914, 72.
110. Ibid., 71–2.
111. ASVe, *CX*, Comuni, Filze, b. 75, no. 147.
112. Ibid., b. 72, no. 184.

10
The Sacrifice

It was mid-June 1559, and Giulia was awaiting Girolamo in Ceneda. This was perhaps the longest time that the couple had been apart since their departure to Crete nine years before. A month or two earlier, she had been ferried with her six small children to the edge of the lagoon, where horse-drawn carriages awaited to take them to their new home in the bishop's castle. The oldest child was seven, the youngest a toddler around eighteen months old. Giulia would have been accompanied on the trip by several servants, and possibly by her father Gian Matteo or one of her brothers. The caravan headed due north over the same roads that Titian had used in the winter of 1548, while Girolamo remained behind in Ca' Barozzi to complete his sentence.

Most of Giulia's life had been spent in urban settings near the sea, and the unfolding Veneto landscape must have come as a revelation. With crops sown soon after the last frost, the countryside was coming back to life after the winter. Although only 40 miles in distance, the trip could have taken two days, with a stopover halfway through near Treviso. The expansive plains approaching the town consisted of a patchwork of small irregular plots in different shades of green, depending on the crop—wheat, sorghum, rye, millet, vegetables—defined by hedges and rows of trees and punctuated by small orchards of fruit trees in full bloom. A first view of newly sprouting wheat fields strewn with red poppies is still an unforgettable experience—for Giulia, receptive to signs and portents, it could have presaged a bright future with a brood of healthy children.[1]

After crossing the Piave River, the little company approached Conegliano—a walled town that spread out around the hilltop fortress that served as the palace of the Venetian podestà. The flat landscape began to give way to rolling hills rising to the north covered by terraces of parallel rows of budding grape vines staked to mulberry trees, a distinctive feature of Veneto vineyards. After the travellers passed Col di Manza, where Titian was building his country villa, the Romanesque towers of Giulia's new home eventually came into view some four miles to the west. Nestled in wooded hills studded with rocky outcroppings, the Castello di San Martino had stood guard in various forms above the town of Ceneda since the eighth century (Figure 5.2). The town now consisted of perhaps 3000 persons with their own citizen councils of nobles, commoners, and rural folk that met in the municipal loggia on the cathedral square.[2]

The Venetian Bride: Bloodlines and Blood Feuds in Venice and Its Empire. Patricia Fortini Brown, Oxford University Press (2021). © Patricia Fortini Brown. DOI: 10.1093/oso/9780192894571.003.0010

At Home in Ceneda

A new classically styled three-tiered marble fountain opposite the loggia would have been a welcome sight to thirsty travellers. It had been constructed as the terminus of a new aqueduct at the behest of Michele in 1555 to thank his subjects for maintaining concord and tranquillity during his absence from the diocese. It remains a prominent, if incongruous, amenity even today. The lower basin, set atop a three-stepped stone base that allowed easy access to the water, was inscribed with the Della Torre coat of arms and an inscription that left no doubt as to the patron:

HOC LATICES MICHAEL COMMUNES DUXIT IN USUS
UNDE BIBAS MUNUS, CENETA, TURRIS HABES
(This water Michele brought into common use:
Wherefore, Ceneda, you have the gift of drink from the [Della] Torre).[3]

Like the decorated wellheads of Venice (and the Bembo fountain in Candia), the fountain was intended to be 'for the convenience of the people as well as an ornament of the city' (Figure 10.1).[4]

The pregnant Giulia, eager to reach her final destination with her charges, would not have tarried long at the fountain. Passing the loggia, the carriages turned right to proceed up the Via Brevia and finally entered the entry courtyard of the Castello di San Martino. Built on the living rock on an outcropping on the side of the mountain, the castle—a sprawling compound of buildings—had been expanded in several campaigns over the centuries. Given its ample footprint, the complex likely housed a large staff of clerics, secretaries, servants, groundskeepers, and guardsmen, in addition to the bishop and his household (Figure 10.2).[5]

Girolamo's young family moved into the bishop's palace. Occupied for more than ten years by a procurator and the support staff in Michele's absence, it was now to be filled with the shouts and laughter of his nephews and nieces. Giulia had a month, or possibly two, to organize the household before Girolamo joined the family in June. It is likely that she set to work immediately, despite her delicate condition. Although this would have been Giulia's first experience living in a hilltop castle, it is unlikely that she spent much time enjoying the garden or the expansive view of the surrounding countryside and the town below afforded by its elevated position. Sansovino later wrote that 'she renounced any recreation and relaxation, since what pleased her much more was the governance of her children, the family, and matters of her home, than to attend to pleasures outside'. We might consider his words a domesticated version of saintly female hagiography, a grand tradition that stressed sacrifice and self-abnegation.[6]

Figure 10.1. Bernardino da Venezia, Marble fountain, 1555. Ceneda, Cathedral square.
The finial rising above the putti supports a metal banderole incised with the Della Torre coat of arms. Photo: author.

Shortly after his arrival, Girolamo would make yet another entry in the *Fedi Battesimali*: 'On Sunday 16 July [1559] at around the 11th hour in the Castello of Ceneda, with the help of God, Ginevra, my third daughter was born to me; on the 23rd she was baptized in the Cathedral church.'[7] This was Bishop Michele's first (and perhaps only) opportunity to preside at the baptismal font for one of his nephews or nieces. Sansovino tells us that the infant was named 'to renew the Lady Ginevra, sister of the Lord Count, a matron no less illustrious for the glorious virtues of her soul, than for the most excellent beauties of her serene and celebrated body, and for having married Signor Giovanni Battista of the most noble house of the Colloredo, who was greatly esteemed and honoured for his prudence and goodness.'[8]

Ginevra's marriage to Giambattista in 1524 had cemented the ties between the Colloredo and Della Torre families. Blessed (like Giulia) with a fertile womb, she had given birth to no fewer than eight sons and six daughters before she was widowed in 1549. Her three eldest children had died by 1559, among them Sertorio, her oldest; her daughter Andriana; and Girolamo, who had so charmed the Queen of England when he was living in exile. Camillo and Carlo were pursuing careers at the imperial court. The hot-headed Marzio was still in exile, seeking vengeance for his father's murder, undoubtedly with his Ginevra's blessing. As

Figure 10.2. Ceneda (Vittorio Veneto). Aerial view of Castello di San Martino. The Via Brevia (now paved) leads in from the left. The original bishop's palace (12–13th century) is the inverted C-shaped complex at the top, flanking three sides of a trapezoid-shaped entry courtyard with a square tower on the north side. A west wing had been added to the southwest corner of the palace and a hexagonal tower to the northwest corner of the courtyard in the 13–14th century. An east wing was added to the southeast corner of the palace at the end of the 15th century to form a large courtyard or cloister that opened to a large garden to the south. The complex would be expanded in 1571 with a curtain wall further to the south anchored at the corners by watchtowers.

with the Della Torre, it fell to just one son, Curzio, to ensure the family's future, and indeed, he would marry Francesca da Porcia the following year.[9] But at this point, he still resided with his mother and the extended Colloredo clan in the Castello di Colloredo da Monte Albano (see Figure 3.3), as well as in the family palace in Udine. Ginevra had no grandchildren as yet, and we might conjecture that she travelled to Ceneda to assist at the birth of her namesake. The fifty-mile trip would likely have taken at least two days, perhaps with stopovers at Spilimbergo and the Castello di Porcia near Pordenone.

Having left Venice behind, Giulia would have to find a new circle of women friends closer by. Titian's daughter Lavinia, whom she may well have known in Venice, is an enticing possibility. She had been living in Serravalle, around 1.5 miles away from Ceneda, since her marriage in 1555 to Cornelio Sarcinelli, a provincial noble. We know little about Lavinia's married life, other than the fact that she had six children. Only one name survives: Giacomino, born around 1560. The family lived in Palazzo Sarcinelli, a handsome sixteenth-century Veneto- style palace in the cent re of town. Between two windows of a room now called the 'camera di Lavinia' is a fresco of a reclining nude, traditionally (and optimistically) considered a work by Titian himself.[10]

With Bishop Michele now back in Ceneda and in no need of a procurator, and the new baby safely born, it would not be long before Girolamo moved his family back to the Friuli, where Giulia would have to adjust to a new residence yet again. But now was not the time.

An Atrocious and Enormous Crime

It would be a long hot summer in the Friuli, without a drop of rain. Tempers were short in Udine, even between members of the same clan. Enter the Colloredos, yet again. On 7 September, the luogotenente, Giambattista Contarini, wrote to Doge Girolamo Priuli: 'This morning I entered the Duomo to hear mass. I heard gunshots behind me, with bullets fired at messer Iseppo di Colloredo, son of Brunoro, who was kneeling in front of the altar of the Corpus Domini. He was shot through and through and died a short time later.' The perpetrator was recognized as Giulio, son of Francesco Colloredo. Contarini suspected that he knew the cause of the assault. He had recently handed down a judgment in favour of Iseppo and against Francesco and his brother Giovanni, who belonged to another branch of the Colloredo family (and were first cousins of Ginevra's deceased husband Giambattista). Their grievance was to be addressed by young Giulio. Accompanied by three Bolognese henchmen, he had hidden behind the altar where Iseppo was accustomed to praying and shot him in cold blood. Also wounding the Venetian capitano, one of the officials who had given chase, the assassins fled the church. They ran to the stable of Francesco's family palace, where saddled horses were ready and waiting. Galloping off, they fired more shots, one of which mortally wounded Contarini's cavalier, a certain Filippo—'a brave and faithful man'—and fled through the nearby Porta di Ronco toward Gorizia, some 25 miles away in imperial territory.

Contarini immediately sent a dispatch to the luogotenente of Gorizia, informing him 'of the atrociousness of this case, which offended the almighty God', and asked him to capture and detain the fugitives should they appear. He also began his own investigation and found 'many swords, broadswords, long and short guns' in the Colloredo palace—indeed, a true arsenal. Inquiries revealed the true planner of the deed: the banished Marzio Colloredo, then holed up in Pavia with other companions. Contarini asks the Ten for the necessary authority to pursue justice for 'such an atrocious and enormous crime.'[11]

Two days later, he writes to the Ten again, pleading for more support:

> Having apprehended the servant who had saddled and prepared the horses for Giulio Colloredo di messer Francesco, I put him to the [torture of the] *corda* after he denied knowing the orders. After he was given the first shake, he confessed the father's [Francesco's] knowledge of the sending of letters back and forth, the planning, the request for horses. I will do what I can, but it is

> necessary for your serenity to give consideration to the security of this city, as well as to those who administer justice.

He admits his frustration (and fear) in apprehending the guilty, 'these Colloredos having such a large following and family network, with hidden factions in the city'.[12]

The Ten threw all the weight of the Venetian government against Giulio and his companions. In a unanimous vote, they demanded that 'those wicked delinquents should be duly punished'. While the obviously guilty Giulio was banned in October, the investigation continued and the wheels of justice ground on slowly. It took another year before sentences of banishment were levied on his servant Gian Giacomo and the elusive Marzio (yet again), with Giulio's father Francesco eventually exonerated.[13]

A Terrible and Almost Unheard-of Time

On the first day of October 1559, Emilio Candido makes another grim entry in his chronicle:

> Note that since the great deluges of May, it has not rained enough up to now to have watered the countryside of Udine sufficiently. Toward the mountains it rained little. The *stradalta* (the area around the old Via Postumia that traversed the low lying plains of the Friuli between Aquileia and Treviso) was almost completely consumed by the great heat; the sorghum fell to the ground from the great drought without ripening to perfection; the millet yielded less than four *stara* (roughly 8 bushels) from 10 fields and was not worth harvesting; there was no buckwheat in the lowlands and very little at the foot of the mountains; there were never so few grapes in human memory; very little hay; turnips were the main foodstuff. The men of the countryside are appalled, and may God protect us from rioting and come to our aid.[14]

It would be another month before a Venetian chronicler could write: 'After 5 months it began to rain on the day of Ognissanti' (1 November) with '*acqua alta* a *braccio* (1.7 feet) high in the streets' in Venice the following day.[15] But it was too late to save the crops. Indeed, the situation was no better in the Ceneda region. The Castello di San Martino would have been well enough provisioned, but the bishop bore the responsibility for taking care of the poor. By mid-November, Girolamo was desperately attempting to provision the city's granaries and petitioned the Council of Ten for permission to import grain. Hoping to exploit his family connections, he also wrote to Francesco Della Torre, then imperial ambassador in Vienna and a distant relative, requesting a licence to bring in grain from Germany.[16]

The weather gods were truly malevolent in these years. The following January it snowed in Venice for three continuous days and the canals froze over, one of just four such occurrences recorded in sixteenth-century chronicles.[17] By February the shortage of foodstuffs in the Friuli reached calamitous proportions; the Dazio da Sal (Salt Office) in Udine successfully petitioned the Council of Ten for permission to extend payment of taxes to Venice over a longer period. Lamenting 'such a terrible and horrendous famine', the Dazio reminded the Ten that the poorest and most miserable people in the countryside lived under the protection of the Serenissima. Most of them had sold their animals for lack of fodder and salt to feed them. Without money to buy sorghum, millet, or salt, many were faced with starvation and total ruin. 'It is a terrible and almost unheard-of situation that prevails at present.'[18]

It seemed that nothing worse could happen, but it did. Candido writes on 4 May 1560:

> The *petecchie* (epidemic typhus) appeared in Udine immediately after the Easter festivities causing great fear, because almost no one escaped, that all died horribly and speedily, nobles as well as commoners, and may God not allow it to continue; and today the ringing of bells as is customary for deaths was abandoned, neither with small bells nor large, as long as this malign influence continues.[19]

The timing of the outbreak was no accident. Recent studies conclude that typhus is 'historically suspected to be responsible for massive mortality in the wake of wars, famines, and migrations'.[20]

Candido reported that spring that 'the most cruel hunger of the present year' exceeded that of the terrible famine of 1527–8 and was even more widespread, afflicting France, Spain, and all of Italy. But the community of Udine would make heroic attempts to feed more than 4,000 peasants who had flocked to the city, as well as its own poor. In a reversal of the normal situation, when the Friuli exported grain to Venice, the Monte di Pietà spent more than 25,000 ducats of its own funds to fill the public granary, buying grain in Venice, brought in by Turkish ships, as well as a great quantity from Germany. The local council attempted to impose rationing and price controls. Only *pane di mistura* was available in bakeries and osterie: bread made with mixtures of whatever grains were available. The peasants in the countryside subsisted largely on herbage and salt. 'It was a most cruel year.'[21]

And yet, it was also a time of contrasts. In the very next paragraph Candido observed that despite the calamities of the past year, the upper part of sala grande in the Castello atop the hill was completed after a campaign that had lasted forty years, and the Luogogenente finally moved in. 'He put in place his insignia or coat of arms with the words *Ioanne Baptista Contareno viro clarissimo Praeto. 1560.*' Once the inside is perfected, 'it will be the most honoured lodging that the Serenissimi Signori would have for their reggimenti'.[22]

Fitting to the Grandeur of the Torriana Family

Girolamo Della Torre had his own honoured lodging to attend to. And despite famine, disease, and civic unrest, he moved the family to his ancestral castle at Villalta at some point that spring or early summer. On 16 August 1560, he made another entry in the *Fedi Battesimali*: 'at around the 13th hour in the Castello di Villalta, my fourth daughter Elena was born to me.'[23] Sansovino tells us that the infant was named Helena 'in place of another Helena of the Lords of Valvasone, a gentlelady of rare beauty of body and mind, and she was the mother of Guido Della Torre, nephew of the Lord Count.'[24] It was a graceful gesture. As we know, Guido had been orphaned as an infant when his parents both died of smallpox in 1546. First raised by his paternal grandmother, Giacoma Brazzaco (widow of Nicolò I Della Torre), until her death in 1551, he was then taken in by his maternal grandmother, Vittoria Strassoldo, wife of Enrico Valvasone and mother of the first Helena. Now around fifteen years old, Guido was the sole heir of his parents' feudal holdings, now administered by Girolamo as executor.

Again, Giulia was tasked with furnishing residences that had not been occupied by the Della Torre family for more than a decade: first Ceneda, and now Villalta and the city palace in Udine. As Sansovino later wrote, 'when she became the wife of the illustrious Signor Conte, she found few, and worn-out ornaments since the house had been many years without the governance of women, because of grave and cruel events of civil disorders accompanied by fires, robberies, and deaths'. But Giulia was diligent: 'In these places, she left three palaces, not only well furnished with the comforts of living, but adorned with rich furnishings, that were both fitting to the grandeur of the Torriana family, and that corresponded much more to the beautiful disposition of these lodgings.' As a result, 'one always had the impression of much magnificence, and [the homes] were always full of illustrious personages'.[25] A lifestyle bespeaking magnificence was expected of a feudal lord. That Giulia, raised in more modest, if comfortable, circumstances, had risen to the challenge of creating a courtly ambience was clearly worth noting. One gets a sense of what it meant to live splendidly from a banquet scene frescoed on a wall in the Castello di Malpaga near Bergamo (Figure 10.3).

The Castello di Villalta, situated atop a mound with expansive views, was not unlike the Castello di San Martino in Ceneda. But in contrast to the bishop's castle, isolated on a mountainside above a proper town with its own citizen council, Villalta was surrounded by fields farmed by peasants who both sustained and were subject to the lords of the castle. The lower Alps were clearly visible to the north. In addition to the rural village below the castle, the Della Torre had suzerainty over the villages of Zucconico (now Cicconico), San Vito di Fagagna, Rivolto, and Cargnacco.[26] In addition, they owned more than thirty fiefs scattered

Figure 10.3. Girolamo Romanino (attr.), *Banquet of Bartolomeo Colleoni in honour of Christian I of Denmark in 1467* (detail), fresco, 1520s (Comune of Bergamo, Castello di Malpaga).

through the central Friuli around Udine and farmed by peasants from whom they collected rents in kind: wheat, rye, oats, fava beans, millet, buckwheat, and sorghum, as well as guinea hens, capons, chickens, lamb and veal shoulders, prosciutto, cheese, and wine. The rents were paid yearly on 16 August, the Feast of the Madonna, to a steward who meticulously documented each payment. If not needed by the Della Torre family, the foodstuffs were sold or sent to relatives; recipients in those years included Vittoria Valvasone, as well as Gian Matteo Bembo and his son Lorenzo. The account books remain in the family archives in Udine to this day, mute testimony to a once thriving family business.[27]

Giulia's new home, her fifth in the past ten years, probably consisted of the castle as rebuilt after the devastation of 1511: the *mastio vecchio*, with its large ground floor kitchen, reception rooms on the first floor above, and bedrooms on the top floor (Figures 3.1 and 3.2).[28] Villalta had been long neglected. Fortunately, the Della Torre clan would be moving in as summer was arriving, and there would be time to make the space more agreeable before the autumn, when chilly winds swept down from the Alps. The resources for grand renovation schemes must have been limited, and Giulia's efforts were probably confined to acquiring furniture and adding accoutrements that were also typical in Venetian palaces: weapon displays (whether for use or exhibition), portraits, and wall hangings, plus carpets for the stone and brick floors.

The refurbishment of Palazzo Torriani in Udine was possibly Giulia's next order of business. The house could well have remained empty since Guido's grandmother Giacoma died in 1551. Several rooms later described as *alla grottesca* may already have been in place, decorated by Giovanni da Udine when the palace was built two decades earlier.[29] But might they have been painted when Giulia was in charge of its refurbishment? The artist had remained close to the Della Torre family, with continuing contacts with Michele or his procurator while Girolamo was in exile, but he departed for Rome in March 1560 and remained there until his death in 1564. New decorations in the palace would thus not have been by Giovanni's hand, but they could have been carried out by one of his followers. And, intriguingly, there was a current model close at hand.

A Place of Retreat

Giovanni da Udine had been much in demand by the Friulian nobility in the 1550s. Among his most notable achievements was the *studiolo* in the Torre di Ponente in the west wing of the Castello di Colloredo, the residence of Girolamo's sister Ginevra. Girolamo and Giulia must have visited the castle in 1560–1 when they were living at Villalta, only five miles away, and admired the recently embellished room. Its barrel vault and lunettes were elegantly decorated in Giovanni's signature style, with stucco cornices and frescoed mythologies, allegories, and grotesques (Figure 10.4).

With a decorative apparatus that was both prescriptive and celebratory, the *studiolo* provided a place of retreat from worldly concerns: fear of the Ottoman Turks; the cursed obligations of vendetta; the ever-present misery of a desperately poor peasantry; loyalties divided between Venice and the empire. The ceiling featured a central tondo in grisaille depicting the *Abdication of Charles V*, who extends his scept re and diadem toward a crucifix on an altar. His imperial coat of arms and motto *Plus Ultra*, with the column of Hercules, on the left, is balanced by armour adorned with the stemma of the Colloredo on the right: i n sum, an allegory of the Emperor's humility and piety on the one hand, and the loyalty of the Colloredo family on the other. The tondo was flanked by four large mythologies inspired by Ovid's *Metamorphosis*, each an allegory of pride and its consequences. A lunette depicting *Peace* burning the weapons of war is countered by the *Triumph of Fame* on the opposite wall.[30]

An eclectic amalgam of humanist culture and feudal values, the programme celebrates the moral compass of a noble family. Its patronage is unknown, but the recently widowed Ginevra is a likely candidate, perhaps in collaboration with her sons and a humanist advisor. She may well have wished to honour the memory of her husband Giambattista, who had served in the armies of Charles V before his assassination on the Grand Canal in 1549, as well as to lay out the precepts of family honour for generations yet to come. Perhaps the program was completed to celebrate the marriage of the thirty-year-old Curzio to Francesca da Porcia in

Figure 10.4. Giovanni da Udine, Allegorical frescoes (detail), Studiolo, Castello di Colloredo di Monte Albano.

Although the room would be badly damaged in the earthquake of 1976, the surviving portions and photographs of the original program reveal a complex iconographical program. This segment of the ceiling features the *Fall of Giants* in the large compartment, with the *Three Graces*, *Hercules and Cacus*, *Hercules and Cerberus*, and *Diana and Actaeon* in the smaller squares. The lunette with *Peace* burning the weapons of war is at the bottom.

March 1560.[31] The *studiolo* decoration would have been a compelling model for the refurbishment of Palazzo Torriani, but in the absence of physical or documentary evidence we may never know.

A Certain Natural Proclivity

With Giulia safely settled in her new homes in the Friuli, her father Gian Matteo was free to take up another post abroad. But now it would be in the Veneto and not across the sea. Elected to the prestigious post of capitano of Brescia on 30 July 1559 at the age of sixty-nine, Gian Matteo had begun his new assignment three months later and set out to improve the city.[32] But this time, he was a reluctant traveller. He later wrote to an acquaintance:

> I came to this city, certainly with the worst disposition, given my age, which is no longer apt for these public offices and dealings. I had devoted to them all my previous years serving my homeland and I thus deemed it was reasonable that my age should receive some respect. But anyway, since that was my lot, I made

> (as they say) a virtue out of a necessity. I came here, then, for entertainment, but also prompted by a certain natural proclivity that I have always had, to embellish and refurbish certain places, whenever and wherever I thought it was needed, as I did elsewhere, I decided to enlarge the square which is in front of the palace where I reside. In this way not only did that part of the town increase its beauty and ornament, according to my desire, but the place also became capable of hosting a parade of people walking and horse-riding, of being the site for the representation of a battle and of welcoming a proper number of soldiers, in all circumstances and in all respects.[33]

But Gian Matteo did not stop there. He also opened a new road, built a fountain, and pursued his antiquarian interests. Excavating in the Piazza del Foro of the old Roman city, his workers unearthed a number of inscribed stones. Among them was a statue thought to be of the orator Marcus Antonius Macrinus. Although it must have been fragmentary at best, Bembo was said to have shipped it back to Venice from Brescia at the end of his term in 1561.[34]

He had been shoring up the family finances over the years with a number of property acquisitions and was ready to retire. In addition to the casa da statio at Santa Maria Nova with its adjacent rental properties, he owned houses in the *contrade* of San Maurizio and San Pantalon, which also produced rental income. His villa at Ponte di Brenta and other country properties in the Padovana provided further revenue, mostly in the form of agricultural products such as wheat, wine, pigs, and geese.[35]

With the exception of Pietro, a cleric, Giulia's brothers continued to pursue careers in public service with an ever-lengthening collective curriculum vitae and brides of their own. Three followed their father's example with activities relating to Venice's Mediterranean empire. Lorenzo, a galley captain since his teenage years and now a father of six children, began a two-year term as capitano of Paphos in Cyprus in 1558. By good fortune, his ducal commission survives, offering us a rare portrait of one of our protagonists. The frontispiece portrays him with a luxuriant black beard and clothed in the lynx-lined red toga of a Venetian senator (Figure 10.5).[36]

Davide, a seasoned ship captain, completed a thirty-two-month term as a chamberlain in the reggimento of Candia in October 1558.[37] Alvise had been elected Patron of the Arsenal the same month, but halfway through his term he would be elected captain of the fleet of six galleys that formed the Guardia of Cyprus, and he was back at sea by December 1559.[38] We will recall the terms of the 1552 dowry contract of his Cretan bride, Magdalena Pasqualigo, that levied a substantial fine on Alvise if he were to take her to Venice before fifteen years had elapsed. If he had adhered to the terms, she might well still be living in Candia in a long-distance relationship kept alive by his stopovers in port. During the intervening years, he had continued to act as her representative in Venice in the interminable legal battle with her relatives over her inheritance. The matter was not yet resolved

Figure 10.5. Commissione of Lorenzo Bembo, capitano of Paphos, from Doge Nicolo Priuli, 1558. MS Typ 330 (Houghton Library, Harvard University).

in 1559, but by 1565 (two years before the end of the injunction), the couple would finally be living together in Venice.[39]

Aside from Sebastiano, an official in the Avogaria, Marco Antonio was the only son to stay rooted to the Veneto and the city of Venice. Once destined for the priesthood, he was recently married to Isabetta Bembo, a wealthy widow who brought him a dowry of 8750 ducats. He had already served as podestà of Castelfranco Veneto and as a master for gold coins in the Zecca, the Venetian mint, and was now beginning a sixteen -month term as one of the three Auditori vecchi, a body that heard appeals from sentences by lower courts.[40] In sum, the family was in the mainstream of the Venetian patriciate, not the richest but not the poorest, and relying on public office, in additional to rental income (and the occasional dowry), to sustain a noble lifestyle.

Indeed, what Gian Matteo may have lacked in material wealth was more than compensated for by his reputation. He had achieved a measure of fame, not only by his tireless labours in Venice's outlying territories, but also from the effusive pen of Francesco Sansovino. The writer had established his own print shop in Venice in 1560 and immediately became the leading publisher of the works of Cardinal Pietro Bembo, Gian Matteo's uncle-in-law and cousin several generations removed.[41] Among the press's publications that year were four volumes of the cardinal's correspondence, one of which featured a series of letters from Pietro to Gian Matteo over a twenty-five-year period.[42] Sansovino prefaced it with a short introduction. Gian Matteo, he writes, 'being a most rare senator, with a great heart, [...] merits memories not only of ink, but [also] of bronze for his great valor, and especially for having done so many and such honoured things for his country, as everyone knows.'[43] Sansovino further promises that as soon as he has collected the memories of Gian Matteo, from his youth to the present day, he would write his biography and make it known to the world.[44] That Gian Matteo was an enthusiastic participant in this enterprise is apparent in a letter that he wrote to Sansovino after reading a book by Nicolò Zeno on the origins of Venice: 'I have found something that you could use to good effect in the story of my life that you have promised to the world... and this is in the said book on page 66.' Bembo suggests that his defence of Cattaro against the Ottoman pirate Barbarossa in 1539 could be fruitfully compared to the struggles of Fastida, the fourth-century king of the Gepidae, against the king of the Ostrogoths.[45]

Sansovino fulfilled his vow, but only in part, to write Gian Matteo's biography with the dedication to his edition of Leonardo Bruni's *La historia universale de suoi tempi*, published in 1561. Here he honoured Gian Matteo with a 2000-word encomium, praising his valour in governing cities in Venice's far-flung territories and in defending them from Turkish aggression. He made particular note of his heroic defence of Zara and Cattaro, his prudence in quelling civic discord in Verona, and his ingenious public works projects in Cyprus, Candia, and Brescia. But that was not all. Sansovino went on to emphasize Gian Matteo's Christian piety: 'in Venice, you lifted up the oppressed, helped the miserable, and with pious and solicitous hands succored the poor of Christ.' In sum, Gian Matteo was to be compared to exemplary Romans for his deeds inside the Patria and beyond: to Numa Pompilio in religion, to Nasica in integrity, to Pompeo in glory, to Cato in gravity, to Cesare in clemency, to Coriolano in patriotism, to Regolo in faith, to Quinto Mucio Scevola in constancy, and to Fabio in continence.[46] The subtext of the message was clear. Not only did Venetians reject the curse of personal vendetta and blood feuds; they also valued mercy, prudence, and reconciliation above retribution.

The Impious Babylon

Not so in the Friuli. While Girolamo Della Torre continued to avoid embroiling himself in the eye-for-an-eye combat of blood feuds and vendetta, friction between the Colloredo and Savorgnan clans continued. The great availability of arms, with virtual arsenals hidden in seignorial palaces and houses of sympathetic bourgeoisie, and the ease in obtaining licences from the Venetian government did not help the situation. The Council of Ten had actually increased such concessions in times of peace, permitting the nobles to tour the city of Udine escorted by a bodyguard of two armed servants to defend themselves from aggression by adversaries. The inevitable result was that at moments of high tension, the entourages swelled, reaching fifteen and twenty persons, 'armed to the teeth'.[47]

Tensions exploded again in July 1561. And not surprisingly, the Colloredo were involved. Francesco Savorgnan della Bandiera encountered Lodovico di Mario Colloredo and several companions in front of the houses of Prospero di Castello in Borgo Aquileia. Savorgnan jokingly poked Lodovico's seventeen -year-old nephew Lelio under his arm and called him 'frascha' (a knavish wag). Lodovico immediately took offenc e. Drawing his sword, and aided by his friends Pietro Strassoldo and Troiano d'Arcano, he mortally wounded Savorgnan. The luogotenente, Gabriel Morosini, reported the incident to the Council of Ten, exclaiming:

> and they are cousins, born of brother and sister...and it appears to me that all the city is disturbed, and I hear a great *bisbiglio* (whispering), much of great import, against the castellans, that could easily give birth to some great disorder, these being proud people.[48]

A few days later, the vendetta erupted. Federico Savorgnan, nephew of the murdered Francesco, challenged and wounded Pietro Strassoldo's son Giovan Giuseppe. The problem as Morosini saw it, was the '*vanità di precedenza*' (the same vanity of precedence that had gotten Girolamo Della Torre into trouble back in 1549). In August Morosini banned the carrying of all weapons for the next six months. In vain. In mid-November, the same Federico, accompanied by his brothers Pompeo and Fabio and numerous armed servants, slaughtered Claudio Colloredo, canon of Aquileia, and his nephew Livio (brother of Lodovico) Colloredo, in front of the Castello di Udine, 'right under the eyes of the Guard and almost in the arms of the Rectors'.[49]

The humanist Cornelio Frangipane wrote to a friend from Tarcento where he had taken refuge after the murder:

> I do not know if one should mourn more over the death of canon Claudio, a man of great valor, or of the cold and lazy justice that has not yet moved, or of the danger faced by all the nobles of this Patria, in whom there would be some radiance of genius and virtue, or of the dangers that even now are still tense, or of our carelessness and our slowness. I am here, having left the impious Babylon to save my life, and others have done likewise, and others while remaining in Udine, are closed up in their houses like Jews on Holy Thursday.[50]

Claiming that the attack on Claudio and Livio had been premeditated and questioning the impartiality of the local officials in Udine, the Colloredo family appealed directly to Venice. In response, the Senate appointed the patrician Paolo Zorzi as *giudice straordinario* (special prosecutor) to prosecute the case. But even fleeing 'the impious Babylon' was no guarantee of safety. Three Savorgnan supporters—the brothers Alessandro, Floriano, and Prospero Antonini, all Udinese nobles—decided to leave town and take refuge in Venice. As they were about to cross the frozen streams of the Tagliamento in late December, they encountered Orazio and Alessandro Colloredo and Troiano d'Arcano who were just leaving Christmas celebrations in the castello of Valvasone. Swords were drawn, the inevitable fight broke out, and of the three Antonini, only Prospero survived. Yet another case was added to Zorzi's brief. In confirmation of Frangipane's charge of 'cold and lazy justice', it would take three years before the perpetrators of the two incidents would be punished, and then only with sentences of perpetual banishment.[51] Country roads, as well as the streets of Udine, remained dangerous places for noble lords, whether castellans or city dwellers.

It was a propitious time for a change of scene for the Della Torre. Pope Pius IV had issued a bull calling for the third convocation of the Council of Trent to open in 1561 on Easter Sunday. But with few delegates appearing by that date, the opening was postponed for six months, and Michele Della Torre arrived in Trent only on 10 October.[52] The implications for Girolamo were obvious: his services as Michele's procurator were again required in Ceneda. The family would remain in the relative safety of Villalta, but Palazzo Torriani—the Casa Grande—in Udine would be rented out for 60 ducats a year.[53] Having put his affairs in order, Girolamo departed for Ceneda.

A Premonition

But shortly thereafter, Girolamo received an alarming letter from Giulia. Again pregnant, she confided that she foresaw her own death the following year. She was less distressed than one might expect. Embracing her untimely demise as God's will, she accorded it the same meticulous attention that she had given to raising god-fearing children, living prudently and industriously, and 'maintaining the household with the most beautiful order'.[54] Was her sense of foreboding based upon a heavenly revelation, preternatural foresight, or disturbing physical symptoms? Sansovino does not tell us. He continues:

> she wished first of all to leave the Friuli for Ceneda, where she must meet with the Lord Count to dispose of all her things. And continually commending her dearest children to her illustrious and most beloved consort, she left ordered and under inventory all the ornaments and utensils of his palaces. And taking leave from relatives that she was able to visit, she predicted that she would not see those places again.[55]

The older boys, Sigismondo and Giulio, aged ten and seven , were of school age and were probably already in Ceneda with their father. That left Giovanni, five; Alvise, four; and their four sisters—Taddea, nine; Marcella, six; Ginevra, two and a half; and Elena, eighteen months—to accompany their mother, along with the servants, on the 50-mile journey by carriage from Villalta over bumpy roads in the dead of winter. The trip would have taken two or three days, with overnight stops, possibly at the castles of Spilimbergo and Porcia. As with the voyage to Candia in 1550, Giulia must have been around six months pregnant. This time the trip would again signal a new beginning, but one of a different sort.

By the end of January, the family were all back together in the Castello di San Martino on the hillside overlooking the town. Giulia continued with her preparations:

> it being the solemn day of the Purification [of the Virgin: 2 February], [she] presented two blessed candles to the Lord Count; she asked him as a gift to her to use them at the end of her life (as these were then used), as if foreseeing that it would not be very distant.[56]

A few days later, Giulia was again in a jostling carriage, but only for a short trip down the Via Brevia and beyond the town, where she would await the arrival of a special visitor: her sister Augusta. Wife of the noble Febo Arnaldi, she had journeyed from Vicenza, some 50 miles to the south.[57] It is possible that the two sisters had not seen each other in more than a decade. Embracing Augusta 'with a demonstration of infinite happiness . . . having desired this for many years', Giulia declared 'that she had come to the time of the final end of her life, which should be in a few days'.[58]

But it would be more than a few days. Whether by chance or by divine providence, the end would come almost two months later, at Easter time. Sansovino writes:

> Having arrived at Holy Week, the Lord Count wished to receive the most Holy Communion, and [asked] the Lady to do the same with all their family. And she begged him with warm affection, that for her satisfaction this should be on Holy Thursday, because she felt that on the day of the most holy Resurrection (Easter Sunday) suggested by the Lord Count, she would not find herself so well disposed to be able to perform worthily that most devoted act, [a wish] with which the Lord Count willingly complied. On Thursday she took that divine sacrament, and on the following day at the hour of 10 in the evening the Lady gave birth to the said daughter, that was followed by a *mola* on Easter Sunday after which she said that the hour of death was near.[59]

Augusta, mother of three sons and three daughters of her own, remained at Giulia's side. An engraving of the *Birth of the Virgin* may give us a sense of the birth chamber, a privileged enclave of women in the bishop's castle (Figure 10.6).

Figure 10.6. Cornelis Cort, *Birth of the Virgin*, 1568 (Amsterdam, Rijksmuseum).
The print is a copy, with alterations, of a drawing by Federico Zuccaro, itself probably a copy of a lost composition by his brother Taddeo, in the Devonshire Collection at Chatsworth.

The exhausted mother lies in a canopied bed, with the midwife and servants bathing the newborn in the foreground. Actual bedrooms of the time were typically furnished with holy protectors: a crucifix above the bed and an icon of the Madonna on the wall. Our Giulia may have been given poultices of coriander seeds to hasten the delivery. Given her piety and trust in God's will, it is unlikely that she had amulets or birth charms, such as prophylactic stones or gems, that were popular at the time. But she surely clutched her rosary and might well have been comforted by other holy objects, even saint's relics, in the chamber.[60]

Girolamo recorded the bittersweet sequence of events in his final entry in the *Fedi Battesimali*. He begins: 'In 1562 on the 29th of March at around the 10th hour - - - was born to me a daughter named Giulia, who is my fifth [daughter], and in order my tenth [child].'[61]

Two details are worth noting. First, there is the discrepancy of the birth date between the two accounts, with Sansovino putting it on Good Friday (27 March) and Girolamo on Easter Sunday (29 March). Allowing that Girolamo's naming of a precise date tends to give him more credibility, we might conjecture that Sansovino wanted to create a more spiritually powerful chronology with two notable dates, in imitation of Christ's crucifixion and resurrection. Second, Sansovino's citation of the tardy expulsion of a *mola* recalls the birth of Sigismondo in Candia. Again, it may have been a case of a twin pregnancy with a mole (extremely rare), or possibly a retained placenta (less rare, but often lethal). Suggestive of the latter, Girolamo's account continues: 'on the 30th [the baby's] mother sustained a continuous fever.'[62]

A Beautiful and Numerous Posterity

But Giulia had an unfinished agenda. Certain that her fever would not subside, Sansovino continues, she first summoned Girolamo and urged him not to grieve, since such was the divine will, reminding him that she had provided him with that 'beautiful and numerous posterity which he had desired more than any other thing of this world'.[63] And, it should be noted, the newborn infant renewed the name not only of her mother, but also of her maternal great-aunt.

Then, calling for her oldest children, Giulia kissed them tenderly and enjoined them to fear and love God, and obey and respect their father—the two most important qualities for them to achieve a long and honoured life.

> [She] then turned to her sister Augusta and said: 'Let us go sister, let us go happily, for God calls us to a happier home,' [words] to which [Augusta] responded that it was not yet her time. Then the Lady Countess, aware of the unhappiness that her sister had taken from her words, added: 'My dear sister, I do not ean you, but me at present, because God [chose] one of us, and I gladly accept changing this poor and fragile life for one that is the blessed and eternal.'[64]

Giulia then began to recite psalms and prayers,

> until afflicted by an attack so grave she was held for dead for the space of some hours by the grieving and lamenting persons around her. But reviving shortly afterwards, she said: 'You do not have to believe that my soul leaves today from this body, and sheds its corruptible vestments, but hold for certain that tomorrow at the hour of nine (midday), always honoured by me with the angelic salutation, it will be called to its highest Maker.'[65]

Sansovino's reference to a seizure—'an attack so grave she was held for dead for the space of some hours'—offers a further clue as to the cause of Giulia's death. Allowing that retrospective diagnoses are problematic at best, we may observe that seizures, convulsions, and coma were characteristic of eclampsia. Had Giulia experienced the symptoms of pre-eclampsia when she foresaw her death several months earlier? These might have included severe headaches, blurred or double vision, light sensitivity, upper abdominal pain, and shortness of breath. Pre-eclampsia, furthermore, is also associated with maternal fever at term.[66] Giulia had by now experienced nine earlier pregnancies and would have been aware of something outside the ordinary.

And yet, she was not yet ready to depart this life, for there was still more to do. The following morning she summoned a faithful servant named Orsa, who had cared for the children in their early years. Comforting her to stay of good mind, Giulia announced that Orsa's daughter and another girl who were both servants in the household would be married to men of good condition the following Sunday, 'by the pious work of the Lord Count'. Girolamo admitted to knowing nothing of the matter, and it appears that Giulia had arranged on her own for him to pay the girls' dowries. When the weddings took place as planned, it was 'not without the marvel of many'. It is worth noting that the strong-willed Giulia, in acting as Girolamo's agent in the negotiation of the dowry contracts, assumed a role that was typically the prerogative of men.

A Miraculous Band of Angels

After her conversation with Orsa, Giulia asked for the two candles given to her by Girolamo back in February and ordered them to be lit. She called for the priests to perform the last rites and surrendered her spirit to God 'with so much fervor, and with signs in her face of a certain jubilation, that everyone understood how content this Lady would be to leave this dark and brief shadow for the bright and infinite light'. In her last words, Giulia described a vision to her sister and others present of 'a miraculous band of angels, who sang and played in such sweet tones, that once could never describe with mortal tongue'.[67]

Girolamo's notation in the *Fedi* concludes: 'on the 2nd of April at midday she died, and she was buried in the Cathedral Church of San Tiziano of Ceneda on the 4th, and on the 5th the baby girl was baptized in the Capella di San Martino in the Castello.'[68]

Again, his succinct account does not capture the full majesty of the occasion. First the women in attendance would have washed Giulia's body and dressed her in her best finery for the burial. This would have been followed by a vigil in the castle, with family members and friends burning candles and keeping watch. Then came the public procession with her casket carried down the Via Brevia to the cathedral in the main square. Typically, a funeral in this period took place on the day after a death, but it may have been delayed on this occasion to allow for a larger crowd and perhaps the attendance of Bishop Michele.[69]

Sansovino elaborates:

> With the most honourable obsequies, and with an infinite concourse of the people, her body was placed in the cathedral church of Ceneda dedicated to the glorious San Tiziano, of which the most Reverend Monsignor Bishop Michele della Torre rector and pastor, by his singular goodness and for the egregious virtues of his mind, was worthy to rule and to shepherd all the Christian flock. We must hold resolutely, that by intercession of that saint, and of all the other elect of God, that innocent soul enjoys the eternal goods of Heaven, where God would ensure that we also, following her pious and Christian footprints, could by his divine mercy be conducted.[70]

Figure 10.7. Master of Ceneda, *Coronation of the Virgin*, 1450. Formerly in the Cathedral of Ceneda (Venice, Gallerie dell'Accademia).

Giulia's spirituality may well have been conditioned not just by sermons and reading the psalms and the lives of the saints, but also by works of art. Indeed, a monumental painting of the *Coronation of the Virgin* held pride of place above the high altar of the cathedral. Complete with a choir of angels and a multitude of saints, the image is strikingly similar to the vision that Giulia had experienced just before her death (Figure 10.7).

Giulia died at the age of thirty , four days after giving birth to her tenth child. Her short life was distinguished by premonitions, dreams and 'signs outside the natural order'. These did not end with her death. Sansovino writes:

> it is a thing of great marvel, that on the same day, and at the same hour of her death, the most valorous Signora Vittoria di Valvasone, who was very much joined in love to the Lady Countess, was advised of this dolorous event [by a mysterious messenger]. At this time, she was 30 miles distant; nor by the great

> diligence that she then used to learn the name of the carrier of such bitter news was it ever possible to find him.[71]

And what of Augusta, whose imminent death Giulia had foreseen? Sansovino confirmed the unhappy prophecy:

> And nonetheless the Signora Augusta, on the second day of July, that was a Thursday, just three months after the departure of the Signora Contessa to the highest good, went there herself, innocent and blameless, so that she had ascended most pure, to find the most beloved sister who had ascended on the same day and hour.[72]

Indeed, genealogies in the Arnaldi family archives recorded Augusta's death on that very day—another sure sign of her sister's privileged engagement with the divine.[73]

The *Vita*

We have drawn heavily on Sansovino's *Vita* of Giulia Bembo, published just three years after her death. What was Sansovino's purpose in writing it? He promises his readers in its opening pages that

> they would have before their eyes a rare example of living well and dying well, and that the memory of such an excellent lady would remain, not like those of many sculpted in bronze and in marble, but in their minds and hearts. Thus compensating for the greatness of the loss received by her death with the pleasant memory of her rare activities, the sadness would be lessened.

A 5000-word *opuscolo* printed on both sides of seventeen octavo-sized folios plus a frontispiece, it is a pamphlet rather than a book, but no less a biography and no less a monument inscribed in minds and hearts (Figure 10.8).[74]

And yet, Sansovino's words do not reveal his motives to write the little monograph in the first place. It has been proposed that Bishop Michele might have suggested it as a 'scritto di rappresentanza' to glorify the Della Torre family.[75] It did do that. Glossing over the family's dark background of vendetta and blood feud violence, it painted a contrasting word picture of the principled Giulia as the luminous exemplar of womanly virtue. And yet, there is no evidence of a personal connection between Michele (or Girolamo for that matter) and Sansovino.

The writer's close relationship to Gian Matteo Bembo is another matter. As we have seen, Sansovino had partly fulfilled his vow to write Gian Matteo's biography with the dedication to his edition of Bruni's *La historia universale*, published in

VITA
DELLA ILLVSTRE
SIGNORA CONTESSA
GIVLIA BEMBA
DELLA TORRE.

IN VENETIA.
Per Domenico, & Gio. Battista Guerra, fratelli.
M D LXV.

Figure 10.8. Frontispiece of Francesco Sansovino, *Vita della illustre Signora Contessa Giulia Bemba della Torre*, Venice: Domenico & Gio Battista Guerra, fratelli, 1565 (Biblioteca Nazionale Marciana).

1561. And yet, alas, the full-scale biography that Sansovino had envisioned never materialized; instead, it would be the daughter Giulia who would be accorded this singular honour. In an ironic twist on the model of the learned daughter nurtured by the learned father, here the pious daughter Giulia, a paragon of Counter-Reformation family values, eclipsed the secular glory of her father Gian Matteo, as well as of her noble husband, Count Girolamo Della Torre, through the medium of print.

Indeed, for the Della Torre, continuity of the bloodline was perhaps more important than fame. Mario Savorgnan del Monte, an erudite Friulian castellan, wrote a letter to the eighty-three-year-old Venetian Alvise Cornaro in 1562, the year of Giulia's death, that admirably articulated the ideology of family renewal, with first names being passed down through the generations. He states that he is one of five surviving brothers out of nine, 'of whom we have made into one alone and that one has made us all '. The third brother was selected by common consent of the others to be married, he explains,

> making him the sole *padrone*; he has up to now six living sons that carry the same names that we carry, in a manner that he, except for one, has renewed everyone, including the father and the two dead brothers, and if we could, by observing your writings (Cornaro's *La vita sobria)*, beg for the long life that you have, we would hope to see ourselves by then to have put forth shoots and be reborn the second and third time.[76]

Or as Sansovino had put it in Giulia's *Vita*: 'in the space of 12 years in which she lived with the Lord Count in all obedience and charity, she renewed both men and women, the major part of the ancestors and herself.'[77]

Notes

1. Tempesta 2013, 279–98; Fassina 1990, 85–92; Candido 1886, 23. My thanks to Dr Paul Meyer for information on spring crops in northern Italy. For a 1690 map of the area, see ASVe, Provveditori sopra beni comunali, Disegni, b. 112, in Peressini 2014, 714.
2. Tomasi 1998, I, 155.
3. Capodagli 1665, 478–9; Bernardi 1845, 253; Bechevolo 1982, 119. Tomasi 2018, 19, 65, 66: the sculptor Bernardino da Venezia was paid for work on the fountain on 5 November 1554, 19 December 1554, 13 January 1555, 12 October 1555, and 30 October 1555. Payments were also made to two stone masons: Bortolo Guerin q. Francesco, called Bortolon in 1553 and on 14 October 1554; and Francesco Guerin q. Florino on 19 September 1555. Tomasi 2014, 63: a *fabbro* (blacksmith), Tiziano Toscano was paid in 1555 and 1556 to repair the *carro matto* that transported stones for the fountain from a quarry at Piné. Baselga di Piné is a comune in the Trentino, located about 12 kilometres northeast of Trento and around 140 km from Ceneda. Although Sartori 2005, 118, stated that the fountain was recently restored, it is again at risk. See Francesca Gallo, 'Si sgretola la fontana di Ceneda " Restauratela prima che crolli",' *La Tribuna di Treviso*, 14 April 2020.
4. See Chapter 8.
5. Cortelletti 2005, 185–201; Bechevolo 1982, 112–18; Tomasi 1998, I, 120.
6. Appendix I: Sansovino, *Vita*, 5v. See Brown 2008, 155–74.
7. ASUd, *AT*, b. 17, fasc. 1, 'Prove storico-genealogiche', 127.
8. Appendix I: Sansovino, *Vita*, ff. 7–8.
9. BCUd, MS Joppi 84, fasc. 27, 'Nota della Nascita di tutta la Figliuolanza del Signor Giambattista di Colloredo e di Lady Ginevra della Torre sua Consorte, scritta di mano del Signor Curzio loro Figlio, e tratta dall'originale'. This compilation of male and female births, recorded by Giambattista's son Curzio, should be considered the most authoritative record of this branch of the family. See Appendix II, Table D. Cf. other published versions of the Colloredo family tree which contain errors: Custoza 2003, tav. VI (secondo ramo); Crollalanza 1875, Tav. VII [terzo ramo].
10. Zagonel 2007, 51–4, states that Lavinia probably died in 1561 after giving birth to her fifth or sixth child. But cf. L Puppi 2004, 38–42, 134–5 nn101, 102, stating that Giacomino was the last child, with documentation suggesting that she died between January 1574 and 27 August 1576. See also Hope 2008, 29–42.
11. ASVe, *CCX*, Lettere dei Rettori, b. 170, no. 242; ASVe, *CX*, Comuni, Filze, b. 76 (11 September 1559); Conzato 2005, 42–3. For the drought, see Manzano 1879, 157.
12. ASVe, *CCX*, Lettere dei Rettori, b. 170, no. 243. For the torture of the cord, see Dumas 1895, 28–32.
13. Conzato 2005, 43; ASVe, *CX*, Criminali, r. 8, cc. 236 r-v (17 October 1559); r. 9, cc. 62v–63r (30 October 1560).
14. Candido 1886, 24.
15. MCVe, MS P.D. C815: Cronaca Veneziana o meglio Zibaldone con molti ricordi meterologici, cc. 13, 15.
16. ASVe, Secreti, r. 7, cc. 110v–111v (10 November 1559). Girolamo and Francesco were six th cousins.
17. MCVe, MS P.D. C815, c. 16.

18. ASVe, *CX*, Comuni, Filze, b. 78, no. 105. For the Salt Office, see Hocquet, 'Venice', 385–94.
19. Candido 1886, 24. For *petecchie*, see references in Chapter 3. See also Daciano 1576, esp. 62–91. Daciano was the communal doctor of Udine [medico fiscio stipendiato] during the plague of 1555–6 and outbreaks of *petecchie* in 1560 and 1572.
20. Bechah et al. 2008, 417–26. See also Alfani 2013, 88–9; Corradi 1867, 188–9.
21. Candido 1886, 25.
22. Ibid.
23. ASUd, *AT*, b. 17, 'Prove storico-genealogiche ', 127.
24. Appendix I: Sansovino, *Vita*, 8r. The term nephew is used here only generically. Guido was actually Girolamo's first cousin once removed on his father's side, as well as his first cousin twice removed on his mother's side—a worthy example of castellan intermarriage.
25. Appendix I: Sansovino, *Vita*, 10v–11.
26. Lazzarini and Del Puppo 1901–3, 1:169.
27. ASUd, at, b. 29, no. 16 [1562–4], 'Estratto del libro delle intrate de Udene del Lord Count Hieronimo Della Torre cavato dal libro del anno MDLXII'. The commodities cited include *formenti, segale, avena et pira, fava, meio, sarasin, sorgo, gallini, caponi, pollastri, persujtti, ocij, lenti, biava, formazo*, and *spalle*. I am assuming that *spalle* [shoulders] refers to lamb or veal.
28. For later phases of construction, see Chapter 12 .
29. See Chapter 4.
30. Custoza 2003, 129–51; Custoza 1996, 34–90; Antonini 1877, 89–93; Maniago 1819, 82.
31. BCUd, MS Joppi 84, fasc. 27. Marzio was still in exile, while Carlo was already in the service of the emperor. See Muir 1993, Muir 1993, 281, arguing that Friulian women were often silent partners in the vendetta exploits.
32. ASVe, *SAV-MC*, r. 3 (1553–62), c. 126.
33. Calvelli 2012, 52–3, with the English translation of a letter written from Brescia by Gian Matteo to Girolamo Faletti, the Este ambassador in Venice, on 1 June 1560, published in Ruscelli 1581, 206–11. See also Damen 2012, 254–5.
34. Calvelli 2012, 54. Rossi 1616, 45–8. The present whereabouts of this statue are unknown.
35. MCVe, MS P.D. c 2706, ff. 9r–10v, citing his declaration for the decima in 1566.
36. Houghton Library, Harvard University, MS Typ 330, Commission of Lorenzo Bembo from Doge Nicolò Priuli, 1558. Lorenzo also served as one of the Dieci Savi in Rialto during these years. ASVe, *SAV-MC*, r. 3 (1553–62), c. 212 (17 September 1558–16 September 1559). For ducal commissions, see Szépe 2018, 155–93, esp. 174–8. For the *dieci savii*, see Hart and Hicks 2017, 209.
37. ASVe, *SAV-MC*, r. 3, c. 170.
38. Ibid., 14, 190; ASVe, *CX*, Comuni, Filze, b. 76, no. 54 (15 December 1559); BMVe, Cod. Ital. VII 553 (=8812), c. 1.
39. ASVe, *Archivio Privato Grimani S. Maria Formosa*, b. 5, filza 457, fol. 27 (10 January 1558 m.v. (=1559). A document dated 30 October 1565 places both Alvise and Magdalena in the parish of San Gregorio in Venice. But Magdalena must have died

shortly thereafter, for a second marriage to Cecilia Priuli q. Antonio, procurator, in 1566 is recorded for Alvise. Barbaro, *Genealogie*, I, 209v–210.

40. Ibid., 37, 79, 102. For the *auditores veteres* or *auditori vecchi*, see Hart and Hicks 2017, 195–6. For the mint, see Stahl 2000, 258 ff. Marco Antonio married Lucietta (or Isabetta) Bembo q. Gaspare in 1557. Gaspare Bembo was Gian Matteo's distant cousin.
41. Bonora 1994, 63 ff; Moz 1985.
42. Bembo 1560a (including seven letters to Gian Matteo Bembo dating from 1537 to 1546); Bembo 1560b; Bembo 1560c; Bembo 1560d. These texts, all published in 1560, were reprinted in 1564 by Comin da Trino di Monferrato. This section is drawn from my essay, Brown 2008, 155–74.
43. Sansovino, in Bembo 1560a, 155.
44. Ibid.
45. Cited by Cicogna, *Ins. Ven.*, IV: 87. Gian Matteo's letter, written from Brescia on 18 August 1560, was published in Sansovino 1565, 109. Bembo refers to Zeno 1558.
46. Bruni 1561, cc.Av, Cr. See also Moz 1985, 101–2.
47. As stated by Bianco 1995, 83.
48. ASVe, *CCX*, Lettere dei Rettori, b. 171, no. 16 (26 July 1561); Conzato 2005, 137; Casella 2003, 123. Cf. Degani 1900, 109–10. Muir 1993, 252, incorrectly states that Lodovico Colloredo was the son of Marzio. For the epithet 'frascha', see Florio 1611, 196. See also Boerio 1829, 254: 'Giovane leggieri e di poco giudizio.'
49. Degani 1900, 110–14, citing Pompeo, Vicardo, and Fabio Colloredo. See also Casella 2003, 123; Veronese 1998, 157–8.
50. Degani 1900, 114. Cf. Antonini 1881, 49 n1 (incorrectly dating the attack to 1549).
51. Degani 1900, 112–14.
52. 'Torre, Michele della (1511–1586)': http://webdept.fiu.edu/~mirandas/bios1583.htm#Torre; O'Malley 2013, 168–76. Pius finally reconvened the Council in the cathedral of Saint Vigilius on 18 January 1562.
53. ASUd, *ADT*, b. 29, no. 16 [1562- 4].
54. Appendix I: Sansovino, *Vita*, 10v.
55. Ibid., 14r.
56. Ibid., 13r–14r.
57. ASVic, Arnaldi, b. 109, Genealogie.
58. Appendix I: Sansovino, *Vita*, 14r.
59. Ibid., 14v.
60. Musacchio 1999, 125–47; Corry, Howard, and Laven 2017, 28, 94–7.
61. ASUd, *AT* , b. 17, f. 169.
62. Ibid. For the retained placenta, see Gordon 2015, 771–90; Burch 2009.
63. Appendix I: Sansovino, *Vita*, 14r–v.
64. Ibid., 15r.
65. Ibid., 15r–v. Cohen and Cohen 2001, 167: 'The None—the Ninth Hour—drifted from the middle of the afternoon toward the middle of the day and gave us our word Noon.' Time-telling was inconsistent in this period, with some systems based upon a twenty-four-hour clock and others on two twelve-hour clocks, based upon sunrise and sunset. The length of the hours might vary by the length of the days.

66. Impey et al. 2001, F170–2. Cf. Gélis 1991, 242–5.
67. Appendix I: Sansovino, *Vita*, 14r–v.
68. ASUd, *AT*, b. 17, 'Prove storico-genealogiche', 127.
69. Cohen and Cohen 2001, 210–13.
70. Appendix I: Sansovino, *Vita*, 17v.
71. Ibid., 17r.
72. Ibid., 15r.
73. Archivio di Stato, Vicenza, Arnaldi, b. 109, Genealogie.
74. Appendix I: Sansovino, *Vita*, 3v–4r. See Brown 2008, 155–74, for a fuller discussion of the *Vita*.
75. Conzato 2005, 183.
76. Savorgnan 1863, 10–11. See Cornaro 1558.
77. Appendix I: Sansovino, *Vita*, 6r.

PART THREE
LINEAGES

11

Wars and Peace

Girolamo, although blessed with 'a beautiful and numerous posterity', was now a grief-stricken widower with nine motherless children. In accordance with the conventions of the day, he would have maintained a dignified restraint throughout Giulia's last days, from her difficult pregnancy and deathbed agonies to her burial. The mourning period, in which he dressed in black, as usual, would last for a year (Figure 11.1).[1] But he had little time to grieve.

Trouble in Ceneda

Just days before Giulia's death, on 21 March 1562, the citizen council of Ceneda had dispatched a delegation to Venice, protesting 'abuses and burdens' imposed by Girolamo as his brother Michele's vicar. The Cenedesi accused him of wishing to make Ceneda a small autonomous principality by forbidding their citizens from appealing his judgments in Venetian courts. At issue was whether the bishop (with Girolamo as his representative) or the Republic had jurisdiction in temporal matters in the diocese. The doge wrote to Michele in Trent on 6 June, acknowledging the bishop's 'prudence and goodness' and expressing his amazement.[2]

Another letter, addressed directly to Girolamo, followed three weeks later: his new regulations should be suspended with no other measure passed until the bishop returned, or the doge would send 'his legitimate representatives' to the city. But Girolamo, his recent loss perhaps hardening his resolve, was not about to back down. He produced a secret papal brief that Michele had obtained from Pope Julius III back in 1551, confirming that although Ceneda was located inside the Venetian dominion, it remained under the temporal, as well as spiritual, jurisdiction of the pope, whose authority was exercised by the Bishop of the Ceneda. Taken by surprise, the Senate was outraged, but took no action until the following spring. Meeting in Trent with two Venetian ambassadors to the Council in March 1563, the ever-conciliatory Michele declared himself a faithful subject of the Republic. The Senate further clarified matters, ordering him to renounce the Apostolic letter and instructing Girolamo to rescind the regulations that had been appealed by the community. Aware that they held a losing hand, the Della Torre brothers saved face by arguing that the brief of 1551 had actually been directed against the Patriarch of Aquileia and the papal nuncio and did not challenge

The Venetian Bride: Bloodlines and Blood Feuds in Venice and Its Empire. Patricia Fortini Brown, Oxford University Press (2021). © Patricia Fortini Brown. DOI: 10.1093/oso/9780192894571.003.0011

Figure 11.1. "Lutto" (Mourning clothes outside Venice), from Cesare Vecellio, *De gli habiti antichi, et moderni,* 1588, c. 166 (Amsterdam, Rijksmuseum).

Vecellio observes: "High-ranking men on the mainland, grieving for the loss of a relative, wear garments similar to the ones shown here, that is a floor-length black overgarment of rough, brushed, unpatterned wool, or of silk, with a long *bavero* made of the same fabric... and they wear black shoes."

Venetian sovereignty in temporal matters. The Council of Ten followed up in June with a decision that any appeals to sentences of the Reverend Bishop of Ceneda and his ministers in civil, as well as in criminal, cases should go to Venice. A constitutional crisis was averted.[3]

The Council of Trent concluded on 14 December 1563 with a long list of substantial reforms. Now free to attend personally to the needs of his bishopric, Michele returned to Ceneda and held a synod, with pastoral visits beginning the following year. With his stewardship marked by charitable works to the poor and strict adherence to Tridentine principles, Michele's reputation for 'prudence and goodness' only grew within the diocese.[4]

A Pamphlet War

As the most violent perpetrators of vendetta were being banished from Venetian territories, the game was changing. Girolamo had paid his dues with ten years of exile and house arrest and stayed on the sidelines. By the early 1560s, the most prominent fugitives were the Savorgnan cousins, Nicolò and Federico, on one side and Marzio Colloredo on the other. But employing their military skills and suppressing their propensity for violence, they became cavaliers and courtiers and learned new ways to pursue the vendetta by proxy.

Indeed, the formal duel was beginning to replace the revenge killings of vendetta as the preferred means to redress conflicts. It emerged as a solution to the 'double bind' in which noble feudatories were placed with the rise of the judicial authority of the state—in this case the Venetian state—over the inhabitants of its territories. On the one hand, personal attacks or insults required retaliation to preserve honour, not just of the individual but of the entire clan; on the other, such retaliation could bring arrest, loss of property, banishment, or even execution. And yet, recourse to the judicial system could well be seen as an abrogation of the obligation of 'honourable vendetta.' All options were undesirable. Even worse, when the offence involved members of the same clan, revenge caused a rupture in kin solidarity. The duel, which arose in the chivalric culture of royal courts, was the answer. Although prohibited by the Council of Trent and abhorred by the Venetian authorities, it promised to replace the savagery of ambushes and street killings by the castellans with a formalized etiquette that involved restraint, focus, and 'honest dissimulation.'[5]

Nicolò Savorgnan, at the court of Emperor Charles V in early 1563, proposed a 'contest of honour' to Marzio to resolve the old feud between their families once and for all. Implicitly, a duel. Marzio, then in Milan commanding the Tuscan forces of Cosimo I de Medici, responded with a challenge on 10 May: a duel between the two of them, each armed with a sword in a closed duelling ground, upon the condition that it would bring a permanent peace, whatever the outcome, to all the families involved: 'thus, we cavaliers with a risk to a few can put an end to the deaths of many.'[6]

Nicolò finally responded from Ferrara two months later, and not with a personal letter but with a printed manifesto. He noted with contempt Marzio's ignorance of proper chivalric etiquette in naming the type of weapon to be used, a prerogative reserved to the challenged individual. Furthermore, he accused Marzio of lying and of sending package bombs to Tristan and Urbano Savorgnan. Instead of a contest of honour, of which his adversary was obviously unworthy, Nicolò engaged in a 'contest of insults.' An exchange of pamphlets and letters ensued, with recriminations and invectives, including charges by Marzio that the Savorgnan had attempted to poison him. In spring 1564, Nicolò's cousin Federico Savorgnan offered to take up Marzio's challenge himself, despite the fact that a strict ban against duelling had just been passed at the Council of Trent.

While arrangements were being made for the duel, Camillo and Federico Colloredo entered the fray, proposing instead that they meet Tristan and Urbano Savorgnan on the duelling field to settle all past scores—but the two Savorgnan refused. The duel between Federico and Marzio was still on. After a first attempt on the banks of the Po River was stopped by soldiers from the Duke of Ferrara, they finally fought it out in an isolated spot on the Ligurian coast, with their seconds remaining on a ship offshore. After both were badly wounded, their seconds intervened and persuaded them to make peace. Marzio embraced Federico and proclaimed: 'the war between us is now over, and in the future, I intend to be your good brother.' But not so fast. The two continued to squabble and the pamphlet war continued, with charges and countercharges. In an artful touch, Federico disseminated notarized statements from several witnesses claiming that Marzio had fought in a cowardly manner.[7]

In February 1565, Marzio published a pamphlet in Brescia that summed up the matter as he saw it. Meticulously compiling a chronology of grievances that stretched back to 1511, he listed seventeen confrontations with the Savorgnan, who had comported themselves dishonourably. Tristan countered on 5 August, challenging Marzio to another duel. But with Marzio on his way to Malta to join Spanish forces defending the island from the Ottoman siege, his brother Camillo offered himself as a substitute. Tristan refused, arguing that duels were meant to resolve issues between specific individuals and not between clans. His position reflected the new code of honour that was replacing the blood feuds of the castellans.[8]

A Fourth Home

Girolamo was spending much of his time in Venice during this period. By 1565 he was renting the upper piano nobile of a palace in the parish of San Silvestro in the sestiere of San Polo—his fourth home, counting those at Ceneda, Villalta, and Udine. His annual rent of 100 ducats was among the highest in the parish. The landlord, Alvise Dalla Gatta fu Marco Antonio, was also living in the house, presumably on the lower piano nobile, with his brother Paolo and widowed mother Julia. Girolamo had a long-standing relationship with Alvise, having named him as one of his procurators before departing for Crete in 1550. The Dalla Gatta (originally called Menor Dalla Gatta), a cittadino family of mercers and comb-makers, owned several other rental properties bringing in substantial rents.[9] Another branch of the family owned a palace near San Salvador, with a courtyard adorned with one of the most elaborate wellheads in the city.[10] Suffice it to say that the family was well off, and suitable landlords, and even associates, for a lordly Friulian count.

On 24 February, Girolamo called a notary to his lodging at San Silvestro to execute the quittance of the dowry of his sister Ginevra, who had died recently. Her son Curzio appeared before the notary on behalf of himself and his brother Carlo, a deacon in Udine, and attested that the dowry had been paid in full. The witnesses included the jurist Sebastian Bravo, who had held office with Gian Matteo Bembo in the Accademia degli Uniti, and a certain Domenico *dicto del dodece portatore*, a bookseller from Florence. Two days later, Curzio's brother Camillo also signed off on the agreement, with Paulo Dalla Gatta and Andrea Bugatto, a citizen of Udine, serving as witnesses.[11] We may note that the transactions took place in Venice, presumably for the convenience of Girolamo, and not in Udine.

What brought Girolamo to Venice in these years? Whether he had ever completed his law studies in Bologna is unknown, but the scanty documentary record suggests that he continued employing skills that he had honed in Ceneda as his brother's procurator and in Crete as *conduttore*—representative—of Cardinal Ranuccio Farnese. In a notarial document executed in Candia on 2 April 1565, Nadal Naviglio, doctor of law and castellano of the Venetian fortress in Candia, elected Girolamo as his procurator in Venice 'to obtain the confirmation and election of his sons and descendants as nobles'.[12] Since Naviglio (or Navilio) was not a patrician surname, Nadal must have been referring to the Cretan, not Venetian, nobility. This curious document suggests that Girolamo had sufficient influence with the Avogaria di Comun in Venice to promise a positive outcome. Similarly, in December 1566, Antonio Nelio, a nobleman of Capodistria and Patriarch of Jerusalem, named Girolamo as his procurator to retrieve 340 ducats in rental income from certain casali owned by the patriarchate in the Kingdom of Cyprus.[13] Girolamo's personal accounts from the 1570s–1580s document a complex financial picture, with substantial holdings in real property that was heavily leveraged with debt.[14] His active engagement in money management, involving connections with Rome and the Mediterranean, may well have called for a base in Venice, rather than in Ceneda or the Friuli.

The record is frustratingly silent on the whereabouts of Girolamo's children in the years after their mother's death. One scenario is that they remained together in the bishop's household in Ceneda, with visits from Girolamo. By 1565, all four boys, ranging in age from seven to thirteen, were of an age to receive an education and learn courtly skills. But what of the five girls, ranging in age from two to eleven years? Was the bishop's castle a suitable environment for their upbringing? They might have been raised in the seclusion of Villalta by trusted servants like Orsa, or, perhaps more likely, in a nearby convent with Girolamo making periodic visits. We will begin to hear more of the children in the 1570s as they come of age, whether for a career for the boys or for marriage for the girls.

The Peace of 1568

After Marzio Colloredo returned to Italy from Malta, the pamphlet war resumed, with him repeating the old allegations and adding new ones. Three Savorgnans—Federico, Tristan, and Nicolò—jointly published a lengthy defence, complete with witness statements, in Ferrara in April 1566. Two years later, Marzio fired back with a class-based rationale of the blood feud, now claiming somewhat defensively that the Colloredo family were the true leaders of the old Strumieri (castellan) faction, for it had a more ancient lineage in the Friuli than even the Della Torre and a more noble lineage than the Savorgnan. He proudly took credit for all the murders committed on behalf of his family, matching each one to an outrage perpetrated in the first place by the Savorgnan. But matters had reached a tipping point. Troiano Arcano, a Colloredo in-law, challenged Federico Savorgnan to a duel. They met on 14 April 1568 in an unfrequented spot between Mantua and Cremona and both died from their wounds on the field of battle. Parity had finally been achieved.[15]

All that remained was to make it official. Concerned about exterior pressure from the Turks, as well as from the emperor Maximilian II, the Council of Ten needed a unified Friulian patriciate. On 15 May, it cancelled all licences to bear arms for the next six months and instructed Alvise Mocenigo, cavalier and procurator (and future doge) to broker a permanent peace between the two factions. First, Mocenigo forbade all the parties from publishing any more hateful polemics, 'because, one can truly say that when the writing of such material began, it quickened the passions and the spread of hatreds more than anything else'. Second, relying on the old principle of collective responsibility, he required all the adult males of the various families—including the Colloredo, Della Torre, Caporiacco, Strassoldo, and Arcano on the one side, and Savorgnan, Torso, Arrigoni, and Antonini on the other—to sign notarized proxies authorizing the head of each clan to sign a peace treaty in their name. The signatories should declare their 'inclination and wish to live in a Christian manner and in peace in the service of God, and of this Dominion'. If anyone in a family broke the peace, the property of all would be confiscated. It was an offer that could not be refused.[16]

During the last three weeks of August, the designated representatives of each family appeared singly and in groups before notaries and witnesses in Udine, Gradisca, Venice, and the castles of Pinzano and Colloredo. By the 29th of the month, nearly all parties had signed when Girolamo Della Torre finally accepted the terms of the treaty on behalf of himself, his brother Bishop Michele, and his sons Sigismondo, Giulio, Giovanni, and Alvise III. Guido Della Torre signed for himself, while Curzio Colloredo signed for his sons and his brothers Carlo, Camillo, and the contentious Marzio, along with several others. Vicardo Colloredo, chamberlain of Ferdinando I, Grand Duke of Tuscany, represented a virtual army from three branches of the family—his brothers Pompeo and Fabio; his distant cousin Mario with his sons Federico, Lodovico, Lelio, and Silla; and another cousin, Francesco, with his sons Giulio, Alessandro, and Brunoro, in addition to a Strassoldo and two Arcanos. Sebastiano Montegnacco and Ettore Caporiacco signed for themselves and 'all of their house'.[17]

The last signature was obtained on Monday 30 August, when Giovanni Maria Gonzaga appeared before a notary on Piazza San Marco to sign a 'true, sincere peace with the magnificent lords Turriani and Colloredi'. He was acting as procurator for Maria, widow of Giovanni Savorgnan, who was guardian of her minor sons Francesco and Federico. It was Giovanni's injury in the brawl in Padua in

1549 that had sentenced Girolamo Della Torre to exile in Candia, and Giovanni's complicity in the murder of Alvise II Della Torre that had likewise sent Giovanni to Zara. Both had returned, chastened, to Venice in 1555 with little taste to pursue the vendetta themselves.[18]

Finally, on the very same day, 30 August 1568, mass was celebrated at the fourteenth hour in the church of San Giovanni Battista on the Giudecca. With all the signatories present, as well as many gentlemen of Venice, Alvise Mocenigo addressed the group:

> Therefore, having to follow peace and reconciliation among all of these Noble Families (the names of which would be too long to repeat), we swear and declare by the authority granted to us that these parties wish that everything said and written [in the pamphlet war] would be null and void as if they had not written such material. And as a sign of a good and loyal peace, everyone should amicably embrace one another, and casting aside and putting into oblivion all past hatreds and passions, promising in the future, with integrity of heart, to employ with words and works all those signs of love and kindness that are used between true and faithful friends.

All the lords present then sealed the Peace of 1568 by embracing and kissing each other on the mouth. This age-old physical act of reconciliation dated back to early feudal times. Likely with a fair amount of 'honest dissimulation', honour was secured on both sides, and the decades-long blood feud had finally come to an end.[19]

The Papal Nuncio

Michele, serving once again as papal nuncio to France, was away from Ceneda for the signing. Appointed by the newly elected Pope Pius V, he had arrived in Paris on 29 May 1566 after a tiring overland journey. He was armed with a brief from the pope: 'If their Majesties believe that Catholicism is the true religion, it is not enough that they profess it and observe it. They must also make their subjects agree with them; otherwise, they will lose, either their throne, or the religion.' The heresy of Calvinism must be fought at every turn, the Huguenots driven out, and the country returned to the orthodox purity of the Catholic church. The immediate publication—and application—of the decrees of the Council of Trent would be the first, and essential, step toward re-establishing religious unity in France.[20]

Although Michele still had friends at the court from his earlier missions, his reception was lukewarm. The British envoy reported back to Queen Elizabeth I of England:

> On the first of June the Pope's Nuncio, Michel De la Torre, Bishop of Ceneda, came in coach from Paris to the Court. No one was appointed to receive him. He dined with a few people of no great account. Afterwards he had audience, the King [Charles IX], Queen Mother [Catherine de' Medici], and others of the Court being present. He recommended to them the Pope's Church, which was sore afflicted, and urged the King to purge himself of the ravening vermin of sectaries and heretics, and also to publish the late Edict of Trent and cause it to be received throughout the realm. The King and Queen gave attentive ear. Nevertheless, a man might now and then easily perceive by the sour countenance the Queen made that she liked not all he had said. After he had saluted divers persons the King made him somewhat too short an answer for so long a demand.[21]

That audience set the tone for Michele's mission. He was frustrated at every turn. When he pushed for full publication of the Tridentine decrees, the king appointed two commissioners to study the matter, one whose orthodoxy was suspect in the eyes of the church and another whom the pope had just declared heretical. When the pope sanctioned French bishops for transgressions, the king declined to apply penalties. When the pope instructed Michele to work for a reconciliation between France and Spain, he dealt clumsily with the situation. Michele had successfully navigated the bureaucracies of the Vatican, but he was out of his depth in international politics. Although royal sentiments would eventually turn against the Huguenots, Michele Della Torre had to be replaced. By the time he was recalled on 12 August 1568, his replacement was already on the road to Paris.[22] Probably much relieved, Michele departed a month later and returned to the obscurity of Ceneda and the welcome news of the Peace of 1568. His name was rumoured as a possibility for nomination as cardinal around the end of the year, but it was not to be, at least by this pope. When Pius V named an unprecedented sixteen in May 1570, Michele would not be among them.[23]

Among the Most Honoured Gentlemen in the City

Nor did Gian Matteo Bembo have much time to mourn his daughter's death during those years. In many ways he was at the top of his game. On 6 January 1563, he would begin a prestigious sixteen-month term as the ducal councillor for Cannaregio. The six ducal councillors, one from each sestiere, were, in Sansovino's words,

> elected from among the most honoured gentlemen in the city since what is required is the grandeur and dignity of magistrates. They sit alongside the Doge, and with him they execute all sorts of business, for the most part private matters

such as giving audiences, reading public letters, granting privileges and other similar matters.

Elected by the Great Council, the councillors were more than just advisors to the doge; they were also his overseers, ensuring that he did not exceed the limited powers explicitly granted him in his *promissione*. In sum, they were intended to keep him in check.[24]

The councillors and the Doge, along with the three heads of the Quarantia, the judicial branch of government, comprised the ten-member Signoria, the apex of the complicated Venetian governmental pyramid. As a microcosm of the capital city, the Signoria represented—and embodied—the Republic itself. The most powerful component of the Collegio, the Signoria set the agenda for the Great Council, received foreign emissaries, and worked with all the councils of government. Its members also sat with the Council of Ten (bringing its actual number to seventeen), an ever more formidable body with legislative and judicial powers annexed to the top of the pyramid.[25]

The walls of the Sala del Collegio, where Gian Matteo shared the podium with Doge Girolamo Priuli and the other councillors, were lined with large votive paintings of the former doges, but there was room for at least one more. In October 1563, the procurators of the Salt Office, the body responsible for the decoration of the Palazzo Ducale, signed a contract with the artist Parrasio Micheli for a votive painting of Doge Lorenzo Priuli to be placed in the chamber. The commission, traditional for doges, was long overdue. Lorenzo, whose wife Zilia Dandolo had been honoured with the sumptuous entry in 1555, had died in 1559 (and replaced as doge—atypically—by his brother Girolamo). The contract specified that the painting should depict 'the Spirito Santo [probably Christ] above a temple richly adorned with architectural columns', with personifications of Fortune and Venetia. The Serene Prince (presumably kneeling before Venetia) is crowned with the ducal corno by a putto 'and accompanied by ten of the Senators who were [present] at his creation, who were among his closest *congionti* (associates)'. The figures were to number sixteen in all. Micheli labelled each senator in his sketch, revealing that the *congionti* included Lorenzo's brother Girolamo (now doge), his brother-in-law Matteo Dandolo (who had withdrawn from the list of candidates in support of Lorenzo), and his arch-rival Stefano Tiepolo (who withdrew his name only when it became apparent that he would not win). They also included Gian Matteo Bembo in the foreground.[26]

This celebration of family and friends, and gracious inclusion of a rival, would have been a satisfying sight to the *primi della terra* whom fortune chose to sit in the Sala del Collegio, the audience hall where ambassadors and foreign princes were received. But that was not all. The walls of the Sala del Maggior Consiglio were also lined with twenty-two painted *istorie* celebrating the Peace of Venice (or Story of Alexander III), one of the most cherished foundation myths of the

Venetian republic. The cycle was begun in 1474 with paintings by Gentile and Giovanni Bellini to replace an earlier rendition that had included works by Gentile da Fabriano and Pisanello. With the canvases commissioned sporadically over the years as funds became available, the new cycle took nine decades to complete.[27]

The final three commissions had been negotiated in January 1562. As Giorgio Vasari writes in his *Lives of the Artists*, 'it had been ordained by the Senate that Jacopo Tintoretto and Paolo Veronese, at that time young men of great promise, should each execute a scene in the Hall of the Great Council, and Orazio, the son of Tiziano, another'. The works were installed some two years later.[28]

One of the notable features of the painted *istorie* was the inclusion of portraits of contemporary figures in events that took place in the historical past. Writing in 1557, Lodovico Dolce had criticized Jacopo's *Excommunication of the Emperor*, completed in 1553, complaining that the artist had

> exceeded the bounds of propriety in a serious way... when he put in so many Venetian senators and showed them standing there and looking on without any real motivation. For the fact is that there is no likelihood that all of them should have happened to be there simultaneously in quite this way, nor do they have anything to do with the subject.[29]

Dolce's criticism fell on deaf ears; the much beloved practice continued as a way of honouring notable citizens in that republic of patrician equals.

When Gian Matteo sat near the Doge on the dais at the end of the Sala del Maggior Consiglio, he would have been gratified to see his own face in Jacopo Tintoretto's *Coronation of Frederick Barbarossa by Pope Hadrian IV in St Peters*. No drawings or copies of Tintoretto's painting survive, but two vague descriptions give us an idea of the composition. Again according to Vasari, 'Tintoretto painted in his scene Frederick Barbarossa being crowned by the Pope, depicting there a most beautiful building, and about the Pontiff a great number of Cardinals and Venetian gentlemen, all portrayed from life, and at the foot the Pope's chapel of music'.[30] Stating that the work was much praised, Sansovino also noted 'portraits of many nobles, with beautiful clothes and beautiful gestures'. He named nine Venetian gentlemen in the painting, Gian Matteo among them.[31]

As we have seen, a book dedication was another way of celebrating contemporaries without breaching the norms of the patrician ethos. Sansovino dedicated his translation of Plutarch's *Lives* to Gian Matteo in 1563, while the paintings were underway. The lengthy homage declared that 'this man showed everyone that even republics oftentimes have men capable of governing empires'.[32]

Gian Matteo's family, despite—or perhaps because of—his many travels, was flourishing. His daughters Augusta and Giulia had made good marriages with mainland nobility. His oldest son, Lorenzo, a galley captain who was frequently at sea, now had five sons and a daughter, thus assuring the continuance of the male bloodline. He had also completed a term in January as one of the three provveditori sopra le galie armade de condennatj, magistrates in charge of the prison galleys, and would be elected in December to the Collegio alla Milizia da Mar, the body responsible for the maintenance and provisioning of the fleet. Alvise, married but childless, was still captaining the galleys of Cyprus and pursuing his wife's legal battle for property on Crete. Marco Antonio, also married and without children as yet, began a term in October as one of the six signori di notte al criminal for Cannaregio. Sebastiano, who never married, was a lawyer in the Avogaria, the civil courts of the Palazzo Ducale. In December, Davide, still a bachelor, was elected proveditore and castellano at Cerigo (Kythera), an island in Greece lying opposite the south-eastern tip of the Peloponnese peninsula.[33]

Pietro, Gian Matteo's youngest son, had followed the example of his famous uncle and namesake and entered the church. He was ordained a priest without completing regular theological studies, perhaps because of family connections. Active at Trent, he became close to the hardliner Cardinal Carlo Borromeo. With Borromeo's support, he was named Bishop of Veglia on 15 January 1564 at the age of thirty and took office ten months later. His diocese, its capital in the city of Veglia (Krk), comprised a number of islands in the Quarner (Kvarner) gulf, off the Dalmatian coast.[34]

It was a time of public triumphs and private sadnesses for the family. Gian Matteo was elected Duke of Candia on 9 April 1564.[35] At first, he was elated—this would be the high point of his career—and accepted the post 'with all promptness, although 74 years old, hoping that the strength of his body would correspond to his ardent desire, and ready soul'. Alas, it was not to be. Several weeks later, on 30 April, the Great Council voted to excuse him, after considering the deposition of the physicians Schili and Bellobuono, attesting to 'the indisposition of his person caused by an inflammation of his legs, that troubles him very much, that forced him with much regret and sadness to supplicate this council…to accept his excuse from going to the regiment of Duca di Candia to which he was recently elected'.[36]

A few days later, on 2 May, Gian Matteo lost a child when Sebastiano died in the family home at Santa Maria Nova at the age of thirty-five. He had been ill for five months.[37] Gian Matteo's brother-in-law Bernardino Belegno died soon after, on 8 June, at the age of seventy.[38] A close neighbour in the parish of Santa Maria Nova, he had served as one of the two required witnesses registering the noble births of Lorenzo's three youngest sons back in the 1550s.[39] More reminders of age and mortality.

And yet, Gian Matteo's affliction did not prevent him from serving on an advisory commission that year to examine how best to divert the River Sile from flowing directly into the lagoon.[40] Nor did it prevent him from accepting another appointment as one of the governatori dell'entrate in July.[41] The family's public image was further burnished by two volumes published by the ever-prolific Sansovino: in 1564 another collection of letters to Gian Matteo from Pietro Bembo,[42] and in 1565 his *Vita delle illustre signora Contessa Giulia Bemba della Torre*. It was a world away from the feudal culture of the Friuli.

Despite the infirmities that denied him a triumphant return to Candia as Duke, Gian Matteo was again elected a ducal councillor for Cannaregio under Doge Girolamo Priuli in January 1566.[43] From Bembo's *decima* (property tax) declaration filed on 28 June, we learn that he was still living in the *soler di sopra* (upper piano nobile) of his *casa da statio* at Santa Maria Nova 'with my sons'—almost certainly the unmarried Davide and perhaps a widowed Alvise. Marco Antonio and his wife Isabetta were living elsewhere and expecting the birth of their first son.[44] The *soler di sotto*, normally occupied by Gian Matteo's son Lorenzo and his family, was rented out for 55 ducats per year. Lorenzo had been serving as capitano of Famagusta, a post held by his father two decades earlier, since August 1565. Given that he had vacated the family home, Lorenzo may have been accompanied by his five sons, aged thirteen to nineteen, as well as his wife Laura if still living; their daughter Marcella was probably already sequestered in a convent. Gian Matteo attests in the declaration, 'when my son returns, I will not rent out this part of the house, nor have I ever rented it out before'.[45]

On 20 August, a year after returning from his Famagusta assignment, his son Lorenzo was elected provveditore generale of the Kingdom of Cyprus.[46] With the island facing the imminent threat of a Turkish invasion, Lorenzo would be sailing into unusually dangerous waters. He must have travelled alone on this occasion, with the rest of the family remaining in Venice. Previously a capitano of Paphos and a perennial sopracomito on the galleys of Cyprus, he was more than familiar with the island. The new appointment was again documented by a handsome ducal commission (Figure 11.2; see also Figure 10.5).[47]

But Pietro, now Bishop of Veglia, was having problems. Like his brother-in-law Michele in Ceneda, he sought to institute a strict observance of the Tridentine reforms. But unlike Michele, he had a heavy hand and soon developed an acrimonious relationship with his constituents. Friction between Catholic bishops and the local population, as well as with the civil authority wielded by the Venetian rectors, was not unusual along the Dalmatian coast, a situation that required more tact than Pietro possessed. In response to complaints by the local priests that he was 'not a sincere judge, but corruptible and greedy' and had made his bishopric, 'which is the house of God, the house of the Devil,' he defended himself in a long letter to doge Girolamo Priuli in July 1566. Deploring the clerics' lack of respect, he lamented: 'The mitre is no longer a mitre, but an object only worthy of being placed and thrown (to say it without shame) in a sewer.' If such charges had been made privately, he claimed, they could have been dealt with. 'But because

Figure 11.2. Commission of Lorenzo Bembo, Provveditore Generale of the Kingdom of Cyprus, from Doge Girolamo Priuli, 1565. MS R.4.30, James no. 659 (University of Cambridge,Trinity College).
In an eloquent statement of Venetian republican values, Justice and Peace stand together in an expansive landscape resembling Cyprus. They are framed by personifications of six virtues in the border (clockwise from upper left): Hope, Charity, Fortitude, Temperance, Prudence, and Faith. The Lion of St Mark at the top is paired with the Bembo coat of arms at the bottom.

they were said publicly in the palace, in the piazza, and in the council, I demand justice from your Serenity with the present letter.' Proudly declaring himself the son of Gian Matteo Bembo, he concluded with a biblical passage 'si me persecuti sunt, et vos persequentur' (if they have persecuted me, they will persecute you).[48] Alas, as we shall see, Bembo's relationship with his flock would not improve over time.

Despite his maladies, Gian Matteo was elected podestà of Padua on 16 August 1568. A highly prestigious office, and not far from Venice, it must have been a tempting prospect, but again, perhaps after considerable soul searching that stretched out over two months, he asked to be excused once again. His failing health may have been one factor in the decision, but another might have been a wish to stay at Santa Maria Nova with his grandchildren.

By December 1569, Lorenzo's own health was in question. Although only forty-nine and at the height of his career, he called the Grand Chancellor of Cyprus to his quarters in Nicosia and dictated his last will and testament. Declaring himself healthy in mind but infirm of body, he wished to put his affairs in order. And to continue to govern the family from beyond the grave. His first concern was for Marcella, his only daughter, who was then being cared for in the monastery of the Ognissanti in Venice. She was to be given a dowry of 4000 ducats if she wished to marry, 'as honorably as possible', or a lesser amount to be determined by the executors if she preferred to enter a convent. The decision was hers.[49]

Lorenzo also left small bequests to his servants and empowered his executor in Cyprus to sell off his possessions, settle his accounts, and send the proceeds to his executors in Venice. Lorenzo had been generous with his own family, with loans to his brothers Pietro (Bishop of Veglia), Alvise, Marco Antonio, and Davide still outstanding; these needed to be recaptured by the executors. Each of his own five sons—Alvise, Andrea, Marco Antonio, Gian Matteo, and Piero—would receive 1000 ducats when he reached the age of twenty years, 'to dispose of and invest as they decide, so that they would have the ability to create something and make some acquisitions.'

The residue of the estate should be distributed equally to the sons and pass from male heir to the nearest male heir, so as never to leave the house of Bembo. Toward this end, Lorenzo makes a request often found in Venetian wills: 'I pray and exhort all my sons to live together, and lovingly, each giving obedience one to the other according to their age, living always with charity and the love of God, and the first who would leave the others should receive 100 ducats less, so that all would have reason to stay together.' It would be a full house at Santa Maria Nova, at least for a time. Marcella, Andrea, and Gian Matteo would all eventually marry, with only the latter producing sons to carry on the family name.[50] The estate, such as it was, would remain intact, at least for a generation.

Senza alcuna pompa

1570 would be a momentous year—for the Bembo family, for the island of Cyprus, and for the Venetian Republic. Retired from public office for the past two years, Gian Matteo fell ill in February. On 22 March he called the ducal notary Cesare Ziliol to his house at Santa Maria Nova and dictated his last will and testament.[51] When he died on 2 June at the age of seventy-nine, the entry in the civic death register noted that he had been experiencing 'an issue of blood' for the past four months—a vague description suggesting a bronchial or gastrointestinal malady.[52] During his last days, he would have been mourning the premature death of his oldest son, Lorenzo, who had died in Cyprus on 16 April, with the news reaching Venice as early as mid-May. Buried in the Latin cathedral of Santa Sofia in Nicosia, Lorenzo would at least be spared witnessing the devastating loss of the city to the Ottomans just five months later.[53]

Let us return to Gian Matteo's testament. Naming the procurator Giovanni Da Lezze, 'whom I've known to be of great valor, just, and loving,' as his executor, he wished to be buried *senza alcuna pompa* (without any pomp) in the humble floor tomb that he had purchased twenty years earlier in the church of San Nicolò inside the monastery of SS. Giovanni e Paolo.[54]

Gian Matteo considered charity an ongoing obligation. Accordingly, the annual income of 10–12 ducats from the *mezzado* (mezzanine) of his rental property at San Maurizio should be used to ransom prisoners each year on Christmas and Easter; if one of his heirs should wish to retain full use of the space, he could make a one-time payment of 200 ducats to invested by the procurators with the proceeds used for that charitable purpose.

Like his son Lorenzo and other patrician men of his time, Gian Matteo was determined to keep the tangible estate assets within the family: 'I wish that all my real property, houses, and villa lands, and those few pieces of silver and furniture acquired with my money, should stay in perpetual *fedecommesso* for my four sons, Lorenzo [then still living], Alvise, Marco Antonio, and Davide, and their legitimate male descendants', with each share to pass on from father to sons. 'The rest, truly, of all my possessions, that will be found beyond those specified in my testament, that is, only the household goods, I leave to Marco Antonio and Davide, my sons, as they have the most need.'[55]

But first there were debts to be paid. Alvise would first have to repay a loan of 1900 ducats to the estate before receiving his distribution, but until then he was free to invest it and enjoy the income. The same conditions held true for the other sons, who were allowed to lend money to each other as long as it remained in the *fedecommesso*. The dowry of Marco Antonio's wife Isabetta should be recovered from the estate and credited to Marco Antonio before the division was made. As her husband, he was entitled to invest her dowry as he saw fit during the course of the marriage, but if he predeceased her, two-thirds (around half of it likely in material goods such as clothing, furnishings, and jewellery) would revert to her as her own property; it thus had to be protected. If the Bembo patriline died out entirely, then the residue of the estate should be given to the hospital of San Giovanni e Paolo 'for the use and aid of the poor'.[56]

While preserving the assets of his estate for the legitimate progeny of his legitimate sons, Gian Matteo also provided for a natural son, Ettor, who must have been born after his wife's death in 1555. He was to be 'governed, taught, dressed, and shod, and the masters who will instruct him should be paid' from the income produced by the estate. The boy was presently in the care of a tutor, but he was given leave to move in with one of his half-brothers—Gian Matteo's legitimate sons—if he chose. The latter were, in any case, collectively obliged to support the boy until he reached the age of eighteen years.[57] These arrangements reflect the harsh reality of an illegitimate birth, for Gian Matteo made no further provision for the boy: no financial settlement, no property, no placement in a religious order, no mention of his mother. We might assume that Ettor's tutor was seeing to his training in some kind of trade or profession, but although he carried the Bembo name, once he reached the age of majority, he was on his own, at least financially.[58] The purity of the bloodline was intrinsically linked to the integrity of the estate.

But what about Gian Matteo's fifth surviving son, Pietro? He was not included in the *fedecommesso*. Since the will had cited a 300-ducat loan extended to 'Monsignore, my son', it is unlikely that it was an oversight. Perhaps he was left out because he was Bishop of Veglia and would produce no legitimate male heirs. Perhaps there was bad blood. For whatever reason, the omission posed a problem which Gian Matteo should have foreseen. According to the Venetian legal principle of 'absolute equivalence' among brothers, all surviving sons (or their male heirs *per stirpes*) should have received the remainder in strictly equal portions.[59]

Predictably, the will was contested the following year. Alvise had died without issue in December 1570, and the lawsuit, filed with the Conservatori delle Leggi in August 1571, involved Pietro, Davide, Marco Antonio, and the sons of the deceased Lorenzo.[60] Because the inheritance had not been made 'pro indiviso', the court was allowed to divide the real estate amongst the four parties. The litigation dragged on until the summer of 1573, when the arbiters, 'wishing to end the differences', proposed a compromise that divided the real property into four parts. Lorenzo's surviving sons (and Gian Matteo's only grandsons as yet)—Alvise, Andrea, and Gian Matteo—would receive the first floor, terrace, and ground floor storerooms of the *casa da statio* at Santa Maria Nova, where they were already living, plus five adjacent rental units on Calle del Forno. Surprisingly, although the youngest surviving son, Bishop Pietro would retain the second floor of the palace, with its storerooms and attic, sharing the common places such as the courtyard and well with Lorenzo's heirs. He too would receive five adjacent rental units.

Dispossessed of the family palace at Santa Maria Nova, the other two sons were allotted equivalent properties elsewhere. Davide, who would marry only in 1577, was given the *casa da statio* at San Maurizio, rented out at the time, and a second *casa da statio* and two apartments at San Pantalon, plus two rental units on Calle del Forno. Marco Antonio, already married, received country properties, including the villa at Ponte di Brenta, with income from grain, wine, and rents, plus four modest apartments on Calle del Forno. But he was still due 850 ducats from his wife's dowry that had been commingled with Gian Matteo's funds. This debt was to be split between the other three parties, at 283 ducats apiece, and paid out to Marco Antonio over time.

The division was well crafted in that each party received his own property that he did not have to share with the others, but suffice it to say that Gian Matteo's will had driven a wedge between the brothers.[61]

A Mercenary Bishop

In contrast to Michele Della Torre, Gian Matteo's son Bishop Pietro was not endearing himself to his diocese in Veglia. Quick to excommunicate those who ignored or contested his rigid decrees, he was roundly detested by the clergy and laity alike. It may be no coincidence that the situation exploded in the summer of 1573 just as Gian Matteo's estate was finally settled. The parishioners complained to the Council of Ten that this 'mercenary bishop' had despoiled their churches of relics and other objects of value. More seriously, seven canons whom Bembo had excommunicated, and not for the first time, were sailing to Venice to appeal his sentence when they were captured by pirates and held for ransom. When the Ten complained to Pope Gregory XIII through the Venetian orator in Rome that the canons had been excommunicated for trivial reasons, the pope responded firmly: 'This judgement is up to us.'[62] On 16 July, the day after receiving the orator's report of the rebuke, the Ten reacted just as angrily. Claiming the right of *ius patronato*, a duty to maintain altars of a church, they enjoined Bembo to restore the chapels of the cathedral in Veglia and to return the church silver that he had taken. They also ordered him to pay the ransoms for the canons captured as slaves and prohibited him from returning to his diocese 'where for the extreme hatred that he has acquired from that populace, some important inconvenience can easily happen.'[63]

A year later, on 10 September 1574, the papal nuncio urged the Republic to allow the bishop to return to his episcopal seat. Bembo, said to have visited his diocese only twice during his tenure, must have returned there at some point, but probably not to stay. For the most part, he governed it from afar, drafting a twenty-two-article *regolamento* (regulation) for the local clergy, with rules for every aspect of their liturgical and personal behaviour. A model of the post-Tridentine reforms and written in the language of the Venetian bureaucracy, it was approved in 1579 by the apostolic visitor, Agostino Valier, Bishop of Verona.[64] Pietro, who had been granted the second floor of the family palace at Santa Maria Nova in the estate litigation, was almost certainly living there for much of the time until his death in 1589, not in Veglia.

The Ottoman Threat

Girolamo Della Torre would have been among the mourners at Gian Matteo's burial, conducted *senza alcuna pompa*, in the monastery of SS. Giovanni e Paolo in June 1570. Gian Matteo had referred to him as *mio caro zenero* (my dear son-in-law) in his testament, and while he did not name him as an executor, we may assume that they had remained on friendly terms. But families live in a larger world. Gian Matteo's death was not unexpected, and any sadness on his passing was overshadowed by ominous news from the Mediterranean. Like any resident of the territory, Girolamo would have been concerned about the Ottoman threat.

Although the Ottoman Sultan Selim II had signed a peace treaty with the Emperor Maximilian II in 1567, the Turks had become increasingly bellicose.

Long eyeing Cyprus as a legitimate Ottoman possession, the Sultan amassed a large war chest, appointed commanders of land and sea forces, and sent an envoy to Venice in March 1570, demanding the surrender of the island or face an attack. The Venetians stood firm, trusting that their new state of the art fortifications would protect Nicosia. Designed by the military engineer Giulio Savorgnan, these consisted of a circuit of high canted walls of packed earth faced with stone punctuated by eleven arrowhead bastions, each named after a leading family of the city, thus converting Nicosia into a star fortress. It would surely withstand any assault.[65]

But not only was Cyprus at risk; so too was the Venetian Terraferma and even Ceneda. Back in 1499, the Turks had swept through the Friuli. Easily crossing the Tagliamento and Livenza rivers, they had reached the village of S. Giacomo di Veglia, a little more than a mile away from the Castello di San Martino. Carrying out a savage massacre of people and property, they took 7000 prisoners 'of every age and every sex' in the surrounding territory. Ceneda was inexplicably spared, but the event created an indelible memory passed down through the generations, and people were terrified that they might not escape this time. In response to the sabre-rattling in Venice, the council of deputies of the Commune of Ceneda voted in March 1570 that 'the Castello di San Martino be fortified to defend itself against incursions by the enemies, reducing it to a defensive fortress'. The councillors were further empowered 'to provide muskets, arquebuses, powder, cannon balls, and everything else judged necessary', and given the 'authority to collateralize or sell public assets' for this purpose.[66]

And yet, Michele Della Torre had just completed three years of pastoral visits throughout the diocese and had other things on his mind. Passed over for cardinal in Pius V's nominations in mid-May, he turned a potential embarrassment into an opportunity and attended to his flock. He convened a second synod in Ceneda on 28 March, the feast day of the translation of the relics of San Tiziano, patron saint of the cathedral, and issued a severe decree against priests who kept concubines or otherwise led a dissolute life.[67]

But things were not going well in Cyprus. On 1 July, the new city walls of Nicosia were not yet complete when Turkish forces landed on the south coast of the island and marched on the city. Three weeks later the siege began. After forty-five assaults, the Venetian forces ran out of ammunition, and on 9 September the Turks breached the walls at the Podocataro bastion, poured in, and massacred 20,000 inhabitants. The Turkish army then moved on to Famagusta with forces that would eventually number 200,000. And yet, even with the city's old-fashioned, if retrofitted, walls, the Venetian garrison with just 8500 men managed to hold out for eleven months. When the city finally fell on 1 August 1571, the Ottoman commander Lala Mustafa Pasha allowed the Christian residents and surviving Venetian soldiers to leave the island, but had the Venetian capitano Marcantonio

Bragadin flayed alive.[68] Lorenzo Bembo might well have shared a similar fate had illness not taken him earlier.

News of the siege reached Ceneda, and the long delayed defensive works ordered for the Castello were finally carried out. A fortified curtain wall complete with crenellations was constructed on its south side overlooking the plain (Figure 10.2). It was provided with two small watchtowers, adorned with carved reliefs—one with the figure of San Tiziano and the other of San Martino, featuring the coats of arms of the city and the bishop. Beneath each was an inscription that stressed the cooperation between Della Torre and his subjects:

MICHAELE TURRIANO EPISCOPO
CIVITAS CENETENSIS AERE PUBLIC EREXIT.
ANNO MDLXXI.[69]
(Erected with public funds of the citizens of Ceneda
By Bishop Michele Della Torre
In the year 1571)

Although Cyprus was lost, the victory of the Holy League (primarily the naval forces of the pope, Venice, and Spain) over the Ottoman navy at Lepanto on 7 October 1571 calmed fears, and Michele could focus again on local matters both secular and spiritual. He continued to endear himself to his subjects with a series of civic reforms. In February 1572, he reorganized the citizen council, which had been described as 'tumultuous and confused', with fifteen councillors elected from each social class—the nobility, the citizenry, and the peasantry—and instituted a new system of elections. A year later, he convoked a third Synod, this time taking aim at clandestine marriages and those consummated before receiving the sacrament—offences forbidden by the Council of Trent. The guilty parties were ordered to stand for 'three feast days at the door of the Church holding a lit candle' and asking people for forgiveness for the scandal they had given them.[70] Michele's religious zeal was accompanied by a political posture more typical of a Venetian subject than a Friulian lord: 'knowing that the freedom to bear arms brought to the troubled souls of many citizens a tendency to brawl, he commanded rigorously that no one should dare to carry firearms through the city.'[71]

All this called for an inscription in the public loggia near the doors to the chancery:

VIVA L'ILLVSTRISSIMA CASA TORRIANA
PATRONA ETERNAMENTE DE' CVORI DI CENEDA
([The illustrious house of the Torriana, benefactors,
lives eternally in the hearts of Ceneda)

According to a seventeenth-century source, the same inscription was affixed to houses of the principal citizens. Not only that: 'Many gentlemen of that city conserved in their homes his portrait from life and spoke of him daily, as a person of virtue and sanctity, conspicuous beyond measure.'[72]

True Tranquillity

Michele surrounded himself with old friends, among them the Bolognese poet Vitale Papazzoni, who had served as his secretary in Rome and had probably taken minor orders. Vitale had also accompanied the bishop to the sessions of the Council of Trent, on his mission to France in 1566, and finally to Ceneda. Michele appointed him Archdeacon of Ceneda in 1569, but he resigned the post four years later in favour of his brother—for his real passion was writing. He was a passionate Petrarchista, a writer of sonnets in the manner of Petrarch, with themes that ranged from missives of platonic love dedicated to noble ladies to whimsical verses about dogs, horses, duels, and the Turkish menace.[73]

Two of Vitale's oldest and dearest friends assembled a corpus of his works and published the volume, unbeknownst to him, in Venice in 1572. Dedicated to Girolamo Della Torre, 'our most respectful illustrious lord', it carried a ponderous title: *Le rime di M. Vital Papazzoni: Tra le quali vi sono alcuni sonetti, Madrigali, Sestine, Canzoni, Capitoli, & Stanze; ad imitation del Petrarca; parte intitolati ad una Madonna Laura: & parte ad alcuni Signori di nobilissimo ingegno dotati.* Said by his editors to have lived a life 'un poco sensuale' in his youth, Papazzoni was praised for redeeming himself by his self-restraint in service of the bishop.

The collection of Papazzoni's poems reads like a chronicle of his times. Some deal with political topics, such as the Battle of Lepanto and the strife between the Catholics and the Huguenots in France. Others describe courtly pleasures. One gets a sense of life in the bishop's castle from a stanza dedicated to an unnamed lady of Ceneda that calls to mind Romanino's frescoes in the Castello of Malpaga (Figure 11.3; see also Figure 10.3):

> No boring thought reigns in us,
> But everyone lives in joy, and in celebration.
> Whoever rides a *gianetto* (a Spanish horse), and who a Corsican,
> Who a Turkish, going for a walk in the forest.
> Often by a valiant Cavalier,
> The lance is also placed in repose between us.
> The delightful hunts, & the banquets,
> With the graceful dances, are almost infinite.
> Then when we return to the Castle,
> We are in the most beautiful and most joyful site
> That was ever formed with the pen,
> Or that is seen in any place in the world.

Figure 11.3. Girolamo Romanino (attr.), Hunting scene (detail), fresco, 1520s. (Comune of Bergamo, Castello di Malpaga).

Other castles are distinct on this side, and on that one,
All around, Cultivated plains, and delicate hills,
Alpine mountains, valleys, and soft meadows.[74]

But more relevant to our story are Papazzoni's verses relating to the Della Torre family: a canzone celebrating Michele's appointment as nuncio to France; an ode to Guido as a Knight of Malta, fighting at Lepanto; and, especially, a sonnet celebrating the Peace of 1568:

FOR THE PEACE MADE IN 1568.
Between the Signori della Torre, Colloredi, & Savorgnani.
True tranquility in the green olive branch
The purest white dove on the crest
Of a *Torre* worthy of empire.
Prophesied to us with a sweet and lively sound.
When having cast aside the ancient hatred
That has smeared blood on more than one path
Now each warrior of three illustrious seeds
Embraces the other with warm fraternal affection
And kissing one another in a humble and slow way
Shows that they are not three, but one blood:
The Torre, the Colloredo, and the Savorgnano

> The crest on the arms of the Della Torre is a white dove,
> with an olive branch in its mouth, & the motto above,
> that says *Tranquillité* in French,
> resonates in Italian as Tranquility and peace.[75]

Different Sides of the Coin

Alas, all was not tranquil in Venice in these years. On 11 May 1574, 'a great dense smoke emerged from the roofs of the Palace, where the doge lives'. It was the first sign of a devastating fire that began in the doge's apartments and swept through the Palazzo Ducale. It gutted the Sala del Collegio, the Anticollegio, the Sala del Pregadi, and the Antipregadi, and ruined the ceiling of the Cancelleria. Gone were the gilt-carved ceilings; the wood panelling, benches, and cabinets (and archives therein); and all the paintings. The votive painting of Doge Lorenzo Priuli in the Collegio that included Gian Matteo's portrait, was, sadly, no more. The smoke was still literally rising from the ashes when another fire broke out on the 22nd of the month, destroying seventy temporary shops that had been erected on Piazza San Marco for the Feast of the Senza.[76]

The next challenge was a state visit; the timing was not optimal. Charles IX, the king of France, died in Paris on 30 May. His brother, Henri of Valois, had been crowned king of Poland in Cracow only in February, but when he learned of his brother's death in mid-June, he prepared to return to Paris to assume the French crown as Henri III. The journey afforded him the opportunity of a visit to the fabled Serenissima. The Venetian authorities were notified on 27 June and the ceremonial experts sprang into action. With less than a month to prepare, and half the Ducal Palace in ruins, the authorities staged the most lavish royal entry of the century, matching, if not exceeding, the visit of Bona Sforza seventeen years earlier (Figure 11.4).

Henri's ten-day visit was marked by a temporary triumphal arch on the Lido designed by Palladio, fireworks, regattas, bull baiting, shopping in the Merceria, a tour of the Arsenale, receptions, masses, exchanges of gifts, banquets, water spectacles, and 'a public festa in the Sala del Maggior Consiglio, where there were two hundred gentleladies of singular beauty all dressed in white *tabino* and *ormesino* and adorned with pearls and an infinite number jewels of the greatest value'. When the king finally boarded a barge that would take him up the Brenta to Padua on Tuesday, 27 July, he sent back a gift to the doge of 'a diamond worth around 1500 scudi' as sign of appreciation and his affection.[77]

But just a year later, a triumphal Venice would soon face one of the greatest trials in its history. Reports of the plague began to circulate through the city in August 1575. While the government initially sought to minimize the threat, it

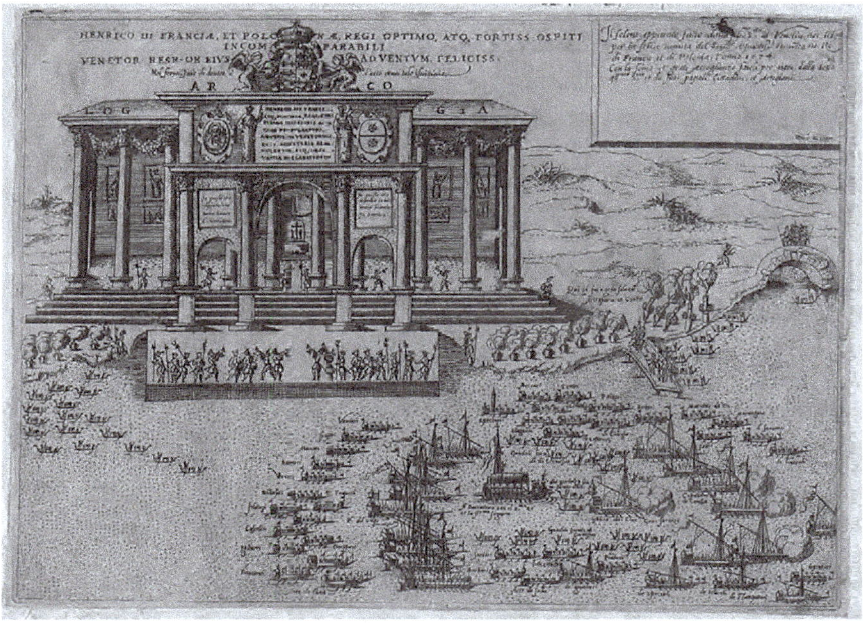

Figure 11.4. Domenico Zenoi, *Entry of Henri III, King of France and Poland, into Venice*, 1574 (Metropolitan Museum of Art).

would prove to be much worse than the epidemic of 1555. Despite the strictest measures to prevent contagion, the death toll mounted daily. Many of the rich fled to their country villas, leaving the magistracies paralyzed. As the epidemic reached a peak in the summer of 1576, the notary Rocco Benedetti described horrific scenes:

> The plague continued, killing more people with every hour that passed, and every day inspiring greater terror and deeper compassion for its poor infected victims. Onlookers wept as these people were carried down to their doors by their sons, fathers and mothers, and there in the public eye their bodies were stripped naked and shown to the doctors to be assessed... It was a fearful sight to see the thousands of houses around the city with doors crossed with wooden planks as a sign of plague. But even more horrifying was the spectacle of so many boats plying continuously back and forth; some being towed by other boats to quarantine at the Lazzaretto Nuovo; some heading out to certain appointed places, loaded up with the mortal remains of the wretched and luckless victims; some returning to the city laden with poor unfortunate widows and orphans who had completed their quarantine... All these things represented a

> sad and sorrowful triumph of death. It seemed all the more horrible and cruel in that it appeared that Divine Justice had sent it deliberately as the other side of the coin to the splendid and sumptuous celebrations held previously...to welcome the Most Christian King of France.[78]

While the plague of the 1570s hit urban centres like Venice and Udine, it largely spared Ceneda and isolated feudal castles in the hinterland.[79] But there were exceptions. A letter to Girolamo dated 24 November 1575 from the Magistrato della Sanità of Gemona, a town in the Friuli around 15 miles north of Villalta, thanks him for his aid in the time of the plague and informs him that an inscription in recognition of his assistance had been put in the loggia of the Palazzo Municipale of the town.[80]

By the time the plague died out in Venice in mid-1577, it had claimed nearly 50,000 victims, some one-fourth of the population. Although the disease had the greatest impact on the poor, who lived in crowded conditions, both the painter Titian and Gian Matteo's son Marco Antonio were among the fatalities.[81]

Just as Venice was getting back to normal, yet another fire broke out in the Palazzo Ducale on 20 December, this destroying the Sala del Scrutinio, the roof of the Sala del Maggior Consiglio, and all the paintings therein, including masterpieces by Titian, his son Orazio, Tintoretto, Pordenone, Jacopo, Gentile, and Giovanni Bellini. Again, Gian Matteo was among the notables whose faces disappeared from the Sala del Maggior Consiglio, along with a great quantity of public records. But tragedy brought opportunity. A new committee of Surveyors was elected, and the rooms were rebuilt and restored to unprecedented splendour by the leading artists of the day in a campaign that went on until the end of the century.[82] The public records and the faces of the earlier generation were gone forever. But Giulia's descendants were establishing another history elsewhere.

Notes

1. For mourning and burial practices, see Martignoni 2005, 99–158 and the outdated, but still eloquent, Ariès 1981, esp. 161–81. For mourning wear, see Rosenthal and Jones 2008, 166.
2. Bernardi 1845, 247.
3. Ibid., 247–9; Conzato 2005, 182–3, 199 n14; Cozzi 1962, 191–3. See also MCVe, MS. P.D. C398, no. 39.
4. Tramontin 1990, 38–9.
5. Brilliantly articulated by Muir 1994, 65–82.
6. Cited by Muir 1993, 264–5; Degani 1900, 119–20; *DBI, s.v.* Colloredo, Marzio.
7. Muir 1993, 266.
8. Muir 1993, 266–8. See also Casella, 2003, 123-30 for these events.

9. ASVe, *X Savi*, b. 135 (1566: San Polo), nos. 259, 335, 336. See also Chapter 5. Cf. ASVe *X Savi*, b. 166, no. 328, Paolo Dalla Gatta's *condicion* which does not name Girolamo as a tenant in 1582, although he states it as his residence in his will of 1589. See Chapter 14
10. MCVe, MS. P.D. c 4/3, Giuseppe Tassini, *Cittadini Veneziani*: 'Albero Menor dalla Gatta'. Paolo's paternal grandfather, Alvise dalla Gatta, was Guardian Grande of the Scuola Grande di San Giovanni Evangelista in 1529 and lent 100 ducats to the Great Council. Sanudo, *Diarii*, 50: 266, 641. For the family palace and wellhead at San Salvador, see Tassini 1879, 126–38; Rizzi 1981, 316.
11. ASUd, *AT*, b. 22, no. 38; ASVe, *NA*, b. 3082 (Nicolò Cigrigni).
12. ASUd, *AT*, b. 6, no. 5 (2 April 1565).
13. Ibid., b. 6, no. 10 (13 December 1556).
14. Ibid., b. 56.
15. Muir 1993, 268–70; Crollalanza 1875, 92–4.
16. Muir 1983, 270–2; Degani 1900, 154–71, with the complete text.
17. Degani 1900, 154–7.
18. See Chapter 9.
19. Degani 1900, 170. See Muir 1993, 270–2, 284–7 for the full lineup of Strumieri and Zamberlani families.
20. Hirschauer 1922, 14.
21. CSP/8, no. 44.
22. Hirschauer 1922, 15–29; Pastor, 18:105–8; Martin 1979, 197–240.
23. Pastor, 17:160–1.
24. Hart and Hicks 2017, 188.
25. Ibid., 187–189; Sinding-Larsen 1974, 126–9. Finlay 1980, 37–44; De Vivo 2007, 33–6. The commissioners representing the Senate in the Collegio were the six Savi del Consiglio [del Pregadi]; five Savi di Terraferma; and five Savi agli ordini.
26. Lorenzi 1868, docs. 608, 761. The other figures were Zuan Capello, Hieronimo Zane, Hieronimo Da Lezze, Marcantonio Foscarini, and Stefano Trevisan. The canvas measured 16.5 × 7 *piedi*. The final payment of 125 ducats was authorized on 28 November 1569. See also Wolters 1987, 108–9; Kleinschmidt 1977, 104–18; Brown 1988 ,219–34; Holt 1990, 123, 139 n40.
27. Wolters 1987, 162–78; Brown 1988, 261–5, 272–9.
28. Vasari, *Vite*, 6:588–9 (in the *Vita* of Battista Franco); Wolters 1987, 169.
29. Roskill 1968, 125; Brown 1988, 219–34.
30. Vasari, *Vite*, VI, 588–9; trans. from Vasari, *Lives*, ed. De Vere, vol. 8.
31. Sansovino, *Venetia*, 1581, c. 132v: 'Et nell'ultimo del Tintoretto stavano, Marchio' Michele Procuratore di San Marco, Michele Soriano Cavaliero, Iacomo Barbo, Pietro Sanuto, et Antonio Longo padre di Francesco, Iacomo Gussoni, Antonio Calbo, Gio. Mattheo Bembo, et Bernardino Riniero fratello di Luigi Procuratore.'
32. Plutarchus 1563, 2r-4v. Cf. Moz 1985, 134, 138. See also Chapter 10 for Sansovino's dedication of Bruni's *La historia universale* to Gian Matteo in 1561.
33. ASVe, *SAV-MC*, r. 4, 41 (Marco Antonio); 174, 205 (Davide); 185 (Lorenzo); ASVe, *MC*, Deliberazioni, Rocca, 1552–65, 136v (Alvise).
34. *DBI, s.v.* 'Bembo, Pietro'.

35. ASVe, *SAV-MC*, r. 4, f. 178: Elected 9 April 1564; excused 30 April 1564; Corner 1755, 2:426.
36. ASVe, *MC*, Deliberazioni, Rocca, 1552–65, c. 141v. The identities of the physicians are uncertain. Neither name appears on the list of graduates of the Studio of Venice (1501–1602) compiled by Palmer 1983, 66–192. But the surname of Schili is intriguingly close to the Scillini present at the birth of Giulia Bembo's first child in Candia. We might conjecture that it was the same person—Gian Matteo's personal physician, who might have accompanied his pregnant daughter to Crete. See Chapter 7. The physicians Prudentio Bellobuono and his sons Propertio and Decio are cited in Venice in 1567: Eamon 2007, 165.
37. ASVe, AC, b. 159, Necrologia di Nobili: '2 Maggio 1564: Sebastiano Bembo amalato mesi 5—S. M. Nova.' Cf. MCVe, Barbaro, *Genealogie*, I, c. 209v, with a death date of 28 March 1564.
38. ASVe, AC, b. 159, Necrologia di Nobili: '8 giugno 1564: Bernardin Belegno di anni 70, amalato mesi uno—S.M. Nova.'
39. ASVe, AV, r. 53, Balla d'Oro 1548–1561, f. 14–14v.
40. Zendrini, *Memorie Storiche*, I, 269. See also Bondesan and Furlanetto 2012, 175–200.
41. ASVe, *SAV-MC*, r. 4, c. 11 (=16). He served 29 July 1564–28 September 1565.
42. Bembo 1564b.
43. ASVe, *SAV-MC*, r. 4 (1562–70), 6. Gian Matteo served 10 January 1566–31 September 1567.
44. ASVe, *X Savi*, b. 131 (Cannaregio, 1566) no. 839. Their son Giovanni Matteo (named after his grandfather) would be born to Isabetta on 4 February 1567.
45. ASVe, *X Savi*, b. 131 (Cannaregio, 1566) no. 839; cf. ASVe, *X Savi*, b. 134 (Cannaregio—1566), no. 1159.
46. ASVe, *SAV-MC*, r. 4, 125; ASVe, SAV-*Sen.*, r. 3, 88v.
47. ASVe, *SAV-MC*, r. 4, 185. Lorenzo served as capitano of Famagusta from 15 August 1565 to 14 August 1567. For the popularity of the Peace and Justice theme, see Szépe 2018, 188–9.
48. ASVe, *Coll.*, Lettere cardinali e altri ecclesiastici, b. 2, filza 2 (11 July 1566); John 15:20; Bonora 2007, 106–9; Kuntz 2001, 53. Pietro served 16 October 1564–23 July 1589, until his death, when he was replaced by his nephew, Giovanni Della Torre (25 September 1589–1623).
49. ASVe, Cancelleria Inferiore, Miscellanea, atti Notai Diversi, b. 66. no. 63 (8 December 1569). Marcella would marry Daniele Tron in August 1575 and had a son; named after his father, he was born in April 1576, probably posthumously. In 1578, she was married a second time, to Ottaviano Contarini, and had three more sons. See MCVe, Barbaro, *Genealogie*, VII, f. 57 (Tron); ibid., MS Cicogna 2499, II, f. 316 (Contarini).
50. MCVe, Barbaro, *Genealogie*, I, c. 210. Gian Matteo married Lucietta della Volpe of Vicenza in 1581 and eventually had eight sons. Andrea married Lucia Arimondo in 1586, but no male births are recorded.
51. ASVe, NT, b. 1259, n. 507 [Cesare Ziliol] (22 March 1570).
52. ASVe, Provveditori alla Sanita', Necrologio, r. 805 (1570–1): 'da uscida de sangue za mesi 4.'

53. BMVe, MS It. VII 14 (7418): Bernardo Bembo, 'Cronica di tutte le case dell'inclita Citta' di Venetia', 68v.
54. For the tomb, which no longer exists, see Chapter 6.
55. ASVe, NT, b. 1259, n. 507 [Cesare Ziliol] (22 March 1570). See similar provisions in the testament of Gian Matteo's wife, Marcella, written in 1547. ASVe, NT, b. 1210.716. Oddly, although both Giulia and Augusta had died in 1562, Gian Matteo mentions the latter in his will: 'Item dechiaro che Augusta fu' satisfatta del legato delli ducati cento che li fu lassato, et ha havuto anche ducati vinticinque de piui da sua madre.' The phrase may have been copied by the notary from an earlier will. Cf. ASVe, Procuratoria di San Marco de Citra, b. 48, Commissaria di Zuan Matteo Bembo fu Alvise of Santa Maria Nova. The practice of entail is the English equivalent of *fedecommesso*.
56. ASVe, NT, b. 1259, n507.
57. Ibid.
58. A Hettor [Ettor] Bembo was an infantry captain in the Venetian forces at Legnago a fortress on the Adige River in Veronese territory, ca. 1582–6. I have found no evidence that this was Gian Matteo's natural son, but the dates fit. See *Relazioni/Legnago*, 62, 68; Cornet 1869, 281. For illegitimate sons of Venetian nobles, see De Vivo 2007, 76–7; Maglaque 2018.
59. See Megna 1991, 285, 294–6, who incorrectly assumed that Pietro was one of the original heirs and made no mention of Alvise.
60. Alvise was elected one of the ten governors of the Collegio della Militia da Mar on 13 June 1570. He died 1 December 1570. His brother David had turned down—'refusato'—the post of capitano of the Borgo of Corfù on 29 October 1570; on 16 April 1571 he would be elected as one of the three Provveditori alle pompe, an unpopular post that enforced the sumptuary laws against inappropriate display. See ASVe, *SAV-Sen.*, c. 99v; ASVe, *SAV-MC*, r. 4, cc. 174, 203.
61. BCV, Cod. P.D./C 2706, ff. 21–8 (26 and 31 August 1571; 13 July 1573); ASVe, *NA*, r. 3290, Marcantonio Cavanis, 1573:II, f. 344–34t (22 June 1573); Brown 2004, 191–5. Cf. Megna 1991, 294–5.
62. Bonora 2007, 108 n44: 'Questo giuditio spetta a noi.'
63. Ibid., 107 n43.
64. *DBI*, *s.v.* 'Bembo, Pietro'. Farlati 1751–1818, 5:210–2.
65. Comescu 2016, 43–52, with further bibliography. Giulio (1510–1595) was the son of Girolamo Savorgnan Del Monte (1466–1529) and nephew of Giacomo (d. 1498), husband of Maria Savorgnan. That made him a first cousin once removed of the violent Tristan. See Casella 2003, 163–71, Tavole 3, 4.
66. Bechevolo 1982, 112, 118–19; Tomasi 1998, I, 120–1 Cortelletti 2005, 199.
67. Hirschauer 1922, 14 n4; Pastor, 17:160–2; *DBI*, *s.v.* 'Della Torre, Michele'; Bernardi 1845, 254–5.
68. Finkel 2007, 160; Manno 1986, 91–137; Pepper 2014, 18–20.
69. Bernardi 1845, 251–2; Cortelletti 2005, 199; Faldon 1993, 138–9. The complete restructuring of the castello would be carried out by Michele's successor, Bishop Marcantonio Mocenigo, in the 1580s.
70. Tramontin 1990, 36–9; Gardi 2014, 151–62. See also Del Col 2014; Del Col 2015.

71. Bernardi 1845, 254–5; Sartori 2005, 118.
72. Capodagli 1665, 479.
73. Bullock 1935, 51–65.
74. Papazzoni 1572, 167r.
75. Papazzoni 1572, 43r-43v.
76. Sinding-Larsen 1974, 1–3; Sansovino 1581, 117v.
77. Della Croce 1574; Benedetti 1574. See also Brown 1990, 136–86; Korsch, 2013, 79–98; Fenlon 2007, 193–215; Fenlon 2013, 99–118; Cooper 2006, 211–27.
78. Benedetti 2001, 117–18. See Preto 1978, esp. 123–40; Crawshaw 2012, 228–31, and *passim*. For the arch, see Cooper 2006, 213–27.
79. Cohn 2010, 253–5; Manzano 1879, 167; Faldon 1993, 139.
80. ASUd, *AT*, b. 17, 132.
81. Both died in August 1576.
82. Sinding-Larsen 1974, 1–3; Sansovino 1581, 117v.

12
Suitable Alliances

Scraps of correspondence from the 1570s offer glimpses of Girolamo and his sons, cousins, and in-laws arriving or departing on horseback or in horse-drawn carriages. Trotting along dirt roads from one castle to another, from one city to the next, they would inhabit a family geography that embraced the city of Venice, Ceneda, the Friuli, imperial territories, and even Muggia, a village on the coast of Istria south of Trieste where the family owned substantial agricultural property.[1]

Girolamo's children were coming of age; it was time to see to their marriages. Although he himself had married a Venetian bride and maintained a residence in Venice, he sought husbands for his five daughters exclusively from the Friulian sphere. As to his sons, two entered the church and two would marry and raise their families in the Friuli.

Taddea

Taddea, the eldest daughter, was the first to marry. On 25 April 1571, shortly after she turned eighteen, a marriage contract was signed with Count Valentino da Valvasone, with the actual wedding taking place nearly a year later, on 15 February 1572, during Carnival.[2] The marriage reaffirmed the already strong ties between the Della Torre and Valvasone families. Valentino, known as Valenzio, was the first cousin of Guido Della Torre, who, we may recall, had been orphaned as an infant when his parents, Nicolò II Della Torre and Elena Valvasone, died of smallpox in 1546. Valenzio was the only son of Elena's sister, Porzia, who had married another Valvasone. Only six years old when his paternal grandmother Giacoma Brazzaco died, the orphaned Guido grew to adulthood in Valvasone with his cousin Valenzio under the care of his maternal grandmother Vittoria Strassoldo Valvasone. The two boys were like brothers, and Guido was the link between the Della Torre and Valvasone clans. Vittoria became one of Giulia Bembo's closest friends, while Girolamo continued to oversee property at Fratta that Guido had inherited from his mother. When Guido became a Knight of Malta in 1569, he had appointed Valenzio as his procurator and he would name him as his universal heir in his testament of 1586.[3] One could not imagine a more suitable husband for Taddea, the first Della Torre bride of her generation (Figure 12.1).

The Castello of Valvasone was conveniently located between Ceneda (around 40 miles distant) and Villalta (less than 20 miles away), on the west bank of the

The Venetian Bride: Bloodlines and Blood Feuds in Venice and Its Empire. Patricia Fortini Brown, Oxford University Press (2021). © Patricia Fortini Brown. DOI: 10.1093/oso/9780192894571.003.0012

Figure 12.1. "Spose del Friuli" (Brides of Friuli and places nearby), from Cesare Vecellio,. *De gli habiti antichi, et moderni*, 1588, c. 217 (Amsterdam, Rijksmuseum).

According to Vecellio, Friulian brides "wear their hair in many shapely little curls framing their forehead and temples and gather the rest of it under a gold net, laden with jewels and precious stones; around this net they tie a strand of large pearls, which they also wear in earrings and necklaces... They wear a gold belt, and the bottom of their gown is banded with gold lace or strips of brocade, with a small train." As an embodiment of family honour, Taddea would presumably have been dressed in a similar manner.

Tagliamento River. Typical of a thirteenth-century castle that had been updated over the years, it consisted of an agglomeration of buildings of various heights and ages encircling a small internal courtyard. Fragments of wall frescoes centuries give us a glimpse of a once courtly environment (Figures 12.2 and 12.3). As with the Colloredo, several branches of the sprawling Valvasone clan lived in the complex. During Taddea's time, the household included Erasmo da Valvasone (1523–93), the most important Friulian poet of the sixteenth century.[4]

Sigismondo

It is not surprising that Sigismondo, Girolamo's oldest son, would seek his fortune in service of the Hapsburgs. The Della Torre investitures as counts of the Holy Roman Empire of 1533 had been reconfirmed with a second diploma by the Emperor Maximilian II on 13 June 1572.[5] Several Colloredo cousins held imperial appointments, and Girolamo was friendly with Francesco Della Torre, a distant cousin who had served as capitano of Gorizia and imperial ambassador in Rome. Francesco had just one son, Raimondo, and a single male heir was a perilous situation. When Francesco's ninth daughter was born in 1559, Girolamo had sent him his congratulations, but allowed that 'the happiness would have been greater if it had been a boy'.[6] By 1575, whether with the backing of a Colloredo or a Della Torre cousin, Sigismondo was pursuing a career at the imperial court in

Figure 12.2. Castello di Valvasone.

Figure 12.3. Castello di Valvasone. Frescoes, fourteenth century.

Graz as the *coppiere* (cup-bearer) of Charles II, Archduke of Austria, son of the Holy Roman Emperor Ferdinand I and brother of Maximilian II. An erstwhile suitor of both Elizabeth I of England and Mary Queen of Scots, Charles had married Maria Anna of Bavaria in 1571 and settled in Graz, eventually fathering fifteen children. Sigismondo enjoyed a warm personal relationship with the archduke, but it became clear that his prospects would be vastly improved if he owned land assets in Hapsburg territory. Landowners whose fortunes were tied to the well-being of the dynasty were held to be the most loyal subjects. Marriage was one of the best ways to acquire land, and the stars were aligned in Sigismondo's favour. Adamo Semetkovitch of Prague, one of Maximilian's courtiers, had died recently, leaving his wife Giovannina Rassauer a very wealthy widow. The emperor brokered a marriage between her and Sigismondo, with the contract signed on 22 February 1575.[7]

When the couple married a year later, Giovannina brought with her two young daughters and a dowry that included the feud of Spessa, complete with medieval castle, in the contea of Gorizia.[8] With the stroke of a pen, Sigismondo had become a feudal landowner in imperial territory. Giovannina died shortly after giving birth to two more children: a daughter, Dorothea, named after her mother, and a son named Carlo (after the Archduke Charles), thus introducing a Hapsburg name into the Della Torre line. Sigismondo, by then well established in Graz as a courtier of the archduke, was once again an eligible bachelor, now with the feudal lands at Spessa inherited by little Carlo under his control. It was time for him to seek another wife. During these years he had become close to Raimondo Della Torre, five years his junior and sole male heir of his father Francesco. Among Raimondo's many sisters, Orsina was held to be an ideal bride. Paying her court, Sigismondo wrote deferentially to his future brother-in-law on 25 November 1580: 'Wishing in this and in every other thing of mine, business, or contract from your very illustrious lordship, to depend, confer and communicate my every thought to you.'[9]

The marriage contract was signed on 6 December 1581. It was a key moment in the life of the Della Torre family. With the wedding, Sigismondo had become a true and proper member of the Gorizian nobility in imperial territory. He was admitted to the Convocazione degli Stati Provinciali of the contea of Gorizia the following year. Although continuing to avow themselves faithful subjects of Venice, the Della Torre were tied ever more firmly to the Austrian house of Hapsburg.[10]

Ginevra

Ginevra must have been the second daughter to marry, probably in 1577, when she was around nineteen years old. The date of her wedding to Count Orazio Polcenigo is uncertain, but clues can be found in a book of daily expenses compiled by Girolamo's factor in Udine. An entry for 12 July 1578 lists a payment for three pair of white *zoccole* (clogs with wooden soles) for Ginevra's sisters Elena and Giulia, who were then staying at the castle of Polcenigo. The reason for their visit becomes clear in a second entry, this dated 27 July, for expenses relating to 'the arrival [in Udine] of the footman of the Illustrious Count Sigismondo who comes from Polcenigo and is going to Gorizia to bring news of the son born to the Illustrious Signor Orazio'.[11] Sadly the child would die. Even more sadly, while the couple eventually had a daughter, Laura, they would produce no male heir.[12]

The Counts of Polcenigo, long participants in the parliament of the Friuli, had been invested with their feudal holdings back in the tenth century. Their castle was located on a hilltop near the Livenza river to the northwest of Valvasone with sweeping views of the valley below. It was around 20 miles from Villalta on a route that led to Ceneda as well as to Venice. The *mastio* where Ginevra gave birth to her son was once fortified with three circuits of crenellated walls, the third encircling what became the borgo below. The original castle is long gone, destroyed by fire in the seventeenth century and replaced by a once imposing villa with a monumental staircase of 366 steps that led down to the town. It too is gone. Only the façade and a ballroom remain today, as fragmentary metaphors of a lost lifestyle of ancestral wealth and privilege.[13]

Elena

The marriage contract between Elena and Lucio Popaite, a noble citizen of Pordenone, was signed on 11 March 1582. Her brothers-in-law Orazio Polcenigo and Valenzio Valvasone, the latter serving as procurator for Guido Della Torre, were signatories to the dowry agreement.[14] In a break from family tradition, Popaite was not a feudal lord with a castle, but he made up for the lack of a title with a palace in Pordenone and large property holdings in the nearby countryside. A widower with three daughters from his first wife Ottavia Mantica, he needed a male heir. Alas, Elena would give him another girl, but no sons. As we shall see in the next chapter, Lucio's disappointment would be to the Della Torre family's advantage in the next generation.[15]

Giulia

Giulia, Girolamo's youngest daughter, was also married off to a noble townsman rather than a feudal lord, again probably in 1582.[16] Her husband, Aurelio da Noal of Treviso, had inherited part of a fortune amassed by his grandfather Alvise Campagnaro. Therein lay a success story. After studying law in Padua, Alvise had distinguished himself as one of the leading attorneys in Venice. He gained Venetian citizenship by privilege and moved in the highest circles. But lacking *cittadino originario* status he found that his opportunities were limited. Already a noble of Noale, he petitioned for admission to the Collegio of Nobles of Treviso and was grudgingly accepted at the urging of Doge Andrea Gritti. In 1540, Doge Francesco Dona named him a cavaliere di San Marco, making him both a noble and a knight. Now known as Alvise da Noal, he monopolized the notarial business in Noale and amassed a fortune in land, primarily by acquiring small properties from clients in distress. By 1542 he was the largest landowner in the Trevigiano. Writing his will in 1556 at the of 84, he forgave half of the debts of his tenants, 'in praise of God and not to make up for any deception that I had ever committed on them'. He left substantial charitable bequests in his will, with his son Giulio (1531–61) the sole heir of the remainder of the estate. When Giulio himself died in 1561, the estate passed on in *fedecommesso* to his three sons, one of whom was Giulia's new husband Aurelio. The couple, who would eventually have two sons and three daughters, would have lived in Ca' da Noal, a handsome fifteenth-century Gothic palace with a frescoed façade facing the Piazza della Cavallerizza in Treviso (Figure 12.4).[17]

Figure 12.4. Treviso, Ca' da Noal, facade.

Giovanni and Alvise

The two youngest Della Torre sons pursued careers in the church. Giovanni sought to follow in his uncle Michele's footsteps. After earning a degree in canon and civil law at the Studio in Padua, he returned to Ceneda as a canon in the diocese, probably in the late 1570s.[18] We will hear more of him further on. We know little of Alvise, also called Luigi, aside from a brief notation in the family records stating that he had joined the Jesuit order. An account book indicates his presence in the Friuli in 1578–9.[19] By the end of 1582, of the nine Della Torre children, excluding the two priests, only Marcella and Giulio were yet to marry.

A Most Noble Gift

Girolamo's preference for Friulian marriages for his children does not tell the whole story. He maintained a wide circle of friends and acquaintances, not only in Ceneda, but also in Venice. And not only clerics, but also writers and intellectuals. Among them was the historian Paolo Ramusio, the precocious son of Giambattista, geographer and publisher of *Navigazioni and viaggi*, an important collection of travel accounts. In 1548, when only sixteen, Paolo had published three eclogues in praise of Cardinal Pietro Bembo, who had died the previous year, and in 1555, the Latin writings of Girolamo Fracastoro, a close friend of both Pietro and Giulia's father Gian Matteo. Paolo's acquaintance with Della Torre must have begun in the late 1550s when Girolamo returned to Venice from Crete.

Paolo was a member of the short-lived Accademia della Fama (1558–61) and like many dedicated Latinists, he was passionately interested in antique inscriptions. In 1583, declaring himself his *antico servitor* (ancient servant), Paolo asked for Girolamo's help in obtaining a piece of ancient spolia with a Roman inscription that a friend had seen under the portico of the palace of Curzio Colloredo in Udine. The stone was not, after all, 'yet being used or of service in any place of that palazzo'. As Paolo put it, he would be 'in perpetual obligation' to the lord count for this favour.

Girolamo was only too happy to intervene with his nephew on behalf of a learned friend. One is reminded of his letter recommending Titian to Cardinal Madruzzo some decades earlier. Now, as then, acting as an intermediary cost little and could only burnish Girolamo's credentials as a man of taste and learning. By 13 April, the gift was confirmed. Paolo wrote to Curzio that words could not suffice to express his affection and gratitude for this 'nobilissimo dono' (most noble gift). He asked that the stone be consigned to his agent, who would send it by road to Portogruaro and thence by barge to Venice.[20] The inscribed stone was later determined to be from Carnia, the northeast corner of the Friuli, once a part of Cisalpine Gaul. After Paolo's death, his heirs conceded it to Giorgio Contarini, who transported it to his residence in Este and thence to the civic museum in the nineteenth century.[21] We might consider it part of Girolamo's legacy and an inadvertent act of historical preservation.

An Expanded Villalta

It was probably during this period that the castle of Villalta underwent a second phase of reconstruction.[22] The old three-story *mastio*, rebuilt after the devastation of 1511 and refurbished by Giulia Bembo, would now be augmented with an imposing east wing and two courtyards that transformed a claustrophobic medieval fortified castle into an elegant villa (Figure 12.5). The façade of the new wing has a Renaissance look, its austere style fitting in surprisingly well with the medieval aspect of the older buildings and the newer battlements. New entrance portals to both the lower and upper courtyards constructed in 1585 were possibly the final phase of the renovation.[23]

Among the remaining traces of the decorative schemes from this period are scenes of rural life and imprese (emblems) frescoed beneath the windows of the

Figure 12.5. Castello di Villalta from the east.

The castle complex was built on two levels, its 14–15th century nucleus on the upper level consisting of the old clocktower, mastio, and courtyard (the latter just visible on the far right). These structures were augmented in the later 16th century by the massive new palace wing built on the track of the old curtain wall that originally closed off the south side of the courtyard (see Figures 2.1 and 2.2). A second upper courtyard, enclosed by a medieval looking crenellated wall in front of the palace, was accessed through a single portal reached by a staircase leading up from a third, lower courtyard or borgo. Protected by a new perimeter wall, it too was accessed through a single portal. The farm buildings now flanking it were probably constructed in the 17–18th centuries.

reception rooms on the piano nobile of the *mastio*. One *impresa* depicts two wind-gods blowing lustily at a rock in the sea, with the motto *MEM[ENTO] SEMPER* (Always remember); another features a peacock, its tail feathers fanned out in full courtship display, accompanied by a scroll inscribed by a phrase in French: *Lealté passe tout* (Loyalty vanquishes all). In sum, an emblematic display of Della Torre family values.[24]

Those values were even more evident in the salone of the new wing, later known as the gallery of the ancestors, a place of representation and the most public area of the castle. A frescoed frieze of coats of arms, garlands, swags, and putti still runs around of the room atop the walls, which were originally adorned with portraits of family members. Among them may well have been the portrait of Girolamo that we encountered earlier (see Figure 5.3). By the end of the sixteenth century, the castle complex was a hybrid monument to ancestral glory and a testimony to an enlightened aristocratic present.

Lord of Himself

These were good years for Michele Della Torre. Far away from the intrigues of Paris and Rome, he remained a figure of some importance in humanist circles in Venice. Paolo Paruta, official historian of the Republic, featured Michele in his *Della perfezione della vita politica*, a treatise celebrating politics as civil discipline, published in 1579. In the dedication, Paruta lays out the premise for his inquiry: 'I feel overtaken by a great wonder, when I consider that there would be such diverse roads that have been followed, and that are followed yet, to reach the same goal sought and desired by all, that is happiness itself.' He then answers his own question: 'Therefore, having already asked the oracle of Apollo by what path man could gain happiness, he responded: "By knowing yourself".'[25]

At issue were the relative virtues of the active versus the contemplative life. Paruta explored the topic in the form of an imagined after-dinner conversation between more than a dozen diplomats and prelates that took place in the palace of the Venetian ambassador, Matteo Dandolo, during the Council of Trent. The event was fictional, but the participants were real; nearly all were Venetian patricians with the exception of Michele Della Torre. After dinner the tables were taken away, 'so, then all together they ascended the staircase and gathered in a large and airy room and here, in a half circle, opposite a window that looked toward the mountains, and having taken their seats, they began to chat about various things.'[26]

They spoke first of embassies and customs in different countries and courts. Della Torre, who had only been listening up to that point, joined in: 'The life of the courts, he said, was always so full of annoyance, that as much time a man spends in one, so much is taken from his life.'[27] The Venetian ambassador Michele Surian countered with a typically Venetian response: 'But whoever wishes to live well, should not think of himself alone, but of the entire city; if it is full of corrupt customs, how could he carry out any virtuous operation?'[28] He extolled the civil life as the way to win dignity and praise; it was indeed the only existence worthy to man. His was an attitude that would have been shared by Michele's now deceased brother in law, Gian Matteo Bembo.

But to that, Michele countered:

> This praise . . . is bought at too great a price, that is, with the servitude of oneself, which is the perpetual companion of civil life. For as soon he begins distinguishing himself among his [fellow] citizens, then everyone's eyes immediately turn upon him, so that not just large and public acts, but also private and small ones, are with great diligence observed of him, so that not at any time can he be lord of himself.[29]

For all his time in the sophisticated milieus of Rome and the French court, Michele was never happier than in Ceneda and the Friuli—as lord of himself. That was soon to change.

Notes

1. See, for example, ASUd, *ADT.*, b. 5, no. 6, Libro delle entrade, 1578–9.
2. ASUd, *AT*, b. 22, Doti uscite, no. 40: 1582. For the Valvasone, see Carreri 1906), 1:107–48, 2:135–61, at 159. Taddea died before 1596; Valenzio contracted a second marriage with Claudia di Collalto on 21 July 1596.
3. For Guido see Bonazzi 1907, 108, citing his induction on 19 February 1569, when he was attached to the Priorate of Venice. Bosio 1629, 869, states incorrectly that Giudo died of pestilential fevers in Cefalonia in 1570, when on a galley in the Venetian armata, en route to Cyprus. But cf. ASUd, *AT*, b. 25, Intrade de Fratti (1572); ibid., b. 5, no. 6, Libro dell'Entrade (1578; and ibid., b. 17, no. 4, Libro dell'Intrade (1582), and ibid., b. 25, Conti et material in Villa di Fratta (1583), referring to Guido as alive and well in those years. The feud of Fratta was located near Portogruaro, around 15 miles south of Valvasone. See Carreri 1906, 1:123–6.
4. Maffei 2005, 178–9; Chiurlo 1937.
5. Lazzarini and Del Puppo 1901–03, 1:167.
6. Conzato 2005, 184.
7. Conzato 2005, 184–6. For the Archduke Charles, see also Morelli di Schönfeld 1855–56, I, 77–8.
8. ASUd, *AT*, b. 25, fasc. 36; Maffei 2005, 3–5. The marriage took place on 16 March 1576.
9. Conzato 2005, 186.
10. ASUd, *AT*, b. 25, fasc. 37.

11. Ibid., b. 5, no. 6, Entrade, 27 July 1578. Cf. www.sardimpex.com/della%20Torre/dellatorre-udine.htm (a genealogy website that is useful but contains many errors), stating that the dowry contract was only signed on 30 September 1578.
12. ASUd, *AT*, b. 17, c. 127.
13. Maffei 2005, 128–9.
14. ASUd, *AT*, b. 17, 79–80, 339–40; ibid., b. 22, 'Doti uscite', no. 39.
15. 'Ce fastu?' 202 n9; ASVe, AV, b. 2940. See Chapter 15.
16. ASUd, *AT*, b. 22, Doti uscite, no. 41—1582: 'Memoria riguardante il Matrimonio della n. S. Giulia, figlia del N. S. Co. Gerolamo di Luigi della Torre, ed il N. S. Aurelio Noali di Treviso.'
17. Rossi 1739, 23–68; Bellavitis 1994, 16–18, 62–8, 109–14. The palace, now part of the Museo della Casa Trevigiana, was badly damaged in the Second World War. See Coletti 1935, 61–2; Giovanni Netto 1988.
18. *DBI, s.v.* 'Della Torre, Giovanni'.
19. ASUd, *ADT*, b. 5, no. 6, Libro delle entrade, 1578–9. Alvise would die in Reggio Calabria in 1587 at the age of thirty.
20. ASDUd, MS Bartoliana, b. 151, 84–5, 88. For Paolo Ramusio, see Cicogna, *Ins. Ven.*, 2, 330–5, 504–5; Fracastoro 2008, lii–liv.
21. *Le antiche lapidi del Museo di Este* 1837, 7–21; Gruterus 1603, 42, no. 4.
22. ASUd, *ADT*, b. 5, no. 6, which documents Girolamo's residence in the castle from October 1578 to January 1579, by which time much of the work may have been completed.
23. Ulmer 1997, 278–309; Miotti 1977, 399–407; Maffei 2005, 274–5. Zucchiatti 1989, 7–36, suggests that the west wing uniting the mastio with the tower was built in the seventeenth century.
24. Stylistically dating to the late sixteenth–early seventeenth century, they must have been commissioned by one or more of Girolamo and Giulia's heirs. For heraldic devices, see Pittoni 1568.
25. Paruta 1982, 505. For an incisive summary of Paruta's thesis, see Viroli 1992, 231–6.
26. Paruta 1982, 511.
27. Ibid.
28. Ibid., 513.
29. Ibid.

13
The Cardinal

A Costly Honour

Pope Gregory XIII created nineteen cardinals in the consistory of 12 December 1583. Michele Della Torre was, finally, among them, 'because of your exceptional rectitude, wisdom, faith, integrity and other virtues of character' (Figure 13.1).[1] Nearly seventy-nine, he was also the oldest among them, and in the eyes of many, the honour was long overdue. Michele's name had already been mentioned in 1566 and 1570, but Vatican intrigues had pushed him aside.[2] The honour would be a costly one. Giovanni Gandini, the pope's Cameriere Segreto, traveled to Ceneda to deliver the red *berretta* personally, and the new cardinal rewarded him, grandly, with a gift of 300 scudi. Some 3000 noble personages would descend upon the city, and the new cardinal was hard put to entertain and house them all. But there was help. The citizen council donated 500 scudi and the clergy of the city and diocese another 400. And yet, that was not enough. Girolamo was constrained to borrow 13,500 ducats against funds on deposit in the Monte Vecchio of Venice and take out private loans elsewhere to underwrite the costs of the celebration.[3]

The city council of Ceneda lauded Michele in a nineteen-page handwritten *Oration*, recited in his presence, extolling his illustrious ancestry and praising his many achievements. But even more important was his character—temperance, judiciousness, modesty, humility, perseverance, piety, hospitality, lack of avarice, and, most notably, his loyalty to Ceneda. Like the ancient Romans Curzio and Fabrizio, 'he had refused the rich gifts and copious presents' offered to him by the French king upon his departure from Paris. 'And when, likewise, he did not wish to abandon the governance of the church committed to him [in Ceneda] for the Archbishopric of Milan and the Bishopric of Piacenza in exchange for what was offered, even if very rich and very opulent.'[4]

The Oration also lauded Michele's brother Girolamo for many of the same virtues, as well as his nephew Giovanni,

And finally, one more passage in a very long and repetitive peroration summed it all up:

> imitator of his honourable vestiges, whose virtue and modesty, and laudable customs clearly demonstrate how much should be expected of him; and also his other very distinguished nephews, who with the generosity of their spirit, in

The Venetian Bride: Bloodlines and Blood Feuds in Venice and Its Empire. Patricia Fortini Brown, Oxford University Press (2021). © Patricia Fortini Brown. DOI: 10.1093/oso/9780192894571.003.0013

Figure 13.1. Bartolomeo Carducci [Bartholome Carducho], Posthumous Portrait of Cardinal Michele Della Torre, 1608 (Kutná Hora, Czech Republic, Gallery of the Central Bohemian Region – Jesuit College).

> their noble appearance and most honourable manners represent the true image of their ancestors.[5]

The fortunes of Ceneda were, indeed, closely entwined with the extended Della Torre family.

> Now, then, for the nobility of his blood, for his own virtue and glory, for the experience that he has given by his valor in the assignments of the most important business of the Holy Church, for the testimony and good example of his honourable life, and for all his laudable works, prizes, and ornaments so robust and evident, [Bishop Michele] has been consequently exalted to that degree and honour that are fitting for so many merits, and that he had already been due for so many years.[6]

The Cenedesi erected a triumphal arch in Michele's honour halfway up Via Brevia beyond which a grapevine covered pergola provided a dignified approach to the bishop's castle. More tangible and enduring than any oration, it was proclaimed *la più bella porta della città*.[7] One is reminded of Palladio's Arco Bollani in Udine, erected in 1556 at the beginning of the pathway that led up to the Castello atop the hill. It had honoured Domenico Bollani, then the Venetian luogotenente and later appointed Bishop of Brescia in 1559. He frequented the same circles at the Council of Trent as Michele Della Torre, who now had an arch of his own.[8]

Indeed, the city of Udine was just as jubilant as Ceneda about Michele's elevation to the Cardinalate. He was, after all, a native son. The cardinal's triumph was the city's as well. The city council proclaimed a jubilee

> for three continuous days and three nights with the pealing of all the bells of the churches, with a solemn mass celebrated in the Cathedral, with the firing of all the cannons and other instruments of war, with firework displays atop the towers and campaniles and in the public piazzas, with the sound of many trumpets and drums and with the highest shouts that demonstrated the inner happiness, which was felt by one and all.[9]

The public loggia was lavishly decorated with carpets and adorned with beautiful festoons between the arches of the columns, with the arms of the cardinal, of the luogotenente, of the *miniscalco* and treasurer, and of the seven deputies of the community.[10]

The deputies promptly dispatched a delegation of three ambassadors to Ceneda to congratulate Michele on his promotion. Among them was Antonio Marchesi, a cittadino merchant, who would soon play an important role in the future circumstances of the Della Torre family. Alas, Michele, suffering from gout and probably other afflictions, was unable to receive them personally. But more welcome was a gift of 2000 ducats voted by the council and carried to Ceneda by Raffaele Belgrado, 'a gentleman of high esteem, an old friend and contemporary of the Cardinal'. Guglielmo Gonzaga, the Duke of Mantua, offered Michele one of his *lettiche* (sedan chairs), 'truly small and of little moment', as a token of his willingness 'to serve him in a matter of greater importance'.[11]

Congratulatory letters, replete with expressions of esteem and affection, poured in from the crowned heads of Europe and Italy. Aside from Gonzaga, these included the Emperor Rudolf II, Henri III of France, the Duke of Savoy, the King of Poland, and the Grand Duke and Duchess of Tuscany, along with cardinals, bishops, prelates, rectors of cities throughout the Venetian dominion, and, not least, the Venetian doge. Copies of 153 such letters survive in the Biblioteca Riccardiana in Florence.[12]

Overlooking any tensions that once existed between the Bishop of Ceneda and the signoria, Doge Nicolò Da Ponte enthused: 'Your illustrious lordship can well understand how many reasons and with how much affection we desired the dignity of the Cardinalate for you.' This was not only because of the Signoria's true affection for the man, but also 'for the universal good of Christianity in whose service you have endured so many fatigues and experienced so many dangers.'[13] Simeone Arnosti, a Cenedese citizen and close friend of Michele's, responded in his name: 'The opportunity remains for him to spill his blood and lose his life for the growth of the Holy Faith of Christ and the benefit of the Holy Church, of which this most ancient and religious Republic has always been a protectress.'[14]

The *Cittadino Porporato*

Michele, although still afflicted with health problems, prepared to journey to Rome in August. Firmly opposing the plan, his doctors convinced him instead to travel to Villalta, where he could enjoy the 'native air' without the stresses of his office. It was not to be. Once word reached Udine, the deputies put together a delegation of leading citizens, including the luogotenente and a contingent of knights, all richly dressed, and rode out to Villalta, just five miles distant, to welcome him. It was an opportunity for another jubilee. They persuaded Michele to visit the city so that he could be properly honoured as their own *Cittadino Porporato* (citizen cardinal). He was first escorted to the sanctuary of Santa Maria delle Grazie, and then to the Castello, where he was greeted by the luogotenente with great festivities. All the church bells began to peal, and news of his coming spread through town. That evening the air was filled with fusillades of artillery fire as a prelude to two more days of celebration. The next morning the streets 'from the summit of the Castello all the way to the Cathedral' were filled with 'every condition of person'. The cardinal was escorted down the Piazzale del Castello, under the Arco Bollani and, passing by the loggia, again adorned with carpets, arrived at the cathedral for another high mass, after which he gave the assembled populace his holy benediction.

Michele was escorted back to the Castello, where he was eager to see the newly completed Sala del Gran Consiglio and Sala della Convocazione, rooms deemed 'worthy to be seen by princes and prelates'. After a long and festive lunch, he descended once again into the city to attend vespers at San Francesco, the ancestral church of the Della Torre. But the day was not yet over. He was then conducted to the convent of San Nicolò di Poscolle, where he participated in the feast of the *perdonanza*; then, passing the Portello and the Piazza del Mercato Nuovo, he returned to the Castello for another celebration. The third day began with mass in the crowded church of San Pietro Martire, after which the new cardinal complained of his gout. Still, he soldiered on, visiting the parish church of San Cristoforo to pray and then arriving at the nearby palace of the Brazzaco, his maternal relatives, for lunch. Probably exhausted, he declared his wish to return to Villalta that evening. The luogotenente and the entourage of noble gentlemen returned with carriages 'and a great number of persons on both foot and on horseback' and many trumpets, drums and artillery salutes. Michele finally mounted his *lettica*—perhaps the one sent by the Marchese of Mantua—and was escorted through Porta Villalta by the full entourage for a mile out of town. He did not permit his escorts to accompany him any further, so they dismounted from their carriages and 'after a long compliment they took gracious leave, having received his benediction in the end, and returned to Udine'.[15]

After staying at Villalta for several days, Michele was on the road again, making the familiar 75-mile journey across the flat Veneto plain, past fields with peasants harvesting their spring plantings of wheat, barley, and rye, to Marghera. There he boarded a boat to cross the lagoon to Venice and presumably Girolamo's rental lodgings at San Silvestro. According to Giovanni Giuseppe Capodagli, writing a century later, the 'principal senators and gentlemen of the republic went to his *casa* to escort him to the Collegio, where he was accepted with great acclaim'. Then he returned to the *casa*, with a large escort of Venetian gentlemen and foreigners, and was visited there by Doge Nicolò Da Ponte with all the Signoria on barges. Several days later they granted him the *grazia* to withdraw 13,500 ducats from the Monte Vecchio of Venice against future interest due on the 30,000 florins deposited by his ancestors when they moved from Milan to Udine in the thirteenth century.[16]

Shortly thereafter Michele left Venice and, passing through Treviso and Conegliano, returned to his residence in Ceneda, now his true home. He wasted little time in spending some of the newly acquired funds, for the greater glory not only of God, but also of the Della Torre family. He continued with improvements in the Cathedral, building and endowing two chapels flanking the presbytery, with the obligation of a daily mass to alternate between the two. Adorned with beautiful marbles, one was dedicated to Santa Croce and the other to Saints Paul, Barnabas and Luke, the latter with a gilded wooden tabernacle. He furnished their altars, respectively, with a relic of the True Cross and relics of the dedicatory saints. Above the arch of each chapel was the Della Torre coat of arms and the inscription:

MICHAEL S. R. E. CARDINALIS
TVRRIANVS.

Commonly called the *cappelle turriane*, the chapels would eventually provide a dignified frame for Michele's tomb in the pavement at the foot of the choir.[17]

A Colloredo Marriage

The family had another occasion to celebrate. Girolamo's second oldest daughter, Marcella, was finally betrothed in 1584. Already twenty-eight or twenty-nine years old, she was mature for a first-time bride, particularly in comparison with her sisters.[18] One is reminded of Giulia Marcello, her mother's aunt and namesake, married at around the same age back in 1529.[19] The delay is hard to explain; perhaps she had been running the household at Villalta or perhaps Michele's elevation to the cardinalate made her a more appealing bride. In any case, the groom, Federico Colloredo, was also late to marry. At least 20–25 years older than Marcella and a major player in his family's blood feud with the Savorgnan, he had—as we know—a distinctive, if checkered past. This was the Federico who had been exiled from Venetian territories along with Marzio Colloredo in 1552 for the murder of Antonio Savorgnan. And this was the Federico who had pursued a successful career at the Hapsburg court and had written from England to Pompeo Colloredo in 1559, recommending the courtly life to his younger relatives. Indeed, Federico would join his brother Lodovico, a courtier of the Archdukes Ernest and Rudolf, at the Spanish court in 1561, and remained there for much of the next decade. The brothers' distance from the Friuli may well have saved their lives, for a third brother, Livio, would be murdered by Federico Savorgnan in 1562.[20]

The peace of 1568, with the ensuing abrogation of Marzio's ban, inspired Federico to seek a similar accommodation. He had been barred from his homeland in the Friuli for nearly two decades, and life at court may have lost some of its luster. His repatriation campaign began at the Spanish court in December 1571, with the Archdukes Ernest and Rudolf instructing Diego de Guzman de Silva, the Spanish ambassador in Venice, to press Federico's case with the Council of Ten. The Spanish Hapsburgs would be greatly obliged, Guzman told the Ten, if Federico could be granted a safe conduct to travel in Venetian territories. Guzman knew that he was treading on a diplomatic minefield. The Colloredo clan was much hated in Venice, and there was little taste for doing any of them any favours. But the matter was of great concern to the Spanish. The Austrian Hapsburgs and the papal nuncio also joined the campaign.[21]

Finally, after nearly three years of diplomatic entreaties at the highest level, the Council of Ten reluctantly granted Federico a safe conduct in October 1574, but only for five years, and only as a special favour to the Catholic king. The process had to be repeated five years later, and again, after more papal and Spanish diplomacy, the safe conduct was renewed in August 1579.[22] It must have been renewed yet again in 1584 when Federico's betrothal contract was concluded. With his marriage to Marcella, the historical alliance between the Della Torre and Colloredo families was once again reaffirmed. Federico's branch of the family was distant from that of Giambattista, husband of Marcella's aunt Ginevra, but there was another more recent connection. Federico's brother Lodovico had married Perla Polcenigo, niece of Orazio Polcenigo (now husband of Marcella's sister Ginevra), in 1583.[23] That made Ginevra and Marcella not only sisters, but also cousins by marriage several times over.

Two Deaths and a New Bishop

Pope Gregory XIII died on 20 April 1585 and there were high hopes that Michele might be his successor. Many of his admirers, including the Signoria of Venice and the Dukes of Ferrara and Urbino, urged him to travel to Rome for the conclave: 'it was common indubitable opinion, that he would have been infallibly assumed to the Pontificate.' Michele, old and not in the best of health, seems to have cared little about the honour. And yet, against his wishes, he was put on his way to Rome. But as soon as he arrived in Venice, he heard that Felice Peretti, Cardinal of Montalto, had been elected Pope Sixtus V. Probably much relieved, Michele returned to Ceneda.[24]

But his supporters were taken by surprise. The disappointment was particularly great in Udine—the reverse of the elation over Michele's election to the cardinalate the year before. The jurist Cornelio Frangipane wrote a long consolatory letter to the luogotenente, Pietro Gritti, summing up their shared regrets. He cited eight well-known points in Michele's favour, from the nobility of his blood to his lack of avarice and ambition, was well as his service to the papacy over many years—all virtues that qualified him uniquely for the position. That he was of advanced age, no longer subject to 'the ardent spirits of youth', was also held to be a positive factor. But alas, 'now hearing that another was elected, it is necessary to believe that this was an act of Divine Providence, which is incomprehensible.'[25]

Michele died in Ceneda at the age of seventy-five the following year, on 21 February 1586. It was the first Sunday of Lent, a circumstance that might have occasioned remarks among the pious. The Cenedesi felt the loss 'that one can more imagine than describe, thinking of the goodness and sweet governance of this prince and of the prestige that this city received from his greatness'. The citizen council authorized its deputies 'to make all those expenses they deemed necessary to render the funeral rites of this Prelate worthy of his memory'.[26] With a concourse of clergy and citizens, he was buried with *solenissima pompa* in a floor tomb in the crossing of the cathedral of Ceneda—humble in that it was beneath the pavement, but subtly ostentatious in its placement directly in front of the high altar. Looking up, the worshipper encountered a heavenly vision: *The Coronation of the Virgin,* the monumental altarpiece that had perhaps inspired Giulia Bembo's last thoughts of twenty-four years earlier (see Figure 10.7). Flanked by the *cappelle turriane*, the painting provided a magnificent backdrop to what was held to be a *deposito nobilissimo*, its white marble surface inscribed with the Della Torre coat of arms and an inscription, with a red marble border.[27] Numerous encomia were written in his praise (Figure 13.2).

The Cenedesi wasted no time in lobbying for Michele's replacement as bishop. The city council swiftly elected a noble representative, and the cathedral chapter

Figure 13.2. Frontispiece, Adriano Grandi, *Canzone nella morte dell'Illustrissimo Reverendissimo Cardinale di Ceneda, Monsignor Michele della Torre*, Verona: Appresso Girolamo Discepoli, 1586 (Venice, Biblioteca Nazionale Marciana).

The poem was dedicated to Michele's Jesuit nephew Alvise III, who would die in 1587.

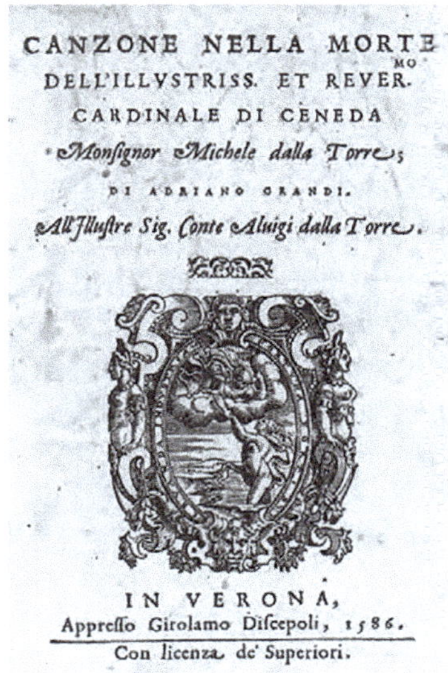

CANZONE NELLA MORTE
DELL'ILLVSTRISS.MO ET REVER.
CARDINALE DI CENEDA
Monſignor Michele dalla Torre;
DI ADRIANO GRANDI.
All'Illuſtre Sig. Conte Aluigi dalla Torre.

IN VERONA,
Appreſſo Girolamo Diſcepoli, 1586.
Con licenza de' Superiori.

chose two canons to travel to Rome to support the election of Giovanni Della Torre, Michele's nephew and son of Girolamo and Giulia. Alas, these best-laid plans went awry. When the three ambassadors arrived at the Vatican just nine days after Michele's death, they were informed that the pope had already appointed Marcantonio Mocenigo (1528–99), a canon of Padua, *cameriere* of the pope, and, importantly, a Venetian patrician, to the position. The pope asked Cardinal Decio Azzolini to respond to the Cenedese delegation. He allowed that the pope had heard of Michele's death with much sadness and mourned the loss to everyone of a lord of such sterling qualities. And even though the successor had already been appointed, after the pope had read all the letters attesting to Count Giovanni's many virtues, 'he was persuaded, knowing that he was raised by his Cardinal uncle, that he would be taken into account for other occasions'.[28]

Giovanni's brother Giulio wrote to their father with the back story. Giovanni's nomination did have the support, he reported, of Cardinal d'Este, Cardinal Farnese, and Cardinal Carafa, among others. But it was strongly opposed by the Republic of Venice, whose case for Mocenigo was presented to the pope by the Venetian ambassador to the Holy See and Cardinal [Agostino] Valier, with the support of Maffeo Venier, the Venetian Archbishop of Corfù, and Cardinal Ferdinando de' Medici, brother of the Duke of Tuscany. The pope decided in favour of the Venetians. Although Mocenigo's appointment was distressing, Giulio counseled his father 'to have patience, taking it all for the best'.[29]

If Girolamo was disappointed, Mocenigo soon learned that he himself should have been careful what he wished for. He arrived in Venice on 14 April on his way to his new diocese to pay his respects to the doge and to thank the Signoria in person for supporting his nomination. Writing to Cardinal Azzolini five days later, he said that he was warmly received and seated next to the doge in the Collegio. But there were storm clouds brewing. The republic was again asserting its jurisdiction over Ceneda, an issue that had only temporarily been laid to rest during Della Torre's tenure. That matter, still unresolved, would be just one of the issues with which Mocenigo had to grapple in his new position.[30]

He reported to the doge on 22 May that after being delayed by high waters, especially of the Piave River, 'I arrived in Ceneda at night so suddenly that I did not know that I was there until the next day'. He immediately ordered 'two solemn processions and prayers to the Lord God, one for the life of the pope and other for your serenity'.[31] On 30 May he wrote to Cardinal Azzolinoi complaining about the dire state of affairs that he found in the city: '*ignoratissimi* priests, who are so bad, that if the seminary whose foundation I will attend to with all my spirit, does not help this Diocese, it will be a truly bad thing.' But that was just the beginning:

> also, the castello, once the most noble habitation of the Bishop and ornament of this city, was certainly falling down and ruined from the foundations, if that good Cardinal still lived a year, by the grace of god, (and whom some were trying to make pope), your lordship would be astonished by the details of his life.[32]

A List of Grievances

By July, the new bishop was battling with the Della Torre survivors over accounts and items that had been removed from the castle before his arrival. The disagreement, which also involved the treasurer of the church in Rome, became so heated that a referee had to be called in. Mocenigo wrote to Giovanni on 11 July with a list of grievances:

> Having arrived in Venice, with the good words that had passed between us, I had forgiven the all the wrongs that Signor Conte Sigismondo, your brother, and Lord Marzio Colloredo, his uncle, had committed, with threats and evil ways to my agents when they took possession of this Bishopric in my name. Just eight days ago one of them was told to watch out for the said Signor Marzio. And I thought to deal with the effects of his harshness with courtesy.[33]

But upon arriving in Ceneda, Mocenigo claims, he discovered a castle stripped of its furnishings and accounts that were incomplete at best and falsified at worst.

> I found that the death of the Cardinal had been concealed for three days, in order to sell 100 stara of wheat for 300 ducats, and all the rest of the grain. I found this by a miracle from a document by the hand of Martino [Giovanni's factor]. Your lordship should know that [these goods] were [still there] after the death of the cardinal, and according to the bull of [Pope] Julius were mine.
>
> I found that 80 walnut stools made by Father Domenico Berti a little before the death of the Cardinal, together with tables, chests, chairs, 40 casks and other things of wood, were taken away. By the bull of Pius V, these belong to his successor, not the heirs,
>
> I found that the ornaments of the chapel, that is, two chalices, one of solid gold; a silver bell; ampules, two of mountain crystal and two of silver; two silver candlesticks; a very richly bejeweled miter, and two others [also] very rich, [were] sent to Venice to the house of Della Gatta. [Furthermore], a case of marked books…candlesticks for use and. a little basin of silver; [and] 70 pieces of silver were sent to Rome; two rings, two crosses, these things, were, I say, all taken away.
>
> I found that Martin, your factor, went looking for many debtors of the Bishop and offered to grant them quittances of all their debt, if they would pay him a tenth part, and many false receipts were made for the obligations of your lordship when the Iconomo (trustee) was created on 23 February 1586 [two days after the cardinal's death]; and the depository of the Reverend Chapter could act against you to have restored to the church what belongs to it.[34]

Mocenigo continues that he would have been content with the 30 scudi that he was able to retrieve from the accounts, and the wine that was his by reason of the papal bulls, and adds that he has already spent 200 scudi of his own funds 'to repair this unhappy castle, which was falling down'. Then he has a change of heart:

> But since it was written to me from every side that I should protect my life from the relatives of your lordship, and that in the chamber of the Signora Ginevra Polcenigo, your sister, it was freely spoken that with iron or with fire or with poison your [relatives] wished to chase me from this castle; I know this, for letters from the most honoured persons that I have near me say it clearly. I confess that my mind is changed and [I am] endeavoring to get back what belongs to the Bishopric with more rigor, which I would not have done; I ordered the retrieval of some chests and very old chairs from a house, which, with the crosses of the churches, had been hidden there.

> Having had an inventory made, all by the hand of a notary, I ordered Martino to render me an account of the administration, as also I decided to write to your lordship to give back to me the miter, vestments, crosses, and candlesticks of the chapel, which things, notwithstanding this, I will receive more gladly with an accord than with litigation, and that would be regarding the goods.[35]

Mocenigo then turns his attention to Girolamo Della Torre:

> Your lord father is unhappy about two things. One that I have taken the wines consigned to your creditors; the other that I would have taken goods bought by him and Count Guido, not by the Cardinal.
>
> To the first I say, my lord, that it is false because I have [only] taken from your vicar 17 barrels of wine, which were sent to the house after the death of the cardinal. Nor is he entitled to the... money lent to the Cardinal to pay the courier when he brought the news of the cardinal's hat...
>
> As to the furnishings, I say to your lordship that those were furnishings of the Castello which after the death of the cardinal were hidden in a house, about which I sent the authentic list to the Treasurer, telling him that they pertained to the seminary; nonetheless I will give 20 scudi to whoever wishes them, and I would also give them to your lordship, although by the bull of Pius V they are mine... But take care, your lordship, that you would not [try to] change the mood of creditors to wish to be paid above the spoils sent to Rome, which (I will well prove) are worth more than 6000 scudi.
>
> Nonetheless, to put an end to this business and so that you know my courteous mind, I say that if it pleases the Reverend Signor Treasurer, my lord, I will surrender what the two above cited bulls give me, I will also surrender the benefice of the grace made me by Our Lord, and I will give to your lordship what you wish.
>
> But your patrimony has not yet been given to me, Signor Conte; I do not want to pay the debts of the Cardinal in that I have the inconvenience of paying my own, and with this I make an offer to your lordship.[36]

Giovanni Della Torre, then in Rome, responded to Mocenigo by the end of the month. 'Your letter of the 12th raises two issues: one of dissatisfaction of my [family], and the other with the debits and credits, although they are mixed together. Of the first, I repute it more imagined and fomented than true, nor have I ever wished to know otherwise.'[37]

Of the accounts Giovanni declares that he knows little, since they were not reported to him:

> Thus, I cannot respond to one or the other if not superficially. And beginning with the first, I have not heard any rumor made in this court, if not about a

> memorial given some months ago by Count Giulio my brother in which he simply pleaded that His Serenity [the pope] should command that he be obeyed in all things; and that this was done after your reverend lordship (also the first to arrive in Venice) had presented another, which seemed intended to give His Serenity a bad opinion of my [family] rather than accurate information that your reverend lordship could have had of the fact. After that this has never been talked about except that I have confidentially spoken with Monsignor Reverend Treasurer, wishing to allay all rancor that could come from this affair. As to Count Sigismondo, my brother and Signor Marzio my cousin, I know very well how much honour and modesty they have brought, in this as in all their other actions, and therefore it is not necessary that anyone should presume to call them into doubt, nor to make the world believe the opposite.[38]

Giovanni reassures Mocenigo that he hopes for his success in the diocese and that he is certain that this will be the case 'without too much fatigue, given the people's good will and desire and the fact that the church had been administered so well for so many years'. But he wishes to make one point clear:

> I want your lordship to know, regarding a matter which pertains to me, that I have never designated the post as a hereditary thing (which I am not sure would even seem legitimate);...and of this I call on God as my witness.[39]

Giovanni knows little about the credits and debits, since he has never concerned himself much with the accounts. But again, he wants to put the record straight:

> I tell you that it is not as was said, that among the silver that was removed from the Castle after the death of the Cardinal of blessed memory, that there were solid gold goblets, nor were there jeweled miters of great price.[40]

Mocenigo is encouraged to get fuller information from the priest Mondino as to whether there were other silver objects which the new bishop should have. Giovanni also wishes to correct the record regarding 'the 80 stools that you tell me were made by the Reverend Priest Domenico Berti; they do not arrive at that number by a long shot, not being more than 36'.[41]

> Concerning the other goods that I took into my house I do not know how one can say that they were hidden, since (so to say) there were carried here to my house by all the people of Ceneda in the daytime and not the nighttime, so that one can apply that proposition 'one who does evil hates the light.' And the Reverend priest Giovanni Antonio knows this well, and many other witnesses worth of faith who were present.[42]

That was, of course, not the end of it. Mocenigo, still not satisfied, writes on 6 August to the Venetian Alvise Belegno: 'No man lives today more travailed than me, finding myself hit from one side by the reverence and love owed to His Serenity [presumably the doge], from the other by a fear not to lose the grace of the Serenity of Our Lord [presumably the pope].' The lament is worth noting because Alvise, who seems to have been Mocenigo's friend and confidant, was—curiously enough—the nephew of Giovanni Della Torre's maternal grandmother, Marcella Marcello Bembo, and thus Giovanni's first cousin once removed.[43] The complex web of family ties could still be unravelled by divided loyalties rising from the age-old conflict between feudal and republican values.

Embattled on Two Fronts

The Della Torre were embattled on two fronts: financial worries, highlighted by the Ceneda situation, on the one hand; and Giovanni's future in the church on the other. For two other attempts at arranging his promotion to an important position had also fallen through. Sigismondo had been hopeful that his brother might be named bishop of a proposed new bishopric of Gorizia, but the plan was premature, and the territory remained an archdeaconate. Then, Giovanni Caligari, Bishop of Bertinoro and the papal nuncio to the imperial court at Graz, lobbied the Curia to have Giovanni named as his successor, but that too came to nothing. Finally, the pope delivered on his promise to keep Giovanni in mind and appointed him as a *cameriere d'onore*, a stepping stone to higher office.[44]

Girolamo Della Torre wrote to the pope from Villalta on 16 September:

> I truthfully confess that in the 82 years that with God's help I have lived in this world, I have never had more happiness and consolation than learning that Your Sanctity has taken for your servant and *cameriere* my son, Count Giovanni... so not being able to come in person, because of my age and indisposition, I humbly thank Your Sanctity for such a favor.[45]

But every silver lining had a cloud:

> When I was believing to spend my life and old age in some repose and contentment, it has now been overtaken by the death of the Cardinal, my brother, with so many other disturbances; it is incumbent on me to pass it as best I can, but what bothers me more is seeing that the Monsignor of Ceneda, the modern bishop, troubles me and my house about those furnishings given by me and bought by our patrimony for the Lord Cardinal my brother, and of his own authority appropriated for himself the wines and the credits left upon the death

> of the said Cardinal, not wishing to satisfy some debts contracted in life by this Cardinal, and he does not wish to pay for the funeral expenses, something that the Holy Church is accustomed to do for every prelate; so much more that my brother consumed his life and property in the service of the Holy See.[46]

Girolamo finally gets to the point in the next paragraph:

> Therefore I have taken measures to implore your sanctity that you would not wish to allow us to be travailed by the said Monsignor, but that you would deign (his having the possession of the wines and credits that amount to more than two thousand ducats) to also satisfy him and to pay some debts which the Cardinal had incurred in life, that in addition to paying for the wines, you would also pay for the funeral expenses, which amount to a thousand ducats in all, nor would you try to repossess the furnishings conceded by me in life to the Cardinal and bought in part with his own patrimony from which I have had to spend much to maintain him in the service of the Holy See in Rome, at the time of Paul III, and at the time of Julius III, and Paul IV in France two times and in Perugia, in Trento, and other places. That in truth I can say to your sanctity it has been the ruin of me and my children, that beyond our alienated possessions we still pay interest of more than 1500 ducats [each year].

Signing the letter with a shaky hand, Girolamo concludes:

> I thus implore your Beatitude to take into consideration my just arguments, the merits of my dead brother and these my elderly years, so that this life that remains to me could be employed more happily in service of God, and of your sanctity, to whom, humbly kissing your Holy Feet, I pray to the Lord God, for a long, happy, and contented life, and the augmentation of the state.
>
> I also swear that all I am left with are two sapphire rings, one white and the other blue, which blue I had given to the Cardinal and the white was given him by a gentlelady, his relative.[47]

A deposition with the full bill of particulars, written in the same hand and apparently appended to the letter, is worth quoting in full:

> That the illustrious Signor Conte Girolamo della Torre has furnished the Castello of Ceneda with his own goods and patrimony.
>
> That the said Signor Conte bought the silver of Bertoldo Valvasone and the said part of his own that he had in the house and bought in Venice.
>
> That the Signor Conte Girolamo had from the Signoria of Venice 13,500 ducats which were the property of the Casa Della Torre with the diminution of income

> for 24 years of 600 ducats a year, of which the major part has been spent for the use of Monsignor Illustrissimo Cardinale, after his promotion to Cardinal.
>
> That the said Signor Conte Girolamo has always helped the Monsignor Illustrissimo Cardinale while he was in the service of the Holy See in Rome as in France and Perugia, that he has done so with a great sum of money and erosion of his revenues.
>
> That the Monsignor Illustrissimo Cardinale did not have another ecclesiastical benefit other than the Bishopric of Ceneda, and that diminished by 500 scudi of pension.
>
> That the Bishopric of Ceneda did not ascend to the sum of 2500 scudi of revenue.
>
> That the Signor Cardinale had always had a very copious household, of gentlemen as well as other servants and a good number of horses, dispensing infinite alms to monasteries of monks and nuns and to other needy persons.
>
> I Girolamo della Torre swear that from the time that the Signor Cardinal Della Torre my brother, of good memory, came to the residence of his bishopric of Ceneda from Pope Paul III, of happy memory, he never made any expense on furnishings of any sort; but always I have accommodated him in all his needs at the expense of my patrimony, except for two bed canopies, one of *pavonazzo* (royal purple) cloth and the other of *pavonazzo tabi* (heavy purple-colored silk), I having furnished the entire castle of Ceneda, with whatever was necessary of silver, furnishings of the rooms, beds, carpets, linens and every other thing that one wishes necessary for the said castle, just as I have always done while he served the holy see, in Rome, as in two times in France, and in Perugia, for a space of 50 years with the expense of 125,000 scudi and more, and for all the goods that one finds in Rome, there has not been spent any of the revenue of the Bishopric of Ceneda…but of our own patrimony, that all I affirm with an oath.[48]

Girolamo's appeal for restitution and reimbursement dragged on and would not even be resolved by the time of his own death.

Mocenigo's troubles, of which the dispute with the Della Torre was only one issue, continued. Writing to the pope's *datario* (almoner) in Rome, on 27 September, he refers to continuing friction with Venice over his secular authority in Ceneda and complains of malign spirits who 'invent diabolical things against my reputation' and of spies who 'observe minutely all my actions'. He concludes: 'I am tired by now of so many annoyances, that continually gnaw at my heart like termites, I consider that it would be better for my peace to abandon every hope and retire in a hermitage with my books, than to live in such misery.'[49] Nor did he endear himself to citizens and nobles of neighbouring communities. Signing his edicts as *Principe*, he was soon embroiled in conflicts with the inhabitants of Tarzo, the Counts of Porcia and the Rangoni of Cordignano, as well as the

Sarcinelli of Serravalle over borders and territorial rights. To rebuild the castle, he created new enemies by imposing heavy taxes on the Cenedesi. Some of them tore down a wall inscribed with the emblem of Saint Mark and blamed him for it. In December Mocenigo writes to Camilla Peretta, sister of Sixtus V: 'I know very well that I was born under a certain constellation that in the conclusion of all my dealings, incredible difficulties come to me most of the time.'[50]

Despite the dozens of panegyrics written in Michele's praise, Girolamo and his sons might well have complained about the same constellation. For the dispute with the pope was only one aspect of a larger financial problem. Indeed, the Della Torre faced considerable challenges going forward.

Notes

1. 'inter primos [occuruit] ob tuam eximiam religionem, prudentiam, fidem, integritatem ceterasque virtutes quibus praeditus.' Cited by Tramontin 1990, 43–4.
2. J. Lestocquoy 1966, 34–6. Ugo Boncompagni, Gregory XIII, was pope from 13 May 1572 to 10 April 1585.
3. Bernardi 1845, 256–7. For the loan, see ASUd, *AT*, b. 2, colto VI, fasc. 4, no. 13.
4. ASUd, *AT*, b. 2, colta VI: 'Della Città di Ceneda Oratione All'Illustrissimo et Reverendissimo Cardinal dalla Torre' (unnumbered pages): [c. 14].
5. Ibid., [c. 16].
6. Ibid., [c. 18].
7. Bernardi 1845, 256 and Bechevolo 1982 both state that the arch was built in 1584. But cf. Capodagli 1665, 480, citing an inscription on the arch which suggests that it was built before Michele was elevated to the Cardinalate: 'TERTIUS agnoscens TVRRIS decora ala, vetusta, virtutisque Memoriae. MICHAEL morumque Tuorum, Paulus Honorato dedit haec tibi sceptra tenere.'
8. Cicogna, *Ins. Ven.*, IV, 452; Cairns 1976, 62–79; Puppi 1989, 148.
9. ASUd, *AT*, b. 2, colto VI, fasc. 4 (21 March 1584).
10. Ibid.
11. Capodagli 1665, 481–2; ASUd, *AT*, b. 2, colto VI, fasc. 4.
12. Biblioteca Riccardiana, Florence, MS 1184, 300r-336v, cited by Tramontin 1990, 44.
13. Tramontin 1990, 45.
14. Ibid. For Arnosti, see Bernardi 1845, 257.
15. Capodagli 1665, 484–5.
16. Ibid., 485–6. See also Chapters 3, 4, and 14.
17. Capodagli, 485–6; Tomasi 1998, I, 146.
18. ASUd, *AT*, b. 22, Doti uscite, no. 43—1584,'Memoria riguardante il Matrimonio della N. S. Marcella figlia del N. S. Co: Gerolamo di Luigi della Torre col N. S. Federico Co: di Colloredo;' ASUd, *AT*, b. 17, 216–17. For typical marriage ages for women, see Cohen and Cohen 2001, 202: 'Everywhere, nearly all women became wives (and sometimes even widows) by the age of twenty-five.'
19. See Chapter 1.

20. Muir 1983, 252; Conzato 2005, 66, n121, 103–5, 108–9; ASVe, *CX*, Comuni, c. 83 (2 January 1561 m.v [=1562]).
21. Conzato 2005, 103–5, 108–9.
22. Ibid., 105.
23. Ibid., 183; Custoza 2003, Tav. 5.
24. Capodagli 1665, 487; Bernardi 1845, 258; Antonini 1881, 31–3.
25. Antonini 1881, 33.
26. Bernardi 1845, 259, citing Mondini, 146.
27. Capodogli 1665, 487–8; Sartori 2005, 118–19.
28. Bernardi 1845, 264–5.
29. ASUd, *AT*, b. 2, colto VI, n. 15, fasc. 4 (2 March 1586).
30. MCVe, MS Cicogna 2241: Registro de lettere de Prencipi, et d'altri negotij secreti et di cose pertinenti alla giurisditione del vescovato di Ceneda, 5v-7v (19 April 1586).
31. Ibid., 22v.
32. Ibid., 23r.
33. Ibid., 27r (11 July 1586).
34. Ibid., 27v.
35. Ibid., 28-28v.
36. Ibid., 28-28v.
37. ASUd, *AT*, b. 2, colto VI, no. 13 (undated, but it must be between 13 July 1586 and 30 July 1586).
38. Ibid.
39. Ibid.
40. Ibid.
41. Ibid.
42. Ibid.
43. MCVe, MS Cicogna 2241, 31v (6 August 1586). Alvise, a lawyer, was the son of Bernardino Belegno and Maria Marcello, sister of Marcella, and thus Giulia Bembo's first cousin. See MCVe, Barbaro, *Genealogie*, I, 193–4.
44. Bernardi 1845, 264–5; *DBI*, *s.v.* 'Della Torre, Giovanni', 567.
45. ASUd, *AT*, b. 2, colto VI (16 September 1586).
46. Ibid.
47. Ibid.
48. Ibid.
49. MCVe, MS Cicogna 2241, 51 (27 September 1586). The datario, the pope's distributor of alms, was Monsignor Giovanni Evangelista Pallotta, who would be elected archbishop of Cosenza on 11 September 1587. See https://webdept.fiu.edu/~mirandas/bios1587-ii.htm.
50. MCVe, MS Cicogna 2241, 89 (18 December 1586). For Peretta, see Dennis 2016. In the end, the sum total of Mocenigo's tenure was positive. He eventually rebuilt the castle with a substantial subsidy from the pope, and finally established the seminary that Michele had hoped for but had not been able to complete. See Bernardi 1845, 264–9; Sartori 2005, 122–4.

14
Retrenchment

With Michele's death, the family had not only lost the key stronghold in Ceneda that it had enjoyed for four decades. Even worse, as is evident from the unpleasantness with Mocenigo, it was also heavily in debt. It was time to scale down.

A Disposable Asset

Aside from Villalta and the feudal lands throughout the territory that produced considerable farm income, the family's main disposable asset was Palazzo Torriani and the family compound in Udine. Behind the palace was a courtyard and a huge garden. The plot, which occupied an entire city block, was bordered by a second *casa grande* with stables, with three *case* and three *cassette* occupied by tenants (Figures 14.1, 14.2, and 14.3; see also Figure 4.1).[1]

The palazzo, courtyard, and garden were rented to the Cavalier Gabriele Vando of Sacile, probably since 1573. But what about the second *casa grande* on the site? Since it did not have a tenant listed, it is possible that the Della Torre had been using it as the business office for the dispersed family properties and as a base for short stays. While official transactions, such as contracts, were transacted at Villalta, purchases of supplies and payments to staff were managed at a site in Udine, as attested by an account book for 1578–9. It lists daily expenses and the comings and goings of Girolamo and his sons, as well as their servants and horses, typically en route to and from other sites—Colloredo in the north; Cargnacco, Padua, and Venice in the south; Gorizia, Spessa, and Muggia in the east; Ceneda, Valvasone, Polcenigo, and Villalta in the west.[2]

But all this could be managed elsewhere, even in rented quarters. The compound was prime real estate that would bring a good price. And there was an eager buyer: Antonio Marchesi, a cittadino merchant with a bottega in Mercatovecchio 'at the sign of Jesus'. His father Martino, an immigrant from Germany, had built a fortune trading in all kinds of merchandise, from iron and other metals to apothecary supplies, and had sought to bring the silk industry to Udine. He had also won profitable contracts to furnish the granaries of Udine and Cividale and to collect duties for silk in Conegliano and the Patria del Friuli, and eventually the same for salt. Martino was, in sum, an entrepreneur par excellence.

The Venetian Bride: Bloodlines and Blood Feuds in Venice and Its Empire. Patricia Fortini Brown, Oxford University Press (2021). © Patricia Fortini Brown. DOI: 10.1093/oso/9780192894571.003.0014

Figure 14.1. Palazzo Torriani of 1540, ink drawing made after 1589. Facade on Borgo Strazzamantello. ASUd, Archivio Della Porta, B. 12.

The façade of the main *casa grande* featured a five-arched ground level portico typical of palaces in the Venetian Terraferma. The central trifora with a balcony on the piano nobile level served as a frontispiece for a salone flanked by smaller chambers. The mezzanine floor above was illuminated by smaller windows; a single dormer window in the roof provided light for the attic, used as a granary. The trapezoid-shaped plan of the ground floor at the upper left reveals a double staircase leading from the atrium up to the salone. The palace is flanked by two open courtyards with rusticated portals and walls topped with decorative crenellations. Visible behind them are buildings, some of them rentals, that border the site. The tall building on the right may be the second *casa grande*.

He had amassed a fortune, and the family was lacking in just two things: a seigneurial palace in Udine and noble Udinese status. The first would help achieve the second. Martino's son Antonio was determined to give the family the presence it deserved. One of the three orators dispatched to Ceneda by the Udinese community to congratulate Michele upon his election to the Cardinalate, he was already well known to the Della Torre family.[3]

Pressed for funds, Girolamo wasted little time. He called his notary Antonio Callegarini to his residence in Venice on 20 March 1586—barely a month after Michele's death—and drafted a contract of sale. Three weeks later, on 10 April, Girolamo's son Sigismondo and cousin Guido met with Antonio Marchesi in the castello of Villalta, along with Camillo and Giovanni Battista Caimo, two noble Udinese brothers who acted as intermediaries. After Camillo copied out the accord, it was signed by the three principals—Marchesi, Guido, and Sigismondo, as his father's procurator—and witnessed by Camillo's brother Giovanni Battista, a medical doctor.[4]

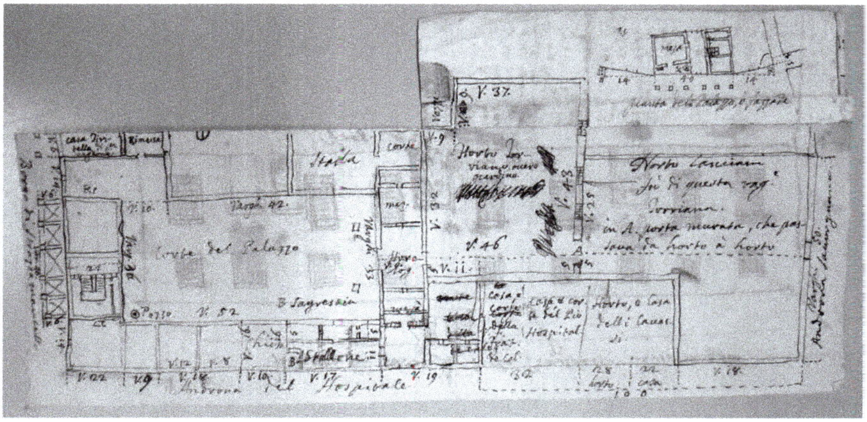

Figure 14.2. Palazzo Torriani compound in 1589. ASUd, Archivio Della Porta. B. 12. (Udine, Archivio di Stato).

The casa grande (1540) is on the far left. The loggia with the clocktower (labeled *Horologio*) at the opposite end of the *Corte del Palazzo*, bisects the property in the middle. The gardens are on the right. A row of houses, a stable (Stallone), and a chapel (*Chiesa*) with its sacristy (*Sagrestia*), are aligned along the Androna del Hospitale on the bottom of the plan. Additional buildings and another stable (*Stalla*) border the courtyard at the top of the plan.

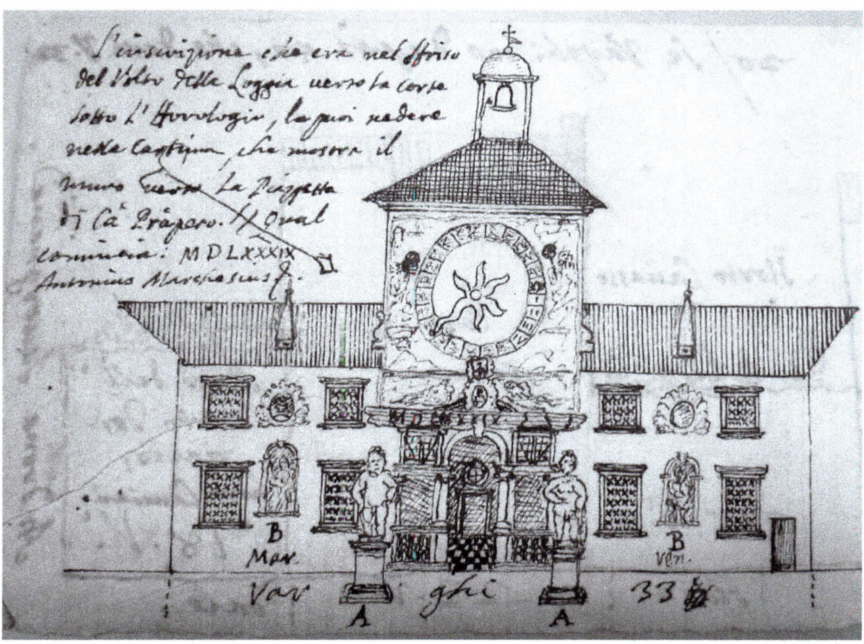

Figure 14.3. Loggia in Palazzo Torriani compound in 1589. ASUd, Archivio Della Porta. B. 12 (Udine, Archivio di Stato).

The contract called for a payment of 8900 ducats, to be disbursed in instalments over the next five years. A reimbursement of 215 ducats to Vando for improvements that he had made to the property brought the total to 9115 ducats. Marchesi made a down payment of 1700 ducats to the Della Torre and ȧdvanced 50 ducats to Vando.[5]

The contract was finalized a year later, on 27 April 1587, again at Villalta. Sigismondo and his brother Giulio signed it on behalf of their father, still in Venice, and their brother Giovanni, who was in Rome. Guido had died the previous November. Already credited with his down payment of 1700 ducats, Marchesi now paid an additional 1200 in accordance with the instalment plan. But the payment was made not to the Della Torre but to Giacomo Ragazzoni, a wealthy merchant with palaces in Venice and Sacile, in Vando's name. For we now learn that the Della Torre were in debt to Vando for that amount in loan instruments dating to 1573 and 1576. We might conjecture that this sum had been used for dowries or for improvements at Villalta. Marchesi also paid an additional 165 ducats directly to Vando himself; when added to the 50-ducat deposit paid the year before, it amounted to the 215 ducats cited in their separate agreement.[6]

Marchesi was ready to move in, but there was a problem. Vando was not ready to move out. He claimed that the Della Torre had agreed to allow him six months to vacate the premises after the contract was finalized. Further arbitration was necessary. Marchesi and Vando met in the vestibule of the main palazzo on Via Strazzavillan on 4 June. They agreed to abide by the decision of a mediator whom both trusted: Fulvio Arcoloniano, a feudal lord, 'who by his pure courtesy had interposed himself'. His compromise contained five points.

First, Vando agreed to renounce the accord made with Della Torre allowing him to remain in the house for six months. Second, he would permit Marchesi to take possession of the casa grande, cassette, stables, courtyard, and other areas. Importantly, he would allow Marchesi to carry out construction work in the said house 'and bring in stones and lime and other materials for his needs without being impeded, and to build stalls, storerooms and whatever he finds necessary'. Third, the income from the rental houses and the warehouses for wine and grain would go immediately to Marchesi, who would become the sole landlord. Fourth, Vando could continue to occupy the rooms that he was presently living in for up to three and a half months without paying rent, and in the meantime he should find another house so that his present lodgings would be empty and free after that time. Fifth, during this grace period, Vando was also allowed to enjoy the stables and all the fruits of the cultivated garden, with the obligation that he could not plant anything new. Finally, Vando was obliged to take good care of any improvements made and to consign them to Marchesi at the end of the time period. Arcoloiano, clearly a skilled negotiator, gave each party enough to be satisfied.[7]

With that knotty issue sorted out, on 6 August, in the castle of Villalta, Reverend Giovanni added his own signature to the agreement of 22 April, and

Marchesi declared himself ready to pay in advance the 500-ducat installment due in October. As requested by Girolamo, with the consent of his sons, this would go not to the Della Torre but directly to Giacomo d'Attimis [d'Attems], capitano of Gradisca, another creditor of the family. The massive debt was being whittled down.[8]

Un magnificentissimo e sontuosa palazzo

Marchesi could not wait to get to work on the property. In just two years' time, with the help of his wealthy and cultivated wife, Lidia Sasso, he would transform it into an impressive center of hospitality and the arts. It was later described as *un magnificentissimo e sontuosa palazzo*. The main palace, some of its rooms already adorned with grotteschi, was brought up to date and further embellished. In the ground floor atrium, a door flanked by marble statues of Adam and Eve opened to a grand staircase leading to the sala on the piano nobile. As guests ascended the steps, they could admire the stone bas-relief bust of Antonio's father Martino on the vault. A touching expression of filial piety, it carried the inscription:

Martino Marchesio
fidei animique candor
et rerum gerendarum usu viro insigni
Antonius F. pientiss.
monumentum hoc dicavit
Vix. Ann XLIV. Obiit. Ann. MDLXIX. VI. Febr.
(To Martino Marchesi,
a man remarkable for the brilliance of his faith and courage,
and for his practical experience,
his most pious son Antonio dedicated this monument.
He lived 44 years. He died on 6 February 1569)[9]

But that was just one distinctive feature of a luxurious interior of more than twenty rooms. The poet Muzio Sforza celebrated the palace in his *Rime* (1590), a collection of poems dedicated to Antonio. He enthused over fireplaces and door frames of coloured marbles, wallcoverings of gilded leather, damask, velvet, and silk, and rooms filled with precious objects, such as gilded vases, paintings, and other admirable items. One of the most impressive rooms was Antonio's *studietto* with a ceiling painting featuring Cupid and Psyche.[10] The painting noted by Muzio was, in all likelihood, *The Coronation of Hebe*, a canvas by Veronese and his studio, now in the Isabella Stewart Gardner Museum (Figure 14.4).[11]

It is easy to see why Muzio could have misunderstood the subject matter. The work presents an exuberant, and somewhat confused, vision of some fifty

Figure 14.4. Veronese and workshop, *Coronation of Hebe*, oil on canvas, 1580s? Originally in Palazzo Torriani (Boston, Isabella Stewart Gardner Museum).

Olympian gods floating on clouds–sitting, standing, conversing, and music-making—against a blue sky. In the centre, Mercury presents Hebe to her parents, Jupiter and Juno, as she assumes the role of cup bearer to the gods. The little room provided an admirable setting for a patron ambitious to make his mark on Udinese society.

Atypically, Antonio's wife Lidia had her own studio. Praising the beauty of her mind that matched the beauty of her body, the Udinese poet Giuseppe Bratteolo would dedicate his *Rime*, a collection of poetry, to her: 'You are the ornament and the splendor not only of the Sasso family, from which you left, and of the Marchesi, in which you entered, but also of Udine, your Patria, of the Friuli and of all Italy.' He elaborated: 'You are accustomed to withdraw every day into your rich and precious studio, adorned with copious, well-chosen and beautiful books of all sorts; and remaining there for a good space of time, you learn now from this, now from another author, the precepts of living well and joyfully.'[12]

Antonio's ambitious plans were not confined to the palace. He enclosed the north side of the big courtyard with a *barchessa* (stables) and the south with a row of apartments flanking a family chapel dedicated to San Martino and topped by a belltower. But the most striking feature was a loggia at the end of the courtyard facing the rear façade of the main palace. An even larger belltower, this with a clock on its face, rose in the centre block above an elegant entrance portal with steps leading into the loggia and beyond that into the garden. Visitors approaching the loggia would be welcomed by a portrait bust of Antonio himself set inside a conch shell niche in the frieze above the portal (see Figure 14.3 above). An inscription documented the completion of the building and celebrated its young patron: *MDLXXXIX, Antonius Marchesius aet. Suae annorum XXXVII* (1589. Antonio Marchesi, at 28 years of age). Stucco statues of Mars and Venus, said to be by Alessandro Vittoria, were placed in niches in the walls flanking the entrance; above each was another shell niche which must also have contained busts, perhaps of Antonio's wife Lidia and their only son, Giovanni Martini. But that was not all. Also flanking the portal were free-standing monumental stone statues of Hercules and Cacus, once attributed to Jacopo Sansovino. The palace, with its courtyard and loggia, would become a cultural centre for the literati of Udine, welcoming nobles and foreigners alike to concerts, poetry readings, and theatrical performances, and even chivalric tournaments.[13]

Known for His Culture and His Liberality

For all that, when Antonio had embarked upon his ambitious project in 1587 the Patria was in turmoil yet again. The harvest was poor that year, and by fall the city was suffering from a terrible famine. An astute businessman just like his father, Antonio now had the opportunity to distinguish himself as a valuable member of the community. In October, relying on his contacts in Germany and elsewhere, he signed an agreement to fill the city's granaries and supply the bakeries with grain. The following March, even before his new loggia was finished, he presented himself to an assembly of 196 citizens in the municipal council hall of Udine and petitioned to be granted noble Udinese status. He was worthy of the honour for several reasons: he was very rich, he owned a remarkable palace, he was known for his culture and his liberality, but above all he had managed to supply not only the city, but also the entire province, with a great amount of grain in a most difficult year, '*cum omnes trepidarent, ne passim homines fame essent perituri*' (when all were alarmed that everywhere people would die of hunger). After months of deliberation, Antonio's petition was approved by the seven deputies of the city on 24 January 1589. Cornelio Frangipane, appointed to recite the text of investiture, found a comparison in classical antiquity. He likened Antonio to Pompey, who had brought in grain from Sicily in time of famine to save his fellow citizens of Rome.[14]

The luogotenente, Bernardo Nani, approved the decree in March 1589: 'because it was made manifest to everyone how abundantly the Noble Messer Antonio Marchesi has satisfied the obligation and most importantly the duty... of maintaining the supply of bread... to this city.' He affixed his seal with the words:

> Praising highly the diligence and the work executed by the Noble Messer Antonio and his virtue by which these people in such a calamitous year received an incomparable benefit and utility, so that we were relieved from a great weight of those worries that the rectors are accustomed to have about the provision of wheat.[15]

To Avoid Scandals and Inconveniences

Bereft of the family palace, Girolamo Della Torre was tying up loose ends. The Venetian Senate had passed a law in December 1586 requiring all feudatories to verify their titles and investitures. This was followed on 29 May 1587 by the appointment of three noble Provveditori sopra i Feudi to administer the new law. On 3 August, in the midst of the famine, Girolamo's procurator, Giacomo Caimo, presented proof of his investitures to the luogotenente. Girolamo declared himself and his three sons—Sigismondo, Giulio, and Giovanni—and their descendants as feudatories, with civil and criminal jurisdiction over the castle of Villalta and its annexed villages, authority that 'I have exercised through my predecessors from ancient times up to the present day'. He swore the 'oath of fidelity in my name and those of my sons, and to do at all times what good and faithful vassals are due to their lord'.[16]

The famine was still raging on 12 September when Girolamo sat down with two of his chamberlains in the *camera cubicularum* of the castello of Villalta. His brother Michele and cousin Guido had died the year before; he had just sold the family palace in Udine in April; he had duly recorded his investitures; and he would turn eighty-five years old in November. It was time to put his house in order. Perhaps mindful of the prolonged litigation over the estate of his father-in-law, Gian Matteo Bembo, he wrote:

> I, desirous long before my death to see my property divided between my sons, so that each would know his separate share, in order to avoid scandals and inconveniences that could occur between them when I am dead, and so that they would have the occasion to be united of mind and loving one another, [and] seeing that they have been discussing these blessed divisions with each other for three or four years and have never been able to come to an conclusion, therefore it appears to me appropriate to assume this duty as patron of

> said faculty, to make such division so that everyone would know his own share, according to my wishes, ensuring that each part would be equal without any diminution.[17]

Girolamo's son Alvise, the Jesuit priest, had died earlier in the year in Reggio Calabria at the age of thirty. That left Sigismondo, Giulio, and the priest Giovanni to share the estate. After consulting with his chancellor Alvise Callegaris, Girolamo divided his properties into three parts, entitled Cargnacco, Villalta, and Muggia. The brothers were allowed to trade properties between one another as long as the total amounts remained equal.

Each would be credited with one-third of the 30,000 ducats on deposit in the Monte Vecchio in Venice, and each would also receive a one-third share of the payments remaining from the sale of the palace compound in Udine to Antonio Marchesi. Some property and funds would remain undivided: the monies in the Monte Vecchio, a house in Padua that brought in 60 ducats in rent each year, and the Ronco di Rosazzo. The latter, then as now, was a centre of viticulture. As Marin Sanudo had written in his *Itinerario nella Terraferma* of 1483, 'Here there are perfect wines...and, it is said, they are the best in Italy.'[18] The Della Torre heirs would presumably be the proprietors *pro indiviso* of this precious resource in perpetuity.

But with benefits came obligations. Each son was henceforth responsible for the taxes, interest, and debts related to his own share. And each was obliged to send Girolamo 400 ducats per year as long he lived. There were also some common debts that they should share equally. If by chance the family should lose its appeal to be reimbursed for the costs of Bishop Michele's funeral, the brothers would be responsible for them in equal shares, as well as for the sum of 2000 ducats incurred by Giovanni's trip to Rome.

Intended to be scrupulously fair, the divisions clearly required much thought and effort, with the assignments seemingly tailored to the needs of each son.

The first part, entitled Cargnacco, went to Giovanni, a cleric who did not need a large family residence. A country property around 10 km south of Udine, the fief had been under the jurisdiction of the Della Torre since 1479 and produced a variety of grains, legumes, and wine. The family administered it from afar, with appointed officials and judges. They had built a house there at some point, but it was inhabited by retainers, and they rarely visited except to collect the tithes and rents. The annual revenues from agricultural products farmed by around thirty families amounted to some 854 ducats.

The second part, entitled Villalta, went to Giulio, who must have expected to marry at some point in the future. In addition to the castle, the property included a cluster of tiny hamlets: Blessano, Gradisca di Sedigiano, Nespoledo, Pasian, Sclaunicco, Reana, Villanova, Villorba, Faedis, San Vito di Fagagna, Buia, Barazetto, Nogaredo di Prato, Ragogna, Rodeano, Susans, San Daniele, Ciconicco, Moruzzo, Fagagna, and Plasencis. Here the crops and animals yielded around 693 ducats per year. To equalize this portion with the first, an additional 160 ducats of revenue were added from rentals in Udine and scattered properties at Basaglia Penta, Gravuzze [?], Codroipo, Chiavali, Bressa, and Carpenedo.

To Sigismondo went the third part: Muggia, a fief on the coast of Istria that primarily produced oil and salt. The assignment made sense, since his residence in the Goriziana was only 30 miles from the property. Since the property yielded only 550 ducats in annual revenues, an additional 303 ducats would come from the Friulian villages of Bicinicco, Favis, Gonars, Lauzacco, Lavariano, Mortean [Mortegliano], Pozzo, Piancada, Rivignano, Sedegliano, S. Stefano, Tissano, Torsa, Selarnico [?], and Zugliano.

But then came the division of the debts and obligations, which were of three sorts: debts with interest, called *livelli*; debts without interest, called *debiti particolari*; and *incarghi*, largely payments in kind—wheat, rye, sorghum, chickens, and the like—to landowners such as the Abbey of Rosazzo and the Church of Trensano.

The *livelli* added up to a staggering 17,450 ducats, owed mostly to individuals, requiring annual interest payments of 1224 ducats. The share to be paid by each son amounted to an average of 336 ducats per year. The *debiti particolari*, which carried no interest, came to 4490 ducats, with each son's share of 1496 ducats having to be repaid eventually.

In sum, although rich in property, and despite the funds in the Monte Vecchio, the family was heavily in debt. The total debt of nearly 22,000 ducats was more than double the 10,000 the family had owed when Girolamo had sailed off to Crete in 1550. What did this mean for the three brothers? Of their annual incomes from rents and agricultural products (around 850 ducats each), nearly half (336 ducats) went to required interest payments. After each had paid Girolamo his allowance of 400 ducats per year, there would be little left over. Although the yearly installments of 1000–1500 ducats from Marchesi until 1591 would help, the creditors of the *debiti particolari* would have to be patient. And perhaps additional creditors would have to be found.[19]

Remaining active and in close touch with his sons, Girolamo moved around between Venice and their several residences. These now included Padua, where Giovanni had been appointed to the prestigious position of canon of the cathedral on 16 April 1588.[20] Girolamo's letter to Sigismondo on 12 June 1589, written by a scribe and signed by him in a shaky hand, leaves no doubt that the old patriarch was still in charge. Staying at the time at Villalta, presumably with his son Giulio, he asks for the loan of a carriage and horses for a visit to Spessa and other places:

To the illustrious Count Sigismondo Della Torre, *figlio carissimo*:

> This morning, with a little good weather appearing after so much bad, I have now decided to send for the carriage with the horses and another four horses for the servants, Zanut and the others present, and I would like to go first to

> Colloredo for a single day, and then another day to Udine to visit the Signor Luogotenente. Then I will come to Cargna, and then together with Count Giovanni, I will come to stay with you for four or five days to see Signora Orsina and the children. And immediately after returning to Villalta I will send back the horses and the carriage if they are needed, because having spent so much time in Venice and Padua, I intend to pass these two months...here in Villalta, and then return to Venice and to Padua...Also, with the carriage you should send me an experienced man to drive it and...a lackey to guide it...And with every comfort I will say nothing more for now, waiting to chat more comfortably in Spessa. Between now and then stay healthy with all the family.[21]

The Last Word

Unexpectedly, good news would arrive the following month. Girolamo's brother-in-law, Pietro Bembo, the unpopular Bishop of Veglia, died at the age of fifty-five. As a canon in Padua, Girolamo's son Giovanni was admirably well situated for further promotion. Again, the Venetians had other ideas, but this time, over their opposition, the pope gave the office to Giovanni.[22] One of Girolamo's most fervent wishes was finally satisfied. Just two days later, he called his Venetian notary Antonio Callegarini to his lodgings in the house of Paolo dalla Gatta in Venice. 'Healthy in mind and intellect, but somewhat aggrieved in body because of my old age', Girolamo decided to draft his last will and testament. He named as his executors 'my dear sons, Count Sigismondo, Count Giulio, and Count Giovanni, at present Bishop of Veglia, together with [whoever may be] the Luogotenente of the Patria del Friuli at the time, who would be superior to my said executors in executing this my last will'. Aware, as always, of post-mortem family disputes, he ensured that there would be an impartial arbiter.[23]

He made special bequests of 100 ducats each to Alvise Callegaris, his chancellor in Udine, 'for the good service that he has given me', and to Valentin Bassi, 'who presently serves me, for his long and faithful service'. To Flaminio Rosai, if still in his employ at the time of his death, went 50 ducats in addition to his salary. Likewise, Zanut da Ciconis would receive 25 ducats if still serving him or one of his sons.

Wishing to be buried in the family tomb chapel in San Francesco in Udine, he left the monastery an endowment of 100 ducats for a memorial service for his soul to be held in there *in perpetuo* on the anniversary of 'the day that I have departed this present life'. The monastery of Santa Maria Maddalena in Villalta would receive a legacy of 500 ducats for a *mansionario* in the Church of San Leonardo.

Girolamo enjoined his three sons to honour the division of property and debt obligations made in 1587. Any son who contested the distribution was obliged to pay an additional 500 ducats to the monastery of Santa Maria Maddalena, with the monies overseen by the luogotenente and by any other son or sons who did honour his father's wishes. These funds would be invested to pay for an additional friar to celebrate a special mass every Friday, Saturday, and Sunday, and on all the feast days. The three sons were counselled to live together in love, peace, and charity, and to use as a model their father and his own brothers who had lived together in charity and love, even though they had separated their property.

Finally, as per tradition, the residue of the estate should pass from legitimate male heir to legitimate male heir through the generations. As required by law, the notary asked whether Girolamo wished to leave anything to the pious places of Venice, or to the shamefaced poor, or for the redemption of slaves. He responded that he preferred not to, wishing to do whatever appeared right to him in Udine.[24]

Girolamo died six months later in Venice at the age of eighty-five, on 25 March 1590, a day that was pregnant with meaning for Venetians. Not only was it the feast day of the Annunciation of the Virgin; it was also the mythical birthdate of Venice itself. Girolamo's body was temporarily deposited at the Frari, close to that of his brother Alvise II. In accordance with his own wishes, Girolamo's remains were taken to Udine for burial in the family chapel in the monastery church of San Francesco. But as we know, Alvise II's body remains even today in a provisional tomb, high on the wall of the Frari, a tangible memory of a violent moment in the lives of the Della Torre in Venice.[25] The story of the Bembo and Della Torre families does not end there. Once closely intertwined by Girolamo's marriage to his Venetian bride, the ties began to unravel as each line followed its separate destiny.

Notes

1. Corbellini 1990, 18–20; Faccioli and Joppi 2007, 63.
2. ASUd, *ADT*, b. 5, no. 6, Libro delle entrade, 1578–9.
3. Corbellini 1990, 18–20; Molà 2000, 239; Tagliaferri 1969, 55–6.
4. ASUd, Archivio Notarile, b. 6357 (11 June 1586 to 26 January 1589), Marius Pictorius de Martinis [Mario Pittorio], Instrumentorum Liber.
5. Ibid.
6. Ibid. See also *DBI, s.v.* 'Ragazzoni, Giacomo'.
7. Ibid.
8. Ibid.
9. ASUd, *ADP*, b. 8; ibid., b. 12, 'Disegni di Palazzo Torrian sulla Piazza Torrian'. See also Joppi 1890, 124–6; Prampero de Carvalho 2003, 33–4; Prampero de Carvalho 2005, 7–14; ASDUd, MS Bartoliana, b. 52/2, Carte Della Torre, c. 60.
10. Sforza, *Delle Rime,* dedication.
11. Hendy, *European and American Paintings*, 284–5; Pignatti 1986, 31–7; Goldfarb, *The Isabella Stewart Gardner Museum*, 108–9; Brilliant and Ilchman, *Paolo Veronese*, 155. The original location of the painting is uncertain, but the description of a ceiling

painting in the inventory of 1675 is suggestive. A two-storey-high room in the mezzado on the north side of the garden loggia is described as 'Soffitado in pittura di tella tutto in un sol Quadro con pitture assai belle antiche'. See Prampero de Carvalho 2005, 63–4.

12. Bratteolo 1597.
13. Joppi 1890, 124–5; Albanese 1984, 211. Hercules and Cacus would be virtually the sole survivors of Marchesi palace complex, aside from Veronese's painting.
14. Corbellini 1990, 20, citing BCUd, Annales, LXIII, 20.
15. ASUd, *AT*, b. 70, no. 16.
16. Ibid., b. 33, no. 6, 3 August 1587. Bishop Giovanni would present the document to the doge on 25 September. See also Manzano 1879, 170.
17. ASUd, *AT*, b. 56, no. 7, 'Divisioni fatte all'Illustrissimo Signor Conte Hieronimo della Torre sopra la revisione fatta dal Cancelier suo Alvise Calligari della sua facolta' alli Illustrissimi Signori suoi Figliuoli Conte Giovanni, Conte Giulio e Conte Sigismondo'. The busta contains three handwritten copies of the document, all essentially the same. Alvise Callegaris was a notary in Udine from 7 September 1584 to 12 November 1610.
18. Sanudo 2014, 434.
19. ASUd, *AT*, b. 56, 'Processi e divisioni tra i Conti Della Torre'. For the properties, see also ASUd, *ADT*, b. 17, no. 42.
20. *DBI, s.v.* 'Della Torre, Giovanni', incorrectly citing Giovanni's birthplace as Bergamo.
21. ASTS, Archivio Della Torre di Valsassina di Duino, b. 258, fasc. 2, 'Documenti di Torriani, del Ramo di Udine e Verona'.
22. *DBI, s.v.* 'Della Torre, Giovanni'; Ciković 2015, 55–70. Pietro died on 23 July 1589. Giovanni was appointed bishop on 25 September 1589.
23. ASUd, *AT*, b. 27 (Cartella 6): Testamenti e Donazioni dei Conti Della Torre (28 September 1589).
24. Ibid.
25. ASU, AC, b. 17, fasc. 1, 'Prove storico-genealogiche della famiglia Della Torre', 130–3; Brown 2013b, 137–59.

15
The Legacy

What was the legacy of Girolamo Della Torre and Giulia Bembo, his Venetian bride? When Girolamo passed away in 1590, he was survived by eight of their ten children. His nephew, the once violent Marzio Colloredo, died as governor of Siena the following year after a distinguished career in the service of the Hapsburgs and the Grand Dukes of Tuscany.[1] With the Peace of 1568, the marriage of three daughters to feudal lords and two to wealthy city-dwellers, and the sale of the family palace in Udine to a commoner (albeit soon to be noble), it would seem that the Della Torre clan had embraced the new aristocratic code of honour in which wealth and virtuous actions benefiting the public at large rivalled antiquity of lineage.[2]

The Daughters

But lineage still mattered, perhaps more than ever, as well as a legacy of landholdings to pass on down through the bloodline. Setting aside Girolamo's sons for the moment, let us consider the marriages of the Della Torre daughters: Taddea to Valenzio Valvasone; Ginevra to Orazio Polcenigo; Elena to Lucio Popaite; Giulia to Aurelio da Noal; and Marcella to Federico Colloredo. These unions created a spider's web of mutual obligations, melding feudal and urban interests, that determined the fates of future generations. Strategic marriages helped to keep the patrimony intact, at least within the extended family. But they also created fissures, promoting a shift from clan unity against the outside world to fierce infighting within.

Girolamo's cousin and ward Guido Della Torre, in leaving his estate to Valenzio Valvasone, his first cousin (their mothers were sisters), had rejected the Venetian custom of passing the patrimony (aside from dowries) only through male descendants carrying the family name, with collateral male lines favoured over direct female descendants. Valenzio and Taddea would have two sons, both of whom seem to have died young, and four daughters whose names 'renewed' the female lineage on both sides of the family. It was they who would eventually share in Guido's legacy and pass it down to their own children carrying the surnames of their respective husbands: a Brazzaco, a Colloredo, a Strassoldo, and another Valvasone—family names already familiar in the Della Torre pedigree.[3]

The Venetian Bride: Bloodlines and Blood Feuds in Venice and Its Empire. Patricia Fortini Brown, Oxford University Press (2021). © Patricia Fortini Brown. DOI: 10.1093/oso/9780192894571.003.0015

And Valenzio proved to be zealous in protecting the legacy for his daughters. His dealings with his brother-in-law Lucio Popaite are a case in point. When Taddea's sister Elena had married Lucio in 1582, her dowry comprised two parts: (1) one of Guido Della Torre's agricultural properties yielding an annual income of 60 stara of grain, consigned by Valenzio as Guido's procurator; and (2) a commitment of 1000 ducats from her father Girolamo. Lucio enjoyed the income from the farm property only until Guido's death in 1585, when Valenzio claimed it back. The 1000 ducats from Girolamo remained unpaid. After the sale of Palazzo Torriani in Udine to Antonio Marchesi, a frustrated Lucio took two actions. First, he filed a lawsuit against Valenzio to recapture the real property, which was, by contractual agreement, part of the dowry. Second, he filed a claim against the Signori della Torre for the 1000 ducats. The first matter was resolved by the Venetian Quarantia, which ordered Valenzio to pay Lucio 3250 ducats in return for allowing the property to remain in Valvasone hands. That Valenzio chose this option, albeit reluctantly, suggests that feudal land was more valuable than cash. But the 1000 ducats remained unpaid, probably because so many other creditors were ahead of the line for the proceeds of the sale of Palazzo Torriani. And yet, a remedy was eventually found with another marriage and a little creative bookkeeping.

In 1598 Lucio negotiated a marriage between Paola, a daughter from his first marriage (to Ottavia Mantica), and Sigismondo Della Torre's firstborn son Carlo (albeit a nephew of Lucio's own wife Elena). Lucio consigned the debt of 1000 ducats to Paola's dowry and remained free of other obligations. Carlo was now his own father's creditor for at least part of his new wife's dowry.[4] This convenient outcome would have important consequences for the family patrimony when Lucio wrote his will some thirty years later.[5]

Marcella, the Della Torre daughter who had married Federico Colloredo in 1584, died childless at Villalta in the 1590s. Federico had purchased the fiefdom of Dobrovo, comprising a castle atop a mountain with its surrounding villages near Gorizia, from the Count of Ottemburg, for the goodly sum of 16,300 florins in 1591. After Marcella's death, he moved there to live with his brother Lodovico and his family. Lodovico's wife, Perla Polcenigo, was the daughter of Valenzio Valvasone's sister Felicita. In the tangled web of endogamous Friulian marriages, that made Perla not only Federico's sister-in-law, but also his second cousin twice removed by marriage. The brothers remained active in imperial circles and rebuilt the old castle in grand Renaissance style in the first decade of the seventeenth century.[6] Federico also became close to Sigismondo's son Carlo, who had married Paola Popaite in 1598. When Carlo wrote his will in 1607, he would name the Colloredo brothers, Federico and Lodovico, as guardians of his children.[7]

The Sons

At least two of Girolamo's three surviving sons seemed destined for greatness. Giovanni, as Bishop of Veglia, was well positioned for higher honours in the church. Sigismondo, based in the Castello of Spessa in Gorizia, was becoming a prominent player in imperial politics. Giulio, by contrast, remained close to home. While he spent some time in service of the Hapsburgs, he was soon back at Villalta.

Giovanni

Bishop Giovanni had drawn up an inventory of his possessions in 1590, shortly after his father's death, and prepared to move to his island diocese off the coast of Dalmatia. His share of the estate was surely enough to set up a suitable residence in the bishop's palace in Veglia. In addition to tapestries, carpets, storage chests, linens, a wealth of silverware, and other household essentials, he listed no fewer than five clocks and a number of paintings. These included portraits of his father Girolamo and Cardinal Michele plus a small picture of the King of France.[8] Giovanni kept a low profile for the next five years, dealing with an aggrieved clergy after the contentious tenure of his predecessor (and uncle) Pietro Bembo. Then in November 1595 Pope Clement VIII appointed him apostolic nuncio to the Swiss cantons. He was travelling into another minefield. Not only was the region divided between Protestants and Catholics; it was also divided linguistically between German and French-speaking cantons. Moreover, it was caught in a diplomatic tug of war between France and Spain. The area had been without papal representation for a long period and there was considerable resentment over the non-payment of Swiss troops by Gregory III—some 40,000 scudi—for a military campaign in France.[9]

Giovanni was instructed to defend the authority of the pope and the Roman church and to institute Tridentine reforms. But, erroneously thought to be pro-French, he was not trusted by the Spanish and he himself doubted whether he had sufficient diplomatic skills to carry out the mission. He delayed his departure, lingering for several months in Padua, but after a briefing by Federico Borromeo in Milan he finally set forth. After crossing into Switzerland in early April 1596, he made his residence in the Catholic stronghold of Lucerne. Much like his uncle Michele, his energies were directed toward reform of the clergy and enforcement of the decrees of the Council of Trent. He travelled tirelessly, reinforcing Catholic dominance in the French-speaking areas in the south. He was less successful in suppressing Protestant tendencies in the German-speaking areas in the north. During his tenure, he also made an effort to maintain a

Figure 15.1. Andrea Vicentino, *Madonna of the Rosary*, with Pope Pius V, St. Dominic, and the Queen of Cyprus, c. 1600 (St. Kvirin, Krk, Croatia).
The painting, given to the church by Bishop Giovanni Della Torre, celebrates the Christian victory over the Ottoman Turks in the Battle of Lepanto in 1571.

presence in his diocese of Veglia, donating several significant gifts to the cathedral. These included a silver reliquary bust and silver pyxis containing relics of its patron saint, San Quirino, that had been given him by Duke Wilhelm V of Bavaria; an antependium embroidered with the Della Torre coat of arms; and Andrea Vicentino's *Our Lady of the Rosary*, an altarpiece commemorating the Battle of Lepanto (Figure 15.1).[10]

Sigismondo

Less than six months after his father's death, Sigismondo would lose his protector and promoter, the Archduke Charles II. Carlo Morelli di Schönfeld, the nineteenth-century historian of Gorizia, recorded the archduke's death: 'He died [on 1 September 1590] after twenty-six years of governing in Graz, mourned by his subjects. The states of the county having been invited to the funeral, which was celebrated with magnificence, Sigismondo Turriano carried the gonfalone of our province.' Seven other nobles, including a Strassoldo and another Della Torre, carried the casket. Five years later, Sigismondo was elected luogotenente of the contea of Gorizia. Morelli observes: 'Well versed in the legal sciences, he was the vigilant guardian of the most essential things that contribute to the happiness of a province.'[11]

Although a Venetian subject by law, with a Venetian mother, Sigismondo's primary allegiance was to the emperor. In his testament of 4 June 1595 he even stated that his property in the Friuli, although held in *fedecommesso* with his brothers, could be alienated 'in case of an opportunity to transport our possessions all together from the Venetian Dominion to the illustrious House of Austria.'[12] He was rumoured to be a leading candidate for appointment as imperial ambassador to Rome, but it never happened. Perhaps it was a matter of finances. Chronically in debt, Sigismondo repeatedly asked for loans from his brother-in-law Raimondo. Aware that his uncle Michele's costly, if prestigious, posts as Bishop of Ceneda, papal emissary, and cardinal had eroded the family patrimony, he may have been relieved, even if disappointed. Indeed, the wealthy Raimondo himself would run up huge debts as the emperor's ambassador to Venice.[13]

And yet, the Hapsburgs found another way to use Sigismondo's talents, and probably resources as well. Toward the end of 1596, he was appointed imperial representative to Transylvania and became a key player in the empire's war with the Turks, who had resumed hostilities three years earlier. The fragile alliance with Transylvania, a buffer zone between Istanbul and the Hungarian front, was at risk. Sigismondo was sent out to the Italian courts, as well as to Prague, Vienna, and Graz, to seek help in maintaining it. He had an impossible task, and by 1598, despite his talent in building consensus, the alliance fell apart. Sigismondo's personal life was also strained by his extended absences. Orsina, by now a mother of ten, was gravely ill and sent letter after letter accusing him of neglect; his son Carlo was reckless and disobedient; and his economic situation was worse than ever. After a frustrating trip to inform the pope of the developments, Sigismondo finally returned to Gorizia, probably early in 1599.[14]

Despite special masses celebrated at Loreto, Orsina died soon thereafter, but Sigismondo did not mourn her passing for long. Dynastic concerns were on his mind. His two oldest children were now married: Dorothea (with a generous dowry worth 4297 ducats) to Baron Federico Lantieri, in 1597; and Carlo to Paola Popaite, in 1598.[15] Sigismondo envisioned that Carlo, as heir to the Rassauer holdings at Spessa, would carry on the family line, while he wished (one might say ordered) his sons by Orsina to remain unmarried. Nicolò should serve the house of Austria as a Knight of Malta or a Teutonic knight; and Girolamo, who had a crippled leg, would become a cleric. But Sigismondo did not intend to remain single himself. In July 1599 he proposed marriage to the much younger Margherita Lenkovich, daughter of Raimondo Della Torre's sister Maria and, as such, his own niece. Raimondo, still ambassador in Rome, was not happy about it. But Sigismondo obtained permission from the girl's father and was determined to proceed, with or without a papal dispensation. His seven daughters by Orsina, he argued, were in need of womanly attention. The marriage took place probably in October, with Lodovico Colloredo representing the absent Raimondo. It was followed early the next year by the marriage of Sigismondo's daughter Torriana to Federico Lantieri's brother Gaspare.[16]

Giulio

Yet another wedding, this with portentous implications for the family, took place in 1600. On 13 August, Sigismondo I's brother Giulio, then forty-six years old, married Caterina Marchesi. Also known as Catella, she was the gifted sixteen-year-old daughter of Antonio Marchesi, the proud owner of the former Palazzo Torriani in Udine. Perhaps Giulio had just been waiting for her to come of age. The marriage of Caterina's brother Giovanni Martino to Lucina Savorgnan, the granddaughter of the sister of Tristan Savorgnan, had been celebrated at the palace in 1595 with festivities worthy of visiting royalty.[17] Caterina was just ten years old at the time and something of a prodigy, reminiscent of Giulia Bembo's mother Marcella Marcello. Caterina's tutor, the poet Giuseppe Bratteolo, described her as 'a young girl of the liveliest spirit, of the most profound memory, and (what is more important) most desirous of learning the arts and liberal sciences'. Already proficient in Latin and vernacular letters at the tender age of twelve, she too was a poet, and Bratteolo included seven of her poems in his collection of poetry published in 1597.[18] Caterina's own wedding to Giulio five years later was also preceded by several weeks of concerts and jousts and celebrated in a richly decorated Palazzo Marchesi.[19]

Sigismondo

It was not long before Sigismondo was on the road again and neglecting his young bride. The Turks captured the Hungarian fortress of Kanizsa near the present border with Austria on 20 October 1600. Austria, Gorizia, and even Italy were at risk. Sigismondo was ordered on yet another diplomatic mission, this time to mobilize other Italian princes and to ask the pope to send reinforcements. Hastening back from Rome to report to the archduke in Graz, Sigismondo attempted to ford the Isonzo river near Gradisca. His carriage overturned and he drowned, not yet fifty years old, on 7 June 1601.[20] As an aside, we might observe that his unfortunate death disproved the old wives' tale that a child born with a caul enjoyed a special protection against drowning (Chapter 7). More significantly, with no children

Figure 15.2. Portrait of Bishop Giovanni Della Torre, 1606. (Padua, Museo Civico).

born from Sigismondo's third marriage, Carlo, then around twenty-four years old, became head of the Gorizian branch of the family. His first son, Sigismondo II, would be born to his wife Paola Popaite on 3 November.[21] Had the infant's grandfather and namesake survived, he would have rejoiced that his male line would continue.

Giovanni

After eleven years of prudent, if not spectacular, diplomacy in Switzerland, Giovanni was granted honorary Roman citizenship, along with his five nephews, in February 1606, and concluded his assignment in June.[22] The honour may have inspired the commission of his portrait (Figure 15.2).

The following year Giovanni completed a manuscript, *Descriptio Helvetiae*, now in the British Museum. Richly illustrated with watercolours of city views, figures, and coats of arms, it offers a detailed account of the history and customs of the Swiss cantons. Although some of the miniatures depend on earlier prints, they were made with a skilled hand. One would like to think it was Giovanni's.[23]

The Udinese Line

26 and Caterina had two sons and a daughter—Alvise IV, Ginevra, and Giulio II–in short order before Giulio died at Villalta in 1603. Three children in three years, thus establishing the Udinese branch of the next generation of the family. Little Giulio's name suggests that he was born posthumously. Perhaps only her husband's untimely death spared Caterina the fate of Giulia Bembo, our Venetian bride who had died at the age of thirty after bearing ten children. But marriage and motherhood meant the death of something else. As had happened with so many other gifted maidens of the time, they signalled the end of Caterina's poetic aspirations. Only one of her poems was published after her wedding.[24] And yet, she did continue to write letters in an elegant, clear hand, and her correspondence with her husband's brother Bishop Giovanni offers us a glimpse of the constraints faced by women in that period.

With his brothers Sigismondo and Giulio now deceased, Bishop Giovanni became the oldest male member of the combined Della Torre family, which now had two lines. Carlo, in his early twenties, was effectively head of the Gorizian line, but the Udinese line—now consisting of the nineteen-year-old Caterina, two toddlers, and a newborn—lacked a Della Torre protector. It was a role that Giovanni welcomed and would gradually assume from afar.[25] The castle of Villalta was less than an ideal home for Giulio's city-born widow, and she moved back to Udine with the children to live with her parents, Antonio and Lidia, in Palazzo Marchesi. But Antonio soon died, with her brother Giovanni Martino inheriting the palace. Although Lidia still lived there as well, Caterina was unhappy with the situation and suspected that her finances were being mishandled by Giulio's procurators. In 1608, she wrote to Bishop Giovanni, then in Veglia:

> I have not yet decided whether to stay here in the house of my brother, nor do I know where to retire. I am more than ever harassed to remarry, but I only want to remain with my children. When I understood that your lordship wanted to protect me, as you once offered to do, I was not at liberty to do as you desired. I do desire, and will always desire, to please you; and although I know that Signor Count Carlo and Signor Curzio were ordered by your lordship to provide for these matters, they are however both so much occupied with their own affairs, that although they have good intentions, they cannot attend here, so that your presence is necessary to be able to lend a hand in everything, because when you give me the courage and authority... I promise to live with my children; I will attend to their wellbeing, and their faculty will increase. And truly it is necessary

> that your lordship should first use your authority to deal with past disorders, with the major part of [their] money being in the hands of this one and that, so that their resources would not be so much diminished and could be retrieved when one wishes and restored to a good state…I remain then awaiting your advice, even more your coming.[26]

We do not have Giovanni's response, but subsequent letters indicate that he has taken responsibility for Caterina's two young sons who were sent away for their education. Referring to Alvise IV, the eldest, in a letter of January 1611, she writes: 'I was hoping to be comforted by knowing that he was well and would be learning; now I understand completely the contrary; patience in this as in my other travails I commend to the hands of God… nevertheless I care for the wellbeing of my son more than any other thing.' And she is heartened by the news that little Giulio II is doing very well.[27] Although young girls were often educated in convents, we may hope that Caterina's daughter Ginevra remained with her in the palace.

When Caterina's brother Giovanni Martino died in 1613, he followed the principle of more or less equal treatment of his heirs in his testament. Since he had no living children, the Marchesi properties were divided between his three sisters. To Ortensia (or more precisely to her husband, Orazio Manin) went a house in Piazza Nuova; to Antea (or, again more precisely, to her husband, Fulvio Savorgnan) went a house in the contrada of Poscolle plus 100 ducats. But to the widowed Caterina, because she already had sons, went Palazzo Marchesi and, with her mother Lidia, the residue of the estate. As the most visible symbol of family identity, the house—again to become Palazzo Torriani—was to be passed from male heirs to male heirs in perpetuity, even though they carried the Della Torre (and not the Marchesi) surname. Caterina and Federico Savorgnan, Giovanni Martino's father-in-law, were to serve as executors.[28]

Alas, the bequest did not resolve Caterina's travails. Her mother Lidia writes to Bishop Giovanni in 1614 that her once bright and lively daughter is now suffering from melancholy.[29] The cause of her distress is not spelled out, but in all likelihood it relates to the management of the feudal properties. Several letters from Caterina to the bishop, written in 1616, recount a tale of woe. Her maternal uncle Andrea Sasso, also a poet, has just died; without his protection, 'our poor house will be the target of fate'. Due to stormy weather, the grain and wine crops are destroyed at San Vito; animals have died there, as well as at Villalta and Tissano; rents cannot be collected; expenses are high; and the factors have engaged in various schemes so that she does not know who to trust. 'Consider, your lordship, how I find myself thinking that it would be better to be dead than with the burdens that I have on my shoulders. Because I see that if God does not help me very soon in these labyrinths, I will lose my mind and my body.' In another letter she exclaims, 'I believe the miseries of this calamitous year will never end'.[30]

It was a bad year in the Friuli, generally, with the War of Gradisca having broken out in November 1615. Venetian forces were pitted against the Archduke Ferdinand on a battlefield that stretched from the Friuli into Istria. Families, many with properties in both Venetian and imperial territories, were divided. Udinese nobles generally supported Venice, while most of the castellans, particularly the Gorizian contingent, aligned themselves on the side of the Austrians. On the one hand, Carlo di Sigismondo, Caterina's nephew and erstwhile protector, was fervently pro-imperial. Although the grandson of Giulia Bembo, a Venetian noblewoman, he reportedly remarked: 'I would rather live and die a little less than poorly in that war under the house of Austria, than very rich under the Republic.'[31] On the other hand, his (distant) cousin Francesco Strassoldo, although he had served the archduke since childhood, became a well-compensated captain in the Venetian army.[32]

With the war concluded in Venice's favour in 1617, the early years of the 1620s were eventful for Caterina's family. Her son Alvise IV, then twenty-one, signed a marriage contract on 18 February 1621, with Sofonisba Antonini, whose father Giacomo had captained Venetian troops in the war. Sofonisba had grown up at the family estate at Rosazzo (where the Della Torre owned property in *fedecommesso*) and brought with her a most welcome dowry of 10,000 ducats. The pair had been promised to one another for a decade, and the nuptials unfolded over a two-year period. The marriage was registered on 13 February 1622, less than a month after Caterina's mother Lidia had passed away, but Sofonisba only moved into Palazzo Torriani a year later. Recording the notable events of her life in her diary, she wrote: 'On 10 March 1623: Note how the lord count took me to his house here in Udine.'[33] The poet Giuseppe Salomoni celebrated the marriage with an epithalamium, presenting the young bride with a daunting prospect. From her womb, he promised, would issue a new Giulio, a new Giovanni, Michele, and Raimondo, a new Lidia and Caterina, a new Girolamo, Francesco, Antonio, Jacopo, Alfonso, Daniele, Sofonisba, Felicita, and Bianca—a posterity 'doubly adorned with matrons and heroes'.[34]

Bishop Giovanni died in Padua also during the early months of 1623. He had given a relic of a fragment of the True Cross to the Cathedral of Padua in 1617 and was buried there in the Cappella di S. Croce in the crypt.[35] Alvise IV's mother Caterina Marchesi had again lost a powerful protector. In October of the same year, at only thirty-eight, she decided to remarry and signed a marriage contract with the Venetian partisan Francesco Strassoldo, but the union does not seem to have been finalized.[36]

Like his new father-in-law, Alvise IV would become an accomplished condottiere, the first in his direct line since Alvise I, his great-grandfather and namesake, who had been murdered in Udine back in the Cruel Carnival of 1511. The young Alvise IV led a cavalry troop against Spanish forces in Valtellina in 1624 and commanded a company of ninety horsemen in the siege of Mantua in 1628. By the end of the decade, Sofonisba would give birth to three children—Lucina, Giulio, and Girolamo.[37] With a third son, named Michele (henceforth Michele III), born later, Alvise IV had renewed a good part of the ancestral line. His mother Caterina lived on at least until 1638, when she wrote her testament leaving him Palazzo Torriani.[38] He inherited his father Giulio's estate as well, which included a half-share in the feud of Villalta and other properties. When his daughter Lucina married Marcantonio Locatelli, 'a gentleman worth half a million in gold', in 1649, the family future would seem secure.[39] But expenses were high, and mounting debts would lead to a crisis less than two decades later.

The Gorizian Line

In the meantime, parallel events were unfolding in Sigismondo's branch of the family. His son Carlo had died shortly after the conclusion of the War of Gradisca, leaving eight children. Having sided with the archduke in the conflict, he had put their rights to feudal properties in Venetian territory in jeopardy. These included his share of the feud of Villalta. The Republic demanded that the felonious feudatories swear their fealty to the Republic, and Carlo's three sons were forced to grow up quickly. On 26 February 1619, Sigismondo II, the eldest, requested (and was granted) investiture of the Friuli properties for himself and his brothers, Michele II and Simone. Then, on 13 June, Sigismondo II ensured the continuity of the bloodline, signing a marriage contract with Marzia Sbroiavacca. He was not yet eighteen. The following year, he and his brothers, as Carlo's male heirs, joined their father's half-brother, Girolamo, in guaranteeing the dowry of their father's half-sister, Emilia, to Baron Gaspare Vito of Dorimbergo. Michele II died the same year, while Simone would remain single.[40]

Sigismondo II and Marzia had a son, naming him Carlo (henceforth Carlo II) after his paternal grandfather, in the 1620s. Lucio Popaite, the child's great grandfather, wrote his will in 1630. He left his extensive properties in Noale, Oderzo, Pedrina, and Pordenone—a bequest that came to be known as the *eredità Popaite*—to the boy, with rights of primogeniture, and set into motion a fateful chain of events that would haunt the family for generations.[41] After Marzia's death, Sigismondo II married Anna Maria Savorgnan in 1638 and eventually had eight more sons and three daughters. When he wrote his own will in 1643, he followed his grandfather's example, but went several steps further. In addition to the traditional *fedecommesso*, with the provision that the Della Torre properties remain undivided, he ordered that Carlo II, again with rights of primogeniture, should control the entire estate. Sigismondo II enjoined all his other children 'to give the same obedience to Count Carlo II, that they would give to the testator, their own father'. Of the sons, only Carlo II should marry, but he should support his brothers with family resources as they pursued careers in the military or the church. Finally, he ordered 'that they [his sons] should never be divided at any time, but must always stay together in good union and brotherhood, and Count Carlo would be the absolute governor of all his faculties'.[42] Vain hope.

This was a far cry from the strategy followed by Girolamo Della Torre back in 1587. We will recall that he left some property in *fedecommesso*, but meticulously divided most of the family feudal holdings, and debts, between his three surviving sons, with the proviso that they be allowed to exchange properties of equal value if they wished. It was also a far cry from the common practice of simply leaving property to the male heirs in common, with them enjoined to live peaceably in 'Comunella', with the intention of promoting clan unity. Primogeniture may have been intended to do the same, but with the illiquidity of landed properties, it often had the opposite effect.[43]

Carlo II would marry Eleonora Colloredo in 1647 and eventually have three sons—Lucio, the *primogenitor* (named after Popaite); Sigismondo III; and Girolamo II—and a daughter, Giulia. Carlo II was destined for a turbulent life. His father's testament had already created tensions and jealousies between him and his half-siblings. Beyond that, born into a feudal culture still marred by vendetta and warring factions, he was wounded in a surprise attack by Dario Neuhaus and Odorico Petazzi, both members of the rival Neuhaus faction in 1650. Exclaiming that it was an act 'without precedence, unimaginable not just for enmity, but also for pure bestiality', he took swift revenge, ordering his retainers to murder Petazzi the following year.[44]

When his father Sigismondo II died in 1654, Carlo II became the sole proprietor of the *eredità Popaite*, as well as a share of the Della Torre patrimony. He was now the father of young children and a rising star in Gorizian politics, but he could not escape the factional violence that had plagued the territory for more than a century. Indeed, although he was appointed capitano and governatore of Trieste in 1666 and capitano of Gorizia by the emperor the following year, the vendetta flared up again with another attempt by members of his faction to assassinate a Neuhaus. Sporadic acts of violence continued, with provocations, ambushes, poisonings, and banishments. Indeed, Carlo's troubles were not over. They would become ever more complicated.

Palazzo Torriani Up for Auction

The Udinese branch of the family had its own challenges. Michele III, the youngest son of Alvise IV and Sofonisba, had married the fifteen-year-old Sulpizia Florio in 1663, with their wedding inspiring the usual effusive poetic tributes.[45] As with Alvise IV's mother Sofonisba, the bride was taken home to Palazzo

Torriani only two years later. Michele III seems to have died shortly thereafter, while Sulpizia remained in the palace. Although she was wealthy, a humiliating disaster was in the offing. Alvise IV's heirs—Michele III (before his death) and his brother Girolamo—had been unable to pay their father's tax obligations and were required to consign part of their properties to the state. While they retained their half-share of Villalta and other feudal possessions held jointly with the heirs of Sigismondo II, Palazzo Torriani was an obvious target. In 1667, it was put up for auction in the public loggia of Udine. Giovanni Ferro, a Venetian noble, stepped forward and bid 2500 ducats in the name of his brother Lazzaro. The price was a steal. The wealthy Ferro family had bought its way into the Venetian patriciate just five years earlier, upon the payment of 100,000 ducats. A seigneurial palace in Udine would be further validation of their new aristocratic status.[46]

But at the same time its loss would also be a blow to the prestige of the Della Torre clan. Family honour was at stake. Carlo II, now 'absolute governor' of the *eredità Popaite* and the patrimony of the Gorizia branch of the family, took swift action. He offered properties in Noale and its territories of equal value to Ferro in return for the palace. Income-producing country property was surely a better investment than a city palace with expensive upkeep, and Ferro accepted. The young Sulpizia, Michele III's widow, was allowed to remain in the palace, complete with full rights to a carriage and six horses, until she remarried, at which time the property would revert to Carlo II's branch of the family. Upon Michele III's death, Carlo II had also wrested full control of Villalta from his father's brother Simone.[47]

Sulpizia was not a widow for long. On 2 March 1669, in one of the most lavish wedding celebrations of the day, she married Torrismondo Della Torre, grandson of Raimondo Della Torre and Ludovica Hofer and ninth cousin of her deceased husband Michele III. The festivities took place in her family's palace, Casa Florio, with concerts, banquets, and a joust in which the groom and his noble guests took part. The event was memorialized by a deliciously entitled epithalamium: *Serto pomposo et immortale tessuto di fiori odoriferi colti dalle muse negli amenissimi giardini di Parnaso per coronare i felicissimi imenei dell'Ill. Sig. T. Della Torre e S. Contessa Torriana nata Floria* (Pompous and immortal wreath woven of fragrant flowers gathered by the muses in the most pleasant gardens of Parnassus to crown the most happy nuptials of the...). After the joust, the couple paraded through the streets of Udine with a long cortege of ladies and knights to the city walls, and thence to their new home in the Castelnuovo in Sagrado, near Gradisca.[48] With Sulpizia safely married, Palazzo Torriani again returned to the direct descendants of Girolamo Della Torre and Giulia Bembo.

But what descendants... Carlo II, now in control of a huge Della Torre patrimony that reached from Noale and Pordenone in the west to Istria in the east, was a textbook case of the corruptibility of money and power. In 1670, he leased the palace in Udine to Pietro and Marcantonio di Prampero for six years. An inventory of the furnishings made at the time describes more than twenty rooms, luxuriously furnished with paintings, sculpture, draperies, tapestries, vases, mirrors, beds, and chairs upholstered in leather or silk, with many such pieces adorned with the coats of arms of both the Della Torre and Marchesi families. Among the noteworthy objects in the grand salone on the piano nobile, the notary listed:

> Six paintings above the doors with portraits of the Torriani Cardinals, Patriarchs, and Bishops, with carved frames, some gilded . . . two portraits of the King of France and his brother . . . a great gilded lantern . . . two wooden figures of Moors, entire, on pedestals . . . a painting above the fir table, with two figures of a man and woman, both almost nude, and the woman holds a golden casket and chain in her right hand.

And in the adjacent chamber on the northwest corner:

> a fireplace of red marble and gilded frames on the walls . . . A large painting without a frame with a portrait of a woman with two little boys on the right and a girl on the left . . . A large octangular mirror surrounded by eight small pictures with little figures, in a black pear-wood frame, with green silk cords and buttons with tassels of gold thread . . . a large desk of pear-wood with ivory insets with nine little drawers with pergoletti, that one pulls out, and in the center a little door, with a lock and key.[49]

Alas, Carlo II's volatile character finally caught up with him. He was arrested the following year for seducing and abducting the wife of a high imperial magistrate and participating in a felonious conspiracy against the Emperor Leopold I. As the historian Morelli put it, he had fallen into 'a labyrinth of disgraces'. He was imprisoned in the Fortress of Schlossberg in Graz.[50]

Fraternal Feud

If Carlo II was bad, his three sons—Lucio, Girolamo II, and Sigismondo III—were worse (Figure 15.3).

In March 1681, Lucio agreed to pay Sigismondo III an annual allowance in turn for sole control over the administration of the family properties. But Lucio was no match for his other brother. In November of the same year, Girolamo II persuaded Lucio to cede him his rights of primogeniture to their father's patrimony and the *eredità Popaite*. Lucio would receive in turn an allowance of 5000 German florins annually. Sigismondo III, in a separate agreement, swore never to marry, and was promised one thousand ducats per year. In 1687, Girolamo II

Figure 15.3. Lucio, Sigismondo, and Girolamo, sons of Carlo II Della Torre, 18th century. BCUd, Fondo Principale, MS 541, cc. 25, 26, 27 (Udine, Biblioteca Civica "Vincenzo Joppi").

Lucio, depicted with a faint sketch of Villalta in the background, was possibly poisoned by his brothers. Sigismondo, father of Lucio Antonio, was murdered by Girolamo.

consolidated his control with a contract with his father Carlo II, still languishing in prison at Graz. He died there in March 1689 without executing a will.[51]

The relationship between Girolamo II and Sigismondo III reached breaking point in 1690, when their brother Lucio died in Udine without heirs, 'with certain signs of poison'. Sigismondo III was living in Venetian territory and Girolamo II in the Austrian possessions. Although both held numerous hereditary titles—imperial marshal, baron, count—of various jurisdictions, neither was satisfied with his share of the properties and each wanted more. On 15 January 1691 the Venetian Council of Ten ordered the two to come to an agreement within the month or Sigismondo III would be exiled to Zante and Girolamo II to Corfù for two years. The threat does not seem to have been carried out, and litigation continued. Sigismondo III, needing liquid funds, was not without imagination. Despite his promise never to marry, he took a Venetian bride, Cecilia Mocenigo, in 1691 and settled down, presumably in the castle of Villalta and Palazzo Torriani in Udine.[52] In 1692/3 he put *The Coronation of Hebe*, the ceiling painting in Palazzo Torriani attributed to Veronese, up for sale. After offering the work repeatedly 'for many and many months', he finally sold it to two Venetian dealers for 900 ducats. The painting was stripped from the ceiling, causing damage to one corner, and taken to Venice and put into storage. In 1695, Girolamo II, Sigismondo III's infuriated brother, contested the sale, arguing that the painting had only been lent to the dealers in order to have a copy made. They were enjoined from selling the painting or moving it elsewhere, but it was never returned to Palazzo Torriani.[53]

The fraternal feud continued, growing ever more contentious. Girolamo II was further angered by the birth of Sigismondo III's first son Lucio Antonio in 1695, with the boy becoming heir to half the Della Torre estate. In 1696 the Council of Ten again sought to separate the two brothers, relegating Girolamo II to Venice and Sigismondo III first to Udine and then to the fortress of Legnago. On 27 August, Girolamo II appeared before the heads of the Ten and accused his brother of violating the terms of the relegation and of committing acts of violence in Udine and Noale. The Venetian authorities began an inquest in Udine on 5 September, calling upon any person to appear who had been 'aggravated in any way by Count Sigismondo Della Torre and having any knowledge of any excess or violence practiced by him against the life and substance of subjects'.[54]

Depositions attesting to Sigismondo III's conduct were obtained from priests, deacons, and judges; from the peasants of Villalta, Ciconicco, Cargnacco; and from residents of Udine, Pordenone, Pedrina, Monfalco, Codroipo, and Noale. Among other outrages, he was accused of demolishing the houses of several humble merchants in Udine in order to have a better view from the family palace. The process took nearly a year. Finally, on 7 August 1697, the Council of Ten banished Sigismondo III from Venetian territories with a large bounty on his head and confiscated all his properties. If captured, he would be beheaded. Many of his retainers, as well as his personal secretary and his *bravi*, were condemned to perpetual banishment from the Venetian state. His confiscated goods were put up for auction on 1 September, but there were no offers. Fear of retribution from members of the family may well have dampened the enthusiasm of any potential buyer. Girolamo II stepped forward at the third auction, held on 17 December, and offered 3000 ducats for his brother's properties. But then his own mother, Eleonora, intervened, stating that she wished to secure the property for Sigismondo III's young children, Lucio Antonio, Carlo, and Eleonora, 'out of pity'. Her offer of 3050 ducats was accepted by the Ten on 9 January 1698.[55]

The conflict between the brothers remained unresolved. A blood feud of another sort. Girolamo II had himself been banished for murdering a gardener and had been hiding out in his castle in Spessa in imperial territory. Although the Republic had also sought to deprive him of the income from his holdings in Venetian territories, his wife Claudia Arrigoni had acquired the fiefs of Villalta and Cargnacco and was collecting his share of rents by proxy. He wanted more and resolved to take the matter into his own hands. On the evening of 15 November 1699, in company with a well-armed contingent of his *bravi*, he rode to the castle of Villalta where Sigismondo III had holed up in defiance of his sentence of banishment. Concealing his identity, Girolamo II called his brother into the open and fired his arquebus, mortally wounding him before the horrified eyes of the victim's children and his wife Cecilia. She testified to the Council of Ten that both her husband and his brother Lucio felt defrauded by Girolamo II, who aimed to make himself 'absolute Padrone of all the faculties of the family' and had tricked his father (Carlo II) into giving him the properties in Austrian territory, the most precious possessions of the Casa.[56] She suspected that Girolamo II had wanted to kill her children as well, aiming 'with the massacre of these innocents to unite the remainder of the faculty, just as he had usurped Ziracco and Spessa with damage to them'. The grisly affair was a grim preface to (and harbinger of) the turbulent life of the four-year-old Lucio Antonio.[57]

On 28 May 1700, the Ten banished Girolamo II yet again, under penalty of beheading if captured, and his goods confiscated. But he escaped Venetian justice once more by fleeing back to Austrian territory where his political connections protected him. Although the prestige and power of the Della Torre in the Venetian Friuli had waned after the peaceful deaths of the first Girolamo Della Torre and his brother Bishop Michele in the late sixteenth century, it had only strengthened in the Austrian Friuli with the service to the imperial court of the first Sigismondo and his descendants. For a time, Girolamo II was virtually untouchable. Even though he had shot his own brother in cold blood, the Convocazione degli Stati Provinciali absolved him of the crime and he continued to enjoy the support of the Gorizian nobility.[58]

The Bad Seed

Sigismondo III's orphaned sons, Lucio Antonio and Carlo III, became heirs to the *eredità Popaite*, largely properties in Noale and Pordenone, and shared *pro indiviso* with Girolamo II's sons, other holdings including the castle of Villalta and Palazzo Torriani in Udine. They also became heirs to a toxic heritage of violence. Their widowed mother Cecilia sent them to Venice to be educated at a Jesuit college around 1707, but the secular lures of the big city proved to be more compelling than a religious education. Although only twelve at the time, Lucio Antonio (henceforth, Lucio)—handsome, wealthy, arrogant, and angry—soon found interests better suited to his tastes: womanizing, bullying, and spending lavishly. He moved back to Villalta and surrounded himself with a band of *bravi*. Eager to display their power, they terrorized the countryside, threatening and extorting tributes from peasants, seducing and raping their daughters with impunity.[59]

In 1712, although Lucio was only seventeen, Cecilia sought to settle him down by arranging a marriage with the sixteen-year-old Eleonora Madrisio, daughter of Count Giovanni Enrico Madrisio, castellan of San Martino del Friuli. Lucio's sister, also named Eleonora, had recently married the bride's brother, Rizzardo. The dowries of both Eleonoras would be equal. The double union of two great families: what could be better?

A festive wedding took place in the castello of Madrisio on 29 March, two days after Easter Sunday. In contrast to his bride Eleonora, said to be 'rather homely', Lucio was a fine figure of a man—tall, blonde, with grey eyes, an aquiline profile, and sensual lips—and, unfortunately, as irresistible to women as they were to him.[60] The young couple moved into Villa Pedrina, one of the Della Torre family's rural properties in the open countryside just south of Pordenone (Figure 15.4).[61]

Figure 15.4. Azzo Decimo (Pordenone), Villa Pedrina.

Built in the second half of the sixteenth century by the noble Cappellari della Colomba family, the villa had been acquired by the Della Torre as part of the *eredità Popaite*. After Carlo II's death in 1689, it became the property of his three sons. According to some sources, Lucio had already moved there with his mother and two siblings after his father's murder at Villalta in 1699.[62]

Although its façade has suffered the ravages of time, the villa still projects an image of solidity, strength, and grandeur. One wall of the salone had been frescoed in 1689, with an architectural perspective composed of two columns flanking an arch offering a view of a fictive garden with a fountain under a leafy arbour.[63]

And now Villa Pedrina would house the next generation. But Lucio proved to be as overbearing and self-indulgent at home as he was in public. Eleonora, 'the most graceful, kind, and accomplished lady that nature could send forth', was soon a most unhappy bride. Lucio's long-suffering mother Cecilia died during that period in her 'noble and delicious home' in Pordenone—perhaps, according to rumours, from poison administered by Lucio himself. Around that time, he and his brother entered into full possession of their father's property. Learning that some of the Venetian possessions had escaped from the family's hands during his mother's regency, Lucio set out to regain control. Still a teenager, but now the swaggering lord of Villalta and Noale, he assembled some four hundred rowdies—virtually a private army—who adopted a distinctive uniform: a wide-brimmed hat with a green rosette and a green and black shoulder strap

With spectacular bravado, he oversaw a wide range of abusive activities carried out by his followers throughout the countryside and frustrated the Venetian authorities: smuggling, refusing to pay suppliers, intimidating shopkeepers, demanding tolls to travel on public roads, conceding licences to bear arms, refusing to pay tithes and taxes.[64] During these years, although he neglected Eleonora for the most part, he fathered three children in rapid succession: Cecilia, Lucio Sigismondo; and Carlo.[65]

Although banished twice from Venetian territories in perpetuity in 1716—by the Council of Ten on 20 April and by the podestà of Treviso on 15 October—with a sentence of lifetime in prison if captured, Lucio was undaunted and continued to shrug off such annoyances. Distancing himself from the Veneto would only show weakness to his followers. Eleonora was in despair. Returning home unexpectedly, Lucio came upon her sharing her desperation with a priest. Irate, he threw his baton at her, accidentally fracturing the skull of little Carlo, nursing at her breast. Lucio was, from all accounts, defiantly unrepentant, and, indeed, simply annoyed at the hysterical weeping of his wife.[66]

Crimes of *lèse-majesté*

Lucio's arrogance seemed to have no end, and few repercussions. The turning point came in 1717. Travelling to Venice for Carnival, he defiantly removed his mask and frequented the *ridotti* (gambling establishments) and other public places. On Giovedì Grasso, 4 February, he paraded around Piazza San Marco in a carriage drawn by six Croatian horses. It was a far cry from the Giovedì Grasso of 1511, when the youth's sixth-great-grandfather Alvise I had been murdered by the followers of Antonio Savorgnan in Udine. Indeed, Lucio roamed through the city with an escort of fully armed followers, consorting with women and violating nuns. He seduced a willing Rosalba Valier, wife of a government official, and, after emptying her house of jewels and personal effects, persuaded her to flee with him, causing 'scandal and universal murmuring'. But still, the government did not act.[67]

Lucio returned to Pordenone and then moved on to Udine, continuing to encourage acts of violence and defiance. The luogotenente complained that he had occupied Palazzo Torriani, with a number of his followers, 'scandalously allowing himself to be seen not only throughout the city, but being driven with odious ostentation on the back of his carriage'.[68] On 17 May Lucio lined up his men in front of the palace 'in the form of a *spalliera* (espalier)' as a votive procession passed by. The intimidating message was clear. On 10 June he was in Treviso, chasing the local capitano out of a tavern where he had taken refuge from a rainstorm. Six days later he arrived in Padua, conspicuously dressed in red, for the feast of Sant'Antonio in a six-horse carriage accompanied by around forty well-armed henchmen. They stormed a house that lodged a contingent of soldiers brought in by the Venetian podestà to maintain the peace. A gun battle ensued, and this time Lucio and his personal army got the worst of it. One of his men was shot dead and two were hanged in Piazza delle Erbe. But Lucio eluded capture yet again. Disguised as a Benedictine monk, he fled to Villalta and then to Gorizia in Austrian territory.

The Serenissima had finally had enough. On 16 July 1717, Lucio was again banished from Venetian territory. But now, if he defied the ban, he would be beheaded between the two columns on the Piazzetta of San Marco. A bounty of 2000 ducats was offered for his capture in Venetian territory, and 4000 for his apprehension 'in alien lands'. His assets, 'both movable and stable'. were confiscated, and he was stripped of all his titles. Palazzo Torriani, one of the family's most cherished possessions, was condemned to be razed to the ground. The sentence was announced on 19 July from the steps of the public loggia of Udine to a large crowd of citizens. But the palace was still occupied. Several of Lucio's cousins had moved into the compound—presumably Girolamo II's children—and did not take the ban seriously. They were soon routed by a company of soldiers sent down from the castello. The palace had to go.[69]

After the most precious objects were hauled away, the luogotenente struck the first blows. A crew of some two hundred masons and carpenters called in from throughout the city completed the demolition, sparing only the church of Santa Barbara (Figures 15.5 and 15.6). The garden was sold to the Savorgnan della Bandiera family. The colossal marble statues of Hercules and Cacus were hauled to Piazza Contarena and erected opposite the civic loggia in front of the church of San Giovanni near Giovanni da Udine's fountain. The space where the palace once stood was renamed Piazza del Fisco and a column of infamy erected with the inscription: 'Lucio Della Torre, banished by the Excellent Council of Ten for the gravest crimes of *lèse-majesté*.' It is worth noting that Lucio's many transgressions were summed up in the term of *lèse-majesté*: offences against the dignity of the [Venetian] state. His open defiance was more damning than the underlying crimes.[70]

Atrocity of Such a Misdeed

The worst was yet to come. Lucio, devoid of funds, had fled to Gorizia. Arriving on 21 June 1717, he took refuge with (ironically) his father's assassin, his uncle Girolamo II. Although accompanied by Rosalba, he had the audacity to plead for compassion from the Council of Ten, citing his 'abandoned spouse and abandoned children' who had remained in Noale. His supplication fell on deaf ears, and he soon wore out his welcome in Gorizia. Abandoning Rosalba, he was accused of seducing two local noblewomen and of stealing jewellery and gold

Figure 15.5. Palazzo Torriani before 1717. Street facade of the main palace (lower left) and three views of the facades facing the interior courtyard, 18th century. BCUd, Fondo Principale, MS 541, c. 29 (Udine, Biblioteca Civica "Vincenzo Joppi").

Figure 15.6. Column of infamy in Piazza del Fisco and Demolition of Palazzo Torriani in 1717. Pencil drawing, 18th century. BCUd, Fondo Principale, MS 541, c. 30 (Udine, Biblioteca Civica "Vincenzo Joppi").

from others. In July 1718 the capitano expressed his alarm to the imperial authorities, fearing the presence of Lucio's contingent of *bravi* as a destabilizing element. More importantly, the youth's desire to recapture part of the family patrimony from his uncle was a threat to alliances between local families. In September he was ordered by imperial decree to leave Gorizia and Gradisca. Characteristically, he ignored the order, and it was repeated in November and again in December. Finally departing in January 1719, he travelled through Austrian territory from one town to another for the next two years, relying on the network of noble families and distant relatives and again wearing out one welcome after another by his ceaseless womanizing. He spent four months imprisoned in the castello of Lubljana for deflowering the daughter of an imperial baron of Klagenfurt. Unable to regain a share of the family patrimony from the sons of Girolamo II, who would die in 1720, he resorted once again to banditry. He returned to the Friuli with some of his men and other noble exiles and again terrorized the countryside.[71]

Lucio finally found refuge in late 1721 with the uncle of his long-neglected wife Eleonora: Count Rizzardo Strassoldo, who lived in Palazzo Strassoldo in Farra d'Isonzo with his wife Mariana and their teenage children, Ludovica and Nicolò. Lucio made himself at home. He first seduced Mariana and then Ludovica, who became pregnant. Mariana was distraught, and a furious Nicolò demanded that Lucio marry his sister to save her reputation. But what about Ludovica's cousin Eleonora, to whom he was already married? A plot was hatched in early 1722 while Count Rizzardo was away in Venice. Nicolò was to travel to Noale with the ostensible mission of inviting Eleonora to join Lucio in Farra for Carnival since he was banned from Venetian territory. In fact, the intention was otherwise. Nicolò would murder her on the road and throw her body in a ditch. Lucio would be free to marry, and who would be the wiser?

Nicolò set off on horseback on 2 February with Orsola Sgognico, a house servant (and his mistress), who was dressed in men's clothing. The unsuspecting Eleonora greeted them warmly when they arrived. She invited Orsola to sleep in her bedroom while Nicolò stayed in the next room. After several days, Eleonora declined to accompany the two back to Farra, saying that she had promised to spend the holiday at San Martino with her brother Rizzardo Madrisio, husband of Lucio's sister, also named Eleonora. He had long been trying to distance his own sister from her abusive husband.

Nicolò quickly formulated a change of plan. On 8 February, he rose at the crack of dawn and saddled the horses. With Orsola busy in the kitchen, he crept into the bedchamber while Eleonora was still asleep and fractured her skull with three blows of his pistol. As with her newborn son several years before, the unfortunate Eleonora did not survive. Nicolò ran to the kitchen and wiped his bloody hand on Orsola's apron. He quickly took leave of the elderly servant who had bridled their horses, telling him that he did not wish to disturb the sleeping Eleonora. The two galloped post haste back to Palazzo Strassoldo in Farra. Thinking themselves safe in imperial lands, out of the Republic's reach, they celebrated their success with Mariana and Lucio the following night at a festive carnival ball.[72]

Eleonora's bloody corpse was discovered by the servant, and the news spread like wildfire. It soon reached the victim's uncle Giambattista Colloredo, the imperial ambassador in Venice, who informed the Council of Ten and sent word to Vienna. Rizzardo Strassoldo, Nicolò's father, wrote immediately to Rizzardo Madrisio, Eleonora's brother, expressing his outrage over 'the atrocity of such a misdeed'.[73] Significantly, both men rejected the age-old remedy of private vendetta and called upon the sovereign authorities—the emperor and his representatives in Gradisca—to administer justice. An outraged Ten empowered the podestà of Padua to investigate, but their jurisdiction applied only to Venetian territories. And yet, this time, there was no place to hide. An indignant Emperor Charles VI immediately ordered the capitano of Gradisca to arrest Lucio, Mariana, and Nicolò forthwith, along with Orsola and Ludovica.[74]

But Palazzo Strassoldo was well fortified. After the initial siege, with mortal injuries to three soldiers, reinforcements of 150 men were sent in with eight pieces of canonry. An all-out battle ensued that lasted three nights and two days. Finally, on 17 February, the last day of carnival, Lucio surrendered and was taken in a cart to the Castello of Gradisca. The three women held out for another day but gave themselves up when the soldiers planted four cannons at the sides of the house and threatened to destroy it along with the inhabitants. Nicolò was discovered hiding in a subterranean chamber where ice was kept. On the first day of Lent, all four were transported to Gradisca for trial. On 24 February, Count Antonio Prata wrote to Rizzardo Strassoldo, praising 'this capture... so much needed to determine the truth, for we must trust in these exemplary achievements'.[75]

Stripped of All Honours

The Della Torre and Strassoldo clans were among the most powerful in the Austrian Friuli. While the wheels of justice moved slowly in Vienna, they moved swiftly in Venice. On 16 March the Council of Ten banished Lucio, Mariana, and Nicolò from the Venetian dominion. If any should violate the ban, bounties of 2000 ducats each were offered if any were captured in Venetian territories and 4000 if outside, plus other emoluments. The family palace in Noale was to be 'immediately demolished to the foundations'. The site should remain empty and a conspicuous column erected with an inscription:

Lucio dalla Torre Bandito capitalmente li 16 marzo 1722 per proditoria commissione d'Omicidio essequito con tradimento dal Co. Nicolò Strassoldo et Orsola Sgognico.

(Lucio Della Torre banished capitally on 16 March 1722 for treasonous commission of homicide with betrayal by Count Nicolò Strassoldo and Orsola Sgognico)

But clarification was necessary. Three weeks later, at the behest of the influential Strassoldo family, the Ten modified the inscription to specify Nicolò's parentage. With the addition of his patronymic, it now read: 'Co. Nicolò figlio del Co. Rizzardo Strassoldo da Farra' (Count Nicolò son of Count Rizzardo Strassoldo da Farra). The honour of the many other Nicolò Strassoldos was at stake.[76]

In Vienna, the trial dragged on for more than a year, with Lucio vigorously protesting his innocence and putting all the blame on Nicolò. To no avail. On 16 June 1723, the emperor signed a sentence condemning Lucio, Mariana, and Nicolò to torture and a public execution. Lucio was 'to be stripped of all honors, prerogatives, nobility, titles and privileges [without prejudice to his son and brother], slashed twice on the breast with burning pincers, rotated alive [on the wheel], and then decapitated on a high stage and his head put on a mast'.

The sentence reached the tribunal in Gradisca on 26 June and was carried out on a platform in the courtyard of the Castello on 3 July. Some 130 witnesses, between soldiers and local people, were present. An anonymous onlooker described the event in excruciating detail, from the torture with burning pincers to the decapitations. A repentant Lucio was the first to die. Accompanied by two Franciscan friars, he asked forgiveness from God and from all those he had offended, kissed the crucifix, and ascended the steps of the platform on his knees. Spared the ordeal on the wheel at the last minute, he was duly beheaded. When the executioner held aloft the severed head, 'a thunder was heard from the crowd that reached down to the Isonzo'.[77]

Mariana was 'tortured with pincers on the right arm' and beheaded. The most painful punishment was reserved for Nicolò. First his right hand, with which he had held the pistol to batter the poor Eleonora, was lopped off and thrown onto on the platform. He was then torn twice by pincers, and finally his left hand was severed simultaneously with the decapitation. Like Lucio, he was spared the wheel. The corpses of the two men were displayed on the wheels, their heads atop the masts, for two days. Mariana's body, her severed head on her belly, remained on the platform. The servant Orsola, although found to be innocent of the crime, was ordered to be present at the execution and condemned to serve a year without pay in the hospital of the fortress wearing leg-irons. As to the young Ludovica whose pregnancy had inspired the unsavoury affair, she was still nursing Lucio's illegitimate son, born to her in prison. She was sentenced to life in a convent of the Convertite and her son was consigned to a wet nurse in Gradisca to be raised. The boy was literally erased from the Strassoldo and Della Torre lineage. Perhaps the most important lesson to take away from the tragic affair is that public justice had replaced the personal vendetta among the feudal lords of the Friuli.[78]

Figure 15.7. Della Torre and Villalta coats of arms, with a banderole inscribed with 'Tranquilité'. Entry portal, Castello di Villalta.

The Castello di Villalta was abandoned and became something of a haunted house, with rumours of subterranean escape passages, abducted maidens and midwives, trapdoors and vertical shafts into which enemies could be thrown, and Lucio's ghost prowling the walls at night. And yet, the Della Torre coat of arms remained above the entrance with its motto in French: '*Tranquillité*' (Figure 15.7).[79]

Redemption

Lucio had brought shame and dishonour to the Della Torre family, one of the most ancient, powerful, and distinguished in the territory. His brother Carlo III and his cousins, the sons of Girolamo II, were banished. When the Emperor Charles VI arrived in Gorizia to attend a solemn mass on 5 September 1728, they were denied the usual honour of preceding him with a sword in hand. Would the sins of the father be revisited upon Cecilia and Lucio Sigismondo, Lucio's twice-orphaned children? With effort, the reverse was true. Raised by their maternal uncle Rizzardo Madrisio, the brother and sister overcame what might generously be considered a disadvantaged childhood. Cecilia would marry the noble Riccardo de' Portis of Cividale and disappear from the pages of history. But more consequentially, Lucio Sigismondo went on to recapture much of the patrimony and restore the good name of the bloodline created by Girolamo Della Torre and Giulia Bembo, his Venetian bride, back in the sixteenth century.[80]

Marrying the sixteen-year-old Elisabetta di Spilimbergo in 1742 at the age of twenty-seven, Lucio Sigismondo pursued a multifaceted strategy that joined an illustrious past to a respectable present and promising future. It was a double wedding, with Elisabetta's sister Claudia marrying Pietro Valvasone di Maniago at the same time. Count Daniele Florio, another relative, celebrated the unions with a poem. The brides' maternal grandfather was Antonio Prata, who had written the consolatory message to Rizzardo Madrisio twenty years earlier. The feudal support network was intact.[81]

Lucio Sigismondo would settle down with Elisabetta in Palazzo Popaite-Torriani in Pordenone and have no fewer than twelve children, nine of whom survived to adulthood. Following traditional custom, the children's names unapologetically renewed the ancestors and themselves. Indeed, the first born, Lucio Rizzardo, carried the names not only of his father and his doting great uncle, thus honouring both sides of the family, but also of his disgraced grandfather.

Around 1740, Lucio Sigismondo built a private oratory at Villa Pedrina, dedicated, fittingly enough, to the Holy Family. A cupola above the choir is frescoed with the Trinity and the Virgin in a golden sky surrounded by clouds and frolicking putti. Seated in the clouds around the base are four Old Testament prophets, the four Evangelists and the four Doctors of the Church. Beneath the dome an elegant altar carved from various marbles features an altarpiece of the Holy Family with Saint Anthony of Padua. But that was not all. A wooden choir protected by a grate was mounted high on the wall facing the altar. It is decorated with twelve Old Testament and six New Testament episodes painted by several artists in reddish grisaille on octangular and rectangular panels. The iconographic programme celebrates the progressive triumph of Christian truth over pagan ignorance.[82] In sum, the story of Lucio Sigismondo's life.

By 1768 his family was complete. Although they were living comfortably in Pordenone, the destruction of the family palace in Udine still rankled. The loss was addressed that year with the purchase of Palazzo Maseri-Manin, a seigneurial palace complex built in the sixteenth century, just steps away from Piazza del Fisco, a now empty square. The prestigious new residence had all the amenities of the old one, including chapel, stables, courtyard, and huge garden, plus a medieval tower. Renamed Palazzo Torriani, it would remain in the family until the late twentieth century.[83]

Passionately interested in genealogy, Lucio Sigismondo searched back into the years before his father's disgrace for more honourable members of the lineage. An entry dated 1769 in the records of the cathedral of Ceneda listed a donation of 14 ducats 'for vespers and mass for the deceased Monsignore Cardinal Della Torre'.[84]

The gift offered an early glimpse of a larger project that bore fruit some six years later in an *Albero Genealogico* drawn on a large folio sheet now in the family archive in the Archivio di Stato of Udine. It displays the male bloodline, beginning with Nicolò Della Torre, father of the Alvise I who lost his life on Giovedì Grasso in 1511, and ending with Lucio Sigismondo himself. High offices, such as *cavaliere aurato*, or chamberlain to the emperor, or cardinal, or cupbearer to the archduke of Austria, were duly indicated under the relevant names. Notarized by a certain Pietro Bombardieri in Pordenone on 14 November 1775, the chart was intended to be an official document. The notary attested that it corresponded to 'carte autentiche' possessed by Lucio Sigismondo and affixed his notarial seal. The document was countersigned by Francesco Bonlini, the Venetian procurator and capitano of Pordenone and its jurisdictions.[85]

That was only the beginning. Lucio Sigismondo continued to track down information on the family. By 1781 he was in contact with Count Daniele Concina, a historian and bibliophile in Udine, and Domenico Ongaro, a priest attached to the Colloredo family, about a curious tomb monument in the Frari in Venice (see Figures 5.6 to 5.8). Collaborative research by the three revealed that the five coats of arms on a painting above the casket were held to be 'without a doubt of the Della Torre of that time'. It became clear that the tomb had been created to house the body of the abbot Alvise II, assassinated on the Grand Canal in 1549. And that Alvise II's brother Girolamo (Lucio Sigismondo's fifth great-grandfather) was undoubtedly the patron of the tomb, most likely in collaboration with his father-in-law Gian Matteo Bembo. They concluded that the monument was probably meant to be temporary, with the body to be eventually transported to Udine for burial in San Francesco. But, as we know, Girolamo was exiled to Crete the following year. When he returned to Venice in 1559, priorities must have changed, and the tomb (and Alvise's body) remained in place. It was then forgotten for more than two centuries, even by the family.[86]

Rewriting History

In 1797, after the fall of the Venetian republic to the French, Lucio Sigismondo also sought to regain his disgraced father's property that had been confiscated in the first decades of the century. The French commander Jean-Baptiste Bernadotte, headquartered in Udine, was most accommodating. The Castello di Villalta, still abandoned, and other properties were finally restored to the family. Even more important symbolically, the column of infamy on Piazza del Fisco was demolished on the night of 28/29 July, with the stones consigned to the Della Torre.[87]

But that was not all. The colossal statues of Hercules and Cacus that had been moved from Palazzo Torriani to Piazza Contarena in 1717 were fitted up with new inscriptions, making it appear that the confiscations were donations. It was an audacious (some might say shameless) act of historical revisionism:

LUCII SIGISMUNDI
AC UNIVERSAE A TURRE
VALLIS SAXINAE GENTIS URBIS HUIC ET LOCO
MUNUS AETERNUM
MDCCCIIC
(From Lucio Sigismondo
and all the Della Torre of Valsassina
for the eternal benefit
of this city and place
1798)[88]

And who were these Della Torre of Valsassina? Between marriages and titles of nobility, the family had acquired no less than thirty-four coats of arms.[89] Lucio Sigismondo had worked tirelessly to put the family archive in order, documenting every title, honour, and distinction of a bloodline that stretched back for centuries. Already at the age of eighteen, he had compiled a bibliography entitled '*Notizie istoriche raccolti da diversi scrittori nell'anno 1733 che parlano della Famiglia Torriana*'. This formed the basis for a comprehensive five-hundred-year prosopography of the Della Torre line, completed in 1798. It contains an entry, ordered by first name, for every member of the family, both male and female, from Napo Della Torre (d. 1278) to Lucio Sigismondo himself, with bibliographical references on births, marriages, honours, offices, deaths.[90]

The entry on our Girolamo, who had died in 1590, praised his strength, virtue, and courage against all odds:

> Having begun from the cradle to experience misfortunes, over the years, being served with a high and admirable fearlessness of mind, he trampled manfully on all the insults of contrary fortune. He always led a civil and modest life, with a keen desire to benefit all, demonstrating in his actions [that he was] adorned with heroic gravity and affability, so that one cannot believe that those who knew him would not love him.[91]

Sansovino's *Vita* of Giulia Bembo is also cited, 'from which one gathers how much virtue, prudence and Christian wisdom with which this most noble lady was endowed, such that one can propose her as an example to ladies of her station'.[92] But, again, that was not all. A separate document, compiled in 1799, listed the '*Dignitari e Ecclesiastici della Famiglia Della Torre*' over the past five centuries: one pope, eleven cardinals, five patriarchs, nine archbishops, sixteen bishops, fifteen prelates, and five generals of monastic orders. To this was appended a list of eleven non-ecclesiastics, entitled '*Persone morte in concetto di santità*' (Persons who died in a state of holiness). Among them was Giulia Bembo Della Torre, the only female among the ninety-two so honoured.[93]

Lucio Sigismondo died in 1804 at the age of eighty-nine, passing on a recouped patrimony to his heirs. Although his large family would seem to have ensured continuance of the line, of his nine sons, two died in infancy, three entered the church, two remained single, and only two married. Lucio Rizzardo, his eldest, divorced his first wife and married Claudia Frangipane in 1799; they had only one child, a daughter, Elisabetta, who died in 1813. Fabio, Lucio Sigismondo's youngest, married Claudia's sister, Teresa, and had two sons: Lucio Giuseppe, who died at the age of two; and Lucio Sigismondo II, his grandfather's namesake, born in 1808. The latter married Teresa Boschetti in 1837, and his only child, a daughter also named Teresa, was born the following year. She was the single survivor of a line founded six centuries earlier who still carried the proud surname of Napo Della Torre. Marrying Count Fleury Felissent of Treviso in 1864, Teresa had a son named Sigismondo, and two daughters, Caterina and Teresa, thus 'renewing the [first] names of her ancestors and herself'.[94]

Notes

1. *DBI, s.v.* Colloredo, Marzio;' Leicht 1907, 34–9. He died on 4 February 1591.
2. See, for example, Povolo 2009, 245–71; Veronese 1998, 153–98.
3. See Carreri 1906, 1:107–48; 2:159.
4. ASUd, *AT,* b. 23, no. 28 (after 1 Feb 1598).
5. 'Ce fastu?,' 202n9, citing ASVe, AV, b. 2940. See also Gianni, 'Un testamento, 866n32; and Crollalanza 1875, 177–8.
6. Crollalanza 1875, 95–6, 177–8; Conzato 2005, 108–18. Now in Slovenia, Dobrovo is around 15 km northwest of Gorizia.
7. ASUd, *AT,* b. 56, 2v.
8. ASUd, *AT,* b. 3, no. 16: 'Vescovo di Veglia Giovanni della Torre, Inventorio delle robbe di Mons. Illustrissimo Della Torre, 1590.'
9. *DBI, s.v.* 'Della Torre, Giovanni, 570.
10. Ciković 2015; Ciković and Jazbec Tomaić 2018. See also Čapeta Rakić and Capriotti 2017, 175–85.
11. Morelli di Schönfeld 1855–56, I, 77–8; II, 365.
12. ASUd, *AT,* b. 7; Veronese 1995, 209.
13. Conzato 2005, 186–7, 200–201 nn 27, 28, 31. See also *DBI, s.v.*. 'Della Torre, Raimondo.'
14. Ibid., 191–2.
15. BCUd, MS DT.162, Enrico Del Torso 1902; ASUd, *AT,* b. 22, Doti uscite, no. 44 (11 April 1597): 'Patti Dotali tra il N. S. Barone Federico di Lantieri, e la N. S. Dorotea della Torre, figlia del N. S. Co: Sigismondo I, qm Gerolamo della Torre.' For Carlo's marriage to Paola Popaite, see Conzato 2005, 205, n. 60.

16. Conzato 2005, 193, 205 n61; ASUd, *AT*, b. 22, Doti uscite, no. 45 (14 October 1607). The Lantieri brothers were sons of Lorenzo, who had participated with Sigismondo in the Archduke's funeral in 1590 See also
17. Battistella 1927–28, 87–8; Sachs 1915, 128–9. Joppi 1890, 125, states that Lucina was the daughter of Federico Savorgnan, son of Giovanni Savorgnan del Torre and Maria di Pagano Savorgnan (Tristan's sister). But cf. Casella 2003, Tav. 7, indicating that Lucina was actually the daughter of Federico's sister Giovanna Savorgnan Strassoldo (with an incorrect death date of 1567 for Lucina). In either case, Lucina would be the granddaughter of Maria di Pagano.
18. Bratteolo 1597. See also Valentinelli 1861, 47, 324, 353; Cox 2008, 144, 329, n.59; Cox 2011, 13–15, 262.
19. Sachs 1915, 129.
20. Conzato 2005, 194.
21. ASUd, *AT*, b. 17, 328.
22. *DBI*, *s.v.* 'Della Torre, Giovanni,' 570.
23. British Museum, London, Add. MS 18285. See Giddey 1950; Jenny-Squeder 1952
24. Cox 2011, 14–15.
25. *DBI*, *s.v.* 'Della Torre, Giovanni,' 570. ASUd, *AT*, b. 17, 161, 216. His testament, written in Padua on 24 July 1609, was updated with a codicil on 3 Oct. 1622.
26. ASUd, *AT*, b. 3, no. 1 (28 Nov. 1608). Carlo and Curzio were Caterina's cousins. Carlo was the son of Sigismondo Della Torre, brother of her husband Giulio; Curzio was the son of Ginevra Della Torre Colloredo (Sigismondo and Giulio's aunt).
27. ASUd, *AT*, b. 3, no. 2 (21 January 1611).
28. Faccioli and Joppi 2007, 160–1, 311–12; Corbellini 1990, See also ASUd, Archivio Manin, b. 170, with Giovanni Martino Marchesi's testament ordering that a tomb be built at a cost of 1500 ducats in the church of San Francesco in which he would be buried along with his father, wife, and two daughters who had predeceased him.
29. ASUd, *AT*, b. 3, no. 3 (8 December 1614).
30. Ibid., b. 3, no. 6 (9 July 1616); ibid., no. 8 (16 August 1616).
31. Capodagli, 235; Trebbi 1998, 264. See also Gaddi and Zannini 2007.
32. Conzato 2005, 255–256, nn 23, 24, 260. Strassoldo's great-great-grandfather Ettore was the brother of Carlo's great-great-grandmother Taddea Strassoldo Della Torre.
33. Casella 2015, 1071–2, citing ASUd, *AT*, b. 79, c. 1v–2r.
34. Salomoni 1626, 110–117.
35. *DBI*, *s.v.*. 'Della Torre, Giovanni,' 570.
36. Capodagli 1665, 235–6; Conzato 2005, 255, n.23. The dowry contract was signed on 30 October 1623, but there is no record of a marriage. For Strassoldo, see www.sardimpex.com/Strassoldo/Strassoldo di Graffemberg e Suffumberg.asp.
37. Casella 2015, 1072, citing ASUd, *AT*, b. 79, 3r–4v. Sofonisba wrote that her firstborn child, presumably Lucina, was born in Rosazzo and that Giulio and Girolamo, 'il secondogenito e il terzogenito,' were born in Udine. She had returned to Rosazzo in November 1630 because of the plague, 'con doi puti et una puta et giera grosa.' She gave birth in January 1631 to a son, Giovanni, who lived only eight days. Alvise IV's brother had died childless by 1526.
38. Corbellini 1990, 21n24, citing ASUd, *AT*, b. 56.
39. Casella 2015, 1072, citing ASUd, *AT*, b. 79, 2v.

40. Conzato 2005, 277–8, 326–7; ASUd, *AT*, b. 22, Doti uscite, no. 47 (18 July 1620).
41. ASVe, *AC*, b. 2940; ASUd, *AT*, b. 7; Ce fastu?,' 202 n9; Gianni 2014, 866 n32; Crollalanza 1875, 177–8.
42. Veronese 1995, 202–203. For Marzia as the mother of Carlo, see ASUd, *AT*, b. 17, 328; Morelli 1855–56, I, 101–103. But cf. De Martin Pinter 2013, 3, with a family tree incorrectly showing Carlo as the son of Sigismondo II's second wife Anna Maria Savorgnan. However, cf. ibid., 4, referring correctly to Anna Maria as Carlo's *matrigna*, or stepmother. See also Casella 2003, 184–185, n. 30.
43. Veronese 1995, 203–204.
44. Bonfio 2006, 79. See also De Martin Pinter 2013, 7. Reminiscent of the old Della Torre and Colloredo rivalry with the Savorgnan clan, the lineup now was between the Neuhaus family on one side and the noble Del Mestri, Manzano and Della Torre families on the other, each side with followers that crossed family lines.
45. Capodagli 1665.
46. Corbellini 1990, 21, n.24, citing ASUd, *AT*, b. 41. Michele III wrote his will in 1665 and must have died shortly thereafter.
47. See ASUd, *AT*, b. 56, for an undated adjudication made shortly after Michele III's death. Simone died on 26 October 1668.
48. Published in Udine in 1669 and cited by Sachs 1915, 129–30.' For the Della Torre villa at Sagrado, see Virgilio 2003, 110–113. See also Romanello 1997, 81–2. Torrismondo, Count of Duino, later served as imperial ambassador to Venice and was the dedicatee of several operas. See Selfridge-Field 2007, 181, 195–6, 215, 221–2. For the Duino branch of the family, see Notizie sul castello di Duino,' 1902, 197–9.
49. Prampero de Carvalho 2005, 7, 55–6; ASUd, *ADP*, b. 12.
50. Veronese 1995, 201–2; De Martin Pinter 2013, 3–4, 18, n.12, citing ASUd, *AT*, b. 46, fasc. 2, 'Processo del Tattimpoch'; Morelli 1855–56, I, 102.
51. De Martin Pinter 2013, 3.
52. Veronese 1995, 205–6.
53. Hendy 1974, 284–5; Pignatti 1986, 31–7. The case worked its way through the courts and was finally adjudicated by the Quarantia Civil Vecchia in 1710, by which time one dealer had died and the other had sold his interest to another investor. The painting was located in the palace of Angelo Querini in 1776 and was eventually sold to Isabella Stewart Gardner in 1899.
54. Veronese 1995, 206.
55. Ibid., 206–207.
56. Veronese 1995, 204–205.
57. Ibid., 208; *DBI*, *s.v.* 'Della Torre, Lucio,' 593; Molmenti 1898, 219–20; Zucchiatti 2003, 82; Spessot 1951, 20–1.
58. Veronese 1995, 209–10.
59. Marcotti 1888, 50–1, a fictionalized romance based upon primary documents. It appears to be more fact than fiction but should be read with caution. Cf. the review by Rigonat 2016.
60. Ibid., 61–2; Zucchiatti 2003, 140.
61. Marcotti 1888, 64.
62. Goi 2016; Maffei 2005, 73–4, PN 009: Villa Cappellari della Colomba, della Torre, Pedrina, Pisani-Santin, Comparin.

63. Goi 2016, 59–61. According to a document dated 11 May 1689, Lucio, the brother of Sigismondo, Lucio Antonio's father, was the patron.The painters were Giovanni Antonio Torri and a certain Antonio Ramanoti. See also Maffei 2005, 73–4.
64. Di Lenardo, 'Torre (della) Lucio Antonio (1695–1723).'
65. Marcotti 1888, 72.
66. Molmenti 1898, 220–1. *DBI, s.v.* 'Della Torre, Lucio,' 594, states that this is the first-born child. This is unlikely if the incident actually happened in 1716.
67. *DBI, s.v.* 'Della Torre, Lucio.' 595; Spessot 1951, 21.
68. Veronese 1995, 214, citing ASVe, Inquisitori di Stato, b. 1057.
69. Molmenti 1898, 224–5; *DBI, s.v.* 'Della Torre, Lucio,' 596; Spessot 1951, 21.
70. Cont 2014, 30; Veronese 1995, 216: 'Lucio della Torre bandito dall'Eccelso Consiglio di Dieci per gravissime colpe di lesa maestà;' *DBI, s.v.* 'Della Torre, Lucio,' 596; Joppi 1890, 124–6; ASUd, *ADP* 12.
71. *DBI, s.v.* 'Della Torre, Lucio.' 596; Spessot 1951, 22.
72. 'Istoria della vita e tragica morte del Co. Lucio della Torre,' 1892, 67–8; *DBI, s.v.* 'Della Torre, Lucio,' 596; Spessot 1951, 22. Rizzardo's wife, Mariana Malvicchia, was of humble origins.
73. Cont 2014, 40, citing ASUd, *AT,* sez. 1, b. 44 (9 February 1722).
74. *DBI, s.v.* 'Della Torre, Lucio.' 596; Cont 2014, 39–40.
75. Cont 2014, 40, citing ASUd, *AT,* Sez. 1, b. 44.
76. Molmenti 1898, 233–34.
77. Zucchiatti 2003, 82.
78. Cont 2014, 39–40. See also *DBI, s.v.*, 'Della Torre, Lucio,' 597; 'Istoria della vita e tragica morte,' 66–73; Piutti, 'Il Conte Lucio,' 83–91; Molmenti 1898, 228–35; Spessot 1951, 22–8; Veronese 1995, 219–21. See also Marcotti 1888, esp. 277–304.
79. Zucchiatti 2003, 82–4, 133–43; Lain 1892; Lazzarini and Del Puppo 1901–03, 2:168–73.
80. *DBI, s.v.* 'Della Torre, Lucio,' 597; Piutti 1892, 83; Di Lenardo, 'Torre (della) Lucio Antonio;' Cont 2014, 36, citing ASUD, *AT,* sez. I, b. 44. See also Marcotti 1888, 305–14.
81. For Florio's poem, see Valentinelli 1861, 255, 354, 359, nos. 1874, 2625, 2665.
82. Goi 2016, 61–9. The ceiling painting and several of the Old and New Testament scenes are attributed to Pietro Feltrin, a provincial painter from Pordenone, and the altarpiece to the Bellunese painter Giovanni Battista Lazzarini.
83. Rizzi 1985, 106–10.
84. ASVe, Soprintendenti alle decime del clero, Condizioni, b. 75, no. 873, 7 (4 April 1769).
85. ASUd, *AT,* b. 17, fasc. 10; cf. Fasc. XXIV.3.
86. See Brown 2013b, 137–59; ASUd, *AT,* b. 19, fasc. 7, Letter from Lucio Sigismondo Della Torre to Don Domenico Ongaro, Pievano di Colloredo (16 October 1781); Cicogna 1854, 507–508. An almost identical list of arms is cited for the Signori della Torre, but without any mention of the tomb, in Francesco Sansovino 1580, 193-193v. See also Ch. 5 above.
87. Joppi 1890, 125–6; 'Il Palazzo dei Torriani demolito nel 1717 1892;' De Piero 1983, 248–50. The empty site once occupied by Palazzo Torriani, and now back in Della Torre hands, had been temporarily turned into a municipal market for chicken, fish and meat. The plot would be sold to the Antivari family in 1812. It is presently Piazza XX Settembre.

88. Joppi 1890, 124; Rizzi 1985, 110. Villalta remained abandoned until 1905 when the family sold it to Giovanni Battista Storti of Cessalto. See Maffei 2005, no. 084.
89. Lazzarini and Del Puppo 1901–03, 1:168.
90. ASUd, *AT*, b. 16, no. 16; ibid., b. 17, fasc. 1: Prove storico-genealogiche della famiglia Della Torre.'
91. ASUd, *AT*, b. 16, 161–2.
92. Ibid., b. 17, 131.
93. Ibid., b. 2. colto 5, *Dignitari e Ecclesiastici della Famiglia Della Torre*, Fasc. 1, Ms. 3955 (2), c. 43. Girolamo's uncle Isidoro, who died in the Cruel Carnival of 1511, was also cited in the list of *Persone morte in concetto di santità*.
94. Rizzi 1985, 110–11; Boccardo 1887, 499; Valentinelli 1861, 365, nos. 2743–2745. Lucio Sigismondo's son Monsignor Michele Della Torre, a canon in Cividale, was a noted scholar and archaeologist. He persuaded the Hapsburg emperor Francesco I to finance archaeological excavations in the area intended to prove the Roman origins of the city. The finds became the nucleus for the modern Museo Archeologico di Cividale del Friuli. See De Santi 2012.

Epilogue

The destinies of the descendants of Girolamo Della Torre and his Venetian bride, Giulia Bembo, were shaped by a feudal culture based on blood and soil that would gradually transition to a culture with respect for the rule of law. The Castello di Villalta was sold in 1905, passing through several hands before its purchase by Sergio and Maria Gelmi di Caporiacco in 1999. They were, as it happens, among the last survivors of the original owners of the castle, the ancient Caporiacco family, whose descendants had sold their remaining shares of the property to Girolamo Della Torre and his brothers back in 1530.[1] An eloquent reminder of a long-gone feudal culture, Villalta had come full circle. It is now a courtly venue for weddings, concerts, and conferences. The Della Torre family archive, lovingly organized by Lucio Sigismondo in the eighteenth century, was given to the Comune of Udine in 1963 by the son-in-law of Teresa Della Torre Valsassina Felissent.[2]

The male descendants of Giulia's father Gian Matteo remained servants of the Serenissima, distinguishing themselves as galley captains and officials in Venice's maritime empire, stalwart defenders, for the most part, of Venetian republican values. Their futures were also shaped by a culture of urban sophistication. Antonia Padoani (1640–1720), the estranged wife of Gian Matteo's great-great-grandson Lorenzo Bembo (1637–1703), became a celebrated composer and opera star.[3] Ca' Bembo on Campiello Santa Maria Nova and Villa Bembo at Ponte di Brenta were passed on down through Gian Matteo's male heirs to Pellegrina Bembo, the daughter of his great-great-great-grandson Lorenzo, and the last survivor of the direct Bembo line. She married Roberto Boldù in 1752 and died in 1797, the same year as the fall of the Republic. With Pellegrina's death, the properties passed out of the Bembo line to her son Lorenzo Boldù.[4]

In a sense, geography is destiny. But so, too, is biology. And despite the efforts by both the Della Torre and the Bembo families to preserve the patrimony through a succession of male heirs, the last survivor in the direct line of each was a daughter.

Notes

1. Zucchiatti 2003, 84–5; Zucchiatti 1989, 30–4; Del Torso 1902; http://www.castellodivillalta.it/; https://www.facebook.com/castellodivillalta/.
2. Di Lenardo, 'Torre (della) Lucio Antonio'.
3. Fontijn 2006.
4. De Checchi 2005.

The Venetian Bride: Bloodlines and Blood Feuds in Venice and Its Empire. Patricia Fortini Brown, Oxford University Press (2021). © Patricia Fortini Brown. DOI: 10.1093/oso/9780192894571.003.0016

APPENDIX I

Francesco Sansovino, *Vita delle illustre signora Contessa Giulia Bemba della Torre*. Venice: Domenico & Gio Battista Guerra, fratelli, 1565. *(English translation by the author)*[1]

//c. 2r//To the renowned Signora Costanza Rangona Fregosa

Francesco Sansovino

Among the dearest and most valued things of the illustrious Signor Conte Girolamo Della Torre, one I esteem most highly is the exemplary life of the most noble Signora Giulia Bemba his consort.

In order to consider the delight and utility that can be drawn from the souls of chaste, virtuous, and prudent ladies, I have judged that it would be worthwhile to put it into light, so as not also to detract from the due glory of such an illustrious lady, and turning my mind to whom I should dedicate such a laudable work, worthy before all the others your glorious name came to mind. For this reason, just as the Signora Contessa Giulia beyond//c. 2v//her actual countenance was in our age rare for grandeur of soul, for nobility of morals, and for the most prudent governance of family affairs, so too your illustrious signora for true zeal of the holy religion, and for noble desire of virtue, and for greatness of spirit, is a luminous example for our times. You then would collect the most precious fruits scattered in these few pages of the many virtues of the Signora Contessa with that loving affection, with which I always love you, and although I am most certain, that this gift would be most dear to you, because she was greatly loved and honoured by you, nevertheless I allow myself to believe that it will add some part of satisfaction, both because today one sees more rarely the examples of those marvelous gifts, which were infused by heaven in the blessed soul of that truly illustrious Signora, and because in reading the present brief history, you will see as in a clear mirror the most beautiful image of her soul.

//c. 3r//

Life of the renowned Signora Contessa Giulia Bembo della Torre

In the bosom of the most noble and magnificent city of Venice, among those families who for nobility are the most famous and illustrious, resides the Bembo, no less for the valor of many excellent gentlemen, both in civil government and in arms, who are celebrated and famous for their antiquity, and also for the honoured memory of the most noble subjects living in the documents, nevertheless we have the most renowned Signor Gian Matteo Bembo, Senator,//c. 3v//second to no other in our times, in whose breast so must prudence and so much valor resides. Then especially it is known, that in the year 1539 he had the virtue of defending the very important city of Cattaro against the numerous and strong Turkish armata, and today he is seen in the highest magistracies that he has had continually in the most powerful Republic.

To this Signor, then, and to the most renowned Signora Marcella, descended from the honoured family of the same name (who in the true faith and in the strength of her mind was very equal to her husband, and endowed with the most happy genius, that with much praise she learned both the Greek and Latin tongues) was born in the year 1532 the Signora Giulia. Her beautiful deeds and lamentable death are again our intention to recount at present, so that many [readers], seeing how admirable she was, living and dying Christian, would have before their eyes a rare example of living well//c. 4r//and dying well, and finally, that the memory of such an excellent lady would remain, not like those of many sculpted in bronze and in marble, but in their minds and hearts, and compensating for the greatness of the loss received by her death, with the pleasant memory of her rare activities, the sadness would be lessened.

Being born of such generous progenitors, she was raised with such noble breeding, that at a most tender age she gave the clearest indication in all her actions of her high and singular intelligence. Thus observing, and imitating the valor of her mother in both words and deeds, everyone noticed, that she was obliged, not just to become illustrious in every virtue, but that behind the splendor of her virtues she must follow many great women in their thoughts and their actions to honourable and glorious ends. Nor was she less the true and legitimate heir of her mother in the singular gifts of her mind than in the considerable beauty of her body. Conforming as much to her most distinguished mother in her//c. 4v// inward virtues as in her outward presence, she was put by her in the constant governance of the house as she came out of her childhood. Once beyond it, she formed a body so beautiful and gracious, that she induced reverence and love in those who beheld her.

This lady was tall in stature, of healthy and strong complexion, beautiful in all her actions, happy in expression, and gracious in manner and affable in every way, so that joining together her natural majesty with a mature delightfulness, rendered her most dignified and agreeable to everyone.

Having reached the age of 18 years, she was by divine providence more than human council (as one could comprehend from many signs) joined in marriage with the illustrious Signor Count Girolamo Della Torre, who by both regal descent and truly rare virtue, with which he was adorned, is held by everyone in great esteem. Thus, all who knew them//c. 5r//could reasonably believe and hold that this most happy union was ordained in heaven in demonstration of a proportionate correspondence of one to the other. For those who with the same good will and the same sincerity of mind were joined together, would likewise be of equal valor, of equivalent virtue, and with compatible beautiful qualities balanced between them. Moreover this heavenly inclination was apparent, because the news spread through the Friuli, and through the environs of the Cenedese, where the Signor Conte then resided as Luogotenente of his brother, the Reverend Monsignore Michele, Bishop of Ceneda, that he had taken a gentlelady of the Bembo family as a wife four months earlier. Since the [Count] would have thought to marry someone, this Signor Conte, and other worthy gentlemen of the Friuli and the Cenedese gave ample credence to such rumors. And in confirmation of this it happened, that such a word was raised in a time when the most able//c. 5v//father of the Signora Contessa was Capitano of the government of the most noble city of Famagosta and of the ancient Kingdom of Cyprus, and it is to be believed that without his express order and commission that it would not then be concluded, and not even negotiated. But after the return of Signor Gian Matteo to Venice, he having diverse requests to marry his daughter, and seeking divine counsel as a Christian, heard the mass in the church of San Francesco and was inspired by the majesty of God to put the Signor Conte before any other, [a decision] with which two of his oldest sons concurred, both having attended the mass with a similar experience. And major evidence that this was a special superior disposition, was (and not without marvel of many witnesses), that several [other] honoured parties [brides] were offered to Signor Conte, for whom human counsel exerted every argument, but not only were their efforts in vain, but from what happened then it seemed that although his dearest friends and relatives had urged him to marry//c. 6r//one of the three most noble ladies in Italy, it was the will of God that he did not consent to this. [Rather], adding the glorious fame of the illustrious father to the great reputation and singular valor of the most prudent mother of the Signora Contessa, he quickly acceded to this [union], almost certain that from such noble plants should be born precious and dear fruits. Indeed, as it happened, none of the three ladies who had been proposed, was ever blessed with children after they married, a principle defect of unhappiness in marriage. [It would have been] particularly unhappy in the illustrious house of the Signor Conte, who had remained the only one [of his line] from whom one could hope for a legitimate posterity of children. Indeed, this union was very fecund, for in the space of 12 years in which she lived with the Signor Conte in all obedience and charity, she [Giulia] renewed both men and women, the major part of the ancestors and herself, because she gave birth to 5 males and 5 females, all living at present [sic] by the grace of God. The first born was called//c. 6v//Lodovico, his name referring to the two Luigis, one the father and the other the brother of the Signor Conte, both of holy customs and truly exemplary goodness.

These children then were born without any defect either of mind or of body, and of a beautiful manner and healthy and of such noble and excellent intellect, that no less for the virtue that appeared in their tender years, as for the fecundity of the womb, and for the mature governance of the said Lady, this illustrious house has had a precious gift and a rich treasure, and in the birth of three of them were seen certain signs outside the natural order, signifying (as one reads in many ancient and modern writers) of some notable event noted in similar appearances. This was observed in the second son born in the kingdom of Candia, and called Sigismondo, to renew the names of the Reverend Patriarch of Aquileia with the lordship of all the Patria del Friuli, and of the illustrious brother of the Signor Conte, because during his birth//c. 7r//the right arm came out first, before any other part of his body, and then with his face all covered with something like a veil, and with a great mass as large as the infant.

After this in Candia, the first of the daughters was born, named Tadea, because this was the name of the most prudent mother of the Signor Conte, which one month before she was born was heard (I vow that it seems incredible but it is true) her voice from her mother's womb, with the greatest admiration of those persons worthy of faith who heard it.

To the third of the sons, born likewise in Candia was given the name Giulio at the request of the mother, who highly desired it, because in this way she also provided to perpetuate her memory in the house of the Torre.

Having then returned to Venice, she had her second daughter, who by common agreement was called Marcella, in honour of her maternal grandmother, who was as we said above was a matron of the highest virtue.

The fourth of the sons followed with the name Giovanni, to represent the//c. 7v//magnanimous Lord Giovanni, brother of the Signor Conte, valiant warrior, and who under the most happy military discipline of the illustrious and famous Francesco Maria, Duke of Urbino, was with much love and honour, nourished and raised. The said Giovanni first saw the light in Venice, and also he was heard to send a loud voice outside his mother's body a few days before his birth, some present who remained stupefied and confused by the novelty of the thing.

He was followed by another male, who was given the name Luigi for the venerated memory of his excellent and religious uncle, brother of the Signor Conte, who was in his times an example of true goodness, and in the most pleasant Ceneda was born the third daughter, called Ginevra, to renew Signora Ginevra, sister of the Signor Conte, a matron no less illustrious for the glorious virtues of her mind, as for the most excellent beauties of her body, renowned and famous, and who//c. 8r//married the Lord Giovan Battista of the most noble house of Colloreta, who for prudence and goodness was greatly esteemed and honoured.

The Signor Conte having then moved with all the family to the Friuli, this lady gave birth in his castle in Villalta to the fourth daughter, called Helena in place of another

Helena of the Lords of Valvasone, a gentlelady of rare beauty of body and mind and who was the mother of the Signor Conte Guido Della Torre, nephew of the Signor Conte.

Having then returned to Ceneda, she had the fifth and last [daughter], from whose birth she died, so that also in this lady the maternal name of Giulia was renewed. These are all the most noble branches of the most happy trunk by order here described, who growing along the way with the favor of God, and with much care of their wise father, give certain hope of having to produce from time to time most gentle fruits, and that these would not have cause to deviate from the ancient lineage from which they issued and descended, and that in the virtues they will resemble those//c. 8v//whose names they carry, so that the Signora Contessa put great study and infinite diligence in raising her children, that they would not suffer any defect, so much in body as in the institution of their minds, that they would be under fear of God and reverence of their parents, and endowed with beautiful manners and excellent customs, and moderate in living and in dress, from which two things depend abstinence from the major sins, and from the most serious faults, so that being raised so virtuously, one cannot conceived in the mind (although great of some), such a high hope, that would not become major, considering the prudent paternal continuation of the road under the most excellent preceptors of the worthy understanding of the sciences and the strong exercise of the body.

The Signora Contessa was not only of entire and perfect chastity, so much that her religious confessor had to affirm many times that he had not ever found her culpable of any mortal sin, but//c. 9r//she was also to all other women of our time the most renowned mirror of continence, disdaining any manner of pomp and of excessive ornaments, and of games and parties, to which she never put any affection or care as a young girl, as I will show in its place and time, so that being a bride, and she had to go to Candia with the Signor Conte, where he was sent by the excellent Council of Ten, she obliged him with many prayers to be content that she, disposing of the gold, the jewels and the embroidery, dressed herself in simple clothing, appearing appropriate to her, that since the mind was in travail on that unfortunate occasion, the clothing of her body should also be modest and re-worn; and not content with this, by her own election she fled vain worldly pleasures, that at times the Signor Conte was constrained for the satisfaction of relatives and friends to persuade her, and almost in a certain way to modestly force her, because she renounced any recreation and relaxation, since what//c. 9v//pleased her much more was the governance of her children, the family, and matters of her home, than to attend to pleasures outside, part truly, as among other noble and principal things, a duty more than any other of every wise and honoured mother of the family.

But of major importance and reputation to this Lady was that she had a soul so invincible and a constancy so strong, that at the same time she surpassed her youthful age and the fragility typical of her sex. She gave an example of this when the Signor Conte had to go to Candia, because not only was she not dismayed to go among so many travails and perils of sea, including corsairs, but rather she opposed with the greatest efficacy the plan that the Signor Conte had to leave her at home, imploring him that he should take her with him, because she gladly faced with him every fortune, that she did not want to stay without him in any sort of comfort, and that such was her innermost desire she made clear in boarding the ship,//c. 10r//because accompanied by all her relatives and friends, who were not without tears, lamenting her departure, she was always cheerful, and with dry eyes showed her joyful mind, and her disposition to suffer major accidents of ill fortune, that were not the present ones, as she soon demonstrated with great liberality on the voyage. Because when their ship reached Sasino, some ships of corsairs were discovered, which put not a little fear into everyone on the ship, whereas this Lady with an intrepid heart, who filled everyone with marvel and consolation, commented to the Signor Conte, who already had armed himself for defense, that for the love that he had for her she asked a special grace: that she would rather suffer death at his own hand, if by chance they fell into the hands of the enemies, than for him to allow her to go into such a vile servitude.

Concerning the governance of her entire household, she showed herself just and prudent in every matter, because treating each//c. 10v//according to his merits and conditions, she never failed to exhort each one to his duty, adding charitable reminders of their deficiencies, putting the most diligent care to their infirmities and their needs, and with the most beautiful order maintaining in the house the necessary commodities of life and living for everyone, and not only at due times dispensing the supplies, but what is more laudable above every other thing, recognizing the service of each with so many signs of generous liberality, that she was by everyone with a sincere heart and true love completely obeyed and served.

Of the notable industry then of this Signora in procuring with advantage the provisions for a home, where one always had the impression of much magnificence, and which were always full of illustrious personages, and of her great astuteness in employing these [provisions], and of her diligence in conserving them, one can understand no less from the order of living splendidly than from the most honourable furnishing//c. 11r//of all the rooms (although these were in many diverse places), that is in Udine, in Ceneda, and in Villalta. In these places, she left three palaces not only well furnished with the comforts of living, but adorned with rich furnishings, that were both fitting to the grandeur of the Torriana family, and that corresponded much more to the beautiful disposition of these lodgings. For when she became the wife of the illustrious Signor Conte, she found few, and worn-out ornaments since the house had been many years without the governance of women, because of grave and cruel events of civil disorders accompanied by fires, robberies, and deaths.

But with all that she was of the most prudent industry in the governance of the family, nonetheless she always had her soul turned to God, since she said that those who founded their plans on the instability of this frail and fleeting world, loved more the mirror, than their face, and rather followed the shadows//c. 11v//than the true body. Concluding in sum that God alone was our certain and secure good, with the highest and Christian judgment she discerned in the allurements of the present life the truth of the eternal, and supported by contemplation of the celestial treasure, she knew the means and followed the ways by which one walks to his creator, so that among the others she always employed those [means] that are usually derive from the riches of Christian charity, willingly dispensing to the poor and to needy persons the necessary aliments of life, and aiding with opportune remedies the conservation of their honour.

And if we would like to discourse on all her activities, we will find that the edifice of her holy words was no less beneficial than the fruitful example of her good works, because she revered and observed beyond measure the precepts of God, that beyond the ordinary practice of others, this most religious Signora frequented the sacraments of confession and of communion, nor did she ever leave any day, in which she was able, that she would not wish to be present at the divine//c. 12r//sacrifice of the mass. And always desirous of hearing the word of God, she disposed of every other care to feed the mind with those gentle concepts, and intent with all her spirit and humility of her heart spent the due hours in holy works, and was most observant in the fasts. And where her earthly strengths did not extend themselves, she compensated with a ready spirit and satisfied with a benign heart, both what was more acceptable to God than her affectionate will. And we must believe, what to her would also be of major merit with his Majesty, both how much more this most Christian lady was revealed to be kind, and how often were the occasions to exercise charity and other pious works, and for this not without reason she was known by all, and called mother and nurse of the poor.

And because the Signora Contessa knew that two things make our life worthy of admiration and imitation, that is prudent deeds and wise words, there are many who marveled that both in one and in the other she was singular. And among those,//c. 12v//she was very often accustomed to discourse with her domestics about the vanity of human things. She said that human opinions being nothing but a dream, it was necessary to reawaken the intellect for the mind not to drowse in these vain pleasures, which deprive us of that certain and eternal good, which is promised to vigilant and Christian souls. For example, one time a noble gentle lady went to visit her, and having found her most intent on a precious piece of needlework, and having been with her to work for a good amount of time, she said, 'Signora, you never chat, nor do you ever say "let's walk through this delightful garden".' To this she graciously responded, 'This world, oh my dear relative, is not a market of words, but of works of the spirit, and of the body, and these are the pleasures and enjoyments of true gentleladies.' Being then another time visited by another gentle lady, who, seeing her alone intent on other works, said to her, 'Signora Contessa, how is it that your ladyship is so alone?' To this she responded: 'I believe //c. 13r// that I am never alone,' and that living far from idleness she has continually before her the eyes, and in her hands the necessary things and proper works.

With these holy and miraculous steps, Signora Giulia Bemba della Torre passed through the pilgrimage of her life. With this most holy and prudent rule of living, and with these more divine than human manners, she traversed all her verdant years to the age of 30, in which she was accustomed to master mundane thoughts and vain designs, that in the others forward, and finally through these glorious studies hastened to final goal. Appearing to approach it, (I believe by divine inspiration) she prepared with all her heart, and with her mind disposed, that she demonstrated the solid and firm hope, that she had founded in the mercy of God, and the secure altar?, that kept her conscience pure and immaculate, so that she was worthy to foresee her death a year before it occurred. Thus it happened that pregnant with her last//c. 13v//daughter, she wished to first leave the Friuli for Ceneda, where she must meet with the Signor Conte to dispose of all her things, and recommending continually her dearest children to her illustrious and most beloved consort, she left ordered, and under inventory all the ornaments and utensils of his palaces, and they took leave from relatives, who could visit. She predicted that she would not see those places again. Having then reached Ceneda, what was the major indication of this? That it being the solemn day of the Purification [of the Virgin: 2 February], having presented two blessed candles to the Signor Conte, she asked him as a gift to her to use them at the end of her life (as they were then used), as if foreseeing that it would not be far distant. And a few days after, coming to visit her the magnificent and valorous Signora Augusta her sister, she went outside Ceneda to meet her, and with a demonstration of infinite happiness, embraced her sister. She said to her, that having desired this for many years, that she had come to the time of the final end of her life,//c. 14r//which must be in a few days. But having arrived at Holy Week, the Signor Conte decided to receive the most Holy Communion, and [asked] the Signora to do the same with all their family. And she with warm affection, asked him that for her satisfaction that this should be on Holy Thursday, because she felt that on the day of the most holy Resurrection suggested by the Signor Conte, she would not find herself so well disposed to be able to perform worthily that most devoted act, with which having the Signor Conte willingly complied. On Thursday she took that divine sacrament, and on the following day at the hour of 10 in the evening, the Signora gave birth to the said daughter, that was followed by a mass on the day of Easter. After that, she said that the hour of her death was near, but that she desired very much to see the Signor Conte again, and to discuss something with him. He came into her presence, and she replied with maternal affection what she had told him other times about the care of their beloved children, urging him affectionately not to give way//c. 14v//to overpowering sadness for her premature departure from this life, since such was the divine will. Conforming oneself to it must chase away every worry from his Christian breast, and all the more so since he could hope more for her from the goodness of God, with her change to a better life; besides, he had reason to remain consoled with the things of the world, himself seeing that beautiful and numerous posterity which he had desired more than any other thing of this world, that he might by the singular grace of God long and happily enjoy them, as his heart had felt in his holy prayers.

With these words, and in similar other ways comforting the distressed Signor Conte, she called to herself all her oldest children; tenderly kissing them. She did not enjoin them, other than to fear and love God, to do anything other than to obey and respect their father, knowing that it was more importantly only due and proper of good children, who are usually the mothers//c. 15r//and conservators of all the virtues, and generous good manners; so likewise, one could not look for anything other than the said two qualities for them to achieve a long and honoured life.

Then she turned to her sister and said these words to her: 'Let us go sister, let us go happily, for God calls us to a more happy home,' [words] to which [her sister] responded that it was not yet her time. The Signora Contessa, aware of the displeasure that her sister had taken from her words, added: 'My dear sister, I do not mean you, but me at present, because God [chose] one of us, and I gladly accept changing this poor and fragile life for one that is the blessed and eternal.' And nonetheless the Signora Augusta, on the second day of July, that was a Thursday, just 3 months after the departure of the Signora Contessa to the highest good, went there herself, innocent and blameless, so that she had ascended most pure, to find the most beloved sister who had ascended on the same day and hour.

With these high thoughts, with these holy arguments, and with these prudent warnings of the harbor of salvation, with//c. 15v//a great heart, full of spirit, and with a happy face, [Giulia] began to say the psalms and to recite prayers, and to invoke humbly our blessed Lord Jesus Christ, supplicating his divine Majesty to deign to accept her soul, never ceasing to repeat that sweet name of Christ, while recommending to him the interior being into those most holy hands, which had been located in the transient skin of the exterior being, until afflicted by an attack so grave she was held for dead for the space of some hours by the grieving and lamenting persons around her. But reviving shortly afterwards, she said:' You do not have to believe that my soul leaves today from this body, and sheds its corruptible vestments, but hold for certain that tomorrow at the hour of nine, always honoured by me with the angelic salutation, it will be called to its highest Giver.'

The following morning having summoned a faithful servant named Orsa, who was very affectionate to the house and in particular to the small children, whom she had//c. 16r// cared for in their early and tender years, she comforted her to stay of good mind. She predicted that a damsel daughter of hers, together with another, who were both in the service of the Signora Contessa, the following Sunday by the pious work of the Signor Conte would be married to persons such that they would have the greatest reason to render thanks to God, to remember her words, and finally to pray to the Signor Conte every happiness. On the day announced by the Signora Contessa, both of them were joined in matrimony to men of good condition, [the Count] then swearing on his conscience, that he had not known anything of this matter before the Signora his consort had announced it. This was not without the marvel of many, who were privy beforehand to the words of the Signora Contessa.

In saying this the Signora thought of the two candles given to her by the Signor Conte, that she was holding in repose, and ordered them to be lit, and asked for herself extreme unction. While the priests performed their office, she remaining//c. 16v//with a sincere mind up to the last breath, always responded with so much elation of her spirit to God, with so much fervor, and with signs in her face of a certain jubilation, that everyone understood how content this Signora would be to leave this dark and brief shadow for the bright and infinite light, displaying her joyful soul to be shortly made a citizen of Heaven and then taken by the angels to present herself on foot to that Lord, from whom alone every true and perfect consolation depends, as she affirmed to her sister, and to others there of having seen a miraculous band of angels, who sang and played in such sweet tones, that once could never describe with mortal tongue.

So in the year of our Redemption 1562, on the second day of April, on Thursday at the hour of nine in Ceneda, in the 30th year of her life, this most noble Signora rendered her blessed soul to her creator, with universal sadness and pain to all those who having known her, knew//c. 17r//how much she was both valorous and modest and full of all those worthy qualities, that are required of every honourable matron, so that she was by many famous intellects celebrated in the Latin and volgare tongues. And it is a thing of great marvel, that on the same day, and at the same hour of her death, the most valorous Signora Vittoria di Valvasone, who was very much joined in love to the Signora Contessa, was advised of this dolorous event. At this time, she was 30 miles distant; nor by the great diligence that she then used to learn the name of the carrier of such bitter news was it ever possible to find him.

With the most honourable obsequies, and with an infinite concourse of the people, her body was placed in the cathedral church of Ceneda dedicated to the glorious San Tiziano, of which the most Reverend Monsignor Bishop Michele della Torre rector and pastor, by his singular goodness and for the egregious virtues of his mind, was worthy to rule and to shepherd all the Christian flock. We must//c. 17v//hold resolutely, that by intercession of that saint, and of all the other elect of God, that innocent soul enjoys the eternal goods of Heaven, where God would ensure that we also, following her pious and Christian footprints, could by his divine mercy be conducted.

Notes

1. A pdf of the original Italian text is available online at: https://books.google.com/books?id=K3dSAAAAcAAJ&printsec=frontcover&source=gbs_ge_summary_r&cad=0#v=onepage&q&f=false.

APPENDIX II

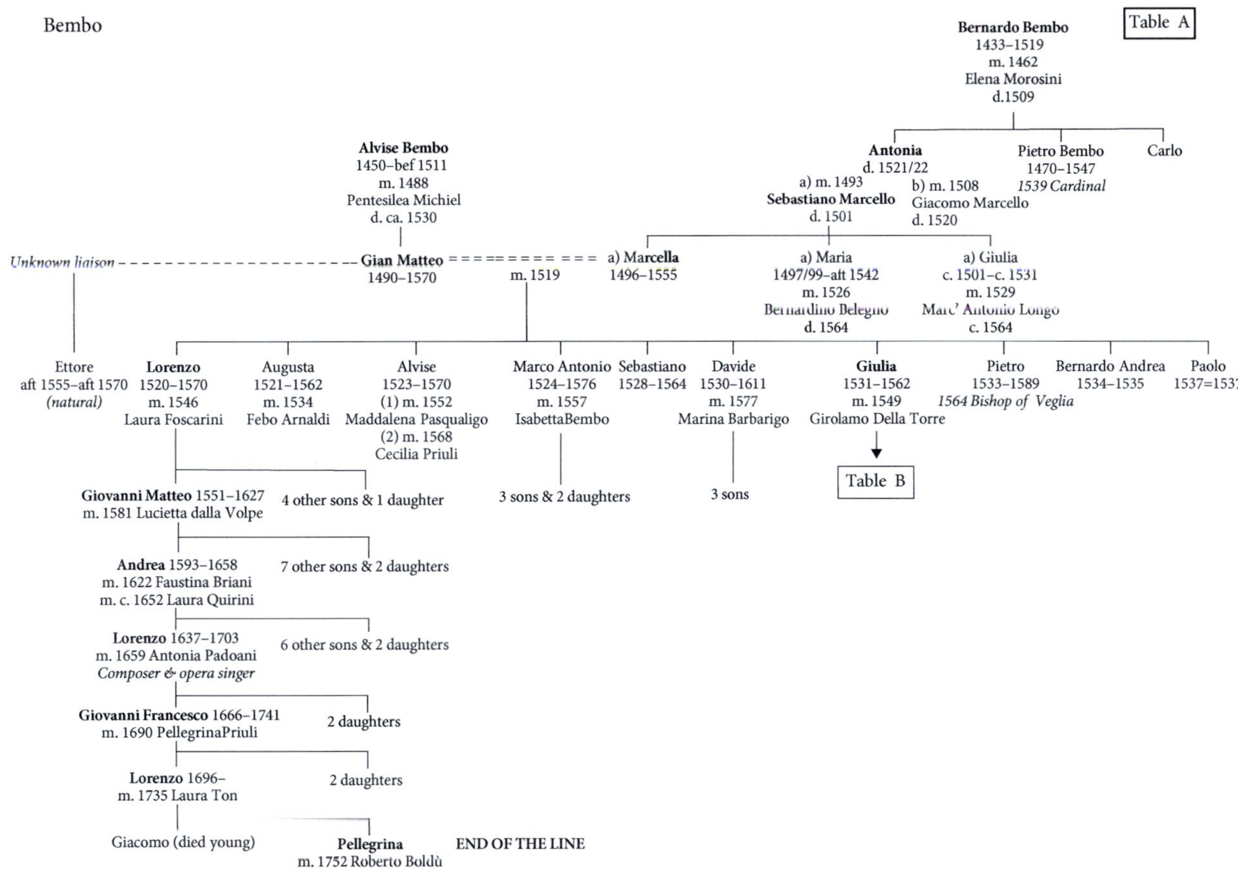
Bembo
Table A
Bernardo Bembo 1433–1519 m. 1462 Elena Morosini d.1509
Antonia d. 1521/22
a) m. 1493 Sebastiano Marcello d. 1501
b) m. 1508 Giacomo Marcello d. 1520
Pietro Bembo 1470–1547 1539 Cardinal
Carlo
Alvise Bembo 1450–bef 1511 m. 1488 Pentesilea Michiel d. ca. 1530
Unknown liaison
Gian Matteo 1490–1570
m. 1519
a) Marcella 1496–1555
a) Maria 1497/99–aft 1542 m. 1526 Bernardino Belegno d. 1564
a) Giulia c. 1501–c. 1531 m. 1529 Marc' Antonio Longo c. 1564
Ettore aft 1555–aft 1570 (natural)
Lorenzo 1520–1570 m. 1546 Laura Foscarini
Augusta 1521–1562 m. 1534 Febo Arnaldi
Alvise 1523–1570 (1) m. 1552 Maddalena Pasqualigo (2) m. 1568 Cecilia Priuli
Marco Antonio 1524–1576 m. 1557 IsabettaBembo
Sebastiano 1528–1564
Davide 1530–1611 m. 1577 Marina Barbarigo
Giulia 1531–1562 m. 1549 Girolamo Della Torre
Pietro 1533–1589 1564 Bishop of Veglia
Bernardo Andrea 1534–1535
Paolo 1537=1537
Table B
3 sons & 2 daughters
3 sons
Giovanni Matteo 1551–1627 m. 1581 Lucietta dalla Volpe
4 other sons & 1 daughter
Andrea 1593–1658 m. 1622 Faustina Briani m. c. 1652 Laura Quirini
7 other sons & 2 daughters
Lorenzo 1637–1703 m. 1659 Antonia Padoani Composer & opera singer
6 other sons & 2 daughters
Giovanni Francesco 1666–1741 m. 1690 PellegrinaPriuli
2 daughters
Lorenzo 1696– m. 1735 Laura Ton
2 daughters
Giacomo (died young)
Pellegrina m. 1752 Roberto Boldù
END OF THE LINE

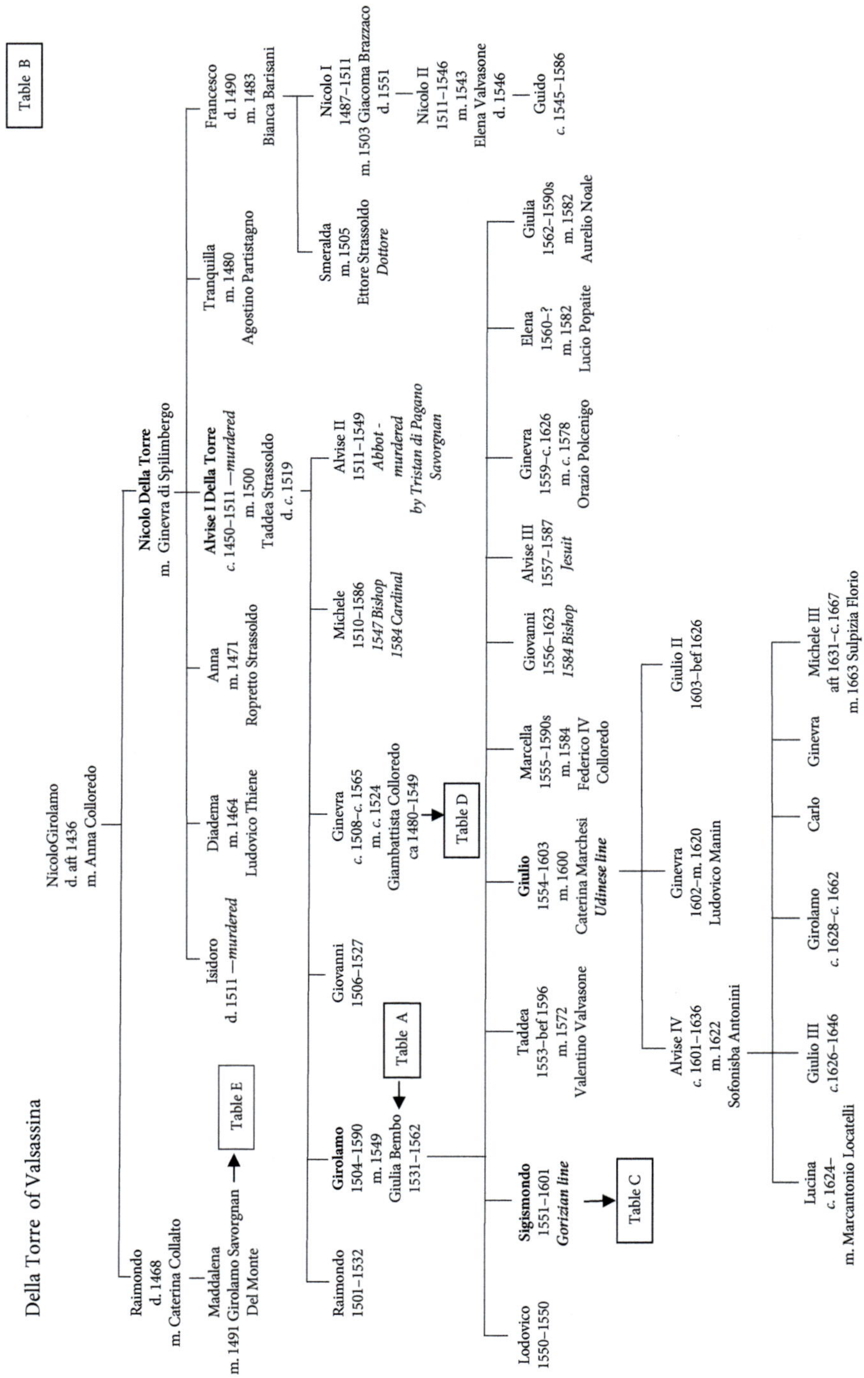

Della Torre of Valsassina
Table B
NicoloGirolamo
d. aft 1436
m. Anna Colloredo
Raimondo
d. 1468
m. Caterina Collalto
Nicolo Della Torre
m. Ginevra di Spilimbergo
Maddalena
m. 1491 Girolamo Savorgnan
Del Monte
Table E
Isidoro
d. 1511 —murdered
Diadema
m. 1464
Ludovico Thiene
Anna
m. 1471
Ropretto Strassoldo
Alvise I Della Torre
c. 1450–1511 —murdered
m. 1500
Taddea Strassoldo
d. c. 1519
Tranquilla
m. 1480
Agostino Partistagno
Francesco
d. 1490
m. 1483
Bianca Barisani
Smeralda
m. 1505
Ettore Strassoldo
Dottore
Nicolo I
1487–1511
m. 1503 Giacoma Brazzaco
d. 1551
Nicolo II
1511–1546
m. 1543
Elena Valvasone
d. 1546
Guido
c. 1545–1586
Raimondo
1501–1532
Girolamo
1504–1590
m. 1549
Giulia Bembo
1531–1562
Table A
Giovanni
1506–1527
Ginevra
c. 1508–c. 1565
m. c. 1524
Giambattista Colloredo
ca 1480–1549
Table D
Michele
1510–1586
1547 Bishop
1584 Cardinal
Alvise II
1511–1549
Abbot -
murdered
by Tristan di Pagano
Savorgnan
Lodovico
1550–1550
Sigismondo
1551–1601
Gorizian line
Table C
Taddea
1553–bef 1596
m. 1572
Valentino Valvasone
Giulio
1554–1603
m. 1600
Caterina Marchesi
Udinese line
Marcella
1555–1590s
m. 1584
Federico IV
Colloredo
Giovanni
1556–1623
1584 Bishop
Alvise III
1557–1587
Jesuit
Ginevra
1559–c. 1626
m. c. 1578
Orazio Polcenigo
Elena
1560–?
m. 1582
Lucio Popaite
Giulia
1562–1590s
m. 1582
Aurelio Noale
Alvise IV
c. 1601–1636
m. 1622
Sofonisba Antonini
Ginevra
1602–m. 1620
Ludovico Manin
Giulio II
1603–bef 1626
Lucina
c. 1624–
m. Marcantonio Locatelli
Giulio III
c.1626–1646
Girolamo
c. 1628–c. 1662
Carlo
Ginevra
Michele III
aft 1631–c. 1667
m. 1663 Sulpizia Florio

Della Torre – *Gorizian line*

Table C

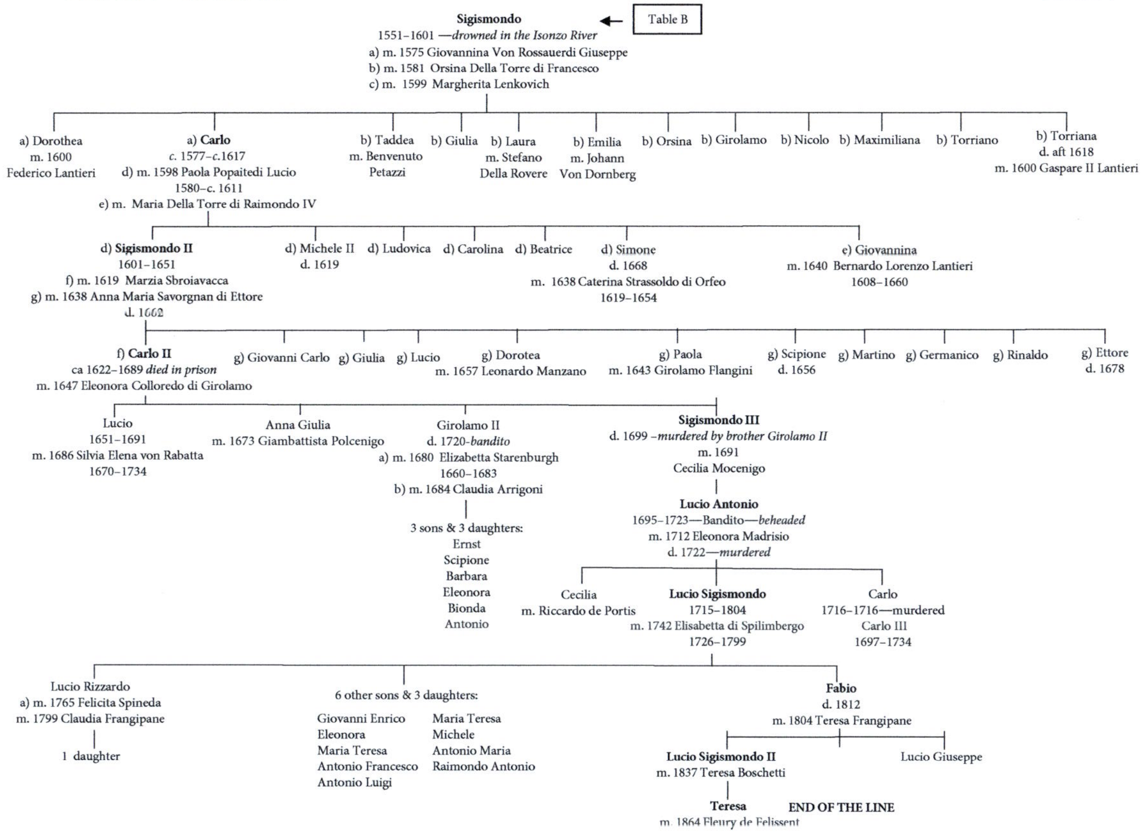

Table D

Colloredo

Giambattista Colloredo
ca 1480–1549—*murdered by Tristan di Pagano Savorgnan*
m. *c.* 1524
Ginevra Della Torre → Table B
c. 1508–*c.* 1565

- Sertorio 1525–1548
- Andriana 1526–1561, m. 1543 Giulio Sbroiavacca
- Girolamo 1527–1557, *Exiled 1549*
- Fulvia 1529-aft 1567, m. Giuseppe Strassoldo
- Marzio 1530–1591
- **Curzio** 1531–1612, m. Claudia Strassoldo, m. 1560 Francesco Porcia
  - 5 sons & 11 daughters:
    - Sertorio Matteo
    - Ginevra Anna
    - **Giovanni Battista Emilio** m. Emilia Porcia
    - Ginevra Silvia
    - Colloreda Virginia Maria
    - Violante Berenice Andriana
    - Orazio Sergio
    - Ginevra Vittoria
    - Bartolomea Fontana Maria
    - Ottavia Maria Laverne
    - Bernardo Sertorio
    - Lucia Maria
    - Valentina Maria
    - Pio Joseffo Carlo
    - Elizabetta Groaura
- Carlo 1532–1574
- Vittoria 1534–1555
- Orazio 1535–1564
- Tadea 1537-aft 1567, m. Ascanio Porcia
- Camillo 1539–1610
- Pio 1541–1542
- Floretta 1542–1573
- Julia 1544-aft 1567

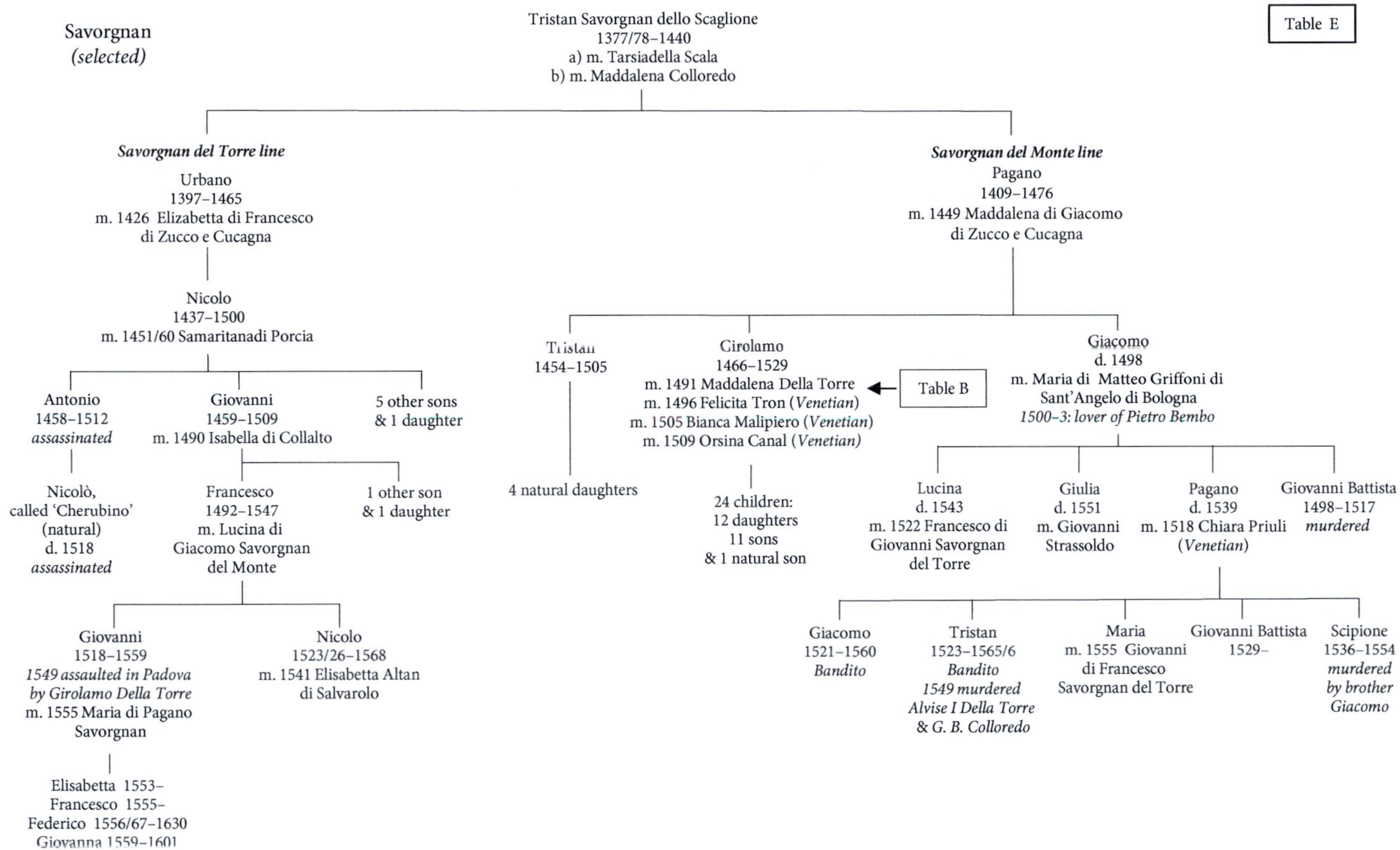
Savorgnan
(selected)
Table E
Tristan Savorgnan dello Scaglione
1377/78–1440
a) m. Tarsiadella Scala
b) m. Maddalena Colloredo
Savorgnan del Torre line
Urbano
1397–1465
m. 1426 Elizabetta di Francesco
di Zucco e Cucagna
Nicolo
1437–1500
m. 1451/60 Samaritanadi Porcia
Antonio
1458–1512
assassinated
Giovanni
1459–1509
m. 1490 Isabella di Collalto
5 other sons
& 1 daughter
Nicolò,
called 'Cherubino'
(natural)
d. 1518
assassinated
Francesco
1492–1547
m. Lucina di
Giacomo Savorgnan
del Monte
1 other son
& 1 daughter
Giovanni
1518–1559
1549 assaulted in Padova
by Girolamo Della Torre
m. 1555 Maria di Pagano
Savorgnan
Nicolo
1523/26–1568
m. 1541 Elisabetta Altan
di Salvarolo
Elisabetta 1553–
Francesco 1555–
Federico 1556/67–1630
Giovanna 1559–1601
Savorgnan del Monte line
Pagano
1409–1476
m. 1449 Maddalena di Giacomo
di Zucco e Cucagna
Tristan
1454–1505
4 natural daughters
Girolamo
1466–1529
m. 1491 Maddalena Della Torre
m. 1496 Felicita Tron (Venetian)
m. 1505 Bianca Malipiero (Venetian)
m. 1509 Orsina Canal (Venetian)
Table B
24 children:
12 daughters
11 sons
& 1 natural son
Giacomo
d. 1498
m. Maria di Matteo Griffoni di
Sant'Angelo di Bologna
1500–3: lover of Pietro Bembo
Lucina
d. 1543
m. 1522 Francesco di
Giovanni Savorgnan
del Torre
Giulia
d. 1551
m. Giovanni
Strassoldo
Pagano
d. 1539
m. 1518 Chiara Priuli
(Venetian)
Giovanni Battista
1498–1517
murdered
Giacomo
1521–1560
Bandito
Tristan
1523–1565/6
Bandito
1549 murdered
Alvise I Della Torre
& G. B. Colloredo
Maria
m. 1555 Giovanni
di Francesco
Savorgnan del Torre
Giovanni Battista
1529–
Scipione
1536–1554
murdered
by brother
Giacomo

Bibliography

Primary texts

Amaseo, Leonardo and Gregorio, with Giovanni Antonio Azio. *Diarii udinesi dell'1508 a. 1541*, ed. Antonio Ceruti. Monumenti storici, 3rd ser., vol. 2, Cronache e diarii, vol I. Venice, 1884.

Barozzi, Francesco. *Descrittione dell'isola di Creta (1577/8)*, ed. Stephanos Kaklamanes Herakleion, 2004.

Bassano, Alessandro. *Dichiaratione dell'arco fatto in Padova nella venuta della Serenissima Reina Bona di Polonia*. Padua, 1556.

Bembo, Pietro. *Delle lettere da diuersi Re, et principi, et cardinali, et altri huomini dotti a mons. Pietro Bembo*, ed. Francesco Sansovino. Venice, 1560a.

Bembo, Pietro. *Delle lettere di m. Pietro Bembo, a prencipi, signori et suoi famigliari amici scritte [...]*, ed. Francesco Sansovino. Venice, 1560b.

Bembo, Pietro. *Delle lettere di m. Pietro Bembo, a prencipesse et signore et altre gentili donne scritte [...]*, ed. Francesco Sansovino. Venice, 1560c.

Bembo, Pietro. *Delle lettere di m. Pietro Bembo, a sommi pontefici, a cardinali et ad altri signori et persone ecclesiastice scritte[...]. Con la giunta della Vita del Bembo, descritta per il medesimo*, ed. Francesco Sansovino. Venice, 1560d.

Bembo, Pietro. *Delle lettere di M. Pietro Bembo, a suoi congiunti et admici, et altri gentili huomii vinitiani scritte*. Venice, 1564a.

Bembo, Pietro. *Nuoue lettere famigliari di m. Pietro Bembo scritte a m. Gio. Mattheo Bembo suo nipote, hora senatore prestantis. nella rep. venetiana*, ed. Francesco Sansovino. Venice, 1564b.

Bembo, Pietro. *Delle lettere di M. Pietro Bembo*. 5 vols. Verona, 1793.

Bembo, Pietro. *Lettere*, ed. Ernesto Travi. 4 vols. Bologna, 1987–93.

Bembo, Pietro. *History of Venice*, ed. and trans. Robert W. Ulery, Jr. 3 vols. Cambridge, MA and London, 2009.

Benedetti, Rocco. *Le feste et trionfi fatti dalla sereniss. Signoria di Venetia nella felice venuta di Henrico III. Christianiss. Re di Francia. Et di Polonia*. Venice, 1574.

Benedetti, Rocco. 'The Plague of 1575–7', 117–19. In *Venice: A Documentary History 1450–1630*, ed. David Chambers and Brian Pullan. Toronto, 2001.

Bergamaschi, Pietro Francesco. *Breve notizia istorica del Pontificio & Imperial Ordine de' Cavalieri Aureati o' sia Dello sprone d'oro antichissimo tra tutti gli ordini cauallereschi laicali e regolari della Chiesa militante*. Turin, 1695.

Bodenham, Captain Roger. 'Voyage to Scio in 1551 A.D.', 1–5. In *Voyages and Travels Mainly during the 16th and 17th Centuries*, ed. C. Raymond Beazley. Westminster, 1903.

Bosio, Jacomo. *Dell'istoria della sacra religione et illustrissima militia di San Giovanni Gierosolomitano*. Rome, 1629.

Bratteolo, Giacomo. *Rime di diversi elevate ingegni de la città di Udine, raccolte da Giacomo Bratteolo et dedicate a l'illustre Signora Lidia Marchesi*. Udine, 1597.

Bruni, Leonardo. *La historia universale de suoi tempi di M. Lionardo Aretino [...]*. Venice, 1561.

Calendar of State Papers Relating to English Affairs in the Archives of Venice, Volume 5, 1534–1554, ed. Rawdon Brown, 270–80 (London, 1873). *British History Online*: http://www.british-history.ac.uk/cal-state-papers/venice/vol5/pp270-280.

Calendar of State Papers Foreign: Elizabeth, Volume 8, 1566–1568, ed. Allan James Crosby, 78–97, no. 444 (London, 1871). British History Online: http://www.british-history.ac.uk/cal-state-papers/foreign/vol8/pp78-97.

Candido, Emilio. *Cronaca Udinese dal 1554 al 1564*, ed. Vittorio Joppi. Udine, 1886.

Capodagli, Gio. Giuseppe. *Corona d'applausi poetici di rime volgari, e latine nelle nozze dell'illustrissimo sig. co. Michele fù dell'illustriss. sig. co. Luigi della Torre, di Valsassina, e del s.r.i. signor di Villalta, etc. e dell'illustrissima signora Sulpizia figliuola dell'illustriss. sig. Sebastiano Florio patritio Udinese*. Udine, 1663.

Capodagli, Gio. Giuseppe. *Udine illustrata da Molti suoi Cittadini così nelle lettere, come nelle armi famosi, e non tanto per dignità Ecclesiastiche, e secolari*. Udine, 1665.

Cappellari Vivaro, G.A. *Il Campidoglio veneto, in cui hanno l'armi, l'origine la serie de gl'huomini illustri et gli arbori della maggior parte delle famiglie*. BMVe, MS, it., cl. VII, 8307 (=18).

Cergneu [Cergnocco], Giovanni Battista. *Cronaca delle guerre dei Friulani coi Germani dal 1507 al 1524*, ed. V. Joppi and V. Marchesi. In *Cronache Antiche Friulane*. Udine, 1895.

Colloredo, Agostino di. 'Cronache Friulane, 1508–1518'. *Pagine Friulane* 2:2 (1889): 5–6.

Cornaro, Alvise. *Trattato de la vita sobria del magnifico m. Luigi Cornaro nobile Vinitiano*. Padua, 1558.

Corner [Cornaro], Flaminio. *Creta Sacra, sive, De episcopis utriusque ritus Graeci et Latini in insula Cretae*. 2 vols. Venice, 1755 (repr. Modena, 1971).

Corner, Flaminio. *Notizie storiche delle chiese e monsasteri di Venezia e di Torcello*. Padua, 1758.

Daciano, Gioseffo. *Trattato della peste e delle petecchie*. Venice, 1576.

Da Porto, Luigi. *Lettere storiche di Luigi Da Porto vicentino dall'anno 1509 al 1528*, ed. B. Bressan, Florence, 1857.

Della Croce, Marsilio. *L'historia della publica et famosa entrata in Vinegia del serenissimo Henrico III. Re di Francia, et Polonia*. Venice, 1574.

Dolce, Lodovico. *Dialogo della institution delle donne*. Venice, 1547.

Egnazio, Battista. *De exemplis illustrium virorum Venetae civitatis atque aliarum gentium*. Libro IV. Venice, 1554.

[Elia de Pesaro]. 'Voyage ethnographique de Venise a Chypre: Lettre d'Élie da Pesaro datée de Famagouste, 18 octobre 1563', ed. and trans. Moise Schwab. *Revue de géographie* (1879): 206–28.

Emiliani, Marcantonio, and Lapro. *Cronaca Udinese dal 1532 al 1616*. Udine, 1881.

Fabri, Felix. *The Book of the Wanderings of Brother Felix Fabri in Palestine and Arabia*, trans. Aubrey Stewart. 2 vols. London, 1892.

Farlati [Farlato], Daniele. *Illyrici sacri*. 8 vols. Venice, 1751–1818.

Flacchio, Engelbert. *Genealogie de la très-illustre, très-ancienne et autrefois souveraine maison de la Tour, où quantité d'autres familles trouveront leur extraction & parentage*. 3 vols. Brussels, 1709.

Florio, John. *Queen Anna's New World of Words, or Dictionarie of the Italian and English Tongues*. London, 1611.

Fracastoro, Girolamo. *De sympathia et antipathia rerum*, ed. Concetta Pennuto. Rome, 2008.

Gaeta, Franco, ed. *Nunziature di Venezia*. 19 vols. Rome, 1958–.

Gerola, Giuseppe. 'Una descrizione di Candia del principio del seicento'. *Atti della Accademia Roveretana degli Agiati*, ser. 3, 14 (1908): 269–81.

Giusti, Vincenzo. 'Trattato della peste d'Udene dell'anno 1556', ed. Vincenzo Joppi. *Pagine Friulane* 12:8 (1900): 122–6.

Gruterus, Janus. *Inscriptiones antiquae totius orbis Romani*. [Heidelberg], 1603.

Guazzo, Marco. *Cronica di M. Marco Guazzo ne la quale ordinatamente contiensi l'essere de gli huomini illustri antiqui, & moderni, le cose, & i fatti di eterna memoria degni, occorsi dal principio del mondo sino a'questi nostri tempi*. Venice, 1554.

Guicciardini, Luigi. *The Sack of Rome*. New York, 1993.

Hart, Vaughan, and Peter Hicks. *Sansovino's Venice: A Translation of Francesco Tatti da Sansovino's Guidebook to Venice of 1561*. New Haven and London, 2017.

Hoby, Thomas. *The Travels and Life of Sir Thomas Hoby, Kt. of Bisham Abbey, 1547–1564*, ed. Edgar Powell. London, 1902.

Labalme, Patricia Hochschild, and Laura Sanguineti White, eds, with translations by Linda L. Carroll. *Venice, Cità Excelentissima: Selections from the Renaissance Diaries of Marin Sanudo*. Baltimore, 2008.

Leggi Criminali del serenissimo Dominio Veneto.Venice, 1751.

Lemay, Helen Rodnite. *Women's Secrets: A Translation of Pseudo-Albertus Magnus's* De Secretis Mulierum *with Commentaries*. Albany, 1992.

Lemnius, Levinus, et al., *Occultes merveilles et secretz de nature*. Paris, 1574.

Lemnius, Levinus. *The Secret Miracles of Nature: In Four Books*. London, 1658.

Lestocquoy, J. ed. *Correspondance des nonces en France, Dandino, Della Torre et Trivultio, 1546–1551; avec des Documents relatifs à la rupture des relations diplomatiques, 1551–1552*. Rome, 1966.

Magno, Alessandro. *Voyages: 1557–1565*, ed. and trans. Wilfred Naar. Paris, 2002.

Mazzuchelli, Giammaria. *Gli scrittori d'Italia, cioè notizie storiche, e critiche intorno alle vite, e agli scritti dei letterati italiani*. Brescia, 1760.

Mercurio, Scipione Girolamo. *La comare o ricoglitrice di Scipione Mercuri cittadino romano, medico della magnifica communità di Lendenara, divisa in tre libri*. Venice, 1595.

Morosini, Domenico. *De bene instituta re publica*, ed. Claudio Finzi. Milan, 1969.

Moryson, Fynes. *An Itinerary: Containing His Ten Years Travel Through the Twelve Dominions of Germany, Bohemia, Switzerland, Netherland, Denmark, Poland, Italy, Turkey, France, England, Scotland and Ireland*. London, 1617.

Newett, M. Margaret, ed., *Canon Pietro Casola's Pilgrimage to Jerusalem in the Year 1494*. Manchester, 1907.

Occioni-Bonaffans, Giuseppe. "Sei documenti tratti dall'archivio privato del Conte Lodovico Della Torre Valsassina." *Archeografo Triestino*, n. s. 5, fasc. 1 (1877): 66–73.

Pagratis, Gerassimos D. *The Reports of the Venetian Baili and Provveditori of Corfu (16th century)*. Athens, 2008.

Papadaki, Aspasia. *Cerimonie religiose e laiche nell'isola di Creta durante il dominio veneziano*, trans. Giorgio Pelidis. Spoleto, 2005.

Papadopoli, Zuanne. *L'Occio (Time of Leisure): Memories of Seventeenth-Century Crete*, ed. and trans. Alfred Vincent. Venice, 2007.

Papazzoni, Vital. *Le rime di M. Vital Papazzoni: Tra le quali vi sono alcuni sonetti, Madrigali, Sestine, Canzoni, Capitoli, & Stanze; ad imitation del Petrarca; parte intitolati ad una Madonna Laura: & parte ad alcuni Signori di nobilissimo ingegno dotati. Con parimente alcune Rime de' detti Signori all Autore*. Venice, 1572.

Paruta, Paolo. 'Della perfezzione della vita politica'. In *Storici e politici veneti del Cinquecento e del Seicento*, ed. Gino Benzoni and Tiziano Zanato, II: 491–642. Milan and Naples, 1982.

Piccolomini, Alessandro. *Della grandezza della terra e dell'acqua*. Venice, 1561.

Pilot, Antonio. 'Gli "Ordini" dell'Academia Veneziana degli Uniti (1551)'. *Ateneo Veneto* (1912): 193–207.

Pittoni, Battista. *Imprese di diversi prencipi, duchi, signori, e d'altri personaggi et huomini letterati et illustri*. Venice, 1568.

Plutarchus. *Le vite de gli huomini illustri greci et romani, di Plutarco Cheroneo... tradotte nuouamente da m. Francesco Sansouino [...]*. Venice, 1563.

Relazioni dei Rettori Veneti in Terraferma. I. Patria del Friuli. Milan, 1973.

Relazioni dei Rettori Veneti in Terraferma. VIII. Provveditorato di Legnago. Milan, 1977.

Reynalde, Thomas. *The Birth of Man-kinde; Otherwise Named, The Woman's Book, by Thomas Reynalde, Physician 1560*, ed. Elaine Hobby. Surrey, 2009.

Ridolfi, Carlo. *The Life of Titian*, ed. Julia Conaway Bondanella et al. University Park, 1996.

Ridolfi, Carlo. *Le maraviglie dell'arte, ovvero le vite degli illustri pittori veneti e dello stato*, ed. Detlev Freiherr von Hadeln. 2 vols. Rome, 1965.

Rossi, Giovanni Battista. *Memorie di M. Luigi Campagnari cognominato da Noale, Nobile Trivigiano, Avvocato Veneto, Cav. e Fiscale della Signoria nel Secolo XVI*. Venice, 1739.

Rossi, Ottavio. *Le memorie bresciane, opera istorica et simbolica*. Brescia, 1616.

Rösslin, Eucharius [Eucario Rhodion]. *Libro nel qual si tratta del parto de lhuomo: e de tutte q[ue]lle cose, che cerca esso parto accadeno, e delle infermita che po[sso]no accadere a i fanciulli: co[n] tutti i suoi rimedii posti particolarme[n]te*. Venice, 1538.

Ruscelli, Girolamo. *Le imprese illvstri con espositioni et discorsi del Ser. Ieronimo Rvscelli*. Venice, 1566.

Ruscelli, Girolamo, ed. *Lettere di principi, le quali o' si scrivono da principi, o' a' principi o' ragionan di principi*. Venice, 1573.

Ruscelli, Girolamo, ed. *Lettere di principi, le quali, o si scrivono da Principi, o a Principi, o ragionano di Principi. Libro Terzo*. Venice, 1581.

Salomoni, Giuseppe. *Delle rime, parte seconda*. Venice, 1626.

Sansovino, Francesco. *Cronologia del Mondo divisa in tre libri*. Venice, 1580.

Sansovino, Francesco. *Delle cose notabili della città di Venetia*. Venice, 1561.

Sansovino, Francesco. *Il Segretario*. Venice, 1565.

Sansovino, Francesco. *Venetia città nobilissima*. Venice, 1581.

Sansovino, Francesco. *Venetia citta nobilissima*, ed. Giustiniano Martinioni. 2 vols. Venice, 1663.

Sansovino, Francesco. *Vita delle illustre signora Contessa Giulia Bemba della Torre*. Venice, 1565.

Sanudo, Marin. *De origine, situ et magistratibus urbis Venetae, ovvero, La Città di Venetia (1493–1530)*, ed. Angela Caracciolo Aricò. Milan, 1980.

Sanudo, Marin. *I diarii*, ed. Rinaldo Fulin et al., 58 vols. in 59. Venice, 1879–1903.

Sanudo, Marin. *Itinerario per la Terraferma veneziana*, ed. Gian Maria Varanini. Rome, 2014.

Savorgnan, Mario. *Del governo della sua famiglia. Lettera a Luigi Cornaro*. Udine, 1863.

Sforza, Bartolomeo Ridolfi. *Vita di Giacopo Foscarini*. Venice, 1745.

Sforza, Muzio. *Delle Rime, Parte Prima*. Venice, 1590.

Sharp, Jane. *The Midwives Book or the Whole Art of Midwifry Discovered*, ed. Elaine Hobby. Oxford, 1999 [orig. pub. London, 1671].

Spanakes, Sergius. 'Relazione del Nobil Huomo Zuanne Mocenigo ritornato provveditore generale del regno di Candia presentata nell' eccellentissimo consillio 17 Aprile 1589'. In *Mnemeia tes kretikes istorias* [Monuments of Cretan history], I, Heraklion, 1940.

Spilimbergo, Roberto di. *Cronaca de' suoi tempi, del 1499 al 1540* (Nozze Serravallo—De Concina). Udine, 1884.

Strassoldo, Soldoniero di. *Cronaca di Soldoniero di. Strassoldo dal 1509 al 1603*, ed. Ernesto Degani. Udine, 1895.

Susannis, Pagano de. 'Della peste fu a Udene l'anno 1556', ed. Vincenzo Joppi. *Pagine Friulane* 12:7 (1899): 106–8.

Thiriet, Freddy. *Regestes des deliberations du Senat de Venise concernant la Romanie*. 3 vols. Paris, 1958–61.

Vasari, Giorgio. *Le vite de' più eccellenti pittori, scultori ed architettori* (1568), ed. Gaetano Milanesi. 9 vols. Florence, 1878–85.

Vasari, Giorgio. *Lives of the Most Eminent Painters, Sculptors and Architects*, trans. Gaston du C. De Vere. 10 vols. London, 1912–15.

Vecellio, Cesare. *Habiti antichi, et moderni di tutto il mondo: di nuovo accresciuti di molte figure: vestitus antiquorum, recentiorumque totius orbis*. Venice, 1598.

Venier, Gabriele. *Relazione della Patria del Friuli presentata all'eccellentissimo Collegio dal Luogotenente Gabriele Venier il di 18 dicembre 1539*. [Nozze Bertolini-Bigaglia]. Udine, 1858.

La venuta della serenissima Bona Sforza et d'Aragona Reina di Polonia et Duchessa di Bari, Nella Magnifica Città di Padova, a ventisette di Marzo con l'entrata nella inclita città di Vinegia, il di 26 Aprile 1556, et la sua partita per Bari. Tratta da una lettera scritta all'Illustre S. Mario Savorgnano. Venice, 1556.

Von Harff, Arnold. *The Pilgrimage of Arnold von Harff, Knight, from Cologne: Through Italy, Syria, Egypt, Ethiopia, Nubia, Palestine, Turkey, France and Spain, which he Accomplished in the years 1496–1499*, ed. and trans. Malcolm Letts. Farnham, 2011.

Vives, Juan Luis. *The Education of a Christian Woman: A Sixteenth-Century Manual*, ed. and trans. Charles Fantazzi, Chicago, 2000.

Weinrich, Martin. *De ortu monstrorum commentarius. In quo essentia, differentiae, causae, & affectiones mirabilium animalium explicantur*. [Leipzig], 1595.

Zeno, Nicolo. *Dell'origine di Venetia et antiquissime memorie de i barbari, che distrussero per tutto 'l mondo l'imperio di Roma [...]*. Venice, 1558.

Secondary texts

Albanese, Angela. 'Alcuni contributi alla biografia di Bartolomeo Ratti.' *Rivista Italiana di Musicologia* 19:2 (1984): 206–33.

Alberghina, Francesco. 'I Domenicani dei Santi Giovanni e Paolo a Venezia. Analisi delle iscrizioni lignee della biblioteca del convento.' Tesi di laurea. Universita Ca' Foscari, Venice, 2016.

Alfani, Guido. *Calamities and the Economy in Renaissance Italy: The Grand Tour of the Horsemen of the Apocalypse*, trans. Christine Calvert. Houndmills, 2013.

Alfani, Guido, and T. Murphy. 'Plague and Lethal Epidemics in the Pre-Industrial World.' *The Journal of Economic History* 77:1 (2017): 314–43.

Ambraseys, N., and I. Karcz. '*Terra Motae*: The Earthquake of 1546 in the Holy Land.' *Terra Nova* 4 (1992): 254–63.

Andretta, Stefano. 'Della Torre, Giovanni.' *DBI* 37 (1989). http://www.treccani.it/enciclopedia/giovanni-della-torre_%28Dizionario-Biografico%29/.

Antonini, Prospero. *I Baroni de Waldsee e Walsee i di Mels i signori di Prodolone e di Colloredo: Accenni genealogici e note storiche*. Florence, 1877.

Antonini, Prospero. "Cornelio Frangipane di Castello, giureconsulto, oratore e poeta del secolo XVI." *Archivio Storico Italiano* 8 (1881): 19–64.

Arbel, Benjamin. 'Supplying Water to Famagusta: New Evidence from the Venetian Period', 651–6. In *Proceedings of the First International Congress on Cypriot Studies: Gazimağusa, 20–23 November, 1996*, ed. Emel Doğramacı, William Haney, and Güray König,. Famagusta, 2001.

Arbel, Benjamin. 'Venice's Maritime Empire in the Early Modern Period', 125–254. In *A Companion to Venetian History, 1400–1797*, ed. Eric R. Dursteler. Leiden, 2013.

Arbel, Benjamin. 'Daily Life On Board Venetian Ships: The Evidence of Renaissance Travelogues and Diaries', 183–219. In *Rapporti Mediterranei, patriche documentarie, presenze veneziane: Le reti economiche e culturali (XIV–XVI secolo)*, ed. Gherardo Ortalli and Alessio Sopracasa. Venice, 2017.

Arfaioli, Maurizio. *The Black Bands of Giovanni; Infantry and Diplomacy during the Italian Wars (1526–1528)*. Pisa, 2005.

Ariès, Philippe. *The Hour of Our Death*, trans. Helen Weaver. New York, 1981.

Arrizabalaga, Jon, John Henderson, and Roger French. *The Great Pox: The French Disease in Renaissance Europe*. New Haven, 1997.

Bacchion, Eugenio. *Il dominio veneto su Corfù (1386–1797)*. Venice, 1956.

Baiocchi, Angelo. 'Contarini, Alessandro.' *DBI* 28 (1983). http://www.treccani.it/enciclopedia/alessandro-contarini_(Dizionario-Biografico).

Barnby, Henry. 'A Voyage to Cyprus in 1563.' *The Mariner's Mirror* 56:3 (1970): 309–14.

Bartolini, Elio. *Giovanni da Udine, III. La vita*. Udine, 1987.

Bassi, Elena. *Palazzi di Venezia*. Venice, 1976.

Battagia, Michele. *Delle accademie Veneziane: Dissertazione storica*. Venice, 1826.

Battilotti, Donata. 'Gianantonio Venier', 211–12. In *I tempi di Giorgione*, ed. Ruggero Maschio. Rome, 1994.

Battilotti, Donata, and Maria Teresa Franco, 'Registi di committenti e dei primi collezionisti di Giorgione.' *Antichita Viva* 17 (1978): 58–86.

Battistella, Antonio. 'Un mercante Friulano del '500.' *Pagine Friulane*, Anno XV, no. 9 (30 May 1903): 131–3.

Battistella, Antonio. 'I vecchi teatri Udinesi.' *Atti della Accademia di Udine*, ser. 5, 7 (1927–8): 77–99.

Battistella, Antonio. *Udine nel secolo XVI*. Udine, 1932.

Baumgarten, Paul Maria. 'Majordomo.' In *The Catholic Encyclopedia*, vol. 9, New York, 1910. http://www.newadvent.org/cathen/09556c.htm.

Bayer, Andrea, ed. *Art and Love in Renaissance Italy*. Exhibition catalogue, Metropolitan Museum of Art. New York, New Haven, and London, 2008.

Bechah, Yassina, Christian Capo, Jean-Louis Mege, and Didier Raoult. 'Epidemic Typhus', *The Lancet Infectious Diseases* 8:7 (July 2008): 417–26.

Bechevolo, Rino. *Il Castello di San Martino—Vittorio Veneto*. Vittorio Veneto, 1982.

Bell, Rudolph M. *How to Do It: Guides to Good Living for Renaissance Italians*. Chicago and London, 1999.

Bellavitis, Anna. *Noale: Struttura sociale e regime fondiario di una podesteria della prima metà del secolo XVI*. Treviso, 1994.

Bellavitis, Anna. 'Patrimoni e matrimoni a Venezia nel Cinquecento', 149–60. In *Le ricchezze delle donne: Diritti parimoniali e poteri familiari in Italia (XIII–XIX secc.)*, ed. Giulia Calvi and Isabelle Chabot. Turin, 1998.

Bellavitis, Anna. 'Family and Society', 319–51. In *Companion to Venetian History, 1400–1797*, ed. Eric Dursteler. Leiden, 2013.

Bellavitis, Anna, and Isabelle Chabot. 'People and Property in Florence and Venice', 76–85. In *At Home in Renaissance Italy*, ed. Marta Ajmar-Wollheim and Flora Dennis. London, 2006.

Belmont, Nicole. *Les signes de la naissance: Étude des representations symboliques associées aux naissances singulières*. Brionne, 1971.
Beltrame, Francesco. *Cenni illustrative sul monument a Tiziano Vecellio*. Venice, 1852.
Beltrame, Carlo, ed. *Ships and Shipyards: Proceedings of the Ninth International Symposium on Boat and Ship Archaeology, Venice 2000*. Oxford, 2003.
Beltramini, Guido, Davide Gasparotto, and Adolfo Tura, eds. *Pietro Bembo e l'invenzione del Rinascimento*. Venice, 2013.
Benzoni, Gino. 'Della Torre, Lucio.' In *DBI*, 37 (1989). http://www.treccani.it/enciclopedia/lucio-della-torre_(Dizionario-Biografico).
Benzoni, Gino. 'Della Torre, Luigi.' In *DBI*, 37 (1989). http://www.treccani.it/enciclopedia/luigi-della-torre_(Dizionario-Biografico)/.
Benzoni, Gino. 'Della Torre, Niccolò.' In *DBI* 37 (1989). http://www.treccani.it/enciclopedia/niccolo-della-torre_(Dizionario-Biografico).
Benzoni, Gino. 'Della Torre, Raimondo.' In *DBI* 37 (1989). http://www.treccani.it/enciclopedia/raimondo-della-torre_(Dizionario-Biografico)/.
Benzoni, Gino. 'Martinengo, Girolamo.' *DBI* 71 (2008). http://www.treccani.it/enciclopedia/girolamo-martinengo_(Dizionario-Biografico).
Benzoni, Gino. 'Priuli, Lorenzo,' *DBI* 85 (2016). http://www.treccani.it/enciclopedia/lorenzo-priuli_(Dizionario-Biografico).
Bergamini, Giuseppe. 'Bernardino Da Morcote (1450–1542).' *Dizionario Biografico dei Friuliani*. http://www.dizionariobiograficodeifriulani.it/bernardino-da-morcote-b-bortolini/.
Bergamini, Giuseppe, and Buora, Maurizio. *Il Castello di Udine*, Udine, 1990.
Bernardi, Jacopo. *La civica aula Cenedese con li suoi dipinti gli storici monumenti e la serie illustrata de' vescovi*. Ceneda, 1845.
Bertolizio, Giorgio.*Dogi: Nullità al potere*. Rome, 2013.
[Bertolla, Pietro]. 'Note storiche Friulane', *Pagine Friulane*, 14:3 (10 November 1901): 47.
Besta, Enrico. *Il senato veneziano (origine, costituzione, attribuzioni e riti*. [Miscellanea di storia veneta, ser. 2, 5]. Venice, 1899.
Bianco, Furio. *1511 La 'crudel zobia grassa' Rivolte contadine e faide nobiliari in Friuli tra '400 e '500*. Pordenone, 1995.
Bianco, Furio. '*Mihi vindictam*: Aristocratic Clans and Rural Communities in a Feud in Friuli in the Late Fifteenth and Early Sixteenth Centuries', 249–73. In *Crime, Society and the Law in Renaissance Italy*, ed. Trevor Dean and K.J. Lowe. Cambridge, 1994a.
Bianco, Furio. *Le terre del Fiuli: La formazione dei paesaggi agrari in Friuli tra il XV e il XIX secolo*, Mantua-Verona, 1994b.
Bistort, Giulio. *Il magistrato alle pompe nella Republica di Venezia*, Bologna, 1912.
Blair, R.G. 'Vagitus Uterinus. Crying in utero.' *The Lancet* 4:2, Issue 7423 (Dec. 1965): 1164–5.
Blanton, Lucas S. and Walker, David H. 'Rikettsia prowazekii (Epidemic or Louse-born Typhus)', 191. In *Mandell, Douglas, and Bennett's Principles and Practice of Infectious Diseases*, ed. John E. Bennett et al. Philadelphia, 2015.
Boccardo, Gerolamo. 'Torriani o Della Torre.' In *Nuova Enciclopedia Italiana*, vol. 23. Turin, 1887.
Boerio, Giuseppe. *Dizionario del dialetto veneziano*. Venice, 1829.
Bonazzi, Francesco. *Elenco dei Cavalieri del S. M. Ordine di S. Giovanni di Gerusalemme*. Naples, 1907.
Bondesan Aldino, and Paola Furlanetto. 'Artificial Fluvial Diversions in the Mainland of the Lagoon of Venice during the 16th and 17th Centuries Inferred by Historical Cartography Analysis.' *Géomorphologie: Relief, Processus, Environnement (Alluvial geomorphology in Italy)* 18:2 (2012): 175–200.

Bonfio, Alessandra. 'Una faida di metà Seicento. Rivalità nobiliari nella Patria del Friuli e nel Goriziano.' *Giornale della deputazione di storia patria per il Friuli*, 86 (2006): 77–116.

Bonner, Elizabeth. 'Vatican Secrets: Some Unpublished Correspondence of Sixteenth-Century Papal Nuncios at the French Court.' *The Innes Review* 53:1 (Spring 2002): 60–78.

Bonora, Elena. *Giudicare i vescovi. La definizione dei poteri nella Chiesa postridentina*. Bari, 2007.

Bonora, Elena. *Ricerche su Francesco Sansovino*. Venice, 1994.

Bowd, Stephen D. *Renaissance Mass Murder: Civilians and Soldiers during the Italian Wars*. Oxford, 2018.

Braida, Giuseppe. 'Un Colloredo in Inghilterra nel 1559.' *Memorie storiche Forogiuliesi* 10 (1914): 70–7.

Braudel, Fernand. *The Mediterranean and the Mediterranean World in the Age of Philip II*. trans. Siân Reynolds. 2 vols. 2nd rev. ed. New York, 1976.

Brilliant, Virginia, and Frederick Ilchman, eds. *Paolo Veronese: A Master and His Workshop in Renaissance Venice*. Sarasota, 2012.

Brown, Clifford M. 'Cardinal Sigismondo Gonzaga (1469–1525). An overlooked name in the annals of collectors of antiquities.' *Xenia*, 21 (1991): 47–58.

Brown, David Alan, and Sylvia Ferino Pagden, *Bellini, Giorgione, Titian, and the Renaissance of Venetian Painting*. Washington and Vienna, 2006.

Brown, Patricia Fortini. *Venice and Antiquity: The Venetian Sense of the Past*. New Haven and London, 1996.

Brown, Patricia Fortini. *Venetian Narrative Painting in the Age of Carpaccio*. New Haven and London, 1988.

Brown, Patricia Fortini. 'Measured Friendship, Calculated Pomp: The Ceremonial Welcomes of the Venetian Republic', 136–86. In *All the World's a Stage: Art and Pageantry in the Renaissance and Early Baroque*, ed. Barbara Wisch and Susan Scott Munshower. University Park, PA, 1990.

Brown, Patricia Fortini. *Private Lives in Renaissance Venice: Art, Architecture and the Family*. New Haven and London, 2004.

Brown, Patricia Fortini. 'Education and Children in the Home', 136–43. In *At Home in Renaissance Italy*, ed. Marta Ajmar-Wollheim and Flora Dennis. London, 2006.

Brown, Patricia Fortini. 'The Exemplary Life of Giulia Bembo Della Torre', 155–74. In *Philanagnostes: Studi in onore di Marino Zorzi*, ed. Chryssa Maltezou and Peter Schreiner. Bari, Venice and Cologne, 2008.

Brown, Patricia Fortini. 'Becoming a Man of Empire: The Construction of Patrician Identity in a Republic of Equals.' In *Architecture, Art, and Identity in Venice and Territories, 1450–1750: Essays in Honour of Deborah Howard*, ed. Nebahat Avcioğlu and Emma Jones, 231–49. London, 2013a.

Brown, Patricia Fortini. 'A Death in Venice: The Forgotten Tomb of Alvise Della Torre.' *Artibus et Historiae* no. 67 (XXXIV) (2013b): 137–59.

Brown, Patricia Fortini. 'Pietro Bembo e l'arte della diplomazia', 37–47. In *Pietro Bembo e le arti*, ed. Guido Beltramini, Howard Burns, and Davide Gasparotto. Venice, 2013.

Brown, Patricia Fortini. 'Portare l'acqua allo Stato da Mar', 108–11. In *Acqua e cibo a Venezia. Storie della Laguna e della Città*, ed. Donatella Calabi and Ludovica Galeazzo. Venice, 2015.

Brown, Patricia Fortini. 'Ritual Geographies in Venice's Colonial Empire', 43–89. In *Rituals of Politics and Culture in Early Modern Europe: Essays in Honour of Edward Muir*, ed. Mark Jurdjevic and Rolf Strøm-Olsen. Toronto, 2016.

Brown, Patricia Fortini. Review of *An Intimate Empire: Renaissance Venice and its Mediterranean World*, by Erin Maglaque. *Journal of Early Modern History* 23 (2019): 269–70.

Brown, Rawdon. *Ragguagli sulla vita e sulle opere di Marin Sanuto*. 2 vols. Venice, 1837.
Brundage, James A. *Law, Sex, and Christian Society in Medieval Europe*. Chicago, 2009.
Brundin, Abigail, Deborah Howard, and Mary Laven. *The Sacred Home in Renaissance Italy*. Oxford, 2018.
Brunelli, Giampiero. 'Ragazzoni, Giacomo.' *DBI* 86 (2016). http://www.treccani.it/enciclopedia/giacomo-ragazzoni_%28Dizionario-Biografico%29/
Brusegan, Marcello. *La Grande Guida dei Monumenti di Venezia: storia, arte, segreti, leggende, curiosità*. Rome, 2005a.
Brusegan, Marcello. *I palazzi di Venezia*. Rome, 2005b.
Bullock, Walter L. 'Vital Papazzoni: Whimsical Petrarchista of the Cinquecento.' *Italica* 12:2 (June 1935): 51–65.
Buora, Maurizio. *Guida di Udine: arte e storia tra vie e piazza*. Trieste, 1986.
Burch, Druin. 'When Childbirth Was Natural, and Deadly.' *Live Science*, 10 January 2009. https://www.livescience.com/3210-childbirth-natural-deadly.html.
Burghartz, Susanna. 'Covered Women? Veiling in Early Modern Europe.' *History Workshop Journal* 80 (2015): 1–32.
Burkle-Young, Francis A., and Michael Leopoldo Doerrer. *The Life of Cardinal Innocenzo del Monte: A Scandal in Scarlet*. Lewiston, NY, 1997.
Burns, Howard, Cristoph Luitpold Frommel, and Lionello Puppi, eds. *Michele Sanmicheli: architettura, linguaggio e cultura artistica nel Cinquecento*. Vicenza, 1995.
Byars, Jana. *Informal Marriages in Early Modern Venice*. New York, 2019.
Byrne, Joseph Patrick, ed. *Encyclopedia of Pestilence, Pandemics, and Plagues*. Westwood, CN, 2008.
Cairns, Christopher. *Domenico Bollani, Bishop of Brescia: Devotion to Church and State in the Republic of Venice in the Sixteenth Century*. Nieuwkoop, 1976.
Calabi, Donatella. 'Il regno di Candia e le "fatiche" del governo civile: le "cento città", le popolazioni, le fabbriche pubbliche,' 97–106. In *Venezia e la difesa del Levante da Lepanto a Candia 1570–1670*, ed. Maddalena Redolfi. Venice, 1986.
Calabi, Donatella, and Paolo Morachiello. *Rialto: le fabbriche e il Ponte, 1514–1591*. Turin, 1987.
Calimani, Riccardo. 'Gli editori di libri ebraici a Venezia', 55–62. In *Armeni, ebrei, greci—stampatori a Venezia*, ed. S. Abbiati. Venice, 1989.
Calore, Andrea. 'Note sul monumento ad Alessandro Contarini nella Basilica del Santo,' Il Santo 28, fasc. 1 (1988): 71–9.
Calvelli, Lorenzo. *Cipro e la memoria dell'antico fra Medioevo e Rinascimento*. Venice, 2009.
Calvelli, Lorenzo. 'Archaeology in the Service of the Dominante: Giovanni Matteo Bembo and the Antiquities of Cyprus', 19–66. In *Cyprus and the Renaissance (1450–1650)*, ed. Benjamin Arbel, Evelien Chayes, and Harald Hendrix,. Turnhout, 2012.
Camescasa, E., ed. *Da Raffaello a Goya . . . da Van Gogh a Picasso: 50 dipinti dal Museu de Arte di San Paolo del Brasile*. Milan, 1987.
Camuffo, Dario. 'Freezing of the Venetian Lagoon since the 9th Century A.D. in Comparison to the Climate of Western Europe and England.' *Climatic Change* 10 (1987): 43–66.
Canosa, Romano. *Il velo e il cappuccio: monacazioni forzate e sessualità nei conventi femminili in Italia tra Quattrocento e Settecento*. Rome, 1996.
Cantù, Cesare. 'Recenti lavori di erudizione storica.' *ASI*, ser. 3, 19, no. 79 (1874): 130–60.
Čapeta Rakić, Ivana, and Giuseppe Capriotti. 'Two Marian Iconographic Themes in the Face of Islam on the Adriatic Coast in the Early Modern Period.' *Ikon* 10 (2017): 169–86.
The Cardinals of the Holy Roman Church: http://cardinals.fiu.edu/cardinals.htm.

Carnevale, Diego. 'Dalla morte pensata alla morte vissuta. La storiografia sulla morte dall' "età dei classici" all' "esplosione" odierna.' *il Palindromo* 9 (2013): 75–91.

Capretti, Flaviano. 'Nota sui nobili Schillini.' *Brixia Sacra* 3 (1912): 302–5.

Cargnelutti, Liliana ed. *Giovanni da Udine*, II. *I Libri dei Conti*. Udine, 1987.

Carmichael, Ann G. 'The Last Past Plague: The Uses of Memory in Renaissance Epidemics.' *Journal of the History of Medicine* 53 (1988): 132–60.

Carreri, F.C. 'Breve storia di Valvasone e de' suoi signori dagli inizi al 1806.' *Nuovo Archivio Veneto*, n.s., 11 (1906): I: 107–48; II: 135–61.

Carson, Rebekah Anne. *Andrea Riccio's Della Torre Tomb Monument: Humanism and Antiquarianism in Padua and Verona*, Ph.D. diss., University of Toronto, 2010.

Carson, Rebekah Anne. 'The Quintessential Christian Tomb: Saints, Professors, and Riccio's Tomb Design.' *Renaissance Studies* 28:1 (2013): 90–111.

Casella, Laura. *I Savorgnan: la famiglia e le opportunità del potere (secc. 15.–18.)*. Rome, 2003.

Casella, Laura. 'Donne aristocratiche nel Friuli del Cinquecento tra strategie familiari e conflitti di fazione', 89–128'. In *Donne di potere nel Rinascimento*, ed. Letizia Arcangeli and Susanna Peyronel. Rome, 2008.

Casella, Laura. 'Il confine quotidiano. Scritture di donne in Friuli tra Cinque e Settecento', 1057–72. In *Il genere nella ricerca storica*, ed. Saveria Chemotti and Maria Cristina La Rocca, I. Padua, 2015.

'Ce fastu?' *Rivista della Società filologica friulana* 71 (1995): 202.

Cevese, Renato. 'L'architettura vicentina del primo rinascimento.' *Bollettino del CISA Palladio*, 6:2 (1964): 201–3.

Chambers, D.S. 'The Enigmatic Eminence of Cardinal Sigismondo Gonzaga.' *Renaissance Studies* 16:3 (Sept. 2002): 330–54.

Chastel, André. *The Sack of Rome, 1527*, trans. Beth Archer. Princeton, 1983.

Chojnacki, Stanley. 'Identity and Ideology in Renaissance Venice: The Third Serrata', 263–94. In *Venice Reconsidered: The History and Civilization of an Italian City-State, 1297–1797*, ed. John Martin and Dennis Romano. Baltimore and London, 2000.

Chojnacki, Stanley. *Women and Men in Renaissance Venice: Twelve Essays on Patrician Society*. Baltimore, 2000.

Chiurlo, Bindo. 'Valvason, Erasmo da', *Enciclopedia Italiana* (1937). http://www.treccani.it/enciclopedia/erasmo-da-valvason/

Cicogna, Emmanuele A. *Delle inscrizioni veneziane*, 6 vols in 7. Venice, 1824–53. (repr. Bologna, 1969).

Cicogna, Emmanuele A. 'Del preteso sepolcro in Venezia di Francesco Carmagnola.' *Rivista Contemporanea* 2 (1854): 507–13.

Cicogna, Emmanuele A. 'Intorno la vita e le opere di Marcantonio Michiel, patrizio veneto della prima meta del secolo XVI.' *Memorie dell'I. R. Istituto veneto di scienze, lettere ed arti* 9 (1860): 359–426.

Ciconi, Giandomenico. 'Udine e sua Provincia.' In *Grande Illustrazione Lombardo-Veneto fino ai tempi moderni*. 5 vols. Milan, 1858–61.

Ciković, Danijel. 'Reliquiario di San Quirino presso la Cattedrale di Veglia (Krk): donazione del duca Guglielmo V di Baviera al vescovo Giovanni della Torre.' *Zbornik z umetnostno zgodovino, Art History Journal*, n. s., 51 (2015): 55–70.

Ciković, Danijel, and Iva Jazbec Tomaić, '*Tutti li sudetti paramenti hanno l'arma de Sua Signoria Illustrissima et Reverendissima*...: Donazioni pubbliche e private del vescovo di Veglia, Giovanni della Torre.' In *Public and Private Commissions: Donors and Works of Art in the Northern Adriatic during the Early Modern Period*. Rijeka, 2018.

Cini, Luigi. 'Passaggio della regina Bona Sforza per Padova nell'anno 1556', 27–65. In *Relazioni tra Padova e la Polonia. Studi in onore dell'Università di Cracovia nel VI centenario della sua fondazione*. Padua, 1964.

Clough, Cecil H. 'Love and War in the Veneto: Luigi da Porto and the Story of Giulietta e Romeo', 99–127. In *War, Culture and Society in Renaissance Venice: Essays in Honour of John Hale*, ed. David S. Chambers, Cecil H. Clough, and Michael E. Mallett. London and Rio Grande, Ohio, 1993.

Cohen, Charles. *The Art of Giovanni Antonio da Pordenone: Between Dialect and Language*. 2 vols. Cambridge, 1996.

Cohen, Elizabeth S., and Thomas V. Cohen. *Daily Life in Renaissance Italy*. Westport, CN and London, 2001.

Cohen, Thomas V. 'The Macrohistory of Microhistory.' *Journal of Medieval and Early Modern Studies* 47:1 (2017): 53–73.

Cohn, Samuel Kline. *Cultures of Plague: Medical Thinking at the End of the Renaissance*. Oxford, 2010.

Coletti, Luigi. *Catalogo delle cose d'arte e di antichità di Treviso*. Rome, 1935.

Colloredo Mels, Pierluigi Romeo di. *Rodolfo di Colloredo: Un feldmaresciallo italiano nella guerra dei trent'anni*. Zanica, 2016.

Comescu, Dragoş. *Venetian Renaissance Fortifications in the Mediterranean*. Jefferson, NC, 2016.

Comune di Venezia, *Venezia e la peste 1348/1797*. 2nd ed. Venice, 1980.

Concina, Ennio. 'Città e fortezze nelle 'tre isole nostre del Levante', 184–220. In *Venezia e la difesa del Levante da Lepanto a Candia 1570–1670*, ed. Maddalena Redolfi. Venice, 1986.

Constant, Caroline. *The Palladio Guide*. Princeton, 1993.

Cont, Alessandro. 'Banditismo nobiliare di primo Settecento: il castellano friulano Lucio della Torre in lotta per la propria sopravvivenza.' *Dimensioni e problemi della ricerca storica* 2 (2014): 27–46.

Conzato, Antonio. 'Per un profilo della nobiltà friulana nel Cinquecento: tra permanenza e partenza.' *Studi veneziani*, n.s., 41 (2001): 99–179.

Conzato, Antonio. *Dai castelli alle corti: Castellani friulani tra gli Asburgo e Venetia 1545–1620*. Verona, 2005.

Coolidge, W.A.B. *The Alps in Nature and History*. New York, 1908.

Cooney, Mark. *Warriors and Peacemakers: How Third Parties Shape Violence*. New York, 1998.

Cooper, Tracy E. *Palladio's Venice: Architecture and Society in a Renaissance Republic*. New Haven and London, 2006.

Corbanese, G.G. *Il Friuli, Trieste e l'Istria : grande atlante storico-cronologico comparato*. Bologna, 1983.

Corbanese, G.G. *Atlante Storico-Cronologico comparato*. Bologna, 1987.

Corbellini, Roberta. 'Le dimore dei Torriani, tra presenza e assenza', 11–23. In *Fortificazioni e memorie del Friuli centrale attraverso i secoli*, ed. D. Frangipane. Udine, 1990.

Cornet, Enrico. *Paolo V. e la Repubblica veneta. Giornale dal 22 ottobre 1605–9 giugno 1607*. Vienna 1859.

Corradi, Alfonso. *Annali delle epidemie occorse in Italia dalle prime memorie fino al 1850. Parte II: Dal 1501 a tutto il 1600*... Bologna, 1867.

Corry, Mary, Deborah Howard, and Mary Laven. *Madonnas & Miracles: The Holy Home in Renaissance Italy*. Cambridge, 2017.

Cortelletti, Monica. 'Il Castello di San Martino a Ceneda attraverso la stratigrafia edilizia', 185–201. In *Castelli del Veneto tra archeologia e fonti scritte*, ed. Gian Pietro Brogiolo and Elisa Possenti. Mantua, 2005.

Cowan, Alexander. *Marriage, Manners and Mobility*. Aldershot and Burlington, VT, 2007.

Cox, Virginia. *The Prodigious Muse: Women's Writing in Counter-Reformation Italy*. Baltimore, 2011.

Cox, Virginia. *Women's Writing in Italy, 1400–1650*. Baltimore, 2008.

Cozzi, Gaetano. 'Paolo Paruta, Paolo Sarpi e la questione della sovranità su Ceneda.' *Bollettino dell'Istituto di Storia della Società e dello Stato Veneziano* 4 (1962): 176–237.

Cozzi, Gaetano. 'Domenico Morosini e il "De bene instituta re publica".' *Studi veneziani* 12 (1970): 405–58.

Cozzi, Gaetano. 'Authority and the Law in Renaissance Venice', 293–345. In *Renaissance Venice*, ed. J.R. Hale. London, 1973.

Cozzi, Gaetano. *Ambiente veneziano, ambiente veneto: saggi su politica, società, cultura nella Repubblica di Venezia in età moderna*. Venice, 1997.

Crawford, Francis Marion. *Gleanings from Venetian History*. London, New York, 1907.

Crawshaw, Jane L. Stevens. *Plague Hospitals: Public Health for the City in Early Modern Venice*. Farnham, 2012.

Crollalanza, Giovanni Battista. *Memorie storico-genealogiche della stirpe Waldsee-Mels e più particolarmente dei Conti di Colloredo*. Pisa, 1875.

Crowe, J.A., and G.B. Cavalcaselle. *Titian: His Life and Times*. London, 1877.

Custoza, Gian Camillo. *Colloredo: una famiglia e un castello nella storia europea*. Udine, 2003.

Custoza, Gian Camillo. *Giovanni da Udine la tecnica della decorazione a stucco alla 'romana' nel Friuli del XVI secolo*. Udine, 1996.

Dacos, Nicole, Caterina Furlan, and Liliana Cargnelutti. *Giovanni da Udine. I. 1487–1561*. Udine, 1987.

Darovec, Darko. *Vendetta in Koper 1686*. Koper, 2018.

Del Col, Andrea. 'La morte dell'inquisito nel castello di Ceneda, 11 maggio 1570. Il processo contro Vincenzo Bertoldo.' *Archivio Storico Cenedese* 1 (2015): 45–82.

Del Col, Andrea. 'Un territorio sotto l'Inquisizione: Conegliano e la diocesi di Ceneda nel Cinquecento', 35–49. In *Un Cinquecento inquieto. Da Cima da Conegliano al rogo di Riccardo Perucolo*, ed. Giandomenico Romanelli and Giorgio Fossaluzza. Venice, 2014.

Dal Prà, Laura, ed. *I Madruzzo e l'Europa, 1539–1658: i principi vescovi di Trento tra Papato e Impero*. Milan, 1993.

Damen, Giada. 'The Trade in Antiquities between Italy and the Eastern Mediterranean.' Ph.D. diss., Princeton University, 2012.

Da Mosto, Andrea. *L'archivio di stato di Venezia: Indice generale, storico, descrittivo ed analitco*. 2 vols. Rome, 1937.

Da Mosto, Andrea. *I dogi di Venezia nella vita pubblica e privata*. Milan, 1960.

Davidson, N.S. 'Sodomy in Early Modern Venice', 65–81. In *Sodomy in Early Modern Europe*, ed. Tom Betteridge. Manchester, 2002.

Davis, Robert C. *Christian Slaves, Muslim Masters: White Slavery in the Mediterranean, the Barbary Coast, and Italy, 1500–1800*. Houndmills, 2004.

Davis, Robert C. 'The Geography of Gender in the Renaissance', 19–38. In *Gender and Society in Renaissance Italy*, ed. Judith C. Brown and Robert H. Davis. London and New York, 1998.

Davis, Robert C. *Holy War and Human Bondage: Tales of Christian-Muslim Slavery in the Early-Modern Mediterranean*. Santa Barbara, 2009.

Davis, Robert C., and Garry R. Marvin. *Venice, the Tourist Maze: A Cultural Critique of the World's Most Touristed City*. Berkeley, 2004.

De Checchi, Franco. 'Il complesso di Villa Bembo-Boldu e l'Oratorio della B. V. Di Loreto a Ponte di Brenta.' *Padova e il suo territorio* 20, fasc. 188 (Nov–Dec. 2005): 9–12.

De Conti, Vanni. *Il Fascino di Giulietta e Romeo tra storia e leggenda*. Youcanprint.it, 2016.

De Martin Pinter, Albina. 'Reti di donne sul confine friulano. Lettere femminili nell'archivio Della Torre (XVII secolo).' *Mélanges de l'École française de Rome—Italie et Méditerranée modernes et contemporaines* 125:1 (2013).

De Piero, Giuseppe. *I borghi e le piazze dell'antica città murata di Udine nella storia e nella cronaca*. Udine, 1983.

Degani, Ernesto. *I partiti in Friuli nel 1500 e la storia di un famoso duello*. Udine, 1900.

Del Torso, Enrico. 'Dello stemma dei signori di Villalta.' *Pagine Friulane* 14:3 (30 Nov. 1902): 42–3.

Dennis, Kimberly L. 'Rediscovering the Villa Montalto and the Patronage of Camilla Peretti', 55–73. In *Wives, Widows, Mistresses, and Nuns in Early Modern Italy: Making the Invisible Visible through Art and Patronage*, ed. Katherine A. McIver. London, 2016.

De Santi, Chiara. 'Il Museo Archeologico di Cividale del Friuli. Dalla fondazione agli sviluppi attuali. I parte.' *Forum Iulii* 36 (2012): 93–122.

De Vivo, Filippo. *Information & Communication in Venice: Rethinking Early Modern Politics*. Oxford, 2007.

De Vivo, Filippo. 'Walking in Sixteenth-Century Venice: Mobilizing the Early Modern City.' *I Tatti Studies in the Italian Renaissance* 19:1 (2016): 115–41.

Di Lenardo, Lorenzo. 'Torre (della) Lucio Antonio (1695–1723).' In *Dizionario biografico dei Friulani*. http://www.dizionariobiograficodeifriulani.it/torre-della-lucio-antonio-1695-1723/.

Dionisotti, Carlo. *Carteggio d'amore (1500–1501)*. Florence, 1950.

Donati, Andrea. *Paris Bordone. Catalogo ragionato*. Soncino, 2014.

Dumas, Alexandre. *Celebrated Crimes*. Vol. 5, trans. I.G. Burnham. Philadelphia, 1895.

Dunn, Peter M. 'Eucharius Rösslin (c 1470–1526) of Germany and the Rebirth of Midwifery.' *Archives of Disease in Childhood—Fetal and Neonatal Edition* 79 (1998): 77–8.

Eamon, William. 'The Canker Friar: Piety and Intrigue in an Era of New Diseases', 156–76. In *Piety and Plague from Byzantium to the Baroque*, ed. Franco Mormando and Thomas Worcester. Kirksville, MO, 2007.

Eatough, Geoffrey. *Fracastoro's Syphilis*. Liverpool, 1984.

Edler, Florence. 'The Van Der Molen, Commission Merchants of Antwerp: Trade with Italy, 1538–44', 78–145. In *Medieval and Historiographical Essays in honour of James Westfall Thompson*, ed. James Lea Gate and Eugene N. Anderson. Chicago, 1938.

Eisenbichler, Konrad. 'Charles V in Bologna: The Self-Fashioning of a Man and a City', *Renaissance Studies* 13:4 (1999): 430–9.

Ercole, Guido. *Duri I banchi! Le navi della Serenissima 421–1797*. Trento, 2006.

Faccioli, Giovanni Tommaso, and Antonio and Vincenzo Joppi. *Chiese di Udine (ms. Joppi 682° della Biblioteca Civica di Udine)*, ed. Giuseppe Bergamini, Paolo Pastres, and Francesca Tamburlini. Udine, 2007.

Faldon, Nilo. *Diocesi di Vittorio Veneto*. Padua, 1993.

Fassina, Michele. 'Il mais nel veneto nel Cinquecento: Testimonianze iconografiche e prime experience colturali.' In *L'Impatto della scoperta dell'America nella cultura veneziana*. Rome, 1990.

Fenlon, Iain. *The Ceremonial City: History, Memry and Myth in Renaissance Venice*. New Haven and London, 2007.

Fenlon, Iain. 'Rex Christianissimus Francorum: Themes and Contexts of Henry III's Entry to Venice, 1574', 99–118. In *Waterborne Pageants and Festivities in the Renaissance: Essays in Honour of J. R. Mulryne*, ed. Margaret Shewring. London, 2013.

Ferraro, Joanne. 'Childhood in Medieval and Early Modern Times', 61–77. In *The Routledge History of Childhood in the Western World*, ed. Paula S. Fass. Abingdon, 2012.

Filippini, Nadia Maria. 'The Church, the State and Childbirth: The Midwife in Italy during the Eighteenth Century', 152–75. In *The Art of Midwifery: Early Modern Midwives in Europe*, ed. Hilary Marland. London and New York, 1993.

Fincati, L. 'La nobiltà veneziana e il commercio marittimo.' *Rivista marittima* 10 (1878): 5–25.

Finkel, Caroline. *Osman's Dream: The History of the Ottoman Empire*. New York, 2007.

Finlay, Robert. *Politics in Renaissance Venice*. New Brunswick, 1980.

Fontijn, Claire. *Desperate Measures: The Life and Music of Antonia Padoani*. Oxford, 2006.

Forbes, Thomas R. 'The Social History of the Caul', 119–32. In *The Manner Born: Birth Rites In Cross-Cultural Perspective*, ed. Lauren Dundes. Walnut Creek and Oxford, 2003.

Fossaluzza, Giorgio. 'Qualche Recupero al Catalogo Ritrattistico del Bordon.' In *Paris Bordon e il suo tempo*. Treviso, 1987.

Frith, John. 'Syphilis—Its Early History and Treatment until Penicillin, and the Debate on its Origins.' *Journal of Military and Veterans Health* 20:4 (2012): 49–58.

Franzoi, Umberto. *The Prisons of the Doge's Palace in Venice*. Milan, 1997.

Franzoi, Umberto. *Le prigioni della Repubblica di Venezia*. Venice, 1966.

Freis, A., M. Elsässer, C. Sohn, and H. Fluhr. 'Twin Pregnancy with One Fetus and One Complete Mole—A Case Report.' *Geburtshilfe und Frauenheilkunde*, 76:7 (2016): 819–22.

Fulin, Rinaldo. *Diarii e diaristi veneziani*. Venice, 1881.

Furlan, Caterina, and Paolo Casadio, eds. *Pomponio Amalteo: pictor sancti viti, 1505–1588*. Milan, 2006.

Gaddi, Mauro, and Andrea Zannini, eds. *Venezia non è da guerra: l'Isontino, la società friulana e la Serenissima nella guerra di Gradisca (1615–1617)*. Gradisca d'Isonzo, 2007.

Gamulin, Grgo. 'Opere in edite del rinascimento', *Arte Veneta* 27 (1973): 265–8.

Gandini, Clemente. *Tiziano: Le lettere*. Pieve di Cadore, 1977.

Garafolo, Luigi. 'I Della Torre nel XV secolo. Matrimonio e famiglia in nuovi documenti.' Tesi di laurea. Università di Udine, 2002.

Garcia Villoslada, Ricardo. *Storia del Collegio romano dal suo inizio (1551) alla soppressione della Compagnia di Gesù (1773)*. Rome, 1954.

Gardi, Andrea. 'Friulani al servizio del papa (XV-XVIII secolo)', 151–62. In *Per Furio. Studi in onore di Furio Bianco*, ed. Alessio Fornasin and Claudio Povolo. Udine, 2014.

Garnett, Geoff P., et al. 'The Natural History of Syphilis: Implications for the Transmission Dynamics and Control of Infection.' *Sexually Transmitted Diseases* 24:4 (April 1997): 185–200.

Geanakoplos, Deno J. 'Erasmus and the Aldine Academy of Venice: A Neglected Chapter in the Transmission of Graeco-Byzantine Learning to the West.' *Greek, Roman and Byzantine Studies* 2, no. 2/3 (1960): 107–34.

Gélis, Jacques. *History of Childbirth: Fertility, Pregnancy and Birth in Early Modern Europe*, trans. Rosemary Morris. Cambridge, 1991.

Georgopoulou, Maria. 'The Meaning of the Architecture and the Urban Layout of Venetian Candia: Cultural Conflict and Interaction in the late Middle Ages.' Ph.D. diss., University of California, Los Angeles, 1992.

Georgopoulou, Maria. 'Private Residences in Venetian Candia.' *Thesaurismata* 30 (2000): 95–126.

Georgopoulou, Maria. *Venice's Mediterranean Colonies: Architecture and Urbanism*. Cambridge, 2001.

Gerola, Giuseppe. 'Una descrizione di Candia del principio del seicento.' *Atti della Accademia Roveretana degli Agiati*, ser. 3, 14 (1908): 269–81.

Gerola, Giuseppe. "I Francescani in Creta al tempo del dominio veneziano." *Collectanea Francescana* 2:3 (1932): 301–25.

Gerola, Giuseppe. *Monumenti veneti nell'isola di Creta*. 4 vols in 5. Bergamo, 1905–32.

Gertwagen, Ruthy. 'The Concept of Ports in the Medieval Eastern Mediterranean: Construction and Maintenance on Crete to the End of the Fifteenth Century.' *International Journal of Maritime History* 12 (2000): 177–241.

Giannetto, Nella. *Bernardo Bembo: umanista e politico veneziano*. Florence, 1985.

Gianni, Luca. 'Un testamento, una famiglia, una villa. I signori di Prata a Fiumicino.' *Atti dell'Accademia San Marco* 16 (2014): 857–74.

Giddey, Ernest. 'La "Helvetiae descriptio" de Jean della Torre (1607).' *Zeitschrift für schweizerische Geschichte—Revue d'histoire suisse* 30 (1950): 267–70.

Gilbert, Josiah. *Cadore or Titian's Country*. London, 1869.

Ginzburg, Carlo. *The Night Battles: Witchcraft and Agrarian Cults in the Sixteenth and Seventeenth Centuries*, trans. John and Anne C. Tedeschi. Baltimore, 1983.

Gleason, Elizabeth. 'Confronting New Realities. Venice and the Peace of Bologna, 1530', 168–84. In *Venice Reconsidered. The History and Civilization of an Italian City-State, 1297–1797*, ed. John Martin and Dennis Romano. Baltimore and London, 2000.

Gluzman, Renard. 'Between Venice and the Levant: Re-Evaluating Maritime Routes from the Fourteenth to the Sixteenth Century.' *The Mariner's Mirror* 96:3 (2010): 264–94.

Gluzman, Renard. 'Resurrection of a Sunken Ship: The Salvage of the Venetian Marciliana that Saved Cattaro from Barbarossa.' *Archivio Veneto*, ser. 6, 8 (2014): 29–78.

Goi, Paolo. 'Villa Pedrina (Della Torre) a Tiezzo di Azzano Decimo.' *AFAT* 35 (2016): 59–69.

Goldfarb, Hilliard T. *The Isabella Stewart Gardner Museum: A Companion Guide and History*. Boston, 1995.

Gordon, Charlotte. *Romantic Outlaws: The Extraordinary Lives of Mary Wollstonecraft and her Daughter Mary Shelley*. New York, 2015.

Green, Monica H. *Making Women's Medicine Masculine: The Rise of Male Authority in Pre-Modern Gynaecology*. Oxford, 2008.

Green, Monica H. 'The Sources of Eucharius Rösslin's "Rosegarden for Pregnant Women and Midwives" (1513).' *Medical History* 53 (2009): 167–92.

Greene, Molly. *A Shared World: Christians and Muslims in the Early Modern Mediterranean*. Princeton, 2000.

Greer, John Michael. *Circles of Power: Ritual Magic in the Western Tradition*. St. Paul, MN, 1997.

Grendler, Paul. *The Universities of the Italian Renaissance*. Baltimore and London, 2002.

Grendler, Paul F. *The Roman Inquisition and the Venetian Press, 1540–1605*. Princeton, 2015.

Gross, L. 'How the Plague Bacillus and Its Transmission through Fleas were Discovered: Reminiscences from My Years at the Pasteur Institute in Paris.' *Proceedings of the National Academy of Science*, 92:17 (15 Aug. 1995): 7609–11.

Guerrini, Paolo.*Un celebre famiglia Lombarda: I Conti di Martinengo—studi e ricerche genealogiche*. Brescia, 1930.

Grubb, James. *Provincial Families of the Renaissance: Private and Public Life in the Veneto*. Baltimore, 1996.

Grubb, James. *Family Memoirs from Verona and Vicenza (15th–16th Centuries)*. Rome, 2002.

Hacke, Daniela. *Women, Sex and Marriage in Early Modern Venice*. Aldershot, 2004.

Haraguchi, Jennifer. 'Fedele Cassandra (1465?–1558).' *Italian Women Writers, University of Chicago Library*, 2003 (http://www.lib.uchicago.edu/efts/IWW/BIOS/A0015.html).

Hendy, Philip. *European and American Paintings in the Isabella Stewart Gardner Museum*. Boston, 1974.

Hellman, Alfred M. *A Collection of Early Obstetrical Books*. New Haven, 1952.

Hirschauer, Charles. *La politique de St Pie V en France (1566–1572)*. Paris, 1922.

Hochman, Michel. 'Schiavone disegnatore', 111–20. In *Splendori del Rinascimento a Venezia: Schiavone tra Parmigianino, Tintoretto e Tiziano*, ed. Enrico Maria Dal Pozzolo and Lionello Puppi. Milan, 2015.

Hocquet, Jean-Claude. 'Venice', 381–415. In *The Rise of the Fiscal State in Europe, c.1200–1815*, ed. Richard Bonney. Oxford, 1999.

Hoffman, G. 'Il pensiero religioso nelle donazioni e nei testament dei Veneziani di Creta.' *La Civiltà cattolica* 10 (1944): 220–6.

Holt, Stephen. 'Paolo Veronese and his Patrons.' Ph.D. diss., University of St Andrews, 1990.

Hook, J. 'The Destruction of the "New Italia": Venice and the Papacy in Collision.' *Italian Studies* 28 (1973): 10–30.

Hope, Charles. 'Titian as a Court Painter.' *Oxford Art Journal* 2 (1979): 7–10.

Hope, Charles. 'The Early Biographies of Titian', 167–97. In *Titian 500*, ed. Joseph Manca. Hanover, NH, 1993.

Hope, Charles. 'Titian's Family and the Dispersal of His Estate.' In *Late Titian and the Sensuality of Painting*, ed. Sylvia Ferino-Pagden. Venice, 2008.

Howard, Deborah. *Jacopo Sansovino: Architecture and Patronage in Renaissance Venice*. New Haven and London, 1975.

Howard, Deborah. 'Venetian Galleys as Domestic and Ritual Space.' *Artibus et Historiae*, no. 81 (XLI) (2020): 63–78.

Humfrey, Peter. *Titian*. London and New York, 2007.

Humfrey, Peter, and Allison Sherman. 'The Lost Church of San Niccolò ai Frari (San Nicoletto) in Venice and its Painted Decoration.' *Artibus et Historiae* 72 (XXXVI) (2015): 247–81.

Impey, L., et al. 'The Relation between Pre-Eclampsia at Term and Neonatal Encephalopathy.' *Archives of Disease in Childhood. Fetal and Neonatal Edition* 85:3 (2001): F170–2.

[Anon.], 'Istoria della vita e tragica morte del Co. Lucio della Torre.' *Pagine Friulane* 5:5 (1892): 66–8.

Jenny-Squeder, Daniel. 'Zu den Illustrationen des Werkes Helvetiae descriptio des Johann della Torre (1607).' *Stultifera navis* 9 (1952): 152–9.

Joannides, Paul. *Titian to 1518: The Assumption of Genius*. New Haven and London, 2001.

Johnson, Eugene J. 'A Window in the Venetian Mint and the Libreria di San Marco.' *Journal of the Society of Architectural Historians* 69:2 (2010): 190–205.

Joppi, Vincenzo. 'Descrizione del palazzo Marchesi in Udine e sua demolizione nel 1717.' *Pagine Friulane* 3:8 (1890): 124–6.

Judde de Larivière, Claire. *Naviguer, commercer, gouverner: Économie maritime et pouvoirs à Venise (XVe–XVIe siècles)*. Leiden, 2008.

Kazhdan, Alexander, ed. *The Oxford Dictionary of Byzantium*. Oxford and New York, 1991.

Kassler-Taub, Elizabeth. 'To Dwell Upon a Holy Hill: The Venetian Ascent to Imperial Power in Sixteenth Century Udine.' Senior thesis, Princeton University, 2010.

Kent Francis William, with Patricia Simons. 'Renaissance Patronage: An Introductory Essay', 1–9. In *Patronage, Art, and Society in Renaissance Italy*, ed. Francis William Kent et al. Oxford, 1987.

Kidwell, Carol. *Pietro Bembo: Lover, Linguist, Cardinal*. Montreal, 2004.

King, Margaret L. *Women of the Renaissance*. Chicago and London, 1991.

Klapisch-Zuber, Christiane. 'The Name "Remade": The Transmission of Given Name in Florence in the Fourteenth and Fifteenth Centuries', 283–309. In her *Women, Family, and Ritual in Renaissance Italy*, trans. Lydia G. Cochrane. Chicago and London, 1985.

Kleinschmidt, Irene. 'Gruppenvotivbilder venezianischer Beamter (1550–1630) im palazzo dei Camerlenghi und im Dogenpalast.' *Arte Veneta* 31 (1977): 104–18.

Korsch, Evelyn. 'Renaissance Venice and the Sacred-Political Connotations of Waterborne Pageants', 79–98. In *Waterborne Pageants and Festivities in the Renaissance: Essays in Honour of J. R. Mulryne*, ed. Margaret Shewring. London, 2013.

Krohn, Deborah L. 'Marriage as a Key to Understanding the Past', 9–15. In *Art and Love in Renaissance Italy*, ed. Andrea Bayer. New York, New Haven, London, 2008.

Kuntz, Marion Leathers. *The Anointment of Dionisio: Prophecy and Politics in Renaissance Italy*. University Park, PA, 2001.

Kushtagi, P., and T. Hegde. 'Unusual Twins: A Case of Intrauterine Pregnancy with Complete Molar Pregnancy.' *The Internet Journal of Gynecology and Obstetrics*, 10:2 (2008).

Labalme, Patricia H. 'Sodomy and Venetian Justice in the Renaissance.' *Tijdschrift voor Rechtsgeschiedenis* 52 (1984): 217–54.

Labalme, Patricia H., and Laura Sanguineti White, with Linda Carroll. 'How to (and How Not to) Get Married in Sixteenth-Century Venice (Selections from the Diaries of Marin Sanudo).' *Renaissance Quarterly* 52:1 (1999): 43–72.

Lain, P. 'Tradizioni sul Conte Lucio Della Torre.' *Pagine Friulani* 5:7 (1892): 110–11.

Lambrinos, Kostas. 'La condizione giuridica e sociale della donna patrizia nella Creta veneziana (sec. XVI–XVII)', 89–96 In *Spazi, poteri e diritti delle donne a Venezia in età moderna*, ed. Anna Bellavitis, Nadia Maria Filippini, and Tiziana Plebani, Verona, 2012

Lambrinos, Kostas. 'Identity and Socio-Economic Mobility in Venetian Crete: The Evolution of a Citizen Family (Sixteenth Century).' *Mediterranean Historical Review* 29:1 (2014): 57–70.

Landé, Carl H. 'Introduction: The Dyadic Basis of Clientelism', xiii–xxvii. In *Friends Followers and Factions: A Reader in Political Clientelism*, ed. Steffan W. Schmidt et al., Berkeley, 1977.

Lane, Frederic Chapin. *Ships and Shipbuilders of the Renaissance*. Baltimore and London, 1934.

Lane, Frederic Chapin. 'Venetian Shipping during the Commercial Revolution', 22–46. In *Crisis and Change in the Venetian Economy in the Sixteenth and Seventeenth Centuries*, ed. Brian Pullan, London, 1968.

Lane, Frederic Chapin. *Venice: A Maritime Republic*. Baltimore, 1973.

Lauber, Rosella. '"In casa di messer Pietro Bembo." Riflessioni su Pietro Bembo e Marcantonio Michiel', 441–464. In *Pietro Bembo e le arti*, ed. Guido Beltramini, Howard Burns, and Davide Gasparotto, Venice, 2013.

Lauber, Rosella. '"Il vero oracolo di Vinegia tutta": il Bravo di Tiziano e Giovanni Antonio Venier, muovendo l'animo al firmamentum.' *Studi Tizianeschi* 2 (2004): 11–30.

Laven, Mary. *Virgins of Venice: Broken Vows and Cloistered Lives in the Renaissance Convent*. New York, 2003.

Laugier, Marc Antoine. *Storia della repubblica di Venezia dalla sua fondazione sino al suo fine*, 12 vols. Venice, 1832.

Lavarda, Sergio. 'Banditry and Social Identity in the Republic of Venice. Ludovico da Porto, his Family and his Property (1567–1640).' *Crime, Histoire & Sociétés / Crime, History & Societies* 11:1 (2007): 55–82.

Lazzarini, Alfredo, and Giovanni Del Puppo. *Castelli Friulani*. Udine, 1901–3.

Le antiche lapidi del Museo di Este. Padua, 1837.

Lechi, Fausto. *Le dimore bresciane in cinque secoli di storia. III. Il Cinquecento nella città*. Brescia, 1974.

Leicht, P.S. 'Martio Colloredo Governatore di Siena.' *Memorie storiche forogiuliesi* 3 (1907): 34–9.

Lloyd, Christopher. *Italian Paintings before 1600 in the Art Institute of Chicago: A Catalogue of the Collection*. Chicago, 1993.

Lorenzetti, Giulio. *Venice and Its Lagoon*, trans. John Guthrie. Trieste, 1994.

Lorenzi, Giambattista. *Monumenti per servire alla storia del Palazzo Ducale di Venezia... Dal 1253 al 1600*. Venice, 1868.

Lowe, Kate. 'Visible Lives: Black Gondoliers and Other Black Africans in Renaissance Venice.' *Renaissance Quarterly* 66:2 (2013): 412–45.

Lucchese, Enrico. 'Joseph Heintz il giovane autore della Pianta della città di Udine con aggiornamento su alcuni dipinti della Galleria d'Arte Antica e in regione.' *Udine Bollettino della Civiche Istituzioni Culturali*, ser. 3, 9 (2003–4), 43–58. Udine, 2005.

Lucco, Mauro. '"Ut dicitur Paridis Bordoni...", ovvero Viaggi in Provincia di un pittore veneziano', 173–92. In *Studi e ricerche in memoria di Laura Bentivoglio*, ed. Sergio Cluat, Feltre, 1985.

Luzio, Alessandro. 'Isabella d'Este e il sacco di Roma.' *Archivio storico Lombardo*, ser. 4, 10 (1908): 5–107.

Maffei, Sergio Pratali. *Ville venete: la Regione Friuli Venezia Giulia*. Venice, 2005.

Maglaque, Erin. *An Intimate Empire: Renaissance Venice and Its Mediterranean World*. Ithaca, 2018.

Magno, Alessandro Marzo. *Bound in Venice: The Serene Republic and the Dawn of the Book*. New York, 2013.

Malanima, Maria Rosa Pardi. 'Colloredo, Marzio.' In *DBI* 27 (1982). http://www.treccani.it/enciclopedia/marzio-colloredo_(Dizionario-Biografico).

Maltezou, Chryssa. 'The Historical and Social Context', 17–48. In *Literature and Society in Renaissance Crete*, ed. David Holton, Cambridge, 1991.

Maltezou, Chryssa. 'Byzantine "Consuetudines" in Venetian Crete.' *Dumbarton Oaks Papers* 49 (1995): 269–90.

Mancini, Matteo. *Tiziano e le corti d'Asburgo: nei documenti degli archivi spagnoli*. Venice, 1998.

Mandelli, Vittorio. 'Francesco Janis (Francesco da Tolmezzo).' *DBI* 62 (2004). http://www.treccani.it/enciclopedia/francesco-janis_(Dizionario-Biografico)/.

Maniago, Fabio di. *Storia delle Belle Arti friulane*. Udine, 1819.

Maniago, Fabio di. *Guida d'Udine in ciò che riguarda le tre belle arti sorelle*. San Vito al Tagliamento, 1839.

Manno, Antonio. 'Politica e architettura militare: le difese di Venezia (1557–1573).' *Studi veneziani* 11 (1986): 91–137.

Manno, Antonio. *I Mestieri di Venezia: Storia, arte e devozione delle corporazioni dal XIII al XVIII secolo*. Cittadella, 1995.

Manzano, Conte Francesco di. *Annali del Friuli: ovvero, Raccolta delle cose storiche appartenenti a questa regione*. Udine, 1879.

Marcotti, Giuseppe. *Il conte Lucio*. Milan, 1888.

Maretto, Paolo. *L'edilizia gotica veneziana*, 2nd ed. Venice, 1978.

Maretto, Paolo. *La casa veneziana nella storia della città dalle origini all'Ottocento*. Venice, 1986.

Marinelli, Sergio, and Angelo Mazza, eds. *Paolo Piazza. Pittore cappuccino nell'età della Controriforma tra conventi e corti d'Europa*. Verona, 2002.

Marson, Luigi. *Guida di Vittorio e suo distretto*. Vittorio Veneto, 2005.

Martin, Andrew John. 'La bottega in viaggio. Con Tiziano ad Augusta, Füssen e Innsbruck (1548): domande e ipotesi.' *Studi Tizianeschi* 4 (2006): 99–108.

Martin, A. Lynn. 'Fabio Mirto Frangipani and Papal Policy in France: The Case of an Independent-minded Nuncio.' *Archivum Historiae pontificiae* 17 (1979): 197–240.

Martignoni, Andrea. '"Requiescat in pace." Il destino dei morti tra fragile pace ed eterno riposo alla fine del Medioevo', 99–158. In *La pace fra realtà e utopia* (Quaderni di storia religiosa, XII). Verona, 2005.

Mayernik, David. *Timeless Cities: An Architect's Reflections on Renaissance Italy*. Boulder, CO, 2009.

Maylender, Michele. *Storia delle accademie d'Italia*, 5 vols. Bologna, 1926–30.

Mazza, Marta, ed. *Lungo le vie di Tiziano: i luoghi e le opere di tiziano, Francesco, Orazio e Marco Vecellio tra Vittorio Veneto e il Cadore*. Milan, 2007.

Mazzotti, Giuseppe. 'Itinerario Tizianesco da Venezia a Pieve di Cadore', 107–15. In *Titianus Cadorinus: celebrazioni in onore di Tiziano, Pieve di Cadore, 1576–1976, atti*, ed. Ugo Fasolo, and Michelangelo Muraro. Pieve di Cadore, 1982.

McClive, Cathy. 'The Hidden Truths of the Belly: The Uncertainties of Pregnancy in Early Modern Europe: Society for the Social History of Medicine Student Prize Essay 1999, Runner-up.' *Social History of Medicine* 15:2 (Aug. 2002): 209–27.

McKee, Sally. *Uncommon Dominion: Venetian Crete and the Myth of Ethnic Purity*. Philadelphia, 2000.

McKee, Sally. 'Domestic Slavery in Renaissance Italy.' *Slavery & Abolition* 29:3 (2008): 305–26.

Medioli, Francesca. 'To Take or Not to Take the Veil: Selected Italian Case Histories, the Renaissance and After', 122–37. In *Women in Italian Renaissance Culture and Society*, ed. Letizia Panizza. Oxford, 2000.

Megna, Laura. 'Comportamenti abitativi del patriziato veneziano (1582–1740).' *Studi Veneziani, n.s.*, 22 (1991): 253–323.

Meijer, Bert. 'Titian and the North', 498–557. In *Renaissance Venice and the North: Crosscurrents in the Time of Bellini, Dürer and Titian*, ed. Bernard Aikema and Beverly Louise Brown. Milan, 1999.

Messina, Francesco. 'Del Monte, Innocenzo.' *DBI*, 38 (1990). http://www.treccani.it/enciclopedia/innocenzo-del-monte_(Dizionario-Biografico).

Miller, William. *The Latins in the Levant, a history of Frankish Greece (1204–1566)*. London, 1908.

Miller, William. *Essays on the Latin Orient*. Amsterdam, 1964.

Miotti, Tito. *Castelli del Friuli: Gastaldie e giursdizioni del Friuli centrali*. Udine, 1977.

Molà, Luca. *The Silk Industry of Renaissance Venice*. Baltimore, 2000.

Molmenti, Pompeo. *I banditi della Repubblica Veneta*. 2nd ed., Florence, 1898.

Molmenti, Pompeo. *La storia di Venezia nella vita privata dalle origini alla caduta della repubblica*. 3 vols. Bergamo, 1905–8.

Monacelli, Susanna. 'Il doge Francesco Venier dal ritratto al sepolcro.' *Venezia Cinquecento*, 18, no. 36 (2008): 43–64.

Moncada, Valentina. 'The Painters' Guilds in the Cities of Venice and Padua.' *RES: Anthropology and Aesthetics* 15 (Spring, 1988): 105–21.

Monreal, Ruth, 'Eppur lo dice! Come si trasmette la sifilide nel poema didattico di Girolamo Fracastoro.' *Studi Umanistici Piceni* 23 (2003): 179–89.

Monumenta spectantia historiam slavorum meridionalium, VIII. Commissiones et relationes venetae, II. Zagreb, 1877.

Morelli di Schönfeld, Carlo. *Istoria della Contea di Gorizia*. 4 vols. Gorizia, 1855–6.

Mori, Elisabetta. 'La Malattia e la morte di Isabella Medici Orsini.' *Roma moderna e Contemporanea* 13 (2005): 77–97.

Moroni, Gaetano. *Dizionario di erudizione storico-ecclesiastica da S. Pietro sino ai nostri giorni*. 103 vols. Venice, 1840–61.

Morresi, Manuela. *Jacopo Sansovino*. Milan, 2000.

Moz, Adriano. 'Francesco Sansovino, A Polygraph in Cinquecento Venice: His Life and Works.' Ph.D. diss. University of North Carolina at Chapel Hill, 1985.

Mueller, Reinhold C. 'Greeks in Venice and "Venetians" in Greece: Notes on Citizenship and Immigration in the Late Middle Ages', 167–80. In *Ricchi e poveri nella società dell'Oriente Grecolatino*, ed. Chryssa Maltezou, Venice, 1998.

Mueller, Reinhold C. *The Venetian Money Market: Banks, Panics, and the Public Debt, 1200–1500*. Baltimore and London, 1997.

Muir, Edward. *Civic Ritual in Renaissance Venice*. Princeton, 1981.

Muir, Edward. *Mad Blood Stirring: Vendetta & Factions in Friuli during the Renaissance*. Baltimore, 1993.

Muir, Edward. 'The Double Binds of Manly Revenge in Renaissance Italy', 65–82. In *Gender Rhetorics: Postures of Dominance and Submission in History*, ed. Richard Trexler. Binghamton, NY, 1994.

Musacchio, Jacqueline Marie. *The Art and Ritual of Childbirth in Renaissance Italy*. New Haven and London, 1999.

Nalezyty, Susan. *Pietro Bembo and the Intellectual Pleasures of a Renaissance Writer and Art Collector*. New Haven and London, 2017.

Nagel, Alexander. *Michelangelo and the Reform of Art*. Cambridge, 2000.

Netto, Giovanni. *Guida di Treviso*. Trieste, 1988.

Norris, Rebecca. 'Women on the Edge: The "Saletta delle Dame" of the Palazzo Salvadego in Brescia', 115–34. In *The Music Room in Early Modern France and Italy: Sound, Space and Object*, ed. Deborah Howard and Laura Moretti. Oxford, 2012.

Occioni-Bonaffons, Giuseppe. 'Notizia dell'Archivio private del comm. Lodovico Della Torre Valsassina in Friuli.' *Archivio Storico Italiano*, ser. 3, 11:2 (1870): 260–1.

Occioni-Bonaffons, Giuseppe. 'Sei documenti tratti dall'archivio private del Conte della Torre Valsassina.' *Archeografo Triestino*, ser. 2, 5 (1877/8): 51–75.

Occioni-Bonaffons, Giuseppe. *Bibliografia storica friulana dal 1861 al 1885*. Udine, 1887.

O'Connell, Monique. *Men of Empire: Power and Negotiation in Venice's Maritime State*. Baltimore, 2009.

O'Connell, Monique, and Eric. R. Dursteler. *The Mediterranean World from the Fall of Rome to the Rise of Napoleon*. Baltimore, 2016.

Ohler, Norbert. *The Medieval Traveller*, trans. Caroline Hillier. Woodbridge, 1995.

O'Malley, John W. *Trent: What Happened at the Council*. Cambridge, MA, and London, 2013.

Oryshkevich, Irina. 'Accommodating Jews in the New Jerusalem: The Roman Ghetto in the Renaissance', 23–8. In *Present and Future Memory: Holocaust Studies at the Italian Academy 2008–2016*, ed. Barbara Faedda, New York, 2016.

Ossa, Juliana. 'Cassandra Fedele.' *Project Continua* (March 22, 2015): Vol. 1: http://www.projectcontinua.org/cassandra-fedele/.

'Notizie sul castello di Duino', *Pagine Friulane* 14:12 (27 July 1902), 197–9.

'Il Palazzo dei Torriani demolito nel 1717.' Pagine Friulane 5:5 (1892): 72–3.

Palladio degli Olivi, Giovanni Francesco. *Historie della Provincia del Friuli*. 2 vols. Udine, 1660.

Palmer, Richard. *The Studio of Venice and Its Graduates in the Sixteenth Century*. Padua-Trieste, 1983.

Papadaki, Aspasia. *Cerimonie religiose e laiche nell'isola di Creta durante il dominio veneziano*, trans. Giorgio Pelidis. Spoleto, 2005.

Park, Katharine. 'Managing Childbirth and Fertility in Medieval Europe', 153–66. In *Reproduction*, ed. Nick Hopwood, Rebecca Fleming, and Lauren Kassell. Cambridge, 2018.

Parry, Seth. 'Fifty Years of Failed Plans: Venice, Humanism, and the Turks.' Ph.D. diss., City University of New York, 2008.

Partner, Peter. *Renaissance Rome, 1500–1559*. Berkeley, 1976.

Paschini, Pio. *Il Cardinale Marino Grimani ed i prelati della sua famiglia*. Rome, 1960.

Paschini, Pio. 'Il mecenatismo artistico del Cardinal Marino Grimani', 79–88. In *Miscellanea in onore di Roberto Cessi*. Rome, 1958.

Pastor, Ludwig Freiherr von. *The History of the Popes from the Close of the Middle Ages*, 40 vols. London, 1891–1953.

Pattenden, Miles. *Pius IV and the Fall of the Carafa: Nepotism and Papal Authority in Counter-Reformation Rome*. Oxford, 2013.

Pepper, Simon. 'Defending the Frontiers of Venice: Fortification and Defensive Strategy in the Friuli before Palmanova', 3–28. In *L'architettura militare di Venezia in Terraferma e in Adriatico fra XVI e XVII secolo*, ed. Francesco Paolo Fiore. Florence, 2014.

Peressini, Andrea.'La palladiana villa Zeno a Cessalto centro amministrativo di un'azienda vitivinicola nelle terre dei dogi tra cinque-seicento', 168–93. In *Il vino nella storia di Venezia: Vigneti e cantine nelle terre dei dogi tra XIII e XXI secolo*, ed. Carlo Favero. Venice, 2014.

Piamonte, Giannina. *Venezia vista dall'acqua: Guida dei rii di Venezia e delle isole*. Venice, 1992.

Piana, Mario, and Wolfgang Wolters, eds. *Santa Maria dei Miracoli in Venice: History, Architecture and Restoration*. Venice, 2003.

Pianca, Vittorino. 'A Vittorio Veneto. Arte, storia, memoria.' *Il Flaminio: Rivista quadrimestrale di studi vittoriesi* 10 (1997): 5–14.

Pignatti, Terisio. 'Veronese and *The Coronation of Hebe* at the Gardner Museum.' *Fenway Court* (1986): 31–7.

Pignatti, Terisio, and Guido Pedrocco. *Veronese*. 2 vols. Milan, 1966.

Pillinini, Giovanni. 'Bembo, Pietro.' *DBI* 8 (1966). http://www.treccani.it/enciclopedia/pietro-bembo_(Dizionario-Biografico).

Pincus, Debra. *The Arco Foscari: The Building of a Triumphal Gateway in Fifteenth Century Venice*. New York, 1976.

Pinkerton, MD, J.H.M. 'Kergaradec Friend of Laennec and Pioneer of Foetal Auscultation.' *Proceedings of the Royal Society of Medicine* 62 (May 1969): 477–83.

Piutti, G. G. 'Il Conte Lucio.' *Pagine Friuliane* 5: 7 (18 Aug. 1892): 83–91.

Pirovano, Carlo, and Monica Minonzio. *I Della Torre. Dalla Contea di Valsassina alla Signoria di Milano*. Gorle (Bergamo), 2004.

Povolo, Claudio. 'Feud and Vendetta: Customs and Trial Rites in Medieval and Modern Europe. A Legal-Anthropolcgical Approach.' *Acta Histriae* 23, no. 2 (2015): 195–244.

Povolo, Claudio. 'Honour and "Virtù" in a Sixteenth Century Aristocratic Republic', 245–71. In *Andrea Palladio and the Architecture of Battle*, ed. Guido Beltramini. Venice, 2009.

Prampero de Carvalho, Marisanta di. *Giovanni da Udine, architetto e la sua attività udinese: un inventario del 1670 con le ricchezze dell'abbattuto palazzo Torriani di contrada Strazzamantello (ora piazza XX Settembre)*. Udine, 2005.

Prampero de Carvalho, Marisanta di. *Perchè Giovanni fu sepolto al Pantheon? Giovanni da Udine con Bramante e Raffaello*. Udine, 2003.

Preto, Paolo. *Peste e società a Venezia, 1576*. Vicenza, 1978.

Promis, C. 'Biografie di Ingegneri Militari italiani dal secolo XIV alla metà del XVIII.' *Miscellanea di Storia Italiana*, ser. 1, 14 (1874): 103–26.

Pullan, Brian. 'Wage-Earners and the Venetian Economy, 1550–1630.' *The Economic History Review*, n.s. 16:3 (1964): 407–26.

Pullan, Brian. *Rich and Poor in Renaissance Venice: The Social Institutions of a Catholic State, to 1620*. Cambridge, MA, 1971.

Puppi, Lionello. *Andrea Palladio: The Complete Works*. Milan, 1989.

Puppi, Lionello. *Per Tiziano*. Milan, 2004.

Quattrocchi, Ed. 'Pietro Bembo: A Renaissance Courtier Who Had His Cake and Ate It Too.' *Caxtonian: Journal of the Caxton Club of Chicago* 13:10 (Oct. 2005): 1–5, 10.

Radcliffe, Anthony. 'The Illness of the Professor/The Soul of the Professor in the Fortunate Woods', 373–4. In *The Genius of Venice: 1500–1600*, ed. Jane Martineau and Charles Hope. London and New York, 1984.

Ranieri, Paola. 'La Chiesa di San Sebastiano a Venezia: la rifondazione cinquecentesca e la capella di Marcantonio Grimani.' *Venezia Cinquecento* XII, No. 24 (2002): 5–139.

Ravid, Benjamin. 'The Venetian Government and the Jews', 3–30. In *The Jews of Early Modern Venice*, ed. Robert C. Davis and Benjamin Ravid. Baltimore and London, 2001.

Renier Michiel, Giustina. *Origine Delle Feste Veneziane*. 6 vols. Milan, 1829.

Richardson, Frank. *Andrea Schiavone*. Oxford, 1980.

Rigonat, Davide. 'Il Conte Lucio di Giuseppe Marcotti: un romanzo storico tra ipocisia e corruzione nel 1700.' In his *La Biblioteca Dimenticata: due anni di ricensioni sparse*, 2016.

Rizzi, Alberto. *Scultura Esterna a Venezia: Corpus delle Sculture Erratiche all'aperto di Venezia e della sua Laguna*. Venice, 1987.

Rizzi, Alberto. *Vere da Pozzo di Venezia—The Well-Heads of Venice*. Venice, 1981.

Rizzi, Aldo. 'Il palazzo Torriani nella città e nella storia', 85–113. In *Palazzo Torriani a Udine*, ed. Francesca Gentile. Milan, 1985.

Robertson, Clare. *'Il Gran Cardinale': Alessandro Farnese, Patron of the Arts*. New Haven and London, 1992.

Rogers, Mary, and Paola Tinagli. *Women in Italy, 1350–1650: Ideals and Realities. A Sourcebook*. Manchester and New York, 2005.

Romanello, Marina. 'Le spose del principe: una storia di donne.' In *La casa secolare delle zitelle in Udine: 1595–1995*. Milan, 1997.

Romano, Dennis. *Housecraft and Statecraft: Domestic Service in Renaissance Venice, 1400–1600*. Baltimore, 1966.

Romano, Dennis. *Patricians and Popolani: The Social Foundations of the Venetian Renaissance State*. Baltimore and London, 1987.

Romano, Dennis. 'Gender and the Urban Geography of Renaissance Venice.' *Journal of Social History* 23:2 (Winter 1989): 339–63.

Romano, Dennis. *The Likeness of Venice: A Life of Doge Francesco Foscari, 1373–1457*. New Haven and London, 2007.

Rosenthal, Margaret F., and Ann Rosalind Jones. *The Clothing of the Renaissance World: Europe, Asia, Africa, the Americas: Cesare Vecellio's Habiti Antichi et Moderni*. London, 2008.

Rosand, David. *Titian*. New York, 1978.

Rosand, David. *Myths of Venice: The Figuration of a State*. Chapel Hill & London, 2001.

Roskill, Mark. *Dolce's 'Aretino' and Venetian Art Theory of the Cinquecento*. New York, 1968.

Ross, Sarah Gwyneth. *The Birth of Feminism: Woman as Intellect in Renaissance Italy and England*. Cambridge, MA, 2009.

Runciman, Steven. *The Sicilian Vespers: A History of the Mediterranean World in the Later Thirteenth Century*. Cambridge, 2012.

Ryder, George H. 'Vagitus uterinus.' *American Journal of Obstetrics and Gynecology* 46:6 (Dec. 1943): 867–72.

Saccomani, Elisabetta. 'Le grottesche venete del '500.' *Atti dell'Istituto Veneto di scienze, lettere ed arti* 129 (1970–1): 293–343.

Sachs, Alice. 'Le nozze in Friuli nei secoli XVI e XVII.' *Memorie storiche forogiuliesi* 11 (1915): 73–138.

Sánchez, Magdalena S. '"I would not feel the pain if I were with you": Catalina Micaela and the Cycle of Pregnancy at the Court of Turin, 1585–1597.' *Social History of Medicine* 28:3 (2015): 445–64.

Sanfilippo, Matteo di. 'Della Torre, Michele.' *DBI* 37 (1989). http://www.treccani.it/enciclopedia/michele-della-torre_(Dizionario-Biografico).

Santarelli, Daniele. 'Paolo IV,' 1164–6. In *Dizionario storico dell'Inquisizione*, vol. 3, ed. Adriano Prosperi, with Vincenzo Lavenia and John Tedeschi. Pisa, 2010. https://edizioni.sns.it/it/testi-online/dizionario-storico-dell-inquisizione-332.html

Sardella, Pierre. *Nouvelles et speculations a Venise au debut du XVIe siècle*. Paris, 1948.

Sartori, Basilio. *A Ceneda con S. Tiziano vescovo e i suoi successori (712–2005)*. Vittorio Veneto, 2005.

Savini, Fabia. 'Antonio Savorgnan.' *Memorie storiche forogiuliesi* 27–9 (1931): 265–305.

I Savorgnan e la Patria del Friuli dal XIII al XVIII secolo (exhib. cat.). Udine, 1984.

Scarabello, Giovanni. *Carcerati e carceri a Venezia nell'età moderna*. Rome, 1979.

Schulz, Anne Markham. *Niccolò di Giovanni Fiorentino and Venetian Sculpture of the Early Renaissance*. New York, 1978.

Schulz, Juergen. 'The Houses of Titian, Aretino, and Sansovino.' In *Titian: His World and His Legacy*, ed. David Rosand, 73–118. New York, 1982.

Schulz, Juergen. *The New Palaces of Medieval Venice*. University Park, PA, 2004.

Scrinzi, Angelo. 'Un sarcofago arcaico antropoide della collezione Boldù.' *Atti del Reale Istituto Veneto di scienze, lettere ed arti* 59 (1899–1900): 505–17.

Secchi, Sandra. 'Bembo, Giovanni Matteo.' *DBI* 8 (1966). http://www.treccani.it/enciclopedia/giovanni-matteo-bembo_(Dizionario-Biografico).

Seitz, Jonathan. *Witchcraft and Inquisition in Early Modern Venice*. Cambridge and New York, 2011.

Selfridge-Field, Eleanor. *The Calendar of Venetian Opera: A New Chronology of Venetian Opera and Related Genres, 1660–1760*. Stanford, 2007.

Setton, Kenneth. *The Papacy and the Levant*. IV:1, *The Sixteenth Century to the Reign of Julius III*. Philadelphia, 1984.

Sexton, Kim. 'Political Portico: Exhibiting Self-Rule in Early Communal Italy.' *Art Bulletin* 97 (2015): 258-78.

Shearman, John. *The Early Italian Pictures in the Collection of Her Majesty the Queen*. Cambridge, 1983.

Simbula, Giulia. 'Cronaca di una morte dimenticata; intervento sull'opera "Tomba Di Alvise Della Torre," dipinto a tecnica mista su tavola del xvi° secolo.' Diploma accademico di II livello in restauro, Accademia di Belle Arti Aldo Galli, Como, Italy, 2019.

Sinding-Larsen, Staale. *Christ in the Council Hall: Studies in the Religious Iconography of the Venetian Republic*. Spoleto, 1974.

Smith, Constance I. 'Heraclitus and Fire.' *Journal of the History of Ideas* 27:1 (1966): 125–7.

Smith, Denis Mack. *Victor Emanuel, Cavour and the Risorgimento*. London and New York, 1971.

Spessot, Francesco. 'Il "Boia" al Castello di Gradisca: L'esecuzione capitale di tre "nobili" delinquenti (3 luglio 1723).' *Sot la nape* 3:4–5 (1951): 18–28.

Stahl, Alan. *Zecca: The Mint of Venice in the Middle Ages*. Baltimore, 2000.

Steriotou, Ioanna. 'The Venetian Walls of Chandax in the XVI–XVII Century.' *EN Bulletin* 56–7 (2003): 42–56.

Strataridaki, A., E. Chalkiadiakis, and N. Gigourtakis. 'The Historical Development of Water Supply to Iraklion, Crete, Greece from Antiquity to the Present', 471–2. In *Evolution of Water Supply Through the Millennia*, ed. A. Angelakis. London 2012.

Stratico, Giambattista, and Francesco Marcolini. *Delle principali febbri tifiche di Udine nel secolo XVI*. Venice, 1837.

Svalduz, Elena. 'Per il polittico di Castello Roganzuolo: la 'casa de messer Tician in Col de Manza', 48. In *Lungo le vie di Tiziano: i luoghi e le opere di tiziano, Francesco, Orazio e Marco Vecellio tra Vittorio Veneto e il Cadore*, ed. Marta Mazza. Milan, 2007.

Svalduz, Elena.'Il territorio veneto prima di Palladio: l'inedito diario di viaggio di Giovanni di San Foca (1536)', 129–36. In *Palladio 1508-2008 Il simposio del cinquecentenario*, ed. Franco Barbieri, Donata Battilotti, and Guido Beltramini. Venice, 2008.

Szépe, Helena Katalin. *Venice Illuminated: Power nd Painting in Renaissance Manuscripts*. New Haven and London, 2018.

Tagliaferri, Amelio. *Struttura e politica sociale in una comunità veneta del '500 (Udine)*. Milan, 1969.

Tampa, Mircea, et al. 'Brief History of Syphilis.' *Journal of Medicine and Life* 7:1 (2014): 4–10.

Tagliaferro, Giorgio. 'Madonna col Bambino in gloria e santi Andrea e Pietro', 54–60. In *Lungo le vie di Tiziano: i luoghi e le opere di tiziano, Francesco, Orazio e Marco Vecellio tra Vittorio Veneto e il Cadore*, ed. Marta Mazza. Milan, 2007.

Tamburlani, Francesca. 'Contributo per la storia dell'insediamento ebraico a Udine degli anni 1496–1556: le fonti della Biblioteca Civica "Vincenzo Joppi" e dell'Archivio Notarile Antico', 39–66. In *Gli Ebrei nella storia del Friuli Venezia Giulia: Una vicenda di lunga durata*, ed. Mariam Davide and Pietro Ioly Zorattini. Florence, 2016.

Tassini, Giuseppe. *Alcune delle piu clamorose condanne capitali eseguite in Venezia sotto la Repubblica: memorie patrie*. Venice, 1866.

Tassini, Giuseppe. *Alcuni palazzi ed antichi edificii di Venezia*. Venice, 1879.

Tassini, Giuseppe. *Curiosità veneziane*. Venice, 1915.

Tedesco, M.T. 'Andamento demografico della nobilita veneziana allo specchio delle votazioni nel Maggior Consiglio (1297–1797).' *Ateneo Veneto* 27 (1989): 119–64.

Tempesta, Tiziano. 'Veneto', 279–98. In *Italian Historical Rural Landscapes*, ed. M. Agnoletti. Dordrecht, 2013.

Tentori, Francesco. *Udine*. Rome-Bari, 1988.

Thiriet, Freddy. *La Romanie Vénitienne au Moyen Age. Le développement et l' exploitation du domaine colonial vénitien (XIIe—XVe siècles)*. Paris, 1959.

Thode, Henry. *Frangipane's Ring: An Event in the Life of Henry Thode*, trans. J. F. C. L. London, 1900.

Tockner, K. 'The Tagliamento River: A Model Ecosystem of European Importance.' *Aquatic Sciences* 65 (2003): 239–53.

Toffolo, Francesca. *Art and the Conventual Life in Renaissance Venice: the Monastery Church of Santa Caterina de' Sacchi*. Ph.D. diss., Princeton University, 2005.

Tognotti, Eugenia. *L'altra faccia di Venere: La sifilide dalla prima età moderna all'avvento dell'Aids (XV–XX sec.)*. Milan, 2006.

Tomasi, Giovanni. *La Diocesi di Ceneda. Chiese e uomini dalle origini al 1586*. 2 vols. Vittorio Veneto, 1998.

Tomasi, Giovanni e Silvia. 'Gli artigiani dei metalli', 13–106. In *Economia e Commerci nelle Prealpi Venete (sec. XIII - sec. XX) vol. 2--Convegno Nazionale 24 maggio 2014*, ed. Centro vittoriese di ricerche storiche. Vittorio Veneto, 2014.

Tomasi, Giovanni and Silvia. 'Gli artigiani della pietra e dell'argilla', 9–86. In *Economia e Commerci nelle Prealpi Venete (sec. XIII – sec. XX) vol. 2 – Convegno Nazionale 15 aprile 2018*, ed. Centro vittoriese di ricerche storiche. Vittorio Veneto, 2018.

Tondro, Maximilian. 'Memory and Tradition: The Ephemeral Architecture for the Triumphal Entries of the Dogaresse of Venice in 1557 and 1597.' Ph.D, diss., 2 vols University of Cambridge, 2001.

Tramontin, Silvio. 'Il Vescovo Michele Della Torre e il Concilio di Trento.' *Archivio Veneto* 30:6 (1990): 9–46.

Trebbi, Giuseppe. *Il Friuli dal 1420 al 1797. La storia politica e sociale*. Udine, 1998.

Truant, Giuseppe. *Pomponio Amalteo e le sue opere*. Pordenone, 1980.

Tzobanaki, Chrysoula. *Marine Trilogy of Khandax: The Ports, the Shipyards, the Fortress on the Sea (Koules)*. 3rd ed. Heraklion, 1998.

Ulmer, Christoph. *Castelli friulani: storia e civiltà*. Udine, 1997.

Valcanover, Francesco et al. *Pittura murale esterna nel Veneto: Venezia e provincia*. Venice and Bassano del Grappa, 1991.

Valentinelli, Giuseppe. *Bibliografia del Friuli*. Venice, 1861.

Vanin, Barbara, and Paolo Eleuteri. *Le mariegole della Biblioteca del Museo Correr*. Venice, 2007.

Vanni, Andrea. *Fare diligente inquisitione—Gian Pietro Carafa e le origini dei chierici regolari teatini*. Rome, 2010.

Veronese, Giuliano. 'Signori e sudditi nelle terre feudali della repubblica veneta nel '500' *Acta Histriae* 7 (1998): 153–67.

Veronese, Giuliano. 'Violenza e banditismo nobiliari in Friuli tra Seicento e Settecento: il conte Lucio Della Torre.' *Ce fastu? Rivista della Società filologica friulana*, 71 (1995): 201–21.

Vianello, Savina, ed. *Le Chiese di Venezia*. Venice, 1993.

Vidali, Andrew. 'Il patriziato tra vendetta, ritualità processuale e amministrazione della giustizia. Venezia, inizio XVI.' *Acta Histriae* 24 (2016): 43–62.

Vimercati, Antonella, et al. 'Two Cases of Complete Hydatidiform Mole and Coexistent Live Fetus.' *Journal of Prenatal Medicine* 7.1 (2013): 1–4.

Vincent, Alfred L. 'Money and Coinage in Venetian Crete, c. 1400–1669: An Introduction.' *Thesaurismata* 37 (2007): 267–326.

Virgilio, Gianni. *Andar per castelli: itinerari in Friuli Venezia Giulia. I castelli del mare e delle acque/2*. Udine, 2003.

Viroli, Maurizio. *From Politics to Reason of State: The Acquisition and Transformation of the Language of Politics 1250–1600*. Cambridge, 1992.

Wyatt, Michael. 'Renaissances', 1–16. In *The Cambridge Companion to the Italian Renaissance*, ed. Michael Wyatt. Cambridge, 2014.

Virgilio, Gianni. *Andar per castelli: itinerari in Friuli Venezia Giulia. I castelli del mare e delle acque/2*. Udine, 2003.

Visceglia, Maria Antonietta. 'The Pope's Household and Court in the Early Modern Age', 239–64. In *Royal Courts in Dynastic States and Empires: A Global Perspective*, ed. Jeroen Duindam, et al. Leiden and Boston, 2011.

Vollo, Benedetto. *I Savorgnani*. Venice, 1856.

Von Einem, Herbert. *Michelangelo. Translated by* Ronald Taylor. London, 1959.

Von Ranke, Leopold. *The History of the Popes During the Last Four Centuries*. 3 vols. London, 1913.

Walker, Jonathan. '*Bravi* and Venetian Nobles.' *Studi veneziani* 36 (1998): 85–114.

Werner, Monika. L'immagine di Bona Sforza nella letteratura italiana del Cinquecento', 168–93. In *Bona Sforza donna del Rinascimento tra Italia e Polonia*, ed. Gerardo Cioffari. Bari, 2000.
Wethey, Harold E. *The Paintings of Titian. Complete Edition. I. The Religious Paintings*. London, 1969 [=Wethey, Titian, I].
Wethey, Harold E. *The Paintings of Titian. Complete Edition. II. The Portraits*. London, 1971 [=Wethey, Titian, II].
Wethey, Harold E. *The Paintings of Titian. Complete Edition. III. The Mythological & Historical Paintings*. London, 1975 [=Wethey, Titian, III].
Williams, Edgerton Ryerson. *Plain-Towns of Italy: The Cities of Old Venetia*. Boston and New York, 1911.
Wolters, Wolfgang. *La scultura veneziana gotica (1300–1460)*. Venice, 1976.
Wolters, Wolfgang. *Storia e politica nei dipinti di Palazzo Ducale*. Venice, 1987.
Wyatt, Michael. 'Renaissances', 1–16. In *The Cambridge Companion to the Italian Renaissance*, ed. Michael Wyatt. Cambridge, 2014.
Yotopoulou-Sicilianou, Elly. 'The Turks in Corfu. The Effects of the Turkish Sieges on the Town's Form', 49–57. In *Corfù: Storia, spazio urbano e architettura XIV–XIX sec*, ed. Ennio Concina and Aliki Nikiforou-Testone. Venice, 1994.
Zagonel, Giampaolo. 'Palazzo Sarcinelli a Serravalle', 51–4. In *Lungo le vie di Tiziano: I luoghi e le opera di Tiziano, Francesco, Orazio e Marco Vecellio tra Vittorio Veneto e il Cadore*, ed. Marta Mazza. Milan, 2007.
Zagonel, Giampaolo. 'Il passaggio per il Veneto (con sosta a Conegliano) della Regina Bona di Polonia nel 1556', 63–72. In *Feste, giochi e musica tra Piave e Livenza (sec. XIV–sec. XX), Convegno Nazionale 21 maggio 2016*. Vittorio Veneto, 2016.
Zamperetti, Sergio. *I piccoli principi: Signorie locali, feudi e comunità soggette nello Stato regionale veneto dall'espansione territoriale ai primi decenni del '600*. Venice, 1991.
Zanotto, Francesco. *Il Palazzo ducale di Venezia*. 4 vols. Venice, 1853–61.
Zannini, Andrea. 'L'impiego pubblico', 415–63. In *Storia di Venezia. IV. Il Rinascimento. Politica e cultura*, ed. Alberto Tenenti and Ugo Tucci. Rome, 1995.
Zendrini, Bernardino. *Memorie Storiche dello stato antico e moderno delle lagune di Venezia*. 2 vols. Padua, 1811.
Zorzi, Alvise. *Venezia scomparsa*. Milan, 1984.
Zorzi, Elda. 'Il soggiorno padovano di due regine di Polonia (sec. XVI e sec. XVII).' *Padova e la sua provincia*, n.s., 8:4 (1962): 22–34.
Zucchiatti,Valter. *Castello di Villalta*. Udine, 2003.
Zucchiatti, Valter. 'Cenni storici sulla costruzione del Castello di Villalta.' In *Castelli del Friuli-Venezia Giulia: studi e ricerchi*, no. 8, 7–36. Udine, 1989.
Zucchiatti, Valter. 'A proposito della datazione del disegno quattrocentesco del castello di Villalta.' *Memorie Storiche Forogiulesi* 64 (1984): 65–8.

Index

Note: luogotenente refers to the Venetian Luogotenente della Patria del Friuli

Figures are indicated by an italic "*f*", respectively, following the page number.

For the benefit of digital users, indexed terms that span two pages (e.g., 52–53) may, on occasion, appear on only one of those pages.

Abano Terme 127, 203
Accademia degli Uniti 164–6
  Dodici Nobili 166, 181–2
  Mariegola 165–6, 165*f*, 166*f*
Accademia della Fama 285
Adige, river 71, 275n.11
Adrian VI, pope 11–12, 55
Adriatic Sea 4–5, 48, 139–40, 155–6, 159n.16, 183–4, 188
Aegean Sea 137
Agnadello 26
Alexander VI, pope 4
Alexandria 97, 138, 143–4, 169–70, 195
Algiers 137, 170
Aliprando, Giacomo 59–60
Alps 20–1, 43, 48, 52, 58, 70, 92, 201–2, 229–30
Alviano, Bartolomeo d', condottiere 26
Amadi, Giovanni 68
Amalteo, Pomponio, painter 92
Amaseo, Leonardo, diarist 27–30
  Gregorio, diarist 30–44, 49–50, 53, 55–9, 61, 72
andar a cappello 197–8
angaria 80, 172
antiquities 171–2, 174–5, 211, 233, 285–6
Antonini, family 256
  Alessandro 236–7
  Floriano 236–7
  Prospero 236–7
  Sofonisba 329–32
Antonio, Giacomo, Bishop of Cremona 53–4
Arrigoni, Claudia 335–6
Arte de Depentori 189
Aquileia 51–2, 58–60, 227, 236
Aquileia, Patriarch of 20–1, 53–4, 69, 88, 156, 251–2, 357
Arbel, Benjamin 140–1
Arcano, family 256
  castle of 39–40
  Troiano d' 235–7, 255–6
Archinto, Filippo, papal nuncio 200
archontes 147–8
Arcoloniani family 37
Ariis, Savorgnan castle 192
Arlato, Girolamo 34
Arnaldi, family 116, 243
  Andrea 116
  Cinzia di Andrea (natural) 116
  Dorothea, wife of Andrea 116
  Elena, mother of Andrea 116
  Febo (Deifebo) di Andrea (natural) 116, 238
Arnosti, Simeone, citizen of Ceneda 292–3
Arrigoni, family 256
  Claudia 335–6
Assisi 79
Attimis, Giacomo d', capitano of Gradisca 310–11
Auditori vecchi 234
Augsburg 91, 93–4
Augustino, Pietro, notary 178
Avogadori 211
Avogaria di Comun 234, 255, 260–1
Azzolino, Decio, cardinal 296–8

Balkans 195
banditi 102, 209–11, *see also* banishment
banishment 22, 44, 51–3, 95–7, 102–3, 128–9, 155, 163, 168, 180, 192, 209–11, 214–15, 227, 236–7, 252–3, 331, 335–6, 339, 342, 344–5
banquets 32, 57–8, 62, 119–20, 123, 164–5, 203, 207, 213, 229, 230*f*, 270, 272, 332
baptisms 74–5, 80, 149–52, 156, 158, 179, 183, 192–4, 208–9, 214, 224, 241
Barbarigo, Vittore, luogotenente 82
Barbarossa, Frederick, emperor 260
Barbarossa, Hayreddin, Ottoman admiral 115–16, 118–19, 137, 223, 234–5
Barbo, Gian Francesco, podestà and capitano 103
Barcelona 72–3

Bari (Puglia) 138, 201, 207–8
Barozzi, Francesco 175
Baselga di Piné (Trentino) 245n.3
Bassi, Valentin 317
Becaris, Costanza de', wife of Giovanni da Udine 74
Beccadelli, Ludovico, cardinal 128–32, 176–7, 182
Belgrado, Raffaele 292
Belegno, Alvise 302
  Bernardino 12, 14, 120, 122–3, 261
  Vincenzo 12
Belli, Onorio 175
  Valerio (medalist), medal of Pietro Bembo 6*f*
Bellini, Gentile 259–60, 274
  Giovanni 152, 259–60, 274
  Jacopo 274
Bellobuono, physician 261
Belloni, Antonio, Udinese notary 55, 76–7, 81–2
Bembo, family 115, 353
  Alvise (d. 1501), father of Gian Matteo Bembo 17n.24, 134n.31
  Alvise di Gian Matteo (1523–1570), sopracomito 11, 177–9, 205, 233–4, 262, 264–6
    lawsuit of 178–9, 233–4
    marriages of 177–8, 205, 246n.39, 260–2
    as sopracomito 178–9, 261
  Antonia di Bernardo (d. 1521/22) 3–8, 10–11, 15
  Augusta di Gian Matteo (1521–1562) 11, 122–3, 196, 238–40, 360–1
    marriage of 116–18, 260–1
    death of 240, 243
  Bernardo di Alvise 13, 17n.24
  Bernardo Andrea di Gian Matteo 133n.9
  Bernardo di Nicolò (1433–1519), humanist diplomat 3–5, 8, 10
  Bartolommeo di Bernardo (natural) 4–5
  Carlo di Bernardo 4–5, 7
  Davide di Alvise 13, 17n.24, 125
  Davide di Gian Matteo (1530–1611) 11, 17n.24, 136–7, 178–9, 233–4, 260–2, 264–5
  Elena di Pietro 15
  Ettor di Gian Matteo (natural son) 265
  Gian Matteo di Alvise (1490–1570) 8–10, 207, 211–13, 222, 230
    Accademia degli Uniti 163–6
    antiquarian interests of 174–5, 211, 233
    audit of accounts of 197–8
    death of 264
    decima of 262
    health of 261, 263–4
    and Francesco Sansovino 234–5, 243–4, 260, 355
    and Girolamo Della Torre 113, 117–23, 125–7, 163, 229–30, 267, 314, 346, 356–7
    marriage of 8–10
    marriages of children 113, 116–17, 119–23, 260–1
    offices and career of 115–16, 125, 197–8, 211, 235, 262
      Brescia, capitano of 232–3
      ducal councillor 258–9, 262
      Candia, capitano grande (generale) of 169–77, 183–4, 197–8
      Candia, Duke of, elected 261
      Capodistria, podestà and capitano of 136, 211
      Cattaro, rettore and provveditore of 115–16, 118–19, 137, 171–2, 198, 211, 234–5, 355
      Famagusta, capitano of 125, 136–7, 171–2, 174–5, 211
      Padua, elected podestà of 263
      Verona, podestà of 115–16, 125, 197, 211, 235
      Zara, Count of 118, 136, 235
    and Pietro Bembo 8–14, 114–15, 117, 120, 125, 136–7, 198, 234–5, 261–2
    and the poor 166–7, 172–3, 265
      see also Accademia degli Uniti
    portraits of, in Palazzo Ducale 259–60, 272, 274
    properties of 265–6
      see also Venice, Ca' Bembo; Villa Bembo-Boldù
    testament of 264–6
    tomb of 125, 264
    water projects of 173–5, 174*f*, 261
      see also Accademia degli Uniti; Marcello, Marcella di Sebastiano
  Giulia di Gian Matteo (1531–1562) 14, 136–7, 158, 184, 192–3, 196, 214–15, 229, 347–8
    appearance of 113–14, 121–2, 356
    births of children 149–50, 156–8, 179–80, 183, 192–4, 208–9, 213–14, 239–40, 356–8, 360–1
    childhood and adolescence of 136–7, 355–6
    Candia, life in 147, 149–53, 156–8, 171, 179–80, 183–4
    Candia, voyage to 132, 358–9
    Ceneda, life in 222–6, 238–41, 359–62
    character of 355–9
    charity of 359, 361

death of 237–40, 360–2
dowry of 119, 183
domestic activities of 223, 229–31, 237, 358–9
Friuli, life in 237–8, 359–61
funeral of 241–2, 362
marriage of 113–16, 260–1, 356–7
piety of 179–80, 237–40, 347–8, 358–62
pregnancies of 125–6, 132, 141–2, 149, 179–80, 192, 207, 213, 223, 237–8, 360–1
surrogate portrait of 114
wedding 119–23
see also Della Torre, Girolamo di Alvise
Isabetta (or Lucietta) di Gaspare, wife of Marco Antonio 234, 265
Lorenzo (Quintilio Lorenzo) di Gian Matteo (1520–1570), sopracomito 10–11, 130–1, 136–7, 183, 229–30, 233, 260–2
Famagusta, capitano of 262
Paphos, capitano of 234*f*, 262
children of 263–4, 266
death of 264
marriage of 117
Cyprus, provveditore generale of 262, 263*f*
testament of 263–4
Lorenzo (1637–1703) 353
Lucilio di Pietro (1523–1532) 11–13
Maddalena, wife of Girolamo Savorgnan del Monte 22–3
Marcella di Lorenzo 263–4
Marina di Alvise 13
Marco Antonio di Gian Matteo (1524–1576) 11, 136–7, 234, 260–2, 264–6, 274
Pellegrina di Lorenzo 353
Pietro di Bernardo (1470–1547), cardinal 3–7, 56, 114–15, 118–19, 198–9, 234–5, 285
portrait medal of 6*f*
History of Venice 44
Pietro di Gian Matteo, bishop of Veglia 136–7, 261, 264, 266–7
Paolo di Gian Matteo 133n.9
Raimondo 22–3
Sebastiano di Gian Matteo (1528–1564) 11, 136–7, 234, 260–1
Torquato di Pietro (1525–1595) 11–13
Ursina di Francesco 282, 316–17, 324–5
Benandanti 157–8
Benedetti, Rocco, notary 272–4
benefices 6, 11–12, 73, 300
Bernardino da Venezia, sculptor 224*f*, 245n.3
Berti, Domenico, Cenedese priest 299, 301
Bianchino, Zuanne 35–6
Bibbiena, Bernardo, Cardinal 8
Bidernuccio (Bidernutio), Alfonso, dottore 130–1
blood feud 96, 98, 101, 146, 167, 235–6, 243, 254–7, 294–5, 335–6
see also Peace of 1568; vendetta
bloodline 4, 10, 13–14, 57, 151–2, 192, 213, 244, 260–1, 265, 320, 330, 344–7
see also lineage
Boccastorta, Andrea 34
Bodenham, Roger 155
Boldù, Roberto 353
Bollani, Domenico, luogotenente, bishop of Brescia 200–2, 204, 291–2
see also Udine, Arco Bollani
Bonlini, Francesco, Venetian capitano of Pordenone 345–6
Bombardieri, Pietro, notary of Pordenone 345–6
Bologna 11–12, 70, 72–3, 76–7
University of 59–60
see also Peace of Bologna
Bonfio, Reverend Deacon 149, 156, 179
Bono, Carlo 145
Bordone, Paris, attrib., *Count Girolamo Della Torre* 89*f*
Bonifacio di San Bonifacio of Verona, condottiere 68
Borgia, Cesare, cardinal 4
Lucrezia 6
Borgo, Teodoro del, condottiere 36
Borromeo, Carlo, cardinal 261, 322–3
Boschetti, Teresa 348
Bosdogan Cadì 164
bounties 43–4, 51–3, 102, 180, 339, 342
Boza, Sebastian 183
Bragadin, Marcantonio 268–9
Bratteolo, Giuseppe, poet 312, 325
bravi 30–1, 167, 168*f*, 335–41
Bravo, Sebastiano, jurist 130–1, 254
Brazzaco, castle of 37, 39–40
family 19–20, 73
Giacoma (d. 1551), wife of Nicolò I Della Torre 37, 77, 130–1, 163–4, 229, 279
Brenta, river and canal 11–12, 94–5, 117, 118*f*, 205, 212, 233, 266, 272, 353
brides xxi, 7–8, 12–15, 24–5, 52, 121, 122*f*, 128*f*
Brescia 62, 146–7, 181–2, 232–3, 235, 254, 291–2
Piazza del Foro 233
Saletta delle Dame 146–7
Breydenbach, Bernhard von, *Peregrinationes in Terram Sanctam* 144*f*

Brugnera, castle of 38–9
Bruni, Leonardo, *La historia universal de suoi tempi* 235, 243–4
Bruno, Giuditta, wife of Teseo Colloredo 38
Bugatto, Andrea 254
Bucintoro 205–7, 212–13

Caimo, Camillo 308
  Giacomo 314
  Giovanni Battista 308
Calergi (Kallergis) family 147–8, 177–8
  Andrea 177–8
  Caterina 177–8
  Matteo 179
Callegarini, Antonio, Venetian notary 308, 317
Callegaris, Alvise 315, 317, 318n.7
Caligari, Giovanni, bishop of Bertinoro and papal nuncio 302
Calimano Ebreo, moneylender 96–7. *See also* Jews
Calvinism 257
Campagnaro, Alvise, *see* Noal, Alvise da
Canal family 24–5
Candia (Crete) 143, 144*f*, 171*f*
  aqueduct 174
  arsenals (shipyards) 144, 171*f*, 173, 197
  Bembo fountain 173–5, 174*f*
  book burning 177
  bull-baiting 176
  Ca' Querini 146–7, 153
  carnival 176
  casali (rural villages) 153–4, 177–8, 255
  Cazamba 173–4
  Cortina Bembo 171*f*, 172
  ducal palace 145, 171, 171*f*, 176–7
  earthquake 145
  Greater Council 177
  Greek and Latin relationships 149–53
  Greek Orthodox church 148, 150–1, 176
  harbour 143–4, 173
  Ierapetra (Gerapetra), castello of 175
  Kairatos, river 173–4
  Knossos 173–4
  Martinengo bastion 146–7
  nobility 147–9
  pageantry 152–3, 170, 176
  palace of the capitano 171
  peasantry 154, 157–8, 172–3
  port 173
  Porta del Molo 152–3
  Rocca al Mare 143, 173
  Ruga Maistra 145, 147, 152–3
  Sabbionara Bastion 172, 197
  San Francesco 151–2
  social and political hierarchy 147–8
  San Marco, ducal church 152–3, 177
  St Mary of the Angels, Orthodox cathedral 150–1
  St Titus, Catholic cathedral 150–1, 156
  San Giovanni 176
  San Pietro 176
  San Salvatore 174–6
  Standia, island of 173
  Venetian reggimento 145, 147–8, 197, 233–4
  villani 172–3
  walls and fortifications 144–5, 171–3, 184
  women in 153
  see also Candia, Jews in
Candida, Aloisa, wife of Giacomo da Spilimbergo 38
Candido, Emilio, diarist 204, 227–8
  Francesco 30–1, 53
  Zuan Battista 32
Canea (Chania) 143
Capodistria 115–16, 136, 211, 255
Caporiacco, castle of 39–40
  family 84n.36, 256, 353
  Ettore 256
  Giovanni Giacomo 53
  Girolamo 167
  Mainardus 53
  Sergio and Maria Gelmi di 353
Capello, Febo, secretary 103
  Zuan 275n.26
Capodagli, Giovanni Giuseppe, historian 294
Cappello, Francesco, provveditore 27–8
  Giovanni, cavaliere 202–3
  Vincenzo, admiral 137
Caprarola 79
Carafa, Antonio, cardinal 297
  Carlo 200
  Gian Pietro, cardinal 176–7, 198–9
    see also Paul IV, pope
  Giovanni 219n.46
Cargnacco, fief 229–30, 307, 315, 335–6, 347–8
Carlo Emanuele I, Duke of Savoy 150
Carnia 285–6
cardinals 4, 123–5, 176–7, 198–9, 260, 290, 297, 347–8
Carducci, Bartolomeo, *Posthumous Portrait of Cardinal Michele Della Torre* 291*f*
carnival 5–6, 19, 30–7, 62, 81, 94–5, 176, 279, 338, 341–2
  balls 32, 38, 176, 341–2
Carpaccio, *Departure of the Betrothed Pair* 139*f*
Carpi, Marco da 167

castellans 19–20, 23–6, 28–32, 34, 40, 43–4, 53, 57–8, 66–8, 71, 80–1, 94–5, 200–1, 236–7, 252–4, 329
Castello, Jacomo de 28, 31
Castello, Prospero di 235–6
Castelnovo, fief 68–9
Castelfranco Veneto 234
Catalina Micaela of Spain 150
Cattaro 115–16, 118–19, 137, 171–2, 195, 198, 211, 234–5, 355
caul 157–8, 195, 325–6
cavalieri aureati (counts palatine) 71–3
Cefalonia 143, 288n.3
Cellini, Benvenuto 74
Ceneda 87–90, 222, 268, 307
  aqueduct 223
  bishopric of 87–90, 131
  Calle Maggiore 92
  Castello di San Martino 87–8, 87*f*, 90, 92, 214–15, 222–3, 225*f*, 241, 255, 268–9, 298, 306n.50
  citizen council 251–2, 268–9, 296
    Oration praising the Della Torre 290
  Colle San Paolo 92
  municipal fountain 223, 224*f*
  municipal loggia 87–8, 88*f*, 90, 92, 269
  ecclesiastical authority 87–90
  relationship with Venice 87–90, 251–2
  San Tiziano, cathedral 87–8, 92, 241–2, 268, 294, 296
  Via Brevia 87–8, 223, 238, 241, 291–2
Cenedese 92, 97–8
ceremonies 57–9, 72, 152–3, 176, 201, 212, 272
  see also processions
Cergneu, Francesco de 31–2
  Giambattista di Francesco 32–4, 41, 44
Cergnocco, castle of 39–40
Cesare da Roma 98, 102
Charles II (1540–1590), archduke of Austria 216, 280–2, 323–4
Charles V (1500–1558), emperor 57, 60, 73, 91, 208, 215–16, 231, 253
  armies of 57, 60, 70–2
  coronation of 70
  patronage of Titian by 91–2, 94
  triumphal progress of 70–3, 201–2
  see also Hapsburgs
Charles VI (1685–1740), emperor 342–5
  see also Hapsburgs
Charles VIII (1470–1498), king of France 23
Charles IX (1550–1574), king of France 258, 272
childbirth 10–11, 14, 39, 48, 56–7, 80, 116–17, 146–7, 149–50, 156–8, 179–80 183, 191–4, 193*f*, 208–9, 213–14, 224–5, 238–40, 239*f*, 282–3, 329–30, 334–5, 356–8, 360–1
Chios 155
Chiusa (Veneto) 71
Ciconis, Zanut da 316–17
Cisternin, Alberto, de Spilimbergo 80–1
Cividale 21, 307–8, 344–5, 352n.94
Clement VII, pope 60–1, 66, 74
Clement VIII, pope 322
coats of arms 50*f*, 90, 103–4, 147, 150–1, 166*f*, 173, 174*f*, 184, 223, 224*f*, 228, 231, 263*f*, 269, 287, 294, 296, 322–3, 326–7, 332–3, 344, 344*f*, 346–7
Codroipo 29–30, 169, 315–16, 335
Col di Manza 92, 222
Collalto, family 19–20, 24, 97–8
  Claudia di 288n.2
  Marc'Antonio, count 59–60
Collateral General 68
Collegio 16n.10, 259–60, 294, 298
  and Apollonia Lang 126–7
  appearances before 5, 10, 23–4, 26, 29–30, 41–2, 59, 128–9, 182
  and Bona Sforza 203, 207–8
  reports to 27–8, 76
  see also Venice, Palazzo Ducale, Sala del Collegio
Collegio alla Milizia da Mar 260–1
Colleoni, Bartolomeo 230*f*
Colloredo, family 27–8, 43, 73, 167, 226–7, 256
  Agostino, priest 43, 53
  Alessandro di Mario 236–7, 256
  Andriana di Giambattista (1526–1561) 57, 80, 224
  Antonio 37–8
  Bernardo 130–1, 153–4
  Brunoro di Francisco 256
  Camillo di Giambattista (1539–1610) 82–3, 224, 254, 256
  Carlo di Giambattista (1532–1574), deacon 224, 254, 256
  Claudio, canon 78, 83, 169, 236–7
  Curzio di Giambattista (1531–1612) 57, 224, 231–2, 254, 256, 285–6
  Eleonora di Girolamo 331, 335
  Fabio 256
  Federico (d. 1511) 36
  Federico IV di Mario 167–8, 215–16, 256, 294–5, 321
  Francesco di Tommaso (1535–1579) 226–7, 256
  Fulvia di Giambattista (1529–aft 1567) 57
  Giambattista (ca 1480–1549) 48, 58, 80–1, 83, 94, 96–8, 130, 295, 342

Colloredo, family (*cont.*)
and the blood feud 52–3, 55–6, 81, 83, 94
marriage to Ginevra Della Torre 57, 96–7, 224–5
military career 48, 231–2
murder of 98, 105*f*, 130, 163
petitions to Council of Ten 80, 82–3, 97
Giambattista (1654–1729), imperial ambassador 342
Giovanni di Iseppo 167
Giovanni di Tommaso 226
Girolamo di Giambattista (1527–1557) 57, 82–3, 94, 106–7, 224
banishment 95–8, 216
at the court of Elizabeth I 216
and the blood feud 94–6
Girolamo di Albertino 43, 55
Girolamo di Federico 55, 64n.32
Giulio di Francesco 226–7, 256
Gregorio 43
Iseppo di Brunoro 226
Lelio 235–6, 256
Lodovico di Mario 235–6, 294–5, 321, 324–5
Livio di Mario 236–7, 294–5
Mario 256
Marzio di Giambattista (1530–1591) 57, 82–3, 215–16, 256, 294–5
banishment of 168, 214–15, 310–11
and bishopric of Ceneda 298, 300–1
and blood feuds 98, 167–9, 180, 224–7, 252–7
military career of 254, 320
and the pamphlet war 254–6
Nicolò di Albertino 53, 55
Orazio 236–7
Pinosa, mother of Teseo 37–8
Pompeo 106–7, 167, 215, 256
Sertorio di Giambattista (1525–1548) 57, 82–3, 224
Silla di Mario 256
Teseo di Albertino (d. 1511) 30–2, 35, 37–8
Vicardo di Girolamo 256
Colloredo di Monte Albano, Castello di 37, 57, 58*f*, 224–5
Studiolo, frescoes 231–2, 232*f*
Cologna Veneta 4
Colombatto, Francesco 35–6
Colonna, Giulia Gonzaga 114
Compiègne, France 102–3
Concina, Daniele, Count 346
conclave 124, 198–9, 296
concubines 11–12, 268
Conegliano 71, 92, 202–3, 222, 294, 307–8
Conservatori delle Leggi 266
Constantinople 137, 142–4, 155, 203
Latin Patriarch of 97, 128, 153–4, 183
Contarini, Antonio, patriarch 6–8, 41–2
Carlo, Venetian orator 57–8
Francesco 145
Giambattista, luogotenente 226, 228
Giorgio 285–6
Marcantonio, Venetian ambassador 70–1
Ottaviano 276n.49
convents 7–10, 14–15, 79–80, 136–7, 194, 196, 255, 262, 343
Cordignano 304–5
Corfù 4–5, 140, 142–7, 170, 183–4, 277n.63, 334
Cornaro, Alvise 244
Benedetto 177–8
Caterina, Queen of Cyprus 138, 323*f*
Pietro 178
Corner, family 159n.31
Giacomo 52–3
Marin 101
Cornetto, Sebastiano, piper 36–7
corsairs 132, 136–7, 142–5, 155, 169–70, 184, 358–9
Cort, Cornelis, *Birth of the Virgin* 239*f*
Costa, Giovanni Francesco, *Course of the River Brenta* 118*f*
Council of Ten 27–8, 56, 61, 80, 131, 142, 180, 207–10, 259, 266–7, 335–6, 342
and appeals and petitions 68–9, 78–9, 96–100, 128–9, 180–3, 190–1, 216–17, 227–8, 295
and banishments 51–3, 95–6, 102, 168, 192, 210–11, 215, 227, 236–7, 334–6, 338–43
and bounties 43, 51–2, 128, 168, 180, 236
decisions of 120–1, 129–30, 182–3, 197–8, 210–11, 217, 252, 295
and licenses to bear arms 62, 82–3, 154–5, 235–6, 256
edicts and orders of 13, 31–2, 49, 55, 100–3, 106–7, 126, 163–4, 167, 169, 177, 209–10
sentences of 22, 39–40, 43, 52, 94–6, 146–7, 168, 334–6
summons by 30, 95
trials by 95–6
see also licences to bear arms
courtesans 4, 6–8, 13, 71, 80
Crema, Antonio da 178
Cremona 103, 255–6
Croce, Baccio della, papal standard-bearer 74–5
Cruel Carnival of 1511 19, 31–7, 42*f*
compensation for losses from 66–9, 73
See also Giovedì Grasso

Cuccagna family 51
Cyprus 61, 138, 153, 197, 233–5, 255, 263–4, 263*f*, 267–9, 323*f*, 356–7
  Famagusta 109n.60, 115–16, 125, 136–7, 140, 171–2, 174–5, 211, 262, 268–9
  Guardia of 233–4, 260–2
  Nicosia 263–4, 267–9
  Paphos 233, 234*f*, 262
Cusano, castle of 39–40

Da Lezze, Giovanni 264
  Hieronimo 275n.26
Dandino, Girolamo, cardinal 128–30
Dandolo, Giovanni 178, 205
  Giovanni Antonio 126–7
  Matteo, Venetian ambassador 101, 123–5, 205, 212–13, 259, 287
  Zilia, dogaressa (wife of Lorenzo Priuli) 212–14, 259
Da Riva, Alvise, capitano grande of Candia 145
Dalla Gatta, family. 254
  Alvise 130–1, 254
  Julia, widow 254
  Paolo 254, 317
Da Ponte, Nicolò, doge 52–3, 55
della Rovere, Ercole 52–3, 294
  Francesco Maria I, Duke of Urbino 56, 61
della Torre(Ambrogina Faustina) Morosina 7, 10–12, 14
  Mariola 7
Della Torre, family 21, 256, 353
  cavalieri aureati 72–3
  fiefs 229–30, 314–17
  Gorizian line 325–7, 329–48
  granted title of Counts of Valsassina 72–3
  indemnification for financial damages of 1511 66–9, 73
  investitures 73, 280–2, 314
  lineage 56, 61, 69–70
    see also bloodline
  petition for *grazia* of Venetian patrician status 69–70
  granted Venetian citizenship 69
  titles of 347–8
  testaments of 76–7
  Udinese line 327–33
    see also Udine, Palazzo Torriani
  Alvise I di Nicolò (c. 1450–1511) 19, 22–4, 27–31, 34, 53–4
    marriage of 24
    military career of 23–4, 26, 69–70
    murder of 35
  Alvise II di Alvise I (1511–1549), cleric 48, 54, 61, 96–7
    assassination of 97–100
    honorary Roman citizenship 90–1
    titles 72–3
    tomb in the Frari 103–6, 104*f*, 105*f*, 125, 345
  Alvise III di Girolamo (1557–1587), Jesuit 214, 237–8, 256, 285
  Alvise IV di Giulio (c. 1601–1636), condottiere 327–32
  Anna, sister of Alvise I 24
  Carlo di Sigismondo 282, 321, 324–5, 327–30
  Carlo II di Sigismondo II 330–3
  Carlo di Lucio Antonio (1716–1716) 337–8
  Carlo III di Sigismondo III (1697–1734) 335
  Cecilia di Lucio Antonio 338, 344–5
  Diadema di Nicolò 80
  Dorothea di Sigismondo 282, 324–5
  Elena di Girolamo (b. 1560) 229, 237–8, 283, 321
  Eleonora di Sigismondo III 335
  Elisabetta di Lucio Rizzardo 348
  Emilia di Sigismondo 330
  Fabio di Lucio Sigismondo 348
  Francesco di Nicolò (d. 1490) 22, 24
  Francesco di Giovanni Febo (1518–1565) 101
  Francesco di Vito (1508–1586), capitano of Gorizia 103, 280–2
  Gastone (Cassono) (d. 1318), Archbishop of Milan and Patriarch of Aquileia 69
  Ginevra di Alvise I (ca. 1508–ca. 1565) 25, 37, 96–8, 224–5, 231–2
    dowry of 254
    marriage of 57
  Ginevra di Girolamo (1559–c. 1626) 224, 237–8, 282–3, 299, 320
  Ginevra di Giulio 327–8
  Giovanni (1506–1527) 25, 37, 55–6, 61, 69–70
  Giovanni (d. 1501), capitano of Gorizia 63n.29
  Giovanni Francesco di Giacomo 53–4
  Girolamo (d. 1506), Veronese professor of medicine 104
  Girolamo di Alvise I (1504–1590) 19, 25, 27, 37–9, 48, 51, 81, 94–6, 101, 180–3, 198–9, 229, 237–44, 251, 267, 270, 302, 316–18, 347
    appeal to Pope Sixtus V 302–5
    appeals and petitions to Council of Ten 78–9, 96, 98–9, 128–32, 163–4, 215–16
    childhood 19, 25, 27, 37–9, 48, 51
    priesthood 60–1, 84n.31, 93
    death and burial 318
    division of properties 314–17
    dueling 59–60, 214–15, 252–4

Della Torre, family (*cont.*)
Fedi Battesimali delli Conti Della Torre 149, 156, 179, 183, 193, 208–9, 214, 224, 229, 239, 241
fight in Padua 94–6
finances 96–7, 130–2, 183, 255, 303–4, 314–17
and Gian Matteo Bembo 113, 117–23, 125–7, 163, 229–30, 267, 314, 346, 356–7
and Giovanni da Udine 74–5, 77, 93, 153–4, 198
grazia of safe conduct from Council of Ten 180–3
sentence (fines) 163–4
lauded by citizen council of Ceneda 290–1
legal studies 59–60, 255
letter to Cardinal Madruzzo 93
life in Candia 144–8, 150–5, 158, 178, 183–4
lineage 53–4
see also bloodline
marriage negotiations 106–7, 113, 116–19
marriages of children 279–85, 294–5
Peace of 1568 256
portrait 89*f*, 91
procurator in Ceneda 90–3, 237–40, 251–2
rent collector (*conduttore*) in Candia 153–4, 198
residence in Venice of 254, 317
testament of 317–18
titles of 72–3, 90–1
trial and sentence of exile to Candia, of 95–6, 128–32, 163
voyage to Candia 131–2, 137–46
wedding of 55–6
see also Bembo, Gian Matteo di Alvise; Bembo, Giulia di Gian Matteo
Girolamo II di Carlo II 331, 333–6
murder of Sigismondo III 335–6
Girolamo di Alvise IV 329–30
Girolamo di Sigismondo 324–5
Giovanni di Girolamo (1556–1623), bishop 208–9, 237–8, 256, 285, 296–7, 310–11, 315–18, 326–30, 326*f*
apostolic nuncio to Swiss cantons 322–3
as bishop of Veglia 317, 322–3
death of 329
Descriptio Helvetiae 326–7
dispute with Marcantonio Mocenigo 298–301
as head of Udinese line of family 327–8
honorary Roman citizenship 326
Giulia di Girolamo (1562–1590s) 239, 241, 282–6
Giulia di Carlo II 331
Giulio di Alvise IV 329–30
Giulio di Girolamo (1554–1603) 183, 237–8, 256, 297, 314–18, 325, 327–30
marriage 325
Giulio II di Giulio (1603–bef 1626) 327–8
Guido di Nicolò II (c. 1545–1586) 80, 96–7, 123, 130–1, 163–4, 230–1, 283, 300, 310, 314, 357–8
as Knight of Malta 258, 279
properties of 229, 256, 279, 308, 320–1
Isidoro (d. 1511) 22–5, 31, 33, 53–4
murder of 34–6, 68–9
Lodovico di Girolamo (1550–1550) 149–52
Lucio di Carlo II 331, 333–4, 334*f*
Lucio Antonio di Sigismondo III 334–46
banishments 338–9, 342–3
condemnation 342–3
execution 343
marriage 336–7
Lucio Giuseppe di Fabio 348
Lucio Rizzardo di Lucio Sigismondo 345, 348
Lucio Sigismondo II di Fabio (b. 1808) 348
see also Boschetti, Teresa
Lucio Sigismondo di Lucio Antonio (1715–1804) 337–8, 344–6
descendants 348
genealogical pursuits 345–8, 353
marriage 345
see also Udine, Palazzo Maseri-Manin, Pedrina, Villa; Spilimbergo, Elisabetta di
Lucina di Alvise IV 329–30
Marcantonio (d. 1511), professor of medicine 104
Marcella di Girolamo (1555–1590s) 193–4, 237–8, 294–5, 321
see also Savorgnan, Federico IV di Mario
Maria di Vito 324–5
Michele di Alvise I (1510–1586) 37, 39, 54, 73, 82, 95–6, 101, 217, 237, 290–305
as bishop of Ceneda 87–90, 156, 180–1, 205, 214–15, 251–2, 268, 270–2
as cardinal 290–6, 303
candidacy for papacy 55
celebrations in Udine 292, 293–4
congratulatory letters 292
panegyrics about 290, 296, 305
triumphal arch 291–2
Council of Trent, at 237, 251–2, 269
death and burial of 296, 345–6
featured by Paolo Paruta 287–8
honorary Roman citizenship 90–1
inscriptions 223, 269–70, 274, 294, 305n.7
majordomo to Pope Paul IV 198–200

    papal court 74–5, 78–9, 90–1
    papal nuncio to King of France 90–1, 96–7, 102–3, 128, 257–8, 271
    papal vice-legate to Perugia and Umbria 180–1
    portrait of 291*f*
    titles 72–3
    at Villalta 293–4
    see also Ceneda, Castello di San Martino
  Michele III di Alvise IV 329–32
  Moschino, brother of Gastone 69
  Nicolino di Moschino 69
  Nicolò di Giovanni Febo (1489–1557), capitano of Gradisca 103, 113, 126
  Nicolò I di Francesco (1487–1511) 24, 28–33, 54
    death of 35–6, 229
  Nicolò II di Nicolò I (1511–1546) 48, 61, 79, 279
  Nicolò di Sigismondo 324–5
  Ottolino di Moschino 69
  Pagano II (d. 1241) 104
  Raimondo (1501–1532) 25, 37, 39, 53–6, 58, 61, 68
  Raimondo di Francesco di Vito 280–2, 324–5, 332
  Sigismondo di Girolamo (1551–1601) 156–8, 237–8, 280–2, 298, 300–2, 315–18, 322–5
    marriages 280–2, 324–5
    service to Hapsburgs 280–2, 324
    testament 324
  Sigismondo II di Carlo (1601–1651) 325–6, 330–1
  Sigismondo III di Carlo II 331, 333–6
  Simone di Carlo 330, 332
  Smeralda, wife of Ettore Strassoldo 39, 48, 79
  Taddea di Girolamo (1553–bef 1596) 179–80, 237–8, 279–80, 321–7
  Teresa di Lucio Sigismondo di Fabio 348, 353
    see also Felissent, Fleury, Count
  Torriana di Sigismondo 325
  Torrismondo 332
  Virginia 80
del Monte, Giovanni Maria, *see* Julius III
del Monte, Innocenzo 182
Dieci Savi in Rialto 246n.36
Diedo, Pietro 94–5
Dillingen 102
Dobrovo, fief of 321
  Giovanni, doge 69
Dolce, Lodovico 15, 260
Dolomites 92
Donato, Francesco, doge 82, 90, 102
dowries 5, 7–9, 12–14, 22–4, 53–4, 57, 74, 80, 96–7, 117, 119, 177–8, 196, 233–4, 240–1, 254, 263–6, 282–3, 310, 320–1, 324–5, 329–30, 336
Dragut Reis, Ottoman admiral 155–6, 170, 183–4
drought 77, 227
ducal councillor 212–13, 258–9
duels, duelling 59–60, 168*f*, 253–4, 270

earthquakes 40–3, 42*f*, 48, 50–1, 53, 58*f*, 66, 145, 171, 232*f*
Elijah of Pesaro, Jewish merchant 140–1, 143
Elio, Antonio, bishop of Pola 102–3
Elisabeth of Valois 150
Elizabeth I, queen of England 215–16, 257–8, 280–2
Emo, Leonardo, luogotenente 52
Emo, Zuane, luogotenente di Patria del Friuli 22
eredità Popaite 330–4, 336–7
Ernest, archduke of Austria (1553–1595) 294–5
Este 285–6
  family 4
  Alfonso I d', Duke of Ferrara 6
  Alfonso II d', Duke of Ferrara 100–1
  Ippolito II d', cardinal 205, 297
  Isabella d' 4
executions 52, 343

Fabri, Felix, German priest 138
factions 19–20, 22–3, 30–3, 44, 53, 55–6, 80–3, 124, 167–8, 199–201, 227, 255–6, 331
  see also blood feud; vendetta
Fagagna 39–40, 229–30, 315–16
Famagusta, *see* Cyprus
famine 60–3, 96, 102–3, 149, 172, 200–1, 204–5, 208, 228, 313–14
Farnese, Alessandro, *see* Paul III
  Alessandro di Pier Luigi (1520–1589), cardinal-nephew 123–4, 128, 297
  Pietro Alvise 319n.18
  Ranuccio di Pier Luigi (1530–1565), cardinal and Latin Patriarch of Constantinople 79, 97, 128, 153–4, 198, 255
Farra d'Isonzo
  Palazzo Strassoldo 341–2
fedecommesso 196, 265–6, 283–4, 324, 329–31
Fedele, Cassandra 206
Felissent, family 353
  Fleury, count 348
  Caterina 348
  Sigismondo 348
  Teresa 348

Feltrin, Pietro, painter 351n.82
Ferdinand II
 as archduke of Austria 57–8
 as emperor 216, 280–2, 329
Ferrara 4–6, 26, 100–1, 253, 255–6
 Duke of 100–1, 207, 254, 296
Feretto, Giovanni Battista 130–1
Ferro, Giovanni 331–2
 Lazzaro 331–2
Florio, Daniele, count 345
 Sulpizia 331–2
Fontana, Giovanni, architect 53
Foscari, Francesco, vice-doge 205
 Marcantonio 79
Foscarini, Alvise 133n.19
 Giacomo, capitano da mar, proveditor general 133n.19, 148
 Laura 117
 Marcantonio 133n.19, 275n.26
Foscolo, Andrea, luogotenente 57–8
Fracastoro, Giovanni, Veronese physician 104, 125, 198, 285
France 23–4, 26, 60, 90–1, 96–7, 123–4, 128–30, 181, 228, 257–8, 270–2, 303, 322
Frangipane Christoph, condottiere 126–8
 Claudia 348
 Cornelio, Udinese lawyer 80, 236, 296, 313–14
 Teresa 348
Fratta 79–80, 279
Frattina, Leonardo 32
 Zuan Leonardo della (d. 1511) 35–6

Galinetta, Fantin 209–10
 Menega, wife of 209–10
galleys 8, 10, 106–7, 117, 131–2, 137–42, 202, 260–1
 Barbara, seizure of the 169–70, 183–4
 of Beirut and Alexandria 6–7, 10, 97, 129, 131–2, 138, 140–1, 169–70, 183–4
 of Candia 178–9
 carrack (*carraca*) 138
 galleass, great galley 140
 see also sea voyages
Gandini, Giovanni 290
Gemona 37–9, 71, 201–2, 274
Genoa 70, 72–3
Gentile da Fabriano 189, 259–60
Gerolamo da Ferrara 98, 102
Giberto, Gian Matteo 60
Gioseffo da Muggia 204
Giovanni Antonio, priest in Ceneda 301
Giovanni da Udine (Giovanni Ricamatore), artist 20*f*, 53, 66–8, 71–2, 77, 93, 156, 230–2
 allegorical frescoes in Castello di Colloredo 231–2, 232*f*
 pension from Pope Paul III 74–5, 78, 153–4, 198
 Antonia, sister of 75
 Raphaiello, son of 74–5, 214–15
 Michelangelo, son of 156
Giovedì Grasso 19, 32–7, 41–3, 55–6, 61, 69–70, 145, 167, 176, 338, 345–6
 see also Cruel Carnival of 1511
Giovio, Paolo 211
Giustiniani, Antonio, luogotenente di Patria del Friuli 28–9
Il Gobbo De la Torre, *see* Della Torre, Nicolò II
godparents 74–5, 80, 85n.42, 150, 156, 158, 179, 193–4, 214
Gonzaga, Alvise 103
 Eleonora 146–7
 Ferrante, governor of Milan 103, 205
 Francesco II, marquis of Mantua 6
 Giovanni Maria 256–7
 Guglielmo, duke of Mantua 292
 Lodovico, duke of Sabbioneta 146–7
 Zuan Lodovico 59–60
Gorizia 26–7, 30, 54, 72, 103, 167–8, 226, 280–3, 302, 307, 321–6, 331–2, 338–41, 344–5
 Convocazione degli Stati Provinciali of 282, 336
Gradenigo, family 160n.51
 Alvise, luogotenente 30–2, 41
 Pietro 18n.53
Gradisca 30–1, 36, 254, 256, 325–6, 332, 339–43
 Castello of 342–3
 War of 329–30
grain, granaries 57, 61–2, 71, 76–7, 96, 137, 141, 145, 171–2, 183, 188–9, 200–1, 204, 208, 212, 227–8, 266, 290–1, 310, 313–15, 321, 328
 see also harvests
Grandi, Adriano, *Canzone nella morte dell'Illustrissimo Reverendissimo Cardinale di Ceneda, Monsignor Michele della Torre*, frontispiece 297*f*
Graz 280–2, 302, 323–6, 333–4
Great Council 259–61
Gregory XIII, pope 266–7, 290, 296
Griffoni, Matteo, de Sant'Angelo of Urbino (condottiere) 16n.10
Grimani, Domenico, cardinal 88, 181
 Giovanni 88
 Marcantonio 106
 Marino, cardinal 58–9, 88–90
Gritti, Alvise, Provveditore Generale of Corfù 142
Gritti, Alvise, Duke of Candia 197
 Andrea, doge 66–8, 73, 283–4

grotteschi 66, 77, 230–1, 311
Guazzo, Marco, Paduan chronicler 174–5
Guerin, Bortolo q. Francesco (stone mason) 245n.3
Francesco q. Florino (stone mason) 245n.3
Guise, Cardinal de 124
Guzman de Silva, Diego de, Spanish ambassador 295

Hapsburgs 19–20, 150, 231, 280–2, 294–5, 320–5, 339–41
court of 70, 73, 91, 93–4, 150, 215, 224–5, 253, 280–2, 291–2, 294–5, 302, 336
imperial armies and troops of 26–7, 29–30, 32–3, 42–3, 51, 57, 61, 70–4, 103, 113, 126
fiefs and territories of 20*f*, 26–8, 43, 54, 103, 226, 279, 282, 329, 335–7
see also Charles V; Charles VI; Philip II
harvests 25, 200–1, 204, 313–14
see also grain, granaries
Heintz il Giovane, Joseph, attrib., *View of Udine* 21*f*, 67*f*
Henri II, king of France 129–30
Henri III, king of France 272–4, 273*f*, 292, 303
Henry VII, emperor 69
Henry VIII, king of England 60
Hofer, Ludovica 332
Mattia 101
honour 32, 37–8, 54, 56–7, 59–60, 78, 123, 167, 320
horses 71, 78, 94–5, 102, 131, 199, 201–2, 226–7, 270, 279, 303, 307, 313, 316–17, 332, 338–9, 341–2
Huguenots 257–8, 270
Hungary 11–12, 70, 216

imprese 208, 211, 286–7
investitures 53–4, 73, 76–7, 280–2, 313–14, 330
Ionian Sea 137, 143
Istria 3, 20*f*, 279, 316, 329, 332–3

Janis da Tolmezzo, Francesco 35, 37–8, 42, 55
Jesuits 110n.75, 214, 216, 219n.46, 285, 297*f*, 315, 336
Jews 140–1, 199
in Candia 177
in Rome 200
in Udine 204–5, 236
in Venice 176–7
Julius II, pope 11–12
Julius III (Giovanni Maria del Monte (1487–1555)), pope 124–5, 128–9, 156, 176–7, 180–2, 198–9, 251–2, 303

Klontzas, Maneas, View of Candia 171*f*
see also Candia (Crete)
knights, knighthood 55–6, 63n.29, 71–3, 91, 198, 208, 283–4, 293, 324–5, 332
see also *cavalieri aureati*
Knights of Malta 79, 109n.43, 271, 279, 324–5, 332
Knights of St John of Jerusalem 11–12, 56, 155–6
see also Knights of Malta

Lala Mustafa Pasha, Ottoman commander 268–9
Lando, Giovanni, capitano grande of Candia 145, 155, 197
Pietro, doge 82
Lang, Apollonia 126–8, 132; *see also* Frangipane, Christoph
Matthias, cardinal of Gurk 126
Lantieri, Federico, baron 324–5
Gaspare, baron 324–5
Lazzarini, Giovanni Battista, painter 351n.82
League of Cambrai 26, 113, 126
League of Cognac 60
Legnago 277n.58, 334–5
Lemnius, Levinus, *Occulta naturae miracula* 157
Lenkovich, Margherita 324–5
Leo X, pope 7, 9–12, 66
Lepanto 3
Battle of 159n.17, 269–71, 322–3, 323*f*
Leopold I, emperor 333
lèse-majesté 52, 338–9
Lesina 138
Leva, Antonio de 71–2
Liabordo di Mels 167
Libavius, Andreas, German physician 179–80
licence to bear arms 62, 66–8, 73, 80–3, 154–5, 200–1, 235–6, 256, 337–8
lineage 14, 24–5, 39, 53–7, 69–70, 255–6, 320–2, 343, 358
see also bloodline
Livenza, river 268, 283
Locatelli, Marcantonio 329–30
Lizza Fusina 94–5, 127, 205–6
London 215–16
Longo, Antonio 275n.31
Marc'Antonio (d. ca 1564) 14
Loredan, Andrea 39–40
Francesco 166*f*
Leonardo, doge 25, 126–7
Lovadina 97–8
Loyola, Ignatius 109n.46
Lubljana (Istria) 30, 339–41
Lucerne 322–3

Luciani, Sebastiano (del Piombo) 74–5, 153–4
Luciscischo, Paolo 59–60
luogotenente, *see* Patria del Friuli, luogotenente

Madrisio, castle of 39–40, 336–7
  Eleonora di Giovanni Enrico 336–8, 341
  Giovanni Enrico 336
  Rizzardo di Giovanni Enrico 336, 341–2, 344–5
Madruzzo, Cristoforo, cardinal, Bishop of Trent 93, 285–6
Magistrato alla Sanità 209
Magno, Alessandro 138–40, 153
Maino, Ambrogio di, Milanese knight 53–4
Mala Zompicchia (Friuli) 29–30
Malipiero, family 24–5
mal italiano, *see* syphilis
Malpaga, Castello di 229, 230*f*, 271*f*
Malta 155–6, 254–6
Malvicchia, Mariana, wife of Count Rizzardo Strassoldo 341–3
Maniago, family 169
Maniche, Hercole dale 131
Manin, Giulio 101
  Orazio 328
Manini, Francesco 83
Mantica, family 202
  Ottavia 283, 321
Mantua 6, 26, 59–60, 72–3, 255–6, 329–30
Manutius, Aldus 164–5
Marcello, family 24–5
  Giacomo di Giovanni (d. 1520) 6–7, 10
  Giulia di Sebastiano (c. 1501–c. 1531) 4–5, 7, 11–14, 195–6
  Marcella di Sebastiano (1496–1555) 3–4, 7, 10, 206
    death of 193–4
    dowry 8–9, 196
    marriage to Gian Matteo Bembo 8–10
    pregnancies and childbirths of 10–11, 14, 133n.9
    testament of 194–6
    servants of 195
      see also Bembo, Gian Matteo di Alvise
  Maria (Marietta) di Sebastiano (1497/99–aft 1542) 4, 7
    marriage 12–13, 120
  Pietro, procurator 12–13
  Sebastiano (d. 1501) 3–5
Marcellus II, pope 198–9
Marchesi
  Antea di Antonio 328
  Antonio di Martino, Udinese merchant 292, 307–15, 321, 327
    granted noble Udinese status 313–14
    refurbishment of Palazzo Torriani 311–13
  Caterina (Catella) di Antonio 325, 327–9
  Giovanni Martino di Antonio 325, 327–8
  Martino 307–8, 311
  Ortensia di Antonio 328
Marghera 294
Maria Anna of Bavaria 280–2
Mariza, servant 195
marriage strategies 15, 24–5, 39, 52, 56–7
Martinengo, Antonio, count 146
  Girolamo, count, governor general of the militia of Candia 146–7
  Scipione 146
Masari family 169
Master of Ceneda, *Coronation of the Virgin* 242, 242*f*, 296
Maximilian I (1459–1519), emperor 19, 23–4, 26, 30, 43–4, 126
Maximilian II (1527–1576), emperor 256, 267–8, 280–2
Medici, Catherine de', queen mother of France 258
  Cosimo I de' 253
  Fernando de' 297
Meldolla, Andrea, *see* Schiavone, Andrea
Mella family 166*f*
Mercurio, Scipione 157
Merlo, Giovanni, *Vero e real disegno della inclita cita di Venetia* 215*f*
Micheli, Parrasio, votive painting of Doge Lorenzo Priuli 259
Michiel, Francesco, luogotenente 167
  Maffeo, luogotenente 82–3
  Marchiò, procurator 275n.31
  Marco 59–60
  Marin 59
  Pentesilea (mother of Gian Matteo Bembo) 17n.24, 134n.31
  Pierina 134n.31
midwives 150–1, 151*f*, 153, 156–7, 238–9, 239*f*
Milan 23–4, 53–4, 60, 69, 94, 103, 127, 150, 167–8, 253, 294, 322–3
militias 23, 29–33, 146–7, 167
Mirandola 100–1
Misoch, Count of 53–4
Mocenigo, Alvise, cavalier, procurator and doge 256–7
  Cecilia 334–8
  Marcantonio, Bishop of Ceneda 296–302, 304–5
Mondino, priest in Ceneda 301
Modon 4–5
Modone, Thomas da 178

Mohammed 179–80
mole (*mola*) 157, 238–9
Monemvasia 137
Monfalcone 30–1
Sebastiano 30–1
Montegnacco, Sebastiano 256
Montemerlo, Monsignor 129–30
Montereal, Antonio 80–1
Monte Vecchio 69, 74, 78–9, 290, 294, 300, 315
Monticolo, Giovanni 55, 80–1
Monticolo, Nicolò 55
Montona (Istria) 3
Monza 55, 80–1
Morelli di Schönfeld, Carlo, historian 323–4, 333
la Moreta, slave 195
Morosini, family 148
Domenico, Venetian ambassador 180–1
Elena (d. 1509), wife of Bernardo Bembo 4–5
Gabriel, luogotenente 236
Pietro, luogotenente 101
morbo francese, *see* syphilis
Morcote, Bernardino da, stonemason 75
Moruzzo 37, 39–40, 315–16
mottos 98, 165, 167, 208, 231, 271, 286–7, 344, 344*f*
mourning 5, 44, 104, 251, 252*f*, 264, 296–7, 323–4
Muazzo, family 159n.31
Muggia, fief 279, 307, 315–16
Muir, Edward 19
Münster, Sebastian 211

naming practices 11, 14–15, 39, 48, 54, 151, 156, 192–3, 208–9, 240, 244, 320, 329–31, 345, 348, 357–8
Nani, Bernardo, luogotenente 314
Navagero, Bernardo 200
Nauplion 137
Naviglio, Nadal 255
Neacademia (New Academy) 164–5
Nelio, Antonio, Patriarch of Jerusalem 5
Neuhaus, Dario 331
Nicosia, *see* Cyprus
Noal, Alvise da 283–4
Aurelio di Giulio, da 283–4
Giulio di Alvise, da 283–4
see also Treviso, Ca' da Noal
Noale 283–4, 330–42
nobility, Cenedese 89–90, 269
Cretan 147–9, 152–4, 178, 255
Friulian 19–20, 24–5, 36–8, 52–6, 58–9, 69, 72–3, 79–80, 90, 96, 101, 118–19, 123–4, 127, 231, 261, 282, 290, 296, 345, 347
Venetian 13, 55–6, 84n.18, 115, 115*f*, 122*f*, 147, 154, 190–1, 255, 355
nuns 7–8, 14–15, 194, 203, 303, 338

omens 30–1, 38, 41–2, 91, 157–8, 179–80, 222, 237–43
Ongaro, Domenco, priest 346
Orsa, servant 240–1, 255, 361
Ortelius, Abraham, *Patria del Friuli* 20*f*
Osoppo, Savorgnan castle 202–3
Ottomans 4–5, 23–4, 26, 56, 70, 137, 142, 146–7, 155–6, 164, 169–70, 231, 234–5, 254, 256, 262, 264, 267–70, 323*f*, 324–6
Ovid, *Metamorphosis* 231

Padua 11–12, 14, 18n.53, 52–3, 82–3, 94–9, 117, 168, 181–2, 201, 216, 256–7, 263, 272, 283–5, 307, 315–17, 322–3, 329, 338–9, 342
Basilica del Santo 95
Ca' Cornaro 203
cathedral, Cappella di S. Croce 329
Loggia 203
Odeo 203
Piazza delle Erbe 338–9
plague in 201, 204, 209–10
Ponte Corbo 95
Porta Portello 203
Santa Sofia, bridge of 203
state visit of Bona Sforza 201–3, 207
Strada Larga 95
Palladio, Andrea 272, 291–2
Palma Vecchio 152
pamphlet war 252–7
papal court 4, 60–1, 74–5, 78, 82, 88, 90–1, 199–200
Papadopoli, Zuanne 148, 153
Papazzoni, Vitale, poet 270–1
Partistagno, family 19–20, 24
Girolamo 130–1
Paruta, Paolo, *Della perfezione della vita politica* 42–4
Pasqualigo, Giovanni 177–8, 205
Magdalena di Giovanni 177–9, 233–4
Passerino, Pietro 37
Pastor, Ludwig 124, 200
Patria del Friuli 5, 95–6, 227, 285–6, 307–8
luogotenente of 20–2, 26–34, 36, 41, 52–3, 55–9, 66, 67*f*, 71, 73, 75–6, 80–3, 94, 101, 120, 163, 167, 169, 180–2, 200–1, 204–5, 210–11, 214, 217, 226, 236, 291–4, 296, 314, 316–18, 338–9
map of 20*f*
parliament of 25–6, 53, 78, 283

Patriarch of Aquileia 20–1, 53–4, 58–9, 69, 156, 251–2, 357
patronage 71, 76–7, 91, 93, 223
Patron of the Arsenal 233–4
Paul III (Alessandro Farnese, 1468–1549), pope 74, 79, 90, 93, 114–15, 123–4, 181–2, 199–200, 206, 303–4
Paul IV (Giovanni Pietro Carafa, 1476–1559), pope 198–200, 208, 212, 303
  as cardinal 176–7
Pavona, Bernardino 34
Paxos 143
Peace of Bologna 70
Peace of 1568 255–8, 271, 295, 320
Peace of Venice 259–60; *see also* Tintoretto
peasants 19–20, 23–6, 28–30, 32–5, 49, 51, 62, 72, 80, 96, 147–8, 154, 157–8, 172–3, 200–1, 228–31, 269, 294, 335–6
  revolts 27–8, 37–40, 43, 48–9
Pedrina 330–1, 335
  see also Pordenone, Villa Pedrina
Peretta, Camilla 304–5
Peretti, Felice, Cardinal of Montalto, *see* Sixtus V, pope
Perosa 61
Pers (Friuli) 37–40
Pesaro, Bartolomeo 95–6
Peschiera 30
Petazzi, Odorico 331
petecchie, *see* typhus
Philip II (1527–1598), king of Spain 94, 150, 200, 212
  see also Hapsburgs
Piave river 92, 97–8, 222, 298
Pieve di Cadore 92
piezara 100, 127
Pinzano, castle of 101, 256
pirates 144–5, 169–70, 195, 266–7; *see also* corsairs
Pisanello, Antonio 259–60
Pius V (Antonio Ghislieri, 1504–1572), pope 257–8, 268, 299–300, 323*f*
plague 40, 42–3, 48, 62, 117, 188, 192–3, 201, 204–5, 209–12, 272–4, 349n.37
Plutarch, *Lives* 260
Podocataro, Livio, Bishop of Cyprus 97
Poland 201–3, 272, 292
Polcenigo, castle of 282–3, 307
  counts of 4–5
  Orazio, count 282–3, 295, 330–1
  Perla 295, 321
    see also Della Torre, Ginevra di Girolamo
Popaite, Lucio 283, 320–1, 330–1
  Paola 321, 324–6
  see also Della Torre, Elena di Girolamo; *eredità Popaite*; Pordenone, Palazzo Popaite–Torriani
Pole, Reginald, cardinal 124
Porcia, castle of 224–5, 237–8
  counts of 304–5
  Francesca da 224–5, 231–2
Pordenone 26, 39, 126, 201–2, 224–5, 283, 330–3, 335–9, 345–6
  Palazzo Popaite–Torriani 337–8, 345
  Villa Pedrina (Azzo Decimo) 336–8, 337*f*
  oratory 345
Pordenone, Antonio, painter 274
portents, *see* omens
Portinari family 202–3
Portis, Riccardo de', of Cividale 344–5
Porto, Francesco da, of Vicenza 68
  Luigi da 36, 39, 42–3, 56
    Historia novellamente ritrovata di due nobili amanti 56
Prague 280–2, 324
Prata, Antonio, count 342, 345
Prampero, Andrea 37–8
  Marcantonio di 332–3
  Pietro di 332–3
Prealpi Trevigiani 92
pregnancy 10–11, 37–9, 125, 138, 142, 149, 157, 179–80, 203, 237–40, 341
premonitions, *see* omens
primogeniture 179, 330–1, 333–4
Priuli, Cecilia di Antonio procurator 246n.39
  Chiara 56, 192, 210–11
  Girolamo, doge 212–13, 226, 229–30, 259, 262–3, 263*f*
  Lorenzo, doge 95–6, 208, 212–14, 259, 272
  Nicolò, doge 234*f*
processions 41–2, 77, 119–20, 150–3, 170, 176, 212–13, 241, 298, 338–9
  see also ceremonies
Procuratori di Citra 79
Provveditori alle pompe 277n.60
Provveditori alla Sanità 210–11
Provveditori sopra i Feudi 314
Provveditori sopra monti 197–8
Provveditori sopra le galie armade de condennati 260–1

Quarantia Civil e Criminale 15n.1, 62, 321
Quarantia Civil Nuova 15n.1
Quarantia Civil Vecchia 350n.53
Quarantia Criminale 16n.10
Querini, Angelo 350n.53

Querini, family of Crete 147
Marco 146
Nicolò 146
Palma, wife of Nicolò 146
Zuane 146
Quintilian (Roman rhetorician) 11

Ramusio, Giambattista, *Navigazioni and viaggi* 285
Paolo di Giambattista 285–6
Rangoni, family 304–5
Guido, condottiere 71
Raphael Sanzio (artist) 66
Ragusa 155, 183–4
Rason Vecchie 78–9
Rassauer, Giovannina 280–2
Raynaldo, spicer 28–9
reconciliation 27–9, 31–2, 70, 83, 129, 216, 235, 257–8
Reeuwich, Erhard 144*f*
relics 152, 174, 238–9, 266–8, 294, 322–3, 329
Renier, Alvise, Duke of Candia 152–3, 177–8
rental payments and income 25, 51, 97, 141, 146, 153–4, 183, 233–4, 254–5, 262, 265–6, 294, 308*f*, 310, 315–16
Rettimo (Rethymo) 143
revenge 42–4, 90, 97–9, 155, 252–3, 331
see also blood feud; vendetta
revenge narrative 34, 51–2, 54
Rhodes 56
Riccio, Andrea, *Death of the Professor*, bronze relief 104, 106*f*
Riccio, Nadal 96–7
Rigala, Giovanni, notary 59–60
riots 32–9, 49, 52, 68–9, 227
Roganzuolo, castle of 92
Romanino, Girolamo, attr.
Banquet of Bartolomeo Colleoni in honor of Christian I of Denmark in 1467 230*f*
Hunting Scene 263*f*
Rome 4, 7, 10, 60, 66, 72–5, 78–9, 82–3, 90–1, 93, 101, 123–5, 128–30, 154, 176–7, 198–200, 230–1, 266–7, 296–7, 300, 303–5, 310, 315
Campo dei Fiori 176–7
ghetto 200
Inquisition 176–7, 198–200
Sack of 61, 66, 69–70, 198–9
Vatican Palace 66
Villa Farnesina 66
see also papal court
Rondolo, Beltrame, patriarchal vicar 35
Rovere, Ercole della 52–3, 55, 82
Rosai, Flaminio 317
Rosazzo 316, 329, 349n.37
Ronco di 315
Rösslin, Eucharius, *Libro nel qual si tratta del parto de lhuomo* 144, 150, 156–7
Rudolph II (1552–1612), archduke of Austria and emperor 294–5
Russea, Zuane 146
Rustem Pasha, Grand Vizier 169–70

Sacile 71, 202–3, 307, 310
Sala Beg, Ottoman admiral 169–70
Salomoni, Giuseppe, poet 329
Salvarolo, castle of 39–40
San Daniele (Friuli) 39–40, 71, 202–3, 315–16
San Giacomo di Veglia 92
Sanmicheli, Gian Girolamo 144–5, 172
Michele 142, 144–5, 171–2, 203
Sansovino, Francesco 103–4, 113–15, 119, 121–2, 132, 189, 234–5, 260
Vita della illustre Signora Contessa Giulia Bemba della Torre 223–4, 229, 237–45, 355
frontispiece 244*f*
Sansovino, Jacopo 88, 152, 188–9, 313
Santa Maura (Lefkada) 143, 170
Sanudo, Francesco, luogotenente 169, 180
Marin, Venetian diarist 3–5, 8, 10, 13, 19–20, 22, 26, 30, 41–2, 44, 52, 57–62, 68, 71, 126–7, 211, 315
Pietro 214
Sarcinelli family 304–5
Cornelio 92, 194–5, 225
Giacomino 225
see also Serravalle, Palazzo Sarcinelli
Sasino 142, 358–9
Sasso, family 312
Andrea, poet 328
Lidia, poetess 311–13, 327–9
savi agli ordeni 16n.10, 275n.25
savi di Consiglio 16n.10, 275n.25
savi di Terraferma 16n.10, 275n.25
Savorgnan, family 20–2, 190–1, 256
Fulvio 328
Savorgnan dello Scaglione, Federico 22
Tristan 22
Savorgnan della Bandiera, branch 339
Fabio 236
Federico 236, 252–3, 255–6
Francesco 235–6
Pompeo 236
Savorgnan del Monte, branch 22
Anna Maria di Ettore 330–1
Costantino di Girolamo (d. 1534) 73
Germanico di Girolamo (1554–1597) 94

Savorgnan del Monte, branch (*cont.*)
Giacomo (d. 1498) 5, 22–3
Giacomo di Pagano (1521–1560) 81, 83, 131, 192, 210–11
Giovanni Battista di Giacomo (1498–1517) 52–3, 55–6
Giovanni Battista di Pagano (b. 1529) 81
Girolamo (1466–1529) 5, 22–5, 27–8, 44, 52, 56, 61, 66–8
Giulia di Giacomo (d. 1551) 52–3
Giulio di Girolamo (1510–1595), military engineer 73, 265
Lucina di Francesco Savorgnan del Torre 325
Lucina di Giacomo (d. 1543) 56–7, 191–2
Maria, wife of Giacomo 5–6, 32, 56, 81
Maria di Pagano, wife of Giovanni Savorgnan 191–2, 256–7
Mario di Girolamo (1511–1574) 73, 81, 244
Pagano di Giacomo (d. 1539) 56–7, 192
Scipione di Pagano (1536–1554) 81, 192
Tristan di Pagano (1523–1565/6) 81, 83, 94, 155, 253–6
attack on Grand Canal (1549) 97–100
condemnation and pursuit by Council of Ten 101–3, 128
Savorgnan del Torre, branch 22, 73
Antonio di Nicolò (1458–1512) 22–3, 25–31, 42–4
assassination 43–4
enmity with the Della Torre 22–3, 25, 27–8
populist strategies 23, 25–6
military service to Venice 26
involvement in Cruel Carnival of 1511 28–31, 68–9
Antonio di Bernardino (1526–1552) 167–9
Bernardino di Giovanni (1495–1556) 52, 73, 101, 169, 180
Elisabetta di Giovanni (b. 1553) 191
Francesco di Giovanni (1492–1547) 52, 56, 73, 81, 191–2
Giovanni di Nicolò (1459–1509) 52
Giovanni di Francesco (1518–1559) 94–5, 98, 128, 130, 163–4
denunciation to Provveditori della Sanità 209–11
family 191–2, 256–7
petition for clemency 190–1
Lucina, granddaughter of Maria di Pagano 325
Nicolò di Antonio (natural), known as Cherubino (d. 1518) 26, 51–3
Nicolò di Francesco (1523/26–1568) 95, 98, 128, 163–4, 252–3, 255–6
Urbano di Bernardino (1538–1595) 253–4
Sbroiavacca, Ascanio 34
Giulio 80, 82–3, 130–1, 184n.3, 204–5
Marzia 330–1
Schiavone, Andrea, attrib., Tomb of Alvise II Della Torre 104*f*, 105*f*, 106
Schili, physician 261
Scillini, physician 149–50, 160n.58
scodella (broth bowl) 193*f*
sea voyages 135n.76, 136, 138–9, 170
activities on 139–41
dangers and hardships of 138
living conditions on 140–2
Selim II, Sultan 267–8
Semetkovitch, Adamo 280–2
Senate 10, 12–13, 44, 52–3, 68, 89–90, 101–3, 118–19, 125, 169–70, 178–9, 183–4, 201–7, 211, 214, 236–7, 251–2, 260, 275n.25, 314
Serravalle 91–2, 225, 304–5
Palazzo Sarcinelli 225
Setton, Kenneth 170
Sforza, Bona, Queen of Poland 201–3, 202*f*, 205–8, 272
Gian Galezzo, Duke of Milan 201
Muzio, poet 311–12
Sgognico, Orsola, servant 341–3
Shakespeare, William, *Romeo and Juliet* 56
Sigismond II, King of Poland 201
Signoria 5, 16n.10, 22–3, 27–31, 37–9, 41, 52, 56, 69–71, 80–1, 89–90, 95, 101, 117, 126, 128, 205–7, 259, 292–4, 296, 298, 303
Signori di Notte 15n.1, 260–1
Sinan Pasha, Ottoman admiral 155–6
Sixtus V (Felice Peretti, 1521–1590), pope 296–8, 300–2, 304–5
slavery 137, 142, 195
smallpox 80, 123, 229, 279
Soldonieri, Lucretia 38
Soldoniero 38
sopracomito 3–5, 117, 178, 262
Spain 3, 26, 70, 150, 205–6, 212, 216, 228, 258, 269, 322
Spessa 282, 307, 316–17, 322, 324–5, 335–6
Spilimbergo 48, 71–2, 201–3, 224–5
castle of 38–40, 71–2, 237–8
family 19–20, 24, 73
Alessandro 73
Bartolomeo di 71–2
Claudia di 345
Elisabetta di 345
see also Della Torre, Lucio Sigismondo
Giacomo da 31, 38

Ginevra di 54
Giovanni Enrico da 43–4
Irene of 114
Odoardo di 71–2
Roberto di, chronicler 71–2
Sterpo, castle of 27–30, 43
Strassoldo 30
castle of 81–2
family 24, 256, 320, 323–4, 342–3
Bernardo 130–1
Ettore, brother of Taddea 24, 39, 48, 51, 53–4, 57–8, 77, 79, 81–2
Francesco 25–6, 130–1
Francesco, di Sopra 329
Giovan Giuseppe di Pietro 236
Giovanni, brother of Taddea 52–3
Ludovica di Rizzardo 341–3
Marco Antonio 81–2
Nicolò di Rizzardo 341–3
Pietro 236
Rizzardo, count 341–3
see also Malvicchia, Marianna; Farra d'Isonzo
Ropretto 24
Taddea (d. 1519), wife of Alvise I Della Torre 24, 37–9, 48
Vittoria 79–80, 164, 229–30, 242–3, 279, 362
see also Farra d'Isonzo, Palazzo Strassoldo; Udine, Palazzo Strassoldo
Strumieri 19–20, 22–4, 28–36, 43–4, 53 68, 94, 255–6
sumptuary laws 22, 212, 277n.60
Suleiman the Magnificent, Ottoman Sultan 137, 169–70
Surian, Antonio, patriarch 7–8
Giacomo, podestà of Ceneda 89–90
Michele, Venetian ambassador 287–8
Susanna, Beltrame, Udinese noble 76–7
Susans 315–16
castle of 39–40
Sustris, Lambert 91–2
Switzerland 322–3
syphilis 3–5, 143

Tagliamento river 38, 48, 71, 101, 201–2, 236–7, 265, 279–80
Terraferma 15, 20*f*, 81, 87–8, 201–3, 211, 217, 268, 308*f*, 315
Tarzo 304–5
Theatine order 198–9
Tiepolo, family 24–5
Francesco 13
Stefano, captain general of the sea 178, 259
times of day 247n.65
Tintoretto, Jacopo 114, 260, 274
Coronation of Frederick Barbarossa by Pope Hadrian IV in St Peters 260
Excommunication of the Emperor 260
Titian (Tiziano Vecellio), painter 72–3, 79, 91–4, 114, 189, 194–5, 222, 225, 274, 285–6
casa da statio in Venice 194–5
caseta in Col di Manza 92, 222
Cecilia, wife of 194–5
and Charles V 91–4
and Girolamo Della Torre 93
Lavinia, daughter of 92, 194–5, 225
paintings 94
Ecce Homo 91–2
Portrait of a Lady (possibly after Titian) 114*f*
portraits 93–4
San Girolamo in Penitence 194–5
Venus 91–2
Virgin and Child in Glory with Six Saints 79
titles 25, 51, 55–6, 69, 72–3, 76–7, 84n.18, 90–1, 118–19, 135n.62, 149, 283, 347
Tolmezzo 26
Torso, family 256
torture 95, 226–7, 343
Toscano, Tiziano, blacksmith 245n.3
Tranquillité 271, 344, 344*f*
Transylvania 324
Trent, Council of 123, 156, 180–1, 200, 237, 252–3, 257–8, 261–3, 267, 269–70, 287, 291–2, 322–3
Trevigiano 283–4
Trevisan, Domenico, Bailo 169–70
Marcantonio, doge 181
Stefano 275n.26
Treviso 71, 91, 201–3, 222, 227, 283–4, 294, 338–9, 348
Ca' da Noal 281*f*, 283–4
Palazzo Brazza 202–3
Piazza della Cavallerizza 283–4
Trieste 26–7, 279, 331
Tron, family 24–5
Daniele 276n.49
Truchsess, Otto von, Prince-Bishop of Augsburg 94, 102, 205
Turks, *see* Ottomans
typhus 61–2, 228

Udine 20–1, 21*f*, 67*f*, 71, 76, 256, 292, 294
Aquileia Nova 58–9
Arco Bollani 291–3
class divisions 20, 53, 55–6
Borgo Aquileia 235–6
Borgo Strazzamantello 77
Casa Florio 332

Udine (*cont.*)
Castello 20–1, 20*f*, 33–4, 36, 41, 53, 57–8, 75, 228, 293–4
clock tower 66, 77
column of infamy 339, 340*f*, 346
columns 20*f*, 75
Comune of 353
Consiglio del Comune 55–6, 61, 75
Duomo (cathedral) 20*f*, 36, 40–1, 74–5, 83
factions 180, 214, 235–7
fountains 67*f*, 77, 173–5, 174*f*, 339
Jews 204–5
Lazzaretto at San Gottardo 204
Loggia del Leonello 20*f*, 57–8, 66, 75, 76*f*, 292, 339
Mercatonuovo 75
Mercatovecchio 66, 75, 307–8
Monte di Pietà 228
Palazzo Brazzaco 293–4
Palazzo Marchesi, *see* Palazzo Torriani, 1587–89 refurbishment
Palazzo Maseri-Manin (renamed Palazzo Torriani) 345
Palazzo Savorgnan (destroyed 1549?) 27
Palazzo Strassoldo 24, 48
Palazzo Torriani 321, 329–33, 338–9
destroyed 1511 27, 32–4, 41, 48
demolition 1717 339, 340*f*
reconstructed 1540 20*f*, 77, 80, 96–7, 230–1, 237, 307–11
façade 308*f*
refurbished 1587–89 311–13, 325, 327–8
ground plan 309*f*
inventory of 332–3
loggia 309*f*
San Martino, family chapel 313
statues of Hercules and Cacus 313, 339, 346–7
Piazza Contarena 20*f*, 66, 75, 77, 78*f*
piazza del comun 66
Piazza del Fisco 339, 345
Piazza del Mercato 58–9, 293–4
piazza del vin 66
Piazza San Giacomo 77
Piazza Nuova 328
Piazzola del Borgo del Feno
plague in 40, 42–3, 48, 61–2, 204–5
Porta di Poscollo 30–1
Porta Villalta 293–4
Porticato di San Giovanni 20*f*, 75, 78*f*
Porto Grazzano 77
Poscolle, contrada of 328
San Cristoforo 293–4
San Francesco, church and monastery 20*f*, 22–4, 27, 41, 61, 77, 103, 293–4, 317
San Giacomo 58–9, 75
San Giovanni Battista 20*f*, 66, 75, 339
San Nicolò di Poscolle 293–4
San Pietro Martire 293–4
Santa Barbara 339
Santa Maria delle Grazie 293
San Tomasso 35
Via Gemona 74

vagitus uterinus 179–80
Valaresso, Gabriel 145
Valier, Agostino, bishop of Verona and cardinal 267, 297
Rosalba 338–41
Valtellina 329–30
Valvasone 29–30, 279, 283, 307
castle of 19–20, 39–40, 236–7, 279–80, 280*f*, 281*f*
family 24, 279–80, 321, 357–8
Bertoldo 303
Elena (Helena) (wife of Nicolò II Della Torre) 79–80, 229, 279
Enrico 79–80, 229
Erasmo da, poet 252
Felicita 321
Jacomo 161n.85
Pietro, di Maniago 345
Porzia 279
Valentino (Valenzio), count 279, 283, 320–1
Vittoria, *see* Strassoldo, Vittoria
Vando, Gabriele, cavalier 307–10
Vasari, Giorgio 74, 260
Vecellio, Cesare 91–2, 121, 125–6
De gli habiti antichi, et moderni 100*f*, 115*f*, 122*f*, 168*f*, 252*f*, 280*f*
Lavinia, *see* Titian
Orazio 91–2, 260, 274
Orsa, sister of Titian 194–5
Tiziano, *see* Titian
Veglia (Krk) 126, 261–3, 266–7, 322–3
vendetta 15, 19, 27–8, 30–2, 37–8, 40–2, 55–6, 80–3, 96–100, 102, 127, 145–6, 166–9, 191, 231, 235–7, 243, 252–4, 342–3
see also blood feud; Peace of 1568
Venetian Republic 19–20, 23, 26, 39–40, 44, 60, 69, 89–90, 144–5, 148, 203, 211, 213, 251–2, 258–60, 264, 287, 292–3, 297–8, 329–30, 355
armies of 56, 81–2
fall of, in 1797 345–6
Veneto 20*f*, 87–8, 87*f*, 88*f*, 92, 117, 222, 225*f*, 232–4, 294
Venice
Arsenale 272
Beccaria 188–9, 212–13

Biblioteca Marciana 188–9, 212–13
Biri Grande 194–5
Ca' Barozzi 213–16, 215*f*, 222
Ca' Bembo 8–9, 9*f*, 13, 121, 125–6, 189, 194–6, 211, 262, 266–7, 353
Ca' Corner della Ca' Grande 189
Ca' del Duca 212
Ca' Dolfin 189
Ca' d'Oro 189
Ca' Morosini (now Hotel Ca' Sagredo) 189, 190*f*, 192–3, 196, 207–9, 214
Calle del Forno 266
Campiello Santa Maria Nova 8–9, 9*f*, 353
Campo Santa Sofia 190
fondaco (grain warehouse) 188–9
Fondaco dei Tedeschi 126, 189
Giudecca 205–6, 212, 257
Grand Canal 41, 119–20, 123, 128, 147, 188–90, 214, 215*f*
  assassinations on 98–9, 106, 168, 190–2, 214, 216, 231–2, 346
  festivities on 206, 212–13
lagoon 188
Lazzaretto Nuovo 209, 273–4
Lazzaretto Vecchio 209
Libreria, *see* Venice, Biblioteca Marciana
Loggetta 213
Loggia dei Mercanti 190
Madonna dei Miracoli 194
Malamocco, port of 188
Merceria 272
Ognissanti, monastery of 263–4
Palace of the Duke of Ferrara 207
Palazzo Ducale 95–6, 98, 106, 113, 119, 121, 123, 125–6, 149, 165–6, 188, 190, 207–8, 213, 272
  Anticollegio 272
  Antipregadi 272
  armoury of the Council of Ten 217
  Avogaria 260–1
  Camera del Tormento 95
  Cancelleria 272
  Cannaregio, sestiere of 258, 260–2
  corte del palazzo 100, 100*f*, 113, 120, 127, 213
  fires in 272, 274
  portico of 62
  Sala del Collegio 207–8, 259–60, 272
  Sala dei Pregadi (Senate) 272
  Sala delle Teste 181
  Sala del Scrutinio 274
  Sala del Maggior Consiglio (Great Council Hall) 213, 259–60, 272, 274
  Scuderia del Doge 100
  Torresella 126–7
Palazzo Grimani 74–5, 93
Palazzo Querini 109n.46
plague in 188, 192–3, 201, 209–12, 272–4
Piazza San Marco 41–2, 52, 62, 77, 102, 212–14, 256–7, 272, 338
Piazzetta 102, 188–9, 212–13, 339
Ponte della Paglia 126, 207–8
Punto della Dogana 206, 214
Rialto 62, 153, 176–7, 189–90, 211
Rio dei Gesuiti 194–5
Rio di Palazzo 121
Rio San Giovanni Grisostomo 121, 189
Riva degli Schiavoni 188
San Barnaba 212
San Biagio 205, 212
San Canciano 194–5
San Francesco della Vigna 117
San Giorgio d'Alga 205
San Giovanni Battista alla Giudecca 257
San Marcuola 98, 102, 117
San Marco, treasury of 217
San Maurizio 266
San Moisè 214
San Nicolò dei Tolentini 198–9
San Nicolò della Lattuga, convent 79–80
San Nicolò di Lido 207–8
San Pantalon 233, 266
San Polo, sestiere of 254
San Salvador 8, 208, 254
San Sebastiano 106
San Silvestro 254, 294
Santa Caterina, convent 7–10, 14, 136–7
Santa Croce 102
Santa Maria Gloriosa dei Frari 79, 103, 152, 318
  Tomb of Alvise II Della Torre 103–6, 104*f*, 105*f*, 125, 214, 346
Santa Maria Nova 123, 188, 194–5, 214, 233, 261–4, 266–7, 353
Santa Sofia 189–90, 192–3, 207
Sant'Elena, island of 207–8
San Trovaso 4–6
SS Giovanni e Paolo, monastery of 125, 152, 267
  Cappella di San Nicolò 125, 264
  hospital of 265
weather 41, 94–5
Torre dell'Orologio 77
visit of Bona Sforza to 205–8
wellheads 174, 254
Zecca 188–9, 212–13, 234
Venier, family 148
  Andrea 178
  Francesco, doge 73, 166, 181–2, 205–8
  Gabriel 76

Venier, family (*cont.*)
  Giovanni Antonio, cavaliere 120, 122–3
  Maffeo, archbishop of Corfù 297
  Marco Antonio 130
  Sebastian, duke of Candia 145, 152–3
Venzon, Venzone 32–3, 53–4, 58, 71–2, 202
Vergon, Zamberlani ringleader 35–6
Veroli, bishop of 60
Verona 30, 56, 71, 104, 115–16, 125, 181–2, 197, 211, 235, 267
  Arco dei Gavi 203
  San Fermo Maggiore 104, 106*f*
Veronese, Paolo 260
  and his studio, *The Coronation of Hebe* 311–12, 312*f*, 332, 334
Via Postumia 227
Vicentino, Andrea, *Our Lady of the Rosary* 322–3, 323*f*
Vicenza 62, 68, 71, 116–17, 122–3, 238
  Palazzi Arnaldi 117
Vienna 43, 57–8, 70–1, 215, 227, 324, 342–3
Vieste (Puglia) 183–4
Villach 43–4, 53, 71, 81
villani, *see* peasants
Villalta 53, 73, 78, 237–8, 274, 279–80, 283, 307, 315–16, 328, 331–2
  Castello di 19, 25, 27, 48, 49*f*, 50*f*, 84n.36, 145, 255, 284*f*, 293–5, 302, 307–8, 310–11, 314, 316–17, 321–2, 327, 334–9, 344, 344*f*, 346, 353, 357–9
    destruction and sacking of 37, 39–40, 48, 68
    expansion of, in late 16th century 284*f*, 286–7
    rebuilding of, after 1511 48–51
    refurbishing of, after 1560 229–31
  fief of 73, 314–16, 329–32, 335–6
  peasants of 37, 335
  San Leonardo, church 317
  Santa Maria Maddalena, monastery 317–18
Villa Bembo–Boldù, at Ponte di Brenta 117, 118*f*, 233, 266, 353
Villa Noniana (Villa Bozza) at S. Maria di Non 11–12, 118*f*
Vittoria, Alessandro 313
Vives, Juan Luis, *De Institutione Feminae Christianae* 5

weddings 8–10, 12–15, 24, 80, 119–23, 122*f*, 146–7, 191–2, 240–1, 279, 282, 325, 331–2, 336–7, 345, 353
Weinrichius, Martin, German physician 179–80
Wilhelm V, Duke of Bavaria 322–3

Zamberlani 20, 22–3, 31–5, 53
Zane, Hieronimo 275n.31
Zante (Zakynthos) 143, 334
Zara (Zadar) 4–5, 115–18, 128, 136, 146, 163–4, 171–2, 190–1, 196–7, 211, 235, 256–7
Zarathustra 179–80
Zen, Caterino 95–6
Zeno, Nicolò 234–5
Ziletti, Giordano 175
Ziliol, Cesare, notary 264
Ziracco 335–6
Zobia Grassa, see Giovedì Grasso
Zoppola, castle of 39–40
Zoppola, Giovanni Giorgio 43
Zorzi, Bartolomeo 145
Zorzi, Giacomo, canon of Cividale 97–8, 101
Zorzi, Paolo 236–7
Zuccaro, Federico 239*f*
Zuccaro, Taddeo 239*f*